you

DOROTHY

JEB

NEIL

GEORGE, JR.

MARVIN

GEORGE

Love to the
Humphrys —
George + Bar

From the Bush family to your family with a prayer for peace, for love, for happiness

#8-5000 LONGMONT, HOUSTON, TEXAS 77027 • 5161 PALISAD... ...ASHINGTON, D...

For a Very Merry Christmas and a Happy New Year

GEORGE AND BARBARA BUSH AND

GEORGE JR.   JEBBY   NEIL   MARVIN   DOROTHY

LET US LIGHT UP YOUR TREE WITH WISHES FROM THE BUSHES

MY FATHER
MY PRESIDENT

MY FATHER
MY PRESIDENT

A PERSONAL ACCOUNT OF THE LIFE OF

GEORGE H.W. BUSH

DORO BUSH KOCH

WARNER BOOKS

NEW YORK   BOSTON

Warner Books
Hachette Book Group USA
1271 Avenue of the Americas
New York, NY 10020

Visit our Web site at www.HachetteBookGroupUSA.com.

Printed in the United States of America

First Edition: October 2006
10 9 8 7 6 5 4 3 2 1

Warner Books and the "W" logo are trademarks of Time Warner Inc. or an affiliated company.
Used under license by Hachette Book Group USA, which is not affiliated with Time Warner Inc.

Library of Congress Cataloging-in-Publication Data
Koch, Doro Bush
   My father, my president : a personal account of the life of George H. W. Bush / Doro Bush
Koch.—1st ed.
      p.   cm.
   Includes bibliographical references and index.
   ISBN–13: 978-0-446-57990-2 (regular ed.)
   ISBN-10: 0-446-57990-4 (regular ed.)
   ISBN-13: 978-0-446-58020-5 (large print ed.)
   ISBN-10: 0-446-58020-1 (large print ed.)
  1. Bush, George, 1924– 2. Presidents—United States—Biography. 3. Koch, Dora Bush, 1959–
4. Children of presidents—United States—Biography. 5. Daughters—United States—Biography.
6. Bush, George, 1924—Family. I. Title.
   E882.K63   2006
   973.928092—dc22
   [B]   2006020984

Book design by Giorgetta Bell McRee

For my father . . .

6-15-14
Happy Father's Day!
To a wonderful
husband —
father —
+ PaPa RV!
love Ya!
Gewonne

Contents

viii CONTENTS

Foreword

I am so delighted and honored that Doro asked me to write the foreword for *My Father, My President*. This is a very important book. It is her story about her father—it's our story, a story of laughter and tears, births and deaths, friends and family. It is a love story, written by the daughter of one of the kindest and most decent men in the world, who also happened to become the forty-first president of the United States—my husband, George H. W. Bush.

Doro Bush Koch is the best-kept secret in America. Not very many people know that George and I have a daughter. We hear a lot about the men in our family, but not enough about the women. While George's father, Prescott Bush, certainly was his role model in many ways, some of the greatest influences in George's life have been the women in our family—his mother, his wife, his daughter, his daughters-in-law, and his granddaughters. Not to mention all the talented women who have worked with him over the years. There's a reason why George Bush asked Doro to write this book. I am thrilled that people will now know George Bush through the eyes of a wonderful woman.

Although I've been told I am the first woman since Abigail Adams to be both a wife and a mother to a president, Doro is the only woman ever in our nation's history to live to see both her father and her brother become president. (Abigail Adams's daughters, named Abigail and Susanna, did not live long enough to see their brother become president.) There is only one woman in American history who could have written *My Father, My President*, and that woman is Doro.

She's written her own narrative about her father's life, which spans all the major events of the second half of the twentieth century and beyond—from World War II and the Cold War to Desert Storm and Hurricane Katrina. You'll see George Bush the elder statesman and diplomat, but you'll also meet George Bush the businessman, the adventurer, the sportsman, and the funniest man I know. Most important, you'll see him as father and grandfather, working hard to raise our family despite the glare of the media and the rush of events.

Our life with Doro began in the 1950s. George and I were living in Texas and had four beautiful, wild sons; we would have taken a fifth with joy, but in our hearts we were longing for another daughter. Our second child, Robin, had died of leukemia in 1953. Robin was named after my mother, Pauline Robinson Pierce, who had died in a terrible car accident that nearly killed my father as well, only weeks before Robin was born. It was a very sad time in our lives. Even in our pain, we knew that we wanted another girl in our family. George especially did.

In August 1959 my Aunt Charlotte Pierce came to Houston to help with the boys, and I went into Memorial Hospital and had a beautiful healthy little girl. We named her Dorothy Walker Bush after George's wonderful mother. The name Dorothy means "gift from God," and Doro was—and is—just that.

My Aunt Charlotte came into my hospital room and told me that when the nurse held up Doro at the window of the nursery, George put his head against the glass and tears flowed down his face. I know sons are supposed to be for their dads . . . and girls for their moms. That may well be true, but my heart fills with love when I think of the joy all six of our children brought us each in their own way. Every dad should have a daughter as loving, thoughtful, and sensitive as ours—and, I should add, as funny.

Doro was at college and wanted to help her dad when he first ran for president in 1979, so it was her idea to leave school and work in the campaign office. George told her that she honestly could not go to the office and sit around as the candidate's daughter. To our great surprise, Doro left Boston College (which she returned to after the election was over) and enrolled in a nine-month secretarial course that went right through the hot summer. She said that she would work her heart out for her dad. That meant a lot to us.

I remember her wearing stockings, a skirt, and a neat blouse all that hot summer while I spent much of the summer in and out of lovely cool Maine. I know she worked hard, like she said she would. To this day, she'd do anything in the world for her dad—including writing this book.

There is a very special relationship between Doro and her dad, and I hope between Doro and her mom. I love and adore our boys, but they don't always understand like Doro does. Doro has a way of looking at the world like no one else in our family—sweet, empathetic, and seeing the humor in it all. Her brothers don't just want to have her around, they *need* to have her in their lives.

Doro started this project by borrowing our Christmas card list and writing to everyone on it, asking for stories about George. It snowballed from there, because the response was overwhelming: hundreds of people responded by snail mail, e-mail, BlackBerry messages, phone calls, you name it. Many stories were laugh-out-loud funny, some were so poignant you'd get a lump in your throat reading them. A few had perfect recall of every detail, and others were foggy with time. Over and over, people told Doro stories she'd never heard before, often of quiet good deeds George had done over the years that no one knew about. Even in the midst of crises, he has always made time for the personal touches—some little, some big—that can make all the difference in someone else's life. These stories speak to George's love of his friends and family.

Through and through, *My Father, My President* is about loyalty. Doro has shown us her dad's loyalty to the principles he was raised with; his fidelity to his friends who have carried him through good times and bad; his trueheartedness in always wanting to do what is right, no matter what the personal cost; and his faithfulness to our family—not just to our sons and daughter but to all the grandchildren, aunts, uncles, and cousins whom he loves so much.

Loyalty is something learned by example and motivated by love. You can't teach loyalty; it is natural. My dad once told me there were really only three things you can give your children that count: the best education available, a good example, and all the love in the world. That was very wise advice. We tried to do all these things. George was better at it than I was, probably because he is the most honest, caring person I know. From his example, our children have learned loyalty, and Doro has all the same sweet loyal instincts he has.

All of our children feel joy with the successes—and sorrow in the pains—of the others. They look out for each other, and they are proud of each other's accomplishments. Life in our family has had its ups and downs—both private and public—like all families. We've made our share of mistakes, and no one in our family is perfect. Politics may sound glamorous, but we've lost a lot of campaigns along the way and seen a lot of heartache. Some of the rough times we've been through could have driven us apart. The important thing is that we stuck together, and we're thankful for that.

Life in politics has certainly given me a few extra wrinkles and gray hair. One time I was asked to be the keynote speaker at the National Plastic Surgeons Convention. I was afraid they'd rush the stage, eager to get their hands on me. Many times I've received letters in the mail with suggestions for new hairstyles, hair colors, and improvements to my wardrobe. If I had a nickel for every fashion "tip" I've gotten, I'd be a millionaire! But my philosophy is that the wrinkles show where the laughs have been, and my white hair is, well, the inspiration for the name my kids bestowed upon me, the Silver Fox.

The only way I know how to be is to be myself. The only way I know how to parent is to parent the way I have been for sixty years. I don't want to be remembered for the number of my children who have been elected to office, or succeeded in business, or raised money for charities. My yardstick for success as a mother is how many of my children are kind, honest, decent people who work hard and serve others. That's the only way I know to measure success in life.

George and I are very proud that all of our children still want to come home. That is our greatest accomplishment. That's the greatest accomplishment of any parent.

The three things I hope you take from reading this book are the importance of family, of love, and of loyalty, for those are the essence of George Bush.

Barbara Bush
April 2006

Introduction

It was the Fourth of July, 1939, and my father had just turned fifteen years old. He was on summer vacation, listening over the radio in Kennebunkport, Maine, when first baseman Lou Gehrig stepped up to the microphones in Yankee Stadium. Facing a terrible death from ALS—now known as Lou Gehrig's disease—Gehrig said with tremendous grace and courage, "Today, I consider myself the luckiest man on the face of this earth."

It's no coincidence that Lou Gehrig is my father's hero. Dad played baseball—first base, in fact—just like the Iron Horse. I remember Dad saving the postage stamps with Gehrig's image on them, on the first day of their issue, for his grandchildren. For as long as I can remember, he's had the same philosophy as Lou Gehrig: he considers himself the luckiest man on earth. He enjoys every minute to the fullest. I'm sure you've seen the photos of him skydiving, playing "speed golf," and traveling halfway across the world with his former political rival Bill Clinton to raise money for tsunami victims.

My father has lived a remarkable life and has lived it with great humility. And it is a uniquely American life. Long before he became president, he lived through a large measure of modern American history, and he kept his moral compass throughout. It's true that no one chooses their family, but he was tremendously blessed to be the son of Prescott and Dorothy Bush, just as I am lucky to be the daughter of George and Barbara Bush.

As his only daughter, I'll do anything in the world for him. Anyone who's met him knows how infectious his enthusiasm is . . . how he draws you into whatever his project is at the time . . . how hard it is to say no to that twinkle in his eye.

And so I couldn't turn him down when, in March 2005, he sent me the following e-mail. He had just returned from a meeting at the Bush Library at Texas A&M University with Patty Presock, perhaps his closest assistant when he was president.

> Dear Doro,
>
> Today, Patty Presock came to our Library Advisory meeting. She made a suggestion that she thinks is exactly right for you.
> When she worked for me she kept some very personal, very special files. She told me she did this because some day she thought you might want to look these files over and then write a book about what is in them.
> I have not seen the files. But I suggest, if you are at all interested, that you call Patty. It would be a fun project. This may not interest you at all but if it does I would be thrilled for you to undertake it. Bobby's sister-in-law, Tricia, could be your researcher.
>
> Just a thought from your devoted Dad

I wrote him back right away, immediately accepting the project. After I hit the "send" key, however, at once I felt excited and worried.

I was excited to help bring to life a side of Dad that most people don't know. The idea of writing a book about his life around never-before-seen private files was instantly enticing. It just felt right.

I was also worried that I wouldn't do Dad justice—that somehow I would let him down, and let down my mother and brothers as well.

For many years, even before my father's presidency ended, people who knew and loved him urged him to write his memoirs either for history's sake or for the sake of his own "legacy" (a word that makes him wince ever so slightly). Invariably, Dad would just shake his head, smile, and say something like, "I think I'll leave that to the historians."

Ben Bradlee, the distinguished editor of the *Washington Post*, once referred to news coverage as the "first rough draft of history." No doubt every president feels that the draft was rougher in some spots more than others. The man my mother married and the father my brothers and I grew up with is a man of uncommon grace, humility, humor, and wisdom, but this was not always conveyed in the pages of the morning newspaper or on the nightly newscasts.

Even when cast in a positive light, the image of Dad captured by the media was never three-dimensional—and as a result, the man we knew was not the man that the vast majority of Americans saw. After all, there is more to a president's life than what happens behind the desk in the Oval Office or in front of the cameras.

My Father, My President is written from the perspective of not only a daughter but also of our family and Dad's legions of friends. Captured in these pages are insights and stories from the people who know my father the best and who shared so many dramatic, historic, and poignant moments in his life.

Within a week of my e-mail exchange with Dad, I sent hundreds of letters to his associates, contemporaries from the world stage, and even his political opponents. The response was overwhelming. In fact, the reaction was so tremendous that I received a response to my letter before I even sent it out! I had shared a draft of the letter with Dad, who couldn't wait for the final version before distributing it to a ton of people. The next thing I knew, the first of many letters arrived with a story quite literally from the end of the earth: Arthur Milnes, a reporter who met Dad during a fishing trip to the remote Canadian Northwest Territories, described how a guest fishing column my father wrote had affected his career.

What followed were several trips to the Bush Library to review his personal papers and other files that no one had ever seen. Together with my sister-in-law Tricia Koch, I also interviewed over 125 people and collected hundreds of letters.

Working on this book project is the most meaningful thing I have ever done. It gave me a legitimate excuse to spend more time with Mom and Dad—to call them and e-mail them. I also spent most of the summer of 2005 in Maine with them—not tough duty, I confess. There I got in the habit of getting up early and walking next door to my parents' house, having a cup of coffee with them, and starting my day visiting with Dad. I would tell him of my progress going through the stacks of material that I was amassing.

At first, Dad was very enthusiastic about the project and we had great fun reminiscing about the past—both that of the country and of our own family. But as the days wore on, I began to sense that he was losing his enthusiasm. I wondered to myself why he was reacting like this, but couldn't bring myself to ask him. What if he had changed his mind about the book and couldn't bear to tell me?

I thought of Jean Becker, his chief of staff, who is like a sister to me. "Let's run it by Jean" is a phrase often uttered in the Bush family. So I went to her and said, "Jean, I'm really worried because Dad was completely enthusiastic about the project and now I sense there's some hesitation there." She told me not to worry, that she would look into it and get back to me.

The next day, Jean approached me. "Your father loves the project. He still thinks it's a great idea. But he's worried about one thing." She paused for a moment, her voice grave but her eyes twinkling. "He's just worried the book is going to be too much *about him.*" After a stunned silence, we both broke out laughing. It was just so typical of him. If nothing else, Dad is humble, a trait he inherited from his mother.

As president, Dad didn't care much about his image. Coming from the "greatest generation," he was more concerned with action and results—not flowery words or a made-for-TV wardrobe.

Advisers routinely counseled him how he should dress in neutral tones and present himself; but to be candid, my father didn't think it mattered whether he wore a red or a blue tie during a debate.

Historians seek the truth as they see it, but the viewpoint they offer isn't necessarily the whole picture. True, a daughter may not have either the expertise or the objectivity of a historian, but a historian doesn't know a father the way his daughter does. For those parts of Dad's life that took place before I was born, or while I was away at school, I reached out to people who could fill in stories from those years. Many of their experiences with Dad were consistent with mine, but they added a new perspective.

You'll hear the voices of his friends throughout the book, and my hope was to include as many of them as I possibly could. *My Father, My President* is not the whole story, but an important piece of it. My story is partial, in both senses of that word, but it's the story I've witnessed—one that I have lived. It won't be objective—how could it be?—but it will be true, I promise you that.

I am deeply grateful to my father for this rare opportunity he has offered me—to delve into his remarkable life. He used to call his own mother "one of God's most special people," and the phrase easily applies to him as well. To that, let me add a special word of thanks and love to my extraordinary mother, without whom neither this book nor Dad's life would be nearly as colorful, meaningful, or fun.

Doro Bush Koch
Bethesda, Maryland
April 2006

MY FATHER
MY PRESIDENT

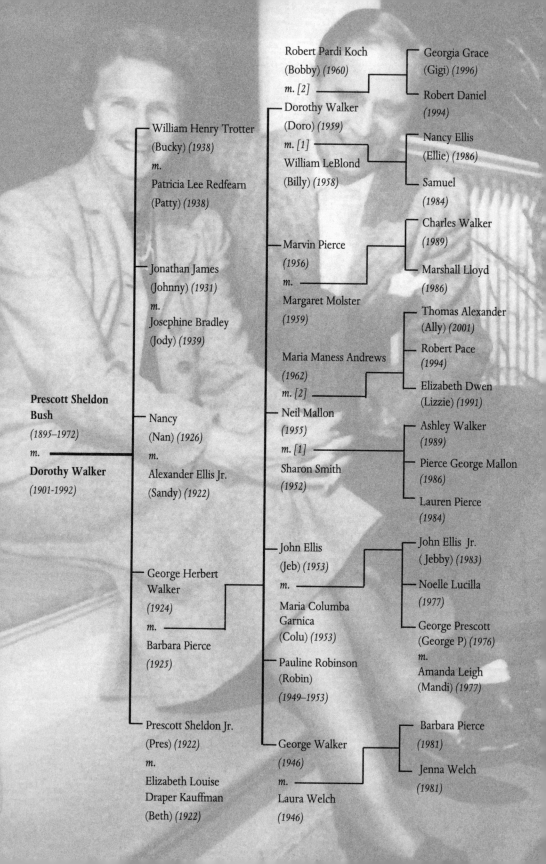

Prescott Sheldon
Bush
(1895–1972)

m.

Dorothy Walker
(1901-1992)

William Henry Trotter
(Bucky) *(1938)*
m.
Patricia Lee Redfearn
(Patty) *(1938)*

Jonathan James
(Johnny) *(1931)*
m.
Josephine Bradley
(Jody) *(1939)*

Nancy
(Nan) *(1926)*
m.
Alexander Ellis Jr.
(Sandy) *(1922)*

George Herbert
Walker
(1924)
m.
Barbara Pierce
(1925)

Prescott Sheldon Jr.
(Pres) *(1922)*
m.
Elizabeth Louise
Draper Kauffman
(Beth) *(1922)*

Robert Pardi Koch
(Bobby) *(1960)*
m. [2]
Dorothy Walker
(Doro) *(1959)*
m. [1]
William LeBlond
(Billy) *(1958)*

Marvin Pierce
(1956)
m.
Margaret Molster
(1959)

Maria Maness Andrews
(1962)
m. [2]
Neil Mallon
(1955)
m. [1]
Sharon Smith
(1952)

John Ellis
(Jeb) *(1953)*
m.
Maria Columba
Garnica
(Colu) *(1953)*

Pauline Robinson
(Robin)
(1949–1953)

George Walker
(1946)
m.
Laura Welch
(1946)

Georgia Grace
(Gigi) *(1996)*
Robert Daniel
(1994)

Nancy Ellis
(Ellie) *(1986)*
Samuel
(1984)

Charles Walker
(1989)
Marshall Lloyd
(1986)

Thomas Alexander
(Ally) *(2001)*
Robert Pace
(1994)
Elizabeth Dwen
(Lizzie) *(1991)*

Ashley Walker
(1989)
Pierce George Mallon
(1986)
Lauren Pierce
(1984)

John Ellis Jr.
(Jebby) *(1983)*
Noelle Lucilla
(1977)
George Prescott
(George P) *(1976)*
m.
Amanda Leigh
(Mandi) *(1977)*

Barbara Pierce
(1981)
Jenna Welch
(1981)

Chapter 1

THE END DEPENDS UPON THE BEGINNING

"His mother was greatly responsible for much of Poppy's athletic success. He thoroughly enjoyed the battle and was always a true sportsman. Never a showboat nor a glad-hander—in victory or defeat. His joy was in playing aggressively within the rules."

—Dad's Andover schoolmate and lifelong friend
Frank "Junie" O'Brien

My name is Doro Bush Koch. My parents named me Dorothy Walker Bush, after my father's mother. No one knows exactly when I got the nickname Doro, but I've been called that as long as anyone can remember. And as long as anyone can remember, my father, George Herbert Walker Bush, has lived his life by certain standards, by a certain set of rules, and with a certain way of doing things that go a long way toward explaining the man he is today. As I set out to tell this story about him, and our family life together, it only seems fitting to start with the person who had the most influence on him: his mother and my namesake, Dorothy Walker Bush. My brothers and I called her Ganny.

Ganny was born in 1901, the daughter of George Herbert Walker, a successful St. Louis businessman and community leader who, among other things, helped organize the 1904 St. Louis World's Fair. The Walkers valued faith, family, and friends, but they also believed in the old adage about public service, "To whom much is given, much is expected." In fact, it might surprise you to know that a century ago Dad's namesake was considered to be the power behind the Democratic Party in St. Louis, Missouri.

Ganny married my grandfather Prescott Bush on August 6, 1921, at the church of St. Ann's by the Sea in Kennebunkport, Maine; two years later, they moved from St. Louis to Columbus, Ohio, where my grandfather worked for the Hupp Products Company. He left a few months later, in November 1923, to become president of sales for Stedman Products of South Braintree, Massachusetts—and seven months later, on June 12, 1924, Dad was born.

Dorothy and Prescott Bush raised their five children in Greenwich, Connecticut—Prescott Jr. (Uncle Pres), Dad, Nancy (Nan), Jonathan (Johnny), and William (Bucky)—with a strict set of rules. Dad's youngest brother, my Uncle Bucky, put it this way: "Mother was very hands-on, quite strict, but in a loving way. She got involved, and she participated. She wanted to make sure that you didn't sit around much. So if you weren't studying, you better be doing something physical or running around the house, because she didn't like idle hands."

My father and his mother had a special bond, and to read many of his letters home to her during World War II is to glimpse what his brother Johnny calls a relationship where "a lot of it was laughter, a lot of it was just joy." Still, she never made any of her children feel inferior in any way—she loved them all the same.

"She made me feel like I was her favorite daughter-in-law," my mother said to me once. "Of course, I know I wasn't. But she made me feel that way."

To give you a better idea of what my grandmother was like, let me share a letter that Dad wrote about her for a school project in 1996 for my daughter Ellie:

Dear Ellie,

I am thrilled you are doing a paper on your great-grandmother. She was the most loving, kind person in the whole wide world. She never hurt anyone's feelings. She always tried to see the other guy's point of view.

So, first, her qualities of character were the best. She loved my Dad with a passion and she gave all five of us, her own kids, far more attention and love than we'd ever deserve.

She'd always go to games, and she loved to participate in the parents' games.

She was the pitcher and Captain of the mother's baseball team that played us when we were in Greenwich Country Day. She was a great athlete—the best of all her friends. She would always hit a home run in those games. Then, too, she was the fastest runner—she'd win the mothers' race every year.

Her best sport was tennis. At age 17 she was the runner up in the National Girl's singles tournament being held at the Merion Cricket Club in Philadelphia. But she never bragged about that.

Once in the 30's her brother, my Uncle Louis, brought a very famous woman player up here to Maine. Uncle Lou set up the match for Mother to play her. Mother played her and beat her. At the end of the match Mum's feet were literally bleeding. She won all kinds of Club tennis championships at the Greenwich Field Club, the Kennebunk River Club, and others too.

She taught us all about sportsmanship—some by bawling us out when we were bad sports, and some by example. She never complained or found excuses when she lost.

She was a fine golfer, too. A really good golfer—with a great short game, and a competitive spirit to match.

Once, when she was little, she tied her brother, Herbie, to the stone posts out here at Walker's Point, for she didn't want him to follow her downtown.

She crewed for her father, your Great-Great-Grandfather G. H.

Walker (Bert) on his 21' sailing boat, the "Giggle On." He'd make her get way up on the bow as ballast when the sea got rough during a race. She loved it.

Once she swam from the pier here at the Point all the way around to the boat club. Her Uncle Joe Wear followed her in a row boat just to be sure she didn't get a cramp and have to stop. She made it easily.

One time my friend Bill Truesdale, way back about 1935, said something to me I'll never forget—he said, "I wish my mother was like yours!" Isn't that something, Ellie? All my friends loved my mother and respected her too. She was so kind to them.

Once I used an ax—Mum had told me not to do it. I cut myself on the leg—a deep cut. I lied to her about what happened. But she knew I was lying. She didn't spank me and she got me to admit, on my own, that I had not told the truth and that I had used the ax when she told me not to. She explained to me about never lying. Now I am 72. Then I was 6 or 7. I have never forgotten.

Mum was always trim—a fairly small woman, always in great shape though. And oh how she loved my Dad.

Oh, yes, when she was around 18 she was presented [as debutante] at the Court of St. James in London. A lot of girls did that in the old days. She had to curtsy to the king.

She grew up in St. Louis, Missouri, and her family came to Maine every summer.

Mum was religious, not pious—but a Christian that knew her Bible and was lifted by her faith. She'd read to us the Lesson of the Day before our meals. She went to church without fail on Sundays. But more than that she lived her faith—teaching not just family but so many friends, too, by her example, by the way she lived her own life. Once Billy Graham, near the end of Mum's life, went over to the Bungalow [in Kennebunkport] to have breakfast. They read the Bible together. She told me afterwards that those 45 minutes were about the "most glorious time" in her life. She admired Billy's commitment to Jesus and to God, and she loved his message.

Oh yes, she played the piano pretty well, too.

I saw my Mum a few hours before she died. I was President then. I flew up to Greenwich to see her one last time. She was breathing with great difficulty—fighting "the good fight with all her might." But, Ellie, I knew for sure that she would go to heaven; and I also knew that she looked upon death not with fear but with joy. She told me over and over again that she knew she would be with my Dad in heaven. During that last visit she was struggling to breathe, struggling for life; but I knelt by her bed and literally prayed that God would take her to heaven right then.

I hope your presentation goes well, for you will be telling your classmates about one of God's truly special people.

I love you, Ellie.

Devotedly,

Gampy

As I read this, it's remarkable how alike Dad and his mother were—both were captain of the baseball team, played tennis, and were religious but not pious. There was, however, one exception. While everyone in his family has been musically inclined, Dad can't play the piano or carry a tune. He claims that there was a "genetic power outage" in his case when it came to music. To this day, however, he still talks about his days singing in the "double octet" in grammar school—usually comprised of sixteen voices. "Often we were undermanned," Dad once noted with great pride, but no one really believes that he sang.

"If he did, he mouthed it," Bucky confided recently, "and that was before his voice changed."

Dad's father, Prescott, was a successful businessman who later served as U.S. senator from Connecticut from 1953 to 1963. My grandfather, of course, was also an important influence on Dad, who describes his father this way: "Big. Strong. Principled. Respected by all who knew him. A leader. Wonderful sense of humor. Once, a guy told a dirty joke in the locker room at the club and Dad walked out on him. He loved my mother very much. He was a great example to everyone in the family, all Ganny's brothers particularly. He was a great golfer—scratch handicap. Champion. Played tennis well. Had his own quartet until he died, almost. Singer in the Silver Dollar Quartet. He was just a wonderful warm guy. Now, he wasn't cozy like Mother. We felt close to him, but not in the same way. He was more the discipline guy."

Years later, Dad recalled, "Mother had gotten a call from a neighbor two miles away. I remember it well. The phone call came in, and Mother said, 'Did you boys do this?' We said, 'Yes.' She told my brother and me, 'Well, your father is going to have to handle this.' We walked into our den in Grove Lane, and he picked up a squash racket, and I thought, 'Oh God, this is it. We've had it.' And he threatened us with it, and said, 'Now, you go over to the Williams' house, you go over and apologize.' So we got out of there, scared to death. Ran as we started, then the closer to the Williams' house we got, we became very terrified and slowed down. We had to knock on the door and say that we were very sorry that we had paid their beautiful daughter ten cents to run naked across the floor. We got out with our lives on that one, but we were sixth graders at the time—natural hormonal urges you get, I guess."

After graduating from Yale, my grandfather served as a field artillery captain in World War I before returning home to enter the business world. As a partner in the Brown Brothers Harriman firm on Wall Street, he took the train every day from his home in Greenwich to his office in Manhattan. During the 1930s, Dad remembers, his father would forgo drinks in the club car of the train with his contemporaries and, instead, go into town and serve as moderator of the Greenwich town meetings. Dad was a teenager by then, and seeing his father serve as unofficial mayor of Greenwich made a big impression.

"He led by example," Dad said. "He ran the meetings, and in everything he did he was the leader. He wasn't a power-hungry guy, it was just leadership. Because of his leadership, things gravitated to him—people would ask, 'How will Prescott Bush feel about this? What'll he vote for?'"

Betsy Heminway, who grew up with my father in Greenwich, remembers my grandfather as "the most extraordinary man. If I ever thought of someone that looked like a statesman, it was Prescott Bush. He would walk in a room and there was a presence."

Dorothy, Prescott, and their five children lived in a big Victorian house on Grove Lane. Upstairs, there was a Singer sewing machine which Ganny used to mend the children's clothes, and a radio as well. There my Aunt Nan and Ganny would listen to the New York Philharmonic on Sunday afternoons, while the boys would play outside and my grandfather would nap. During the week, they'd also listen to Edward R. Murrow before dinner.

Dad's Greenwich years were filled with sports. A Ping-Pong table sat in the front hall, and a tiddlywinks game had a permanent home in the living room. The Bush children tobogganed and skied on the hilly front lawn in the winter, and in the summer they played catch and touch football in the backyard. For team games such as football and baseball, they'd squeeze through the hedge to the neighbor's bigger yard.

One Christmas, my Uncle Bucky received a labyrinth game—a wooden box with a maze and holes on top, and handles on the sides to maneuver the marble. Because he was so young, however, Bucky had to stop playing with it that first night and go to bed at 7:00. Dad, who was fourteen years older than Uncle Bucky, came down to breakfast the next morning and spied the game.

"What's this?" Dad asked his younger brother, wanting to know how it worked. Bucky put the marble on top and proceeded to drop it twice through the first or second hole.

"Well, I've never seen anything like that before," said Dad.

"Want to try it, Poppy?" asked Bucky. (Dad was called "Poppy" because he reminded everyone of his maternal grandfather, George, who was known simply as "Pop.")

Sure enough, Dad ran the marble all the way to the end and

won. Amazed, Bucky asked him to do it again. Dad even bet him a dollar he could do it again, and did. Later, Bucky told his older brother Johnny, "You know, I can't believe it—the guy had never seen this thing before."

"Bucky," said Johnny, "he'd been up practicing all night!"

Dad's father attended Yale with a man named Neil Mallon, who went on to be a very successful businessman in the oil industry and whom the Bush children all called Uncle Neil. Mom said Mr. Mallon "was like Santa Claus" to my father and his siblings. To them, she said, "he was a big man" despite his small build.

One day when he was young, Dad and Uncle Neil were playing catch in the yard—"no great athlete, Uncle Neil," Mom added—when Dad accidentally threw the ball through the windshield of his father's new car. Uncle Neil turned to Dad and said, "Poppy, let's go tell your father."

Dad was scared, and when it came time to confess to the crime, Uncle Neil spoke up first: "Prescott, I made a very bad throw and smashed your windshield." Dad remembered it clearly, and said to me nearly seven decades later, "He was perhaps the nicest man I ever met." Later, when Dad went into the oil business, Uncle Neil would come to have almost as much influence on Dad as his own parents.

★   ★   ★

When he was thirteen, Dad joined his older brother Pres at Phillips Academy in Andover, Massachusetts. Located on a hilltop twenty-one miles north of Boston, the academy was founded in 1778, making it one of the nation's oldest boarding schools.

My Uncle Johnny told me of a time at Andover when a few of the senior boys were ordering the "preps," or new boys, around. They started picking on a smaller boy named Bruce Gelb, ordering him to carry a heavy chair up the stairs to someone's room.

"So Bruce is struggling to carry this chair, and they're laughing at him, and your father just walks across the place and says, 'Look,

I'll take this side, and you take that side . . .'" Dad helped him carry the chair, and Bruce never forgot it.

Years later, after he became president of Clairol, Inc., head of USIA, and ambassador to Belgium, Bruce Gelb told a reporter, "They say there are no heroes for young teenagers in our society. But I can tell you, at age fourteen and a half, I had my own personal hero, a guy that hated bullies, and it was George Bush."

Andover "was a huge influence in my life," Dad told an interviewer years later, "more so than college." Frank "Junie" O'Brien, one of Dad's schoolmates at both Andover and Yale, agrees. He thinks that the faculty at Andover taught, advised, coached, and socialized with the impressionable high school age boys, while students at Yale were older, more independent, and had less interaction with their teachers. Junie O'Brien was so influenced by it he became a high school teacher himself, serving on the faculty at Groton School for thirty-two years.

When he was fourteen years old, Dad was confirmed at Andover and his mother gave him a small blue Bible as a confirmation gift. She wrote the words to an old hymn inside for him:

> *I would be true, for there are those who trust me,*
> *I would be pure, for there are those who care,*
> *I would be strong, for there is much to suffer,*
> *I would be brave, for there is much to dare;*
> *I would be friend to all, the foe, the friendless,*
> *I would be giving and forget the gift.*
> *I would be humble, for I know my weakness;*
> *I would look up, and laugh and love and lift.*

Andover's school mottoes were *Finis origine pendet*, "The end depends on the beginning," and *Non sibi*, "Not for self." Those philosophies fit with my grandparents' emphasis on honesty, loyalty, generosity, modesty, sportsmanship, and becoming what the students there called an all-rounder.

That family philosophy was spelled out in a letter that Dad came across a few years ago. Generations later, it reminds me that the values of our family have remained the same. The letter was written by my great-grandfather George Herbert Walker as he was steaming out of New York Harbor past the Statue of Liberty on a ship to France. It was dated May 22, 1920, and addressed to his four youngest children. To me, it clearly spells out our family's creed—one that my grandmother and her siblings embodied throughout their lives:

> *Please remember now each and every one of you that Father counts on you to do your best and he knows you will . . . Always remember too, my dear boys, that you are gentlemen and not muckers and that your word is your bond and inviolate.*
>
> *I am very proud of you all, for I see you all developing along the right lines. Thanks to your own good sense and to your dear Mother's teachings. Go on and you will live to become useful men and good citizens. Use your heads. Be good losers and winners too, play fair, and if in doubt, give the other fellow the benefit of it, and you will also grow to be good sportsmen, than which there is nothing finer. Give me a man who is one, and I will show you a man of high character and principles.*
>
> *I did not mean this letter to be a preachment and nothing that I have said is either original or new, but it is the truth and it is the unmutable law . . .*
>
> *Herbie, you have come along in fine shape and I know you are going to continue.*
>
> *Jim, you have always been gentle and you too will continue to come along.*
>
> *John, my boy, your character is in the making and a great part of your future depends on how you control yourself now. Make your mind control and think before you act and I am sure that you too will come along.*
>
> *Louis, you are still too young to judge, but remember this, old*

man, no boy will ever be what I wish him to be unless he knows what the truth is and sticks to it, through thick and thin.

I love you all dearly and I am proud of my boys. I send to each of you a heart full of love, ever yours through trouble and through life. Devotedly, Father.

My father forwarded this letter to all of us when he came across it a few years back—thinking we'd get "a great big kick out of it." Reading it brought a smile to my face. I particularly liked the part about not being "muckers." My Uncle Louis, the youngest one listed at the end, turned out to be the wild one of the bunch—and also gave our family many warm and funny memories.

For example, after my grandfather Prescott had graduated from Yale, he continued to be active in the Yale Glee Club Associates. They had an annual dinner at which they'd all sing. Uncle Louis couldn't carry a tune, but he considered the dinner a big deal and was dying to attend. According to Uncle Johnny, Lou kept pestering my grandfather to bring him to the dinner—but to no avail.

"Absolutely not, Lou," my grandfather firmly stated. "It's for former Glee Club members only."

The night of the dinner came, and at one point a waiter tapped my grandfather on the shoulder to offer him a drink. Prescott turned around to find Uncle Lou in a waiter's suit, working at the dinner!

★   ★   ★

Years later, in 1940, while Dad was in his junior year at Andover, he got a bad staphylococcus infection in his arm that nearly killed him—there was no penicillin available in those days. According to his sister, Nan, Dad would have graduated at age sixteen but for his six-week stay at Massachusetts General Hospital and a long recovery afterward.

The headmaster called Dad's parents and suggested he repeat

the year, so Dad spent a fifth year at Andover and graduated at age seventeen. This gave him more time for sports, as well as an easier year in terms of his classes. Dad became captain of the baseball team and of the soccer team, and was manager of the basketball team. (That is, until one day when he was shooting baskets and the coach, Frank "Deke" DiClementi, turned to Dad and said, "Forget being manager—I think I can use you on the team.)"

"That year was the making of George, a changing point," Aunt Nan said years later. "It was a brush with death, brush number one. It was also his fifth year at Andover, where he was the great man—not The Great I Am, but he grew into this great leader on the campus. He was captain of soccer and captain of baseball and did wonderfully in his studies. People admired him. I was terribly popular for a while—everybody wanted to come to our house because they might run into George."

By the way, what Aunt Nan means by "The Great I Am" is a sort of family shorthand we have. "Nobody likes the big I Am, George," my grandmother would say to him. "Don't be talking about yourself." Or, "There were too many 'I's' in that sentence."

Once, Dad told his mother that he'd scored three goals in soccer. She replied, "That's nice, George, but how did *the team* do?" This grew out of a New England Yankee sense of modesty, and in Dad it evolved into a reluctance to speak in the first person, and eventually into a revulsion against appearing to brag in any way or make himself the center of attention.

It's why, years later, he's never written his own memoirs.

Chapter 2

A WARTIME WEDDING

"When you read about the fact that he survived and the others didn't, it's almost like there was some divine hand in what was happening."

—**Norman Schwarzkopf**

On December 7, 1941, Dad was walking across the Andover campus with friends when he heard the news that the Japanese had bombed Pearl Harbor and killed some 2,400 Americans. Like everyone, he was stunned.

In the two years since the German invasion of Poland in 1939, the United States had walked the line of neutrality—and the debate over our role in the emerging conflict had divided our country. After the ninety-minute attack in Pearl Harbor, however, the American people were totally, immediately united. The next day, President Franklin Roosevelt asked for—and the U.S. Congress passed—a declaration of war against the aggressors.

The "sleeping U.S. behemoth" had finally been stirred awake.

Dad was not unique in that he was outraged and wanted to enlist immediately—to join the fight, to do his part. Because he was not yet eighteen, however, he couldn't enlist, so he had to remain in school until graduation. He was so eager to join the fight, in fact, that for a brief period he considered signing up in the Royal Canadian Air Force, where one could get in sooner.

Another fateful event took place a few weeks after Pearl Harbor when Dad went to a Christmas dance with some pals and spotted an attractive girl across the room.

"She was very beautiful," Dad said of the first time he saw Mom. "She stood out—the most beautiful girl out there on the dance floor. I asked somebody who that was. They said, 'Barbara Pierce, from Rye.' And I said, 'Well, I'd sure like to meet her.' She was wonderful."

According to Mom, Dad "breezed in, asked me to dance. My brother, Jim [Pierce], cut in immediately—never danced with me once in his life before—and said, 'Aren't you Poppy Bush? Do you want to play in a basketball game on Thursday night? The prep school boys against the locals?' And the end of the story is, the locals whipped them, but I was so mad at Jimmy Pierce. He said [to Dad], 'When you get rid of her, come over and talk to me.' I mean, it was really terrible."

Mom went to the game that Thursday night, and she and Dad instantly hit it off.

Spike Heminway grew up with Mom in Rye, New York, and he remembers, "Everybody in Westchester County was after her. She was the most popular girl, the best-looking girl you've ever seen in your life. And I'd always heard about George Bush. Then he comes in and sweeps her off her feet, and off they go."

Back at the Bushes' house, Dad's sister, Nan, heard all about Mom. "He said he met a wonderful girl last night, and she was beautiful and funny." She was in a green dress for the holidays, with beautiful brownish-red hair. As their relationship grew, according to Uncle Johnny, "they would just laugh about everything and he would kid her. She always has been a great audience for him, because it takes great confidence to be funny."

Looking back on their courtship, Dad remembered the things he loved most about her: "Her sense of humor. As my mother would say, she was interested in the other guy. She had a great propensity for friendships. She had good friends around, and loved sports."

He added with a smile, "She has strong opinions now. She didn't used to have that so much when she was younger. She didn't express her opinions like she does these days."

As the spring came and Dad was finishing up at Andover, he asked Mom to the senior prom. She wrote him a note in response, from South Carolina, where she was in boarding school:

Dear Poppy,

I think it was perfectly swell of you to invite me to the dance and I would love to come or go or whatever you say. I wrote Mother yesterday or the day before and rather logically, I haven't heard from her, but I'm sure she is going to let me come or go, etc. I'm really all excited, but scared to death, too. If you hear a big noise up there, don't worry, it's just my knees knocking.

"We were starry-eyed puppies," Mom recalled. There were many trips to Rye to call on her. Junie O'Brien, a fellow player on the Andover baseball team, remembers a lull in practice one day when he and Dad were standing just off first base. Dad reached into his right pocket and produced a photo of Mom to show him.

Junie said, "I told him she was a winner, and he said, 'You're telling me. I'm going to marry her.' "

The families heard more and more about each other, and the two fathers got to know each other on the commuter train into New York City, where Marvin Pierce, Mom's father, was president of McCall's Publishing.

After Pearl Harbor, Dad's father went to Andover because my father was thinking of joining the navy. "His father begged him to go on to college and he didn't," Mom recalled. "His father said, 'You can go for a year to Yale like everyone else.' But everyone else from different schools did [enlist], and George went right in. You felt like you just had to do your part."

A few days after graduation from Andover—on his eighteenth birthday, June 12, 1942—Dad enlisted in the navy. He remembers how his father took him down to Penn Station in New York to put him on the train, and told him to write his mother. It was very difficult both for Dad and for his father, who had served in World War I. In fact, my grandfather helped launch the USO organization and became its first chairman at the request of President Roosevelt in 1941.

The navy needed pilots, and had recently changed its requirement for aspiring aviators. They'd only need a high school diploma, rather than completion of two years of college. Dad gladly signed up to be a pilot. "I think I always wanted to fly, and the navy always appealed to me," he told me. "I wanted to go into combat; everyone did back then. It was one of the best decisions I ever made, and yet I was only seventeen at the time."

It was during that first year that he was gone, while he was in basic training in Chapel Hill, North Carolina, that my parents got "secretly" engaged. Actually, my mother said, "Everybody in America knew, except we didn't think so."

They had gotten engaged in the fall during a visit to Kennebunkport and tried to keep it a secret, because they thought people would think they were too young. But as Mom's brother, Jimmy, said to her, "You've got to think we're idiots. I mean, one look at the two of you."

Eventually, their secret came out when a classmate of Mom's at Smith College kept pressuring her to go out on blind dates with boys from Amherst College. Mom kept declining, and finally, she had to admit she was engaged to Dad. She called him and explained, and they decided to "go public."

In 1943 when Dad's ship, the USS *San Jacinto*, was commissioned, Mom and Ganny traveled together on the train to Philadelphia for the ceremony. "Do you like diamonds?" Ganny asked her, and it began to dawn on Mom that Ganny was bringing an engagement ring to Dad. (It turned out to be a star sapphire with diamonds around it.) They had a good time together, and Aunt Nan remembers Ganny returning home and saying, "That girl could talk to absolutely anybody."

The Bush family liked my mom from the start.

"I think they thought, 'We want him happy,' " Mom recalled, and they saw in her that same sense of humor we all enjoy. When Dad told his father of his intentions to marry Mom, Prescott's eyes welled up with tears, one of the few times my father ever saw him cry.

She was only seventeen in the fall of 1942, and Aunt Nan says, "She was just so pretty and tall and slender and funny. They were a twosome." Mom remembers going to visit Dad, who was the youngest among the navy pilots in training. "He said, 'Please tell everyone you're eighteen.' You know how many people asked me how old I was?" she asked me, laughing. "No one."

Shortly after, Dad was shipped out to the Pacific with Mom's name painted on the side of his plane, and their engagement— secret or not—lasted for over two years. "It was very scary when he went, very scary," Mom remembered. "It was particularly terrible for his mother."

The family prayed for Dad at every meal during grace, and at church. And, of course, Ganny would read his letters out loud when they arrived.

★　★　★

After flight training, Dad was assigned to Torpedo Squadron (VT-51) where he flew an Avenger (TBM). He was also VT-51's aerial photographic officer in September 1943—and in the spring of 1944, his squadron was based aboard the newly commissioned *San Jacinto*. The *San Jac* was part of Task Force 58 that participated in operations against Marcus and Wake islands in May and then in the Marianas during June, which included one of the largest air battles of the war. Returning from that mission, in fact, Dad was forced to make a water landing. The crew survived, but the plane did not.

For his book *The Greatest Generation,* Tom Brokaw spoke with

Dad about his obligation as an officer to read the outgoing mail of
the enlisted men, so that no sensitive military information would
be compromised. Dad recalled, "As I did my duty and read the
other guys' mail, I learned about life—about true love, about
heartbreak, about fear and courage, about the diversity of our
great country. The sailors would ask about the harvest or fishing
or the heat in the cities. When I would see a man whose letter I
had censored, I would look at him differently, look at him with
more understanding. I gained an insight into the lives of my ship-
mates, and I felt richer [for the experience]."

The first casualty in Dad's squadron was his best friend and
roommate, Jim Wykes. Jack Guy, who was also in the squadron,
explained to me, "Jim went out and just never returned. And we
never could find him, never could see him. He just left the radar
screen, that was it."

As part of his duties as an officer, Dad often wrote to the families of crew members who were missing or killed in the line of
duty. When Dad wrote to the Wykes family to give them the awful
news, Anna Wykes, Jim's mother, wrote back to Dad:

> The Good Lord answered our prayers. We prayed and hoped
> that Jimmy's roommate or one of his friends would write to us.
> Nothing in the world could bring us more comfort than receiving
> your letter . . . My heart was very sad and it ached and pained. I
> have lost hope of ever seeing Jimmy again . . . Your sincere friend-
> ship and your faith in him brightened things for me. I will remem-
> ber you in my prayers—I asked the Lord to give you health and
> strength, protect you always, and bring you home safe. I shall never
> forget you.

In the Brokaw book, Dad also remembers an incident when he
was standing on the deck of the aircraft carrier when a plane made
a bad landing. As the plane spun out of control, a crew member
standing nearby got chopped up by the propeller. A leg landed
right next to Dad. A chief petty officer sprang into action, ordering

the sailors to swab the deck and get ready for the next incoming plane. Dad still remembers the officer as someone who was able to take charge and function despite enormous stress.

In August, the *San Jac* launched operations against Japanese forces in the Bonin Islands, a volcanic island group five hundred miles south of Tokyo. Dad flew a few sorties as the operation began.

Then came September 2, 1944.

The first eyewitness account ever published of what happened that day came from Lieutenant (jg) Nathaniel Adams. In it, Lieutenant Adams talked about the mission on that hazy morning to knock out key Japanese radio towers on Chi Chi Jima, about 150 miles north of Iwo Jima. Four Avengers went in to bomb the communications center, followed by several Hellcat fighters with machine guns to protect the bombers from antiaircraft fire:

> The sky was now filled with smoke from the exploding shells. In this caldron of fire, Bush took a fatal hit just before he was set to release the four 500-pound bombs. He continued his 200-mile-an-hour dive on the target and released his volley of explosives. I could see his engine flame and then spread to the fuel tanks housed in the wings. As he leveled off and cleared the target area, I followed from above. His plane continued to spew black smoke. It was apparent that the shrapnel had punctured a fuel line. "Get out," I thought, "before you blow up." Our planes were rigged not only to hear communication between planes, but any talk between the pilots of the torpedo bombers and their crews. Just then I heard, "Hit the silk! Hit the silk!" It was George telling Ted White and John Delaney [his wingmen] to bail out. ["Hit the silk" refers to their silk parachutes, and was an expression for evacuating.]
>
> A tremendous amount of black smoke and fire continued to trail from the stricken plane. Even through the smoke, I could see one of the crewmen jump through the exit door near the rear of the plane. George actually was able to turn the plane for that moment to shield the jumper from the slipstream. Whoever jumped had a faulty chute. He drew one of those streamers that furled and never opened. I could see him all the way down as he fell to his death. Whether it was Ted White or John Delaney, we will never

know. One thing I do believe is that whoever remained in the plane was dead. He had time to get out. Shrapnel could very well have killed him during the dive to the target.

Next, Lieutenant Adams described how Dad escaped the burning plane just before it hit the water and exploded in a ball of fire. He was able to get free of his ripped parachute before landing in the ocean, and swam over to a little raft that had been his seat cushion in the cockpit:

> His problems were still far from over. The wind and the tide were moving the raft toward Chi Chi Jima. I think he was only a couple of miles off the south shore. About that time, I saw a number of these little Japanese boats take off from the beach. I guess they were about twenty feet long. My God, it looked like a flotilla coming out to capture George. The raft was drifting right towards his captors. They were closing fast. That's when our four Hellcats took action. I tell you, we dove with all of our 50-caliber guns blazing in each plane and just blew at least a dozen of those boats right out of the water. The rest of them fled for shelter. That put a stop to that threat in one big hurry. It was a hell of a shoot-out.

While Dad had been told about the possibility of being taken prisoner by the Japanese, the odds were against it. Very few airmen ended up as POWs. (It was more common in the army, with soldiers on the ground.) But clearly, Lieutenant Adams was concerned about those boats heading toward Dad for a reason. Years later, rumors of Japanese atrocities were found to be true. In fact, the commanding Japanese general on Chi Chi Jima gave his soldiers the following order: "Worship your emperor with a deep bow. Practice with your bayonet; open the heart and the lungs and let the enemy bleed. As they take their last breath, take out the sword and behead them."

Adams reported that "in some cases the officers took out the livers of selected victims and participated in cannibalistic ceremonies to prove their worthiness as soldiers of the Empire."

Dad wrote back to Lieutenant Adams, thanking him, for "without your covering support I would undoubtedly have been captured, executed and cannibalized." Sure enough, in a war crimes tribunal held after the war, the Japanese officer in charge of Chi Chi Jima was tried and executed, and among the charges was cannibalism. (Dad observed in hindsight that since he only weighed 160 pounds at the time, "I'd have been like an hors d'oeuvre for the poor guy.")

After the fighter planes took out the small flotilla of Japanese boats heading toward Dad, the pilots were concerned they'd run out of fuel, so they returned to their carrier as it headed south to join Admiral William F. "Bull" Halsey's Task Force 38. A periscope came up in the shark-infested waters near Dad's raft, and years later he joked that he "broke the world's hundred-yard freestyle paddling record" as he paddled his raft toward the American submarine that surfaced. The crew of the *Finback* submarine soon rescued him, along with several other pilots from other runs. The remarkable thing about this is that when he was pulled onto the submarine deck from the water, a crew member filmed the rescue.

The next day, Dad typed a letter to his parents telling them of his second brush with death. He sounded so young—he was only twenty—and so worried about his friends John Delaney and Ted White: "There was no sign of Del or Ted anywhere around . . . It bothers me so very much. I did tell them [to evacuate] and when I bailed out I felt that they must have gone, and yet now I feel so terribly responsible for their fate so much right now. Perhaps as the days go by it will all change and I will be able to look upon it in a different light."

Once he received Dad's letter, my grandfather wrote a long letter to Ted White's mother, saying, "Your son was such a wonderful lad and I am so glad that my boy knew him. His letters spoke so highly of him previous to this disaster; and also, of course, his letters written on the submarine are just heart-breaking . . . I can't possibly tell you how unhappy Dorothy and I are about Ted and how deeply we feel for you and your husband."

Dad also wrote to Mom: "I hope my own children never have to fight a war. Friends disappearing. Lives being extinguished. It's just not right. The glory of being a carrier pilot has certainly worn off."

Back then, Dad thought that his guilt about his friends would ease with time, but it didn't. I think it bothered him for years that somehow it was his fault or that there was more he could have done to save them. He has great difficulty—to this day, over sixty years later—talking about it with anyone.

John Magaw, Dad's lead Secret Service agent for many years, immediately noticed Dad's difficulty in discussing this traumatic episode when asked about it early in the 1980 campaign. "I just sensed the emotion in him. So I made a mental note to myself: I'm going to call him wherever he is every year" on the anniversary of being shot down—September 2—"as long as he's alive and I'm alive."

As much as he doesn't like to talk about it, when I asked Dad, he said, "Certainly, you wonder why God spares your life. Why should my two crewmen be killed? And you wonder, why me? Why should my life be spared?"

After being rescued, Dad remembers sitting in the wardroom of the *Finback* with the other pilots while the Japanese dropped depth charges all around the sub. There was a steward as well—"the other guys were scared, but that guy was really panicked," he remembers. They were told to sit there and be still. The Japanese listened for any sound that would give away the sub's location. The real submariners, the ones with "ice water in their veins," weren't that worried about it; but to Dad, this was brush with death number three: "It was scarier for me than being shot at in a plane. I mean, in the airplane, you could control your destiny to a degree and you could see the puffs of smoke, and you knew what the problem was. But in that submarine, we just sat—of course, we hadn't been through it, we hadn't been trained as submariners."

They were just kids, and they didn't have ice water in their veins.

★ ★ ★

Back home, Dad's family heard he had been rescued before they heard he had been shot down. But the confusion was nerve-racking as they all waited for news of his condition. Mom was very distracted at Smith College and enlisted her father's help with teachers: "My poor father . . . was a self-made man, worked his way through college, Phi Beta Kappa, brilliant . . . he would call Ms. Corwin, the student adviser, and say, 'Barbara's fiancé is overseas; and she's so worried . . .' Long story short: I didn't go to class much."

The *Finback* eventually dropped Dad back on Midway Island. He flew in a transport plane to Oahu and then hitchhiked out to rejoin his squadron aboard the *San Jac,* operating over the Philippines. Jack Guy, Dad's friend in the squadron, told me, "When he went back to Hawaii to be reassigned, they gave him the option to go back to the United States or to go back to his old squadron out in the middle of the Pacific and finish up the tour there. He elected to come back out to where we were. We thought he was absolutely crazy. Of course, we told him that. But it showed us this guy had a real dedication to duty."

Then, later, came the news everyone wanted to hear: Dad sent a letter to his parents on December 1, 1944, saying he was coming home. He asked his mother to tell my mom to set the wedding date, and also very politely asked his mother for help planning the honeymoon, saying he'd "hate to fail Bar in my initial effort as an efficient husband." He suggested to Ganny that "Cuba would be nice"—this was almost twenty years before the Cuban missile crisis, and Americans could still travel there freely—but they ended up going to Sea Island, Georgia, instead.

Dad arrived home on Christmas Eve, 1944.

"There were tears, laughs, hugs, joy, the love and warmth of a family in a holiday setting," he remembered. "No reunion could have been scripted more perfectly."

Two weeks after Christmas, on January 6, 1945, Mom and Dad were married in Rye, New York.

"I remember us all in our bridesmaid dresses—in green—and

Bar, beautiful, coming down the aisle wearing our family veil and George, so handsome in his uniform," recalled Aunt Nan. Everyone in the family attended the wedding.

They returned from their honeymoon to Connecticut. Mom recalls her early impression of her new father-in-law: "His [Dad's] father was scary. He was six foot four, a very successful businessman." She remembers sitting at the Bush home as a newlywed, chatting with my grandfather Prescott as she was smoking a cigarette. My grandfather said to her, "Did I ever tell you that you could smoke?" Mom was so taken aback by that, she blurted out, "Well, did I marry *you*?"

My grandfather burst out laughing.

Not long after that, Dad was assigned to a new squadron, and my parents were stationed in a number of posts—Florida, Michigan, Maine, and finally Virginia. Dad's new squadron, VT-153, had received orders to go back to the Pacific, but before they were deployed, World War II officially ended, on August 15, 1945. It was VJ Day, and the streets of Virginia Beach—where my parents were stationed—filled with cheering crowds. "Boy, there was some jubilation around this world," Mom remembered.

She and Dad decided to return to New England so my father could enroll at Yale as part of the largest freshman class in the school's history—about eight thousand students, five thousand of whom were veterans, many of them married.

Dad met a fellow veteran named Lud Ashley there, and eventually, they both became members of a secret society called Skull and Bones. When I asked if people at Yale were aware that Dad had been shot down, Lud explained, "You couldn't turn around at Yale without bumping into guys who had had experiences of that kind. It wasn't big news because that's what happens in a war. Of the fifteen guys in the Bones club we were in, seven were pilots. I'm not sure if five of them weren't shot down somewhere along the line. Your dad's situation was one that most of us said, 'Well, he's lucky to get out alive.' That's the way we thought of it."

That's the way Dad thought of it, too—not that he was some

sort of war hero, but lucky to be alive. To this day, he feels that the true war heroes are the ones who give their lives.

★ ★ ★

While Dad and Mom were at Yale, Uncle Johnny was at a boarding school nearby at the time, not yet in college, and he remembers how much they enjoyed those years. "Life was really fun. They were living in an infinitesimally small apartment at 37 Hillhouse Avenue, and I went and visited them, slept on the couch . . . they were the class of '48, and it was a great football team in the fall of '46, one of Yale's great football teams, and they had all these wonderful veterans playing—big, handsome, rugged guys—and they all knew your dad—all of them. All the couples, the married couples, all kind of centered around them at Yale."

I asked him why that was, why their house was the center of activity—full of football players, even though Dad played baseball and soccer, not football. Uncle Johnny answered, "He was enormously popular. He has that ability to make everybody else funny. It's a unique gift and it kind of centers around being unselfish. He has the ability to tell jokes, but he didn't tell as many jokes as he did create humorous situations in which others would participate."

Mom and Dad spent their weekends going to football games and parties—"we did go to chapel, too," Mom adds—and Mom watched Dad play soccer and baseball.

Soon Mom was pregnant with my brother George. She was working at the student bookstore and brought their dog Turbo to work. With the new baby coming, they knew they'd need to move across campus. "Turbo went to live with the Bushes when we moved," Mom said. "The place we moved to would not take dogs. Now, the place we had lived before wouldn't take babies, and we chose the baby. We decided that was better. We lived in the house with thirteen babies and eleven couples. Our baby, George Walker Bush, arrived on July 6, 1946."

The postwar conditions at Yale—overcrowded and hastily arranged for such a big incoming class of veterans—do sound pretty ramshackle. Three families shared one kitchen with my parents, and unfortunately, somebody in the crowd was obsessed with germs. According to Mom: "We were the mediators in the whole performance, and one would put their child out in the hall on the potty seat, and that just drove the germ person almost to have a stroke." She also remembered one very nice couple with whom they shared these very close quarters: "Half the dining room was our living room, and half the dining room was their bedroom. So we spent quite a lot of time knocking on the wall."

Dad's teammates on the baseball team made him captain in 1948, after Yale had played in the first baseball College World Series in June 1947. So in the spring of 1948, when Babe Ruth presented a manuscript of his book to the Yale Library, Dad, as captain of the baseball team, accepted the manuscript on behalf of the university. Uncle Bucky went up for the occasion and remembers that the Babe looked "real sick."

Dad told one reporter later, "I thought I'd died and gone to heaven," which is what happened to Babe Ruth only a few months later (on August 16, 1948).

Babe Ruth's teammate Lou Gehrig had died a few years earlier, in 1941, and was another of Dad's favorite players. Years later, when a postage stamp was issued in Gehrig's name, Dad sent one to his oldest grandson, Jeb's son George P., with a note that read, "This guy was my baseball hero. Of good character, his decency showed through. He was a team leader—courageous and able. He was a dependable guy—his teammates all respected him . . . You're a Lou Gehrig kind of guy. Devotedly, Gampy."

Dad received academic credit for parts of his military training and graduated Phi Beta Kappa in 1948 after two and a half years. Then he had to decide what to do about a career. He had an offer from his father's Wall Street firm, Brown Brothers Harriman. In fact, Roland Harriman went to my grandfather and said, "We want to make an exception to our policy about nepotism, and we want your permission to talk to your son George." Prescott Bush said okay, but when they asked Dad if he'd like to have a job there, he politely declined.

"He wanted to *do* something," Uncle Johnny later explained. "He'd been in the service and he'd been in all of the challenges that that offered. And he saw himself sitting behind a desk and balancing somebody's checking account. He just didn't want to do it." While Dad did not follow his father into banking, years later, of course, he did follow his father's example by going into public service.

Mom thinks he made the decision long before graduation, while he stood night watch on the *Finback* after being rescued in the Pacific. "Your dad did not want to work in a bank. He wanted to work with something he could put his hands on . . . He decided that on the submarine when at night he'd be on duty looking at the stars. He decided that he wanted to be able to touch it. And so Neil Mallon offered him a job to be trained by Dresser Industries. He could start out at Ideco, a subsidiary of Dresser that sold oil equipment in Odessa, Texas," she said.

Dad took the offer—and soon two future presidents and a First Lady were bound for the frontier.

Chapter 3

GO WEST, YOUNG MAN

> "Midland doesn't have any mountains, it doesn't have any
> oceanfronts, it doesn't have any fishing holes or other similar
> niceties; what it did have were caring transplanted citizens, like
> the Bushes, who pitched in on every effort, from the Boy and
> Girl Scouts to the United Way and most everything in between.
> You can do a lot in a small town if you are willing, and the
> Bushes were—in spades."
> —**Martin Allday,** Dad's first campaign manager

Mom and Dad, with George in tow, took Uncle Neil's advice to
heart when he said, "What you need to do is head out to Texas and
those oil fields. That's the place for ambitious young people these
days." (Years later, Dad would also give credit to Horace Greeley,
the *New York Tribune* publisher whose famous advice to the unem-
ployed was, "Go west, young man.")

By the time he arrived in Texas—via the red 1947 Studebaker
Dad's parents gave him as a graduation gift—he was ready for the
challenge of making his way in the oil business. Dad started at
Dresser Industries as an equipment clerk, which he later described
as "the very bottom of the corporate ladder." He painted oil well
machinery and swept warehouses. He had come out to Odessa

alone, sending for Mom and one-year-old George as soon as he found them all a place to live—which turned out to be a small two-room duplex with a bathroom they shared with their neighbors.

One neighbor—a thirty-eight-year-old woman, who had a twenty-year-old daughter and a three-year-old grandchild—made her living by "questionable means," entertaining a steady stream of men all hours of the day and night.

Dad explained, "I think she was selling her favors and she'd forget to unlock the bathroom, so we would be locked out and we'd have to pound on the door . . . 'Just a minute!' She was not a charming person but not altogether unfriendly. It was a broadening experience. Here comes Barbara Bush out of Rye, New York, and me out of our sheltered environment in Greenwich, Connecticut—except for the navy—and you're knocking on the door, hoping some lady of ill repute lets you into your own bathroom."

Mom noted that they considered themselves lucky in that several of their other neighbors only had outhouses. I guess everything's relative!

Dad worked hard, and as he did, he was absorbing crucial information about the oil business. He wrote home to one friend that "fortunes can be made in the land end of the oil business, and of course can be lost . . . If a man could go in and get just a few acres of land which later turned out to be good he would be fixed for life."

He liked Odessa a lot, he wrote later. "There was an unspoken community code that had to do with the value of a person's word. More often than not, a handshake was all that was needed to conclude a business deal."

After just a year in Odessa, however, Dad was transferred to a job with another Dresser subsidiary, meaning they were moving to California. While in California, they lived in Whittier, Huntington Park, Bakersfield, and Compton. During this time Mom was pregnant with Robin, and Dad was working seven days a week.

While they were in Bakersfield, Mom's brother, Jimmy Pierce, got engaged to Margy Dyer, and upon receiving word of it, Dad wrote to Margy to welcome her into the family. He enclosed a fake "proxy" for her to sign, voting for him as president of the P-I-L Club. It stood for the Pierce-In-Law Club, whose current president was Walter Rafferty, the husband of my mother's sister, Martha Pierce. Dad felt that Walter hadn't provided the kind of leadership that was needed in the club. "I feel under new vital leadership we might progress beyond all horizons . . . We could have uniforms, chartreuse T-shirts, with amber P-I-L in letters on the back and numbers on the front. We could wear 'em at Sunday lunch at the Pierces. We would form demolition squads to harass the unruly in-laws. See, there are thousands of possibilities IF we have the right leadership." He ended by saying that Mom and he were "hoping against hope" to get to the wedding, which they did.

But shortly after the wedding, tragedy struck. Mom's parents were in a horrible car accident, instantly killing her mother, Pauline. Her father was hospitalized, but he later recovered.

Mom had just been to Margy and Jim's wedding in Ohio, and her father advised her not to make the arduous trip home, for fear that something might happen to the baby. Mom took that advice and did not go to her mother's funeral. Dad was able to get the day off from work, and she spent the day with him and their friends the Jenkinses.

"I always wished I had gone home," Mom recalled. "My dad was in the hospital when the funeral service was held. My mother and I loved each other, but I was not her favorite. Mummy and Daddy had just moved into her dream house. She waited a year after they bought it while it was being made totally perfect. My mom always wanted more . . . She felt that the grass was always greener, and would talk about when her ship would come in. She died when her ship had come in. I have always felt comforted by that."

A few months later, Mom gave birth to her first daughter, Pauline Robinson Bush—named for her mother and nicknamed Robin—on December 20, 1949. "Your oldest brother was three and was looking forward to Christmas. He was a joy," she remembered, but "we had moved so much that year that I met the doctor for the first time on the night the baby was born." What a difficult time that must have been for my mother, only twenty-four years old, grieving for her mother, giving birth to her own daughter.

★ ★ ★

The following year, 1950, Dad transferred back to Texas to be a salesman for Ideco, the company he started out with in 1948. They settled in Midland and began making a life there for their growing family. Another friend and fellow Yale graduate, Earle Craig, recalls a group of young families that started socializing together, gathering on Sunday afternoons on the practice athletic field adjacent to Midland High School. The boys and men would play touch football while the girls and young mothers would spread blankets on the grass and gossip and cheer for their team. Mom used to push Robin in a beautiful perambulator, and four-year-old George would hold on to the pram's handle.

Uncle Bucky recalls how many friends they made: "He's always had a gazillion friends. I don't remember when he didn't. The only difference now is that they're famous actors and baseball players and presidents and prime ministers, which they didn't have in Midland, Texas."

He also remembers their ranch house on a nice suburban street that backed up to the Little League park. Uncle Bucky lived with my parents for a while, when George and Robin were little. Bucky would work in the oil fields as a roughneck on a drilling rig, from eleven o'clock at night until seven o'clock in the morning. He'd then go home to sleep and then head over to the park and umpire George's Little League games.

About that same time, the Midland touch football team Dad played on challenged a team from Lubbock to what became known as the Martini Bowl, for obvious reasons. One of Dad's friends, John Ashmun, remembers it well: "The Lubbock group . . . responded with eleven players, plus wives and others, riding to Midland in a beer-loaded bus. This conditioning as well as the highly prejudiced hometown refereeing . . . was the only means by which a Midland victory was claimed." Lubbock also brought three All-American football players, some of whom had gone pro—Bobby Layne, Glenn Davis, and Mal Kanter—but Midland prevailed. There was a barbecue afterward, and Mr. Ashmun remembers "we poured the Lubbockians back on the bus as great losers."

Mom and Dad went to many high school football games. Dad called the Odessa-Midland game "a total experience in itself." He later wrote about it for *America West* magazine: "Whole towns would travel by caravan to neighboring towns to settle bragging rights for the coming year. When the Odessa Broncos took on Abilene or Midland—there wasn't much point trying to talk about anything else."

He also helped coach my brother George's Little League team, the Cubs. Joe O'Neill, who was on my brother's team, says his mother could tell who was playing for the Cubs because they'd always have head injuries. He explained that my dad went out one time to the outfield during practice, "and as the ball would approach he would put his gloved hand behind his back, duck his head, and catch the ball in his glove behind his back. Naturally, we all thought this was the neatest thing and we all tried to imitate it. That is where the bloody scabs on the tops of our heads came in." The kids were getting beaned on the head while trying to catch the ball behind their backs, just like Dad had done.

★ ★ ★

In 1953, my brother Jeb was born. He was named John Ellis Bush, after my father's brother Johnny and my Aunt Nan and Uncle Sandy Ellis. (My brother's initials, JEB, became his nickname.) The year 1953 proved to be a bittersweet one, however, because the same year Jeb was born, three-year-old Robin was diagnosed with leukemia—which in that day was considered very much an exotic, and incurable, disease.

Mom remembers Jeb being a newborn, and Robin waking up one morning and saying, "I don't know what to do this morning. I may go out and lie on the grass and watch the cars go by, or I might just stay in bed." Mom didn't think that sounded like a normal three-year-old, so she took her to the pediatrician, who ran some tests and soon gave them the results: leukemia.

Dad explained to an interviewer years later, "I said, 'What does that mean?' The doctor said, 'Well, it means that she can't . . . she can't live. You can treat her, or you can let nature take its course.' So we treated her. She was very precious."

The diagnosis was bleak from the beginning, and almost immediately, Mom and Dad took Robin to Sloan-Kettering in New York for treatment. Mom stayed with Robin, and Dad commuted back and forth because of his business and of course to be home with George and Jeb.

Looking back, I don't know how they did it. But Dad's college buddy Lud Ashley was a tremendous friend to them. "Where I was working at Radio Free Europe," Lud remembered, "I was just a couple of blocks away from Sloan-Kettering, so I would go there . . . and see if the door to Robin's room was closed. If it was, well, then I figured something was going on in there, and I'd wander around to a nice waiting room overlooking the East River. I'd go out there for half an hour or so and then go check the room again. It was an easy thing to do."

Robin knew who Lud was, he said, "but in all truth, she was a sick little girl. Her eyes didn't sparkle or anything of that kind . . . she had things sticking out of her and really, she wasn't in good shape at all. It was really tough going for her."

"Lud came every night to the hospital," Mom remembered. "He would come up and check on Robin. And he was a huge friend, to a point that a nurse said, 'Well, I saw Mr. Bush last night.' I said, 'You did what?' She said, 'I saw Mr. Bush. He comes every night to visit the baby.' It was Lud; George was in Texas. A couple of times I caught him when I would go out on the porch to have a cigarette—and there would be Lud."

When Robin died on October 12, 1954, my parents gave her body to research. Years later, Dad would still remember that decision, writing about it in his presidential diaries. He recalled how, during Robin's sickness, the family next door—who had also lost a child—turned on the doctor when he asked if they'd donate the child's body to research, in order to save other children's lives. The family's grief came out as bitterness toward the doctor, and Dad and Mom learned a valuable lesson from it.

So after giving Robin's body to science, they stayed for a memorial service, then left immediately for Texas to be with George and Jeb. Later, the hospital unexpectedly contacted them about Robin's cremated remains, which Lud and Ganny went and picked up.

"It may seem strange," explained Lud, "but it didn't seem strange to me, and I don't think it seemed strange to Dorothy either. They had been through a hell of a lot, and it was just a little box of ashes that we're talking about and getting them into the ground. There had been a church service . . . I think they just thought they probably weren't quite up to that."

Robin's death had been devastating to my parents. So they all agreed that Lud and Ganny would bury Robin's ashes in the family plot in Connecticut, which was a tremendous comfort to Mom and Dad. Nearly half a century later, Mom and Dad re-buried Robin's ashes in the plot at the Bush Library in College Station, Texas, where they will be buried as well.

At the time, Dad was teaching a Sunday school class for teens in Midland. One friend, Melinda Cox, remembers that many times, "he arrived disheveled and unshaven, to teach his class. Having no time to prepare the lesson, he would share with these young people his feelings on life, death, war, faith, hope, and despair."

Somehow, after Robin's death, Dad and Mom got past their profound grief. I don't know how except that they turned to each other and clung tightly. They reminded themselves to count their blessings, and at the very top of that list was "faith, family, and friends."

"I have stopped asking 'why?'" Dad wrote to Lud Ashley afterward. "One thing I do know is that when one is worried or suffering or troubled that there are only two things that help—friendships and faith . . . We will have many wonderful memories of people who helped us, but none will exceed in my mind your many gestures of true friendship."

Someone once asked Dad how he reconciled a loving God with what had happened to Robin. He answered by quoting the Gospel: "Suffer the little children to come unto me." After a moment, he continued, "It was inexplicable how this could happen to an innocent child . . . but faith that God works in wondrous, mysterious ways. You get strength from that, strength to cope."

Years later, after I was born, Dad shared memories with me of Robin's brief life, and although I never knew her, she seemed to come to life before my eyes. Many nights my dad would tuck me in, and we would stay up talking about her. "Tell me about Robin," I would say. Tears would stream down his cheeks as he described her blond hair and her curls and how sweet Robin was. I'd ask about when she died, and he'd tell me about going up to New York where she was being treated at Sloan-Kettering and seeing her in the hospital.

He always ended by saying, "She's in heaven now."

More than telling stories, however, my parents turned their pain into something positive. Mom and Dad became active in raising money for cancer research, serving for years—and still do today—on the board of the M. D. Anderson Cancer Center in Houston, which is now a world leader in cutting-edge cancer research. There are several different programs and projects named for Robin, such as the Robin Bush Child and Adolescence Clinic at M. D. Anderson and the Robin Bush Children's Reading Room in the Barbara Bush Library in Spring, Texas.

Dad thinks that if Robin had been diagnosed with leukemia today she would have lived, because of the tremendous advances in cancer research. Childhood cancers like the one that killed Robin have shown some of the largest improvements in the last few decades—today, the five-year survival rate is over 75 percent.

Back in Robin's day, however, almost every childhood cancer was fatal.

My mother says that Robin's death instilled in both her and Dad a compassion that has stayed ever since. There is a sad part of my mom and dad that those of us who have never lost a young child could never understand. There is also a part of them that appreciates every man, woman, and child all the more because of their loss.

Right after I was born in 1959, my father, who was thirty-five at the time, went to meet me in the hospital nursery. Peering through the nursery window, his face pressed up against the glass, he looked at me and began to sob. Tears of happiness over my arrival, as well as, I'm sure, a wave of sadness over the loss of my sister, Robin, who had died six years earlier. Though he was blessed with four healthy sons, there was still a hole left by Robin's death in my father's heart. Mom only told me about this first meeting at the nursery on my birthday in 2005.

I had an inkling of it in an old letter my father had written to his mother, several years after Robin had died and before I was born. My grandmother had kept it until her own death in 1992, when it was given to my mother. It reads in part:

There is about our house a need. The running pulsating restlessness of the four boys as they struggle to learn and grow; their athletic chests and arms and legs; their happy noises, the world embraces them . . . all this wonder needs a counterpart. We need some starched crisp frocks to go with all our torn-kneed blue jeans and helmets. We need some soft blond hair to offset those crew cuts. We need a doll house to stand firm against our forts and rackets and thousand baseball cards. We need a cut-out star to play alone while the others battle to see who's "family champ." We even need someone . . . who would sing the descant to "Alouette," while outside they scramble to catch the elusive ball aimed ever roofward, but usually thudding against the screens.

We need a legitimate Christmas angel—one who doesn't have cuffs beneath the dress. We need someone who's afraid of frogs. We need someone to cry when I get mad—not argue. We need a little one who can kiss without leaving egg or jam or gum. We need a girl . . .

Eventually, they had me, their only living daughter. It's a strange thing to mourn someone you've never met, but my heart still feels heavy when I think of what might have been. As much as I love and cherish all four of my brothers, having a sister would have been wonderful. Nine years older than me, she would have been someone to share all sorts of things with, someone to look up to and seek the kind of advice that only a sister can give.

Perhaps because I grew up without Robin, I was overjoyed to find out that my second child, Ellie, was a girl. On an early prenatal visit, my husband, Billy LeBlond, left the room because the doctor was going to do an ultrasound, which would reveal the baby's sex, and he wanted it to remain a surprise. When he returned and I was smiling and crying, he instinctively knew the doctor had told me I was going to have a girl.

★ ★ ★

In the years after Robin's death, my parents continued to live in Midland. In 1955, my brother Neil Mallon Bush was born; and in 1956, Marvin Pierce Bush came along, named after Mom's father.

At one point, Dad wrote his father-in-law an update from Texas:

Georgie aggravates the hell out of me at times (I am sure I do the same to him) but then at times I am so proud of him I could die. He is out for Little League—so eager. He tries so very hard. It makes me think back to all the times I tried out. He has good fast hands and even seems to be able to hit a little. I got as much a kick out of watching him trying out as I do out of all our varied business efforts. Jeb, the clown, is fine and Neil brings us nothing but happiness. We still miss our Robin. At times Bar and I each find ourselves vividly recalling the beauty and charm of our little girl. Time has

not dulled these happy memories at all. I guess if we had Robin
now we would just have too much happiness.

Dad and Mom had their hands full—raising kids, coaching sports, and working in the oil industry. Dad had decided toward the end of 1950 that it was time to take what he had learned working for other people and put it to use for himself. He went to Uncle Neil Mallon and told him of his plans. Uncle Neil supported him in his decision and made suggestions for starting a new business in the royalty and production end of the oil business. Uncle Neil was quiet and kind, and brilliant in business. On his advice, Dad formed Bush-Overbey Oil Development Company with a neighbor, John Overbey.

As our family grew up, so did Dad's company. That same year, in fact, he merged his company with two brothers, Hugh and Bill Liedtke. The Liedtkes, from Tulsa, Oklahoma, were also a part of the young crowd in Midland who wanted in on the West Texas oil boom. They called their new company, which specialized in land deals, Zapata Petroleum Corporation.

Zapata hit it big when they struck oil at Jameson Field in Coke County, which is still producing oil today. Looking back on that find, Dad wrote, "It was my big break in the business world and the thing that permitted me to finance our kids' education and gave me the financial base to risk going into public life."

By 1954, at the age of thirty, Dad became cofounder and president of a third firm, Zapata Off-Shore, a contract drilling company which was a pioneer in experimental offshore drilling equipment. They named both companies Zapata after the 1952 movie *Viva Zapata!* in which Marlon Brando plays the Mexican revolutionary Emiliano Zapata.

Dad recently recalled the birth and growth of his offshore company:

> In a way, we were pioneers with Zapata Off-Shore, because we made a deal with a man named RG LeTourneau who had de-

signed a revolutionary three-legged offshore drilling rig with rack and pinion design. It was unique. A lot of companies took a look at Mr. Le Tourneau's plans and didn't want to take a chance on it.

That first rig was called the Scorpion, and it was built in Vicksburg, Mississippi, in 1956, along the Mississippi River. I'll never forget going there, and watching these giant earth-moving machines trying to push that rig into the river. It was such a spectacle, in fact, that the entire undertaking drew a crowd—some of whom laughed at what, for a time, appeared to be an exercise in futility. But we got it in the water at last, and took it down to New Orleans for a ceremonial launch, and then out into the Gulf she went.

On the Scorpion's very first location, however, one of the thirty-foot cans at the bottom of one of the legs collapsed. So what did we do? We called Mr. LeTourneau, mildly complaining about all of this. We got him out to the rig, where he stood on the deck to assess the situation. Then he took out a piece of chalk, made a few lines right there on the deck, and told his metal cutters to take out about fifteen feet of the can—basically to cut it in half—which did work.

And with that, we were on our way.

From there, we also pioneered a floating rig, converting a ship for drilling purposes. The first one was called Nola 1. This was in the days before GPS. You couldn't get any positioning to keep it on location, but it worked reasonably well. We sent it down to Mexico, where we did some drilling for PEMEX, the Mexican national oil company. You had to have partners there, so we formed a partnership called PERMARGO and drilled a well.

If you want to see the Nola 1 today, go down now to the Gulf of Campeche. Sixty years after the well was drilled, what's left of the rig is still on the beach, the victim of a hurricane.

After that, we drilled the deepest offshore well at the time between Cuba and the United States for Standard of Cal. For that project, we were based out of Marathon, Florida, in the Keys. The roughnecks were thrilled with this particular location, so we had no problem getting good hands on this project.

When we first started, however, we couldn't get circulation—presumably due to the porous, coral-like material we were dealing with just below the ocean floor. Finally, we got the well down and it was probably the most expensive dry hole that Standard ever drilled.

During my brief time in the offshore business, we also had some international projects of some note.

For example, we drilled the deepest offshore well at the time off the coast of Kuwait. This was also an over-the-side, floating rig effort. Shell drilled it, and we were partnered with Bill Clements's company, SEDCO. This too was a dry hole—but the pay was good, and in a sense we were pioneers there as well.

We also helped Japan Petroleum drill in the Sea of Japan. We had a consulting contract with them, and they came and swarmed all over our rigs in the Gulf of Mexico. Then we went over there as consultants, to help them drill their first hole. They had built a three-legged rig called the White Dragon that bore a tremendous resemblance to the Scorpion, and after they drilled that first well using our expertise we parted ways. They were very nice, and that also proved to be a good contract for us.

We sought contracts in Libya unsuccessfully—this was during the time before Qaddafi. I remember going there. We almost built a drilling rig in Greece. We drilled in Brunei, also partnering with SEDCO on that project. We drilled in Venezuela, in the Gulf of Paria. That was long before Hugo Chavez—the government was more hospitable in those days—then we moved the rig over to Trinidad, where we drilled for Rio Tinto in Trinidadian waters.

It was there in Trinidad that we ended up in a lawsuit with the company we were drilling for, and I went over to England with our lawyers to try and work something out. So much of our money was tied up in this deal, and I was so worried at the time, that I ended up passing out cold on the floor of a hotel room in London. I pushed the button for help, which was conveniently located down near the floorboards, and thankfully a man appeared because I had passed out stark naked—I was shaving at the time, and suddenly felt sick.

The valet came in and helped me into bed, then called a British doctor who said, "You have a bit of food poisoning, old boy." He prescribed that I drink a bit of Coca Cola—which is the exact opposite of what I should have been doing, since in reality I had a bleeding ulcer. The doctor missed the diagnosis.

Unaware of my true condition, I went to my meeting at Lloyd's of London that afternoon feeling very weak, where we conducted our business and I had a touch of sherry with lunch—again, not what I should have been doing given my situation. That night I flew back to New York on the slow-poke planes we had back then, transferred and flew to Dallas; and eventually I made my way back to Midland.

When I got to my doctor, he said, "You're lucky you didn't die. You have a hemorrhaging ulcer."

I learned how to deal with that condition, which was good when other agonizing events would come along—such as trying to be elected president of the United States.

Other memories from my oil days: We always dreaded the onset of hurricane season. Our rigs were not nearly as weather-ready as they are today. When Hurricane Betsy slammed into New Orleans in 1965, it totally wiped out a rig where we had a third of our assets tied up. This was before GPS. I went out with our drilling engineer and rented a little Piper to look for it, but it had completely vanished.

They did eventually find part of it using sonar, but by then it was of no use to us; fortunately, the insurance company made good.

In the fall of 2005, after President Clinton and I surveyed the havoc wreaked in New Orleans and across much of the Gulf Coast by Hurricane Katrina, I continued on to the small town of Cameron, Louisiana—which had been totally leveled by Hurricane Rita, which had followed in the wake of Katrina.

When I got there, I found one building left standing, which had been built with Works Progress Administration money back when Franklin D. Roosevelt was president of the United States. Every house, every warehouse, every library, every school, everything in Cameron was totally flattened. It was a very emotional experience for me, because my mind immediately shot back to 1957 and Hurricane Audrey, which nearly destroyed the town with a twelve-foot tidal surge that killed 600 people who were never told to evacuate. That was my first exposure as a drilling contractor to the devastation caused by hurricanes.

I saw dead bodies being taken out of homes and thrown on a

work boat. I saw animals stranded on tiny strips of land, totally trapped by the water. That experience left a real impression on me.

During this same time, Dad's father ran for, and won, a special election to the U.S. Senate from Connecticut.

Without question, my grandfather's example of public service throughout his life inspired Dad later to run for office himself. Wherever he went, whatever he did, Prescott Bush had plenty of admirers.

"Senators respected him, whether they agreed with him or not. He had friends on both sides of the aisle. He was a gentleman with great dignity," Dad says of his father's public service. During the early 1950s in Midland, Dad ran into Senator Lyndon B. Johnson at a hotel, meeting him for the first time. He introduced himself as the son of Connecticut Senator Prescott Bush, and Senator Johnson replied that Dad's father was the best thing that happened to the 83rd Congress. Dad boldly teased that he was glad to hear that from a staunch Democrat. "Your father and I don't like to be thought of as Republican or Democrat, rather as good Americans!" Johnson said.

Prescott Bush ran for the Senate after a successful career on Wall Street. He didn't start out in life as a politician—and neither did Dad or my brothers Jeb and George. It's just not the way our family looks at politics. My grandfather Prescott passed down the idea that you would only run for office after you had built a financial base—*then* it was time to give back and go into public service.

When Prescott Bush first ran for the Senate in 1950, he lost by only a thousand votes. Then the man who beat him in the Senate race and became senator from Connecticut, Brien McMahon, died in office. Prescott won the special election to fill that seat in 1952— the year Dwight Eisenhower was elected president in a landslide— and then served out the rest of McMahon's term and was reelected in 1956.

During that special election in 1952, a photographer arrived at the Bush home in order to take some campaign publicity shots of the family. Uncle Johnny remembers how the man suggested that Prescott and Dorothy pose in the kitchen together, with Dorothy preparing dinner and Prescott peeling potatoes. "That's a great idea," teased my dad, who was visiting from Texas. "Somebody show Dad where the kitchen is."

An interesting footnote: When I spoke to former Massachusetts governor Michael Dukakis for this book, he told me that while he was an undergraduate at Swarthmore, he attended the Washington semester program at American University. It was the fall of 1954, and he was in the gallery of the United States Senate the day that Senator Joe McCarthy was censured. He saw my grandfather Prescott stand up and speak out against McCarthy.

"That was not an easy vote, let me tell you, and he stood up," remembers Dukakis. "He was active in Planned Parenthood in the late forties in Connecticut, too. That was not an easy thing to do, in a heavily Catholic state. My sense of your family really started with him.

"Joe McCarthy may be the single most important reason I got into politics, because I couldn't stand the guy. I thought what he was doing was terrible," Dukakis continued. "I cannot exaggerate how tough it was for good people in politics to stand up and take this guy on. In some cases they were defeated—Millard Tydings was a Democratic senator from Maryland and he took McCarthy on and got beaten, because of it. It was hysteria sweeping the country. To have some folks—particularly on the Republican side of the aisle—stand up and say, 'This is wrong,' was very, very important."

My grandfather was a popular senator, known as an advocate for fiscal responsibility including the line-item veto for the president. He had other firm convictions as well.

"When he was first elected in 1952, he vowed to get out of the Senate before he turned seventy," said Dad. True to his word, in

1962, at the age of sixty-seven, Prescott Bush announced he would not seek reelection to the Senate and returned to Wall Street.

★ ★ ★

In 1959, right before I was born, Zapata Off-Shore split from Zapata Petroleum Company. My dad took control of Zapata Off-Shore, and our family moved to Houston. By this time, my mother was an expert in packing and moving a household, but with four boys and another child on the way, it couldn't have been easy.

Soon after arriving in Houston, Dad joined the Houston Country Club and paired up with a recent University of Texas Law School graduate named James Baker as his doubles partner in tennis. Another lifelong friendship—one that would help influence the course of global events in the decades to come—was forged.

Secretary Baker remembers with a smile how the tennis pro at the club, Hector Salazar, "would throw points so that it looked like we were doing a lot better than we were. He would play 'customer tennis,' and I'm not sure your dad ever really accepted the fact that that was happening. He's competitive."

Even if Dad was in denial over Hector's generosity on the court, Secretary Baker recalled how Dad more than returned the favor off the court.

"Hector didn't have much money, and the rest of us didn't have much either," Mr. Baker said. "Your dad decided we needed to get a pot together to buy a car for Hector. I remember thinking that I couldn't afford to pay the upkeep on my car, but anyway, I think he was successful in getting a car for Hector."

Dad passed the hat quietly among Hector's many fans so the tennis pro wouldn't have to take the bus to work anymore.

After settling into our new life in Houston, Dad began to actively pursue another interest of his—politics. Mom was not surprised when Dad agreed to run for Harris County Republican Party chairman in the fall of 1962 after a group of his contemporaries urged him to do so.

In the early 1950s, Dad had actually gotten his first taste of local politics in Midland. "There were no Republicans in those days in West Texas," Dad told an interviewer once. "I mean, there just weren't any. Barbara and I ran the first primary ever held in Midland, Texas. Republican primary. And as God is my witness, three people voted all day long in the primary: Barbara, me, and some drunk Democrat, saying, 'Is this where you go to vote?' "

The campaign was covered by, among other media outlets, a neighborhood newsletter hand-printed by my brothers: Jeb (ten) was editor, and Neil (eight) and Marvin (six) were reporters. "Mr. Bush is running for chairman of the Republican Party," the newsletter reported matter-of-factly. "He has four sons and a daughter. He urges everybody to vote for him."

Harris County, being very large, was comprised of more than 270 precincts, and Dad insisted on visiting every last one of them. That race marked the beginning of my father's signature style of campaigning—leave no hand unshaken, no letter unwritten, no speech unspoken.

Thankfully, it paid off: My brothers were able to report that "Mr. Bush wins unanimously as head of Harris County Republicans."

He was on his way.

Neighborhood Round-Up   Feb. 23, 63

Staff

Editor: Rob Kerr
Co-Editor: Jeb Bush
Reporter: Randy Svanson
Reporter: Stewart Bates
Reporter: Ren Thad Grundy
Reporter: Marvin Bush
Reporter: Neil Bush
Reporter: Bill Thawley

Sports

Prob. Winner	Margin	Prob. Loser
Baylor	6	Arkansas
Loyala Chicago	10	Houston
Texas	3	S.M.U.
Texas A&M	13	T.C.U.

Games of Sat.

Games of Tues.

S.M.U.	3	Arkansas
Texas A&M	7	Baylor
Texas Tech	4	T.C.U.

Features

Doug Osborne, who is coach and teacher in 5th grade Math at St. Johns, is going to be the Rice Baseball coach for the 1963 season. We hope he helps the Rice team a bit.

LISTEN!!

Boys and girls from 5 years of age to 12 years can enter a Duncan Top Contest! It will be held at 283 Maple Valley in the Driveway, Saturday, March 1, 1963, at 2:00 is when it will be held. The winner will receive a free Duncan Top!

Newcomers

New Neighbors

The La Rues, who live on Broad Oaks, have moved in. They have 2 children.

The Galaghers are building a house on the corner of Broad Oaks and Briar Drive. They have 5 children.

The DeMontronds have moved in. They have 3 boys.

A Joke

AMP! Something's gone wrong with my old shaving brush.

LITTLE BILL! That's funny. It worked perfect yesterday when I painted my bike with it.

Adds?

For 5¢ you can fill this space, SU-2/2.44

Mr. Bush wins, unanimously as head of Harris County Republicans,
¡Buna Bs!

For the man who has everything
¡Buna Bs! call SU-2.44

The staff of the Neighborhood Round-Up was able to report that Dad was elected chairman of the Harris County Republican Party.

Chapter 4

JUMPING INTO POLITICS

"That's one that his mother taught him: never gloat when you win. When you don't gloat when you win, you don't tend to pout when you lose. There's a fine balance in life and he found that balance."

—Alan Simpson

My earliest memory of my father goes back to when I was five years old, in 1964. After serving as Harris County Republican Party chairman, he was running for the U.S. Senate from Texas against the incumbent, Senator Ralph Yarborough. Yarborough was a legend in Texas, out of the liberal wing of the Texas Democrats. There had been a split among the state Democrats in those days—in fact, President John F. Kennedy had gone down to Dallas to try to patch things up on that fateful day in November 1963. Yarborough was there in Dallas for the president's visit, and many believe that his ongoing feud with right-wing Democrats led to Yarborough sitting in the second car, rather than up front with the president in the first car. Conservative Governor John Connally was in the president's car, and he, too, was shot that day but survived.

Yarborough had been elected the junior senator from Texas in

1957, joining Lyndon B. Johnson, who was the senior senator. Smilin' Ralph, as everyone in Texas called him, had a reputation for aligning himself with the national party rather than with his colleagues from Texas. As a Republican, my father saw an opening as Yarborough continued to distance himself from the moderate-to-conservative state Democratic Party. Of course, I don't remember this firsthand; I only learned about it as an adult. All I knew at the time was that Dad was running for Senate.

I do remember my parents being very busy and there always being a lot of people in and out of our house. There seemed to be a lot of hustle and bustle, things moving very quickly from a small child's point of view. I also remember photographs being taken of us children with a baby elephant—a live baby elephant and we were sitting on it! As a five-year-old girl, getting to ride on top of a baby elephant was like living a dream. I didn't even know what the Republican Party was, much less that the elephant was a symbol of the GOP and a donkey the Democrats.

At one point that fall, my brother Marvin remembers seeing Dad's smiling face on a billboard. He felt proud, confused, a little intimidated—and for the first time realized that maybe "our lives might be different from the other kids in school."

Marvin also remembers walking into our house on Briar Drive in Houston in 1964 and seeing "bodies all over the place." Of course, he meant *live* bodies—campaign volunteers making posters in just about every room. There was a core group that came over to the house pretty regularly to work on the campaign, usually on weekends, drawn by Dad's charisma as well as the free burgers and hot dogs my parents supplied.

The Black Mountain Valley Boys out of Abilene, Texas, usually joined Dad on the bus during that campaign. They would go into small towns, set up on their flatbed truck, and play music. Then Dad would get off the bus and make speeches to whoever had gathered.

In the end, my father lost the election. My brother George, who was eighteen at the time, was driving to the "victory" party when he heard on the radio that Dad had lost. He remembers feeling devastated. It's something that every political family must learn to cope with—the disappointments that go with the territory.

For his part, my dad was disappointed but remained optimistic. He told us all we'd win the next time around.

I could sense the tension, and I remember all the unhappy faces. As a five-year-old, I couldn't possibly understand that he made quite a credible showing given that Lyndon Johnson was the 1964 Democratic presidential nominee running against Republican Barry Goldwater, in the aftermath of President Kennedy's assassination. Having Johnson at the top of the ticket certainly didn't hurt the Texas Democrats, nor did the fact that Johnson was the heavy favorite. Dad, as a relative newcomer, could be proud of how well he had done.

A week after the election, Dad wrote to Richard Nixon, who had been the losing Republican candidate for president in 1960 against John Kennedy. Nixon had campaigned for Dad and then returned to his New York law firm, when Dad wrote to him: "We got whipped, and whipped soundly, but out of the gloom on November 3 there are some bright spots." He pointed out the magnitude of the Johnson landslide, and its long coattails in Texas. Johnson beat Goldwater by some 700,000 votes, but Yarborough beat Dad by only 300,000. The Bush campaign, moreover, polled over 1.1 million votes, the most any Republican in Texas had ever gotten until then. He thanked Nixon for his campaign visit, adding, "You really got under Ralph's skin, and he kept going around after this visit saying 'I really am effective' and 'my colleagues really do like me.' In fact, he ran in a few left-wing colleagues to prove his point."

As much as Dad loved running for office, the people he had met in Texas were even more important to him. Here's a letter I recently received from Bessie Liedtke, the wife of one of Dad's business partners at Zapata, describing what happened on election night:

This is from my heart. My mother and I were very, very close. She died the very day George H. W. Bush lost the senatorial election to Ralph Yarborough. He took the time to call and console me about

my mother, and this was a time when he had to be very disap-
pointed about his own loss. He probably does not remember doing
this, but this speaks volumes to me about the kind of man he is and
I shall never forget it.

Dad returned to Zapata after the election, and in September of
the following year, 1965, Hurricane Betsy barreled into the Gulf of
Mexico. The oil industry sustained over $100 million in damages
from the storm, $5.7 million of which was due to the loss of a
highly successful Zapata offshore drilling barge called Maverick.
While three other Zapata rigs survived the storm, Maverick vanished in the hurricane without a trace. This was very upsetting
news to Dad, because Maverick's disappearance meant the loss of
a major drilling contract, as well as plans for a proposed merger.

Taylor Blanton, a longtime friend of our family, expanded on
Dad's recollections of that storm and remembered visiting with
Mom when Dad returned from looking for the rig. "I remember
him saying it was impossible for this rig to have just disappeared
completely, but they had flown back and forth over the area until
they were sure it was not there, and had just disappeared underwater. No shouting, no cursing, no anger—just dejection and sadness
at losing something so vital to Zapata and to his business future,"
Taylor told me.

Taylor became a fixture at our house during his college years,
and he remembers Jeb, Neil, and Marvin skinny-dipping on hot
summer nights in our pool in Houston. "When your parents
wanted them to get out and go to bed, your dad would yell, 'Here
come the Vanderhof girls!' and the boys would grab towels and
run inside" to avoid being seen by the neighborhood girls.

Taylor also remembers how Dad and Mom performed many
kindnesses behind the scenes, ones that few people know about to
this day: When a friend lost her life savings in a scam, they gave her
money to replenish her lost nest egg; when a local businessman's
company began to fail, they gave him financial help; when the vice
chairman of the county Republicans suffered a cerebral hemor-

rhage and began to have financial troubles, Mom and Dad stepped in to help. And when Taylor graduated from college, practically penniless, Mom and Dad surprised him with a VW Beetle. I remember being in the garage when he found the car with a giant card on it, signed by all of us.

★   ★   ★

After what he calls his "spectacular lack of success" in the 1964 Senate race, Dad decided to run for Congress in 1966 to represent the 7th District. This time, he won against Frank Briscoe.

It was during this race that Don Rhodes reappeared in our lives. Don was working as a night clerk at a convenience store and first began to volunteer in his free time for Dad's unsuccessful Senate race—he'd do all the "grunt work" that no one else would do, such as going to the post office, posting yard signs, and checking the mailing lists. When Dad lost the 1964 race, Don disappeared. But when Dad announced his second bid, Don came back, this time to be hired full-time. He has remained one of Dad's most loyal friends and employees.

"He's been with me ever since, and now he's part of our family," Dad says.

It was during these years of campaigning in Texas, when my brothers and I were very young and my parents had to spend hours away from home, that Paula Rendon came into our lives as well. Actually, it was the year I was born, 1959, that my mother answered an ad in the newspaper seeking a sponsor for a woman who wanted to come to the United Sates and work. Paula came from Cuernavaca, Mexico, where her husband had left her with three small children to raise. It took a lot of courage for her to come to America as a single mother and make a life for her family—as well as ours. She remains, like Don, a big part of our family today.

Paula is like a second mother to us. She took over when my mother was busy helping my dad. She fed the five of us, cared for us, and taught us Spanish—all while raising her own family at the same time.

When I was about twelve years old, I was very round, and I couldn't find any clothes that fit my shape. Paula made some for me.

Today, at age eighty-four, Paula still runs my parents' household, which, given the amount of friends and family coming and going, is no easy feat. She is a gifted flower arranger and is famous for her pies and jalapeño jelly, but doesn't give up recipes easily. Paula came to stay with me when Sam was born, and she planted a garden in my yard while the baby was napping. She continues to love my children, as well as my nieces and nephews, the same way she loved us growing up. Paula stands just under five feet tall, and as the children grow, they all see if they can measure up to her—in more ways than one.

At the time of Dad's 1966 congressional race, I was still quite young—only seven—and again, my memories are more like snapshots in my mind. I remember filming campaign commercials in our backyard and going to St. Martin's Church in Houston, where our friends congratulated Dad on his win. While there were lots of handshaking and hugs to go around, I was scared and nervous about leaving my home for Washington, D.C.

Dad, two of my brothers, and I went to Washington on our own. My brother George was at Yale, and Jeb stayed at Kinkaid High School in Houston, then switched to the same boarding school Dad and George had attended, Phillips Academy in Andover, Massachusetts. Mom was still packing up our house in Houston when school started for Neil, Marvin, and me in Washington.

My parents bought a house on Hillbrook Lane in Northwest Washington from Senator Milward Simpson of Wyoming, Senator Alan Simpson's father. Alan Simpson recalls it being a beautiful home with a hedge in the front yard which Senator Estes Kefauver, Adlai Stevenson's running mate, drove through one time when he was drunk. Senator Simpson remembers his parents' real estate settlement, or lack of one: "They sold their home on Hillbrook Lane to George and Barbara on a handshake. The brokers were all irritated, the lawyers were irritated. Everybody was irritated. They said, 'But you have to have a broker and a lawyer and a real estate agent!' That was typical Bush and typical Simpson."

When my brothers and I arrived at the house, Dad told me that he had heard that across the street there was a little girl who was going to be in my same class at National Cathedral School.

One of the things I was most worried about was whether my new classmates were going to wear short socks or long socks. In Texas, we wore short socks, but I had heard that in Washington some girls wore kneesocks. I became fixated on that, as eight-year-old girls might do. Because I was really fretting about the sock situation, my dad went over and introduced me to the neighborhood girl in my class, Olivia Crudgington, who went by "Libby" back then. He first suggested that we be friends, and then he straight out asked her what kinds of socks she and the other girls in class wore.

Some girls might have been embarrassed by this, but my dad had a way about him that endeared him to everyone. I always thought he was the most fun of any of the dads, very charming and loving, and Libby and my other girlfriends thought he was movie-star handsome.

Tragically, a few years later when I was in boarding school and my parents were heading to China, where my dad was to be the U.S. liaison representative, Libby's father died. Dad wrote her a note, which she told me she has never shared with anyone except her late husband. She has kept the note in her dresser drawer for years, along with a photo of Dad on his boat, which he had enclosed:

Dear Libby,

Here's a little souvenir (it may seem a little egotistical to send it to you—I hope not).

Anyway, you see, I love you and don't want you to forget me when I go to China on October 17th.

We are thrilled over the future—wouldn't it be great if you could come see us someday.

We go see Doro in about eight days—I miss her.

Lib, let's make a deal—ok? If you ever need help or free advice (it would probably be worth what you paid for it!) from an old man that loves you—count on me—now, in the future, always. You are my very special friend—send us a letter to China some day. Love ya.

GB

"Your father could have been a gas station operator and it would have meant the same to me," Libby said. "It was an act of pure generosity that meant the world to me then, as it does now."

Dad was the only adult who wrote Libby a note when her father died.

As for my mother, someone apparently forgot to tell her that a congressman's term was two years—rather than two months—when we first arrived in Washington. She insisted on dragging us, and any visiting Texans, to every monument, battlefield, and museum she could find within striking distance of our new home that first summer. Marvin laughs, looking back at that time: "I'm not sure whether it was Neil or me who finally broke the news to her that we would rather spend some time with our new friends than climbing the steps of the Washington Monument with visitors from the 7th Congressional District of Texas."

While Mom was entertaining constituents and keeping the household running smoothly, Dad was getting his sea legs in Congress. True, his own father had been a U.S. senator, but not until Dad had moved to Texas as an adult. He had never really been to Washington much before that, except for an occasional visit to his father's Senate office.

When my father arrived in Washington in the late 1960s, it was a very busy, hectic time to be a member of Congress. The Vietnam War, the assassinations of Martin Luther King Jr. and Robert

Kennedy, the civil rights movement—so much was going on in our nation.

Because Dad's schedule was jam-packed, Sundays took on an even greater importance to our family. It was when we went to church and had a Sunday lunch with the whole family and various friends and neighbors. The late congressman Sonny Montgomery, a Democrat from Mississippi, came over regularly. Supreme Court Justice Potter Stewart and his wife, Andy, lived on our street. Andy was one of Mom's closest friends, and much to my humiliation, they used to walk the dogs in their bathrobes around the neighborhood. (My children now suffer the same humiliation when I walk our dog in my bathrobe!)

Looking back now, I can see that even in his early political years Dad was more than just a witness to the history that was unfolding. He was an agent for change. For example, on April 10, 1968, Dad voted to pass the very controversial Housing Rights Act of 1968 (aka the "Open Housing Bill"), which was the last of the three great civil rights bills of the 1960s.

Taylor Blanton explained to me, "It's hard to believe today, but in 1964 'equal rights for all' was not something very often mentioned by candidates in either party in Texas or the South." The day before the House was to vote on the Housing Rights Act, Martin Luther King Jr. was buried. You can imagine the atmosphere at the time.

According to the House of Representatives Postal Service, Dad received more mail that year than any other member of Congress—and much of it ran heavily opposed to this bill. The volume of mail was so high, in fact, that Dad had to hire extra staff to fold and stuff envelopes, with every staffer working one late night a week on mail duty—including Dad, who stayed late every Wednesday night to help answer angry constituents' letters.

There were phone calls, too. Allie Page Matthews, who worked for Dad at the time, remembers an African American female staffer, Velma Johnson, who was fielding some of the phone calls.

"She was on the phone and tears were coming down her face. He took the telephone out of her hands and said, 'I don't know who this is, but this is George Bush and don't you ever call this office and talk to a member of my staff like that again.'"

A front-page headline in the *Houston Chronicle* from the time reads "Bush's Life Threatened over Rights Vote," referring to another caller who had made a death threat against Dad because of the vote. The *Chronicle* quoted my father as saying that some of the mail was filled "with hatred and venom. That anyone would resort to this kind of talk makes me ashamed I'm an American." Dad was adamant that voting for passage was the right thing to do.

On Wednesday, April 17, a week after that historic House vote, Dad flew to Houston to face his constituents who had objected to the bill. When he was introduced to the angry crowd at Memorial High School, he was met with a house full of boos. He wasn't shaken. He quoted Edmund Burke: "Your representative owes you not only his industry, but his judgment; and he betrays, instead of serves, you if he sacrifices it to your opinion." He reminded the four hundred people in attendance that their freedom and the principles by which they lived were being defended by "Negroes" (then the politically correct term) in Vietnam. "Somehow it seems fundamental that a man—if he has the money and the good character—should not have a door slammed in his face if he is a Negro or speaks with a Latin American accent. I see a ray of hope, not a handout or a gift, for Negroes locked out by habit and discrimination." He turned the crowd around, and, the *Chronicle* reported, Dad "received a standing ovation at the end of his address."

An interesting aside: President Bill Clinton first became aware of my father in 1966, when he was a senior at Georgetown University and clerking for the Senate Foreign Relations Committee. "My first impression of him was, he was a Republican who moved to Texas by choice and wound up voting for a civil rights bill—the open housing bill. I didn't know anything about his district, but I couldn't help wondering whether it hurt him or not. It really meant a lot to me . . . I grew up in the segregated South, and civil rights was the animating issue of my life when I was a young man. So I thought, now who is this guy who gets elected to Congress in Houston on the Republican ticket and votes for civil rights? I loved it."

An old friend of Dad's, Dan Gilcrist, remembers going with Dad to an African American church in Houston a year or so after the housing vote. According to Dan, Dad had a standing invitation to Sunday services whenever he was in the district, because the members of the parish genuinely liked him. So one Sunday morning, he and Dan were sitting in the middle of a large congregation when the preacher introduced Dad and began discussing how much my father had done for the parish. With all this praise, Dad leaned over and quietly asked for Dan's pen, then made out a check, returned the pen, and waited for the collection plate to be passed.

But then the preacher didn't stop: he got more and more excited, listing more and more details of Dad's life, and even began to sweat—and it became clear that this was not just an introduction but an entire homily on Dad. Meanwhile, the parishioners were joining in with a chorus of "amens" and "right ons." Dan noticed Dad looked more and more uncomfortable. Dan said, "Then George, considering the amount on the check vis-à-vis the homily, leaned over to me and with a pained look on his face, pulled out his checkbook and said, 'Let me see that pen again.'"

As his stand on that civil rights bill illustrated, my father always took the lead in helping others, not just when it was politically convenient for him. Jimmy Allison, one of Dad's best friends, who worked for the 1964 Senate campaign and who was campaign manager for the 1966 congressional campaign, lived at our house in Houston for three months. He remembers that before running for Congress, Dad had decided that he should sell his interest in Zapata Off-Shore Drilling Company because it could pose a conflict of interest if he was elected to office. So he made it known that he was interested in selling his share. He found a group ready to buy, and one morning, while sitting in his office, the phone rang. It turned out to be the foreman of one of the offshore rigs telling Dad that the prospective buyers had come for a tour and then made it clear that they were planning on getting rid of some of the employees. After Dad hung up with the foreman, he called the buyers right then and told them that part of the deal meant keeping his old employees on the job. Less than a week later, he sold his stock in Zapata to another company that agreed to those terms—but for far less money.

Jimmy also recalled how Dad struck up a running correspondence with a constituent named Paul Dorsey who was not a supporter of my dad in the 1966 campaign and had written to express his opposition. Dad thought the man's letters showed him to be a man of intelligence and integrity. So Dad wrote to him over the course of a year and a half, trying to bring him around—which he ultimately did.

Looking through the stack of letters, I found quite a bit of advice to Dad, including: "If you should ever appear on TV with LBJ, don't look too damn happy about it." He would also enclose newspaper clippings—dozens sometimes—including one letter to the editor of the *Houston Post* from Mr. Frank Jungman in which he predicted that the next Texan to be president "will be personable, likable, hardworking George Bush." Dorsey wrote cynically, "Is this fellow on full or part-time payroll?"

What Dorsey didn't tell my father was that while he was exchanging letters, he was also dying of cancer. Dad found out. And what my father didn't tell Dorsey was that he secretly sent money to his hospital to pay the medical bills.

Paul Dorsey never found out.

★   ★   ★

By early 1968, Dad's two-year term was nearing its conclusion. Since he was running unopposed, he didn't have to campaign hard in his district. Instead, he went on the road for the Nixon-Agnew ticket. Nixon had campaigned for Dad when he was running for Congress in 1966 and had gone all around the country speaking on behalf of many other challengers. He made a lot of friends for himself by doing that, since in the fall of '66, the GOP elected land-slide numbers to the House of Representatives. Later on in 1968, Nixon asked Dad and a handful of others to be his surrogate speakers. My father recalled being surprised at the request and found it "rather flattering for a new congressman."

It was no surprise to some of the people around Dad. Jimmy Allison, then Dad's administrative assistant in Congress, went to dinner with a young man named Pete Roussel one night. "We were closing the deal for me to come work for Congressman Bush," Pete remembers. "We had dinner down on Sixth Street in Austin. As we parted, I turned into the night, and as I did, Jimmy called back to me. He said, 'Pete, stick with George. Someday he's going to be president.' And mind you, he was talking at that point about a second-term congressman, a statement which I never forgot."

Jimmy died in his mid-forties, well before my father became president—but later when Dad became president, he asked Jimmy's son, Jay, to be his personal aide.

Soon, it was reported that Dad was on Nixon's short list of vice presidential choices, suggested for the job by President Eisenhower, according to rumors. Nixon strongly considered Dad but ultimately decided that four years in Congress from a safe Texas district didn't merit a place on the national ticket. Dad felt that was a fair enough assessment. He also started to think about his next run for public office.

At President Nixon's 1969 inauguration, some people were surprised that Dad went to the airport to see President Johnson off. No one was more surprised than LBJ himself, who did a double take when he spotted my father in the crowd. His widow, Lady Bird Johnson, recalled that day: "Through the years, I have been the recipient of so many generous messages of love, support, and encouragement from George Bush—mostly handwritten! But engraved on my heart is a cold January 20 in 1969 when Lyndon and I said our farewell to Washington and departed for Texas. There in the crowd at Andrews Air Force Base was George Bush . . . George

Bush is not only a strong Republican but he is a very warm and caring man who wrote the book on friendship!"

No other Republican officeholder was there. This was a time when most Republicans were at the parade following the Nixon inauguration—after all, their party was taking power for the first time in a decade—but after speaking with his longtime friend and assistant Rose Zamaria, Dad chose to be there to say farewell to a fellow Texan, a man with whom he often disagreed but always respected.

The longtime White House correspondent for *Time* magazine, the late Hugh Sidey—who came to be a great friend of my father's over the years—remembers the two competing events in the days before the "split screen" on CNN. "On Richard Nixon's inauguration day in 1969, the White House press corps was all staked out at the Capitol and around behind the inaugural stand at the White House to record the new president's every move. We at *Time* magazine were all fixed up with telephones and portable TV sets so we would not miss a beat. I recall sometime after the swearing-in of Nixon passing one of the tiny television screens and seeing a live shot from Andrews Air Force Base as former president Lyndon B. Johnson was preparing to fly back to Texas. He was being bid farewell by Republican Congressman George Bush, a fellow Texan. But it was such a unique gesture at that level of power I can recall pausing to watch the brief encounter, and to put it in the back of my mind that this new person—obviously climbing the political ladder with unusual grace and good humor—was one to watch."

President Johnson told my father that day that if he ever needed anything, to be sure to call on him. A year went by, and it was time to start thinking about what his next move would be, politically speaking. Dad wanted to run for Senate, but his friends were urging him not to. Dad was the first freshman congressman to serve on the powerful Ways and Means Committee in sixty-three years—and his friends were convinced that he was in an enviable position that would only get better with time.

But Dad had a nut to crack, and it was another run at his old opponent Ralph Yarborough. The politics were complicated, and Dad turned to an unlikely ally for counsel, remembering President Johnson's invitation to visit his ranch in the Texas Hill Country. So Dad asked LBJ for his advice about whether he should run for the Senate. President Johnson said, "Let me put it to you this way: the difference between the Senate and the House is like the difference between chicken salad and chicken shit!"

The meeting at the Johnson ranch, which was supposed to be secret, got leaked to the newspapers and attracted some negative press for the ex-president. Dad didn't care for himself but didn't want to cause any political embarrassment for the former president in his Democratic circles. Like his own father, Dad was always someone who believed that Democrats and Republicans should and could work together. This Texas-style bipartisanship also surfaced in my brother George's administration as governor.

In 1970, Dad took President Johnson's advice and went for the chicken salad.

Chapter 5

BAKER AND BENTSEN

"Friendship means a lot to George Bush. His loyalty to friends, I think, is one of his defining personal strengths . . . Loyalty goes up, and loyalty goes down . . . He likes to say, 'Where would we be without friends?' He is right. In the end, our lives are defined by our family, our faith, and our friends."

—**James Baker**

By 1969, Dad's old adversary and a fierce opponent of Lyndon Johnson, Ralph Yarborough, was coming up on the end of his second term in the Senate and was going to try for a third. Because LBJ was still such a large figure in Texas—he had just published his memoirs and was building the Johnson Library in Austin—Dad had gone to the former president to see if he would actively oppose Dad's candidacy. Once LBJ had been consulted, my father felt there was nothing to stop him from throwing his hat in the ring.

James Baker was a recent widower, and Dad was trying to help get his mind on something else. Mary Stuart Baker had died young from cancer. Before she slipped into a coma two weeks before dying, Mom and Dad had gone to visit her and ended up being the last people outside of her own family to see her alive. Because of

Robin's death, Mr. Baker had felt he could lean on Dad when he was first told that Mary Stuart didn't have much of a chance. After Mary Stuart died, her husband was absolutely heartbroken.

"I was depressed and somewhat at loose ends, and it was George who helped me get back on my feet," Secretary Baker said, remembering how Dad asked him to join his second Senate campaign. "He did it for one reason: he did it out of friendship, and he did it because he's the most considerate person I have ever met. He did it to give me something to occupy my mind other than my grief. He reached out to a friend in time of need because that's the kind of person that George Bush was and is."

At the time, Baker had a law practice in town, and he remembers the exchange he had with Dad about joining the campaign:

"Well, George," Mr. Baker said, "that's a great idea except for two things. Number one, I don't know anything about politics, and number two, I'm a Democrat."

Dad said, "Well, we can fix that latter problem."

They did, and Mr. Baker got religion right then and there.

Dad had an excellent chance to win the seat because Yarborough's position was a lot less certain than it had been during the 1964 campaign. Most important, perhaps, Richard Nixon, a Republican, occupied the White House in 1970. That would help.

The situation dimmed considerably, however, when Lloyd Bentsen, a conservative Democrat who was Dad's age—and was also a handsome, well-respected businessman—announced that he would challenge Yarborough for the Democratic nomination. Bentsen made his announcement on January 9, and Dad, not one to be scared off by the possibility of a formidable opponent, declared his candidacy four days later.

Today, of course, Texas is one of the redder "red states," but back in 1970 you might say it was one of the more yellow "yellow dog" states—meaning it was dominated by Democrats. In fact, when John Tower won the special election for the U.S. Senate in 1961—filling then–Vice President Johnson's seat—he was the first Texas Republican elected statewide since 1870.

During the 1970 Democratic primary, Bentsen waged a very aggressive campaign, attacking Yarborough from the right, calling him a radical and an ultraliberal, running a conservative campaign in a conservative Democratic state. It worked. Bentsen carried the Democratic primary with 812,000 votes, while Dad won the Republican primary with 87,000 votes.

A win is a win, but the fact remained: the GOP was outnumbered ten to one.

My brother George, who was twenty-four at the time, remembers driving with Dad the day Lloyd Bentsen beat Ralph Yarborough. To George, the whole campaign seemed to change in an instant. There was a stunned silence—then Dad, always the optimist, said, "We can win this one."

George had graduated from Yale and was serving in the Texas National Guard. When he had time off, he would jump in a car and travel around to various Texas counties campaigning for Dad—not easy in a state with 254 counties. That experience made a lasting impression on George. It gave him practical campaign experience in Texas, working to build the state Republican Party. But he also became "emotionally involved," as Dad later put it.

That year, 1970, saw the completion of the World Trade Center, the death of four students at Kent State who were killed during a protest of the U.S. invasion of Cambodia, and Simon and Garfunkel were at the top of the music charts. I was eleven, attending National Cathedral School in Washington, taking tennis and piano lessons, and hanging out with my friends. Dad and Mom went back and forth to Texas to campaign, and when they were there, I stayed at my friend Libby Crudgington's house.

In my young mind, the fact that Dad was once again running for office meant there would be a flurry of activity and campaigning that would involve us as a family—participating in campaign ads, attending rallies, making posters. Mom campaigned with him and needlepointed "Bush" labels for straw handbags, which we both carried. The "Bush Belles," a group of female volunteers from across Texas, would campaign with my parents and hand out literature at all the stops. They wore blue and white outfits with sashes, straw hats, and scarves that were red, white, and blue with stars and that said "George Bush" on them. They campaigned for Dad in all three of his Texas campaigns, and in their heyday there were sixty-six Bush Belles. My parents still keep in touch with some of the Belles, many of whom volunteer in his Houston office today.

At one point during the Senate campaign, while George was stationed at Moody Air Force Base in Georgia, Dad called him up and said he was throwing a party for Frank Borman, one of the first American astronauts to circle the moon, at the Alibi Club in Washington. The Alibi Club is a tiny hole-in-the-wall kind of place in town, not far from the White House. Dad thought George would get a kick out of meeting the astronauts, since George was in training to become a pilot himself.

Dad also suggested that George bring Tricia Nixon along, who was roughly the same age as George and living at the White House. This suggestion is typical of Dad—he is always planning parties, getting groups of people together, and playing the part of the serial matchmaker (with a decidedly mixed record!).

Arriving home from Georgia, George drove to the White House in Mom and Dad's brand-new 1970 purple Gremlin with denim seat covers. (Author's note: I checked, and the denim seat covers did indeed "come standard" on the 1970 Gremlin.) He remembers taking the elevator to the second floor and meeting Tricia in the family quarters.

From there, George and Tricia got in a Secret Service car—leaving behind that very stylish Gremlin. They had a "nice time," he recalled, despite the fact that she asked him not to smoke. They reportedly got back to the White House at a reasonable hour.

President Nixon wasn't home when George picked Tricia up, but in hindsight George now knows how Barbara's and Jenna's boyfriends must feel about their dates' father being the president of the United States. He's been there himself.

Years later, incidentally, my mother and I went to a wedding shower for Tricia Nixon, during her engagement to Ed Cox.

Despite the fact that Ed didn't smoke and he didn't drive a purple Gremlin, Tricia seemed very happy.

A final postscript to this story: In 2005, I attended a dinner at the White House that the president and First Lady hosted in honor of Prince Charles of Great Britain and his new wife, Camilla, the duchess of Cornwall. It was a fun night, with my parents and my brothers attending. Prince Charles gave a wonderful toast, in which he said the first time he came to the White House, during the Nixon administration, they were trying to marry him off to Tricia Nixon. I gave the president a big smile. Prince Charles doesn't know they have that in common!

Whenever George's National Guard schedule would permit, Dad enjoyed having George along with him on the campaign bus. As for George, I'd say the 1970 race was one of the reasons he became so involved in Dad's later presidential campaigns—he loved traveling with Dad.

★   ★   ★

In the end, running against a conservative Democrat in Texas in 1970 proved to be an insurmountable challenge—and Bentsen won with 53.4 percent of the vote. Dad made a solid showing for a Republican, but it was still a tough loss. (The Harris County campaign run by James Baker, incidentally, was more successful. Dad won 60 percent of the vote there, where both candidates lived.) Mom remembers that at the last minute, an initiative involving sales of liquor by the drink was put on the ballot, "and that caused a huge Democrat turnout" particularly in East Texas, a part of the state that is solidly Democratic.

Pete Roussel, who had been on the campaign staff, analyzed Dad's race: "When Senator Yarborough was upset in the Democratic primary by Lloyd Bentsen, you didn't have the ideological difference that had been anticipated in that race. Nevertheless, in typical George Bush fashion, he ran a truly energetic and all-out campaign . . . One of the things he was up against was at that time a pretty powerful Democratic Party in Texas. Lloyd Bentsen was not only out there campaigning; Lloyd Bentsen had a very popular former Texas governor campaigning for him named John Connally, and he had a very well known former president named Lyndon Johnson who was living in Texas then campaigning for him. Late in the campaign, President Nixon came to Texas and campaigned in East Texas and Dallas for George Bush. In the end, though, Bentsen prevailed."

Pete also remembers the day after Dad lost: "Here's a man who'd just gone through a grueling race for the Senate, giving it everything he had. It would have been the natural thing for many of us to sit around and feel sorry for ourselves. That's kind of the way I was feeling. I went down to his office the next day, and what was he doing? When I walked in, he was on the phone calling people, trying to get jobs for the people in that campaign who were all out of jobs now. And I thought to myself, 'I'll walk down the street with my back broken to help this guy,' based on that. It was such a typical act of kindness and loyalty by him."

Marvin sized it up afterward: "He and Bentsen agreed on too many things, and, at that time, Texas was a solid Democratic state. I blamed it on President Nixon. I thought that if he worked harder for Dad's campaign, Dad would have won in a landslide."

I, too, took it hard. On election night, when I heard the news, I burst into tears.

"What's wrong?" someone asked.

Through my tears, I answered dejectedly, "I'm the only person in the fifth grade whose dad doesn't have a job."

The *Houston Chronicle* documented the scene in an article titled "Bush Concedes, Wishes Bentsen 'Best of Luck'":

> A little girl stood weeping in the corner, nestled in the arms of her older brother. He seemed to be fighting to keep back the tears. Their political candidate had just conceded the race. This poignant scene summed up the reaction of all the supporters of the two children's father, George Bush, who had just publicly recognized his loss to Lloyd M. Bentsen Jr. in the race for the U.S. Senate.

I'm not sure which of my brothers the article was referring to, but one of George's roommates said George was also tearful on election night. As the evening wore on, they both got sadder and sadder. But he took his cues from Mom and Dad, telling a reporter years later, "I learned that life goes on. I draw a lot of lessons from my dad. Since Mom and Dad didn't think life was over, I didn't either. I remember how gracious he was in defeat. I would have felt otherwise."

He added, "Dad was given a second, or a third, life and he went on. Good people go into politics. They sometimes win. They sometimes lose . . . It tells us there is something bigger than elections. Maybe that's the big lesson I learned from 1970."

Senator Bentsen, for his part, went on to serve for more than twenty years in the U.S. Senate, and ran on the 1988 Democratic ticket with Governor Michael Dukakis against Dad and Senator Dan Quayle. Eventually, Senator Bentsen left the Senate to be secretary of the treasury in the Clinton administration.

Senator Bentsen looked back on that 1970 Senate race in a letter to me before he died. He remembered being invited by Dad to the vice president's house early in 1981 for lunch after church. "After a delicious lunch, I was near the vice president while looking around at the happy crowd, and I said, 'I think I did you a favor back in '70 in that Senate race.' And he said, 'Well, Lloyd, I guess you did—but I just didn't understand it at the time.'"

Chapter 6

ELOISE AT THE WALDORF

"President Bush taught me how valuable personal contact and human tenderness are to the job of diplomacy. He once told me, 'The first call you make to someone should not be to ask them for something.' It was the accumulation of small gestures of kindness, he believed, that built a relationship of trust between leaders and enabled them to work effectively together."
—**Condoleezza Rice**

After losing the Senate race, Dad returned to Washington to finish out the last few months of his term in the House of Representatives. As has always been his way, he immediately turned his attention toward the future, rather than dwelling on the past. He thought about becoming U.S. ambassador to the United Nations and approached President Nixon about that position, then held by Ambassador Charles Yost. "I was fascinated by the politics of the U.N., the vote-getting and the contacts to be made," Dad told me. "Even though Ambassador Yost was a senior career diplomat, the political forum which was the U.N. was not best for him and certainly not for Nixon, so he was asked to resign." Moreover, President Nixon was under attack in New York City because the

Republican mayor, John Lindsay, did not like the president. Dad liked the idea of representing the Nixon administration in New York.

President Nixon, however, had his own plans for Dad: making him a special assistant to the president. Dad said that, of course, he would abide by whatever decision the president made, but he thought the U.N. job would be a better fit. It certainly would better serve President Nixon, who had no advocate in New York City. So Nixon relented, and within four months of that defeat in the Senate race, we were on our way to New York City.

Since we were leaving Washington for New York City in the middle of the school year, the disruption became a social emergency for a sixth grader like me. Desperate times call for desperate measures; and just as Henry Kissinger made a secret trip to China, I made my own secret trip to Ed Curran, the headmaster at the National Cathedral School. Now, normally, I would have been mortified at the mere thought of doing such a thing, but in this instance I somehow mustered the courage to ask if I could board at the school instead of accompanying my parents to New York.

Mr. Curran sensed this was a big step for me—having never seen me before in his office—and as he was a friend of my parents', he let them know I was having trouble adjusting to the idea of leaving. Still, all three said no to the idea of a sixth grader boarding anywhere, and so that was the end of that.

Fortunately, Secretary Kissinger's trip was more successful!

When Dad was sworn in as U.N. ambassador in February 1971, I started attending the U.N. International School in Manhattan along with the children of the other diplomats. By this time, my brothers George and Jeb were already living on their own, and Marvin and Neil were at boarding school—Marvin at Phillips in Andover, Massachusetts, and Neil at St. Albans in Washington, D.C. So it was just Dad, Mom, myself, and Paula Rendon, our housekeeper.

The official United Nations ambassador's residence is located in the Waldorf-Astoria Hotel—at Fiftieth Street and Park Avenue—on the very top floor. Our apartment was number 42A, on the forty-second floor, and the apartment itself was big and beautiful, consisting of nine rooms, five of which were bedrooms, and a forty-eight-foot living room that was used to host large official receptions. There were high ceilings, handsome old woodwork, working fireplaces, and big windows with beautiful views of New York City. One thing I remember about the apartment was that the flagship store of Steuben glass loaned Mom a stunning collection of Steuben to display in the ambassador's residence.

Having never lived in an apartment before, I genuinely felt like I was living as Eloise at the Plaza—from the Kay Thompson book. Eloise lived at the Plaza Hotel on Fifth Avenue, and her rule was, "Getting bored is not allowed!"—and that sounded good to me. I rode the elevators constantly and made friends with Lettie and Mary, two of the elevator operators. I remember doing my homework sitting on the pull-down stool in the Waldorf elevator. Lettie and Mary would even let me turn the elevator crank now and then. I also remember eating hamburgers at Oscar's, the hotel coffee shop that's still there today, and bringing my friends there for snacks.

It was just one big adventure. My visiting girlfriends and I would explore the hotel and check out the parties and whatever else was going on. As a young and impressionable girl, of course, being around all that high fashion at the Waldorf had an effect on me. One day, for example, I decided I needed to buy a particular pair of red and green suede shoes that had a bit of a platform heel. I thought they were the greatest. Soon after, one of my cousins, Peggy Peters, a buyer for Bonwit Teller, came to visit. She took one look at them and told me they looked like bowling shoes. I loved them anyway.

During this tour of duty at the Waldorf, one of my best friends, Jodie Dwight, came to stay with us. Jodie's house was near ours in Kennebunkport, and during the summers Dad would pull up in the boat outside her house and honk the foghorn. She'd come running down the beach, dive into the water, and swim out to us. We'd haul her into the boat and off we'd go—the three of us.

By the time Jodie came to visit us in New York, she and I were at that precocious age when you pull innocent pranks on people like calling up random stores and asking them if they've got Prince Albert in a can (*well, let him out!*). Of course, this was well before the days of caller ID. Can you imagine being asked if your refrigerator was running, and seeing the caller ID: "UN Ambassador's Residence"?

Another key detail about our apartment at the Waldorf: it was U-shaped, so if you were to stand in one arm of the U and look across and down, you could see right into the apartment below on the other arm of the U. I mention this because, one particular day, Jodie and I just happened—very innocently—to look across and down into the apartment below ours, and there, lying on the bed, was a naked man.

Naturally, two sixth-grade girls found this to be hysterically funny. Quickly, we got a piece of string, a Magic Marker, and a piece of cardboard and made a sign that said "Hi there." We ran around to the arm of our apartment directly over his window and dropped our sign-on-a-string out the window. Jodie began lowering it down while I ran around to the windows on the other side of the apartment to see what would happen.

Just then a woman—I assume the naked man's wife—encountered the sign, then hurried over to their window and shut the shades in a panic. By now we were laughing so hard we were crying. When we finally calmed down, we went and found Dad and confessed our anonymous little prank. He sounded stern: "Do you realize that everyone knows the U.S. ambassador to the United Nations lives on the forty-second floor?" We could tell he was trying to keep a straight face.

When I didn't have friends like Jodie visiting, however, life got a little lonely. It was hard to make new friends, and sometimes I felt like an only child. It was the first time I was without at least a couple of my brothers. Despite that, I loved our time in New York because I got to do so many fun and interesting things with my parents, like go to the theater. One of the biggest stars on Broadway, Carol Channing, also lived at the Waldorf during this time, and I was fascinated by her long fake eyelashes and wigs. Carol came to our apartment several times for parties, and because I knew she had been in *Hello, Dolly!* and *Thoroughly Modern Millie,* I became hooked on musicals. During our year in New York, I saw *No, No, Nanette; Pippin;* and *A Little Night Music,* among others.

★ ★ ★

Although living at the Waldorf had its Eloise-like moments, that time period wasn't totally idyllic. Reality set in when my grandfather—my father's father, Prescott Bush, who lived in Greenwich, Connecticut, and worked in New York—began to get a bad cough. Within a short time, my grandfather was diagnosed with lung cancer and admitted to Memorial Sloan-Kettering, where Mom was a volunteer and where Robin had been treated. This was before CAT scans, MRIs, and all the other diagnostic tools we have today.

In my grandfather's case, there was almost no hope from the start.

Dad visited him nearly every day at the hospital and would come home heavy with grief. One night, he told me that he ran his fingers through his father's thin hair and how sad that made him feel because he always had such thick hair. Less than a month after his symptoms emerged, he died, on October 8, 1972—almost eighteen years to the day after Robin. I remember watching *Love Story* on TV right after he died and crying my eyes out, just sobbing, because of all the sadness in our home.

Recently, Dad told me that shortly after his father's death, a family friend committed suicide after receiving a diagnosis of terminal cancer. His wife said to Dad, "Why couldn't he die with courage, like Prescott Bush did? Why did he have to take the selfish way out?" Dad explained to her that her husband had spared his family the agony of a long-drawn-out cancer death. "But she put Dad up as the example of how you do it, how you face death with courage," my father said.

Richard Nixon had been an admirer of my grandfather's—some said he considered my grandfather a "political mentor." When his nomination for vice president in 1952 was in jeopardy, for example, Nixon consulted my grandfather before giving his famous "Checkers speech." On the occasion of my grandparents' fiftieth wedding anniversary in 1971, President Nixon sent a nice note mentioning Dad: "I welcome the opportunity to tell you personally what you undoubtedly hear not only from friends in Connecticut but across the country about the strong leadership that George provides in his sensitive and demanding duties at the United Nations. He is indeed his father's son."

For my grandfather's funeral, President Nixon once again reached out—sending flowers from the White House and a warm note, written the day after my grandfather had died. Given my grandfather's illness and death, we were all even more grateful for Dad's appointment to the United Nations, as it allowed us to be so close to him at the end.

I recently came across my grandmother's eulogy of my grandfather, in which she said, "When he stood at the altar fifty-one years ago and promised to 'keep thee only unto her as long as you both shall live' he was making a pledge to God that he never for one moment forgot, and gave to his wife, the most joyous life that any woman could experience. As a father, he believed in necessary discipline when the occasion demanded, but was always loving and understanding. As the children grew older he respected each as an individual, ready to back any decision thoughtfully reached, and giving advice only when sought." That statement is equally true of my father.

★   ★   ★

Uncle Pres and Dad in 1924, the year Dad was born.
(GHWB Personal Collection)

Dad as a little boy. (GBPL)

Dad and his brothers Jonathan and Prescott Jr.
in Kennebunkport, Maine, late 1930s. (GBPL)

Dad at Andover, 1937–1938. (GBPL)

Mom at age twelve: Little did she know how much fishing would figure in her future! (GBPL)

Dad as captain of the 1940
Andover soccer team. (GBPL)

Yale's baseball team. Dad [seated, far left] was captain of the team and played first base, although he always said that he was "all field, no hit." Sitting just to his right is Junie "Dad" O'Brien. (GBPL)

My grandfather, "Gampy." He was an avid sportsman and a scratch golfer. (GBPL)

My grandmother, "Ganny."
She was a championship tennis
player and loved competition.
(GBPL)

Dad joined the Navy at age eighteen—
at the time, the youngest Navy pilot to
earn his wings. (GBPL)

Dad in the cockpit of his TBM
Avenger, with my mom's name on
the panel. (GBPL)

September 2, 1944:
Dad is rescued by
the Navy submarine
USS *Finback*.
(GBPL)

Mom, at nineteen, and Dad, age twenty, were married on January 6, 1945, in Rye, New York. (GBPL)

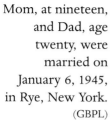

Mom and Dad with Turbo, their first dog, in 1945. (GBPL)

Ganny and Gampy's twenty-fifth wedding anniversary, 1947, Kennebunkport, Maine, on Walker's Point. Back, left to right: Beth (holding baby Kelsey), Prescott Jr. (holding Prescott III), Bucky, Gampy, Dad, Uncle Sandy Ellis. Front: Uncle Jon, Ganny, Mom (holding "Georgie"), and Aunt Nan. (GBPL)

Dad reads a bedtime
story to George, 1948.
(GBLP)

Cowboy George W.
(GBPL)

Robin, summer of 1953. (GBPL)

Mom with George, Jeb, and Neil
on Christmas morning, 1956.
(GBPL)

Ganny, Dad, George, and Robin, 1953. (GBPL)

Dad and me in Houston, Texas, 1959. (GBPL)

My favorite picture of my four brothers the summer I was born, 1959:
Marvin, Neil, Jeb, and George. (GBPL)

Bathtime for Dad, Neil, me, Marvin, and Jeb, 1963. (GBPL)

Our entire family the year I was born, 1959, in Houston, Texas. George and Jeb stand behind Neil, Dad, me, Mom, and Marvin. (GBPL)

Ganny, Dad, and me at the River Club in Kennebunkport, Maine, 1962. (GBPL)

Jeb and me in our Easter finery, 1963. (GBPL)

We were all happy to get off the elephant used in this campaign shot because his hair was prickly! (GBPL)

Dad campaigns for the Senate from the back of a flatbed truck. (GBPL)

ELECT GEORGE
BUSH
U. S. SENATE

Dad on the 1964 campaign trail with the Bush Belles. (GBPL)

Our family in Houston, Texas, early 1960s. (GBPL)

Marvin in clown pajamas poses with Mom, who was preparing to go out for the evening, 1962. (GBPL)

June 11, 1962: My grandfather Senator Prescott Bush, former secretary of state Dean Acheson, and President John F. Kennedy all receive honorary degrees from Yale University.
(Yale University Library Manuscripts and Archives)

Mom and me with the needlepoint "Bush Bags" that Mom made for the 1966 congressional campaign. (GBPL)

My brother George at campaign headquarters, announcing the winning votes in the 1966 congressional race. (GBPL)

Kennebunkport, Maine, 1968: Dad and I are twins! (GBPL)

The United Nations job turned out to be the perfect posting for Dad. Today, he still holds a U.N. record: the "hat trick" of attending Security Council meetings as ambassador, vice president, and president. Clearly, he not only enjoyed it—he also thrived in such settings because of his natural ability to connect with a broad diversity of people.

Years later, General Brent Scowcroft looked back on Dad's tenure at the U.N. and how it helped him later in life. "What did he learn there? He learned the perspective of about 150 smaller states, all of whom had problems that most of us don't even realize. And he used to visit them, he used to talk to them. He used to get their points of view. He used to cultivate them. So when he came to the Oval Office, he knew what they were thinking about, he understood what they were thinking about, and he could empathize and work with them."

This penchant for personal diplomacy began when he started taking individual ambassadors and their wives to Broadway shows, or Mets games, or even to a John Denver concert at Carnegie Hall. At one point, Mom and Dad took the British foreign minister, Sir Alec Douglas-Home, and his wife and the British ambassador, Sir Colin Crowe, and his wife to an Audubon Society bird sanctuary for some bird-watching, only to find it closed for the day. Dad helped Mom, Lady Crowe, and Lady Home over the fence, along with the rest of the group. They were accosted by security men and their dogs but were not arrested.

Dad's friend Spike Heminway remembers when Dad took a group to a Mets game, and Spike became worried when Dad went for a hot dog and never came back. He got up to investigate, only to find Dad alongside the busy hot dog vendor, helping him hawk hot dogs to hungry Mets fans.

A coveted ticket at the time was for the first *Godfather* film. Mom remembers the long lines of people in Manhattan waiting to see it—"miles long around every theater, the big thing to do." So Dad got one of the theaters to host a special screening, and he invited all the ambassadors and their wives—essentially the entire General Assembly.

"I was shocked at the movie," said Mom, who was surprised and upset at the glorification of the Mafia and the portrayal of a violent, high-crime America. "Here we are inviting all these foreign dignitaries. So we came out of the theater saying to them, 'Don't worry, it's only a movie.'"

But as Mom and Dad were downplaying the film, the guests left the theater to find a newsstand in front carrying an early edition of the next day's paper. The headline read "Five Mob Members Killed in New Jersey."

"Right in front of the whole theater," Mom laughed. "How could we have done that?"

It was a busy year at the U.N. for Dad, featuring several highly publicized Security Council debates on air hijackings, apartheid in South Africa, the Cold War, the U.S. contribution to the U.N. budget, and the Israeli attack against Lebanon.

Adding to the drama of that year, shots were fired into the Soviet mission to the U.N., hitting an apartment where a young family was living. The Jewish Defense League, which was led at the time by a radical rabbi named Meir Kahane, issued a press release the next day applauding the shooting. As Dad prepared to walk to the U.N. building shortly afterward, Rabbi Kahane, standing in the lobby of the U.S. Embassy, approached him, saying he wanted to "talk." He wanted Dad to listen.

"I told him when they condoned the shooting that I had 'heard' enough," Dad recalled. "I stepped past him and was led across to the U.N. by security people." Kahane eventually took his extremist followers and moved to Israel, but returned to New York in 1990 and was assassinated by his political opponents.

Also in 1971 was the India-Pakistan War, which was very important policywise because of the Cold War. "India was much closer to Russia, and Pakistan was much closer to us," Dad recalled. "It was kind of tense. I think the Pakistanis always felt that we were a little shaky. They knew that Washington was where the decisions were made, not at the U.N. The question we faced at the time was whether we were tilting in favor of Pakistan or India. Kissinger was driving the policy and said we were tilting toward Pakistan."

Dad remembers the then-president of Pakistan, Zulfikar Ali Bhutto, addressing the General Assembly during the war. Bhutto gave a "very strong" speech, then "took his speech out, ripped it apart, threw it down, and stormed out. Real powerful. I got to know Bhutto. In fact, later when I was in China, on the way back to Washington one time for consultations, we flew west from China toward Pakistan. We were Bhutto's guests and stayed in a little guesthouse there."

Sadly, Bhutto was thrown out of office during a 1977 military coup and executed two years later. His daughter, Benazir, later became prime minister of Pakistan.

Without a doubt one of the most important U.N. votes during Dad's tenure took place on October 25, 1971, when the People's Republic of China was admitted and Taiwan was kicked out of the United Nations. Until that vote, Taiwan had held the China seat, representing the communist mainland, known as the People's Republic of China, as well as the nationalist Republic of China on Taiwan.

The compromise my father supported was called the dual representation policy, in which there would be one China but with two votes. It failed 55–59, and my mother remembers being in the General Assembly audience that day and seeing the Taiwanese ambassador walk out of the United Nations, "back straight and head held high," while people from one of the missions at a third world country turned to Mom, jeering and spitting at her.

Tom Lias, one of Dad's aides who watched the vote from the gallery of the General Assembly, witnessed the Taiwanese ambassador's exit as well. "He had, from the standpoint of international politics, been humiliated, and so had his country. The world organization was really throwing them out." As the ambassador made his way across the Assembly hall, Dad "ran to get around to the back of the hall so he could go to that ambassador and put his arm around him and sympathize with him . . . It's another example to me of the kind of compassion that Ambassador Bush had at a time of stress." Lias continued, "There was not as much blood spilled at the United Nations as there might have been if some really nasty, really pro–Red China U.S. ambassador had been sitting there, who would have let the Nationalist China guy walk out and sort of diplomatically thumb his nose at him as he left. That's not in the Bush character to do that."

Anti-Americanism was running high. Arthur Fletcher, a former member of the U.S. delegation, looked back on the situation: "Ambassador Bush had to face the music, so to speak, and take the brunt of the bitterness that had built up over some twenty years because the People's Republic of China had not been able to join. They felt that we had kept them out. And although George certainly hadn't had anything to do with keeping them out, he had to stand in front of the gun when the final decision was made.

"When the vote was taken," Fletcher continued, "well over two-thirds of the delegates really showed their wrath toward the U.S., with some of them coming down in front of our area of the U.S. and hissing at the American delegation. I thought George handled himself superbly that night, and in fact, throughout that entire period. He proved to me that he could function under the gun without showing any signs of stress or strain. He seemed to anticipate that it was going to be a rough ride for a while, but that he could ride it out. He was a source of inspiration for the rest of the American delegation at that time."

What was complicating the situation was that while Dad was trying to round up votes in support of our longtime ally, Taiwan, President Nixon was secretly seeking to improve relations with mainland China. Nixon was motivated by two goals: to contain a potential nuclear threat and to take advantage of the animosity between the Chinese and the Soviets and basically open another front in the Cold War against the Soviet Union. (Canada and other Western allies had opened diplomatic relations with Communist China earlier during the Nixon administration, so the tide was changing internationally.)

In July 1971, President Nixon directed Secretary of State Kissinger to embark on a "secret trip" to Peking, to pave the way for a public visit by the president in February 1972. It was between these two trips, in October 1971, that the dual representation vote had taken place, giving the People's Republic of China a seat at the United Nations.

In notes dictated a week after the vote, my dad thought the warming relations between the United States and Mao Zedong had something to do with losing the Taiwan vote. "The minute the president announced his trip to Peking, the race to Peking was on," Dad wrote, referring to other countries who saw how the tide was turning toward China and away from Taiwan.

I asked Dad about Kissinger's secret trip. "It made my job rounding up votes for the status quo—for our dual representation policy—almost impossible," he said. "Kissinger kind of got angry with me when he got back, asking, 'What happened with the vote?' I told him, 'It was very difficult, when you were over there.' He knew that. Everybody in the General Assembly knew it. When they heard [that Kissinger was in China], it affected their vote."

Fifteen countries abstained from that historic vote, many after assuring Dad of their support.

The press was also a factor in the vote, alleging "undue pressure" and arm-twisting by the American delegation, which Dad felt was completely untrue. As it was, he felt terrible about losing the vote, like he'd let the Taiwanese people down, and was dismayed at the level of anti-American sentiment that had come about as a result.

★   ★   ★

As seriously as Dad took his work, he has never taken himself too seriously. In late 1970, *New York* magazine published an article by ABC sportscaster Dick Schapp with the headline "The Ten Most Overrated Men in New York." The ten men were: McGeorge Bundy, who had been national security adviser to Presidents

Kennedy and Johnson; Terence Cardinal Cooke, archbishop of New York; Ralph DeNunzio, head of the New York Stock Exchange; Sanford Garelik, New York City Council president; Senator Jacob Javits; Gabe Pressman of NBC; Arthur Ochs "Punch" Sulzberger, publisher of the *New York Times;* Steve Smith, husband of Jean Kennedy Smith; Broadway producer David Merrick; and finally, the U.S. ambassador to the United Nations, George Bush.

Dad was amused to be named on such a list, and decided it would be fun to throw an "overrated party." So he promptly sent a letter to each of his listmates—addressing each as "Dear Most-Overrated Mr. Garelik" or whatever—inviting them to cocktails at the U.N. ambassador's residence. He told them he thought it might be fun to get together, adding, "I'd like the chance to look you over to see why you are so 'overrated.' " He also included the article's author, Dick Schapp (who was brave enough to attend), and a few friends and fellow diplomats "so we can have an international judgment as to who is indeed the most overrated of them all."

Mom remembers that Senator Javits "wouldn't come, because he didn't think it was funny, but it was great fun." During the party, Dad jumped up on a chair and gave a dramatic reading of the article, adding funny comments about each man and himself. At one point, my mother overheard the Russian ambassador asking a friend who was more familiar with Western culture, "Vat is dis *'overrated'*?"

My parents hosted an endless string of receptions—entertaining constantly—as it came with the job. The big parties were fun and I'd come in for a while and see people, and then go off and do my homework. But my favorite part of our daily routine was going to school in the morning, because I got to spend uninterrupted time with Dad.

At first, I was taking public transportation to school, but unbeknownst to me, the CIA had received intelligence information that a radical Arab terrorist organization, Black September, was planning some sort of an attack against Israelis or Americans in New York. The CIA feared that our family might be a target, and they specifically wanted me to be driven to school rather than continue taking public transportation.

(By the way, the CIA's concerns were well founded. In September 1972, terrorists associated with Black September stormed the Munich Olympics and eleven Israeli athletes were killed.)

Dad had a driver who drove him to the U.N. mission every day in a black limo, but I was mortified at the idea of showing up in a limo—so they had Jerry Aprile, my dad's driver, switch to a more innocuous-looking sedan. Jerry was a real New Yorker and he was very funny.

Yet even in the sedan I was embarrassed, and insisted on getting dropped off a block before the school. I was painfully aware of being in the minority as an American student for the first and only time in my life. I remember the feeling of being different and alienated—and I was so focused on my own embarrassment I neglected to notice that most of the other students, who were also children of diplomats, were arriving in black limos!

Being the teenage son or daughter of someone in public life can be unusual because you're aware of the coverage in the press, the riding in the limos, the life in a glass bowl—but you're powerless to do anything about it, and not old enough to have developed a thick skin. To be honest, it can also be a bit lonely, especially if you have to move around a lot as we did. You lose the security that comes with living in one community for a long time. In that regard, my nieces Barbara and Jenna Bush are lucky to be twins and to have each other.

Chapter 7

THE *TITANIC* BOILER ROOM

"As you look back now at that period of 1973 and 1974, and realize how remarkably unscathed George Bush has come out of all that [Watergate], that's as high a tribute as I think you can give any man or woman."

—**Bill Steiger** (speaking in 1978)

In November 1972, shortly after President Nixon was reelected in a landslide victory over George McGovern, he summoned Dad to Camp David to discuss "the future." Dad had served as ambassador to the United Nations for nearly two years by then, but President Nixon had a new idea for making use of my father's talents and party loyalty: the president had asked for the resignation of Kansas Senator Bob Dole as chairman of the Republican National Committee and wanted Dad to replace him. (In fact, President Nixon had requested the resignations of every member of his cabinet as well as of Senator Dole, at the start of his second administration.)

Dad wasn't sure he wanted the job. He clearly loved the U.N. posting and was not ready to leave; but given his instinctive deference to the office of the president, he also knew it might not be his decision. "I always felt that one should do what the president asked of him, unless he was certain he could not do the job," Dad explained to me. (An old friend and colleague from the House, Congressman Bill Steiger of Wisconsin, said years later that he wished Dad would have said no to a president just once.)

Mom was sure he shouldn't take the job because of all the travel involved—the chairman of the RNC spends his time constantly helping candidates in all fifty states—and because she had seen how vicious party politics could be. Interestingly, many of his diplomatic friends thought it was not only a great job but a step up. (After all, the Chinese communists pointed out, Chairman Mao's title was "chairman of the party.") Despite his doubts, and those of my mother, Dad felt he really couldn't turn the president down.

Dad never felt close to President Nixon, but he respected many of his achievements, particularly in the realm of foreign affairs. They had an affable relationship and, before Watergate, one of mutual respect. So in January 1973, just as President Nixon was beginning his second term in office, Dad made the move to the Republican National Committee. We left the Waldorf and returned to Washington, and I, thirteen years old by then, returned to National Cathedral School.

It wasn't until after Dad arrived on the job in January that the Watergate story broke; and, of course, he never would have taken the job had he known what was to come. Barely a month later, in February 1973, the Senate Watergate Committee was established. By April, President Nixon denied he was involved in the break-in and cover-up, and Attorney General Richard Kleindienst had resigned— along with White House aides John Ehrlichman and H. R. "Bob" Haldeman. Then White House counsel John Dean III was fired.

In May, a special prosecutor, Archibald Cox, was named. During the summer that followed, John Dean testified before the Senate Watergate Committee, and Judge John Sirica ordered the White House to turn over the tapes President Nixon had been recording in the Oval Office dating back to 1971.

My father was under enormous strain. Leading a political party whose president was sinking deeper and deeper into a legal, political, and ethical quagmire with each passing day must have been more than most people could have endured.

During his twenty months leading the RNC, Dad kept a diary that reveals the depths of his anguish over what was happening. Reading the entries in order, and knowing the end result, is like watching a car drive off a cliff in slow motion. For example, an early diary entry involves Nixon's conversation with my father about Spiro Agnew's impending resignation on tax evasion charges unrelated to Watergate:

September 16, 1973

He [President Nixon] pointedly asked if John Connally [treasury secretary] could be involved in this matter. It occurred to me immediately that he was considering Connally for Vice-President . . . I get the feeling that within a week or ten days the Vice President will resign. I get the distinct feeling the President is giving top consideration to appointing Connally, who I am sure he feels he can get through both Houses of Congress.

Former Texas governor John Connally—Ralph Yarborough's nemesis who had edged him out of Kennedy's car in Dallas that day—was now the only Democrat appointed to Nixon's cabinet, serving as secretary of the treasury. He had spearheaded the "Democrats for Nixon" effort in Texas, which helped Nixon win Texas as part of the GOP landslide in the 1972 presidential race. After the election—and three months after LBJ's death—Connally became a Republican.

When word of Nixon's leaning toward Connally got to both Republicans and Democrats in the Senate, however, the idea went down in flames. Afterward, Congressman William Whitehurst of Virginia remembered that President Nixon asked every Republican member of the House and the Senate to submit up to three names to him, as possible candidates for the vice presidency. White-hurst submitted Dad's name (so we know Dad got at least one vote). Nixon ended up naming Gerald Ford as his vice president—but also made it clear he'd support Connally for the 1976 Republican nomination.

At about the same time, Henry Kissinger, Nixon's secretary of state and national security adviser, won the Nobel Peace Prize. On October 13, 1973, Dad wrote:

I also couldn't help but think of the irony when Kissinger got the Nobel Peace Prize. Here was Nixon taking all the flack on the war, Kissinger executing his policies, and Henry walking away with a coveted honor. Of course I have great respect for the job Kissinger did—his imagination, his grasp of the situation—but it is also a little ironic.

A week later, on Saturday, October 20, the "Saturday Night Massacre" took place. That night, Attorney General Elliot Richardson refused to fire special prosecutor Archibald Cox, who had sided with the Senate Watergate Committee in demanding that the White House turn over Nixon's tapes. Because the special prosecutor was appointed by the Department of Justice, he answered to the attorney general and could be fired by him—but both Richardson and Deputy Attorney General William Ruckelshaus refused to fire him and resigned in protest. Nixon then named Solicitor General Robert H. Bork as acting attorney general, and Bork went ahead and fired Cox—all this in one night.

Dad, for the most part, didn't let the pressure show. He seemed the same at family dinners and Sunday barbecues, happy at his place manning the grill, making sure everyone had a drink, joking around with his guests. As always, family and friends came first to Dad.

My childhood friend Liz Grundy, who later went on to work for Dad, recalled a time when she was fourteen, at the height of Watergate, when she came to our house for a weekend barbecue with her parents.

"Throughout the afternoon, we noticed that your father was constantly having to interrupt his hamburger grilling to go inside to take telephone calls," she recalled. Liz stayed on to have a sleepover, and the next morning Liz's mom offered to come pick her up.

"Oh no," Dad said. "I have to go downtown, I'll be happy to bring her in."

As it turned out, the barbecue was the same night as the Saturday Night Massacre. "Thus, all the phone calls and the trip downtown to the White House on a Sunday," Liz noted. "In the midst of all this, George Bush still made time to drop off his daughter's friend on the way."

In November, Dad discussed with President Nixon what had happened after Vice President Agnew's resignation in October. Although Nixon had nominated Gerald Ford to replace him, Ford would not be confirmed by both houses of Congress and sworn in until early December:

November 14, 1973

We talked about the Agnew matter. I told him that Barbara and I had supported Agnew and told him about my personal letter from Agnew . . . I told him I was going to call on him. I said I might be criticized for this but I felt an affection for the man. The President indicated I did just the right thing and he told me he himself had bought Agnew his Cabinet chair (which cost $600).

While he wanted to pursue his own political career, Dad told Nixon that he would stay with the RNC job—which he didn't much care for—because he felt the party needed the consistency of his leadership during the beginning of what would become a protracted period of difficulty for the Republicans:

I told him that I had been urged by Connally, Anne Armstrong and others to run for Governor of Texas but that I had decided not to do it now. I felt there was a chance for a Republican to win and it would

*be important, but I felt that my leaving might inadvertently increase
the speculation that I had no confidence in the Administration—it
might add to an air of instability. I mentioned that I was not trying
to equate myself with Ruckelshaus or Richardson. The President
agreed that it would be good to stay on the job. I believe he said
"through the elections." He then said, "You could go into foreign
service which we could arrange very easily, but I think you ought to
come into the Cabinet at that point."*

By this point, I am beginning to feel that as RNC chairman my
father, like Atlas, was keeping the weight of the world on his
shoulders, but just barely:

November 30, 1973

*This job is like walking a tightrope. You want to be fair to the Presi-
dent—you want to accentuate the positive accomplishments of the
President, you want to take credit for them for the Party, but you
want to be darn sure that the people know the Party does not approve of Watergate or its handling . . . Right now after the November elections there are a wide number of comments that the
Republican Party has had it—that we are in for a disaster . . .*

On December 3, 1973, the president publicly disclosed his personal
finances, under pressure from the press. (Nixon had given a speech
to a group of newspaper editors, and during the question-and-
answer session had promised to release his financial record, fa-
mously declaring, "I am not a crook.") As Dad listened to the
lawyers present the figures, he thought of his own father's opinion
about Nixon's financial situation:

December 3, 1973

*. . . I could not help but feel what a difficult thing for a President
to have to lay all this out. I also had the feeling, frankly, that the
President would have been well advised given his net worth not*

to have bought Key Biscayne and San Clemente. It was too big a bite
for a man with that kind of limited resources. I remember Dad
telling me that he worried about this, and I thought, "Oh, how old-
fashioned." But I think now in retrospect, he was right. I also think
about Bar telling me that the President ought to let go of one of the
houses because of the energy crisis.

In the midst of all this, my brother Jeb came to Dad to announce that he wanted to marry Maria Columba "Colu" Garnica
of Leon, Mexico. They had met in Mexico when he was on a high
school program teaching English to schoolchildren. It would be
the first wedding in our family. Dad really wanted Jeb to finish college first—and almost to prove his love for Columba, Jeb not only
finished a year early but graduated Phi Beta Kappa from the University of Texas.

So on February 23, 1974, Jeb and Columba were married in
Austin, Texas. The wedding was very small, just family members.
The ceremony was at the University of Texas in the chapel on
campus. They seemed so young—Jeb, with long hair and a mus-
tache, was only twenty-one years old. "Colu," at age nineteen,
spoke little English at the time, and my main impression of her
was that she was tiny and very beautiful. Dad hadn't met Columba
until the rehearsal dinner at a restaurant called the Green Turtle,
the night before their wedding.

When I asked Jeb recently whether Watergate and the stress it
was placing on Dad in any way cast a pall over his wedding, he answered, "He was gracious and accepting even though I placed this
burden on him—of not even knowing the love of my life until the
night before the wedding . . . No talk of Watergate."

My brother Marvin was the photographer for the wedding, because he was the right price (meaning free) and because, in his
own words, he considered himself "a younger version of Ansel
Adams, armed with my new Minolta camera and a burning desire
to leave my mark on the world as we knew it in 1974."

Here is Marv's recollection of that day:

It was with that sense of heightened self-importance that I volunteered to be the photographer for Jeb and Columba's wedding. Nobody really protested because the ceremony was small and relatively informal and Jeb and Columba were practically kids. So, if they were responsible enough to get married, then maybe I was responsible enough to memorialize the event for both families. Sounds good, right?

The cool thing with my fellow high school photographers was to roll your own film from spools that held hundreds of frames. It appealed to the "starving artist" mentality and was a sign of being a purist. So, in anticipation of Jeb and Columba's wedding, I rolled a few canisters of film and packed them for Austin. I was an "in your face" brand of photographer, snapping pictures at every possible angle and at annoying distances from the subjects. My mom claims that I was snapping photos from the ground (sometimes through someone's legs) at people who were trying to have regular conversation. I think she's exaggerating, but it is probably a fair description to say that I was early in the paparazzi movement. So, for the better part of two days I snapped away, naively imagining that Jeb would forever be grateful to his little brother for the beautiful photo album that would memorialize his special day.

The first moment of panic came when I was in the darkroom, reviewing the negatives from the wedding rolls. The frames seemed too congested with conflicting images. I was hoping that my eyesight was playing games with me, so I printed out one of the frames. That's when the real queasiness hit. As the paper settled into the chemicals in the tray, I began to see the image of a guitar over a picture of my grandmother and my parents. Uh-oh! It hit me like a ton of bricks. I had rerolled previously used film that had been taken at a Frank Zappa concert at the Mosque in Richmond, Virginia. Every single photo of the Bush and Garnica families had either a photo of Frank Zappa and/or members of his band, the Mothers of Invention, superimposed onto their own images. I remember thinking to myself that a Frank Sinatra photo may have been acceptable—not Frank Zappa!

Anyway, I chose the coward's way out—silence. Deafening silence. Radio silence. Aside from a few questions to the effect of, "How did your pictures turn out?" I heard very little about my embarrassing attempt to help my brother out. For the next thirty years, practically nothing was said about the incident. The wedding marked the end of my photography career. Luckily, my mother thought to take one picture of Jeb and Columba with her Kodak pocket Instamatic, and that photo, copied a few times over, is in scrapbooks and on coffee tables in Texas, Maine, and Florida.

The epilogue to the story, never previously revealed to any family members, is that I submitted a picture of the bride and groom (yes, with Zappa) in an art show at school. I called the picture something clever like "Zappa's Bride" and won third prize in the photography category.

★   ★   ★

About a week after Jeb's wedding, seven Nixon aides were indicted for conspiring to obstruct justice—among them Ehrlichman, Haldeman, and former attorney general John Mitchell—and President Nixon was named as an unindicted coconspirator. Within two weeks of that, Dad wrote in his diary about a difficult meeting with the White House chief of staff, Al Haig:

March 13, 1974

He [Haig] started off by being fairly tough and firm with me, telling me that it was getting down to the wire, that if the President was going to survive there had to be an all-out offense, that they were preparing papers and they wanted me to give it full range support. I asked what it was . . . he wanted me to say that I would support it. I thought for a minute—low keyed it and said that in my opinion the President was entitled to advocacy and that if in good conscience I couldn't support what it was that he was talking about then I would resign. I said I felt I probably could but I didn't want to say without seeing in advance what it was.

The White House was putting Dad in a very difficult position, and Dad began to sense an us-versus-them mentality in this discussion with Haig:

> *There was too much, for my thinking, of the feeling that everyone that wasn't supportive was totally against, in other words—turning against the whole Judiciary Committee, the House, we don't have any friends on the Hill—nobody is standing up for us. This went through the whole theme . . . I did get the feeling that Haig goes through a lot of inner turmoil in his own mind. He must have some difficult times with the President though he would never say this to me . . .*

Dad concluded this entry with a statement about the political pressure he was experiencing, in terms of agreeing to the administration's public relations offensive:

> *At this moment I haven't even seen the papers that [speechwriter] Pat Buchanan is putting together—his talking points. They are talking about an all-out offensive—whatever the hell that means. I have called them as I see them so far. Bending, stretching a little here or there, insisting that things that I don't want to put my name on have the White House name on them, not mine. And I am not going to change that, I'm simply not going to do it.*

There were several principles at stake in Dad's mind throughout this time. First, of course, was his integrity and his wanting to do the right thing in this difficult, complicated, and unprecedented time. Second, there was his extreme loyalty—his aversion to "piling on." Third, there was his essential optimism that Watergate would resolve itself and the Nixon presidency would survive. For example, a month later—on April 18, 1974—he wrote of being "heartsick" and of things being "massively fouled up," but then he added that he's "still believing that the evidence on the tapes will vindicate the President but not totally, not clearly, not to get this whole matter behind us. Resignation seems wrong to me still; impeachment, though possible, does not even seem likely right now . . ."

Within a few weeks, he realized he supported resignation, mostly in defense of the presidency as an institution—another principle that was very important to him then, and certainly after he himself went on to serve in the Oval Office. On the night before the House Judiciary Committee's impeachment hearings began, Dad wrote:

May 8, 1974

My own gut reactions are really mixed up. I believe this thing about resignation being bad for the system; and yet for the first time it seems like it might be the only answer. I am not talking about short term politics. I am talking about the Presidency and what has happened to it because of these ugly revelations. Probably they went on before but that no longer seems to be the point.

That summer, in a letter dated July 23, 1974, Dad wrote to my brothers (he thought I was too young to be included) and shared his private thoughts about Watergate as it was nearing its inevitable conclusion. He talked about what a great country America is and how lucky they were to be citizens—but that Watergate was the worst of times, that it reflected "abysmal amorality." He went on for many pages talking about the president and the men who worked in the White House. But it is in the final page of the letter that he draws lessons from Watergate:

Listen to your conscience. Don't be afraid not to join the mob—if you feel inside it's wrong. Don't confuse being "soft" with seeing the other guy's point of view. In judging your President give him the enormous credit he's due for substantive achievements. Try to understand the "why" of the National Security concern; but understand too that the power accompanied by arrogance is very dangerous. It's particularly dangerous when men with no real ex-

perience have it—for they can abuse our great institutions. Avoid self-righteously turning on a friend, but have your friendship mean enough that you would be willing to share with your friend your judgment. Don't assign away your judgment to achieve power.

As RNC chairman, Dad was caught between the proverbial rock and a hard place. Charged with promoting and supporting the Republican Party, he found himself being forced to defend a situation that he eventually found to be sickening. Toward the end of the letter to my brothers, he expressed the toll it had taken on him:

These have been a tough 18 months. I feel battered and disillusioned. I feel betrayed in a sense by those who did wrong and tracked corruption and institutional subversion into that beautiful White House. In trying to build the Party, I feel like the guy in charge of the Titanic *boiler room—one damn shock after another.*

The same day he wrote to my brothers, Dad reflected on Watergate's effects on the Republican Party. He wrote in his diary:

July 23, 1974

These are complicated times. I can't imagine a set of circumstances in terms of Party that are more complicated. I feel frustrated that our programs and our philosophy and the President's magnificent record on war and peace would normally have us riding high even in spite of the problems of inflation. This Watergate thing dominates all the news. It doesn't dominate the concern of the voters. The concern of the voters is still on inflation where of course we have a tremendous problem.

Dad had a difficult job outside of Washington as well, traveling to state party events and having to deal with irate Republicans. Arthur Fletcher, who had been a delegate to the United Nations and then a consultant to the RNC, remembers, "That was not a tenderfoot's assignment, holding the Republican Party together. But George did not apologize, did not back off from the assignment, and I thought he stood the test superbly well. I know of no other national chairman that had to ride out the tide the way he did. And in spite of it—to still get out and raise money, go across the country and talk to a lot of mad, bitter, disgruntled Republicans, and face a hostile press that was asking him some very tough questions—through it all he handled himself very well."

Dad told me he had two stacks of mail. One said, "Why do you keep the party close to Nixon when you know the party per se had nothing to do with Watergate?" The other stack said, "Why are you not doing more to help President Nixon?" Dad continued, "In my speeches to the Republican faithful, I made the point over and over again that the party was in no way involved in the Watergate scandal, but that we should not pull away from Nixon without concrete evidence of wrong-doing."

On July 24, the Supreme Court unanimously ruled that Nixon must turn over the Watergate tapes to the special prosecutor. Over the next several days, the House Judiciary Committee voted to approve articles of impeachment. Dad had a "big picture" conversation with Al Haig, in which he conveyed his concerns as party chairman:

July 31, 1974

Haig stopped short of being critical of me, although I will readily concede the White House probably feels I have not done enough to partisanize it . . . I told him the adverse effects on the Party in terms of money, morale, deterioration of support, of real strong support. I told him that I did not love the President, I respected his achievements . . .

Dad's diary entry on Monday night, August 5, 1974, strikes me as increasingly emotional:

As I dictate this memo at 10:10 p.m. on August 5 I do not feel the Pres-
ident can survive . . . I have decided not to issue a statement, to sim-
ply sit and let the storms swirl around, although give some leadership
to the committee by telling them not to get too far out front. I am torn
between wanting to express my own agony and my own emotion,
and get out front and cry resignation and this is too much . . .

Dad also wrote of a conversation with Al Haig, who made a
sweeping prediction: "He [Haig] predicted the President would
not survive, but that we would look back when were both 80 and
say he had been one of the great presidents of our time . . ."

Now that Dad is over eighty years old, it's time to address whether
General Haig's prediction was on the mark. I asked Dad how he felt
about Nixon and his presidency in retrospect. Here's what he said:

"I got to know him pretty well, and I admired much of what he
was doing and went on to accomplish as a two-term president. I
felt he was very, very smart, but he had a lot of hang-ups. One was
that his disdain for 'Ivy Leaguers' came through loud and clear. He
would single out Ivy Leaguers at cabinet meetings and one could
look around the room and see several Ivy Leaguers at the cabinet
table. As the tapes revealed, he had a rather ugly side in which he
was hypercritical of some groups."

He had a few things to say about the president's men as well:

"I liked Haldeman and Ehrlichman, and I think it was recipro-
cal. [Charles] Colson back then was a tough guy. He has gone on to
really do wonderful things in his prison ministry. I respect him, but
back then did not feel very close.

"John Dean always struck me as an arrogant little creep. He became a big shot. He turned on Nixon, and, of course, much to the
delight of the Nixon-haters, he put a negative spin on a lot of
things about Nixon. He became a hero when he testified before
Congress. He was as guilty as Nixon ever was, but somehow managed to escape a lot of the public disapproval." Then, after further
reflection, he added, "Perhaps some of this visceral anti-Dean feeling I have is because of the way he has attacked your brother."

And as for how he thinks Nixon felt about him:

"I always felt Nixon thought I wasn't tough enough. I lacked the kind of bulldoze-'em approach that some of his lieutenants had. Nixon liked the tough guy. He encouraged toughness and not taking any guff."

My take: Dad stuck to his principles and refused to use his position at the RNC as a bully pulpit to defend and excuse a corrupt president—if Nixon interpreted that as weakness, so be it. We'll leave it up to history to decide whose perception is more accurate.

Dad was very fond of Nixon's family, particularly his daughter Julie, and to this day, the sadness he felt about their suffering is still evident.

"I recall Julie Nixon coming to see me at the RNC headquarters. I was chairman at the time. Julie was desperately trying to rally support for her dad. She asked me if I couldn't help more. At that time, Nixon was sinking fast. Julie obviously felt we could do more. She was very, very nice and she had been terribly hurt by the attacks on her dad, not from the RNC but from the press and many political people, some in our own party. I respected Julie then. I could see she was hurting badly. I ached for her, but there was nothing we could do. I had gone around the country encouraging support for Nixon until it became clear he was going down because of his own false statements."

The toll that political scandals take on family members, particularly the children, is immeasurable. A strange image I remember from that time is of Ann Haldeman, a teenage schoolmate of mine whose dad, H. R. Haldeman, was on the White House staff. I remember her opening her jacket and having all kinds of Nixon-Agnew buttons on the *inside* of her blazer.

As I look back on it, that incident makes me sad. I can understand how Ann wanted to support her dad. Whatever you might think about President Nixon and his inner circle, the children should be unassailable—yet, in some ways, they bore the same brunt of the pain and the shame as did their parents.

When Dad spoke with Al Haig on August 5, Haig had just returned from a weekend at Camp David with the president, along
with his speechwriters Pat Buchanan and Ray Price and White
House press secretary Ron Ziegler. The Supreme Court had just
ordered President Nixon to turn over the White House tapes, and
so Nixon had played the tapes for them over the weekend. At the
Monday morning staff meeting afterward, Haig asked Pat
Buchanan to brief Dean Burch, who was political director at the
White House—and, therefore, liaison to the RNC—as to what was
on the tapes. "That was about 10:00 or 11:00 in the morning and
we just heard it and almost unanimously—nobody really thought
much about it, we just went to the bar—and opened up the bar
and had a drink and toasted the president and that's it, you know,
we fold her up now, it's over," said Dean Burch.

From there, Burch took the transcripts of the tape with him
to brief Dad and John Rhodes, the House minority leader. Rhodes
recalled afterward: "Etched on my memory until I die will be that
morning—it was the Monday before Nixon resigned—when
George Bush and Dean Burch and [White House counsel] Fred
Buzhardt came out to my house. I had a bad case of laryngitis and
wasn't going to the office that day. So they came out to the house
to brief me on the contents of the June 23 tape, the one in which
the president told Bob Haldeman to make sure that the CIA told
the FBI to call off the Watergate investigation for national security
reasons. And George Bush hadn't been briefed either on that, so
we were briefed together. And we both came to the same conclusion, that this was a smoking gun, a clear case of an impeachable
offense. Not only an impeachable offense, but an offense so grave
that you almost *had* to impeach. So we came to the conclusion that
the end of the road had been reached for Mr. Nixon at exactly the
same time." (John Rhodes died in 2003.)

The next day, Tuesday, August 6, 1974, was "a traumatic day,"
Dad wrote, as he sat in on a "grueling" cabinet meeting just two
days before Nixon announced he would resign from office:

The President sat there, strong, determined, announcing his deci-
sion to remain in office and yet unreality prevailed. Jerry Ford reit-
erated his position that because of his peculiar situation he was not
going to involve himself in the President's defense . . . It kind of
cast a pall over the meeting. Haig later told me he thought it was
wrong, the President was clearly shook up. Ford later told me that
he wondered if it had offended the President and how it had gone
over. I told him I thought that he had done the right thing and that I
had told Haig, which I did, that Ford was simply reiterating a posi-
tion he expressed the day before, so that the President would be sure
to know it. Because the President indeed at that meeting was say-
ing we should go all out, be together, be unified, go forward, etc. . . .
His explanation of this awful lie was not convincing. It simply was
unreal, but everybody just sat there.

Later on in the same meeting, Dad felt pulled in two directions, as
he thought of the evidence on the president's tape:

The President looked uncomfortable, once he smiled over to me and
with his lips said, "George," smiled and looked warm and my heart
went totally out to him even though I felt deeply betrayed by his lie
of the day before. The man is amoral. He has a different sense than
the rest of the people. He came up the hard way. He hung tough.
He hunkered down, he stonewalled. He became President of the
United States and a damn good one in many ways, but now it had
all caught up with him. All the people he hated—Ivy League, press,
establishment, Democrats, privileged—all of this ended up biting
him and bringing him down.

In the same entry—they got longer as resignation neared—he
wrote that he'd made it clear to the president (through Haig) that
Nixon must resign. "This era of tawdry, shabby lack of morality
has got to end," he wrote, and called Vice President Ford a "latter-
day Eisenhower":

*He is an Ike without the heroics but he has that decency the country
is crying out for right now. I will take Ford's decency over Nixon's
toughness because what we need at this juncture in our history is a
certain sense of morality and a certain sense of decency. Nixon can
no longer present it. My own views are that the President should get
out and get out now . . .*

Dad also lashed out at the press and the Washington "meat-grinder":

*The incivility of the press had been a paralyzing kind of thing over
the last few months. And now it continues, that blood lust, the
talons are sharpened and clutched, ready to charge in there and
grab the carrion of this President. I am sick at heart. Sick about the
President's betrayal and sick about the fact that the major Nixon
enemies can now gloat because they have proved he is what they
said he is. No credit, no compassion, no healing, simply the meat-
grinder at work. I suppose when it is written one can establish that
perhaps I should have done more, but I am not made up to walk on
the body of a man whom I don't love but whom I respect for his
accomplishments.*

He closed this entry wondering about Rose Mary Woods, the president's secretary:

*I have not seen Rose Woods and I wonder how she feels. The gloom
in the White House is unimaginable, difficult to describe. It is
brought dramatically home that this President is a liar, a total liar
and we cannot face up to it in fairness, in the nation's interest, in
any other way . . .*

Dad's close friend Dean Burch was also in that final cabinet
meeting, which he said had to be the most "surrealistic" cabinet
meeting he'd ever seen:

The whole goddamn world was crashing in on us. The White House was collapsing. And President Nixon came in and just had a regular cabinet meeting. He was saying we were going to do this and we're going to strike that program, we're going to do something else. George had a letter addressed to President Nixon in which he said he felt that he had to resign. And he wanted to bring it up at the cabinet meeting. I felt that he should bring it up, but I didn't think he should bring it up at the cabinet meeting. I just didn't think that was an appropriate place to face a man down and say, I want to read a letter demanding your resignation.

I've never seen such an unhappy man as George was during this period, because now all of us had come to the conclusion that we'd all been lied to for many, many months . . . But George then went in to see the president after that meeting and gave him the letter. He told him that there just wasn't anything left, wasn't any support left, and that he, George, as chairman of the party, sided with those who felt the president had to go.

It was not, in George's case, the idea of jumping on after the man was down. He had stayed with him to the bitter, bitter end. Maybe too long. Maybe George should've bailed out earlier, although frankly, I would have thought a great deal less of him had he done that. Not because of any personal loyalty to Nixon, but I just think that the party chairman, appointed by the president, sticks with him until he himself has made up his mind. George contributed, certainly, to the decision that President Nixon had to make. And he contributed to it well.

Much has been written about that "surrealistic" cabinet meeting, with others present at it each remembering it a bit differently. My dad's diaries note that he spoke up at the meeting—a suggestion had been made for the president to meet with congressional leaders, which Dad strongly advised against because of the confrontational mood on Capitol Hill—and as a result, his asking how expedient a congressional trial of the president would be, should it come to that. Here's what then–Secretary of Health, Education, and Welfare Caspar "Cap" Weinberger wrote to me, shortly before he died:

In the faltering days of the Nixon Presidency, we were having a rather desultory Cabinet meeting. The agenda item concerned a new anti-inflation campaign. President Nixon wanted to support a large scale anti-inflation meeting scheduled for the next week. Your father finally said, "Look, this is quite ridiculous, talking about matters of this kind when the only thing on everyone's mind is whether this Presidency is going to survive." President Nixon glowered and then said, "One thing is certain—I will never resign the Presidency." End of meeting. Your father had again demonstrated firmness and decisiveness and candor. He literally spoke for the whole Cabinet.

The day after that bizarre cabinet meeting, Dad presented President Nixon with the following letter:

August 7, 1974

The Honorable Richard M. Nixon
President of the United States
The White House
Washington, D.C.

Dear Mr. President:

It is my considered judgment that you should now resign. I expect in your lonely embattled position this would seem to you as an act of disloyalty from one you have supported and helped in so many ways.

My own view is that I would now ill serve a President, whose massive accomplishments I will always respect and whose family I love, if I did not now give you my judgment.

Until this moment resignation has been no answer at all, but given the impact of the latest development, and it will be a lasting one, I now firmly feel resignation is best for this country, best for this President. I believe this view is held by most Republican leaders across the country.

*This letter is made much more difficult because of the gratitude I
will always have for you.*

*If you do leave office history will properly record your achieve-
ments with a lasting respect.*

Very sincerely,

George Bush

Dad went to the White House to see Rose Mary Woods. It was
Thursday, August 8, 1974, the day the president had announced he
was going to resign:

*I went over and saw Rose Woods. There was a pall over the entire
White House. I debated about seeing her, but I felt it was a kind
thing to do. I felt she would probably be sore about my resignation
request letter and she was strained at first. Eddie Cox was there the
whole time. Rose had some tears. I told her you'll probably differ
with me, but I am convinced that this is much the best thing for the
President as well as the country. She said, "Yes, I do differ with
you." She was sore with [Senator Bob] Griffin and [Congressman
John] Rhodes and others who have been close friends with the President. She was apparently blind to the enormity of what he had
done. Faithful to the end . . .*

Then, finally, on Friday, August 9, 1974, President Nixon announced his resignation:

*There is no way to really describe the emotion of the day. Bar and I
went down and had breakfast at the White House. Dean and Pat
Burch and the Buchanans were there in the Conference Mess. There
was an aura of sadness, like someone died. Grief. Saw Tricia and
Eddie Cox in the Rose Garden—talked to them on the way into the
ceremony. President Nixon looked just awful. He used glasses—the
first time I ever saw them. Close to breaking down—understand-*

ably. Everyone in the room was in tears. The speech was vintage Nixon—a kick or two at the press—enormous strains. One couldn't help but look at the family and the whole thing and think of his accomplishments and then think of the shame and wonder what kind of a man is this really. No morality—kicking his friends in those tapes—all of them. Gratuitous abuse. Caring for no one and yet doing so much . . .

I went back to the National Committee and addressed them. I tried to identify with the feelings I am sure they all felt—of betrayal and distrust and yet pride. I told them we had been through the toughest year and a half in history and yet I now felt we were coming on an optimistic period. I told them that the President [Ford] asked me to stay on. All in all it was a pretty good meeting although I felt drained emotionally and physically tired.

Having read the diary entries penned during the Watergate era, I was fascinated on the one hand and saddened on the other, to revisit the angst my dad had endured. It amazes me now that when he was with our family, Dad managed to keep his compass as a father throughout it all.

I can't imagine what it would be like to work hard and put yourself on the line for a man who ultimately lies to you. It's ironic because Dad bends over backward to be ethical—anything that even smells of borderline is out of the question with him. So defending Nixon for that time period must have been an enormous disappointment when he found out he was guilty as charged.

Dean Burch talked about whether, in hindsight, Dad should have resigned in protest: "During it all, he was able to keep up the front that everything is working and the system will take care of itself, and yet I know damn well that he must have gone home and thrown up after giving some of those speeches that he had to give to hold the thing together. He was placed in an absolutely impossible position, of course. We all were. We were all stuck in a situation that we just couldn't control. But George had to be up in the front lines all the time, and that was a very difficult place to be.

"George might have done himself some momentary good by bailing out two or three weeks before the end, but the hell of it is I think that would have simply cheapened him, rather than having added to his stature in the long run. That was just not an option that some of us had. We were in too far to make a big pretext of resignation and stomping off in a huff. We were there and we just simply had to play out the hand—and we had no cards. And George was not an elected official and he didn't have a constituency that he had to report back to, so he didn't have that sort of an excuse . . . But I think George played it the hard way, which was to stay."

It wasn't until years later that Dad could look back at the whole episode and find the humor. In the late 1990s, he told an interviewer about a phone call he received at the height of Watergate from Bob Strauss, the head of the Democratic National Committee. Strauss said, "George, your job reminds me of making love to a gorilla." Dad said, "How so?" And Strauss said, "Well, you can't stop till the gorilla wants to."

"And that's the way it was," said Dad. "You had no control over these things. Just happened on and on, and finally, the gorilla stopped and Nixon resigned."

So it doesn't surprise me that Dad would stay in the game, move forward, and take on the next challenge—despite such a profound disappointment. "It never occurred to me to get out of public life because of Richard Nixon's transgressions," Dad said to me. "Even then, I felt I could continue to serve in some way, somewhere."

Chapter 8

LAND OF CONTRASTS

"He went from the United Nations to China, a country just emerging from total isolation, a country with whom the United States had had no contact for about two decades. And we were just trying to feel our way. Here he got the image of a giant awakening: paranoid, jealous, hopeful. And he grappled with the question: How do you work with that? How do you cultivate them?"

—**Brent Scowcroft**

It was August 1974, and we had all been in and out of Kennebunkport that summer, everyone on vacation from schools and jobs. We all watched on television as President Nixon resigned and Chief Justice Warren Burger swore in Vice President Gerald Ford as the thirty-eighth president of the United States. We also watched as speculation built regarding whom President Ford would choose as his vice president.

Dad had arrived at the house in Maine with Pete Roussel, who was his press secretary at the RNC, because the two of them wanted to get out of Washington. The D.C. rumor mill was in overdrive, and each day it seemed there were more reporters calling.

Mom had called Spike Heminway and asked him to keep Dad busy while he was home, to take his mind off things. When Spike arrived at the house one morning, he yelled for Dad and found him upstairs on his knees, fixing a toilet. They moved on from that project to scrubbing the hull of Dad's boat, flipped over on the sandy beach after the tide had gone out. It was there that Pete found the two of them and gave them the word that Nelson Rockefeller's private plane had just taken off from a local airstrip and was heading for Washington, D.C. (The Rockefellers had a vacation home nearby.)

The three of them headed back to the house, where Mom was in the kitchen. Pete, Spike, and Dad sat out on the porch with a small television turned on.

"Well, it's not going to be me," Dad said to Pete.

"How do you know that?" Pete replied.

"Because I haven't heard anything," Dad said. Just then the network anchor broke in on the television. "And now an announcement from President Ford at the White House," said the announcer. The door to the East Room opened and then immediately shut.

"Well, there's been a brief delay of some sort," said the anchor.

At that moment, the phone right next to Dad on the porch rang. It was President Ford, and Dad had a brief conversation with him, then put the phone back down. Dad turned to Pete and Spike and said, "Watch that tube. It's not going to be me." And sure enough, the door opened again, and out came President Ford to announce he had chosen Governor Rockefeller.

Pete remembers a local television crew from the Portland, Maine, station walking up shortly after that, while they were all still on the porch. The reporter stuck a microphone over the railing and said, "Mr. Bush, you don't seem to be too upset about this."

Dad stared at the reporter and then said, "Yes, but you can't see what's on the inside."

It was, of course, an honor to even be mentioned for consideration. Despite the fact that Dad received more votes than anyone else in a poll of Republican National Committee members as a possible vice presidential candidate, he didn't expect to be chosen for the job. Since this was coming on the heels of Watergate, he knew that President Ford needed a vice president who wasn't associated with Washington.

Dad and President Ford had known each other since the 1960s, when Ford was a congressman from Michigan. I asked President Ford about that phone call.

"I was one who always tried to soften the blow, so to speak, and that's why I called your dad," President Ford said. "I thought at the time my administration would be strengthened by having somebody who had some background in state administration. Your dad was a good candidate because of his record, but Nelson Rockefeller had the background as a former governor of New York."

A few days later, on August 22, 1974, shortly after Rockefeller's selection was announced, President Ford invited Dad to the Oval Office to discuss his next assignment.

During this meeting, Dad told President Ford that it was essential he put his own person in as chairman of the RNC, and they both agreed that Mary Louise Smith would be a great replacement. (Mary Louise Smith had been Dad's choice, as she was serving as cochair of the RNC with him. She was a native Iowan with a history of political and civic leadership.)

As for himself, Dad expressed an interest in going into international affairs. To this, the president offered, "London and Paris are open. Would you be interested in either of these?"

Paris and London were two of the top diplomatic postings—it doesn't get any better. They were both plum jobs that come with lots of glamour and perks. Dad responded that while that was very flattering—"beautiful embassies, wonderful challenges," as he put it—he'd prefer to go to Peking, now known as Beijing, China.

"I knew what I didn't want to do. I didn't want to go to a big embassy and be an ambassador," he told me. Because Washington was just opening its relations with Peking—a relationship that was very strained so far—our presence in China was not one of a full embassy, as it was in Paris or London. Technically, it was the U.S.

Liaison Office, or USLO. "I just wanted to do something really different. I'd been through the drill with the Republican National Committee; but I had loved my U.N. days and wanted to get back in foreign affairs. The challenge of China seemed to be like the future—which it certainly turned out to be," he explained.

If Dad could somehow further Washington's relationship with Peking, which he believed he could, then that's where he wanted to be. He felt it would be more challenging in many ways—very different and, not an unappealing factor, very far from Washington. "It was halfway around the world, it was different, and it was the future," he said.

Ford said he'd discuss it with Secretary of State Kissinger. Soon afterward, Dad was told, "China it is."

Dean Burch, who had stayed on as counselor to President Ford, remembered hearing about the meeting from a "shocked" President Ford: "I, along with everybody else, was terribly surprised . . . because I knew that it was within his power to have taken almost any job he wanted . . . he could have been secretary of commerce or something else had he wanted it."

During his time at the United Nations, Dad had become fascinated with China and its place on the geopolitical world stage. Through working on the question of the dual representation policy, Dad had come to better understand not only Taiwan but China, in all its layered complexities. Beyond the vexing question of Taiwan, the normalization of U.S.–China relations depended on several areas of concern: economics and issues of trade; security and concerns over the Soviet expansion in Asia; and democracy and human rights issues.

China in 1974 was at a unique moment in its history. After imperial rule ended in 1911, China's ruling party was the nationalist Kuomintang, which called for parliamentary democracy and moderate socialism. It was led by Chiang Kai Shek and was in a coalition with the communists throughout World War II. But in 1949, Mao Zedong and his Red Army pushed the Kuomintang from the mainland. The nationalists fled to Taiwan and set up the Republic of

China there, which maintained China's seat in the United Nations and on the Security Council until 1971—when the dual representation vote took place while Dad was ambassador to the U.N.

Just before that vote, Henry Kissinger had made his now-famous secret trip to China, which preceded Richard Nixon's historic visit in 1972. Nixon met with Mao while he was there.

In 1966, Mao and his third wife, Jiang Qing, directed the Cultural Revolution in order to fight "bourgeois" values and rekindle the revolution. Thousands were executed in ideological cleansing campaigns, and by the time my father arrived in 1974 the civil unrest had slowed. It wasn't until September 1976—long after Dad and Mom had left—that the Cultural Revolution was declared over with the arrest of the Gang of Four, a group of communist leaders that included Mao's widow, a few weeks after Mao died.

And so, in October 1974, my parents arrived in China. My father became the chief of the U.S. Liaison Office, only the second American to serve as the chief of the USLO, following David Bruce, one of America's most respected diplomats. Relations with the United States were new and very fragile, and Dad loved the idea of being in on the ground floor of it. Mao by this time was an ailing eighty-year-old—although no one knew exactly where he was at one point—and speculation was rife among the diplomatic corps that he was dying. Dad called it "reading the Chinese tea leaves." (The speculation turned out to be true, as Mao died less than two years later, on September 9, 1976.)

Harry Thayer, who was Dad's deputy in China and who had been on the U.N. staff with Dad, noted that the new mission chief was well received when he arrived—in part because of his personal diplomacy during his U.N. days. In addition to the baseball games and Broadway shows he'd invited other diplomats to in New York, Dad hosted the new Chinese delegation at his mother's home in Greenwich, Connecticut, for brunch.

I remember going to that brunch. My grandmother had the children, including the Thayer children, wait on tables—on her terrace. My mom remembers that Ganny had been a widow for only about a month and was wearing black pants and a black top with a beautiful Senate pin that my grandfather had given her. The Chinese were very formal, all wearing suits. I can hear my grandmother's sweet soft-spoken voice responding to them with phrases like, "Isn't that lovely?" I also remember lots of bowing and laughing, and the "ah, ah, ah" that comes when a word is understood.

Dad and Mom were running late because their driver had taken the long way. While we were waiting, the rice got a bit overdone. When the food was served, the Chinese foreign minister took a scoop of rice and then asked politely, "What is this?" Embarrassed, we had to explain it was minute rice. It was so overcooked the Chinese didn't recognize it!

Harry Thayer, Chris Phillips, and some of the other staff from the U.N. mission came out as well, enjoying a nice September day that coincided with the Chinese foreign minister's annual trip to the United States. "It was atypical and unusual" for an ambassador to invite foreign visitors to such a get-together, Thayer said, "and it was the kind of personal touch your dad was very good at."

Harry Thayer also said that the Chinese would have kept a record of Dad's interactions with the Chinese officials at the United Nations. Every conversation that Dad had and everything he did in New York would have been chronicled in that Chinese record, and available to people in Peking who were going to be dealing with him. Luckily, they must have liked what they read in those dossiers: the Chinese and the diplomatic community welcomed him very politely and graciously.

Dad's style was a bit different than that of his sole predecessor, David Bruce, who was more reserved. Before Bruce arrived in Peking, he had been the United States ambassador to France, West Germany, and Great Britain. "Though greatly respected, Ambassador Bruce was discouraged from attending any National Days—every country represented in China had its own national celebration—and we changed that policy," my father said. While Dad, too, had great respect for protocol, he was also very outgoing and eager to make connections with people on a personal level, regardless of rank.

For instance, my father took some heat when he invited one of the CIA's China bureau communications officers to lunch the second day he was there. Some members of the foreign service community grumbled about this, saying, in effect, "You can't do that, you have to have us first." But even those overly preoccupied with protocol couldn't help warming up to Dad pretty quickly.

Harry Thayer remembers bicycling around Peking with Dad, to various national holiday celebrations and assorted occasions, and to church, which was a fifteen-minute bike ride from the embassy. One day, Harry got into a taxicab. When the driver saw that he was American, he made a thumbs-up sign and said, "Bush good!" The word had gotten around among the locals—especially the taxi drivers who would see Dad riding his bike around town and eating at the half a dozen restaurants that were available to foreigners in Peking—that Dad was a good guy, a friend of the Chinese people. Dad brought parties of staff, visitors, and diplomats to all the restaurants open to foreigners, and Harry said it helped build the image that Dad was "as much as an American can be, the man-about-town."

"President George Bush is an old friend of the Chinese people," Jiang Zemin, former president of the People's Republic of China, told me. "He knows China very well and has made enduring efforts to push forward China–U.S. relations and friendship between the two peoples. In the fall of 1974 . . . he made a lot of Chinese friends. Many people were deeply impressed by the photo of President Bush and Mrs. Bush riding bicycles in the streets of Peking. President Bush later assumed many other important positions, but his interest in the growth of China–U.S. relations never receded. He is a main participant in and witness to the process of the bilateral ties over the past thirty-odd years."

Dad devoured everything he could about China: the politics, the history, the culture—and even tried to learn the language, practicing on everyone from the waiters in restaurants to fellow tennis players on the court. He and Mom took very seriously their daily language lessons with Miss Tang, their Chinese language tutor. Because she had been educated in the West, Miss Tang knew her life was in danger during the Cultural Revolution.

"So she was back in her shell," Dad said, because she was afraid of radical students who were known for beating people like her in the streets. "She was wonderful, but very reluctant to talk about herself at first. We stayed in touch with her."

Mom was relishing the fun of a foreign posting together—just the two of them—and saw it as an opportunity to have Dad "all to herself." His previous work schedules hadn't allowed much time for each other: first back in Texas, when he worked so hard to build his business; then in Washington, keeping up with the hectic life of a congressman; and finally as RNC chairman during Watergate. In China, they would be alone for the first time since George W. had been born twenty-eight years earlier.

The older "boys," George and Jeb, were now adults—George studying to earn his master's degree at Harvard, and Jeb married and settling down with Colu in Texas. Marv and Neil were off at boarding school, and soon I would be as well, entering tenth grade.

★   ★   ★

I followed in the footsteps of my grandmother, my Aunt Nan Ellis, and several cousins and chose Miss Porter's School in Farmington, Connecticut. I had applied before my parents knew they were going to China, so my family thought the timing worked out well. Still, I was nervous. When Mom dropped me off, I could barely let go of her. It wasn't just that I was leaving home: it was also that my parents were leaving the country.

While I wanted to go away to school—my brothers had all gone to boarding school—I quickly realized it was not for me. It was an awkward age. I was shy and never really felt I fit in—and though I stayed for three years, most weekends were spent wishing I were with my family.

During that time, Mrs. Freeze, my art history teacher, suggested I study Chinese art, which in a way kept me in touch with what my parents were going through. When I eventually went to China, I was able to identify with much of what I saw because of this art course. Looking back, I appreciate Mrs. Freeze's thoughtful attempt to help me experience China with them from a distance. She must have sensed how much I missed them.

They missed us, too. Even though he was halfway around the world, my dad had a way of making me feel like I was the most important person in his life. Whenever I spoke to him by phone—which wasn't too often, with long-distance calls at five dollars a minute in those days—he always sounded so glad to hear my voice, and it made me feel so loved. To this day, the sound of his voice makes me feel the same way.

When they left for China, our family had to work harder to stay in touch. As a result, we became much closer. Despite the fact that we were all spread out—China, Virginia, Texas, Connecticut, Washington, D.C.—the ties that bind were fast and firm.

★   ★   ★

The fifteen months my parents spent in China, from October 1974 until December 1975, were a very happy time for them personally. There they enjoyed entertaining new friends and immersing themselves in all things related to the "Middle Kingdom."

My father kept a diary, now some thirty years old, which I read for the first time in researching this book. During his time in China, he dictated his thoughts just about every night into a tape recorder. When those tapes were transcribed, the material filled more than three hundred typewritten pages.

While some wondered why Dad would want to go to China when he could have chosen a more comfortable or prominent posting, Dad never regretted his choice for a moment. He saw the glass half-full in one of his first diary entries, where he recounts conversations he had with Henry Kissinger about the posting:

I think in this assignment there is an enormous opportunity of building credentials in foreign policy, credentials that not many Republican politicians will have. Kissinger has mentioned to me twice, "This must be for two years, George. You will do some substantive business, but there will be a lot of time when you will be bored stiff." I thought of Henry and I am sure [of] his role in having Nelson Rockefeller get the VP situation, but I will say that he was extremely generous in telling Chiao Kuan Hua [the chairman of the Chinese delegation to the United Nations when Dad was there, and who now served as Mao's foreign minister] that I was close to the President.

In another of the early entries, Dad asks himself the questions many others must have had on their minds:

In going to China I am asking myself, "Am I running away from something?," "Am I leaving what with inflation, incivility in the press and Watergate and all that ugliness?," "Am I taking the easy way out?" The answer I think is "no," because of the intrigue and fascination that is China. I think it is an important assignment, it is what I want to do, it is what I told the President I want to do, and all in all, in spite of the great warnings of isolation, I think it is right—at least for now . . . hyper-adrenaline political instincts tell me that the fun of this job is going to be to try to do more, make more contacts . . . the fun will be in trying.

Dad's diaries from China are full of entries that begin with phrases like "another beautiful day in Peking," "almost euphoric in my happiness," and "lots to do and lots to learn." Dad noted that his first visitor upon arrival was the head of the Kuwaiti mission. There are many references to new friends at various embassies, "movie nights" at their residence with popcorn and popular American films, and plenty of laughter resulting from language difficulties.

It helped that our cocker spaniel C. Fred went with them, along with seventeen cases of dog food. Dad relates that C. Fred arrived from quarantine upon their entry into the country looking "damned confused" and dirty. (It turned out the more they washed him, the grayer he got. His blond coat turned gray because of the hard water and pollution in the air, as did my parents' clothes and linens.) On the day of the dog's arrival, "four of the help in the back ran away when they saw C. Fred. Bar called him over and had him do his tricks and they were soon out watching him and laughing. Initially they were scared."

The locals were scared because, in those days, dogs were outlawed in Peking—for sanitation reasons, supposedly. I didn't believe it, and assumed that the number of dogs was inversely related to the number of Chinese restaurants there (more on this in a minute). Dad loved to go on morning runs with C. Fred, while Mom frequently took him around town despite all the stares.

Together, my parents explored Peking on foot and on bicycle. They were reluctant to take limos everywhere—especially for short distances—out of consideration for the staff and, really, a sense of adventure. Their stay in China was particularly adventurous when it came to the food. There are references in the diaries to eating sea slugs—a delicacy at twenty-five dollars a pound—chicken blood soup, swallow's spit, and worst of all, upper lip of dog (hence my brilliant theory on the lack of dogs). They loved the food in China and served only Chinese food in their residence. Their favorite restaurant was called the Sick Duck, because it was located next to the hospital. Here's an entry:

Dinner on the twenty-third at The Sick Duck. Course after course of duck including the webbing and the feet, the brain served handsomely.

As Dave Barry would say, I am not making this up.

Mom had a daily tai chi session at 6:00 a.m. and says she did it for several reasons, one of which she described as follows: "It was a way to interact with the Chinese, as well as the people who were below the rank of ambassador. There was almost a caste system. Amazingly old-school."

One of Mom's first outings was to procure bicycles and, subsequently, government licenses for them. The first week, Dad and one of his deputies, John Holdridge, went to a sporting goods store to get a Ping-Pong table "for the kids." They brought back the "Double Happiness" model, which cost $125, compared to the world championship table the salesmen were pushing for $250. Although Dad said the Double Happiness table was for us to use when we visited, he had grown up with a Ping-Pong table in the front hall of his childhood home in Connecticut. He was good.

As Dad began his initial series of diplomatic calls on the Chinese officials and other embassies in Peking, he tried to set a different tone. He made his first call on the acting chief of protocol for the Chinese, telling him that the United States would prefer "frank, informal discussions if possible, that Chiao Kuan Hua [the foreign minister with whom Henry Kissinger had put in a good word] ought not to feel that he should have a formal kind of reception for me of any kind, that I would much prefer a very small meeting where we could talk more frankly. I knew Chiao had many banquets and I felt he didn't need yet another one."

He explained his motives for approaching the protocol chief in this way: "What I was attempting to do was to establish a frank relationship and to try to move out of the normal, diplomatic, stiff-armed, stilted deal. It may be difficult. It may be impossible but I want to keep pushing for it. What I have got that can be helpful in this approach is having been in politics . . . I said that if they wanted to talk about the American political scene I would be prepared to do it from the unique vantage point of having run one of our parties"—something that carried a lot of weight in one-party Communist China. At one point, a Chinese official even referred to him as Chairman Bush, before Dad set him straight about what it meant to be head of the RNC, to great laughter.

The U.S. Liaison Office in China was "a reporting post more than an action post," Dad explained to me recently. "Our experts—there weren't that many of us, just fifteen or so there—would get as much information from other embassies as they could, or any other way they could, and they would report when they came back." So while there were broader policy reasons for the U.S. to open relations with China—promoting free markets and democratic principles, as well as addressing security concerns—the goal of the USLO was to listen and learn, and then report.

Just as Dad's tenure began, the cover of a CIA operative named James Lilley was exposed by columnist Jack Anderson in October 1974.

"It was very embarrassing for me, for him, and for everybody," Lilley said, looking back. "He took it in good stride. I said, 'Boss, I don't think my utility here is going to be indefinite; I think I should eventually leave.' He said, 'Don't rush, take it easy.' So I finally left six months later, on routine home leave. We didn't want these guys who play games in the newspaper to intimidate us."

Lilley added that his final memory of that trip was leaving on the train with his wife, Sally. As the train pulled out of the station, Lilley opened the letter that Dad had written. He and Sally read it, and she began to cry. "It was a very nice note, very moving," he said.

Lilley was chosen by Dad fifteen years later to be ambassador to China, and he has vivid memories of what it was like in 1974 when my father first met Deng Xiaoping, later the leader of the Chinese communists. Americans had a hard time winning the trust of the Chinese, and the feeling was mutual. So much was riding on making some sort of a personal connection, and my father instinctively knew this.

Ambassador Lilley recalled, "When these two men met, Deng—the short, tough revolutionary from Sichuan in central China—and Bush—the tall, ambitious, and smart elitist from America's Northeast—the chemistry was immediate. Deng saw Bush as an American who someday would lead his country, and Bush saw in Deng a major force in China's future. Deng could be very acerbic and your father was very enthusiastic and he couldn't be put down. I think Deng realized your father mattered in Republican politics and he mattered a lot. It was not an intellectual appreciation but a visceral one."

Dad and Mom quickly realized that they wanted to send a

message, of sorts, to the Chinese. They wanted their inclusiveness and warmth, their openness, and their casual, friendly attitude to be symbolic of the U.S. attitude toward China. "We were out—the United States was out being active," Dad told me. They saw how some missions—especially those from Eastern Europe and the Soviet Union—were isolated and, likewise, so were the countries they represented. In his diary, Dad refers at one point to Ambassador Vasily S. Tolstikov of the USSR:

> *Most interesting fellow but he is kind of isolated, living in this massive white marbled palace. There is no thaw there between the Soviet Union and China, or if there is, he damn sure hasn't been clued in on it.*

He enjoyed the Africans and was convinced that one way to learn more about China was through them. Members of the African delegations often came to diplomatic soirees, as he did, "tuxedoless," and were anything but remote:

> *That evening we went to a dinner dance given by Ambassador Akwei of Ghana. He apparently has been a leader in the diplomatic community via dancing. He has a Hi Fi set rigged up, a table overflowing with Western food, a young son whose eyes sparkled . . . and seemed like one of our kids when asked to run the tape recorder or something.*

As he worked to forge friendships with the Chinese, Dad relied on his love of sports—something he counted upon many times over the course of his career. He played a lot of Ping-Pong and tennis with the Chinese—horseshoes came later—and he attended spectator sports on a regular basis, including a very exciting game of hockey between the Soviets and the American kids, a few years in advance of that miraculous game during the 1980 Olympics. "Sports really are marvelous for getting across political lines," he writes, and his own sportsmanlike conduct and athletic charm went a long way toward reinforcing the message he was trying to send. (By the way, he still uses a phrase in his tennis games that he picked up in China: "unleash Chiang"—a reference to Chiang Kai Shek, the nationalist leader exiled on Taiwan—as slang for *Let's start the game and serve the big one.* He had a bit of a weak serve, and it was his way of making fun of it: *Time to unleash Chiang!*)

That year, we still gathered as a family for Thanksgiving, without Mom and Dad. It was too far for either us or them to travel just for Thanksgiving. My brothers and I came from boarding school or college and gathered at the Greenwich home of Spike and Betsy Heminway. "Quite a rowdy Thanksgiving," Spike recalls. "A lot of football watching, everyone on the den floor." We were excited knowing that Mom was coming to join us for Christmas in a few weeks.

Throughout his time in China, Dad was very impressed with the curiosity and friendliness of the Chinese people, yet he also saw their reticence and unreasonableness at times. "It is hard to equate the decency, kindness, humor, gentility of the people of China with some of the rhetoric aimed against the United States," he wrote. As many times as he was approached with respect and humor, he was also assaulted with anti-American, anti-imperialist propaganda.

He called it "the land of contrasts," and the polarity of life there went beyond just the words and slogans:

> *The beauty in many ways. The courteous friendliness of the individuals with whom you do talk. The desire to please in so many ways. And then that is contrasted with the basic closed society aspect of things. Lack of Freedom. Discipline of people. Sending them off to communes. No freedom to criticize.*

At another point, he writes, "You respect the discipline, you respect the order, you respect the progress but you question the lack of gaiety, the lack of creature comforts, the lack of freedom to do something different." He wrote about the daily life: "The contrasts are enormous. There will be a waft of marvelous odors from cooking and then a few yards further some horrendous stench from garbage or sewage." He describes loudspeakers blasting angry propaganda at happy children on the playground, who continued their games with their hands clapped over their ears.

Nowhere was the contrast more clear than when Henry Kissinger came to visit. "He is a man of great contrasts," wrote Dad when the secretary of state arrived in November, along with then–Secretary of Defense Donald Rumsfeld, Brent Scowcroft, who was then the national security adviser, and a few other aides:

There is too much entourage feeling. Too much kind of turmoil. Is he coming? Is he coming? Is he late? Is he late? Nobody is willing to bite the bullet and speak up. Amazing—mixed feeling. Great respect for the man and his accomplishments and yet concern about some of the trappings and some of the ways of handling people. Everyone with him talks about how difficult it is, and yet he can be extremely charming. Pressures on him are immense and the accomplishments immense so one forgives the eccentric things . . . No question about it. People quake, "He's coming. He's coming."

Another entry reads:

Kissinger is an extremely complicated guy. He is ungracious, he yells at his staff . . . and yet all those petty little unpleasant characteristics fade away when you hear him discussing the world situation. He comes alive in public . . . He literally is so alive within, you can see it on the outside very clearly. He is like a politician with the roar of the crowd on election eve, or the athlete running out at the 50-yard line just before the kick off. The public turns him on.

Dad notes Kissinger's "bitching" about the press, but then sidling right over to the press corps to chat. His demands for work to be done, then a lack of follow-through. To Dad, the man was an enigma. Later on, he writes:

I remember one big argument I had with Kissinger the time of the China vote [presumably as to whether Kissinger's secret trip to China had pulled the rug out from under Dad during the dual representation vote] and yet at lunch he graciously turned to Barbara and said that "George is the finest ambassador we've had up there anytime since I've been in government." Very pleasant. Unsolicited and I might add, totally unexpected.

Kissinger was very curious as to what Dad's plans would be after China, politically speaking, and even asked if he was going to run for president in 1980. Dad replied that he couldn't see that far ahead and just wanted to do a good job in China. I noticed that within a few months, however, he has a diary entry that toys with running for governor of Texas:

I have time to think these out. The plan might be to go home after the elections in '76, settle down in Houston in a rather flexible business thing, shoot for the governorship in '78, though it might be difficult to win. Should I win it, it would be an excellent position again for national politics, and should I lose, it would be a nice way to get statewide politics out of my system once and for all.

When Kissinger left just after Thanksgiving, Mom traveled back to the United States to spend Christmas with us. Dad was lonely without her, but his mother traveled to China with her sister-in-law Marge Clement to spend Christmas with him. He took them to embassy dinners and bike riding, which they loved to do—in fact, my grandmother continued to ride well into her late eighties. As he relates their adventures, you can just hear his voice in the Dictaphone:

Gave her a nice twenty minutes or so to shape up, and then we took a long bicycle ride down past the Great Hall of the People. You should have seen the people stare at old momma on the bicycle.

After his mother left, Dad wrote one particularly sad entry, when President Nixon was gravely ill with phlebitis:

> *Dinner alone. Early to bed, troubled by the VOA [Voice of America] report that President Nixon is in critical condition. I remember my last two phone calls with him, the only two I had since he left the White House. I felt like I was talking to a man who wanted to die. Here we are in China largely because of him, and the whole damn thing is sorry.*

My brothers and I made plans to visit China in the summer, and I couldn't wait. For my parents, the winters in China were long and difficult. Everything turned gray and drab. At one point, Aunt Nan went for a visit and spent ten days bicycling around Peking with Mom, before the two of them traveled to the countryside. It was the first time my mother and my aunt really spent any time together, and it cemented a lifelong friendship.

Away at boarding school, I got homesick. On weekends, my friends went home to their parents. Occasionally, I'd get invited along. I missed my parents and my brothers. Dad writes of a letter that arrived from Marvin, saying things were great, but it made Mom sad:

> *Bar sat and cried as she read it . . . I miss the children a lot every day and yet they seem to be holding together. They seem to be getting strength from each other. They spell out their love for their parents. We are very lucky.*

Over the cold winter months, Mom and Dad entertained plenty of people, despite the fact that in those days, you couldn't just travel to China. There were no visas. Any travel by foreigners had to be at the invitation of the USLO. So my dad decided to take advantage of this restriction and bring in the best of the United States and show them the best of China. He invited the heads of

Coke and Pepsi, for example, for visits. He found a way to get people into China who couldn't have done it on their own, no matter who they were.

As friendly and easygoing as Dad was, the when-in-Rome maxim could only be carried so far. One day, the Chinese guard posted at the entrance of the liaison office compound refused entry to one of Dad's expected guests. She was the wife of our consul general to Hong Kong, an American citizen who happened to be ethnic Vietnamese. Despite the American passport, the guard refused to allow her to enter.

As his deputy, Harry Thayer, remembered, when Dad found out, he "absolutely blew his stack" at the Chinese for the effrontery of refusing the admission of an American diplomat. Dad went to the gate and blasted the officer for not letting in this woman, but his tirade did no good. Finally, the Chinese foreign minister was called, and within a few minutes the guard relented. Dad just couldn't tolerate this sort of behavior, particularly when it affected an American citizen.

★ ★ ★

Summer finally came. George arrived in China a week before Marvin, Neil, and I did. Jeb was not able to join us because of a new job at the Texas Commerce Bank—and he and Colu were expecting a baby. Neil, Marvin, and I arrived on June 12, Dad's fifty-first birthday. It was an amazing trip. Dad's diary entry that day reads:

Doro, Marvin and Neil arrived . . . They looked great, giggling, bubbling over with enthusiasm—having enjoyed Honolulu, tired, not seen anything of Tokyo, only one night there and into Peking. They were great. They rushed down and played basketball, rode down to the Great Square. Marvin played tennis and then off we went to the Soup Restaurant, where we had eel and they all loved that. Neil Mallon bought the dinner and it was all pretty good.

Dad's mentor Neil Mallon and his wife, Ann, were visiting, and on the first Sunday we were there, we all went to church. Despite the fact that the Chinese did not allow their own people any freedom of worship, the government did allow foreign diplomats to attend church services every Sunday. My parents were regulars at a tiny church that had a congregation of fourteen people and was located atop the old Bible Society building. The services were conducted entirely in Chinese—except when the foreigners sang the old familiar hymns in the languages of their own countries, with the Chinese ministers singing the same hymns at the same time in Chinese.

While we were there, my parents decided it might be a good idea to have me baptized at the Bible Institute, since I had not been baptized yet. It sounds a little unusual that I was fifteen and still not baptized—but remember, I was the youngest of five in a frenetic family.

Arranging for a baptism in a communist country is no small feat. Dad and Mom were grateful that the Chinese government allowed the service, but that was only after an official meeting. The authorities wondered—understandably—why we wanted to do this, as did I. Mom explained that we wanted the family together for the occasion and just hadn't been able to do it earlier. But I soon discovered a great reason for being baptized at fifteen: you get to pick your own godfather. So I picked one of Dad's funniest and most handsome friends, Spike Heminway. I sent him a telegram right away inviting him immediately to China for the baptism, though I didn't expect him to come.

Spike remembers it as "that wonderful Chinese telegram which we didn't understand." "We were sitting there, in Maine," he said, "and this telegram arrived and it was in Chinese. We said, 'What in God's name is this?'" I had no idea that the telegram would be sent in Chinese. Somehow Spike and his wife, Betsy, found a way to translate it and wrote back—in English—that he couldn't make it. So I telegrammed back a message asking if my brother Marvin could stand in for him. Of course, Spike said okay.

So there we were that day at the service, two awkward teen-agers standing up as replacement godfather and goddaughter. I remember one of the three ministers was from the Church of England and another was a Baptist. There were a number of el-derly Chinese people, taking pictures and smiling, despite the lan-guage barrier. Mom remembers it as a very special, spiritual hour. "A very special day," Dad recalls fondly now, thirty years later.

Welcoming a child into the church is always a joyous occasion; but welcoming a child into an underground church in a commu-nist country is unforgettable—not only to the parents and the child but also to all those who witness it. It sent a glimmer of hope to the Chinese people who were there and to the many others who heard about it. If this little ceremony inspired just one of them to hold out hope that perhaps someday they'd have the freedom to be baptized, that's great. To me, it was one more unique thing about my life—embarrassing at the time, but remarkable looking back on it now.

George, Neil, Marvin, and I took a train ride with Mom to Wuxi and then Shanghai and then to Peitaiho (now known as Beidaihe), a beach resort. Back in Peking on bicycles, we went to Mom's fa-vorite place, the Forbidden City. She knew every nook and cranny. And we visited the Summer Palace and the Ming Tombs and the Great Wall. It reminded me of the days when Dad was in Congress and Mom took us all to see the sights.

One thing that sticks out in my mind regarding all this sightsee-ing was that my brothers were complete oddities to the locals—they towered over the Chinese, and Neil's blond hair made him even more exotic-looking.

A week later, we celebrated George's twenty-ninth birthday be-fore he left China by himself to go back to Harvard. After gradua-tion, he was thinking about returning to Midland, Texas, to try his hand in the oil business. When George left, Dad noted in his diary that George was starting out a little later in life than Dad had, "but nonetheless starting out on what I hope will be a challenging new life for him. He is able. If he gets his teeth into something semi-permanent or permanent, he will do just fine."

Shortly before Neil, Marvin, and I left, my parents threw a wonderful Fourth of July party, complete with hamburgers and hot dogs (ordering hot dog buns all the way from Japan), American beer, and even American cigarettes. Dad spent months preparing for it. "Hot as Hades," Mom remembers, and "the children of Harry Thayer and George Bush cooked and served with complaints." We also helped decorate, with lots of red, white, and blue. It was held at the USLO compound, and quite a big crowd came.

It was not your usual Peking party. The Fourth of July had been celebrated in years past by Dad's predecessor, but Dad's party was reportedly noisier and more active than in prior years. The sound of pounding could be heard throughout the compound on July 3, and when worried staffers came to investigate, they found Dad up on a ladder hammering away, securing American flags and balloons. Dad loves a good party.

At the end of our trip, Dad came up with the idea to send us—just the kids—on the Trans-Siberian Railroad from Peking to Moscow. Dad thought it would be a once-in-a-lifetime opportunity. Besides, how much trouble could a bunch of teenagers get into on a slow train through Siberia?

We boarded the train in China on July 16 for a five-day trip through Mongolia and Siberia and then on to Moscow. Our traveling party was composed of Marvin, Neil, myself, and a friend of mine visiting from school. We had two tiny rooms with two berths, one stacked on top of the other. The very first night, we left our windows open and woke the next morning covered in black soot. The train burned coal, and we were covered in it.

We shared a bathroom with the entire car, and when I went to freshen up, I turned on the faucet and out came the water . . . one drip at a time. I then realized that leaving the window open the first night of the five-day trip was a big mistake.

We traveled through China with Chinese personnel on board and a Chinese dining car. When we got to Mongolia, everything switched over to Mongolian personnel and a Mongolian dining car. While this was being changed over, our rooms were searched and we were asked to show our passports. All of this by Chinese authorities first, then Mongolian, then Russian—in very loud and aggressive voices. All the train personnel—especially in Mongolia and across Siberia—seemed angry and always searching for stowaways or something else. I was very nervous and worried, but nobody else seemed to be.

The train would stop for five or ten minutes at a time in tiny train stations in what looked like the middle of nowhere. (Actually, it really was the middle of nowhere. It was the farthest reaches of Siberia, after all.) At one point, my friend got off the train to buy a loaf of bread and I was a wreck as the train was about to leave without her. She did make it back after some very real angst, but I was too scared to get off at any point along the way. We were told to bring snacks (crackers and peanut butter) and thankfully we did, as we experienced firsthand how food in the Siberian gulags must have tasted.

Neil spent the whole trip studying guidebooks and reading maps and giving us history and culture lessons. I took comfort in peanut butter and crackers. My friend took comfort in Marvin, who by now had a crush on her. Together, the four of us traveled through the countryside in China, across the Gobi Desert and out of Mongolia, then around Lake Baikal—the deepest freshwater lake in the world and nearly four hundred miles long—then across the steppes of Siberia and through the Ural Mountains until we reached Moscow. (When he saw the deepest lake in the world, Neil remembers thinking, "Wow, this is cool . . . but after four days on a train, I guess anything is cool.")

Once we arrived in Moscow, English-speaking Russian "intel" agents met us and we toured the sights they allowed us to see, like St. Basil's Cathedral and Lenin's tomb. "It was surprising that we had the freedom to move around," Neil recalls, adding that it was not nearly as oppressive as China had been. We stayed overnight in an apartment provided by the state, "plain furnishings, simple but clean," Neil remembers, and that we were accompanied by an English-speaking Russian woman who worked for the Soviet domestic security agency.

Before we left, Neil has a vague recollection of Marvin negotiating with the locals to swap Levi's. "American jeans were a hot commodity," he said. (Marvin—whose recollection of this is even more vague than Neil's—is a very successful businessman today, to no one's surprise.)

Russia was gray, and, to my mind, the people at that time looked sour and unhappy. Then we went to Leningrad and saw the beautiful pastel-colored buildings and the Hermitage. While on the train, Neil had announced that his dream was to see the Swiss Alps while drinking wine—underage drinking was legal in Europe—and eating cheese and chocolate in the shadow of the Matterhorn. I think all that Siberian food inspired this vision. When Marvin and my friend decided to head back to the United States together, I was left with Neil and his alpine dream.

When I think back on it, I'm amazed we were allowed to do this on our own. It was typical of the spirit we grew up with—having a mom and a dad who loved a good adventure. I think it was something they would have liked to do, and thought it would be a great idea to send us instead. "I was the oldest of the three of us, and it wasn't like we had an adult companion," Neil recalls. "It was a great experience to feel empowered, to be responsible. The fact that they would allow us to go and encourage us to explore and see the world, in a way, is a metaphor for the way they raised us. They allowed us to grow wings and fly in different directions."

★ ★ ★

Looking back on my parents' fifteen months in China, I see it as a positive period of growth for my family. The photo albums of that time show my parents both looking healthy and happy, in front of the Great Wall of China, the Forbidden City, the Summer Palace. It was a time for my Dad to recharge his political batteries after the difficult, drawn-out months of Watergate, and an opportunity for my parents to be alone together.

Though it was many, many years ago, they still light up when they talk about their time there. The memories are a little less crisp now, but still vivid. Not just the sights, but the smells, tastes, and sounds of China. In one of his final diary entries, Dad tried to record it all, as though he was afraid he might someday forget:

Sounds that I will not forget. The early morning singing in the park—loud and usually very good tenor voices for the most part. The organized cadence of kids marching. The never ceasing honking horns downtown in Peking, the jingle of bicycle bells, the laughter of the children as they play near the park, the blaring of the loudspeakers with the excesses of the propaganda whether it's on a train, in a park, at a building site, wherever. The July and August sound of the crickets.

Chapter 9

A Year at Langley

"For the last fifteen or more years, I don't think I have once seen him speak about CIA when he didn't begin to choke up. There is a special emotion that he has that I've never seen with the Vice Presidency or even the Presidency that in retrospect affects him emotionally. There was this bond made during 1976 that lasts to this day—both on his part and on the part of the folks at the Agency."

—Bob Gates

One day, Dad found himself sitting in the Great Hall of the People in Peking, across the table from Deng Xiaoping. "Ah, I see you are leaving," said Deng with a sly smile on his face. "Have you been spying on me all along?"

Dad laughed remembering it, and said of the Chinese leader, "He had a sense of humor." Deng knew that my father had received a cable from President Ford, asking him to leave China and come home to run the CIA. Dad agreed to it, and soon the story was in the Chinese newspapers. Next thing he knew, Deng Xiaoping was hosting a farewell lunch for Dad and Mom in the Great Hall.

Even though it was just lunch, the other diplomats were amazed. Normally, Dad explained to me, Deng had no contact with ambassadors, only heads of state—"but I wasn't even an ambassador!" Despite the fact that Dad's title was "U.S. liaison to China," Deng knew that Dad was someone he wanted to keep an eye on. A year or so later, when Deng was purged from power, one of Dad's CIA associates, Jim Lilley, remembers writing up a memo about it, saying in effect that Deng may be down but he's not out. He'll be back.

"Your father sensed that himself," Ambassador Lilley told me. "Although Deng was out, we knew he was coming back. And he did come back—roaring back."

Why would Dad have agreed to leave when he was enjoying his posting in China so much? Mom and Dad still talk about how great their time in Peking was. Why go back to Washington? "When the cable came in," Dad remembered years later, "I thought of Big Dad [Prescott Bush]. What would he do? What would he tell his kids? I think he would have said, 'It's your duty.' It is my duty, and I'll do it."

Dad accepted the CIA job, although somewhat wistfully. He wrote to his good friend Congressman Bill Steiger, "I honestly feel my political future is behind me—but hell, I'm 51, and this new one gives me a chance to really contribute."

It was controversial for Ford to name a politician—a former congressman and RNC chairman—to head the CIA. In fact, Senate Democrats stated that they would only confirm Dad if he would agree not to be Ford's running mate the next year, in the 1976 reelection campaign.

James Baker, who went on to become Ford's campaign manager for the reelection, remembers, "I thought it was an outrageous demand and told my friend that it would be a serious mistake to let his enemies dictate the terms of his career path. George disagreed with me. 'This is something the president wants me to do,' he said. 'It's something that interests me and I am going to do it.'"

"One of the great enigmas to me was the decision by President Ford, which I think he made in all good faith, to bring George back and put him in the CIA," said Dean Burch, who was a member of

Ford's White House staff. "It was, I think, the ultimate tribute to George's rectitude that he was thought of for a job like that. It also happened to be the worst thing, politically, that could have happened to him at the time. And then George had the terrible decision as to whether to push for confirmation without taking that blood oath that he wouldn't seek the vice presidency. I know damn well he did not want to lock himself out, but he did, for a number of reasons. I think, first of all, he clearly wanted to be confirmed—he didn't want to be turned down, which is an obvious thing. But secondly, I guess he, down deep, as did I, agreed that the CIA should not be a political resting place." The finale to all this is that President Ford stated publicly he would not select Dad as his running mate. Thus Dad never had to pledge he would not be seeking the vice presidency.

The "great enigma" that Dean Burch referred to was what General Scowcroft called "the grand shuffle," in which President Ford moved several members of his staff and cabinet around. President Nixon had made Henry Kissinger both secretary of state and national security adviser, and President Ford wanted to separate the two jobs, so he put General Scowcroft in as national security adviser. He also wanted William Colby out as CIA director, so he replaced him with Dad; and he wanted James Schlesinger out as defense secretary. Donald Rumsfeld, then White House chief of staff, wanted to move over to be defense secretary, and so Dick Cheney became White House chief of staff, replacing Rumsfeld.

In addition to the congressional Democrats' concerns, some inside the Agency harbored concerns as well: "At the outset there was a lot of nervousness about it—mainly on the grounds that, traditionally, the Agency is not politicized," Angus Thuermer, a loyal CIA man, told me. "It's never been Republican. It's never been Democrat. It just has to call them as it sees them, regardless of who's in power, and it prides itself on its professionalism and not its political status. And your dad having been, at one time, chairman of the Republican National Committee—that carried an impression of a politician, and we had never experienced that kind of leadership before . . . that same thing made it pretty difficult for your dad to get confirmed when he was before the Senate."

Eventually, of course, Dad was confirmed by the Senate.

James Lilley, who returned to the CIA headquarters in Langley, Virginia, after the Jack Anderson column ended his China tour, was happy to hear the news that Dad would be heading the CIA. Moreover, in an agency that values "Duty, Honor, Country" more than most, Dad's military service was appreciated by the agents. As one agent put it, "I'd worked for many navy men before, but never one who had flown fifty-eight combat missions and been shot down."

So not everyone was a skeptic.

Dad stepped into the shoes of William Colby, who had led the CIA during Watergate and the stormy months afterward. The "smoking gun" tape, in which President Nixon directed his aides to have the CIA call off the FBI investigation of Watergate because of "national security concerns," was particularly damaging to the CIA.

In addition, at one point Director Colby had revealed CIA assassination attempts against Fidel Castro, prompting outrage on Capitol Hill. Senator Frank Church, a Democrat from Idaho, and Congressman Otis Pike, a Democrat from New York, had led the charge in investigating the CIA abuses. (Church made such a name for himself in these hearings that he later ran for president in the 1976 Democratic primaries, but lost to Jimmy Carter.)

The Church Committee in the Senate was writing its final report to be published in April, and many of its recommendations changed the way the CIA operates to this day. But first Dad had to deal with recommendations of the Pike Committee in the House, whose final report in January of that year was so outrageous the full House refused to accept it. It ended up being leaked to the *Village Voice* rather than being published in the *Congressional Record*, and it was the talk of the town. The Rockefeller Commission, appointed by President Ford, was also preparing a report with the help of some of its members, including Governor Ronald Reagan of California.

Dad looked back on the hearings: "I still will never forget the effect those young staffers had when they went out there and almost accused everybody there of being a crook—'You know you're guilty, and we're going to find it out!' And it just sent terrible vibrations through the building. That was pretty well wrapped up by the time I got there. People were down. They were discouraged. They wanted a leader who would stand up for them. That's what I did. I was no expert on intelligence, but they knew that I believed in the importance of their mission, the importance of intelligence for the president, and conforming to the law."

On his first day on the job, according to Angus Thuermer, Dad walked into the morning staff meeting with a newspaper in his hand. "What are they doing to us?" he asked as he slammed the paper on the table. Within ten minutes, the fact that he had said "us" was all over the building.

There was pressure on Dad to show that the president was serious about cleaning house at the CIA in the wake of the hearings. "I did make the changes," Dad told me. "I forget how many, but a lot. It's how you do it. You don't have to be confrontational. You have to empathize with the family and say, 'Look, I know this is a change. You just have to work through it.' I made a lot of changes in the top people at CIA, but I did it by getting people new assignments or encouraging some of them to retire."

In July, Dad chose Hank Knoche to be his deputy. Hank had been there since 1953 and been the right-hand man of other directors, so he knew the Agency in a way that would be indispensable to Dad. He was a great athlete—he was a 6'4" center who had been the first pick in the first-ever NBA draft in 1946 before joining the CIA. He was Dad's kind of guy, and he was well respected by the staff.

"I was the inside guy for the most part," Knoche explained afterward. "Director Bush was very busy on the Hill with the Congress, in the White House with the administration, and the consumers of intelligence and the cabinet, and he did a lot of speaking on the outside. This was a new thing for the CIA—the need to explain ourselves publicly. Before, we'd always been a silent service. But the investigations and reviews made it necessary for us to get out there and explain our raison d'être and what we were trying to accomplish. So he did a lot of that."

As a result of the congressional committees' findings, the rules on Capitol Hill had changed for the Agency. According to Knoche, "We had to forge new relationships with Congress and respond to the new kinds of oversight we would be getting both from the executive branch and from Congress; and with your dad having been a congressman at one time and having been close to the White House . . . this put him in an ideal position to help us build new bridges."

My parents went on a morale-boosting trip to Europe right after Dad was sworn in, and they were gone for several weeks. Dad met with leaders of other intelligence agencies. Security was very tight, because a CIA station chief named Richard Welch was assassinated on December 23, 1975, outside of his home in Athens, Greece, right before the Senate voted on Dad's nomination.

Once they returned, Dad plunged into his new job, working long hours. I also recall how my mother started to spend a great deal of time in her room with the door shut. Maybe I should have picked up on this warning signal, but the truth is, it wasn't until Mom's 1994 memoirs came out that my brothers and I learned she had suffered from depression during that CIA period. We had no idea.

Mom hid her depression from everyone except Dad. He tried to convince her to get professional help, but she didn't talk to a doctor about it for many years. I was shocked that this indomitable, dynamic woman thought about driving off the road into the trees. But I also admire her decision later to disclose her problem publicly; no doubt she helped many women struggling with the same condition to seek the help they need.

As it was, I wish I could have helped her when it was happening.

Meanwhile, at work, Dad was a man on a mission. A government official who knew Dad during his CIA tenure said: "Bush was absolutely outraged by what the Congress was doing to the CIA in the worst years of 1974 and 1975 . . . He really felt there was a serious need for somebody who had some public credibility to get to the CIA and help to restore its effectiveness, help repair the damage the Church Committee had been doing. He saw this as a very important mission."

I think that's true. Dad told me, "I loved defending the Agency."

"There were a lot of high-powered people in this country who, at that stage [1975] were wondering whether you could have an intelligence service as a part of a free and democratic society," explained Hank Knoche. "And when your whole career and your whole purpose for being is questioned—well, I think many good organizations would break . . . We did have the feeling we were terribly alone, that there was nobody out there defending us or championing the cause. George brought that to us. He became a champion."

So morale at the CIA was at an all-time low. "Basically, the agency was taking body blows," recalls Bill Barr, a lawyer in the legislative affairs office who accompanied Dad to the Hill for some of his appearances before Congress as the new oversight committees were being formed. Dad immediately did what previous directors had not done: he treated the people who worked there with dignity and respect. He ate often in the employee cafeteria and rode the main elevator instead of the director's elevator. CIA headquarters was located across the river from the White House, and Dad got office space right across from the Executive Office Building for the intelligence staff so they'd have less of a commute for meetings. Moreover, in December 1976, Dad invited Lionel Hampton, the great jazz vibraphonist, to play a concert in "the Bubble"—the auditorium at CIA headquarters—for all employees.

During the Cold War, Dad was very concerned about the Soviet military, and he fostered an objective look at the Soviet threat. "I put into effect a thing called Plan B," he told me. "We had a bunch of ardent—you might say more conservative—analysts look at the same information as the professional analysts looked at and see what they came up with—to see how objective the intelligence was. It was always pretty much the same."

Dad said the debate within the CIA today is the same as it was back then, especially regarding the issue of intelligence—whether it was analysis of the Soviet threat then or North Korea and Iran today: "The question is, how effective is the operation? It's almost déjà vu. Are we getting enough human intelligence? Science and technology has moved forward. Most people would realize that it's a question of analytical work—how good is the analysis?"

With so much to do—dealing with Capitol Hill, assessing the Soviet threat in the midst of the Cold War, "the challenge of managing morale," as he put it—Dad's days were full. On a typical day, he'd get to work at 7:30 a.m., sometimes earlier. He would start in his office, then head to the morning staff meeting, where he would hear reports from the department heads—the directors of intelligence, operations, and science and technology. He did not personally brief the president at the White House on a daily basis—as later CIA directors often did for him when he was president—"but if there was a crisis or something happened, then I'd go down there and take the experts with me."

It was during this busy time that my parents' first grandchild was born. He was named George Prescott Bush after my father and grandfather and is affectionately known as George P. My parents were ecstatic when he was born—we all were. At sixteen years old, I was honored when Jeb and Columba asked me to be George P.'s godmother. After all, I had only been baptized myself about a year earlier. It was a big deal for me.

George P. was the most beautiful baby I had ever seen. Everyone wanted to hold him because he was so soft—with those round baby cheeks, and dimples on the backs of his little round hands. His baby fat turned out to be a valuable asset: when he was about a year old, George P. fell out of a window at Mom and Dad's house in Houston. He crawled over to a floor-to-ceiling window on the second floor of the house, and—in every mother's nightmare—he pushed on the screen and out he went. Thankfully, he landed on a very forgiving hedge and was fine. It was the adults who never quite recovered.

★   ★   ★

When Dad left the CIA at the end of the Ford administration in 1977, there was no discussion of the possibility of his staying on. Being a political appointee rather than a career CIA man, Dad assumed that President Jimmy Carter would want his own man in place. Dad was fine with that—in fact, he recalled recently, "I am profoundly grateful he did not ask me to stay on for a transition." He knew that Carter had run against the "Washington establishment" as a peanut farmer from Georgia and would want a different kind of director. (In fact, President Carter's initial nominee to replace Dad was Ted Sorenson, a JFK speechwriter who had become a Washington lawyer. During the confirmation fight, it came out that he was a committed pacifist. His nomination was withdrawn, and Admiral Stansfield Turner was confirmed as the new director.)

One of the last things Dad did as CIA director was to spend a day briefing the incoming president on intelligence matters. Hank Knoche remembers Dad's day, which started out with a meeting with the budget director; followed by meetings with Vice President Rockefeller and President Ford to tell them he'd be stepping down as CIA director; then a flight to Plains, Georgia, during which Dad told his staff he'd be resigning. When they arrived to meet with President-elect Carter and Vice President-elect Walter Mondale, Dad took a few minutes alone with them first to tell them of his resignation. Then, with both staffs present, he began what was scheduled to be a one- to two-hour briefing but ended up being a six-hour session. Knowing that Secretary Kissinger was going to Plains the next day for his briefings, Dad wrote notes for him on the flight back, then personally delivered them to Kissinger's home at about midnight.

Hank Knoche commented, "When I think back on that day during which George had met with the budget director, the president of the United States, the vice president, the president-elect, the vice president-elect, the secretary of state—through it all there was a true professional continuity and gracefulness. Even though it was a very serious time for him, I was terribly impressed. As a matter of fact, the next day we were so impressed that at our 9:00 a.m. staff meeting I gave him, personally, just about the highest award that the agency has to give, and told the staff what George had done that previous day. It was a very touching moment."

On his last day in office, a note arrived from Dad's secretary at the CIA to my brothers and me, reading, "Today is January 21, and thus your father is no longer with us. He is no longer with us in body, but he will live on here in spirit. He gave us so much." She attached Dad's farewell letter to his fellow CIA employees, which ended with this: "I am leaving, but I am not forgetting. I hope I can find some ways in the years ahead to make the American people understand more fully the greatness that is CIA."

★ ★ ★

Dad was director of Central Intelligence from January 1976 to January 1977. On April 26, 1999, more than twenty years later, I attended the ceremony when they named the CIA complex in Langley, Virginia, for Dad. He joked that Mom had said the only reason they name buildings after people is if they are really, really old or are already dead. In reality, he was deeply touched by such a meaningful honor.

The way my father was treated that day at the CIA ceremony was overwhelming. Former congressman Rob Portman, who sponsored the legislation that named the CIA complex for Dad, said that one CIA official told him that Dad's coming back "will be like Elvis has returned." Dad stayed in close touch with many of his CIA colleagues for years and continued to receive regular intelligence briefings long after he left public office.

Looking back on it years later at the dedication ceremony, Dad said, "I left here some twenty-two years ago after a limited tenure, and my stay here had a major impact on me. The CIA became part of my heartbeat back then, and it's never gone away." He wondered out loud why previous directors had not been chosen as the namesake, instead of him, then started to get emotional when recalling certain agents—Richard Welch and William Buckley—who had died very violent deaths in the line of duty.

Then he said something that, to me, speaks volumes about him: "It has been said by others that patriotism is not a frenzied burst of emotion, but rather the quiet and steady dedication of a lifetime. To me, this sums up CIA—Duty, Honor, Country. It is an honor to stand here and be counted among you."

That day—and every day he was director—Dad walked past "the wall of stars" at CIA headquarters, which commemorates all those who gave their lives in the line of duty. I asked him about it.

"That's the thing about the CIA," he said. "People who serve never sit at the head table or get recognition, and are serving for the right patriotic reasons—belief in service to country. Belief in country." He told me he'd gone to visit a CIA training camp in 2004 and was seated next to an attorney who was in her twenties. "She woke up one day and said, 'I'm not doing anything for my country.' A few months later, she was overseas in a very delicate undercover situation, risking her life. So people are still there who serve for the right reasons. And *that's* what I love about the CIA."

Later, Dad looked back on his departure from the CIA: "I was sad to leave the CIA, a job that I loved. But it was great to get back to Texas. Now my main challenge was to figure out what came next in my life."

Chapter 10

An Asterisk in the Polls

"He was truly an asterisk in the polls. I asked to spend some of our campaign money on political ads during the election for city council and mayor of Boston, so that people would associate the Bush name with something other than Busch Beer. You wanted people to put his name in the context of an election, rather than a beer bash at college."

—**Andy Card**

It was 1977, and Karl Rove called Dad in Houston wanting to stop by and get some job-hunting advice. When Dad was Republican National Committee chairman in the early 1970s, Karl had been chairman of the College Republicans while Lee Atwater served as its executive director. "We were the nineteen-year-old reprobates in the subbasement of the National Committee," remembers Karl, and Dad had laid down the law with the two of them, telling them "not to do anything stupid."

Now it had been a few years, and Karl, married and back in Texas, came to see Dad. "I've got an idea," said Dad. "Why don't you come to work for me?" Dad had just started a political action committee called the Fund for Limited Government to raise money for other candidates, travel around the country, and lay the foundation for a presidential bid in 1980.

Karl accepted Dad's offer; the fund had its first paid employee; and Dad's first campaign for the White House came to life.

Dad and Mom had returned to Texas in 1977 after the Carter inauguration; and Jim Baker had also returned to Houston, after having served as national campaign manager in the 1976 Ford campaign. Mr. Baker had remarried, to the former Susan Winston, and had just run unsuccessfully for attorney general of Texas when Dad called him in 1978 and said, "Let's get going." Jim said he'd love to help but had one problem. He was carrying a $150,000 deficit after his statewide race. Baker was very worried about it: "I need to get rid of that somehow."

Dad reassured him, "We'll take care of that later."

A few months later, during the general election, Dad wrote a letter on Jim's behalf that was sent out to all Baker supporters in Texas. In response, those supporters actually sent in more than the defunct campaign needed to pay off its debts. As he considered what to do with the extra cash, James Baker thought back to the time when his own father had contributed to Senator Prescott Bush's reelection campaign in Connecticut. When Prescott Bush decided not to run for reelection in 1962, he actually returned the leftover campaign money to everyone who had contributed to him.

"My dad was profoundly influenced by that," Baker said. "He used to tell me all the time, 'That's the only politician I've ever known that ever sent any money back.'"

And so James Baker decided to send all the extra contributions back to his donors. "I was really taking a page out of Senator Prescott Bush's book," he said.

With his campaign debt taken care of, Baker signed on as Dad's campaign manager for the presidential campaign. During the 1970s, Baker had paid his political dues, working for the Texas GOP, then entered national politics with the 1976 Ford-Dole campaign. By the time Dad approached him, "I was the only living Republican who had run a national presidential campaign and not gone to jail," Mr. Baker joked. He was referring to John Mitchell, Nixon's campaign manager, who served nineteen months in a federal prison after he was convicted for his role in the Watergate scandal.

At the time, Baker recalled, "Many people came to me and asked, 'What are you doing? John Connally and Howard Baker and Bob Dole will blow this guy [Dad] away. Why are you doing this?' And I said, 'I'm doing it because he's my friend and because I think he'd make an extraordinarily good president.'"

Together, the two of them traveled to California, calling on President Ford first. Dad told President Ford of his plan to run for president, and Baker asked for his blessing as campaign manager. If President Ford had decided to run again—which was still an option at the time—Baker would have felt obligated to help. Ford assured them he would not be running for president and said the whole idea was "perfectly fine." Next, they went to see Governor Reagan. "I can't tell you what I'm going to do," the governor said, "but thank you for the courtesy of coming out and telling me."

Satisfied, Dad and Baker returned to Texas.

Meanwhile, the team Dad had already been quietly putting together began to take shape. Along with Karl Rove, he hired Pete Teeley as his press secretary, an off-the-boat British immigrant who had survived the bombing of London during World War II, moved to Detroit, and graduated from college attending night school. At the time, Pete had just finished a stint as press secretary for Senator Jacob Javits of New York.

My brother Jeb, meanwhile, served as Dad's original traveling aide—a twenty-four-year-old father of two out on the road five days a week. (Eventually, Dad hired David Bates, who was a tennis buddy of Jeb's from Houston just out of law school, and Jeb began traveling on his own, campaigning for Dad in forty-eight out of fifty states.) Another close friend and fellow Texas oil man, Bob Mosbacher, soon became the finance chair. This core group traveled all over the country, testing the waters for a run at the presidency. No cell phones, no faxes, no fancy planes. They crammed into coach seats on airplanes, with their twenty-eight-year-old scheduler, Margaret Tutwiler, sending the itineraries and arrangements by overnight mail along the way.

Even before he was elected to national office and had access to government aircraft, Dad hated waiting in airports. At one point, much to Margaret's chagrin, Dad got a copy of the paperback listing of all airline flights—it was called the OAG—and he would call in suggestions for other flights to Margaret. "It went on all the time," she said.

At first, Dad's candidacy struggled. "It never got anywhere . . . no notoriety or public knowledge because, once in a while, my name would be in a poll and there was an asterisk," Dad told me. The front-runners would typically be listed by name in poll results—Reagan, Dole, Howard Baker, Connally—but then the survey listed 4 percent for "other candidates," Dad being one of them. He was an asterisk at the end of the poll results.

But with more trips into key early states, more local Republican "Lincoln Day" dinners, more state party events, things slowly started to change.

★　★　★

During this time, Dad went to a lunch that James Lilley, his old friend from the CIA, hosted at his home for the chief of the Chinese mission to the United States. Dad knew the Chinese diplomat from his time in China and said to him, "I'll tell you something. I'm running for president." Lilley thought this impressed the Chinese, especially given Deng's feeling that Dad was someone who "mattered" in Republican politics. Shortly afterward, Dad decided to take Deng Xiaoping up on his invitation to return to China for a visit.

The traveling party for this return trip to China consisted of Mom; James Baker; Lowell Thomas, the globe-trotting CBS Radio reporter and his wife, Marianne; Chase Untermeyer, a good friend who had volunteered on Dad's 1966 congressional campaign and today is ambassador to Qatar; Dean and Pat Burch, who had been friends since Dad's days at the RNC; David Broder, the *Washington Post* reporter, and his wife, Ann; Hugh Liedtke, his partner from Zapata Petroleum, and his wife, Betty; and Jim Lilley. They went to Tibet as well and then down the Yangtze River.

The group met with Deng, who was back in power after being purged in 1976. Their meeting took place in the Great Hall of the People, which was where Dad had last met with Deng before leaving to head the CIA. The purpose of the meeting was to offer the Chinese "risk contracts" for offshore oil, which would allow the Chinese government to share the risks of offshore drilling with American companies in exchange for a share of the profits. Ambassador Lilley told me that it was an important symbolic meeting, because it was the first successful linking of American technology and management with Chinese resources and labor, all within the context of offshore oil exploration. It was a breakthrough, and very relevant to the revolutionary economic reforms Deng began to implement the following year.

Dad remembers that it was the first time that the Chinese called him *lao pengyou,* which means "old friend." "They'd toast me as an old friend of China," he explained. "I don't want to come off as bragging, but I really do have a special standing in China . . . They all consider me a friend of China. It's very nice."

★   ★   ★

Back home, my brother George, a businessman in the Texas oil industry, decided to mount a campaign of his own, running for Congress in Texas's 19th District, which stretched from the scrubby desert of the Midland-Odessa region northward into the farm country around Lubbock. The local congressman there, George Mahon, had announced his retirement after forty-three years in office.

My brother remembers meeting early on with the former governor of Texas, Allan Shivers, who flat out told my brother he couldn't win. When George asked why, Shivers explained that he would be facing a strong opponent in Kent Hance, a well-respected man who was more suited to the district than George was.

"I listened to him, said okay, and decided to run anyway," my brother recalled.

My brother campaigned nonstop and won the Republican primary. One of Dad's rivals in the upcoming Republican primaries, Governor Reagan, had endorsed Odessa Mayor Jim Reese, George's Republican opponent. "Dad wasn't particularly pleased about that," my brother recalled. But then Governor Reagan called to congratulate George after he won. George lost that fall, however, receiving 47 percent of the vote in a district that had never elected a Republican to Congress.

Shortly after declaring his candidacy, George also met a librarian and schoolteacher named Laura Welch at a cookout at the home of mutual friends. They only dated for three months before they married, and most of us met her at the wedding. Laura had grown up in Midland, and we all instantly loved her. Marvin said that Laura coming into our family was like Audrey Hepburn arriving at Animal House, yet she fit right in. An only child, she adapted to our family with grace, charm, and humor. George had to promise her that she would never have to give a campaign speech for him. That didn't last very long. Now she's one of the best speakers in our family. As First Lady, she comforted our nation in the wake of 9/11, and her work on education and helping young people has had a positive impact all across our country. Just as important to me, she's a great mom and a great friend.

During this time, I was majoring in sociology at Boston College and got to know John Anderson Jr. His father was a Republican congressman from Illinois who also ran in the 1980 Republican primaries, dropped out, then returned in the fall as an independent. John Jr. and I were friends, and our mutual friends chose sides—in my view, of course, the discerning students chose to support my father. But what are the chances of two college classmates both having dads run for president of the United States?

Riding the bus one day across the campus at Boston College, I noticed a young woman who looked friendlier than my school-assigned roommate from Asbury Park, New Jersey. (My roommate was a follower of the Grateful Dead band whose need for privacy with her boyfriend caused me to spend a tremendous amount of time at my Aunt Nan's house in nearby Lincoln, Massachusetts.)

Wendy West and I became fast friends. When I told her a few months later that I wanted to take a year off from school to volunteer on my dad's campaign, she offered to join me. Worried about how her parents would react, she said to me, "You've got to come with me to tell my parents about your dad and about the campaign. It'll really help my case if you come."

We went to dinner with her parents, and Wendy announced that my dad was running for president. They responded, in unison, "President of *what*?" We laughed because they hadn't even heard of him. It took some convincing, but eventually, Wendy's parents let her take the year off.

Wendy and I joined the campaign team in Massachusetts, whose ranks included state legislator Andy Card, secretary of transportation for my dad and my brother's former chief of staff; Ron Kaufman, a local campaign worker at the time who eventually headed up the Political Affairs Office at the White House during my father's administration; and Andrew Natsios, until recently administrator of USAID. They made me a college coordinator, and I took off on a tour of college campuses—mainly on the East Coast—where I handed out campaign literature and talked to anyone who would listen about why my father would make a great president.

As time passed, I got more comfortable talking to people, at least one-on-one, and that led to the next step: public speaking. In fact, the very first public speech I gave was in Brainard, Massachusetts, at a Republican women's club where the youngest member had to have been in her seventies. It was the friendliest, least intimidating audience you could imagine. From a college student's perspective, of course, they looked really old—all contemporaries of my grandmother—and there couldn't have been a heckler in the crowd.

Nevertheless, when I got up to speak, I literally experienced the sensation of choking. By that, I mean not being able to breathe. I opened my mouth to try to talk about my dad, but was so overcome by emotion and fear that nothing but a few unintelligible sounds escaped my lips. So I had no other choice but to sit down. Thus went was my very first speaking engagement!

★ ★ ★

In early 1979, Dad responded to a note from President Nixon: "I am determined to make an all-out effort for 1980. I start with no name identification and I realize that. I will, however, continue to keep a 'low profile.' I am determined to organize, and organize well, before escalating the candidacy to high levels of public attention."

Why did Dad decide to run for president? Dad had a speech he used to give at the time titled "Why I Want to Be President," in which he said, "Jimmy Carter is not the first president who has failed to provide the strong, inspiring leadership that we so badly need . . . We are now in the late 1970s, and when they end, many will happily say goodbye—goodbye to Vietnam, to Watergate, to recession, to inflation, to the 'me' decade, and to the decline of American influence." Dad talked about the need for new leadership with integrity and enthusiasm, and his desire to be a new kind of president.

"I rather arrogantly felt that I had the credentials," Dad said. (Hugh Sidey, who covered the presidency for years for *Time* magazine, agreed, saying, "He was the most experienced man to be president since the founding fathers, in my judgment.")

Newsweek editor Jon Meacham looked back on Dad's decision and his credentials: "Can you name a former director of the CIA who's a plausible presidential candidate? No, you can't. George Bush knew what he wanted to do and never gave up. To be chairman of the Republican National Committee during Watergate . . . to lose two Senate races, which is so painful. To emotionally keep going—to keep getting back up. The great politicians always do that. Churchill is a great example—he lost more elections than we've had lunches—yet George Bush kept getting back up and running, always with dignity, always with grace. He had no enemies, which is amazing when you think about it. One of the things that's always interested me is with both Nixon and Ford, it never seemed to be in the cards that he wouldn't get an important job. It was always, what important job can we find for you? Because he was a very loyal, intelligent man."

"It took one hell of a lot of courage after having done the jobs he did to step out and run for president when you have no name ID, no ability to really raise a lot of money," James Baker told me. "A candidate is sometimes the lowest form of human life. Everybody's an expert in politics, and it just took one hell of a lot of courage and your dad had that courage."

My sister-in-law Laura has her own theory as to why Dad ran: he was raised by his mother with a love of sports, and "maybe that athletic part of it translates to other parts of life, to running for office. The idea that you would get on the court—those are the people who will step up to the plate and take the licks. There are a lot of would-be presidents and would-be governors that never run for anything." Maybe that explains why two of my sports-minded brothers, George and Jeb, were not afraid to enter the political arena.

Dad formally announced his candidacy at the National Press Club in Washington, D.C., in May 1979. My grandmother was with us that day, and I remember looking over and seeing how proud she was of her son announcing his candidacy for president of the United States. James Baker remembers the lead story in the *Washington Star*, written by Jack Germond and Jules Witcover: "Bush Campaign Peaks on the Day of Announcement."

"We proved them wrong," he says now.

Late in 1979, a friend of Jimmy Pierce (one of my cousins on Mom's side) named Joe Hagin had just graduated from Kenyon College and took a job with Dad. In short order, he went to Florida to work on one of the first straw polls (basically a popularity contest), called the Florida Presidential Preference Convention, in Orlando. Joe shared an apartment with my brother Marvin, and together they hatched an idea for Mom and Dad to host a party for the convention guests and to shake as many hands as possible. The duo rented all the ballroom space they could get in the host hotel.

Joe recalled: "I figured people would be more likely to vote for somebody if they had a picture with them. So we bought three Polaroid cameras and had these really fancy little envelopes made up— *Ambassador and Mrs. Bush welcome you*—so every time he'd stick out his hand, one of the guys would snap a Polaroid picture and we'd slide it into one of these envelopes and hand it to the people."

Whatever they did worked, because the final straw poll vote on November 17, 1979, ended with Dad coming in a surprisingly strong third behind Governor Reagan (who was the favorite going into the poll) and former Texas Governor John Connally. The headline in the *Orlando Sentinel* the next day read "Reagan Takes the Cake, but Bush Takes the Icing."

Dad's campaign didn't stay low-profile after that. "What seemed just impossible awhile before suddenly became possible . . . It just took off," Dad recalls. They went into the Iowa caucuses energized—a core group of staff and volunteers traveled around Iowa with Dad, working at the precinct level. "Just strictly grassroots campaigning," Dad recalls. "We went up there and worked organizationally very hard . . . we had a good Iowa team." It helped that early on, Dad had lined up a base of key supporters in Iowa.

"There was a huge Bush ad in the *Des Moines Register*, which was really quite shocking, because it was like a who's who of the Republican Party in the state of Iowa, and it was quite impressive," recalled Pete Teeley. It was timed to coincide with Dad's announcement of his candidacy on May 1. Local volunteers took him around to "Meet George Bush" town meetings and covered every inch of the state. Sally Novetsky, a county chairman for Dad, remembers Dad speaking without notes, being so warm and friendly with people that she'd tell potential supporters, "Once you've heard and met him, there will be no doubt who you will be for." She was right, and the campaign started picking up converts from other candidates.

Becky Beech, Mom's assistant who hailed from Iowa and was the granddaughter of Mary Louise Smith, Dad's cochair at the RNC, remembers Mom went to all ninety-nine counties in Iowa for small campaign events and coffees—"it was very much retail politics," she recalls.

My brother Marvin spent almost a year in Iowa, working on Dad's campaign. Before the caucuses, he might go to the West Des Moines High School auditorium and give a short speech to several hundred people and from there go to somebody's living room in Cedar Rapids and speak to just ten people.

"I look back many years later and I see friends of mine who work at the family business and contribute to the family company's success. For me, it was really a neat feeling because I felt that I'd always been a taker from Dad. Trust me, I realize that my involvement didn't move the dial in Iowa—but he made me feel like it did, and that gave me a great sense of confidence at a younger age than I might have otherwise," Marvin said.

All the hard work paid off. Dad won the Iowa caucuses. At the victory party at the Hotel Fort Des Moines, Dad called it Big Mo— big momentum—and it "definitely [made me] a contender, Reagan and me . . . that was the biggest breakthrough for me," Dad recalls.

Becky Beech agreed: "People were elated. It was clear that it was extraordinarily significant. You could tell from that night to the next morning how the media attention was shifting directly onto them."

More important, he was no longer an asterisk in the polls.

From there, however, they headed into New Hampshire—and into trouble. "There were false expectations that the Big Mo would sweep us past Ronald Reagan, who was the presumed front-runner," said Andy Card. "The Big Mo lost its momentum in New Hampshire."

In Manchester, the League of Women Voters sponsored a tele-vised debate, and Governor Reagan won over the crowd with his signature charm. Soon after, a controversy arose with a scheduled debate on February 23, 1980, in Nashua, New Hampshire. The local New Hampshire newspaper, the *Nashua Telegraph,* invited Dad and Reagan to debate each other—without any of the other GOP candidates. Dad would have been happy to debate the others as well, but since the newspaper was hosting the event, he felt obligated to abide by their rules. The other candidates—John Anderson, Howard Baker, Bob Dole, and Phil Crane—were all miffed about being left out and showed up anyway. Ronald Reagan backed down and agreed they should be included, but Dad didn't know about this reversal. When the newspaper insisted on sticking with the original plan—and Dad sided with them—some thought he was being rigid.

The Reagan campaign had covered the rental of the hall where the debate took place—and when Reagan attempted to explain why the other candidates should be included, the moderator instructed the A/V technicians to turn off his microphone. "I paid for this microphone, Mr. Green," Reagan thundered defiantly. The audience loved the line (which came from an old Spencer Tracy movie), which has since earned a place in political lore.

Betsy Heminway was in the audience that night. From the Bush campaign's perspective, she said, "It was horrible."

Dad eventually lost the New Hampshire primary, and he has since pointed to that debate as a low point in his campaign. Apparently, so did David Gergen, later a TV commentator and a communications director for President Clinton. Gergen started on Dad's staff in New Hampshire; but after that debate, he packed his bags and left the campaign without saying a word to anyone.

"He just gave up on me," recalled Dad.

Pete Teeley remembers that Dad "stayed in there when, I must tell you, it was pretty gloomy at times. We weren't raising any money. A lot of volunteers that had come to work for us, they all quit. A lot of them went to work for Reagan."

Andy Card was the Massachusetts campaign chair and remembers the morning after the New Hampshire loss. There Dad made the decision that they had to win Massachusetts. "We worked re-

ally, really hard to restore positive momentum and exceed expectations, by carrying Massachusetts," Andy recalled. The momentum
started to pick up again as the campaign moved forward to win in
Michigan and Pennsylvania. Meanwhile, John Anderson decided to
drop out of the Republican race and run as an independent; and
Howard Baker and John Connally chose to just drop out altogether.

In Connecticut, another recent college grad, Tom Collamore,
remembered meeting Dad a few years earlier as a volunteer at a
fund-raiser for the Republican candidate for governor. Even
though Tom was just "a punk driver," as he described it, Dad was
very nice to him—in his estimation "the nicest by far" of all the potential presidential candidates who made their way through Connecticut then. So Tom wrote Dad a note saying, "I'm just a college
kid but if you run for president, I'd love to help you."

He got a nice note back from Dad, but didn't hear anything until
he got a phone call from Malcolm "Mac" Baldrige, an old Yale friend
of Dad's. (Mac would become President Reagan's secretary of commerce on Dad's recommendation, and tragically, he died in a 1987
horse riding accident. I like to remember him as a cowboy from Connecticut.) Mac told Tom, "I've just agreed to chair the Connecticut
campaign for George Bush for president, because I've known George
for a long time," he said. "And they sent me the file from Houston on
Connecticut, and your letter is one of the only things in it, so I
thought maybe we ought to get together and you can help me out."

So Tom joined the "George Bush for President" staff in Hart-
ford, which consisted of one other person at the time in addition
to Mac. Whenever Dad visited the state, Tom served as both
scheduler and director of ground transportation.

The campaign had a big Winnebago, and with Tom behind the
wheel, Dad devoted a week to Connecticut during which he traveled
all over the state in the RV, attending rallies and giving speeches
and visiting coffee klatches. In fact, Dad's first day of Secret Service
protection coincided with Tom's first day behind the wheel of the
RV, with a worried Secret Service agent riding shotgun up front be-
side him.

Miraculously, Tom managed to keep the Winnebago and all its occupants intact for the entire week, and Dad even won the primary. The campaign continued through other states—they won Michigan but lost Texas—and though the long days never seemed to end, everyone with whom I spoke claims to have enjoyed it.

Just about every Bush family member worked on the campaign in some capacity. After losing his congressional campaign, my brother George felt he needed to pursue his business career, but he still helped when he could. Neil and Marvin, both in college, took time off to work as well. Like Marvin in Iowa, Neil spent a lot of time in New Hampshire. Meanwhile, Jeb and Colu, who had moved to Venezuela because Jeb had a job at a bank there, came back to work full-time for the campaign. Jeb continued on the road with the remaining primaries—Pennsylvania, Texas, Michigan, and Oregon—and he remembers being in Portland, Oregon, when Mount St. Helens erupted.

All three of Dad's brothers, Prescott, Johnny, and Bucky, pitched in as much as their schedules would allow—as did Dad's sister, Nancy Ellis, and an army of assorted cousins, nieces, nephews, aunts, and uncles. Of course, none of us worked harder than my mother, who Becky Beech thinks made more appearances than my father did.

Margaret Tutwiler pointedly remembers that the Republican governor of Texas, Bill Clements, did not endorse Dad for the Texas primary. So Don Rhodes, completely on his own, would go out at night in his pickup truck and take down the Clements campaign signs around Houston. "Don was so loyal to your father. He was furious. He'd come in every morning and not talk about what he'd been up to the night before," Margaret recalls.

Occasionally, I got to accompany my father out on the campaign trail, which was a real treat. Dad was a great campaigner—but not because he is an amazing orator. In fact, he's the first to tell you he is not a great speaker on the campaign stump; but Dad was a natural at connecting with people, particularly face-to-face, handshake-to-handshake. The Secret Service told me he had a rule that he'd never just kiss a baby, like many politicians do. He'd always check with the parents first for permission to hold a child, so that families never felt that they were just props in some newspaper photo. He never wanted to offend the parents.

During one primary trip to Nebraska, Dad's bus got lost in a snowstorm. It was late at night, and Dad was sleeping across the aisle from Bernard Shaw, a reporter for the then-fledgling Cable News Network—CNN—who was assigned to Dad's campaign.

"We'd been up for hours," Bernie told me. "I don't know how many stops we'd made. As a joke, we got a pint bottle of bourbon and we put it in your father's lap. Some of us pretended to be asleep and we were restless and turning, what have you, as was he. He woke up and he put his hand on this bottle and he said, 'What the hell is this?' And everybody just started laughing. Some of the still photographers took a picture or two, which never saw the light of day, but he couldn't stop laughing. Sometimes when he laughs really hard, his eyes start watering. He showed a great sense of humor."

★   ★   ★

As the campaign ground forward, Governor Reagan steadily built up more delegates than Dad—and as the momentum began to shift, the money began to run out. James Baker came to Pete Teeley and said, "Pete, we're out of dough and I can't pay you." Pete said, "I don't care. I'll just be a volunteer, and we'll just go through with it." Soon enough, Dad found out that Pete and a number of other staffers had volunteered to go without a paycheck. He called each one of them up and thanked them.

"But what was also amazing is that . . . five or six days later, I was going through the mail and there was a note from your dad," recalled Pete. "And it was about that very subject and it was really something from the heart. He's on the road, he's working like hell, you know—twelve, fifteen, eighteen hours a day—and yet he finds the time to write this lovely note to say thanks *again*. I was really touched by that. I think about it even today."

Other people—Ron Kaufman, who had helped in the primaries, and Paige Gold, a young staffer—later received notes from Dad that also contained checks for their back pay after they went on volunteer status. (Dad held fund-raisers after the campaign ended to pay off his debts, especially to his staff.) "People in the business don't believe me to this day when I tell them that," Ron told me. "In the history of politics it's never happened before."

All the other candidates had dropped out by the Oregon primary, leaving just Dad and Reagan. Yet the writing was on the wall. "At some point, it became clear I had no chance to go further," Dad says. That "some point" occurred at the Holiday Inn at the Columbus airport in Ohio, Joe Hagin recalls. "Reagan had picked up enough delegates that night to put him over the total he needed . . . and I went home and slept for a long time."

Quitting the race would not be an easy decision; but Jim Baker, his campaign manager, convinced Dad that staying in the race was not a good idea, despite his feelings for those who had done so much for him. Baker reasoned that if Dad held out and contested Governor Reagan in his own state of California—which was the next primary—it would add to the antagonism that had naturally built up between the two campaigns. Mr. Baker told Dad, "You know, you would then have no chance at all to get put on the ticket."

Vic Gold—Dad's great friend and campaign speechwriter, who had been press secretary to Barry Goldwater in 1964 and later press secretary for Vice President Spiro Agnew—remembers spending an entire day with Dad, discussing whether to drop out. "It would have been very divisive, and he could see that—but at the same time, when you talk to people years ahead of time and they say they're going to work on your campaign for two years, and then you come up and say, 'Well, I'm not going to campaign there' . . . this was all a part of this decision."

Dad called the entire staff together and asked each one to submit a secret ballot as to whether they thought he should stay in or drop out. He read the notes and came to his decision. "He did the right thing," Becky Beech told me. "He thought it all through. We were all asked to vote, knowing that he had a press conference the next day." Becky voted for him to remain in the race—"fight to the finish"—but "it was sad because everybody thought he could be a great president and could possibly win, but it was clear that the primary was not going in his favor."

After swearing him to secrecy, Dad also discussed withdrawing from the race with John Magaw, his lead Secret Service agent. Dad knew he'd lose his Secret Service protection as a noncandidate, and he wanted the agents to be able to plan accordingly.

Incidentally, John Magaw didn't say a word to anyone, even though the campaign staff knew something was up and kept asking him questions. On May 26, everyone boarded the campaign plane for a previously scheduled stop in Houston, with the usual staff and press contingent. As the plane took off, suddenly music started coming over the loudspeaker in the cabin. It was the Kenny Rogers song "The Gambler" with the line "You've got to know when to hold 'em, know when to fold 'em." The staff didn't see it coming, and the press looked stunned.

"Boy, was that emotional," John Magaw remembers. Then Dad, also having a hard time, stood up in front where everyone could see him. He looked out over the crowd and gave them a quick salute.

After the plane landed, Dad made a statement to the press that he was essentially dropping out: "I have never quit a fight in my life. But throughout my political career—as a precinct worker, a county chairman and national chairman—I have always worked to unite and strengthen the Republican Party," he said. It was in that spirit that he pledged to Governor Reagan his "wholehearted support in a united party effort this fall to defeat Jimmy Carter." He ended with his vision of America "as a strong, purposeful, compassionate nation in need of new leadership for the decade of the eighties."

Pulling out of the presidential race was one of the toughest decisions my father ever made. But it also turned out to be one of the best—if not *the* best—decision of his political life.

Chapter 11

Out of the Clear Blue Sky

"Every week the columnists buried us. Every week we'd lose a primary and they'd say, that's the end of that, and then the next week he'd come back and win one. I remember I said to the fellow from the *Post,* the next time you bury us, you better drive a stake through his heart, because he kept coming back. That was the thing that most impressed the people around Reagan—your father's resilience. He was literally the last man standing. It was just—if you want to win, get George Bush. Reagan understood that."

—**Vic Gold**

After Dad dropped out of the presidential race, Andy Card made plans with his family to go to the Republican National Convention that summer in Detroit. He had been chosen to serve on the platform committee with Dad's friend from Texas, Senator John Tower—and after the convention, the Card family made plans to go camping for a week in Plymouth, Michigan. Andy's wife, Kathy, and their three children had driven all the way out to Michigan from Massachusetts with a car full of camping gear.

"We had our Bush hats on, generating hoopla, floor demonstrations," Andy remembers. Tonight, July 17, was the night Governor

Reagan was going to announce his running mate, and there were reports that he was considering asking President Ford to be his vice president. Since they didn't think Dad was going to get the job, Andy and a crowd of delegates—including John Volpe, former governor of Massachusetts, and Silvio Conte, the colorful Massachusetts congressman—were getting ready to leave the convention early to get a jump on the traffic. Dad was scheduled to address the convention that night, and as soon as he was finished, they'd head out.

Dad, meanwhile, was preparing to give his speech. As he walked over to the convention center with some of his staff, speculation about the number-two spot on the ticket was swirling. Back at the hotel, a group of staffers watched the news on a television set in a hallway.

"It was just about sunset when Ford was being interviewed by Walter Cronkite, and that's where people first got the idea that, wait a minute, they're trying to put a Reagan-Ford ticket together," remembers Vic Gold, Dad's speechwriter. "Suddenly, Cronkite said, 'Would you consider a vice presidency?' And Ford did not give a 'no' answer. See, Ford knew at the time negotiations were actually going on. Cronkite asks, 'How would this be? Would you split the executive authority?' And instead of Ford saying, 'What are you talking about?' Ford actually starts answering questions along that line."

Vic continued, "I'm getting very angry because I said, what in the devil is this guy doing? He's really holding out that he'd consider the vice presidency. Cronkite continued, 'Well, would you take on foreign policy?' And Ford said, 'Well, you have to be delicate about matters like that. After all, Governor Reagan has some pride.' There was a *Washington Post* reporter standing right behind me, and I'm talking to Pete Teeley, and I'm angry. I said, 'Pride? What does that horse's ass know about pride?' The next morning on the front page there's a story about the night in the Bush headquarters, and paragraph three reads: Vic Gold said, 'What does that horse's ass know about pride?' Well, that finished me with Jerry Ford."

(A few weeks later, President Ford was going to ride on the Bush campaign plane. Usually, Vic sat up front with Dad, but when he heard President Ford was coming, he began to pack up his typewriter and move to the back of the plane. Dad asked him where he was going. Vic explained he was moving to the back of the plane because he was sure Dad wouldn't want him around President Ford. But instead, Dad said, "Stay right where you are." So Vic stayed put, Ford came on, and everything was fine. When it was all over, however, Dad turned to David Bates and said with a smile, "Did you notice how quiet Vic Gold was?")

Margaret Tutwiler remembers calling home to her parents, "perfectly furious" at the idea of Ford becoming vice president. "I went to a pay phone and I started crying when I called my father, saying, 'This is wrong, this is horrible. I never want to work in politics again. I want a ticket home.' He said, 'Get ahold of yourself and stay put.'"

James Baker, the 1980 Bush campaign manager and 1976 Ford campaign manager, had actually flown to the convention on President Ford's plane. "We were all very down because Ford being considered was a real story. You had people who had worked for Ford, like Bill Brock and Henry Kissinger and Alan Greenspan, out there lobbying Ford to do this. I just couldn't believe that they were going to go with Ford. Only those of us working in your dad's campaign were against it. We were a tiny band. I mean— what are you going to call him, Mr. President/Vice President or Mr. Vice President/President? It was weird," Mr. Baker told me.

Dad's staff were all fervently praying that the governor would pick the man with the second highest number of convention delegates: George Bush. As they waited for Dad to be introduced for his speech, however, an ABC News reporter came up and said, "Hey, did you hear the news? Ford agreed to the deal. It's a done deal." Unfazed, Dad went out and gave his speech, one that earned him a big ovation. He kept it short, however, because it was Ronald Reagan's night and Dad wanted to just go out there and show his support.

I was in Detroit for most of the convention, there in what Dad would say was a "straphanger" capacity—a reference to a person in the crowd just along for the ride. I do remember helping Jeb and Aunt Nancy make "Bush for VP" signs for use on the floor of the convention, but mostly I hung out with the staff and my brothers. On the evening of Dad's speech, I remember wearing a lavender dress that I had spent entirely too much time picking out.

★ ★ ★

After Dad's convention speech, we all returned to the Pontchartrain Hotel, which was not too far from the Joe Louis Arena. Jeb recalls stopping at the bar with Dad for a beer, and "it was okay until at the bar, the reporters were continuing to say that there were efforts to put President Ford on the ballot."

Dad remembers Jeb saying it just wasn't fair. "Jeb, what do you mean it's not fair?" Dad asked. "You keep your head up, and we're going to leave town. Let's show a little class here. We can't whine about not being picked for vice president. Nobody owes us that. We have to be good sports."

They left the bar and went upstairs—Dad to his room at the end of the corridor, and Jeb to his down the hall. "I was very depressed," Jeb said. David Bates joined Jeb in his room for a Scotch.

Meanwhile, James Baker told Pete Teeley to head downstairs to the press room and "put a lid on it for the night"—media talk, meaning no more news tonight. It was close to 11:00 p.m., and no one had heard from Governor Reagan. So Pete headed to the main floor of the hotel in the elevator.

Just then Dad says, "Reagan—out of the clear blue sky—called me."

James Baker had just finished talking to someone involved in the Reagan-Ford negotiations and had heard that things might break down when the phone rang in Dad's suite. It was the Secret Service calling to tell Dad they were two floors below him if he needed anything.

Dad was wondering what that was all about when the phone rang again. Baker picked it up and announced, "Governor Reagan is on the line." Mom shooed everyone out into the hall. Someone ran downstairs to bring Pete Teeley back up.

"Hello, George, this is Ron Reagan," the front-runner said. "I've been thinking about it, and I wonder if you would be willing to be my vice presidential candidate."

Dad said he would be honored.

Then Governor Reagan asked, "Is there anything about my platform or anything else that might make you uncomfortable down the road?"

As Dad later reflected, it was unusually thoughtful for the front-runner to ask if there was something about *his* positions that might make the number two man uncomfortable—but then Dad already had an idea that Ronald Reagan wasn't your run-of-the-mill politician. Dad said he had no problems and expressed full confidence that they could work together as a team.

The crowd in the hall, meanwhile, had no idea what twist of fate was unfolding. Most were sadly predicting that Reagan was calling simply to inform Dad he had chosen Ford. Vic Gold, I recall, was doing push-ups, which is what he did when he was under stress. (Usually, he would announce that he was quitting as well, but this time he only did push-ups!)

Down the hall, someone knocked on Jeb's door and said Dad wanted to see him. When Jeb entered the suite, he recalled, Dad looked sad. He glumly told Jeb that Governor Reagan had called. Jeb, very distraught, said, "Well, at least he had the decency to let you know that you aren't the VP nominee."

Dad paused, smiled, and then said, "He called to say he wants me to be VP!"

"He put on the big act," remembers Jeb. "I couldn't believe he did that. So then he brought David Bates in and Bates almost collapsed."

Next was Vic Gold, also "having been set up the same way I was," Jeb said. Vic actually started jumping and screaming before going back to his push-ups.

Next, Mom and Dad came to the hall door, very straight-faced, and bid good night to everyone who was standing out in the hall. The group, dejected, started to complain. "What? You can't just say good night!" They wanted to know exactly what the governor had said.

My parents could not continue to keep straight faces, breaking into wide grins and announcing that Governor Reagan had asked Dad to be vice president. "Of course, then there was great rejoicing and backslapping and clapping and everybody was very pleased," Dad remembers.

Shortly after that, there was a loud noise outside as the announcement became public on television that Dad was the VP choice. A big party started in the hallway outside Dad's suite.

Out on the freeway, Andy Card's car full of Massachusetts delegates heard the news over the radio and "we literally did a U-turn on the highway," Andy recalls, and came back to the Convention Hall. "We stayed up all night making signs and posters and getting everything ready with a lot of volunteers."

"I went to the Republican convention in Detroit knowing the vice presidency was a possibility, but I did not expect it," Dad said, looking back. "No one was more surprised than I was when I answered the phone in my hotel suite and Ronald Reagan was on the other end of the line."

Pete Teeley recalls hearing from the Reagan people what had been going on in their suite: "He was asking them if Ford would stand for this or stand for that. And there were a couple of key issues in which Ford was not willing to support Reagan . . . Ford wanted to be able to name certain cabinet secretaries, including defense, state, and treasury. Well, if you take those three, there was nothing else that Reagan could do. He might as well have stayed in California. And in effect what they were trying to do was get Ford to be president and have the power, and Reagan wasn't going to go along with that . . . And apparently, Reagan got mad. And he looked at somebody and said, 'Get me George Bush.' And that was the best call he ever made."

That night, the new ticketmates and their wives agreed to meet for breakfast in the morning and then appear at a joint press conference. Mom and Dad were a little nervous getting ready for the breakfast. They didn't know the Reagans very well, and the heady developments of that night seemed surreal. But when they walked into the breakfast, The Reagans couldn't have been warmer.

As the Reagans and my parents rode down in the elevator to a convention event, the topic of what they were wearing came up—whether their similar ties were color-coordinated.

"That reminds me of the man who passed away and his wife went to the funeral parlor to check on how he'd look for the funeral," Governor Reagan said. "The funeral director showed the woman her husband. She said, 'He looks great. The only thing is, I really always thought he looked better in a blue suit. Is there anything we can do about that?' And the funeral director thought for a second. Then he picked up the phone and said, 'Charlie, can you change the heads on 13 and 14?'"

Thus began a tradition of joke-telling Dad had with President Reagan that continued throughout their White House partnership and beyond. Dad loved collecting jokes, often doing a last-minute sweep for jokes from the staff, to share with President Reagan.

"From there on, I saw this wonderful, warm side of Reagan," Dad said of the 1980 convention. "He was wonderful to work with. I hadn't really known him that well. And he couldn't have been nicer to me."

During the fall campaign, he added, the national campaign staff would give the Bush staff the message of the day, "but Reagan himself never tried to rein me in or rein me out. He never tried to say, 'You've got to try to do this more, or don't do that as much.'"

After the convention, Dad invited the key members of his team to Kennebunkport for the weekend to discuss the fall campaign, along with a group of advisers, and Andy broke the news to his family that the camping trip was off. Within an hour, he packed everybody up into the car and drove east all night long. Kathy, his wife, dropped him off at the gate at my parents' home on Walker's Point.

On a Wednesday in August of that summer, I was in Kenne-bunkport and decided to join a few friends for a picnic in Stage Harbor, borrowing Dad's boat to get there. Dad was out of town, and so I asked Pierce O'Neil, who worked at the local boat club and whom Dad trusted with the boat in the past, to take a group of us out on the water. On the way home, however, we hit a rock which bent the propeller.

"I had that feeling you used to get when you threw a baseball through your parents' living room window," Pierce remembered. He scrambled to find a replacement prop by the time Dad arrived on Friday for the weekend. The best he could do was Saturday at noon, and so on Friday afternoon, he waited on the porch to break the news to Dad.

Sure enough, Dad arrived and, moving quickly, asked Pierce to accompany him while he changed clothes and headed out to the boat. "The butterflies in my stomach were swarming," Pierce said, and he broke the bad news about the prop to Dad. Without a pause, Dad asked, "Is everyone all right?" and then, "How about if we play some tennis?"

"I couldn't believe it! I had broken the man's boat and not one angry or scolding word," Pierce said. "The situation taught me a lesson I have remembered ever since and tried to keep in mind when interacting with my kids and others: keep things in perspec-tive, don't overreact, and think of others."

The next week, while Dad was away, Pierce volunteered to strip all the varnish off the trim of the boat and refinish it—and says he "enjoyed every minute of it!"

That fall, Jim Baker became a senior adviser to the Reagan cam-paign, and Dad's friend Dean Burch was assigned to the vice presi-dential campaign. Mom and Mrs. Reagan campaigned together but soon decided they could cover more ground separately.

Throughout it all, Mom was confident of victory, but the moment it crystallized for her was when she was alone in Michi-gan, watching television. President Carter was on TV denying that he had called Ronald Reagan a racist, but then they played the sound bite of him standing in an African American church suggesting as much.

"That's how I knew," she said. "I said to myself, 'Of course, we're going to win.' I mean, there he was, caught on television. Ronald Reagan was no racist."

On election day, a crowd of young staffers and my brothers played touch football while we waited for the news. That night, Reagan and Dad made a joint appearance at a big campaign party in Peoria, Illinois, the kind that has an oversized map of the United States and a guy on a ladder posting the results. Then Reagan flew to California and Dad to Houston to watch the results.

The final tally: 489 electoral votes for Reagan-Bush and 49 for Carter-Mondale. Seven states went Democratic in 1980. The popular vote was a little less lopsided, with Reagan-Bush at 50 percent of the vote, Carter-Mondale at 41 percent, and John Anderson at just over 6 percent.

That night, Ronald Wilson Reagan was elected the fortieth president of the United States, while my father was elected the forty-third vice president of the United States.

Of course, by this point in his career, Dad had already distinguished himself as having held a series of nationally and internationally significant posts, appointed by two Republican presidents. Along the way, he had also occasionally been mentioned as potential VP material—but that call had never come. Now, thanks to the opportunity afforded him by Ronald Reagan, the 1980 election marked the first time Dad had participated in a national election—the first of four in which he would personally partake. The year opened with him reaching for the top rung on the political ladder; and though he had fallen short of that goal, the year closed with him just a single rung shy. It was an amazing twist of fate that had brought him this far, into the uppermost reaches of the U.S. government.

Just as "the Gipper" had paid his Hollywood dues behind leading actors such as Errol Flynn, Dad too would learn to play a supporting White House role to the main character striding toward the center of the world stage in January 1981.

Chapter 12

MR. VICE PRESIDENT

"I once said that he is a great Vice President, but I know and I've seen that it didn't come easily. George Bush is a man of action, a man accustomed to command. The Vice Presidency doesn't fit easily on such a man. But George Bush is also a patriot. And so he made it fit, and he served with a distinction no one has ever matched. Day in, day out, I've sought George Bush's counsel from the very first day of our administration."

—Ronald Reagan

Life for the Bush family took a fascinating turn when Mom and Dad moved into the vice president's residence. Looking back, I see it as the best of all worlds for my parents because it was like a real home. Unlike the White House, it afforded them privacy. Perched on a hill on the grounds of the Naval Observatory, north of Georgetown on Embassy Row and less than ten minutes from the White House, the Victorian-style house has twelve-foot ceilings, thirty-three rooms, and a terrific wraparound porch. It was originally occupied by the superintendent of the Naval Observatory, but the chief of naval operations liked it so much he took it over.

Eventually, it became clear that the vice president needed an official home because of the increasing security that came with the job. Vice President Nelson Rockefeller was the first vice president to be in the house, but he only used it for entertaining (the truth was, his home on Foxhall Road in Northwest Washington was much grander). Vice President Walter Mondale, his successor, was the first to actually live at the Naval Observatory.

I was in the middle of my college studies the day Mom and Dad moved in, back in school for the winter semester. "Moving into the house was just wonderful and exciting—a whole new dimension in our lives," says Dad. "It was mind-boggling in a sense. And then getting the office in the White House, the one right down the hall from the president in the West Wing; and the great big ceremonial office in the Executive Office Building; and the one up in the Capitol as president of the Senate. So we had all that to get started. It was great."

During the transition, Dad and President-elect Reagan visited Capitol Hill, paying a courtesy call on the congressional Democratic leadership in House Speaker Thomas "Tip" O'Neill's office. When they walked into the room, Dad spied his old friend Dan Rostenkowski and brought President-elect Reagan right over. Dad and Congressman Rostenkowski had served together years earlier on the House Ways and Means Committee, when Dad was a congressman. "Listen, you've got to know this guy," Dad said to Reagan about Congressman Rostenkowski. "He's going to be chairman of the Ways and Means Committee."

At that point, Tip O'Neill was deciding between making Rostenkowski the chairman of Ways and Means or the majority whip and was leaning toward the latter. When Dad introduced him as the next chairman of Ways and Means, Rostenkowski said, Tip O'Neill "almost died." As soon as the meeting was over, O'Neill pulled Rostenkowski aside and said, "What's George Bush doing, saying you're going to be chairman of Ways and Means? You better talk to me first," followed by a tongue-lashing about who was in charge.

Rostenkowski then called Dad and told him about the pickle he was in with the Speaker, and Dad explained that Rostenkowski would be far better off as chairman of Ways and Means than as majority whip, in line behind Jim Wright, who was a young man and would probably be around for a while. "Danny, it's all going to be the economy and it's going to be taxes," Dad predicted about the Reagan agenda. Rostenkowski agreed with him, but asked Dad not to tell anyone else he'd be chairman in public anymore. "He says, well, what's done is done," Rostenkowski said to me. Sure enough, Dan Rostenkowski took the chairmanship shortly after that day, and served for fourteen years, during the Reagan, Bush, and part of the Clinton administrations.

As the 1981 inauguration approached, Mom had gowns made for her by New York designers Arnold Scaasi and Bill Blass. The former had met Mom at an earlier event and told her, with a slightly disdainful eye on her outfit, that he could "make a prettier dress for you."

On inauguration night 1981, Mom and Dad had to appear at each of nine inaugural balls around town, traveling by limo with the Reagans. They'd get introduced to the crowd and then take a little spin on the dance floor. Dad, frankly, has never been much of a dancer— but Mom says at the inaugural he "danced very sweetly at all nine balls, because he knew he should. They were short spins!"

During the inauguration, our entire family was invited to the White House with the Reagans. It turned out to be one of several times that we would be invited to the White House during those eight vice presidential years, mostly for state dinners and other events. We didn't see much of the Reagan kids over the years, though Maureen was very friendly and campaigned a lot for her father. Jeb spent some time with her on the campaign trail and admired her loyalty and tenacity. "She was a great speaker," he remembers. Just like President Reagan.

The Reagan and Bush children shared the common bond of having their fathers become president. All of us know how hurtful it is to have family members criticized publicly, so I've been surprised and taken aback—to say the very least—at how inexplicably bitter Ron Reagan Jr. has been toward my brother George. Ron Jr.

seems to go out of his way to express his contempt for our forty-third president.

As far as our mothers go, Mom and Mrs. Reagan got on quite well, though they are very different people. When I asked Mom if they were fast friends, she replied, "Not fast friends, but friends." Because Mrs. Reagan had never lived in Washington before, Mom instinctively felt she should protect the new First Lady. Soon after President Reagan and Dad took office, in fact, some senators' wives had a meeting to tell Mrs. Reagan how to "skin a cat."

In particular, Mom remembered Strom Thurmond's wife telling Mrs. Reagan what exactly they wanted her to do at some event. "I could see it was irritating her just slightly," Mom recalls. "And I said, 'This is ridiculous. She was a governor's wife and she knows exactly what she's doing.'"

Meanwhile, settling into his office at the Old Executive Office Building, Dad gathered together everyone whom he had hired up to this point. My father put together a great staff, including Admiral Dan Murphy, his chief of staff; Pete Teeley, his press secretary; Boyden Gray, his legal counsel; and later, Don Gregg, his national security adviser. Dad and Boyden didn't know each other yet, but clearly he liked and respected Boyden, as he ended up serving as Dad's chief legal counsel throughout the twelve years of his vice presidency and presidency—a White House record.

That morning, Dad welcomed everybody and gave a little talk. At the end, he said, "One thing I want you all to always remember is this: the first day that you walk through that gate and you don't get a special feeling about where you are and what you're doing, that's the day that you need to go find something else to do."

He was also very serious about supporting the president and his staff. Dad admonished the group never to leak information in the press or say anything against the president's policies. As far as he was concerned, they were one team—and everyone was there to support President Reagan and his agenda.

From the start, Dad and President Reagan began to have lunch together every Thursday, which succeeding presidents and vice presidents have continued to this day. "No agenda. No written notes. Just the two of us," Dad explained to me. "A lot of people would say, well, you're going to see the President, tell him this, tell him that. But I didn't do that, and one of the reasons it continued in a very frank way is that he knew I wasn't going to say, by the way, Mr. President, so-and-so wants you to do this. It was very informal—I felt totally free to say whatever I wanted. Bring in the latest jokes or talk about what he was going to do, like going to the cemetery in Bitburg, Germany."

They'd also share Mexican food, which they both loved—chips and salsa, tortilla soup, or *chile con queso.*

Joe Hagin watched the Thursday lunches develop into something bigger. "He provided a very trusted voice to the president, and he supported the president, who did not have a lot of foreign policy experience. He served as an honest broker and an honest sounding board for the president, because I think the president understood that nothing that the two of them said to each other would ever leak. And that was very important . . . in short order, President Reagan grew to trust him."

Jon Meacham, the presidential historian and *Newsweek* editor, explained to me the impact of what Dad and President Reagan were doing, slowly but surely. "President Reagan was in the midst, with your father's help, of really reorienting the country from what had been a center-left country from 1960 to 1980 to a center-right country, where we still are. When you look at what President Kennedy, President Johnson, President Nixon, President Ford, President Carter were doing, it was all slightly to the left of center. It wasn't crazy liberal, but that's where the dial was. Reagan pushed it back center right, and your father held it there."

★ ★ ★

On March 30, 1981, Dad was off on a day trip, this one to Fort Worth. It was his first visit back to Texas since he had become vice president. Back in Washington, President Reagan had just delivered a speech at the Hilton Hotel across town, and as they were leaving the building to return to the White House, six shots rang out. Not only was President Reagan shot, so was Tim McCarthy, a Secret Service officer; Jim Brady, President Reagan's press secretary; and Thomas Delahanty, a D.C. police officer. John Hinckley Jr., the twenty-five-year-old shooter, was arrested on the scene.

Air Force Two had just taken off from Fort Worth heading to Austin when the word came in about the shooting. They were flying in an old Boeing 707—it had been President Eisenhower's Air Force One—and the onboard television would go black whenever the pilot communicated with ground control, adding to the confusion and suspense about the president's condition. Chase Untermeyer, who was on the VP staff at the time, remembers that after they had decided to return to Washington, a call came in from the president's counsel, Ed Meese, that Reagan had come through the surgery successfully and was out of danger. However, the Secret Service was still uncertain whether there was a larger plot behind the attempted assassination, and wanted Dad to helicopter directly to the South Lawn of the White House for safety.

While Dad was still in the air, Secretary of State Al Haig made his now-famous announcement to the press, "I am in control here," which had something to do with why Dad decided not to take the helicopter to the White House from Andrews Air Force Base. Instead, he choppered to the vice president's house first and then drove to the White House in a secure motorcade.

Dad explained his decision this way: "I didn't want to look like I was president of the United States. I don't know whether they had actually transferred the power to me as president, but clearly, I was next in charge. Al Haig had come up to the press room and said he was in charge here, and it was important to get back and keep the regular order"—which is Dad's nice way of saying that under the Constitution, the "regular order" for succession would be vice president, then Speaker of the House, *then* secretary of state.

Years later, Don Gregg looked back on the whole scene: "The contrast between the way your dad behaved, which was to just move in unobtrusively and there was the sense of continuity, and Al Haig, who was rushing in saying, 'I'm in charge'—it just couldn't have been more striking. A man with a huge ego, in the case of Haig, and a man with great compassion and a great sense of proportion, your father."

Chase observed that from that day forward, many Reagan staffers who had previously treated Dad with "limited enthusiasm" came to trust him.

Dad's concern was with how President Reagan was doing. He wanted to go to George Washington Hospital right away to see the president, but when he heard about the pandemonium there, he decided to send Joe Hagin to check it out first. "I went down that night and it was chaos at the hospital," Joe remembered. "I sent word back that I thought it was not a good time for a visit."

"So we went the next day to the hospital to see President Reagan," said Joe. "The vice president was very concerned about Nancy and the appearance of the whole thing. I was impressed with how calm and collected he was, how determined he was to handle it in the right way and not to be seen as stepping into the limelight."

Pete Teeley went along, too. "We went upstairs and the VP said, 'Well, come on, you can go see President Reagan,'" Pete told me. "I was kind of reluctant to do it—Mrs. Reagan was there and I thought to myself, 'Hell, she's not going to want a bunch of staff guys wandering through.'" So when Dad went into President Reagan's room—he didn't stay long, just enough to say hello and be able to reassure everyone back at the White House that the president was fine—Pete went to visit Jim Brady, a very good friend of his and the president's press secretary. John Hinckley had shot him in the head during the assassination attempt.

"His [Brady's] condition was shocking," Pete told me. "It looked like he had just suffered a terrible beating. And Sarah [Jim's wife] said to me that the doctors wanted him to start recognizing sounds and voices and names, and she had me whispering to him . . . He wasn't making any movements. It was a very sad situation."

The day of the assassination attempt, Rich Bond, Dad's deputy chief of staff, had his own personally devastating experience. Rich and his wife, Valerie, were at Children's Hospital in Washington, D.C., visiting their baby son, Patrick, who had been born prematurely back in December. Patrick had been fighting for his life every day for three months, but then sadly, he died that morning at the hospital. Rich and Valerie were returning to their home with Valerie's parents when Rich got an emergency call through the White House switchboard to report to the office because of the shooting.

"Shock on top of sorrow," Rich summarized, "a long, stressful afternoon and evening." By 11:00 at night, everything was just beginning to calm down and Dad called Rich into his West Wing office, saying he'd just heard the news about Patrick. "I started to cry and he gave me this long, fierce hug, telling me it was going to be okay," Rich remembers. It was okay—the president survived, and another son, Michael Thomas, was born to the Bonds in the fall of the following year.

As 1981 progressed, my parents read in the paper that a cross had been burned in the front yard of a Cameroonian couple serving in Washington with their country's embassy. Without any announcement or press contingent, Mom and Dad just went over and rang the doorbell, expressing their regrets and support to the scared couple.

"I think Dad is drawn to people who are hurting," Marvin added. "He's a natural healer. He doesn't profess to be that, but he has an amazing innate sense of when people are hurting and that's when he'll turn on that attention—whether it's in the form of a beautiful letter or a hug or some unsolicited advice."

★　★　★

The attempted assassination marked a turning point in Dad's relationship with President Reagan. For example, Don Gregg remembers meeting with Dad one Saturday morning after the assassination attempt, when Dad said he found out that the president would be at the White House on a summer Sunday—a prisoner of the "bubble" that presidents tend to live in. Don quoted Dad as saying, "He just feels like a bird in a gilded cage down there. I may ask him to play golf."

When I asked Jim Baker about Dad's relationship with President Reagan, he said, "Well, it matured. At first, it was a little bit shaky. Reagan went to your dad not because he wanted to, initially, but because there wasn't any other possibility. Why? Because your dad had delegates at the convention, and the best way to bring the party together would be to put George Bush on the ticket.

"But your dad quickly overcame any reservations that Reagan had by being an absolutely perfect vice president," Secretary Baker added. "I've said to people over and over, nobody ever performed that job better than your dad, because he knew that he was never supposed to be juxtaposed against Reagan. He was an absolutely superb vice president for Reagan, and they really got along extremely well. It was a very, very close friendship, and I'd say that began the first year."

Jim Baker, President Reagan's chief of staff, was in a good position to watch the relationship grow—he was in the office next door to Dad's in the West Wing, near the Oval Office. He followed Dad's lead to ensure that the normal rivalries between the presidential and vice presidential staffs never took root.

"It didn't happen in our administration," said Baker, "because I was the chief of staff and I know I satisfied the Reagans that I was totally loyal to them; and yet I was in a position to see that the vice president was included in meetings."

As the 1982 midterm elections approached, Dad began to campaign for Republicans in closely contested districts. His very close friend Lud Ashley, a Democrat, was running for reelection for his congressional seat in Ohio, which he had held since 1955. Republicans in Washington had identified Lud's seat as winnable and decided to devote resources—including the vice president—to unseat the incumbant.

"He came out to Toledo and campaigned against me!" Lud laughingly told me. Dad went to the *Toledo Blade* for a meeting of their editorial board, whose members all knew that he and Lud had a long history together—but that didn't stop them from trying to bait Dad into saying something against Lud. Dad looked at them and explained that of course he was campaigning for a Republican-controlled Congress, but added, "If you think I'm going to say one word against Lud Ashley, you're crazy. Have I made myself clear?"

Lud lost the election, and Dad hasn't heard the end of it since.

★   ★   ★

Dad was very happy that the vice president's house was adjacent to a tennis court. He played tennis regularly. He also played paddleball in the House gym with some of the congressmen on the Hill who were involved in the administration's tax reform legislation: Sonny Montgomery, Dad's friend and regular paddleball partner (who would yell "Kill Bubba!" when he tried to put the ball away); Bill Archer, who replaced Dad as the congressman representing Houston and later became chair of the Ways and Means Committee; and Marty Russo, the congressman from Illinois, who was also on Ways and Means.

"We kicked butt," Marty Russo remembers. "Your dad does not like to lose."

On a trip to Australia in 1982, Dad was playing tennis with his old friend John Newcombe and Tony Roche, the former Wimbledon doubles champs, at an indoor court in front of a few dozen spectators. Several times in a row, Tony would lob it to Dad, who would smash it back, and then Tony would drop it right at Dad's feet. The third time, Dad tripped over his own feet and fell down, blood streaming down his elbow.

"You could hear a pin drop," recalls John Newcombe. "The Secret

Service wanted to laugh but dared not. Suddenly, George sprung to his feet and said in a loud voice, 'Don't shoot him! I'm okay.' "

During a trip to Mexico, Dad spied Jim Burch and several of his fellow Secret Service agents playing tennis on their off-duty hours. Dad approached their supervisor, asking if Jim would be allowed to play with him and a pair of local tennis pros. Jim was allowed, and Dad made sure Jim received autographed, official photos of the match when they returned home. Later, Dad tipped Jim off when Dad was scheduled to play different matches with Bjorn Borg, Ivan Lendl, and Tony Roche, so that Jim could arrange to be on duty then and watch the match.

Many times after tennis or running, Dad checked his weight after showering. Ralph Basham, one of his Secret Service agents who went on to become head of the Secret Service and subsequently U.S. Customs and Border Protection commissioner, remembers one time in the locker room. "He would go over and get on the scale. He didn't want any extra weight on him, so he wouldn't even put his glasses on. Then he couldn't read the scale. 'Ralph, come here. I can't read. What does this say?' he'd ask. Of course, then I'd say, 'Well, sir, it's two hundred.' He'd reply, 'Oh no, it can't be. Read that again. It's got to be a bad scale.' "

★　★　★

During the first Reagan administration, my brother Neil and his wife, Sharon—who had met and fallen in love during the New Hampshire primary in 1980—welcomed their first child, Lauren, into our family.

Dad wrote Lauren a note when she was three days old that referred to a photo of her in the paper, "smiling right out there in front of all the world, just like your wonderful Dad has done all his life—even when it hurt." Like Lauren, Neil was always smiling, even though he went through a terrible struggle with learning disabilities as a child. I remember one time in the mid-1980s a letter arrived from a junior high school teacher asking Mom to share some of Neil's struggles with the students, because "they feel like failures." Mom immediately asked Neil to help, and Neil wrote a candid and inspiring note to the teacher:

> *People probably thought I was lazy or didn't care or that I just wasn't very bright. Despite the learning disability, I knew deep down inside I wasn't dumb. The root of my difficulty was a reading problem known as dyslexia . . . I learned that through hard work I could overcome my handicap. I also developed other skills that "smarter" people sometimes have trouble with—a desire to fight for my goals and an ability to get along with people . . . As your students know, life is not always easy and for me it sure didn't seem fair. With the combination of a strong desire to learn, the willingness to work hard, and support from family, friends and teachers, every human has the potential to climb any mountain.*

Neil was diagnosed with dyslexia and got the proper help while he was in high school. Learning to deal with dyslexia changed his life. Today as a result, he works harder, cares more, and enjoys life like few people I know. Although he was working at an energy exploration company when he wrote that letter, he now heads an educational software company.

Neil credits "the magic of Dad's support—combined with Mom's—and they never let me feel like I was different or less able." Mom and Dad found Neil's strengths—basketball, for example—and played to those strengths. "Mom took me to all the assessments and evaluations, but they both gave me the shot-in-the-arm confidence I needed to go through life. Half the battle of a learning disability is not to personalize it—to feel like you're stupid or use it as an excuse."

My brother George agrees that Mom and Dad's love was crucial to his success in life. "I used to tell our girls: 'I love you. There's nothing you can do to make me stop loving you, so stop trying.' In other words, Dad made sure his kids understand that there's this great well of affection available no matter how awful things get."

"Everybody had a shared experience," explains Marvin. "It killed us *all* when we'd read some nasty article about Dad. And in a way that became a rallying cry for all of us to help defend each other, help each other through some very difficult elections. It's been inculcated into our family by virtue of the fact that we spent a lot of time with Dad's family and his siblings. They were very cohesive, very close to each other."

As Marvin explains it, "I think there were fathers who were around more and, to a certain extent, were stifling to friends of mine. Always around and judging the kids. One of the greatest attributes of both of our parents is that they gave us enough rope to make a lot of decisions, and they knew how to pull that rope in when we abused the privilege."

How has our family remained intact despite the constant glare of publicity and Dad's long hours? "You can analyze it all kinds of ways. It's love, period," said my brother George. "If we didn't love each other as much as we do, and love Mother and Dad as much as we do, it would be harder to circle the wagons. People would be going their own way."

★   ★   ★

After the assassination attempt, President Reagan didn't travel much, at least internationally, and Dad stepped in to help in this regard. As a result, his relationships with leaders around the world grew not only in number but in importance.

For example, Dad began a great friendship with Canadian Prime Minister Brian Mulroney, who explained, "When we were in a meeting, President Reagan was in charge. Your dad did what a strong, loyal vice president is supposed to do: he kept his own counsel and shared it only with the president. But then when I'd go to the vice president's house to see him, it was different. He had opinions on everything. I found him entertaining and funny and fascinating, a wonderful guy.

"One day my wife, Mila, and I were there, and we were sitting there having a glass of Coke and a couple of sandwiches," Mulroney continued. "All of a sudden, the doors open and the grandchildren came in. They were crawling all over him. He never missed a beat. He kept talking to me. He enjoyed every second of it. The dogs were running around and, I said to myself, this guy's got his values in the right place."

One of Dad's first official trips as vice president was to size up François Mitterrand, the newly elected president of France. Don Gregg, Dad's national security adviser, was sitting with the two leaders in a very formal dining room when suddenly he spotted two dogs up on their hind legs outside the French doors, pawing to get in. Dad suggested they finish lunch and take the dogs for a romp outside the Elysée. "Your dad was wonderful with the dogs and it was a very, very humanizing moment with Mitterrand, who was otherwise rather cold and withdrawn." With that, another solid relationship was born.

After the Mitterrand meeting, they flew to London to meet with Prime Minister Margaret Thatcher (as well as her husband, Denis, one of Dad's favorite people, who passed away in June 2003). They then flew back to Andrews Air Force Base to spend the night in Washington.

"Got up the next morning, flew to California, went to the Reagan ranch, briefed the president on the Mitterrand visit, and then flew to the Far East," recalled Joe Hagin, who traveled to sixty-two countries with Dad during the vice presidential years. "In a matter of eight days, we were in eighteen of the twenty-four time zones in the world."

When I asked my father what he liked most about being vice president, he said, "I liked being around Reagan, and I liked traveling abroad . . . He was very generous about my traveling to different places. He'd let me take the initiative." Mom's back-of-the-envelope accounting of all of my parents' travel during the vice presidential years comes to 1,629 days spent out of Washington, traveling an estimated 1.3 million miles—about fifty-four times around the world.

During the eight years he was vice president, Dad attended

many funerals. In fact, Jim Baker used to joke that my father's slogan as vice president should have been "You die, I fly." But none were more important in terms of relationship-building than those of the Soviet Union's three leaders: Presidents Leonid Brezhnev, Yuri Andropov, and Konstantin Chernenko, who died within twenty-eight months of each other.

Each time there was a state funeral in Moscow, there would be a long receiving line in one of the grand halls of the Kremlin. Once they reached the end of the receiving line, each world leader would be brought into a private meeting room for bilateral discussions. When Dad would go into the room, no aides or Secret Service were allowed in with him. As a precautionary measure, Secret Service Agent John Magaw would slip a little hand alarm to Dad—a small remote alarm that would transmit a wireless signal to the Secret Service in the hall—to keep in his pocket in case he began to choke on a piece of food, or some other similar situation.

It was assumed that the room in which these bilateral meetings were held was bugged. As other leaders entered the room, they would look at each other and occasionally pass little notes, cleverly working out a sort of code to use when they had to speak out loud. And they got better at it each time, so that they were able to have a conversation without allowing the KGB to know what they were actually talking about. My father enjoyed that enormously—he got a big kick out of seeing these world leaders develop ways of circumventing the audio surveillance.

When President Brezhnev died unexpectedly in November 1982, my parents and the VP staff were on a tour of Africa. They left Nigeria for Moscow, and warmer clothes were sent from Washington with Secretary of State George Shultz—"the highest-ranking deliveryman in the world," Dad said later. Mom and Dad soon found themselves in front of Brezhnev's coffin, paying their respects to Mrs. Brezhnev.

Dad recalled, "The flowers were spectacular. The setting awesome. The music Chopin. Superb." Suddenly, the three hundred strings that had played so beautifully gave way to a military march, and Brezhnev's coffin was positioned behind Lenin's tomb by a tank-puller. "There was no mention of God. There was no hope, no joy, no life ever after, no mention of Christ and what His death has meant to so many," Dad recounted. "So discouraging in a sense, so hopeless, so lonely."

On the way back to Africa, Dad wrote a cable to President Reagan in midair from Moscow to Frankfurt on November 15, 1982, outlining how the funeral had become an opportunity for a bilateral meeting with Brezhnev's successor, Yuri Andropov. And then, vintage Dad, he described the funeral itself to Reagan in terms of their own families: "I at first saw only hostile troops and hostile power. We had a little wait, and I watched the changing of the guard and looked at the faces, and then I saw my sons and yours: George, Jeb, Neil, Marvin, Mike and Ron."

Dad and Mom returned to Zambia after the funeral. Shortly after, they sat down for lunch with their African hosts, and an African clergyman got up and offered a blessing before they began the meal. Dad said, "Oh, I can't tell you how good it feels to have a meal blessed!" He continued, "I've just come from this very dark ceremony in Moscow watching Brezhnev be buried, and the only sign of anything religious was when Mrs. Brezhnev was given a last look at her husband before his coffin was closed and she bent over and kissed him on the cheek and then crossed herself." Back here in the States, I remember how her seemingly tiny religious gesture made headlines—and how it gave many in the West hope for commonality and even peace.

After just fifteen months in office, Leonid Brezhnev's successor, Yuri Andropov, died of kidney failure at the age of sixty-nine on February 9, 1984, and once again, Dad found himself attending the funeral of a Soviet leader. As he had before, he went to the Kremlin for the burial and stayed for a series of bilateral meetings with the new Soviet leader. Andropov's successor, Konstantin Chernenko, was also in failing health when he assumed office and died at age seventy-two just thirteen months later, in March of 1985. He was the last of the Soviet "old guard" leaders, and had already turned over many of his day-to-day responsibilities for running the Soviet empire to a fifty-four-year-old former Politburo member named Mikhail Gorbachev. It was at Chernenko's funeral that Dad met Gorbachev for the first time.

"The minute I met him, I said to myself, 'This man is different,'" Dad recalled years later. "You could tell he wanted a dialogue in a different way from the others. He was his own man; he was charismatic."

He continued: "I remember once Gorbachev flared up when we were talking about human rights . . . and then he calmed down and said, 'We ought to talk about these things. Tell President Reagan I want to discuss any subject he wants.' It was quite a breakthrough, because I was the first one from our country to see him in action in this powerful new job."

Just as he did after the first Soviet funeral, Dad wrote a cable to President Reagan from Air Force Two. Gorbachev was about to become the leader of the Soviet Union, and what strikes me about Dad's letter is his take on Gorbachev's charisma and the effect it might have on members of Congress:

> *One has got to be optimistic that Gorbachev will be better to work with . . . hopefully one will truly "start anew" . . . there is the possibility that his attractive personality will be used to divide us from our allies and to attract more support for old views and themes. I can just see some of our Members of Congress eating out of his hand in wishful anticipation of achieving détente, but giving away too much in the process as we try to figure out who this man really is. It will be an interesting trip, but as the monkey said when he was shot into outer space, "It beats the hell out of the cancer research lab!"*

★ ★ ★

In 1983, Dad and Mom went on an official trip to Europe, to visit the allies and negotiate with the Russians on the issue of intermediate-range missiles. This important trip is memorable not only for the international stakes involved but also because of the massive protests, including two attacks on Dad's motorcade—one in Germany and the other in the Netherlands.

But Dad would not be intimidated or back down.

On June 26, 1983, for example, German Chancellor Helmut Kohl hosted Mom and Dad at an anniversary celebration in the city of Krefeld (North Rhine–Westphalia) commemorating the first wave of emigration from Germany to America 300 years ago.

"For us Germans, and for me as German chancellor, it was a great honor that none other than the American vice president and his wife, Barbara, came to Germany for this occasion," Chancellor Kohl told me. "This occurred at a time when the stationing of midrange weapons was being discussed intensely in the Federal Republic of Germany and was also being protested against in many places. In Krefeld as well, the atmosphere was heightened, and the commemoration was not without disturbances. The lights even went out at times in the hall where we were gathered. But George Bush did not let himself be irritated by it and he gave a splendid speech about German-American relations. What impressed me was the great composure with which George Bush reacted to the disturbances, which were very embarrassing."

Chris Buckley, Dad's speechwriter for two years who today is the editor of *Forbes FYI* magazine and a best-selling author, was also on that trip and remembers events this way:

"He was sent to Europe to about eight or nine European capitals in as many days to persuade the Europeans to accept the placement of Pershing and ground-launched cruise missiles that they themselves had requested. But the Russians had whipped up a big propaganda campaign, and there were marches in European capitals with hundreds of thousands of people demonstrating against America for 'forcing' these missiles on poor little Europe.

Chris continued: "It was a very important trip and he gave one speech in Berlin when we arrived and it basically made the case. The *Times* of London did an editorial about him and said, not a bad speech—which for the English is very good. It was a very testy time. We had to drive through a jeering crowd in London—people giving me the finger, and I gave it right back!! Special relationship? *Special relationship this!* We drove to the Guildhall in London and your father gave the speech and then there was a question-and-answer session. These lefty Brits stood up, most of them with clerical collars on, saying, 'How can you force these missiles on Europe? You're trying to blow up the world and make everything dangerous.' You know, the old pacifist rant. And your dad just looked at this guy and said, 'Wait a minute. Believe it or not, I care about this. *I have kids, too, you know.*' And he absolutely disarmed the crowd. At that moment, standing in the Guildhall, I could tell he was angry, and yet there was even something gentle about his anger. That's how I think of his leadership. He led gently. There's not an ounce of bluster or inauthenticity about him."

★ ★ ★

Early in the morning on October 23, 1983, a suicidal terrorist drove a Mercedes truck, loaded with explosives equivalent to six tons of TNT, at high speed into the headquarters building of a U.S. marine battalion at Beirut International Airport. The explosion killed 241 American servicemen, mostly marines, who were stationed there as part of a multinational peacekeeping force.

President Reagan directed the Marines into Beirut in August 1992 at the request of the Lebanese government to assist, together with French and Italian military units, in supervising the evacuation of the Palestine Liberation Organization. The multinational force was also there to serve as peacekeepers, attempting to help the Lebanese government achieve political stability after years of factional fighting. Sadly, the mission would fail, and Lebanon would again descend into deadly chaos.

The day of the bombing, Dad told President Reagan that he would like to go to Beirut himself. President Reagan agreed, and the next day, accompanied by General P. X. Kelley, then the commandant of the United States Marine Corps, Dad made the trip to Lebanon. They stood there, side by side, in the rubble, watching young marines as they clawed at twisted steel and broken concrete in an effort to find their comrades—hopefully alive.

"It was a sad but meaningful manifestation of *Semper Fidelis*," notes General Kelley. "When we subsequently visited the wounded aboard the USS *Iwo Jima*, I could not help but see compassion and pain on the face of a true hero—one from another war and another generation."

★   ★   ★

When there were breaks in Dad's travel schedule, he and Mom would head to Kennebunkport, Maine, to our family home, which would eventually become known around the world as Dad's summer White House. In the late 1890s, my great-great-grandfather Dwight Davis Walker and my great-grandfather George Herbert Walker bought the peninsula of land that today is called Walker's Point in Kennebunkport. In 1901, they built a big Victorian home on the tip of the land and named it Surf Ledge. These days we all call it the Big House. A second, smaller house built next to it, called the Bungalow, was given to my grandparents Dorothy and Prescott as a wedding present the year after they were married. From the turn of the century onward, the Walkers would escape the summer heat of St. Louis by heading to Kennebunkport; by the 1930s, my grandparents brought their children there for the summer from Greenwich, with Prescott Bush commuting weekends on the overnight train from Greenwich.

There in Maine, my grandmother Dorothy taught my father and his siblings sailing and tennis and bridge. Aunt Nan remembers the sound of the surf on the Maine coast lulling them to sleep at night, and she thinks it continues to help Dad relax. When they were thirteen and eleven, Dad's grandfather George Walker let him and Uncle Pres take out an old boat named the *Tomboy* for hours on end, which began my Dad's love of being on the water.

Aunt Nan says that for Dad, spending time in Kennebunkport became "a very deep and important thing in his life, a real touchstone place."

Dad calls Walker's Point his "anchor to windward."

The famous nor'easter of 1978 damaged thousands of homes along the New England coast, including the Big House. At the time of the storm, Uncle Herbie—George Herbert Walker Jr., my grandmother's brother—owned the house, but when he died shortly afterward, my Aunt Mary decided to sell the house to Mom and Dad.

Since Dad had left the CIA and moved back to Houston, he and Mom had the time and energy to fix up the storm-damaged house. Previously, we had a gray house on Ocean Avenue, facing Walker's Point, which had terrific ocean views as well.

By the time Dad became vice president, he and Mom started entertaining on Walker's Point. At one event, they hosted a dinner for a group of diplomats who had come to visit. Tim McBride, one of Dad's personal aides, recalls that when the group arrived—probably a dozen people—Dad remembered quite a few from his U.N. days, but there were some new faces to him, and he had trouble putting names with them. As he tried to decide where everyone would be seated for dinner, he was having a hard time.

"Go get my Polaroid camera," he said to Tim, referring to the one he had used in China, "and run around and take pictures of all the guests, and those will be the place cards." Tim did exactly that, and Dad carefully arranged the guests by photo.

On one of his first weekends in Kennebunkport as vice president, Dad decided he needed a haircut. Previously, a local barber named Emile Roy had sent a letter to Dad's presidential campaign, volunteering to help after he read an article about Mom and Dad's time in China. After reading Emile's letter, Dad called him up for a haircut (of course, Emile didn't believe it was really Dad on the phone!), and the two have been friends ever since.

"George invited me fishing one time and it turned out to be a chilly day," Emile told me. "I was in a short-sleeved shirt and

George ran back to the house to get me a jacket. He came back with a hat as well and said that he did not want me to lose my head over it. I think he was referring to my toupee!"

In 1983, Mom and Dad invited all of the nation's governors and their families over to Walker's Point for a cookout, when the National Governors' Association held its annual meeting in nearby Portland, Maine. In a scene that could have been right out of the movie *Groundhog Day*, both Governor Michael Dukakis of Massachusetts and Governor Bill Clinton of Arkansas were guests.

"Our daughter, Chelsea, then was three years old," remembers President Clinton. "I took Chelsea up to meet the vice president. I thought, 'Boy, I have such a smart, well-behaved daughter. She'll be great.' I said, 'Chelsea, this is Vice President Bush.' And she shook his hand and she said, 'Where's the bathroom?' And he just laughed. He took her by the hand, introduced her to his mother, and took her to the bathroom. He didn't have to do that. He could have had somebody else take her. He could have pointed it out to me. He did it himself. I never forgot it."

★ ★ ★

During the spring of 1984, Dad was campaigning for the reelection of the Reagan–Bush ticket in Colorado. As Dad walked through the lobby of the Denver hotel where he was staying, he noticed a group of retired baseball Hall of Famers such as Hoyt Wilhelm and Juan Marichal and Whitey Ford. They were there to play in an Old Timers exhibition game that night at Mile High Stadium.

Sean Coffey, Dad's personal aide at the time, remembers Dad stopping to chat with the players assembling for the photo. The players, in turn, started talking baseball with Dad—who had played first base in two College World Series in 1947 and 1948, while at Yale.

The rap against Dad was that he was "all field and no hit," but during a 1948 game in Raleigh, North Carolina, Dad happened to hit a single, a double, and a triple—with a few pro scouts looking on. The scouts approached Dad's coach, Ethan Allen, after the game, but "unfortunately, Coach Allen told them the truth, so the scouts never talked to me much after that," Dad later said. Six of his teammates were signed by the pros instead.

Dad confessed his shortcomings thirty-six years later to the assembled Hall of Famers. Nevertheless, they invited Dad to come to the game that night, and the next thing Dad knows, he's in the locker room at Mile High Stadium. They had him suited up in a uniform, and he was swinging a bat when Pete Teeley found him. "I looked at him and I said, 'What are you doing?'" Pete said. "'These guys play baseball every day even at the age of sixty. You haven't played in years. I don't want you to go out there and make a fool out of yourself.' He got mad as hell about that."

Meanwhile, over the stadium address system, they announced there was a "mystery guest" playing with the team, and Dad came out. The crowd had no idea who he was until the announcers said Dad's name as he went up to bat. Milt Pappas, the great All-Star pitcher, pitched to Dad. Then Dad hit a sharp single to center field and made it to first base.

"The players were delighted, and he was really happy," remembered Sean, who watched from the third base side. Dad was eventually forced out at second to end the inning—at which point he put on a glove and headed out to first base, his old position at Yale.

"The best was yet to come," said Sean, because "who comes up but Orlando Cepeda, who was known for hitting line drives. Sure enough, he hits a rocket down the right field line. If it had hit somebody in the head, it would have taken their head off. As it was, it looked like it was going into the right field corner for a double—but that was before first baseman Bush jumps to his left. He dives for it, knocks the ball down, gets up, scrambles into foul territory, turns around, and lobs a perfect underhand pitch to the pitcher covering first. Orlando Cepeda is out. Mile High Stadium erupted in cheers."

"A Walter Mitty night for me," Dad told one of the interviewers as he came off the field with a smile, referring to James Thurber's mild-mannered character who daydreams of being the fearless hero.

★ ★ ★

In 1983, Joe Hagin went to Dad and told him that while he'd do anything in the world for him, he couldn't travel anymore—together, they'd been on the road for three years without a break. Dad understood, thought about it, and called Joe back to suggest the job of assistant to the vice president for legislative affairs. Worried that he was young and inexperienced in the world of legislation, Joe told Dad he wasn't sure it was the right job for him. The more he found out about it, in fact, the more shocked he was—"a two-rung promotion," Joe called it, with a beautiful office in the Capitol, a good-size staff, and a driver.

"Nonsense, you'll do fine," Dad reassured Joe, explaining that the job involved not much travel but a lot of congressional hand-holding. Then Joe discovered why my father wasn't concerned: "I found out several months later that he had written all one hundred senators a personal letter about me . . . he really invested a lot of time doing all those handwritten notes. People totally welcomed me."

While Joe was working with Democratic senators and congressmen back in Washington, the Democratic Party held its convention in San Francisco, nominating former vice president Walter Mondale for president and Congresswoman Geraldine Ferraro for vice president. Ms. Ferraro was a three-term member of Congress and a former public school teacher who had gone to Fordham Law School at night while raising three children. She was the first woman nominated for the vice presidency by a major party. It was a bold stroke by the Mondale campaign, and it presented a tricky challenge for Dad.

"He was complimentary of my nomination," Ms. Ferraro told me. "One, because it was the politically right thing to do; and two, because your father was a very gracious man."

Looking back, Dad says now, "I was very surprised at her nomination. She had limited experience on the national scene beyond being a congresswoman from New York. I got to know her a little bit during the campaign. I haven't seen her in a while, but I do like her."

There were stories at the time about a tenfold increase in total media coverage of the vice presidential race from 1980 to 1984. What Dad remembers was the challenge of making appearances with Ferraro, because of the crowds she drew.

Ms. Ferraro agreed: "It was mind-boggling to see. Certainly, I didn't expect the response that the candidacy had. It was more the candidacy than it was me. I think probably any woman who got the nomination would have been received very much the same way—and that's in either party. My audiences were as large as President Reagan's and in some instances larger. Forty thousand people would show up—it was the most amazing thing."

Meanwhile, in a bar in Sterling, Illinois, then-Congresswoman Lynn Martin was trying to earn an endorsement from some steelworkers in a late-morning meeting. She paid no attention when the phone behind the bar rang, but then the bartender announced that some wise guy had just called and said he was the vice president of the United States. And then the phone rang again, and the bartender realized, actually, that it *was* the vice president.

"It's for you," he said to the congresswoman.

"So I went to the phone and it was your dad," Ms. Martin told me. 'What are you doing in a bar?' And I said, 'Trying to get votes. What are *you* doing?' He said, 'I'm calling you because I'm going to debate Representative Ferraro and I'd like you to help me prepare.'"

Congresswoman Martin suspects she was chosen because she and Congresswoman Ferraro served on the same House committee, and were both "sharp—if you were being kind, you could say we were 'sharp witted,' but maybe occasionally just 'sharp.'"

Mom thought that Dad might not have been taking the whole thing seriously enough, partly because many of his staff members were telling him everything would be fine. But things might not be fine—"she's going to be tough," Ms. Martin recalled Mom saying to her about Ms. Ferraro in a phone call.

"Your mom said, 'Listen, he's full of himself right now. Cut him down.' I said, 'That's easy for you to say—he's vice president of the United States. This is my career, too, you know.'" Here she was, a young mother and a new member of Congress. But somebody had to be tough—and help Dad get ready for a difficult debate.

One of the things Congresswoman Martin observed is that she had always debated men—but when men debated women, they primarily debated their wives or mothers. They are seldom in the situation my father was in at that time in America. He had to learn to walk the line between his extraordinary politeness and his competitive side. Boyden Gray, head of the debate prep team, remembers, "It was very, very tricky . . . the strategy was he had to win, but he couldn't win too strongly. He couldn't be seen as ganging up on her."

Boyden remembers the first debate rehearsal, which was to have a television camera, a stage, podiums, chairs, the whole set, in a large auditorium in the Executive Office Building. Dad had specifically said he didn't want anyone in the session other than Congresswoman Martin and essential staff.

"I ignored his instruction and invited everybody I could think of," Boyden said. "So we had the place practically filled with Reagan's staff and everything else. When he came in and saw the auditorium two-thirds full, he was furious. *Absolutely furious.* But it was the right thing to do, because it made him take the task seriously. And you know, Lynn Martin gave him a pretty hard time."

Ms. Martin says Mom concedes that Dad was not ready for the first practice debate. He was better by the second, and "he cleaned me up by the third."

A few days later, the two vice presidential candidates met in Philadelphia for the real debate, and no matter what Ms. Ferraro said, Dad kept his cool. He's participated in one vice presidential debate and five presidential debates over the years; nonetheless, he says the one with Ferraro was the most tense.

"I think the press was automatically divided," Dad said. "A lot of the females in the press corps said this was one of us. You could hear 'em clapping."

In fact, there was a press room behind the stage, filled with people whom Dad would call the spinmeisters—the political guys from the Reagan-Bush campaign, like Lynn Nofziger and Lee Atwater. (They were waiting for the end of the debate and one of the rituals of American politics to start—reporters interviewing political operatives in the "spin room." Supporters of each campaign would hold a sign over their head with their candidate's name on it, then roam the room giving sound bites to reporters as to why their candidate won the debate.) While the debate was still going on, Dad's political staffers actually saw the journalists clapping for Ferraro.

"It was a tough one," Dad said.

After all the spin had been captured by the reporters, the media analysts that night declared the debate a tie—which came as a relief to both candidates.

The day after the only vice presidential debate, however, Dad made an appearance before a group of longshoremen, one of whom kept waving a sign that read "You kicked a little ass last night, George!" He kept yelling that same comment at Dad, over and over, from the crowd.

As Dad was getting into his car to leave, the man repeated it again to Dad, this time right next to him. Unfortunately, Dad actually repeated the comment back to the man—not noticing an intrusive boom mike as he climbed into his limo. It was all over the news in no time.

Compounding the situation, shortly afterward my mother was joking with some reporters on the campaign plane, thinking she was "off the record." (Note to reader: never assume you are "off the record" with a reporter.) Mom remembers that one "had needled the president about his elite, rich vice president. It really had burned me up because we all had read that Geraldine and her husband, John Zaccaro, were worth at least $4 million, if not more.

The press were teasing me about it, and I said something like, 'That rich . . . well, it rhymes with rich . . . could buy George Bush any day.'"

By the time it was on the radio news, Mom had called Ms. Ferraro to apologize. By the time it was on the television news, she had called Dad to apologize.

At that point, the media were ready to ambush Mom en route to the next appearance, but before they could, Dad called back with a friend's advice: "Remember Halloween." The poet laureate (we call her the poet laureate of our family because of her skill with rhyming words) marched out smiling and said she had talked to Ms. Ferraro and had apologized for calling her a "witch"—and that the apology had been graciously accepted.

Even today, Geraldine Ferraro is very understanding and gracious about the incident. She says, "Your mother was not the candidate. She was very protective of your father. It didn't figure into the top ten things I worried about. We still kid about it. More than once my girlfriends will remind me, 'You know, Gerry, you rhyme with witch!' It's very funny."

A night or two later, Dad went to a campaign event, and as he got to the podium, he sheepishly apologized to the crowd: "Sorry we're late, but Bar and I were upstairs cleaning our mouths out with soap."

There were other memorable moments from that fall campaign—the critics calling President Reagan the Teflon President; the "Bear in the Woods" ad campaign reminding voters of the Soviet threat; President Reagan not realizing a microphone was live when he joked that the "bombing will begin in five minutes." But in November, President Reagan and Dad won in a landslide, carrying every state except Vice President Mondale's home state of Minnesota. The Reagan-Bush ticket took 525 electoral votes to Mondale-Ferraro's 13.

"My mother was the only person in the entire country who didn't know we were going to lose," Ms. Ferraro remembered. When she called my dad that night to concede the election, Dad unexpectedly invited her to lunch. At her suggestion, Dad brought "his Geraldine Ferraro," Lynn Martin, and she brought "her George Bush," meaning Bob Barnett, a Democratic lawyer who is married to Rita Braver of CBS News.

"I'd have preferred to be the host today, but under the circumstances, I'll take what I can get," Ferraro said. Dad said, "It's a free lunch."

The *Washington Post* reported afterward that they enjoyed salmon steak, asparagus with potatoes, and brownies for dessert, in Dad's ceremonial office in the Executive Office Building.

Bob Barnett remembered that Ms. Ferraro told them she'd lost her luggage on the way back from vacationing in St. Croix after the election. Dad replied that he was very experienced at losing luggage and was, in fact, a fan of bad lost-luggage jokes, and shared this one: A woman comes up to the counter at United Airlines in Washington with three pieces of luggage. She asks the ticket agent, "Can you send one to New York, one to Los Angeles, and one to Hawaii?" The ticket agent replied, "We can't do that!" The woman says, "Why not? You did it last time."

Dad knew that in order to prepare for the debate, Bob had not only researched his speeches and issue papers but had read *The Preppy Handbook*. He'd even bought those striped ribbon watchbands that Dad sometimes wore. When Dad noticed Bob had on a plain leather watchband during lunch, he took his own watch off its watchband and gave the striped one to Bob as a souvenir. He later sent photos of them comparing watchbands, inscribed "To Bob, you preppy, solid watchband stand-in."

"On the day of our lunch," Bob told me, "George Bush was gracious in victory."

The four of them enjoyed a lively lunch, and Dad afterward showed them the desk in the vice president's office with his predecessors' initials carved in the woodwork.

"It's amazing," Ms. Ferraro said later. "I don't think women would do that to the furniture."

Chapter 13

MASTER OF THE SMALL GESTURE

> "Dad invented quality time, as far as I'm concerned. He's a busy guy, but he's such a magnetic personality and so fun to be around that—even though he may have worked fourteen hours that day—it's the one hour you're with him that really makes your day."
>
> **—George W. Bush**

Because January 20, 1985, fell on a Sunday, the public ceremony for President Reagan's and Dad's second inauguration was scheduled for Monday, January 21. That Monday dawned a bright but bitterly cold day—with windchill temperatures reaching as low as twenty below zero. As a result, the public inauguration ceremony was moved indoors to the Capitol Rotunda and was forced to become a semiprivate ceremony. Even the parade had to be canceled.

I remember squeezing inside the Rotunda for the ceremony, with far more people than the fire marshal would have normally allowed. I felt the same sense of swelling pride and emotion as I had four years prior. After the festivities, I remember going back out into the winter cold—back to my life in New England, where I was working in an art gallery.

About an hour after that indoor ceremony, Democratic congressman Marty Russo, a friend of Dad's who was on the House Ways and Means Committee, was going back to his office by way of the House gymnasium. Dad had been sworn in, attended a luncheon, and then decided he had time for a quick game of paddleball that afternoon. He was about to play with Marvin and a cousin when they realized they needed a fourth.

"You and I are going to take these young kids on and we're going to show them," Dad said to Marty, "so suit up." Marty did, and they beat the young men two out of three games.

Once the inauguration weekend was over, Dad settled back into work. Because he was an early riser, Dad would regularly arrive at the White House at 7:00 a.m., while the rest of the White House didn't get started until closer to 9:00. Tom Collamore, the Winnebago driver during the Connecticut primary, had been promoted to the vice presidential staff a few years earlier, and now was on the road constantly with Dad, as assistant to the vice president and staff secretary.

"If it wasn't foreign travel," Tom recalled, "it was strategically picked domestic travel. And so it was six workdays, and then Sunday you were back in Washington to change your laundry and pick up the new materials and go out again. It was that way pretty much [in] '86, '87, '88. It was at least three and a half years. Always a frantic pace."

Tom also remembers that any staff member with any relative in any small town across the country was invited to bring family members to the holding room, prior to an appearance by Dad, just to chat with my parents for a few minutes—"and that filled the staff member's gas tank for another six months."

Ray Siller, a comedy writer who wrote jokes for both Bob Hope and Johnny Carson, came to spend a weekend at the vice president's residence with Mom and Dad. Ray arrived in a cab with heavy suitcases in the trunk. Dad grabbed the luggage and carried them up to the house ("Pretty amazing to have this man as a bellhop," Ray thought) and got him settled in a guest room. At the end of the weekend, my parents stopped by his guest room and Dad asked if the room was okay. Ray said it was.

"Bar, he didn't notice it," Dad said, dejected. Ray *had* noticed it, but was just too polite to say anything. What was "it"? Dad had put fake dog poop in the closet.

On a more serious note, Shirley Green, who worked in Dad's press office for Pete Teeley, went home from work one night to find her home not only burglarized but ransacked. After calling the police, she called Pete Teeley to let him know she wouldn't be in the next day. Pete called Dad, who called Shirley to make sure she was okay. He said, "You aren't going to stay there by yourself tonight, are you? Come stay with us." Shirley said she guessed it was like getting back on a horse after a fall, and she might as well stay there and get used to it. Dad insisted again that she come over to the vice president's residence, and she declined again. "No, really, Shirley," Dad said, "Bar and I'll jump in the car and come get you right now!"

"What a funny moment," Shirley told me, looking back. "He and Bar hadn't 'jumped into the car' to drive anyplace in years! But George Bush's automatic kind and thoughtful—though funny—reaction to a friend in distress was also the only time I nearly broke down in tears."

Marlin Fitzwater, Dad's press secretary during the second Reagan administration, put it this way: "His instinct has always been to do good things without considering political or public benefits. He is the master of the small gesture. I used to call it the small gesture with the grand results." To be sure, little touches went a long way toward building a tremendous amount of loyalty and, I think, were part of a larger effort on my father's part to bring out the best in his staff. And the "grand result" was an effort on everyone's part never to let Dad down or disappoint him in any way.

Chris Buckley, Dad's speechwriter, remembers a morning when there had been a leak to *Time* magazine from someone on the VP staff. The staff knew very well that Dad's cardinal rule was

No leaking. At the daily staff meeting, Dad began by saying how disappointed he was, then adjourned the meeting on the spot. "We all started looking at the floor. It was like being back in school when the headmaster was saying, 'Buckley, it's not that you let the school down, it's that you let yourself down.'"

Trust me, I have been there. My brothers and I never ever wanted to disappoint Dad. One time, Jeb had to confess to something he'd done as a kid—"the statute of limitations has run out so the details aren't as important," he jokes now—but Dad told Jeb he was disappointed in him.

"It was like silence," Jeb recalled. "It was the worst thing he could have said."

My brother George agrees: "There are some basic rules . . . a young person needs to be told there are these rules. He told me that when I was a young guy. He's a man of enormous integrity and great values, and there is no question that you will disappoint him if you do not live up to certain basic standards . . . On the other hand, he's an incredibly forgiving person. He doesn't hold grudges and that's very important."

Mom and Dad visited China in 1986 and were enjoying seeing old friends again. Chinese leaders threw a large banquet in their honor in the third-floor ballroom of one of the newest hotels in the city. My parents and the Chinese dignitaries sat at a long head table, elevated on a riser, across one end of the ballroom. The head table overlooked perhaps fifty or more round tables of Chinese guests, with perhaps two or three Americans, from the vice president's staff, the American embassy, or American businesses, at each table.

The tables were heaping with food and white bottles of Moutai, a special Chinese wine that supposedly had the power to fell a horse in midstride. As the courses began, the Chinese host at each table proposed a toast to their new American friends. The American delegation was immediately fearful. The briefing papers had warned the Bush delegation that Moutai was designed to loosen tongues and embarrass guests. The idea was to toss one's head back and take the entire drink in two gulps, thus complying with the hosts' shouted command, *"Gambe!"* As dinner went on, a lot of Moutai was consumed in this fashion.

By midevening, after Dad and the mayor had exchanged very warm toasts, the conviviality was going so well that Don Gregg picked up his glass of Moutai, left his table, and went to toast his counterpart at another table. Seeing this, a few others around the room followed suit. Unfortunately, among them was a young staffer who picked up an entire bottle of Moutai and began going table to table, or so it seemed, with special toasts for his new Chinese friends. After about three tables, it became apparent that his gait was unsteady, his voice louder than necessary, and calamity could be at hand.

Anyone who knows my parents knows the dangers of that situation. First, any public embarrassment by a staff person that detracts from the success of the mission, or embarrasses the country, is a career-ending move. Second, behavior and protocol are serious parts of diplomacy. And third, Dad believes that good manners are essential, and bad manners are unacceptable. The young aide was about to violate all three.

Marlin Fitzwater noticed that Mom, from her elevated vantage point at the head table, had been watching with obvious disdain as the young man moved from toast to toast. When he arrived at Marlin's table, Marlin pulled him aside and suggested he return to his table and stay seated.

The young man never said a word. He just turned and walked a little unsteadily back to his seat. At the end of the dinner, my parents headed to the elevators as they returned to their room. Dad had sent a message to the aide during the dinner, ordering him to join them at the elevator after the meal. Mom hadn't been the only one watching the *"Gambe!"* performance.

It was no doubt the longest elevator ride of the young man's life. Three people got on. Only two got off. Dad fired the young man and instructed him to take a commercial flight back to Washington. Unfortunately, there were no commercial flights available, so he rode back on the cargo plane with all the equipment.

Marlin looked back on the incident: "It's a reality of the presidency and vice presidency that their personal values and sense of propriety are watched like a hawk by thousands of people throughout the government. Standards are set, limits applied, and codes of conduct are established by the personal actions and attitudes of the officeholder. In this case, it became accepted wisdom that Vice President Bush was a man who countenanced good manners, appropriate behavior, and civilized conduct. It was also understood that if you crossed the line, you would not get off the elevator. George Bush was not afraid to fire people."

Dad never tried to embarrass people with their mistakes. I've never once heard Dad talk about this incident and only learned about it myself from others. As a matter of fact, Dad made sure that it never went on the aide's permanent record. Dad still keeps in touch with the young man, and although the aide was reluctant to speak with me about this incident, he shared many other wonderful memories about Dad. This former aide went on to great success in life.

On a Saturday in July 1985, President Reagan was undergoing surgery on his colon. It was not an emergency, but nevertheless, presidential power had officially been transferred to Dad—but just for the few hours that the president would be unconscious. That same day, coincidentally, Dad invited David Bates and two other friends of his, Jack Sloat and David Cunningham, to the VP residence for a tennis match. At one point in the set, Dad was playing up at the net when Cunningham lobbed a shot to him, causing Dad to back up toward the baseline to get it.

What happened next was never reported at the time: Dad stumbled and fell on his back, bumped his head, and blacked out. The United States may have been without any president at all for a few moments! As he lay on the court not moving, Secret Service agents and a doctor jumped out of the bushes around the court, where they had been covertly watching the whole thing, as his tennis partners rushed across the court.

"He might have had a small blackout. Whether he knew who he

was or what he was doing for fifteen or twenty seconds, I wouldn't swear to it," remembers Cunningham. The agents drove him up to the house—they wouldn't let him walk—with Dad apologizing for breaking up the tennis game.

★   ★   ★

One staff member told me Dad always believed in the better side of us, and I think that was true not only of his family but of his staff, his friends, and his fellow world leaders. The Secret Service, for example, felt that way. Dad had tremendous respect for them and their abilities. He made it a point to thank his agents every night before he turned in, which I'm told is unusual. Dad also protected the agents from unwitting people who asked them to carry bags for him or pass notes to him, telling the unknowing individuals that it wasn't the agent's job.

One time our dog C. Fred got sick in Dad's limo, and as the car pulled up to the vice president's residence, Dad hopped out and the car pulled away. Dad yelled for it to come back, and when it did, he immediately began pulling out the floor mats that C. Fred had soiled. "Sir, we'll take care of that," said Agent Magaw. "No, you won't, absolutely you will not!" replied Dad. "He wouldn't let us touch it," John Magaw said. Dad cleaned off the mats.

Similarly, my cousin Debbie Stapleton remembers fishing with Dad on his boat Fidelity one afternoon when some buoy lines became snagged on the propeller. Dad immediately cut the engine, stripped off his shirt, and dove into the cold Maine water—leaving the Secret Service agent "somewhat aghast," she said. He had the propeller clear before the agent could do a thing.

The agents also remember Dad's punctuality. He never wanted to keep anyone waiting for him—whether it was a world leader, a security detail, or a mom stuck in a traffic jam waiting for the motorcade to race by. Dad thought keeping people waiting was the height of rudeness. My brother George says it's one of the lessons he's learned from Dad. "Be on time. Don't make people wait. If you're late, it's like you're the most important person on the face of the earth. Whether it be on the campaign trail or in personal relationship, it's flat rude."

Tim McBride knew one way to make sure Dad stayed on time at official events. "With eye gestures, I could tell if he'd had enough," Tim said. "But if we were at a big mob reception and he's shaking hands, it's hard to free him up. People want to see him. I'd say, 'Mr. Vice President, we really have to go.' 'Okay, Tim,' he'd say. Then 'Mr. Vice President, we really have to go.' Finally, I'd say, '*Sir, the agents have blocked the streets. The traffic is backing up along the motorcade route.*' He would run to the car, because he was extraordinarily concerned about not inconveniencing all the people out there. "

Funny things happen in motorcades. Dad and Mom had a running joke with the agents whenever people on the side of the road made an obscene gesture at the motorcade. "Look, that man says we're number one!" Or: "Bar, let's put that guy's vote down as undecided."

★ ★ ★

Throughout this time, my brother Marvin had been getting sick and not telling anyone. His wife, Margaret, knew, but the rest of our family had no idea. Finally, he got so sick that he ended up in the hospital, hemorrhaging and losing weight, with a severe case of colitis.

Marvin remembers being so sick that he thought he was hallucinating in his hospital room, seeing Dad outside the door and "this white hair going by in the front and that was Mom." That's when he knew it was serious—they were out in the hall discussing his options so they wouldn't scare him. His organs were shutting down and his vital signs were bottoming out. We were all very worried.

At the hospital, Margaret was by his bedside around the clock.

She remembers Dad staying all day in the hospital room, with a stack of briefing papers and a phone, working from a chair in the corner and keeping an eye on Marvin.

They were newlyweds, practically, and this happened before they had children. Margaret had had her own brush with death years earlier as a child—when she was only five years old, she was diagnosed with ovarian cancer. She told her parents she had a tummy ache, and they believed her. They did exploratory surgery and found cancer in her ovaries and liver. After chemo and radiation, she miraculously survived—but without her ovaries.

When Margaret and Marvin got engaged in 1981, she worried about telling him that she would not be able to conceive and deliver a child. Marvin didn't bat an eye. He immediately said it was no problem: they'd adopt. Ever since, she's been a committed advocate of both early detection of cancer and the joys of adoption. Margaret is, in a word, remarkable.

Marvin meanwhile had a long recuperation in Maine, with Mom and Margaret and the rest of the family taking care of him. The doctors had removed most of his colon, and for the rest of his life, he'd have to wear a colostomy bag on the outside of his body. Marvin was understandably bitter and depressed about the bag, so Dad asked Rolf Benirschke, the former place kicker for the San Diego Chargers, to call Marvin. Rolf had had the same surgery in 1979—and actually wore two colostomy bags—but then played seven more seasons of professional football and retired as the team's highest scorer.

A friend of Rolf's also came to the hospital, a man who was a runner like Marvin. He announced he'd just run a marathon, but Marvin thought, "So what? Who cares?" Then the man lowered his trousers to reveal his colostomy bag. "That was a turning point," Mom said, and soon enough Marvin was up and walking, playing tennis with friends, and reading some terrific books. To this day, Marvin credits that recovery period with his love of reading.

"Margaret and I were on the waiting list to adopt a child. After my surgery, one of the biggest concerns I had was that my surgery would hinder our chances of being able to adopt. And ironically, I was just getting back to work at my office at Shearson Lehman Brothers and Rolf had come over. That was our first chance to really meet each other face-to-face. It was while he was sitting in the office that I got the call from our baby adoption agency that our daughter, Marshall, was born." She had been born on Father's Day, which added to Marvin's joy.

Marvin was well enough to go to Texas and pick up Marshall, who was the first of two wonderful children he and Margaret adopted. Marvin has now helped many other victims of colitis and Crohn's disease, reaching out as Rolf did for him. Knowing that the Speaker of the House, Tip O'Neill, was going to have a colostomy, Marvin called him and helped him on several occasions. In fact, Tip once told my father that Marvin had saved his life.

Marvin explained, "There are a lot of people who can't deal with it. They think they are in a hopeless position after having the surgery. And I'm in the position to help them understand it's just the beginning of their life, not the end of an old one, but the beginning of a new life."

★   ★   ★

In the summer of 1985, Dad received word that in the midst of the famine in Africa, thousands of Ethiopian Jews were stranded in the Sudanese desert after a secret Israeli rescue, Operation Moses, had collapsed. The Israeli operation ended when *Washington Jewish Week* broke the story, and the government of Sudan rescinded its support. Thousands of refugees were stranded as a result.

Meir Rosenne, Israeli ambassador to the United States, went to see Dad and asked him to intervene with the Sudanese government. Dad said yes, and by that fall, he went even further—he committed to a secret emergency airlift to take the stranded Jewish refugees out of the Sudan and bring them to Israel. The CIA was involved in what was dubbed Operation Joshua, and an estimated eight hundred Jews were saved.

"These were Ethiopian Jews, not American citizens," Ambassador Rosenne explained to the press afterward. "I know of no precedent in modern history when a country did what the U.S. did in this case. The debt of gratitude we owe to the U.S. is immense."

Rudy Boschwitz, then a senator from Minnesota and later U.S. ambassador to the U.N. Commission on Human Rights, commented, "For the first time in history, a large group of blacks had been taken from the African continent not for slavery, but for love." Years later, when he was president, Dad asked Senator Boschwitz to negotiate a second airlift as well, named Operation Solomon, in which an additional fourteen thousand Ethiopian Jews were rescued by the Israelis within twenty-four hours.

"It was quite a foreign policy and humanitarian victory," said Senator Boschwitz, a Jewish immigrant who fled Germany in World War II and lost many relatives to the Holocaust.

"He was a good vice president because he so complemented Reagan in the skills he brought to the table, especially in foreign policy experience, which Reagan did not have," Boyden Gray observed. "He added a great deal to Reagan's presidency in terms of governance. But he never wanted to get credit for it, because he knew that wouldn't go over well. He was completely self-effacing about it."

On January 25, 1986, a cold, clear day in Washington, Dad gathered in his West Wing office with Tim McBride to watch the space shuttle *Challenger* and its seven-member crew—including a married schoolteacher and mother of two children, Christa McAuliffe—lift off on a new mission. A minute after clearing the launch pad at Cape Canaveral, however, disaster struck. With millions across the country, including schoolchildren, watching on live TV, a faulty O-ring in one of the solid rocket fuel boosters ignited a massive explosion.

To that point, a total of seven Americans had died in our space program. In a fiery, shocking instant, that number was doubled.

President Reagan immediately asked Dad to go to Florida to console the families, who had gathered at the site of the liftoff.

"Within a few hours, we were on Air Force Two, heading down to meet with the families. That was probably the first major event in which I witnessed your dad's role as a comforter on behalf of the nation," Tim remembers.

Dad still keeps in touch with June Scobee Rodgers, the wife of *Challenger* Commander Dick Scobee, who died that day. "I do remember speaking to the spouses of the crew," says Dad now. "They were all in one room, sobbing and grief-stricken. It was tough since, as you know, my tears flow easily. I did manage to get through it."

In the wake of the *Challenger* disaster, President Reagan gave a memorable speech to the nation where he said farewell to the astronauts who had "slipped the surly bonds of Earth to touch the face of God." For his part, Dad went to comfort the families in person, hugging widows and children in tears.

There were other crises at home. The AIDS epidemic was just starting to be understood by the public, and violent crime was on the rise. Drug abuse was the top issue according to the polls, remembers Boyden Gray, who said that the drug issue led to the first use of the phrase "Trade Not Aid." Encouraging third-world farmers to grow legitimate crops—instead of marijuana or cocaine—became part of the free trade agenda of the administration, and later was the spark for the North American Free Trade Agreement, to which Dad was very committed later during his presidential years.

Admiral Dan Murphy, Dad's original chief of staff before Craig Fuller, helped Dad oversee the South Florida Task Force, which President Reagan then asked Dad to expand nationally into the National Narcotics Border Interdiction System. It brought together many agencies—Defense, CIA, Customs, to name a few—and later became the model for one of Dad's first initiatives as president, the creation of the office of the "drug czar."

My father's experience from his CIA years came in very handy. John Magaw, Dad's Secret Service agent, noticed that when they'd alert Dad to some crisis that had come up through the intelligence reports—whether a threat to him or not—he often already knew about it.

"He understood all kinds of intelligence—whether things came through an informant, or a highly secure source, or a black source," John added. A "black source" is one that is not traceable, yet John says often Dad would know exactly who the black source was because of his CIA experience. "He knew when the intelligence came in, how to evaluate it. He knew the right questions to ask."

Hard-core drug use was rampant by the mid-1980s: cocaine use was at an all-time high in 1985 and '86; and use of a new form of the drug, crack cocaine, was skyrocketing. Boyden remembers, "There was one White House briefing on crack and why it was such a debilitating, addictive drug. There were a lot of people in the room, and they had the leading drug specialists from New York, all the best experts they could find. At one point during the meeting, the vice president asked the experts, 'Now, why is crack so addictive? What is it?' And one person said, 'Well, sir, it's like four orgasms all at the same time.' To which the vice president replied, 'Well, let's not all rush for the door at once!'"

In the midst of his work on big issues such as drug abuse, deregulation, and the Cold War, Dad still remembered that little things mean a lot—especially to his grandchildren. He sent a memo to his personal assistant, Patty Presock, along with a few small toys, telling her to "save these for me to mail to George P. at camp when he gets there. He'll be lonely and this will cheer him up."

But then, on George P.'s first day at camp—before he ever received the gifts—he wrote to Dad:

Dear Gampy,

Here's a poem I made up:

When I look out the window I see my friends
And when they come back Jeff intends,

What are you doing George.
Oh, I'm just writing to my best friend (that's you!)

When one of George W.'s twins, Barbara, was little, Dad took her and Jenna to the circus and bought Barbara a stuffed animal that she named Spikey. One night, when Barbara stayed at the vice president's residence for a sleepover, Mom was putting the twins to bed when young Barbara "threw a total fit," she remembers now. Spikey was nowhere to be found. They looked everywhere in the house, and then Dad organized a search party, including a few Secret Service agents and dogs, to search the grounds.

By the time they returned empty-handed, Barbara had fallen sound asleep. Spikey was recovered unharmed the next morning.

Barbara's mom, Laura, also recalls losing a contact lens down a bathroom drain at the vice president's house early one morning, before the housekeeping staff arrived for the day. Dad came in with some tools, and to her delight, opened the trap beneath the drain and rescued the contact for her. We know he didn't like leaks, but we didn't realize how good he was with drains!

★　★　★

With the 1988 campaign looming on the horizon, Marlin Fitz-water developed a new press strategy for Dad. The plan called for my father to spend more time with the Washington press corps, giving as many interviews as possible, so that a good base of understanding could be established on both sides.

"They all wanted him to say something bad about President Reagan, and he refused to do it," Marlin recalled. "I remember when I first took the job, one of the things he said to me was, he never wanted President Reagan to look over his shoulder and wonder if he was supporting him. If I ever leaked anything to the press or ever in any way contributed to any criticism of the president, I would be fired. And so it was pretty clear what the rule was. Indeed, that's the way he conducted all of these interviews. God bless him, he did something like seventy-five interviews in the two years that I was with him, and I swear seventy-four of them were critical of him. But he kept right at it. And I think it paid off in the end."

Marlin and Dad were on the road one day in 1986, waiting for Dad to be introduced in front of a crowd in a high school gymnasium. The holding room was actually a girls' locker room that had been cleared for the occasion, with pink walls and giant mirrors with Hollywood makeup lights all around them. As they waited, Marlin's phone rang. It was a newspaper reporter asking for a reaction to a story that had just broken—that President Reagan had approved trading arms for hostages in the Middle East, and the proceeds had gone to finance the Contras in Central America. Marlin and Dad didn't know anything about it, and so they decided not to comment.

"I'll always remember the juxtaposition of facing an issue that I knew was going to be with us for a long time—because it was just one of those things that kept unraveling and you don't know what it's about—and having it start off in a pink dressing room with makeup bulbs glaring in our face. An incongruous beginning," Marlin remembered.

Iran-Contra, as it came to be known, always seemed to me to be blown out of proportion, particularly among the Beltway press corps. The revelations unfolded over many years, always like a light drizzle of rain in the background rather than a downpour, as Watergate had been.

Once the story broke, President Reagan appointed a blue-ribbon panel known as the Tower Commission—headed by Senator John Tower, with Senator Edmund Muskie and General Brent Scowcroft—to investigate the allegations.

In its final report, however, the commission cleared Dad of any knowledge of the scheme: "There is no evidence that the Vice President was aware of the diversion. The Vice President attended several meetings on the Iran initiative, but none of the participants could recall his views." To most people, the Tower report closed the book on the whole incident, but not to the press. Reporters continued to hound Dad about it for a long time.

★ ★ ★

In 1985, Billy Graham visited our family in Maine, at the invitation of my parents. While we had all met Dr. Graham before—he's been a friend of our family for years—Dad invited cousins and friends to join us in meeting Dr. Graham for an evening, and then asked Dr. Graham to answer questions and speak to us informally. He graciously accepted and thus began an evening many of us will never forget.

His message of Good News was clear that night, and what made the difference was how humbly he spoke about it and his life of service. I have always been an admirer of Dr. Graham and his genuine and unabashed love of Jesus Christ. His work is done in such a way that many people of other faiths admire his sincerity and determination. There is a gentleness and love that reminds me of my own dad.

I have carried that meeting in the back of my mind ever since, and I think it left a lasting impression on many members of our family. My brother George, for one, has spoken about his encounter with Dr. Graham many times and the far-reaching difference it made in his life.

No one was more thrilled with Dr. Graham's talk that night than my grandmother Dorothy Walker Bush, who was a pillar of strength to us in her faith. Of all the visitors that have come to Kennebunkport, I think Dr. Graham meant the most to her. My dad made this possible for us, and it was one of the greatest experiences that have come with being one of his children.

I have found Reverend Graham to be a great teacher—he brought my religious beliefs to a personal level. In grade school, I had attended the National Cathedral School in Washington, D.C., on the grounds of the sixth largest cathedral in the world. Billy Graham taught me that the majestic God of the cathedral was also my own God, and that I could personally know Him through a relationship with Christ. It was a life-transforming moment for me.

As for my father, I would describe his faith as quiet but deep. He is less likely to speak about his faith but has no trouble living it. My brother George observed, "He's not the kind of guy that sits around and says, 'Well, let me tell you about my faith.' He's like a lot of these kids who went to World War II—his faith was probably enhanced when he was in danger. I remember walking into his bedroom one time and he was reading his Bible. It surprised me. He's like all of us—he's figured out in life that your faith is a walk. But he felt uncomfortable talking about it in the political arena."

★　★　★

While still in college, I started dating a boy from Maine named Billy LeBlond. We met in Kennebunkport, where he worked during the summers—when we were in our sophomore year—and we started dating during the 1980 campaign. I was attending Boston College while Billy, a big, strong, gentle guy from a family of ten kids, was a hockey star at Boston University.

After we graduated, we got married, and not long after we had two beautiful children, the first of whom, Sam, was born on August 26, 1984. I was living in Connecticut at the time, and Sam was delivered at Greenwich Hospital. He weighed ten pounds and was the most perfect baby I had ever seen.

The day after Sam was born, I was lying in my bed resting when the nurse who was attending to me said casually, "That's funny. There are some German shepherds in the driveway, and police cars, and lots of other cars trailing behind . . ." I knew instantly that it was my dad stopping by for a surprise visit. I was overwhelmed with joy that he had come. He had been out campaigning for the '84 elections and had spontaneously decided to come see his new grandchild.

It was at this moment that I suddenly realized I looked like I'd just had a baby! I immediately tried to get up, rush to the bathroom, and get cleaned up—but it was too late. There was a knock at the door, and in Dad came.

"I'm here to see our new baby," he said. So off we went (catheter in tow) down the hall to see Sam. Dad greeted all the doctors, nurses, and new mothers along the way—having photos taken and signing autographs. We reached the nursery, and there we were—Secret Service agents, staff, Dad, and I peering through the glass looking at a giant baby sleeping away.

Dad thought he was as beautiful as I did.

Dad also brought along White House photographer David Valdez to snap some photos, but the nurse on duty would not let Dad and David in the viewing room. Dad, intent on getting photos of the baby, got a Secret Service agent to distract the nurse while David quickly took some photos.

Earlier, I had asked Dad his opinion on names for his grandson, and here's what he wrote in a letter to me. Funny to read today:

> *Names are important. If I were you I would not go for "Herby"—that's a nickname normally and though I would of course be pleased personally, it isn't right to put the emphasis there.*
>
> *Walker—well, maybe. I was called that when they first shipped me off to Country Day at age 5. Mum thought it was better than Poppy. It lasted about 10 days—then it shifted over to Poppy—a burden I bore heroically until, thank God, we went to war with the Japanese and I went to the Navy and I left Poppy pretty far behind. No, Walker LeBlond is a little formal somehow—though don't rule it out entirely.*
>
> *George. I see your point. George W is one of a kind and it wouldn't do at all to have George L be under the undue influence of Uncle "W."*
>
> *Hey, Doro, we're going to love the kid no matter what you call him/her. I for one can't wait.*
>
> *Devotedly—with love to Bill,*
>
> *Dad*

We named our son Sam, which, technically, I could credit to my great-grandfather on the Bush side, Samuel Prescott Bush. However, the truth is, Sam was named after our cat. We liked the name Sam and decided if the baby was a boy, we'd steal the name from him (we renamed the cat). To this day, Sam still says, "Can you believe my parents named me after a cat?"

When our first daughter was born two years later, we named her Nancy Ellis LeBlond for Dad's vivacious sister and my favorite aunt, Nancy Bush Ellis. As for the name Walker, Marvin and Margaret named their second child, and only son, Walker Bush, which sounds much better than Walker LeBlond.

By the end of 1987, shortly after Ellie was born, it was becoming evident that my marriage to Billy wasn't working. At some point, Mom noticed that things weren't going so well and sensed that a separation was on the horizon. She sat me down and said, "I have some advice for you." Mom proceeded to tell me about a divorced couple with a daughter, and how the mother took every opportunity to denigrate the father. The little girl grew up and realized that the father wasn't the monster the mother had made him out to be, and turned against the mother.

It does nobody any good to do that, Mom said, and I took her words to heart.

As it was, no one in my immediate or extended family that I knew of had ever been divorced before, so we were heading into uncharted waters. To add to it all, my father was the vice president of the United States. Most of all, I remember feeling I had let my family down, especially after I saw a sensational piece written about the divorce in one of the tabloid papers. But as always, Dad supported me with unconditional love.

Mom and Dad's first concern, of course, was for our children. Sam and Ellie spent lots of time with them. After I was divorced, I moved to Washington, and whenever Dad went to Maine, he took Sam and Ellie with him so they could spend time with their dad, who was living in Cape Elizabeth, Maine.

Dad's second concern was Billy. After our divorce in 1990, he asked Billy to play golf and made sure that Billy knew he was welcome in our house anytime.

By example, my parents taught me to handle a tough situation in the best possible way. I'll never forget when I later started dating Bobby Koch. Dad invited us over to the White House to have dinner with Sally and Dick LeBlond, my former in-laws, who were in town. I was nervous about the dinner, but somehow Dad made all of us feel welcome. We had a wonderful time, and it helped me stay connected to the LeBlonds, a family I love and admire.

This gesture of kindness was the right thing to do, and Dad instinctively knew that. Mom and Dad helped me understand that I had to be aware of my children and that Billy would always be their dad. They helped me navigate my divorce with dignity.

My parents' lessons have paid off. You could say that dinner was a small gesture with grand results, because Billy remains close to our family to this day.

Chapter 14

POINTER MAN

"Needless to say, I'm not an expert on the Republican Party or, for that matter, winning the presidency. But your dad seemed to me to be the kind of Republican that I admired and respected. He had some balance to him. My sense was he was a good, strong, viable candidate."

—**Michael Dukakis**

The same week that Dad announced his second candidacy for the presidency, on October 12, 1987, *Newsweek* magazine put him on its cover with their infamous headline "Fighting the Wimp Factor." The photo featured my father speeding along on his cigarette boat—one hand on the wheel and the other on the throttle, with a seafarer's scowl on his face, wearing a foul-weather jacket.

In the weeks and months leading up to the announcement, a *Newsweek* reporter named Margaret Warner said she was writing a profile of Dad, and had convinced him that it was going to be a reasonable piece, mostly biographical about our family and how we interact. "So I did something we never did," Dad told me. "I told Mother she ought to talk to her." Thus assured, eighty-six-year-old Dorothy Bush sat for an interview. In fact, we all did—Jeb,

George, Aunt Nan, Mom. We all felt the same way Dad did: "She really won us all over. She was very sweet and very nice."

During my interview with her, I showed Margaret around Kennebunkport a little—and I remember how she kept saying how much she loved my parents, how great they were. In fact, it seemed that everything she asked me about them started with, "Your parents are so amazing. Let me ask you this . . ."

Then the story got published. The article's theme was repeated over and over, with words peppered throughout it like "subservient," "emasculated," and "silly." The word "wimp" alone appeared eight times, and pictures and quotes from my family and Dad's closest friends were manipulated to make it appear as if we all agreed with the author's premise. Even now, reading it almost twenty years later, I'm still struck by how cruel it was.

So shortly after it was published, I called Margaret and asked why she wrote what she did. Margaret began to cry and said that her editor made her put the word "wimp" in all those times, and said that she was very sorry.

But the damage was done.

It still amazes me today that Margaret, or any nameless editor, could use that word about a man who had flown fifty-eight combat missions and survived being shot down at sea—let alone everything else Dad had done in his life to that point.

Democratic Congressman Dan Rostenkowski put it this way: "It used to tee me off to no end in the campaign when they talked about your father as a less than physically adept individual. That son of a gun almost got killed in that airplane disaster, and yet they looked at your father as being somewhat timid. That used to boil me. I think that conclusion drew me closer to your father. I got to like your dad a lot, because I thought that they portrayed him very inaccurately. But then again, I knew him."

Like Congressman Rostenkowski, anyone who knows my father knows better—but that didn't save *Newsweek*'s readers from being treated to a fictional series of insights about Dad that were gained under false pretenses in October 1987.

Years later, incidentally, I saw Margaret at a party, and it made me realize that in politics you do run into the same people over and over. She seemed to avoid me; and if I were her, I suppose I would still be embarrassed, too.

When the "wimp" cover hit newsstands, of course, my brothers and I felt used—and were even more upset than Dad was. Don't get me wrong: Dad was furious. He told me, "It was hard to treat Margaret the same way after what a lot of people felt was a betrayal." Still, it's as Geraldine Ferraro said—it's easier to be the candidate than to be the family. Dad was the one to calm everybody down because he could take it, but the rest of us hated how he was being treated.

Ede Holiday, who was the treasurer of Dad's PAC at the time, says, "I often use that story for my kids—if George Bush ever listened to what other people said about him, he never would have been president. You have to have the strength of character to keep moving when something so unreasonable and unfair happens to you in a public way."

Candidly, we felt the same sense of outrage when conservative columnist George Will later described Dad as "Reagan's lapdog." It was a particularly disdainful observation coming from another Reagan supporter. My father valued loyalty a great deal and had been an unquestionably loyal friend to Ronald Reagan. To have that same trait used against him by one of President Reagan's staunchest defenders was both absurd and petty.

Jon Meacham, now managing editor of *Newsweek*, explained what the press was doing: "It's the nature of the media beast to build somebody up and then tear them down, and then build them up and tear them down again. An important thing to remember about the press is there is no ideological bias. I honestly believe we have a bias toward conflict and a need to change the narrative. That's the problem—it's not that we're liberal or conservative."

Howard Kurtz, the *Washington Post* media critic, agreed: "The media often assign narratives to people in public life and then look for stories or anecdotes to confirm those narratives." So the media narrative at the time was that although Dad may have been the front-runner, he didn't have the "right stuff" to become president.

It was against this backdrop that Dad officially announced his candidacy at the Hyatt Regency Hotel in Houston before most of our family and two thousand supporters—including several astronauts and June Scobee Rodgers, the widow of the *Challenger* commander; a few baseball players from the Houston Astros; and even a professional wrestler named Paul Boesch who was one of the original stars of Wrestlemania.

Of course, many of my parents' friends from Texas were there, along with our family. Lionel Hampton, the eighty-year-old jazz great who had played for the CIA employees years ago, was there, too.

Dad's notes recalling that night were both poignant and funny: "Bar looks beautiful. Thirty-four years ago today, Robin died . . . Lionel Hampton, loyal to the end. Loyal, loyal, loyal . . . The balloon drop that started at the top of the Regency was marvelous," he continued. "For a frightening moment, it looked like a *condom drop*—raw rubber appearing from the ceiling—balloons that had popped during the night. But, then down came the array of balloons . . ."

By the end of the event, he wrote, "The press doesn't understand that there is strength in all of this."

★　★　★

Almost as soon as Dad announced his candidacy, reporters started asking President Reagan if he would endorse my father's candidacy—to which the president said he would not. This surprised and disappointed me, and I wondered why the president was so reluctant given the fact that Dad and he were so close—and by all accounts, Dad was a superb and loyal vice president. There were quite a few GOP candidates in the primaries, and in hindsight perhaps he felt that as head of the party he couldn't do anything until the nomination.

To Dad, however, it was no surprise. "It never occurred to me that he would not support me. There was a lot of speculation in the press that he wasn't going to—which was put out by some of the real right-wing guys. He assured me privately he was for me. Some of our people around me were saying, 'Well, he ought to be out there sooner.' But I wasn't surprised at all. He did what he said he'd do, at his own pace, his own time, and that was all right."

The other announced candidates for the Republican nomination were Kansas Senator Bob Dole, who, like Dad, had served in World War II; former Delaware governor Pierre "Pete" DuPont; President Reagan's former secretary of state and President Nixon's chief of staff, General Al Haig; New York Congressman and former Buffalo Bills quarterback Jack Kemp; and televangelist Pat Robertson, whose candidacy lasted longer than most experts predicted.

For the Democrats, the contenders were former Arizona governor Bruce Babbitt; Senator Joe Biden of Delaware, star of the Senate Judiciary Committee; Massachusetts Governor Michael Dukakis, the son of Greek immigrants in his third term as governor; Congressman Dick Gephardt from Missouri; Senator Al Gore of Tennessee, a late entrant who had his eye on winning Super Tuesday; former senator Gary Hart of Colorado, who lost the nomination to Walter Mondale in 1984; the Reverend Jesse Jackson, who also ran against Mondale in 1984; and finally, the bow-tie-wearing Senator Paul Simon of Illinois.

The media soon dubbed the Democratic candidates the Seven Dwarfs—an unflattering reference comparing them to the much-ballyhooed noncandidacy of New York Governor Mario Cuomo. Governor Cuomo was the subject of a "draft" movement in the press, and he even made fun of his own presidential aspirations at the annual Gridiron Dinner in Washington, saying that Satan had offered him the presidency in exchange for his soul. Cuomo replied, "So what's the catch?"

The national press touted other noncandidates as well—including Bill Moyers, the PBS reporter, and Pat Schroeder, a former congresswoman from Colorado.

Another editorial cartoonist noted that voters looking in their refrigerators that Thanksgiving would find six varieties of fruitcake and one leftover turkey—meaning Gary Hart, who was running again after his 1984 finish. Hart was the presumed front-runner until a photo of him turned up in the *National Enquirer* on the deck of the yacht *The Monkey Business* with Donna Rice, a woman who was not his wife. Hart ended up dropping out of the race, then jumping back in, then dropping out again.

Joe Biden also faltered early. In his case, he was caught plagiarizing parts of a speech by Neil Kinnock, a Member of the British Parliament. Curiously, Biden only used the parts of the Kinnock speech where Kinnock talked about growing up as the son of a coal miner, which Biden was not. The tapes showing Biden's and Kinnock's speeches were put out to the press by Dukakis campaign manager John Sasso, who was fired for his role, and Biden dropped out shortly thereafter.

Dad assembled a top-notch team for his campaign leadership: His national cochairs were New Hampshire Governor John Sununu, who had been active in organizing the grassroots effort in New Hampshire, and Texas Senator John Tower, Dad's friend and chairman of the Senate Armed Services Committee. James Baker, having served as President Reagan's chief of staff and Treasury secretary, was the general chairman. In addition, there was what Roger Ailes called the Group of Six, or G-6, as it came to be known, made up of Nick Brady, the former Wall Street banker and New Jersey senator; Bob Mosbacher, the Texas oilman who ran fund-raising; pollster Bob Teeter; Dad's chief of staff, Craig Fuller; political guru Lee Atwater, who had been instrumental in the 1984 Reagan reelection; and Roger Ailes, a well-known media consultant.

"At the end of the day, when everybody went home, that group would go out to dinner and figure out where we were going next," Ailes remembers.

"Lee would call them 'the adults,'" Ede recalls of the G-6. "Having these 'adults' over the top of the campaign helped everybody not get into trouble. It gave needed maturity to the campaign organization."

Each of us in the family took a role as well. I campaigned in both the primaries and the general election. In fact, Jack Kemp's daughter Jennifer and I became good friends, because often I'd run into the children of the other candidates at events, and it was nice to see a friend in the crowd.

Because I was living in Maine at the time, I also campaigned there some but mostly traveled all over the East Coast and mid-Atlantic states. A campaign worker, Bill Canary, traveled with me and became a close family friend.

My brother Neil worked hard in New Hampshire, and Marvin traveled all over the country. Marvin, in fact, remembers going to Chicago and campaigning there with a Democratic councilman named "Fast Eddie" Verdeliac, who had endorsed Dad.

"We spent some time freezing our rear ends off at a Chicago Bears game, and every person walking by would call out, 'Yo, Eddie, you're my man!'" Marvin recalled. "The guy worked me like a dog—we did about eight events in one day, and the last one was at a raucous union hall. Maybe four hundred fifty people in a room with a capacity of two hundred, and everybody was drinking pretty heavily. By the time I got up there to speak, I was basically screaming in tongues about how great Dad was. Eddie was fantastic. He gave a beautiful tribute to Dad. I couldn't understand a word he said, but it was beautiful."

When I pointed out to Marvin that Fast Eddie's legal clients allegedly had ties to the mob, he said diplomatically, "Well, you meet some colorful people and you get endorsements from unexpected sources."

Jeb resigned as Florida secretary of commerce and campaigned for Dad mostly in Florida and California. He remembers talking to Lee Atwater early on with George, right when Dad hired Lee. "George and I ganged up on him and had a stern conversation with him. We said, 'We don't care what a hotshot you are, we want to know how loyal you're going to be to Dad. If someone threw a hand grenade in this room, all Dad's children would want to be the first to jump on it to save him. Would you do the same thing?' He was a little cocky—all these political operatives are—and we wanted to test his loyalty, his allegiance."

Lee handled it well, and said that if loyalty was a concern, then perhaps George should move to Washington and keep an eye on things. So George moved to a town house in Washington, D.C., with Laura and their four-year-old twins, Barbara and Jenna. Laura remembers, "We picked that town house because we wanted to be really close to the vice president's house. We figured it might be the only time in our lives we'd live in the same town they lived in. It was really a bonding experience for all of us. Until then, Bar and I certainly hadn't been close at all."

Mom and Dad, George and Laura, and Marvin and Margaret had hamburger lunches together every Sunday, despite the fact that they were in the middle of a national campaign.

George took an office at campaign headquarters and became the "loyalty enforcer"—a term he coined in describing his job. "I was a person without portfolio," George said. "I was there really to kind of be Dad's eyes and ears in the campaign. I call it a loyalty enforcer, but also I was there to be in a position where I could help the team stay a team."

"What happened, of course," added Laura, "was George and Lee really developed a friendship."

Lee's friend Karl Rove explained why a "loyalty enforcer" was a necessity on that campaign: "Having been vice president for eight years, your dad was depending on a lot of people who had been for somebody else in the previous eight years and whose interests might be more professional than personal. The people who did it for Nixon and Ford and Reagan were prepared to do it for Bush. Not necessarily out of extreme personal loyalty, but because that was the way you advanced your career in Washington. That's great—but when you get into choppy waters, those people are more likely to be wringing their hands to a member of the press, or pouring out about one of their colleagues, or being indiscreet about campaign activities. Simply because their ultimate loyalty is not to the man himself."

At one point, *Esquire* magazine ran an interview with Lee that featured a photo of Lee in his underwear, which upset George a great deal. The article characterized Lee as "all grit . . . all blood on the floor and don't look back." George recalls, "I called Lee and said, 'This isn't about you. This is a disgrace. And if you think I'm upset, talk to my mother.' He immediately called her and apologized."

George also was the first one to deal with a campaign rumor that Dad had an affair with Jennifer Fitzgerald, his executive assistant in China and at the CIA, telling *Newsweek* in June 1987, "The answer to the big 'A' question is N-O." Years later, in 1992, I stood with my parents at a press conference in Kennebunkport when the issue came up. Of course, it wasn't true. Even Michael Dukakis thought the rumor was outrageous because he fired a staffer, Donna Brazille, for spreading the rumor.

"To hell with all that. I just said, 'Look, we're not going to have any part of that,'" Governor Dukakis told me. "When you decide you're going to go into this business, you've got to decide who you are, what standards you're going to set for yourself and the people around you. If folks get out of line, you can't accept that."

As you might expect, it was incredible to me that Dad was put in such a preposterous position. It was one more example of how people who run for office become public property, and how some people in the media will stop at nothing to bring them down. Where does it stop? The press can say whatever they want, and if you don't go out and deny it, they assume that it's true—and it becomes part of their "narrative."

★   ★   ★

Aside from the nastiness of the campaign rumor mill, I have very fond memories of the 1988 campaign. I suppose we all tend to glorify our "early years," but to me it seems like a different time than the politics of today. There were so many characters running for president, so many twists and turns, and we were all young and enjoying this surreal adventure.

Adding to the romance of it all, my brothers and I were all basically newlyweds, and there were many young grandchildren running around the campaign events. I also remember habitually staying up late to watch *Saturday Night Live*. In fact, that year marked the beginning of Dana Carvey as George Bush. When I asked Dana about the first time he met my father, Dana said, "I think your dad had a really good attitude about it, because he always said [Carvey slips into his impersonation of Dad]: *Comes with the turf. Got to be able to take a few zingers. Not take yourself too seriously.*" In the beginning, Dana said he didn't think there was much to impersonate—"I really didn't pick it up," he explained—and mostly concentrated on Dad's hand gestures, pointing with his right hand into the distance, doing the double hands when he'd say "at this juncture."

But then he moved into what he calls "a Texas sort of lazy, clipped syntax kind of thing that I just went with." He explained to me that he exaggerated the phrase "not going to do it" to become "not gonna do it" and, finally, "na ga do it." "You take little teeny observations of him and then just make them almost a separate character."

My brothers and I saw Dana's impersonation before Dad did—"Look, I don't stay up late like you kids do," he'd say—but he became more familiar with it once he was in the White House.

★   ★   ★

I can't remember when I first met Lee Atwater, but I always liked him. Everyone respected his instincts because he was tough and no-nonsense. I knew that with him on our side, we'd be in good hands politically.

"He had a huge, infectious personality," Marvin remembers. He saw a lot of Lee because Marvin's business office was only a few doors down from campaign headquarters in Washington. Marvin recalled that Lee had little Civil War soldiers on his desk, and he would make his points by moving the soldiers around. Lee was very disciplined, jogging every day, never drinking, and smoking a pack of cigarettes a week—but he only smoked on Fridays.

I also remember how Lee had one of the only cell phones in town—it was as big as a lunch box and he took it everywhere. He was on the cutting edge in those days. (During the 1988 campaign, there was no e-mail or voice mail, no fax machine on Air Force Two, and certainly no BlackBerry or Internet. One campaign staffer, Debbie Romash, remembers doing "the Delta dash"— rushing to the courier service on Delta Air Lines that used the last flight out of Washington every night, to get schedules and briefing books to the campaign team on the road.)

As he looked to the 1988 primary calendar, Dad wanted to erase his 1980 loss in New Hampshire. One of his key people back then had been Andy Card—who had since run, and lost, for Massachusetts governor in 1982. I respect Andy and volunteered on his 1982 race—stuffing envelopes, making phone calls, even passing out bumper stickers with Andy's father one day.

After Andy lost, Jim Baker offered him a job at the White House as liaison to the nation's governors. Andy remembers one advantage of the job was that it allowed him to build close relationships with Republican governors and their grassroots operations in key states, including New Hampshire Governor John Sununu, who had been a Reagan supporter in 1980 and had become the chairman of the Republican Governors' Association in 1987.

Dad and his team were well aware that Governor Sununu's help would be crucial in 1988. "There's a saturation of politics here, and Lee loved that atmosphere. He understood New Hampshire and he used to come up a lot," said Governor Sununu. "The vice president actually felt a little more comfortable campaigning here than in Iowa. New Hampshire is a 'see me, touch me, feel me' campaign state. I estimate that he personally shook hands with about fifty thousand people that year before the primary. I'll bet we had about five thousand Polaroid pictures taken—on the theory that if somebody has a picture of themselves and the vice president on the mantel, they'll work awfully hard to make it a picture of themselves and the president on the mantel."

In 1987, Dad and Lee Atwater met with Andy and convinced him to leave the White House and run the New Hampshire campaign. Andy's wife, Kathy, wasn't too happy about the idea, but he convinced her. "It was a life-changing experience for me," Andy says now, remembering that he saw Kathy only thirteen nights that entire year and slept on a cot in his office in Concord.

Andy also assembled a group called the Freedom Fighters, grassroots organizers who ran operations at the precinct level. They met every Monday at 7:00 a.m. in Concord, "which means some people had to leave Coos County way up north [where the town of Dixville Notch votes first in the primary and gets tremendous media attention] at 3:00 a.m. to get to Concord in time for the meeting," Andy recalls. He told every precinct captain in the state it was not their job to get George Bush elected president, only to get George Bush elected president of their precinct.

"I told them we want to be like Larry Bird [the Boston Celtics legend]—we'd love it if it came to New Hampshire, and we were two points down with ten seconds left in the game. We would be standing outside the three-point circle begging for the ball because we have the confidence that we can sink the three-point shot. That was what our campaign strategy was all about."

★ ★ ★

Of course, the campaign road to New Hampshire first made its way through the Iowa caucuses. Mary Matalin was working at the RNC at the time and had been sent to Iowa as a field worker.

"That was the first emergence of the Christian Coalition," she remembers, referring to supporters of Pat Robertson. "Nobody knew who they were. I kept calling Rich Bond and Lee Atwater, and no one believed me because they hadn't seen it. You had to be on the ground. They couldn't see them in the polling, so we didn't know what their numbers were. We take them for granted now. So we were shadowboxing with the invisible army of the Christian Coalition. We also had Bob Dole in that race. It was not his home state, but he was a farm state guy. He was very organized there."

Given Dad's success in 1980, everyone presumed he would win Iowa again in 1988. But we lost to Dole and Robertson, coming in third. The shock of that loss shot through the campaign. How bad was it? To give you an idea, Atwater fired Mary that night and then called her in the middle of the night to fire her again. Then the next morning, Lee fired Mary for a third time in front of all the field personnel!

When I asked Dad about Lee's reaction the night of the Iowa caucuses, he recalled, "Lee was a tough, elbows-flying fighter. With me, he was always respectful and very supportive. But he'd fly off the handle. He'd get very uptight when things weren't going well. He was an emotional fellow."

"The next morning, I had to go on a Wisconsin trip with the vice president," Mary said. "That primary was going on then, and somebody else told the VP that I was fired. Right there, he said, 'Oh. She's unfired. That's ridiculous. She's not incompetent.' We weren't even that close then."

Lee Atwater's wife, Sally, remembers how gracious Dad was to all the Iowa workers: "Lee said that when your father addressed his campaign workers, he told them he, George Bush, was taking full responsibility for the loss. He wanted the workers to know that he knew how hard they all had worked."

As Mary said, the Iowa loss stunned all of us. Jeb remembers it well: "I was sent to Council Bluffs, Iowa, and the intern who was supposed to be traveling with me, after he saw the king-size whippin' Dad had gotten in the caucuses, left me. Evacuated. So I got a six-pack of beer, walked back on my own to the Motel 6, and watched the rest of the dreary results by myself."

Ede Holiday was the money person for the campaign. The day after we lost Iowa, she called Andy Card at 5:30 a.m. in the campaign headquarters in New Hampshire asking what he needed. In no time, the entire campaign staff went up there on buses to go door-to-door.

"I got up there and Lee Atwater was literally in a catatonic state," Ede said. "He could not speak. He could not breathe. I don't know if he brushed his teeth for three days. He just feared it was the end. He literally could not function. We'd just lost Iowa, and if we lost in New Hampshire, we'd be done. John Sununu, on the other hand, had the biggest smile on his face. He kept saying, 'Don't worry, we're going to win. I guarantee you we'll win in this state. This is what we're going to do.' And he laid it all out."

With less than a week to go in New Hampshire, important decisions had to be made regarding how to spend precious campaign resources—and among Dad's top advisers there were the inevitable, sharp disagreements about how much money to spend. Bob Mosbacher, for example, wanted to save some for down the line, but Lee said to him, "If you don't spend it here, there won't be anyplace to spend it down the line, because we'll be out of the race." Lee decided to front-load the money, betting that Dad would win New Hampshire, South Carolina, and Super Tuesday.

For the entire team, the pressure was on.

All of this played into the decision to run the "Senator Straddle" ad, attacking Bob Dole for flip-flopping on the issues. Dad was not enthusiastic about it but finally decided to do it. "If you can get it on the air, then all right," he said to Mosbacher. Dad was referring to the fact that the ad schedules at all the TV stations had been set, and they were not taking any changes.

Two months before this pivotal primary, however, Governor Sununu had asked Dad to accept an invitation for an interview at Channel 9 in Manchester—the biggest media market in the state. The event was right at the height of the Christmas season, and Dad asked, "Why do we have to do this?" But the governor prevailed, and Dad and Mom went.

The reception turned out to be an all-hands-on-deck event at the station, complete with families. Mom and Dad chatted and posed for photos with family members, reporters, and station management. "They just won everybody over at Channel 9," Sununu remembered.

That gesture would pay off later in the heat of a hotly contested, do-or-die primary. When Sununu was told there was no way to air the "Straddle" ad on Channel 9, he called the station manager, "who obviously had been at that Christmas reception with his children and his wife and had about nine pictures taken. And I said, 'Can you meet me at the station and help me convince your people to change this?' And he said, 'Of course, I'll do that for the vice president.'"

Apparently, Dad made such an impression on the station management that they were very comfortable bending the rules to accommodate what was being asked.

Sununu met the manager after hours, going in with our ads. When the governor saw Dad later, he said, "Oh, by the way, when you asked me three months ago why you had to do that Christmas event, this is why."

Therese Burch remembers campaigning with Dad in New Hampshire, at a truck stop called Cuzzin Richie's. While Dad was visiting with truckers in the coffee shop, the press corps were buying baseball hats in the gift shop that said "Shit Happens" and wearing them to surprise Dad. Of course, he roared with laughter, she said, and then as he was getting ready to leave, a trucker invited Dad to take his rig for a ride. So Dad jumped into the driver's seat, and the reporters all assumed he'd take a spin around the parking lot. "To everyone's amazement, the vice president took off in the eighteen-wheeler Mack truck and headed for the highway. One Secret Service agent, Russell Rowe, jumped on the back of the truck, as the other Secret Service agents and press scrambled to follow," she said. When they got back, Dad thanked the trucker and had a good laugh. "The press and the crowd were all speechless because they couldn't believe he knew how to drive the rig."

It was clear that Dad had to win New Hampshire to stay in the race. "Here we were, like Larry Bird, begging for the ball, with great confidence that we could sink the shot and win," said Andy Card. "And that's what we did." Dad won, this time beating Bob Dole by 15,000 votes and Pat Robertson by a three-to-one margin.

Next came the South Carolina primary, part of Lee's strategy to build the "southern firewall"—sort of an insurance policy to ensure that a conservative was elected in case Iowa and New Hampshire didn't go well. Lee was confident of victory because of his experience in his home state—where he organized college campuses for Strom Thurmond's reelection campaign in 1972 and then did the same for Richard Nixon, before going to Washington as national director of the College Republicans with Karl Rove. Pat Robertson's campaign was stopped cold in South Carolina, and it was a big win for Dad going into Super Tuesday.

That year, 1988, was the first year the parties held the so-called Super Tuesday primaries—the first regional group of primaries ever held—encompassing fourteen states, mostly in the South. The idea, Andy Card explained, was that "if you didn't have momentum going into it, you weren't going to come out of it successfully." Dad won 600 of the 803 delegates that were in play in 1988, to close the gap on the 1,139 needed to secure the Republican nomination. "It was a landslide," remembers Bill Canary, a campaign operative who went on to become special assistant to the president for intergovernmental affairs. He noted that Robertson only won the state of Washington, and that although Bob Dole's best chances were in Arkansas, Oklahoma, Missouri, and North Carolina, "we won them all," Bill said. "It ended the debate as to who would be the Republican nominee in 1988. In the end, it was the Democrats that still were without a clear nominee by March 8."

Among the Democrats, Jesse Jackson won the five Deep South states, Al Gore the five border states, Michael Dukakis won Florida, Texas, and Maryland, and Dick Gephardt won only his home state of Missouri.

At one point, Mary Matalin, a lawyer by training, was sent to Michigan to handle a complicated rules fight having to do with delegates, which ended up in federal court there. Pat Robertson had charged Dad's campaign with buying off Kemp supporters, and held a separate convention to select delegates—despite the fact that the state party chairman did not recognize that rogue meeting. A legal battle ensued, and it came down to a decision by the Bush campaign that had to be made: do we cut a complex deal with the other Republican candidates who had delegates pledged to them, or do we forge ahead in court by ourselves and hope for the best? So Mary came in to brief the campaign's G-6.

"They already didn't like me from Iowa," Mary recalled. "We went through all the arguments, and they were all saying, don't do it, it's too risky. Your father asked what I thought. I thought we should cut the deal. He said, 'Well, I trust her. She's on the ground. She knows what's going on. We're going to do the deal.' That's the way to manage people. Nobody knew what to do. But he had faith in me. That is one of a million stories of why people would work their hearts out for him—because this is not just lip service to loyalty and trust. This is how he behaved."

It turned out it was the right decision—a throw of the dice, she said, a big risk. Dad won Michigan, and soon he had the votes to wrap up the Republican nomination.

★   ★   ★

As the two parties headed to their conventions, tradition stated that the challenger's party would go first and the incumbent last. So the Democratic convention was held first, in July at the Omni Coliseum in Atlanta. It was there that Ann Richards drawled, "Poor George, he can't help it—he was born with a silver foot in his mouth."

Senator Teddy Kennedy followed next, hitting on Iran-Contra and calling out to the crowd over and over, "Where was George?" (A year or so later, Senator Kennedy sent Dad a good-natured note with a photo of a billboard from Milford, Connecticut, which read "Where's George? In the White House, Teddy!!")

It was also in Atlanta that then-Governor Bill Clinton gave such a long and tedious speech that he was nearly booed off the stage. It's still called the "In Conclusion" speech by some, because that's the point in his speech when the crowd cheered loudest. In fact, many observers said that it was the end of Bill Clinton's political career—the first of many times that would be said about him, and not just by my brothers.

So much for conventional wisdom!

In general, I thought the entire Democratic convention was mean-spirited, with the attacks on my father more personal than political. I remember disliking Ann Richards's comments most of all. Politically, I disagreed with almost everything she said. I did, however, like her line saluting women, saying "Ginger Rogers did everything Fred Astaire did, only backward and in high heels."

Dad looked back on it, saying, "It upset me that she was doing that, making it personal like that—but that's the campaign. When George beat her a few years later, I guess you could say he showed her what she could do with that silver foot!"

As his running mate Governor Dukakis chose Dad's old Texas rival Senator Lloyd Bentsen. "I made a lot of mistakes in that campaign. I think one of the things I did well was to go through this [VP selection] process, and it was exhausting. We were all aware of what happened with McGovern and Eagleton," Governor Dukakis told me, referring to George McGovern, the 1972 Democratic nominee who dropped his running mate, Thomas Eagleton, from the ticket after it came out that Eagleton had received electroshock therapy for depression. They went on to lose by what was then the second largest landslide in American history.

So after the last primary in June, Dukakis asked Paul Brontas, his campaign chairman, to begin the process of choosing a VP candidate. "We narrowed the field down to four people: Lloyd Bentsen, Al Gore, Dick Gephardt, and John Glenn," the governor added. "We set up teams, volunteer teams of lawyers and accountants, one for each candidate, who went into their backgrounds, their finances, their stuff over and over again. I met with each of them." He ended up choosing Bentsen because of the geographic balance, his experience on Capitol Hill, and his ability to be a "first-rate president," should the need arise.

The night Michael Dukakis and Lloyd Bentsen officially claimed the Democratic nomination, I remember seeing the split-screen image of the roll-call vote of the delegates, putting them over the top—with the Dukakis family sitting up straight on their hotel room sofa.

Governor Dukakis was very excited to have his eighty-six-year-old grandmother at the convention. He told me about her—how she arrived from Greece at nine years old, lived in the tenements across from a shoe factory, and was the first Greek American woman to attend college in American history, graduating Phi Beta Kappa from Bates College in 1925. She had become a schoolteacher, gotten married, and raised their son in Brookline, Massachusetts.

Mrs. Dukakis was eighty-six; my own grandmother Dorothy was eighty-seven when she attended the Republican convention, to see Dad accept the nomination.

While the Democrats were having their convention, my father and Jim Baker got out of town, heading up to Shoshone National Forest in northwestern Wyoming for a week of fly-fishing. Dad recorded in his diary at the time:

> I have concluded from this trip that I can be very happy in what follows on. If I lose, I don't know what I'll do, but I know I'll be happy. But the main thing is, I'd like to do something to help others . . . I still feel confident that I will win, but the polls are tough . . . I feel rested and my mind is clearer. We'll go back to the rat races; the copies of memos; who has the action on this letter and that; the stacks of paper; the endless criticism; great pressures; and the ugliness; but this little jaunt has proved to me that you can get your soul refurbished.

It's a good thing the trip was reinvigorating, because by the time the Dukakis-Bentsen ticket rolled out of Atlanta, the Democrats were seventeen points ahead in the polls. Suddenly, Dad was an underdog.

In August, the Republican convention was held at the Super-dome in New Orleans. It was exciting and great fun, being on the convention floor, attending the parties, and seeing so many old friends. Ronald Reagan gave a terrific speech, as you might expect, asking Dad to "go out there and win one for the Gipper." The crowd loved it. My sister-in-law Columba seconded Dad's nomination as president, first in Spanish, then in English.

Meanwhile, Jeb's twelve-year-old son, George P., led the audience in the Pledge of Allegiance in front of the entire convention and television viewing audience. According to his father, George P. couldn't have been more nervous. Jeb remembers how his son was "looking like he was going to throw up. He turned white. Didn't have a pulse. So he went out . . . and I was on my hands and knees behind the curtains looking around the corner in case I had to run out. I was thinking, 'He's going to lose it.' So I was going to run out." But George P. did fine, and no one ever saw Jeb hiding off-stage on his hands and knees.

Dad wrote in his diary that week:

> *The kids and the grandchildren were front and center, and they did well. Doro speaking so beautifully for her Mother and also on the convention floor. The boys, all of them, on the television and speaking at the convention, all were terrific. Our family got much more focus. They took the heat well, and they showed great presence and great warmth.*

There was a lot of speculation as to whom Dad would choose as his running mate. About three weeks before the convention, in fact, some of his friends—Fred Malek, the director of the convention, and his wife, Marlene; Jim and Susan Baker; my brother George and Laura; and Vic Gold and his wife—had kicked around a few names in front of Dad, who never said a word and just listened. "It's going to be Kemp—couldn't you sense his reaction?"

Fred remembered saying to Marlene on the drive home. "Of course, I was dead wrong."

I also remember a family dinner right before the convention where we all went around the table and took a guess. Dad sat there, nodding and listening, but never saying a thing. I don't remember any of us being right.

Unbeknownst to us, he had called Dan Quayle, a senator from Indiana, the Monday after the Democratic convention and asked if he'd mind being considered for vice president. Senator Quayle talked it over with his wife that night and then called back to say okay.

"Bob Teeter will be calling you," Vice President Quayle remembers Dad saying. "That was it, until the day of the convention. He didn't interview because he didn't want to put people through that. He knew us all very well, especially the members of the Senate, because he was such a worldly person. In his mind, he knew their capabilities, knew who they were, knew what he needed, and that he didn't really have to do this. Plus, I don't think he particularly liked the process he went through himself, in previous years. He just didn't like it when the cameras would be on six candidates and then it would be down to three. *Why aren't you in the six?* Then the three down to one. *What did you do wrong?* He doesn't enjoy that part with the press. It's his caring side coming out."

On the day Dad was to announce his choice to be on the ticket, the Quayles were eating lunch at Sammy's Steak and Lobster Place on Bourbon Street in New Orleans when the call came in to return to the hotel. They had been eavesdropping on other diners' lunch conversations and actually heard someone say, "I wonder if this guy from Indiana's got a chance."

"So I get back and am told to call Jim Baker," Quayle recalled. "I think, 'Dang it, Baker's got to tell the losers.' I turn on the television and Tom Brokaw says, 'We've just confirmed it's not Jack Kemp. And hang on here, yes, we now have confirmation that it is apparently not Senator Dole.' And so I call Baker and he said, 'Hang on for the vice president.' When the vice president asked,

'Would you?' I said, 'Absolutely.' He said, 'Thank you very much. We'll be a great team. We'd like to keep this a secret. This is your first big assignment.'"

Dad also told the Quayles to come to the Spanish Plaza in New Orleans at 3:45 p.m. for the announcement. Senator Quayle replied, "I don't know where the Spanish Plaza is, but I'll figure it out, don't worry."

That afternoon, a crowd was waiting on the plaza for my parents to steam down the Mississippi aboard a paddleboat named the SS *Natchez,* then land and make the announcement on a stage at the dock. I was on board the *Natchez* as well and had no idea whom Dad would announce.

It was crowded, and Quayle remembered, "No one let me through. They said, 'Who are you?' and I said, 'I'm the senator from Indiana.' 'We don't care where you're a senator from, we're waiting here to find out who is going to be the next vice president.' I said, 'It might be me, guys! Let me through!' Finally, Roger Ailes and Strom Thurmond and Tommy Thompson saw me about fifteen rows back, and they sent the Secret Service to get me to the front row."

When Dad made the announcement, he surprised everyone.

"I wanted somebody young and somebody who had a good record, and he had been working on labor legislation with Kennedy," Dad said as he reflected on his choice of a running mate. "Dan had defeated Evan Bayh and gone into the Senate. He was young and attractive and that's why I wanted him." Dad also liked Senator Quayle because he had a conservative voting record and would bring regional balance to Dad's Texas/New England background.

Dan Quayle gave me his theory on why he was chosen: "I don't think your dad's told anybody how it came down to Dole and myself, but that's my guess. It was a generational choice. I've always compared it to what Eisenhower did in picking Nixon. Because Nixon was actually younger than I was—Nixon was thirty-nine when Eisenhower picked him. Your father had all the credentials, just like Eisenhower. So I knew that I had a pretty good chance, and that he might do something a little unexpected. But you never know. It's a decision of one."

Dad knew that Quayle had served in the Indiana National Guard during the Vietnam War. In fact, a Washington lawyer and Vietnam veteran, Bob Kimmett, had talked with Senator Quayle on behalf of the campaign about his guard service. Kimmett noticed that Quayle's draft number was actually a high number and that even though he would not have been drafted, Quayle decided to go into the guard anyway. Apparently, Kimmett thought it was all right. My brother George, who is only six months older than Vice President Quayle, had been in the guard as well, so it didn't set off any alarms with Dad.

But it did with the press.

"The news media treated him horribly," remembers Dad. "They jumped all over him for his service with the National Guard during Vietnam. Brutal, brutal. And it continues to this day."

As for Marilyn, before there was Hillary, there was Marilyn Quayle. She had been a lawyer in her own right, and together they had a law firm, Quayle and Quayle, in the same building as Dan's father's business. Senator Quayle worked in newspaper publishing, and Mrs. Quayle had a successful law practice. Later, when he became vice president, she put her law practice on hold and considered running for an open Senate seat, but decided against it.

★   ★   ★

The night after the Quayle announcement, Jim Baker asked each member of our family to represent our state delegations—to pay tribute to Dad while announcing that our state had cast all of its delegates' votes for him. We were all so excited—I would announce Maine's votes, Marvin would do Virginia, Neil would do Colorado, Jeb would do Florida, and George would do Texas, putting Dad over the top for the nomination. I remember wearing a red-and-white-checked dress and being very nervous. I practiced my lines over and over again. Somehow, I managed to get the words out without too many malaprops.

"I was pretty fired up," Marvin recalled. "Had a nice suit on and was well prepared, had some nice remarks about Dad. I was candidly a little nervous and was hovering around the Virginia delegation. I had taken the liberty of informing virtually everybody I knew on planet Earth that I was going to be on television, and encouraged them to tune in. Then I realized about halfway through they were doing this in alphabetical order. By the time Virginia came along, there were about four citizens in Guam who were watching on C-SPAN. I appreciated Neil's tribute to Dad—which came after he praised Colorado for being a state—'from the mountains of Aspen to the hills of Breckenridge, from the cow pastures of Durango to the . . .' His speech went on for about fourteen minutes. I don't think that helped my cause much. Once they got to Texas, they timed it in such a way that George, our brother, put him over the top and the balloons were falling around. By the time I got up, the janitors were kind of cleaning up the balloons that had popped hours earlier. You guys were all back in the hotel suite, and you watched me on some sort of internal television feed."

Earlier in the day, Dad had invited Ray Siller, his friend and comedic writer, up to his suite at the Marriott to watch the nomination vote. Ray arrived in the suite expecting to find a big crowd and instead discovered my father alone with all the grandchildren, abandoned by the rest of us and left to babysit all the kids.

"The Bush munchkins seemed heavily caffeinated, flinging their toys on the floor, ricocheting about the room, drivers in a NASCAR race gone terribly wrong," Ray remembers. Dad threatened them all with bedtime, "and from the other room two of the boys responded to the vice president's command by bolting in with space-age weaponry and randomly spraying the perimeter." One kid blasted his grandfather, who then asked Tim McBride to please find a pointer for him to use. Tim found a schoolteacher's pointer—a three-foot-long wooden dowel with a rubber tip—and brought it back to my father, complete with red, white, and blue streamers.

Dad then invented a game called Pointer Man, in which one child would serve as Pointer Man, standing before the bank of television screens and, at the direction of the others, pointing every time a friend or family member appeared on-screen. Then it would be someone else's turn to be Pointer Man. This had the effect of getting the children to sit down and clear a sight line for Dad and Ray to see the televisions. Ray said Dad's job that night reminded him of the plate-spinners on *The Ed Sullivan Show*, juggling the grandchildren while watching history unfold on the monitors.

That night—only one day after the Quayle announcement—Dad said to Ray, "I can't understand the criticism the press is heaping on Dan about serving in the National Guard. Don't know why they're making such a fuss over that. So many at the time fled to Canada."

The next night was my father's acceptance speech for the Republican nomination. According to Fred Malek, "It was do or die," the high point of the entire convention, and he remembers being with Dad, Roger Ailes, Bob Mosbacher, and Lee Atwater in a holding room below the podium about thirty minutes before the speech. "He should have been completely on edge—it was show-time, and unless he delivered, his campaign was likely to sink," Fred remembers, adding that the campaign was still seventeen points down to Dukakis at this point. "To my surprise, he sat there with us watching the convention on TV and traded jokes for half an hour. Never said a word about the speech until he delivered a great acceptance speech."

The truth is, Dad "worked on it over and over," according to his diary the night of the speech. Roger Ailes arrived to help Dad polish up his delivery. Ailes today runs the Fox News Channel, but at the time, he was a New York "image" consultant that the campaign had hired—and that Dad resisted at first. Ailes recalled, "Secretly, he thought all the guys around Reagan were staging him too much. He said, 'I'm already vice president.' I said, 'You're not president—yet.' So even though he didn't like the sort of business I was in, he and I hit it off and had a lot of laughs. He knew I wasn't there to change him and I wasn't there to do anything 'weird,' as he put it."

Recently, I came across Roger Ailes's notes from that night, to help Dad with his delivery of the acceptance speech:

> Listen to the audience . . . Let the equipment do the work— Don't overshout . . . Do not rush . . . Do NOT step on laughs or applause . . . Wait to start next sentence . . . Silence is drama . . . Don't start sentences then have to start them over . . . Eyes that twinkle . . . Absolute total confidence . . . Never furrow brow or look worried . . . Calm—cool—self-contained . . . Give the Best Speech of Your Life—Enjoy it.

"I remember sitting there when the family had all gone to the convention hall . . . I felt calm; I knew what I had to do." Dad was worried that the press had built it "up and up and up—had to do this, had to do that, and it was the biggest moment in my life, which it was; and almost setting expectations so high that they couldn't be matched, and yet they were."

"Great speech. Fantastic acceptance speech," said Jeb afterward. "I took the speech"—literally—"he signed it for me and then I kept it for a while. I had to give it back. Sent it to the library. It was with his annotations."

Peggy Noonan, one of President Reagan's speechwriters, was very helpful to Dad; but Tom Collamore, his personal aide at the time, didn't like the way that Noonan subsequently "made a cottage industry out of taking credit for some of his finest speeches and statements. While she may have been an important wordsmith, the ideas were his. I saw the notes that he wrote reflecting on what he wanted to say in his convention speech and in his inaugural address. Those were his ideas."

Dad sent a memo to Peggy, laying out themes and ideas. In the final speech, he called for a "kinder, gentler" America and saluted Americans who are engaged in community service—"a brilliant diversity spread like stars, like a thousand points of light in a broad and peaceful sky." He jokingly promised to "keep his charisma in check." And he said this: "The Congress will push me to raise taxes, and I'll say no, and they'll push, and I'll say no, and they'll push again, and I'll say to them, 'Read my lips: no new taxes.'" The crowd roared.

By the end of it all, Dad not only closed the gap with Dukakis but left New Orleans two points ahead in the polls.

★   ★   ★

Meanwhile, the simmering feud with *Newsweek* over the "wimp" cover continued. Dad later told me, "I was at the VP house with Jimmy Baker and they said Katharine Graham wanted to come talk about it. Out she came with Rick Smith, who was the editor in chief of *Newsweek,* and Evan Thomas, the Washington bureau chief. They wanted to do a behind-the-scenes book, which they did every year, with Tom DeFrank.

"Baker said, 'This is unacceptable.' I said, 'We're not going to cooperate with them. If *Newsweek* asks a question in a news conference, we'll answer it with no discrimination against them. But we're not going to lean over and discriminate *for* them by giving them the inside, behind-the-scenes story of this campaign. I'm going to tell our people on the campaign not to cooperate with them.' And we did. But I think some did cooperate anyway.

"They came out and said they were terribly sorry about the 'wimp' piece," Dad continued. "Evan Thomas spoke up: 'I was the one responsible for this. I'm the guy that did it.' I have to take it he was showing off for the publisher and owner, Kay Graham. It poisoned my relationship with him."

Later that fall, on a cold Sunday, even snowing a little, Roger Ailes was waiting at Andrews Air Force Base outside Washington when Dad landed in Air Force Two.

Roger was at Andrews because the campaign press office, unbeknownst to him, had earlier agreed to a "campaign profile" of my father by Dan Rather of CBS News, having been assured by the network that it was a standard videotaped piece on the candidate.

Roger had gotten a secret call that morning from someone at CBS News, a young man Roger had helped get a job. "He went to an outside pay phone and he called me and said, 'Look, I'll get fired if they find out I told you this, but the producer of the show is going around the newsroom saying, "We're taking Bush out of the race tonight."'" Here is Roger's account of what happened from then on:

I went out to Andrews to meet him and got in the car with him on the way to the speech. I said, "I've got a tip-off that this is really not a campaign profile, this is really an attack on Iran-Contra. They've canceled half the show. Rather is geared up to go after you." And your dad said, "I've answered those questions a hundred times and they're not going anywhere." I told him I thought this was a real political hit. I didn't think this was like a standard interview.

We worked it out that if it was a standard interview, your dad would do what he always did. And if it wasn't, I said, just say, "Dan, your comparing my career to Iran-Contra is like my comparing your career to the time you walked off the air." The significance of that is, in broadcasting if you leave dead air, that's the equivalent in the military of going AWOL. You just don't do it. Professional broadcasters don't leave their post. Dan had done that in a flap. Some show ran over and he got into a snit. He walked off the air and left six minutes of dead air on CBS. It was probably the most embarrassing moment of his career, because it was the most unprofessional thing he could possibly do.

So I gave that line to your dad. I told him not to use that unless he had to, but if they start down a road you think is unfair, then nail him on this. I think your dad put it in the back of his mind and really didn't think too much about it.

I also found out that Rather was being briefed over the weekend by a Democrat adviser named Tom Donilon, brought in to coach him. I thought that was unfair. That's the first time I had ever heard of a network bringing a guy in to coach an anchor on how to get a politician. That would be like hiring me at that time to go in and coach Tom Brokaw on how to get somebody. It just wasn't done. I don't have that a hundred percent, but I'm told it was true and I think it probably was. I did see Donilon later at the

L.A. debate with Bob Squire [a Democratic political operative] and with Mike Dukakis, so I believe it probably was true.

Your dad and I went to the Senate office and he got ready to go in. I went down the hall and looked in the room where they were going to shoot, and I noticed they had sent an assistant bureau chief over to produce the interview. Normally, they would send a field producer. I'd been around long enough to know that if the assistant bureau chief is there, they're expecting something more important to happen.

I went back and I said, "This looks pretty serious. They're going to play a little package before you go on, and then Dan is going to interview you." And they played this package explaining Iran-Contra. There must have been a factual error or two in it, because your dad got mad. I could see he was looking at it and he said, "That's not right, that's not right." And I thought, "This is good. He's getting cranked up here."

The vice president was ready for bear when the thing started. But he's ever the gentleman, and so he was trying to do the best he could to not get hot about it. Then Dan started boring in on him on Iran-Contra: "Aren't you guilty?" And finally, Dan said something and I gave your dad the signal, *just go for it*. He didn't want to go for it.

My sense at that point was that we could lose this battle. I grabbed the clipboard out of the bureau chief's hand and I wrote WALKED OFF THE AIR. I showed it to him, made a fist, and said, "Go! Go! Just kick his ass!"

Rather must have said something that made him mad. And your dad just unloaded on him. He said, "Dan, comparing this to my career is like comparing your career to the time you walked off the air."

When you go back and look at the tape, it looked like Rather was in the ring. If you slow the tape down, it looks like he took a punch. His head rolls forward. His head comes back, his eyes roll up and come back down. It just looks like one of those old boxing movies where the guy takes a punch. That was pretty much it. It was pretty clear that fight was over and your dad won.

We went back to the holding room and, of course, the calls started pouring in. They were mostly favorable to your dad. Only a few weren't. I heard him on the phone in the background saying,

"Yes, you're right. No, I'm sorry. You're right. I'm sorry." He hung up, and I thought, "Who the heck was that?" I mean, everybody is calling to congratulate him. I said, "Who was that?" He said, "That was my mother. She said that just because that other man was rude was no excuse for me to be."

Looking back, Ailes said that the interview wiped out the "wimp" image, but "I don't think the feud ever went away. It was simmering for ten years. Sometimes your dad says we won the battle and lost the war—because Rather went after him for the next ten years. It came to a head again when Rather went after your brother over his Texas National Guard record. It did not stand up to journalistic standards. You just don't pay somebody for five and a half years to do an investigative piece on news that everybody already has, unless you're out to get them."

★   ★   ★

"Roger did a very good job of recognizing what the press was going to try to do," Governor Sununu remembers. "They didn't want your father to win. Dealing with the 'wimp factor' article and the Dan Rather interview are good examples of Roger planning ahead and letting the president know the kinds of things that would happen."

Along with Sig Rogich, Ailes was also instrumental that fall in creating the campaign's television ads, including ones on the furlough program that Michael Dukakis supported for violent criminals in Massachusetts—they showed a revolving door at a prison with convicts going right out of jail—and the famous "tank" ad, in which Dukakis was photographed in a very large tank helmet. Dad remembers that one as his favorite of all the ads, adding, "Roger Ailes and Sig Rogich get the credit for that ad—it was the best of all."

There had been other good ads earlier in the campaign on both sides. Dick Gephardt aired an ad showing Dukakis urging Iowa farmers to grow Belgian endive as a crop. The Dukakis campaign, for their part, ran an ad showing an acrobat dressed up as Gephardt, doing backflips as an announcer listed his flip-flops on various issues.

My favorite ads, however, were the positive spots. My daughter Ellie had a starring role in one ad, running across a field and jumping into Dad's arms. Ray Siller remembers my father telling him how patient Ellie was during the taping, how she just kept running toward him through a meadow, take after take. That was a great ad. I remember hearing that a prominent Democrat—I think it may have been former Democratic national chairman Bob Strauss—even said, "If I see that ad one more time, I may even vote for the s.o.b."

Although my focus was on Dad and what I could do to help his campaign, other people were focused on Michael Dukakis. I only met Michael Dukakis and his wife, Kitty, once, during that strange dance that takes place after a presidential debate. It's very important onstage as to who puts his hand out first, especially after just being attacked in front of millions. Most of the time, the two families—never having met each other before—have to congratulate each other warmly for the benefit of the cameras. Every move is watched and can easily be misconstrued.

The campaign focused on several issues, one of which was Dukakis's support for the furlough program in Massachusetts—first pointed out by Al Gore in a Democratic debate—in which violent criminals were allowed weekend furloughs, even though they were not eligible for parole.

"I didn't even know Horton's name or whether he was black or white at the beginning," Lee Atwater said afterward. "I only knew he was in prison for a terrible crime. Then I hear this guy was given a furlough. He was in jail with no hope of parole. Why would you let a guy like this out? He had no incentive to go back. And he couldn't get the death penalty [in Massachusetts]. What would be his incentive not to kill and rape? That's why it was such a salient issue with the American people."

It wasn't until October 1988—right before the election—that Democratic Party leaders denounced the furlough issue as racially motivated, but the press immediately disputed this line of attack. Even the *Washington Post* editorialized the next day that it may or may not be relevant to stress the Dukakis furlough record, "but it isn't racist."

Today, after many years of Democrats and the press repeating false information, people mistakenly think the campaign used the Willie Horton story to racially divide people, not to show Dukakis's weakness on crime. (Years later, during the debate over the Bush administration's civil rights bill, Dad sent my brothers and me a briefing paper reiterating the facts of the Horton case, because they had gotten so distorted over the years. His note read, "If anyone raises Willie Horton in some context other than the furlough abuse, flash this true explanation at 'em.")

I asked Dad recently about the whole Willie Horton episode: "I felt we did the right thing. The people at the *Lawrence Eagle-Tribune* won a Pulitzer Prize for the exposé of Willie Horton. It was definitely a crime issue. We got on Dukakis about having this lenient furlough program where he let people out of jail, and here was the best example—a man who was a convicted rapist who went out and raped again when he was on furlough. By the way, he demanded we call him William Horton later, when he was back in jail. Just a humorous aside."

The crime issue was very powerful in 1988, especially after an NYPD officer named Eddie Byrne—he was only twenty-two at the time—was executed by a drug gang in his patrol car. This cold-blooded killing came on orders from a drug kingpin who had wanted his gang members to "kill a cop" as a test of bravery. The incident made headlines nationally, because it illustrated how out of control drug-related violence had become in our cities. In a very emotional ceremony, Eddie Byrne's parents gave Dad his police badge, which my father still has. Shortly afterward, the Boston Police endorsed Dad over Michael Dukakis.

Governor Dukakis looked back on the fall campaign with regret.

"One of the big lessons of 1988 is if the other guy is going to come at you—and people have been coming at people since the beginning of the Republic—you've got to have a carefully thought-out strategy for dealing with that . . . It's very clear that you cannot sit there mute if people are attacking you. And that's what I did. And by the time I woke up to the kind of damage [that] was being done, it was almost irreparable," he said. "It was a judgment call I made, and it turned out to be a very unwise judgment call."

On the positive side, and helping Dad's cause, the economic news was good during the campaign. Seventeen million new jobs had been created in the previous five years; inflation had dropped from 12 percent to 4 percent during the Reagan-Bush administration; interest rates had been cut in half; and unemployment was the lowest in fourteen years.

Lee Atwater had a way of operating, "command focus" as he called it, and it brought discipline and strategy to the campaign. Along with Jim Baker's day-to-day leadership, the campaign hummed along. A good example of both men's impact was the "line of the day" message that they sent out in a fax pyramid—then an emerging technology—that would include the latest campaign developments, quotes from my father, and bulleted issues to about ten thousand campaign workers across the country every afternoon. The idea was that if some precinct captain in Iowa was on *Nightline*, he would have the latest from Bush headquarters. Campaigns in both parties have been doing the same thing ever since, only now by e-mail instead of fax.

Andy Card had been helping with opposition research on Michael Dukakis, and since he knew Dukakis personally from his days in the Massachusetts statehouse, Andy was good at anticipating Dukakis's response to things. He became instrumental in the preparations for the debates. "I first met Dukakis when I was a sophomore in high school," Andy remembers. "I knew he'd been a cross-country runner and a trumpet player and a Boy Scout. He didn't like people in uniforms and ran away from being a Boy

Scout. The year I got elected to the legislature was the year he got elected governor. He was a reformer and a maverick."

The fall debates came—two presidential and one vice presidential. James Baker and Roger Ailes negotiated all the arrangements with the Democrats. "Baker and I would do good cop, bad cop. They thought I was crazy and Baker was sane," said Roger. "I said, 'I want a forty-eight-inch-high podium.' Well, that would have come up to Dukakis's eyebrows. I said, 'Look, my candidate's tall. His eyes focus at forty-eight. We can go to forty-six inches if that will help you.' Well, that got up just under Dukakis's nose. They kept wanting a forty-two. But I kept pushing them to get the taller podium, knowing that it would make him look like Rocky the Squirrel standing back there. Every once in a while I'd go crazy and say something half-obscene and Baker would calm me down. Then he'd say, 'I've got to leave, got to get back to the White House. I'll leave you with Ailes.' And, of course, they'd immediately say, 'No, no, no. That's okay. Don't leave us with Ailes.' We finally negotiated a pitching mound for Dukakis to walk up on, but no cameras back there to actually shoot it, which we agreed to."

Jeb remembers the pitcher's mound: "Instead of having a riser, a step where he could stand up, they built it like a baseball mound, where you could see the pitch. So then he had to get off this little pitcher's mound to shake hands with Dad."

In the pre-debate practices, Dick Darman played Michael Dukakis, and Roger Ailes was the emcee. Ailes and the other campaign strategists urged Darman to be very tough on Dad, and he was. He repeatedly went after Dad for supposedly being "out of touch" with ordinary Americans. He also mixed in some humor—coming out onstage wearing a tank helmet, holding up an ACLU membership card, and standing on a wooden riser.

"But it was evident that I was getting to the VP—and doing so in front of a live audience of family, friends, and advisers. I persisted. He clearly did not like what was happening. Not at all. But he remained cool. When we came to the end of one of the sessions, I knew I had gone too far," Dick said. At the point when he was to shake hands with Dad midstage, Dad walked off the stage "without a word to me or anyone else." Dick walked to his car alone, fearing he'd made a career-defining mistake. But soon enough, Dad thanked him for making him work even harder on debate preparations, and even invited Dick to the election night festivities.

Dad just can't stand debating: "Hated it. It was show business. You look this way and then that way. A lot of cosmetics. We thought we did pretty well in some of the presidential debates, but the next thing you know, out comes Tim Russert or somebody saying we lost the debates. So I hated them," he said to me.

Then the real debates came. Once all the pre-debate preparations were wrapped up, Roger Ailes would spend the last half hour before the debate with Dad alone—"so that nobody else would run in the room and interrupt him or disrupt him or ask him a question he couldn't answer or, frankly, get him in a bad mood," Roger told me. "I wanted to have the last word. I walked him to the stage in Los Angeles so nobody would run up to him and say his house was on fire. Something that would get you totally off."

"Your dad was not happy, I don't think, with his performance in the first debate; but he killed him in the second. He absolutely demolished Dukakis," remembers James Baker.

The fact that Dad was not thrilled with that first debate may explain why my brothers Marvin and George were so nervous before the second debate that they went to a theater near the vice president's residence to watch a movie instead of the debate. Out of sight did not mean out of mind, however: the suspense was such that not once, not twice, but at least three times George anxiously dispatched Marvin to the lobby to call his friend Pat Quinn from a pay phone.

"Marvin called three times, saying 'PQ, now, give it to me straight. Don't sugarcoat it for me, PQ,'" Pat recalled. "When Marvin called the first time, I told him it looked like it was 'about even, don't worry about it.' The longer the debate went on, however, the more positive I felt about the vice president's performance. By their third call I told them, 'This is a home run. He's kicking butt.' "

Hearing the good news, Marv and George immediately left the theater and went back to the vice presidential residence to watch the rest of the debate.

The big break in the debate came when the moderator, Bernie Shaw, asked Dukakis if he'd change his mind about opposing the death penalty if his wife, Kitty, was raped and murdered. Dukakis gave a very unemotional "no" answer to Shaw, and many people now think that one exchange essentially finished off Dukakis's chances of winning. "If I had to do that over again, I'd do less rehearsing," Dukakis told me. "By the time you get to that last month or two, you've been at it for months and months and months and you could really start going robotic."

After that answer, Dukakis's advisers suggested he show some public affection for his wife, which he did. This in turn caused some of Dad's advisers to suggest that my parents also get more romantic. Here was Dad's funny response:

Sweetsie:

> *Please look at how Mike and Kitty do it. Try to be closer in, more—well er romantic—on camera. I am practicing the loving look, and the creeping hand.*
> *Yours for better TV and more demonstrable affection.*

Your sweetie-pie coo-coo.

Love ya

GB

★   ★   ★

At some point in the fall, the Dukakis campaign announced it was pulling out of Florida, in an effort to focus resources on states where they had a fighting chance. Jeb was the state chairman for Bush-Quayle in Florida, and upon hearing the announcement by Dukakis, he arranged for a big rally. "We had a bon voyage party for Dukakis along Biscayne Bay. We had a picture of a boat with all of Michael Dukakis's baggage on it. We were saying good-bye to him as he was leaving the state. And while we were doing that at our campaign rally, there was a guy going back and forth in a small motorboat with a blond boy wearing diapers with a sign that said 'I'm Dan Quayle.' That's how things go in the campaign."

The final two weeks were filled with an endless series of campaign stops. Jeb also remembers traveling on the campaign bus with the Beach Boys and Loretta Lynn, with a lot of stops for them to sing in front of small-town crowds. Still, as we made this final push, everyone was exhausted and not at all sure we were going to win. Dad remembers, "The polls looked pretty good, but there was some last-minute questioning and doubt."

We ended up in Houston for the election night party at the George Brown Convention Center, my entire family gathered with Mom and Dad along with thousands of people. I remember being nervous—literally feeling like I was on pins and needles.

There was a dinner at the home of some friends earlier in the evening, and Joe Hagin remembers the moment when *NBC Nightly News* came on. There were TVs everywhere in the house. Joe remembers what happened next: "It actually shocked us all because it was so early, and Brokaw called the election. So we went to the convention center and, after more results came in, [he] did the acceptance speech and we came back out and I was riding in the police car in the front of the motorcade. Then they said on the Secret Service frequency, 'Timberwolf wants Hagin.'" So Joe jumped out, ran back to Dad's limo, and was offered a job on the spot, to come back from his corporate job in Cincinnati to a White House job in Washington. "Even today, all these years later," he said, "it's all kind of like a fairy tale."

The results were in: Bush-Quayle had received 53 percent of the popular vote and 426 electoral votes; Dukakis-Bentsen had 46 percent and 111 electoral votes. My father had won all but ten states. "I still find it incredible and almost impossible to believe," Dad said. He went to bed that night thinking of all the people who should have been there, not the least of whom was his father.

My father was now president-elect of the United States of America. As you might imagine, I was ecstatic—we all were—but the reality, the historical impact, of what had happened to Dad, and to us, would take time to digest. That night, the full range of emotions cascaded over us; relief, unbridled joy, exhaustion, and a tremendous sense of pride. In the eyes of many, Dad had started his quest for the White House as a marginal Don Quixote-esque figure in a fantastical misadventure; yet, just as he had always striven to complete his mission as a naval pilot, he had also withstood the partisan attacks and barbed pens of the Beltway pundits to make this improbable dream a reality. Even today, the sheer magnitude of what he achieved seems surreal—as if it happened in another lifetime. Yet it did happen, and in due course my father would take his place in history with the other distinguished Americans to precede him into that high office.

The next morning, my parents were flying back to Washington on Air Force Two with a big crowd of family and staff. George and Laura's five-year-old twins, Barbara and Jenna, had stuffed the airplane's toilet with paper, and Mom was in it up to her elbows trying to unclog it. "I couldn't help but wonder if any other First Ladies-elect had spent their first morning unstuffing the toilet," she said.

It was, as Dad's friend Dan Jenkins is fond of saying, "life its own self."

Chapter 15

AGE OF THE OFFERED HAND

"I think [history] will remember him as the man who taught us to keep the peace. George taught us to stay in touch with our allies, and stay in touch with the world, not just when you need them. I think [future generations] will remember him as a peacemaker."

—**Barbara Bush**

Not even the bitter cold of the 1985 inaugural, had it been replicated, could put a chill on the excitement of January 20, 1989. Dad had worked too hard, and come so far, over the past decade—going from an asterisk in 1979 to 1600 Pennsylvania Avenue in 1989. It had been a long, exhilarating climb, and with a lot of help he had finally reached the summit of the "mountaintop of U.S. politics," as he has called the presidency.

The day started with a prayer service at St. John's Church, and Mom and Dad met the Reagans at the White House for coffee before riding up to the Capitol. The morning chill clung stubbornly to our nation's capital that day; and as the president and president-elect rode together, President Reagan recounted how, when he was sworn in as governor of California, "just as I placed my hand on the Bible, the sun came through and warmed it."

For our family, inauguration day 1989 possessed a similar fateful feeling.

As Dad and Mom prepared to walk out onto the West Front of the U.S. Capitol for the swearing-in ceremony, however, something wasn't quite right. Suddenly, Dad turned to Tim McBride, his personal aide at the time.

"Tim, I need my overcoat," he said. "President Reagan is in his, and I don't want to draw this contrast." The day turned cloudy and windy, and although it was mild, Mrs. Reagan was bundling President Reagan up in an overcoat and a scarf.

With the entire Congress, the Supreme Court, the cabinet, a who's who of Washington, and a worldwide television audience awaiting the ceremony, Tim realized he didn't have enough time to retrieve Dad's coat from the car, so he offered up his own topcoat, which happened to be the same size.

"On one of the biggest days of his life, what's he thinking about?" Tim reflected. "The other guy."

Dad's inauguration marked the two hundredth anniversary of the presidency; and it was awe-inspiring to consider that only thirty-nine other men (President Grover Cleveland counts twice!) had preceded my father into that high office. Sitting behind the podium off the center aisle and looking out at the enormous crowd on the National Mall, I realized that so many people across America—and even around the world—would now be counting on Dad to lead them and help them. A small crowd of protesters also gathered on the Mall away from the ceremony, and their presence reminded me that—even on this festive day—there were still those in the loyal opposition determined to challenge Dad at every turn.

I loved standing next to my eighty-seven-year-old grandmother, my namesake, sharing a front-row seat to history. Dad later said how he regretted that his father was not alive when he became president, but the fact that Ganny was there made that remarkable occasion all the more special for all of us.

As the ceremony started, I remember thinking how tall and

handsome Dad looked. People who only know him from their TV set are always surprised how tall he appears in person at 6'2". I also remember looking at the network booths and all the faces that dominated our nightly news. Everyone looked like caricatures of themselves. It seemed surreal to have all those familiar faces in one spot.

But it was real, and as the sun pierced through the breaking winter clouds, I watched my father become the forty-first president of the United States. In one majestic moment, Dad was the leader of the free world.

It was deeply moving to know our country was in such good, decent hands. The family pride that swelled in my heart, however, was accompanied by an undeniable lump in my throat. The presidency in some respects can be compared to a roller-coaster ride. From high atop that initial platform, the new chief executive is inevitably hurled into the ups and downs of life in Washington.

Jon Meacham, the managing editor of *Newsweek*, pointed out an interesting historical footnote from the swearing-in ceremony. While Dad is generally very reserved about public demonstrations of his faith, he opened his inaugural address that day with a prayer. Jon noted that the only other presidents who have done that to date are George Washington and Dwight Eisenhower.

Following the ceremony, Mom and Dad escorted the Reagans to Marine One for their return trip to California. Earlier that day, Dad wrote President Reagan a note with which he enclosed a small image of the White House as a gift:

January 20th

Dear Mr. President and Nancy,

Here's a tiny going away present. You've probably got a thousand of these, but Barbara and I felt this might be a nice reminder of the House you've graced for so long.

I will choke up, I expect, as we say farewell later today—so here goes—

It's been great. I'll never forget all you've done. I'll try to earn
that support.
  Good luck—Love, too!

  George

Meanwhile, the rest of us filed into Statuary Hall, the "Old Hall
of the House," where we were seated for the traditional congressional luncheon. We weren't far from where the 1984 swearing-in
ceremony had taken place, in the Capitol Rotunda. Situated between the House Chamber and the Capitol Rotunda, Statuary
Hall served as the original House of Representatives from 1807 to
1857 as well as the site of six presidential inaugurations—the last
one being in 1850. Today, the semicircular room with its arches and
columns is filled with busts and statues of leaders from all fifty
states and, more often than not, tour groups. In this historic, ornate setting, the Congress saluted the new president and vice president, and the warm toasts offered by the congressional leaders
added to the excitement and hope of the day.

The inaugural parade immediately followed lunch, so everyone
in our family, except Mom and Dad, rushed to the White House
and into the presidential box—the glass-encased reviewing stand
erected on the north side of the White House grounds. Meanwhile, Mom and Dad started to make their way down Pennsylvania Avenue. They were supposed to ride in the limo, but Dad was
eager to greet everyone along the parade route, so he and Mom
would periodically jump out of the car to walk and wave. At one
point, Mom spotted her favorite weatherman, Willard Scott, and
ran over and gave him a quick kiss.

Arriving at the presidential box, Mom and Dad enjoyed watching the 78 floats, 145 parade units, and 10,000 participants pass by.
Dad was particularly excited when a float passed by carrying his
old friend Jack Guy and the rest of the surviving crew members
from his navy squadron, VT51. The kids loved it, too—little blond-
haired blue-eyed Sam had enough energy for everybody, and loved

seeing the parade and running around with his cousins in the re-viewing stand. The only one who wasn't enjoying herself was my daughter Ellie, then aged three, who told me she was starting to feel sick. My heart ached at the sight of her, wearing her brand-new dress we'd bought for the day, and her little cheeks pink with fever. Since we were right in front of the White House, I asked a military aide if we could go inside, and he escorted us up the drive-way and right through the North Portico doors.

I was so worried about Ellie that it took a minute to realize I was in *the* White House, making us the first family members other than Mom and Dad to enter the building on that first day.

It was there that I met the chief usher, Gary Walters, and first experienced how the amazing White House staff somehow makes that very public building feel like a safe family home. In this minor case, Gary called one of the on-call White House doctors, who came immediately to help get Ellie on the mend.

Gary, who is still at the White House today, has likened his job to that of a hotel manager. The White House staff comprises over ninety people, including chefs, housemen, butlers, carpenters, plumbers, electricians, curators, and calligraphers. These dedicated public servants maintain the home of the president, provide for the care of the White House and its grounds, and tend to the endless details that go with the ceremonial events of the presidency. With-out them, the White House simply could not function.

It turned out Ellie only had an ear infection and was going to be fine. Since she was feeling better, we thought it would be all right to leave her and Sam, who was five, with our nanny Eileen that evening while Billy and I joined our friends and attended several in-augural balls, including the one hosted by our home state, Maine.

Attending an inaugural ball is a privilege that few Americans get to enjoy, and I was grateful for the opportunity. But having said that, going to an inaugural ball always sounds more glamorous than it re-ally is: guests are packed into a cavernous room like sardines; you are lucky to see anyone you know; and you have no room to dance!

Of course, Mom and Dad had plenty of room for their quick

spins around the dance floor at each of the fourteen balls they attended—which makes me tired just thinking about it. In fact, Mom's only unpleasant memory of that inaugural weekend was her feet. They hurt the entire time, because she had bought four pairs of twenty-nine-dollar shoes and had them dyed to match her gowns for the various events. The shoes turned her feet whatever color they had been dyed.

"Don't ever buy a twenty-nine-dollar pair of shoes," Mom advises today.

(By the way, after the inaugural, many people started sending Mom tips for changing her hairstyle and hair color. In fact, one citizen sent in computer-generated photos of Mom with a series of suggested hairdos so she could see how she'd look!)

Before we left the White House for the evening's festivities, it was decided that Marvin and Margaret would stay in the Lincoln Bedroom that first evening. Before Marvin and Margaret turned in for the night, however, Gary Walters warned them that it was "definitely a haunted room."

While there were no confirmed ghost sightings that night, Marvin did learn an important historical lesson: "Even though it wasn't Abraham Lincoln's bed, but an actual time-period piece, I discovered people must have been a lot shorter back then because there wasn't a lot of room to navigate," he said. "I think Margaret probably ended up sleeping on the couch, but it was still great."

The next morning, Saturday, January 21, at 9:09, Dad gave his first press conference in the Oval Office. In the very first remarks he made to the press, he talked not about policy, but about his mother, his first guest in the oval office, and what a joy it was to have her in the White House. When the media asked her how she felt, my grandmother responded, "It's the most exciting day of my life—so far."

Then, referring to Ellie as the "points of light kid" from the campaign commercial, Dad briefed Helen Thomas and the White House press corps that he gave his granddaughter some Tylenol at 6:00 a.m., that Ellie had eaten pancakes, and that she was making a quick recovery. It would be normal for Dad to talk about Ellie, but in the Oval Office as president—that was a whole new twist!

That first full day, 250 family members descended on the White House for lunch. Everyone from my siblings and our spouses to Ganny, Aunt Nan, Uncle Bucky, even Uncle Lou—they were all there. Uncle Johnny told me the story that two nights earlier, he had gotten a phone call at his hotel from a woman named Wendy Robbins Rockwell. "Wendy Robbins, my God, I haven't seen you since I got out of Yale," he said. Wendy replied, "I called you because you told me when we were eleven years old that your brother was going to be president of the United States. I just called to congratulate you on being right!"

With presidents in the family, the distant cousins do come out of the woodwork. In fact, we had cousins there that day that I had never laid eyes on and, still to this day, don't know their names.

Dad wanted to have an "open house" on his first day as president, and tours were conducted on a first-come, first-served basis. Some people had waited in line all night to see the mansion—but when Mom and Dad tried to greet the crowd, the line came to a standstill. Mom and Dad didn't want to delay the throngs of people outside in the cold still waiting to get in, so their meet-and-greet couldn't last long.

My grandmother stayed upstairs in the residence most of the day. Because of her frail condition, she had come to Washington on an ambulance plane with a doctor and nurse to see her son become president. The day before, during the inaugural parade, she had come in out of the cold—going up to the Queen's Bedroom to watch the rest of the parade with Billy Graham.

Incidentally, after Ganny returned home to Connecticut, my Aunt Nan called to ask her what she thought of the White House. "Oh, Nannie," my grandmother replied, "it's *much* too big. They're never going to be able to make it cozy. They ought to go back where they were before. It was a much better size for living. They should just use the White House for official things."

★ ★ ★

One of the truly unique features of our democratic system is the seamless, peaceful transfer of power between chief executives. Our Constitution tells us what day and even what time the swearing-in should occur. Geniuses that they were, however, our founders were less helpful on the mechanics of how this transition takes place—how one family's worldly possessions can be moved out of the White House, and another family moved in, in the course of a single day.

That miracle of democracy generally falls to the White House staff and a small army of movers.

The transition went well for Dad. For starters, he was the first sitting vice president to be elected president since Martin Van Buren in 1836—and during his eight years as Ronald Reagan's number two, he had seen firsthand how the institution of the presidency functioned.

Previous vice presidents split their time between the largely ceremonial office in the Old Executive Office Building, now called the Eisenhower Executive Office Building, and their office on Capitol Hill, where they preside as president of the Senate. Dad also had an office located inside the West Wing. This helped when it came time to move his desk into the Oval Office.

President Reagan had used what is known as the Resolute Desk, which was built from the ship timbers of the HMS *Resolute*. Queen Victoria of England presented it to President Rutherford B. Hayes in 1880 as a gesture of friendship between our nations—and the desk had been used by every president from Hayes to Kennedy. It became famous as the Oval Office desk in which the Kennedy children were photographed playing hide-and-seek.

After President Kennedy's assassination, however, President Johnson loaned the Resolute Desk to the Smithsonian and had his vice presidential desk brought over from the Capitol. This started a tradition whereby vice presidents brought their VP desks with them to the White House. Both President Nixon and President Ford followed suit, as did Dad.

Since President Carter had not been a vice president, he brought the Resolute Desk back into use. Presidents Reagan and Clinton also used it, as does my brother George. Dad liked to use the Resolute Desk in his office upstairs in the White House residence.

Dad had a few things on his Oval Office desk throughout his four years: a favorite clock, a photo of my sister, Robin, and, in the top middle drawer, a note from President Reagan that was waiting for him that first day. It came on a playful memo pad stamped "Don't let the turkeys get you down" with a Boynton cartoon drawing of turkeys standing on an elephant at the bottom. President Reagan's note read:

Dear George,

You'll have moments when you want to use this particular stationery. Well, go to it.

George I treasure the memories we share and wish you all the very best. You'll be in my prayers. God bless you and Barbara. I'll miss our Thursday lunches.

Ron

"What a sweet man," Dad said when he found the note. He had it encased in clear Lucite and kept it in his desk drawer all through his presidency. Later, at President Reagan's funeral, Dad referred to this same note in his eulogy: "He certainly never let the turkeys get him down. He fought hard for his beliefs. He led from conviction but never made an adversary into an enemy. He was never mean-spirited."

One more permanent item eventually worked its way onto Dad's desk—roughly eleven months later. After U.S. troops returned from ousting Panamanian strongman Manuel Noriega in

December 1989, Dad and Mom stopped by a San Antonio hospital to visit the wounded soldiers.

Jay Allison, my father's personal aide at the time, remembers Dad coming out of the critical-care unit with a small American flag in his breast pocket. Jay could see that it had been an emotional visit; and for a long time, Dad simply couldn't talk about it.

During that hospital visit, my father had met a severely wounded Army Ranger, nineteen years old, who had been in the first wave of troops landing in Panama. The Ranger handed Dad his flag and said that even if he'd known beforehand that he would lose an arm and a leg in combat—which he did—he still supported the president's decision because it was the right thing to do. Dad kept that flag in the pencil cup on his desk in the Oval Office every day after that—and he promised the Ranger that it would serve as a daily reminder of the personal sacrifice our soldiers make. Later, according to Dad's assistant Patty Presock, when visiting heads of state came to the Oval Office, Dad would ask that a miniature flag from the visitor's country—like the ones guests at the arrival ceremonies were always given—also be placed in the pencil cup.

★ ★ ★

I noticed that something had changed within the walls of the White House that first week. Previously, if I walked down the hall with Dad, we'd navigate our way through the crowd, dodging staff members going to and from meetings. Now, however, people stepped aside for Dad and stood up a little straighter as he passed by. They were not doing this because Dad had changed—but rather out of respect for the office that he held.

Dad also did things a little differently as well. Two interesting observations about Dad's behavior in the Oval Office come from two close colleagues.

Judge William Webster served as director of the CIA under

Dad—and he recalled visiting with Dad one Saturday morning in one of the little cubbyhole offices off the Oval Office. Dad was dressed in a sport shirt and casual clothes, and the two were discussing a matter when Dad realized he had something on his Oval Office desk related to their conversation. The trouble was, he told Director Webster, "I don't like to go into the Oval Office without wearing a coat and tie." He'd have to send Judge Webster the document the next day, Dad decided.

"It reflected a deeply felt respect for the office," the judge later said. "This was just the two of us. He wasn't showing off for the press. He certainly was not trying to show off for me—I'd known him for a long, long time. It's the way he felt, and it's the way he has lived."

Dick Darman, meanwhile, had spent four years in the White House as an assistant to President Reagan before Dad asked him to head the Office of Management and Budget. During the Reagan years, Dick had often been in the Oval Office just before the media were allowed in for one event or another. In such situations, Dick said he was always struck by how quickly and completely Ronald Reagan could focus on the TV cameras and play to them.

"President Bush was different," Dick said. "The first time I was with him when the press entered the Oval Office, the reporters formed the usual semicircle around the president's desk. The TV cameras were in the center facing the president directly. Helen Thomas happened to be at a far end of the semicircle. When she asked the first question, the president turned to her and stayed focused on *her* as he responded. In so doing, he turned his head three-quarters of the way *away* from the TV cameras. From a media-management perspective, that would ordinarily have been considered a mistake. But the president was less interested in the cameras than he was in showing his questioner proper courtesy and respect. He simply did not enjoy the contrivances of the larger media game."

★　★　★

Every incoming president strives to hit the ground running, so to speak, and Dad's White House team started to take shape the day after his victory in November 1988. That first morning after election night, in fact, he had a press conference to announce his opening round of appointments. He tapped his friend and fellow Houstonian James Baker as secretary of state; New Hampshire Governor John Sununu became White House chief of staff; Boyden Gray as White House counsel; and Dad's longtime friend and former congressional aide Chase Untermeyer as assistant to the president for personnel. On the day before—Election Day—Dad asked Lee Atwater to serve as chairman of the Republican National Committee, Dad's old job.

Craig Fuller, former chief of staff in the vice president's office, and Bob Teeter, who had been the campaign pollster, were named cochairmen of the presidential transition. By January, Fuller and Teeter, in turn, helped Dad put in place the remainder of the cabinet appointments. Among others, Dad also asked his trusted friends Nick Brady and Bob Mosbacher to serve as secretaries of treasury and commerce, respectively; former New York congressman Jack Kemp became secretary of housing and urban development; and another former opponent, Senate Minority Leader Bob Dole, saw his wife, Elizabeth, become secretary of labor. Chicago lawyer Sam Skinner became the secretary of transportation. For the post of national security adviser, Dad turned to General Brent Scowcroft, who served in that same capacity in the Ford administration.

Many of these were people I had grown up knowing, and it was not a surprise to see them return to public service in Dad's administration.

This was indeed a "friendly takeover" from the Reagan administration—one Republican president to another—and, perhaps as a result, many of the Reagan staffers thought they were going to stay for another eight years. Yet, no matter how people might agree philosophically, a president needs certain people in certain positions—people that have a feel for the nuances of his agenda and are personally loyal to the president.

"One of the hard things we had to do in the first few months was have a lot of the Reagan people leave," John Sununu recalled, "so we could fill it with Bush loyalists instead of generic Republican loyalists or Reagan loyalists. And you know the president: that kind of thing is generally hard for him to do—he's such a kind man. Besides, that's the kind of job a chief of staff can and should handle for the president—so that's where I developed the reputation for being direct."

During the transition period in December, Dad's chief of protocol, Joseph Verner Reed, also suggested that the president-elect invite the United Nations secretary-general, Javiar Pérez de Cuéllar, to dinner early in his administration as a gesture of friendship to the United Nations. Dad enthusiastically embraced this suggestion and replied, "I want to have Secretary-General de Cuéllar as my *first* dinner guest at the White House."

On January 24, Dad and Mom hosted a dinner party for the secretary-general and more than thirty U.N. officials upstairs in the family quarters. "The gesture, I can assure you, was appreciated not only by the member states' permanent representatives, but also the thousands of international civil servants across the globe who learned about it," Ambassador Reed recalled. "It was a great triumph of international diplomacy for the most senior United Nations alumnus."

Dad's first week in office was a particularly busy one, filled with swearing-in ceremonies for cabinet officers and senior White House staff. When that first Thursday arrived, though, Dad was not so caught up in events that he didn't notice something was missing—and he wasn't alone.

"When we came home to California after George's inauguration," Nancy Reagan remembered, "Ronnie began work in his new office the next day. It was a busy and exciting first week for Ronnie, but when Thursday came around, it just didn't seem to be the same. As Ronnie sat down at his desk to have a sandwich, the phone rang and the White House operator said President Bush was calling. When he picked up the phone, Ronnie heard George's

Our official congressional family portrait, soon after we had moved to Washington, D.C., in 1967. (GBPL)

Dad and his congressional staff: Rose Zamaria, Don Rhodes, Pete Roussel, and Tom Lias. (GBPL)

Christmas in Houston, 1969: Me, Dad, Jeb, George, Marvin, and Neil. (GBPL)

Dad and me in our boat *The Rebel*, 1969. (GBPL)

Family tennis in Kennebunkport. (GHWB Personal Collection)

Dad, me, Marvin, and George in a family game of dominos. (GBPL)

My beautiful mother. (GBPL)

The one and only photo of Jeb and Columba's wedding, February 23, 1974. (GHWB Personal Collection)

Marvin and me at the Ming tombs during our visit to China in 1975. (GBPL)

George W. and me in front of the U.S. liaison office in China. (GBPL)

Marvin and me right after I was baptized in China, 1975. (GBPL)

My dad's mentor, Neil Mallon, and his wife, Ann, visited Dad in China. (GBPL)

Dad frequently rode his bike during his tenure in China. (GBPL)

Our family at one of the Reagan/Bush inauguration events: Neil, Sharon, Laura, George, me, Colu, and Jeb. (GBPL/Cynthia Johnson)

President Reagan plays with our dog C. Fred during a 1981 visit at the vice president's residence. (GBPL/Cynthia Johnson)

Dad and Pete Teeley visit President Reagan at George Washington University Hospital four days after he was shot. (GBPL/Cynthia Johnson)

The Dukakis family visit Walker's Point during a governors meeting that Dad hosted, July 30, 1983. (GBPL)

Dad hosts Geraldine Ferraro (right), Bob Barnett (left), and Lynn Martin for lunch shortly after the 1984 election. (GBPL/Dave Valdez)

Ruth and Billy Graham with George and babies Jenna and Barbara at Walker's Point, 1983. (GBPL)

Paula Rendon, a second mother to my brothers and me. (GBPL)

Dad plays in the Old Timers' Game in Denver, Colorado, 1984. (GBPL / Dave Valdez)

Dad makes a surprise visit to see Sam LeBlond and me, one day after Sam was born, August 27, 1984. (GBPL / Dave Valdez)

Dad uses his Polaroid to take a picture of Sam, Ellie, and Marshall in front of the Christmas tree at the vice president's residence in 1987. (GBPL/Dave Valdez)

Dad with my four brothers at NBC studios in Washington, D.C., June 9, 1986.
(GBPL/Dave Valdez)

My very favorite picture of my dad, taken at Walker's Point, September 1987.

August, 1988: Dad escorts Ganny to church at St. Ann's by the Sea, where she was married in 1921.
(GBPL/Dave Valdez)

Our family at the 1988 Republican National Convention in New Orleans.
(GBPL/Pete Souza)

We won! Watching election returns on TV with Uncle Jon, Uncle Pres, and Dad, November 8, 1988.
(GBPL/Dave Valdez)

Our extended family in front of the South Portico on inauguration day, 1989.
(GBPL/Dave Valdez)

Dad reads the personal note left by former president Reagan that tells him not to let
the turkeys get him down. (GBPL/Dave Valdez)

Mom, Ellie, and me in the White House, the day of Dad's swearing-in.
(GBPL/Dave Valdez)

George and Marvin watch the 1989 Super Bowl in the movie theater at the White House.
(GBPL/Dave Valdez)

The "fish watch" at Walker's Point, August 31, 1989. (GBPL/Dave Valdez)

The BIG TENNIS MATCH: Jeb and Marvin vs. Chris Evert and Pam Shriver.
(GBPL/Dave Valdez)

Dad lost this round of horseshoes, but Ron Jones is jubilant in victory.
(GBPL/Susan Biddle)

Signing the Americans with Disabilities Act on July 26, 1990. Front: Evan Kemp, Dad, and Justin Dart. Back: Vice President Dan Quayle, Reverend Harold Wilkie, and Sandra Parino. (GBPL/Dave Valdez)

Ellie interrupts Dad during a meeting with General Scowcroft at Walker's Point. (GBPL/Carol Powers)

Uncle Lou—"the Uncle of the President"—and Aunt Grace, 1990. (GBPL)

My mom and dad, August 6, 1988, in Kennebunkport, Maine. (GBPL)

friendly voice saying that he, too, was about to eat lunch and it just wasn't the same without him. Ronnie was so touched, and I'll always remember how much that phone call meant to him."

Meanwhile, Dad and Vice President Quayle kept the Thursday lunch tradition alive.

The vice president would discuss the different Washington personalities with Dad. "He'd like to know what was happening on the Hill, for example, in the House and the Senate," Vice President Quayle related. "Behind the scenes, it would help him in his dealings with these various members. He'd get some personal insights on what was really going on."

When Vice President Quayle would return from foreign trips, he said Dad was very interested in what the various foreign leaders were doing—"other than the big topics that came through our communiqués that we'd always write afterwards. He knew all these people, and it would help him in his role as president to have a better appreciation and understanding of the people involved."

"I always looked forward to that time with him," Vice President Quayle added. "Beyond the substantive things, we'd talk about family and joke back and forth. There were always some light moments, but it was a way to kick back and reflect on what was going on."

★ ★ ★

One of the central hallmarks of Dad's presidency had to be the way he forged personal relationships with his fellow world leaders—and during the transition period, President Reagan and President-elect Bush held a historic joint meeting with the foreign leader who figured most prominently in Dad's national security plans as he was preparing to take office: Mikhail Gorbachev.

Gorbachev had come into office in 1985 and taken the world by storm as a new breed of Soviet leader. He seemed more adept at populist, Western-style diplomacy; he had a sense of humor; and he was promising more openness through his glasnost and perestroika reforms of the Soviet political and economic systems.

Dad had first met President Gorbachev at President Chernenko's funeral when Dad was vice president. The next time they spent time together came in December 1987, shortly after Dad declared his second candidacy for president, when President Gorbachev visited Washington to sign the INF Treaty with President Reagan. This treaty would eliminate intermediate and short-range missiles staged in the USSR and Europe—a globally significant development coming just two and a half years into President Gorbachev's tenure.

At the conclusion of a successful three-day summit, Dad rode out to Andrews Air Force Base with Mr. Gorbachev, and their private conversation was indicative of how far our countries' relations had progressed. "It was possible for us to have a conversation that was unprecedented in its candor and willingness," President Gorbachev told me. "Vice President George Bush told me he wanted 'to look over the horizon,' and so we did."

President Gorbachev recalled how the conversation went:

"In the months to come, I will be mostly working on the campaign," Dad said to him. "If things continue to go well for me and I win big in the first primaries, my nomination will be assured . . . If I am elected, I will continue on the course we've set . . . Years ago, it took Richard Nixon to go to China. Now it takes Ronald Regan to sign the INF Treaty and have it ratified. This is a role for a conservative . . . With the Democrats, you would do well overall, but, as we say here, they don't deliver. Although I'll be very busy campaigning, I would be ready to help on some U.S.–Soviet issues, perhaps troubleshooting."

President Gorbachev replied, "I appreciate what you've said, and I value the spirit in which it was said . . . If you become your country's leader, I hope we'll continue our interaction. It is good that you've made clear this intention."

The two then discussed relations with China and agreed that they would be dealing with it without hidden agendas, without trying "to play a card."

"Later, as president, George Bush adhered to that agreement," President Gorbachev recalled.

A year later, on December 7, 1988, President Gorbachev and President Reagan met at Governors Island in New York Harbor—eight hundred yards off the southern tip of Manhattan Island. The event was a public opportunity for President Reagan to pass the baton of Cold War leadership to Dad, who was president-elect by then.

In his book, *A World Transformed,* Dad recalled being "a bit uncomfortable" about that meeting—in particular, about being placed in the "awkward position" of having to weigh [his] role as vice president against his future role as president. President Reagan had been "extraordinarily considerate and kind" to him for eight years, so he "tried to avoid anything that might give the appearance of undermining the president's authority." To the end, Dad was "determined to be a supportive vice president, one who had been—and would continue to be—loyal to his president."

Sadly, President Gorbachev's visit to the United States was cut short the next day by the news of a terrible earthquake that devastated Armenia and killed at least fifty thousand people.

Into this void stepped AmeriCares, a wonderful relief organization started by Dad's grade school classmate Bob McCauley. McCauley planned to send a plane loaded with medical supplies to Yerevan and called to see if any member of the Bush family would like to make the flight. He felt that such a gesture would mean a great deal to the Russian people. So my brother Jeb and his twelve-year-old son, George P., volunteered to go.

"It was really like being in a different world," my nephew George P. told me. "In terms of the total devastation, I'm not sure I can really describe the amount of pain and suffering that we witnessed. Just about every structure was off of its foundation. There were people literally walking through the street with very little clothes on and starving and it was just—I mean, at age twelve, it was the most graphic thing I'd ever seen in my life."

"With tears in his eyes, the son of President-elect George Bush presented candy and gifts today to brighten the Christmas of children injured in Armenia's earthquake," read the lead paragraph in the *Washington Post* article that Christmas Day. "This is probably the greatest Christmas gift I could give myself or my son," Jeb was quoted as saying, referring to their visit with more than six hundred boys and girls in Children's Hospital No. 3 in Yerevan.

"The best thing about that was Gorbachev telling me afterwards that when Jeb went to church in Armenia and shed a tear there, it did more for the U.S.–Russia relationship than anything I could possibly imagine," Dad recalled. "To me, it just seemed like the compassionate thing to do, and Jeb wanted to do it, as did George P."

Upon their arrival home, Dad wrote a letter to George P.:

> . . . Men are not supposed to cry, says convention; but we do and we should and we should not worry when we do.
>
> When Ganny dies I will cry—my Mom—she's 87 now. She has hurt a lot in the last few years and her bones are very brittle and so in a sense it will be a blessing when she goes to God; but I will cry because I love her a lot and I will miss her. I cried when my Dad died. He was a big guy—bigger than your Dad even. He was strong and principled—and, you know, when we were very little we were a little scared of him though we knew he loved us. When he was sick in the hospital I ran my hand through his hair and it felt different than I thought it would. Isn't it odd?—I cried about that.
>
> I cry when I am happy and I cry when I am sad. But when I saw you and your wonderful Dad in that church in Armenia on Christmas Day I cried because I was both happy and sad. I was very proud of you. Don't ever forget what you saw there. Don't ever forget what you participated in. In less than two weeks I will be President of the United States. I know I will not forget what that little trip of yours meant to people all over the world.
>
> You're a good man Charlie Brown and I miss you a lot . . . Tell your Mom and Dad I love 'em. Devotedly,
>
> Gampy

★   ★   ★

As the weeks went by in the new administration, our family began to adapt to life as the First Family. My brother George was thinking about trying to buy the Texas Rangers baseball team; Neil was looking to get out of the oil business and perhaps go into cable television; Jeb was serving on a few boards; Marvin was doing well in the investment business; and I had just taken a new job with the state of Maine tourism office.

Early in 1989, Mom was diagnosed with Graves' disease, a condition where antibodies attack the thyroid gland and cause the eye muscles to tighten, giving the appearance that the eyes are bulging. Graves' disease is not curable, but it is treatable with either radiation or surgery followed by thyroid hormone replacement pills.

It was bad enough that Mom had to cope with this condition, but Dad was also diagnosed with Graves' disease shortly thereafter—and their dog, Millie, came down with lupus, another autoimmune disease. Neither is contagious.

Given the profound improbability of this happening, experts checked the vice president's residence in case there was something in the water or air there—but nothing was ever found. In fact, the most helpful analysis Mom and Dad got came from my brother George, who called Mom and Dad to suggest that "if they would quit drinking out of Millie's water bowl, it never would have happened in the first place."

During the spring of 1989, Millie also had her first and only litter of puppies—thus fulfilling one of Mom's wishes. On a whim, back during the campaign, my mother had made a list of things she wanted to do someday if Dad lost the election. Along with things like touring the French wine country and going on ocean cruises, Mom listed that she wanted their dog to have puppies. Once Dad won the 1988 election, however, Mom realized that the only thing doable on the list was the puppies, so Millie got "married" to Tug, another springer spaniel, who belonged to their good friends

Sarah and Will Farish. Next thing you knew, a slew of six puppies was frolicking around in the Rose Garden—and it seemed as if the entire White House staff was helping to look after them.

Mom and Dad used shredded newspapers for Millie's bed, but the newspaper ink rubbed off onto the puppies and Mom jokingly complained to the newspaper executives about it. The executives responded by sending over reams of clean, unprinted paper!

Another member of our family who was also adjusting to life with Dad in the White House was our Uncle Lou Walker, my grandmother's brother. Uncle Lou was impressed with Dad's new station in life, and was quite pleased when my godfather, Spike Heminway, had business cards printed up for Uncle Lou announcing him as "The Uncle of the President of the United States."

One time, Uncle Lou and my Aunt Grace were in Antigua with some friends, and Donald Trump's yacht came into the harbor to moor. Uncle Lou came up with the idea of seeing if the group could board The Donald's yacht. Everyone agreed, so they piled into a motorboat and sped off. As they neared the yacht, Uncle Lou started yelling up to the deck, "Ahoy there!"

Getting the attention of one of the crew members, Uncle Lou said, "I'd like to come aboard." When the deckhand inquired who he was, Uncle Lou said unabashedly, "I'm the uncle of the president of the United States and I'd like to come aboard with my friends and see the yacht. Is Mr. Trump there?"

The deckhand then answered the "uncle of the president of the United States": "Shove off, fella."

★   ★   ★

Each time a new president enters office, particular attention is paid among the media, on Capitol Hill, across the country, and around the world to what he does during his first one hundred days. This presidential benchmark was first applied to Franklin Roosevelt, who entered office in 1933 during the height of the Great Depression, a period of genuine national crisis. Since then, however, this "first one hundred days" yardstick has been used in the United States and even abroad to measure a national leader's initial progress.

In Dad's case, his first hundred days could be summed up in one word: bipartisanship. Dad counted among his friends dozens of Democrats on Capitol Hill, including his old friend Sonny Montgomery from Mississippi, House Ways and Means Chairman Dan Rostenkowski of Illinois, and others. It helped a great deal to have friends on the other side of the political aisle when you consider that the Democrats controlled both the U.S. House and the U.S. Senate for all four years of Dad's presidency. Compromise would be essential to achieving any meaningful legislation.

To emphasize his desire for bipartisanship, Dad declared that he wanted his presidency to be known as "the age of the offered hand" in his inaugural address. For much of his first two years in office, both Dad and Congress tried to make good on that pledge.

In his first hundred days, in fact, Dad and Democratic leaders in Congress managed to reach a bipartisan budget agreement, as well as a key bipartisan agreement on foreign policy in Central America.

The former Democratic whip in the U.S. House, Tony Coehlo, recalled Dad's first meeting with the congressional leadership:

> After I was elected majority whip [the third-ranking Democratic member in the U.S. House] in 1987, I started attending these leadership meetings—with the top Democratic and Republican leadership of the House and the Senate meeting with the president, the vice president, the chief of staff, and some cabinet officers but not the whole cabinet.
>
> I'm just a dumb little Portuguese kid who milked cows in California, very poor family—and the first time I walked in the room I was overwhelmed, sitting there at the cabinet table with all these people and the president.
>
> When President Reagan came in, we all stand up, of course. He sat down, the rest of us sat down. Then he reached into his breast pocket and he pulled out some three-by-five cards. And he started

reading from the three-by-five cards. I don't remember the specifics, but I remember him saying, "Good morning. It's nice to have all of you here this morning. Today, we're going to discuss three items. One of them is health . . ." at which point he turned the conversation over to whoever the expert at the table was. President Reagan, that I saw, never led the discussion. He always turned it over to other people.

When the conversation on the first item finished, President Reagan continued referring to his notecards. "The second item is on trade," he said, still reading. "I know that you've put in your own bill—and it's a big bill that you intend to push—but we have some ideas and our own legislation. I hope you will listen to it and hopefully we can have some compromises. Leading the discussion on the trade bill will be Secretary of the Treasury Jim"—still reading, turning over the notecard—"Baker . . ."

I'm just sitting there watching all this, and I don't think I said anything. I was just overwhelmed.

Now skip forward two years, to January of 1989—and the first meeting of the leadership for the government. President Bush walks in, and we all stand up. He sits down, and we sit down. He reaches into his breast pocket, and I'm going, "Oh no." He read some notes, then he put them back into his breast pocket and said, "Now I want to sort of set rules for these meetings, and I hope that you will agree with it. We're going to come here, and let's use the hour effectively. There are some things that I want to discuss with you, and there will be things that I'm sure you'll want to discuss with me. And I will lead these discussions. But don't feel restricted. Let's get into a real dialogue. Let's see if we can solve problems."

At that very moment, he got a round of applause from everybody at the table. It was refreshing. President Bush would make sure he knew the subjects that he needed to bring up, then he'd put them back in the pocket—and we'd start a free-flowing discussion. It wasn't always pleasant. We had our share of disagreements, but President Bush moderated the whole thing, and I always felt we got things done.

It worked so well that first year that one time he called a meeting at five in the afternoon. After we assembled, he said, "When we have these meetings, I hope they can remain confidential.

That's hard to say in Washington; but if we're really going to be effective, we've got to be open and trust our colleagues not to go out and repeat them." Everybody basically agreed with that.

Then the president said, "The reason I'm calling this meeting is because I'm about to do something, and I want to let you know before I do it. The critical thing here is that we keep it confidential to maintain the element of surprise."

President Bush wanted us to know he was going into Panama after Manuel Noriega. The great thing is: not only did everybody support him, but after everybody left that meeting nobody said a word. The operation started the next day, and at the next meeting he was extremely complimentary of everybody. We felt good about it. We felt good that people in the room honored that trust and it didn't get out. After that, people felt freer, more open to say things because they trusted the president and he trusted us.

He was a fabulous leader that way.

Even during Dad's so-called honeymoon period, open, frank exchanges in the Cabinet Room were not enough to keep partisanship from rearing its ugly head on occasion.

For example, while most of Dad's cabinet appointments sailed through to an easy confirmation by the U.S. Senate, one was not so fortunate: Dad's nominee to be the secretary of defense, his 1988 campaign cochairman and longtime Texas ally Senator John Tower. Senate Democrats decided to oppose the Tower nomination, tearing into their colleague based on horrible rumors that Tower was very fond of women and alcohol.

Despite the risk of an early political defeat in the Senate, Dad continued to support his nominee, writing a friend at the time: "I have never seen such a campaign of innuendo, vicious rumor and gossip in my entire life."

In fact, about the best thing to come of the entire Tower nomination was the active, positive support Dad received from Bob Dole, the Senate minority leader, who did everything he could to help lead the fight for Senator Tower. Meanwhile, the ugly attacks prompted the nominee to take the extraordinary step of forswearing alcohol if confirmed. Since they were both staying at the Jefferson Hotel during their respective confirmation hearings, Senator Tower went to Transportation Secretary Sam Skinner's room at 11:00 one Saturday night and asked Sam to witness Tower signing a written pledge that he would not drink alcohol if he was confirmed as secretary of defense.

"Senator Tower said he was going on the ABC Sunday show the next day with Sam Donaldson and was going to announce the pledge on national TV," Secretary Skinner recalled.

Senator Tower then took out a piece of paper where he had written down his pledge, and Skinner agreed to sign it. He noticed there was a second signature line, for Dr. Narva, the Senate doctor.

"After he left, I called Boyden Gray and gave him a heads-up," Sam added. "The next morning I watched as he announced the pledge and took it out of his pocket on national TV. I held my breath hoping he would not mention that I had signed it, and when he did not, I breathed a sigh of relief. I could just imagine what the president would say if he heard that his newest cabinet member had witnessed 'the pledge.' "

Sadly, the Tower nomination was voted down in the Senate on March 9, after which Dad nominated Wyoming Congressman Dick Cheney to replace Senator Tower. Dad had first met Cheney in 1969, when Cheney worked for Congressman Bill Steiger, a second-term House member from Wisconsin. Dad got to know him better when Cheney served as President Ford's chief of staff.

"By 1988, I had just been elected the Republican whip at the House, the Republican leader, and I had planned to spend my career in the House of Representatives hoping to someday be the Republican leader," Vice President Cheney recalled. "Then President Bush came along and asked me to be secretary of defense, and I haven't regretted it for a minute."

"He changed my life." The vice president added:

With the Democrats outnumbering the Republicans on the Hill, it was risky for Dad to take a leading Republican House member out of action, but my father clearly believed Cheney would be accepted by his colleagues—and, more important, would do a great job. Cheney subsequently breezed through the Senate confirmation process, served as secretary of defense throughout Dad's administration, and has since gone on to serve with distinction as President George W. Bush's vice president.

Before the Tower nomination battle even began, however, General Scowcroft began a thorough review of U.S. policies around the world, and found that National Security Council internal policies needed improvement. As the NSC and Dad debated the results, it became clear that Dad was uncomfortable with the formal structure of the NSC.

"He wanted to discuss issues more frankly, without a bunch of back-benchers sitting around taking notes," said Scowcroft, so he set up an informal group, which he called the Gang of Eight. The Gang of Eight was comprised of Dad, Vice President Quayle, Secretary of State Baker, Secretary of Defense Cheney, Governor Sununu, General Scowcroft, a note-taker from the NSC staff, and the chairman of the Joint Chiefs, General Colin Powell.

Dad also encouraged open debate, letting his very strong policy officials argue out something in front of him. Between Scowcroft, Baker, Cheney, and Powell, this was not a group of shrinking violets.

"We would argue with each other and get mad at each other," former secretary Powell told me. "Scowcroft and I would be shouting at each other, and Cheney would be mad at me because I'm supposed to be his subordinate—but I've been asked my opinion and I would say something with which he didn't necessarily agree. But the beauty of it was that even though we would have these disputes and arguments, we never lost sight of the fact that we were a team and we worked for the president. And he was good enough to let us argue in front of him without stopping us and without holding anything against us, and then he'd make the necessary decision."

Dad never micromanaged his Gang of Eight, and he purposely chose people who were compatible with each other. "He selected the team not only because of their knowledge and their skills, but because he knew that he could trust them and that they could work with each other," said General Scowcroft. "That's very rare, because most presidents select their cabinet and their NSC and they have no idea how it will work because they're dealing with people who've never worked together."

This foreign policy review prompted criticism from some in the media that the new administration lacked "vision," and also elicited concerns in Moscow.

"At first, I was somewhat concerned that President Bush's administration took 'time out' to reassess relations with the USSR," President Gorbachev told me. "I still believe that we would have been better off without it, for relations between our two countries were already on a firm foundation, which George Bush had helped to create. There were probably some internal reasons for that pause. Be that as it may, subsequent contacts confirmed that the policy of building up U.S.–Soviet relations would continue."

Chapter 16

GREASING THE SKIDS

"I don't think the Oval Office was ever occupied by someone with a deeper and more nuanced understanding of foreign policy than President George Herbert Walker Bush."
—**Brian Mulroney**

In late February 1989, Mom and Dad made their first major foreign trip together, going to Japan for the funeral of Emperor Hirohito, followed by a return visit to China, then Korea. The presidency is an institution steeped in symbolism, and this particular trip made Dad the first president to travel to Asia before Europe. Whether it was intentional or not, this trip set a new tone reflecting Dad's long-held view of Asia in general and China in particular as emerging world powers.

As it turns out, neither the trip to Japan nor the one to China was free of controversy. For example, when the White House announced Dad would attend the Hirohito funeral, veterans' groups around the country were outraged, citing the emperor's actions in World War II. Of course, Dad was also a veteran; and like the fervent anticommunist Nixon going to China in the early 1970s, my father similarly had the moral standing to go to Tokyo in 1989. Dad

argued that it was the right thing to do. He wrote in his diary the
night of the funeral:

> *My mind raced back to the Pacific. I did think of my fallen com-*
> *rades . . . here I was President of the United States, paying respects*
> *to the man who was the symbol of everything that we hated. A man*
> *whose picture was always shown to keep us all together, fighting*
> *hard. Endless pictures of Japanese soldiers cutting off the heads of*
> *prisoners, or firing the coup de grace against thousands as they*
> *were dumped into the graves alive, all in the name of Hirohito. And*
> *there we were, paying tribute to him, a gentle man indeed.*

Emperor Hirohito had helped democracy take root in postwar
Japan by renouncing his divinity and backing the new constitution;
and over the course of Hirohito's sixty-two-year reign, Japan became one of the world's great economies and one of our strongest
allies. After the emperor's funeral in Japan, Mom and Dad continued eastward to China for a brief two-day visit. It was a warm
homecoming for them, seeing old friends and even returning to
the church where I had been baptized over a decade before.

Actually, I had been baptized in a little church atop the old Bible
Society building, but, happily, the congregation had since grown
so large that they had to move into a bigger space. Mom and Dad
remember that the church leaders and members recalled my being
baptized there, and that they considered me to be a member of
their parish, even though I was not along on the trip. The choir
sang "What a Friend We Have in Jesus," which must have been an
emotional experience for them.

This visit to China also afforded Dad a chance to renew his ac-
quaintance with Deng Xiaoping and to express his hope for im-
proved relations between our two nations. While Dad has been a
frequent visitor to China since leaving the White House—making
some sixteen post-presidential visits to date—this February 1989
visit would be his only trip to China as president. Little did he or
even China's leaders know, but events there would soon spiral out

of control, making official contacts between China and the United States very difficult.

★ ★ ★

In late spring of 1989, I was asked to go on a delegation to Taiwan, as a guest of the Taiwanese government. Dad didn't like the idea of a foreign government picking up the tab for a presidential son or daughter, so he said no. But shortly afterward, he asked me to serve on my first U.S. presidential delegation, going to Paraguay for the inauguration of President-elect Andrés Rodríguez. It was an exciting proposition, as Paraguay had been under the dictatorship of Alfredo Stroessner for thirty-five brutal years. Stroessner had been accused of torturing and murdering his political opponents.

Then General Andrés Rodríguez, the army leader, overthrew Stroessner and won the first multicandidate election in many years. (In fact, a new constitution was adopted in 1992.) So these were hopeful times. Never in my wildest dreams did I think I would visit Paraguay, a landlocked country about the size of California surrounded by Argentina, Brazil, and Bolivia.

Our delegation consisted of Senator Larry Pressler (R-SD), Representative John Paul Hammerschmidt (R-AR), Peace Corps Director Paul Coverdell, Tony Salinas of Texas, Elsie Vartanian of New Hampshire, and Jodie Dwight, my childhood friend from Maine.

Jodie and I stayed at the embassy in Asunción with Ambassador Timothy Towell and his family, who could not have been more gracious hosts. While in Paraguay, we also rode the last wood-burning train; we visited a Peace Corps outpost to view an irrigation project; and we went to an *asado*—a Latin barbecue—at a ranch on the outskirts of Asunción. The ranch was reminiscent of Texas—the same vegetation and landscape. There we were treated to delicious Paraguayan fare with lots of sizzling beef.

In fact, the ranch was famous for raising a particular kind of bull, the pride of this ranch. Jodie and I went on a much-anticipated tour to view the bulls; and when we got there, the bulls were the biggest I'd ever seen. (They were so big their "units" were almost touching the ground.) At that moment, immaturity descended and Jodie and I got the dreaded "giggles," which seems to happen to me at the most inappropriate times. We were able to regain a semblance of control and finish our visit, but it's funny after seventeen years the things one remembers.

Far more important, I remember the inauguration of President Rodríguez—and the feeling of freedom that was in the air that day. The Rodríguez family treated us like family, and our delegation sat in the best seats with family and friends everywhere we went. I remember clearly the parade with the military marching by, the flags and the fanfare. The city was dusty and in need of repair, but ripe for the new administration to begin anew. It was a proud moment of political stability in Paraguay, which still has its struggles today.

★   ★   ★

Meanwhile, Dad took an informal—relaxed, even—approach in contacting his fellow world leaders. From the beginning of his administration, he started working the phones, reaching around the globe to call his fellow leaders, many of whom he knew from his days at the United Nations, from China, and from his eight years as vice president. Dad called nearly two dozen world leaders within days of being sworn in as president, no doubt because he wanted to get to know as many of the new ones as possible on a first-name basis.

"When I first came to work at the National Security Council in 1989, I couldn't believe how often President Bush contacted his counterparts abroad," Secretary of State Condoleezza Rice told me. "He would call someone like German Chancellor Helmut Kohl, for example, all the time—just to say that he was thinking about him after reading how Kohl had won some big vote in the Bundestag [the German parliament] or something like that."

"This had never been done before, and in fact some of the foreign leaders thought they were phony calls at first," said Bob Gates, who served as Dad's deputy national security adviser before being appointed director of Central Intelligence. "It was like somebody saying, 'This is Queen Elizabeth calling.' It took probably a year and a half before we had some procedures smoothed out with some of these other people. It went the fastest with the British and the Germans and the French, but it was really funny some of the time when he would reach out and try and talk to some of these leaders, because they just weren't prepared for him."

For example, former Japanese prime minister Toshiki Kaifu told me that on New Year's Day of 1990, at eight o'clock in the morning, the phone rang in his bedroom. It was Dad. "A Happy New Year to you, Toshiki! We have a custom in our country. We say Happy New Year to family members first and then to our friends and relatives. I wish you the best of luck this year, Toshiki. Barbara asks me to give her best regards to you and Sachiyo." The prime minister recalled, "Wasn't I surprised to receive an unexpected call in such friendly terms! I thanked him profusely."

Earlier, in August 1989, Dad had taken Prime Minister Kaifu to the horseshoe pit at the White House before their first meeting, after sensing that his guest was a little tense. "We had a lot of fun," the prime minister remembers. Dad repeatedly called the prime minister by his first name, but given the Japanese custom of showing deference to elders, Prime Minister Kaifu called Dad "Mr. President." But then Dad said with a smile, "Toshiki, my name is George. Say 'George,' won't you?" He put his arm around Kaifu's shoulder, and the prime minister told me he'd never forget that day.

Dad also got to work on our relations with our European allies—some of which were in good shape, but some of which needed attention. For example, General Scowcroft explained the relationship Dad was heading into with the French: "President Reagan and President Mitterrand didn't get along at all. They disliked each other, and used to play tricks with each other to see who would come in last at NATO meetings and be the poo-bah. It was really quite poisonous."

Early on, Dad told General Scowcroft, "I want to fix that." Scowcroft enthusiastically agreed in principle, but was less certain when Dad proposed inviting President Mitterrand to Kenne-bunkport. General Scowcroft wasn't sure someone as stiff and formal as the French president would enjoy the informality of Kennebunkport—but Dad pressed ahead with his invitation.

Since I was living in Maine at the time, Dad asked me to meet the French and American advance teams several weeks ahead of the visit to show them around Walker's Point and the cottage where President Mitterrand would be staying. On a cold, overcast spring day, I led an army of advance men—it seemed like hundreds of them—to my grandmother's house, which was right next door to my parents' house on Walker's Point. My grandmother's sum-mer house, called the Bungalow, was where the president of France would stay.

The Bungalow is a one-story house with ocean views on all sides, but it is also simple and modest. It was no Versailles, but it was filled with happy memories. It had very few amenities—and a furnace was not one of them. We walked into the house, and since it had been closed up for the winter, it was very cold and damp. The French took one look around and, with eyebrows raised, began talking among themselves in French, making tsk-tsk noises and starting sentences with *Mon Dieu!* Instead of Louis XIV arm-chairs, they encountered a living room full of well-worn summer furniture.

To aggravate an already tense situation: As we walked down a hall to the master bedroom, I showed them the master bath. Sit-ting on the toilet seat was an "extender"—an elevated seat with handles that makes sitting easier for an older person. The French advance man in charge asked me what it was. I tried to explain, in the most delicate way possible, as the man's previously quizzical face soon betrayed his great horror.

Quickly, I moved the tour to the bedroom, where several Frenchmen inspected the bed the president would sleep in. They took one look at Ganny's hospital-style bed—the kind that goes up and down with a remote control—and firmly announced it would not do. It was clear at that moment that I had lost them. They said they would have to arrange for a different bed for President Mitterrand.

When the Mitterrands finally arrived, Mom and Mrs. Mitterrand spent a day in Portland, and I arranged a luncheon for them at the home of Betsy and Chris Hunt in Cape Elizabeth, Maine. After lunch, we took Mrs. Mitterrand out in a boat in Casco Bay—which has literally hundreds of islands, big and small—so she could experience the beautiful rugged coast of Maine. We also went to the Museum of Fine Arts in Portland, where there were many dolls the French had sent as a thank-you after World War II.

Dad and Mom treated the Mitterrands like family. "It was a foreign policy coup," said General Scowcroft. "From that time on, Mitterrand never disagreed fundamentally on anything the president really wanted. We could not have made a better move, because of all the things we had to do with the French in the last days of the Soviet Union—it just couldn't have happened."

Also invited to Maine for this breakthrough visit was Walter Curley, who was set to leave in two weeks for his post as our ambassador in Paris. "It was a weekend of substantive discussions, plus some fun," Ambassador Curly later recalled. "I must admit that if you want to get set up well when you get to Paris, have the president of the United States introduce you in his own house to the president of France with his arm around you. It indicated to the French president and to his senior colleagues my access to the Oval Office and to Secretary Baker. This awareness was extremely useful throughout my term in France."

★   ★   ★

In May 1989, while the administration's strategic review was still under way, Dad sent Secretary Baker to Moscow to meet with

President Gorbachev. It was the first time Secretary Baker had been to Moscow and the first time he would confront a Soviet leader one-on-one. Their agenda encompassed three main topics: Dad's active interest in developing a constructive relationship between superpowers; his desire for a sensible, peaceful resolution to the conflict in Central America (Nicaragua); and the possible timing for a summit meeting between the two superpower leaders.

"The diplomatic mission was crucial to the president because we wanted perestroika to succeed," Secretary Baker explained. Dad was extremely anxious to hear from Baker immediately after the meeting; in fact, he wanted to hear from Secretary Baker even if the secure communications broke down.

Just in case, he told Baker to call him and, if the meeting went very well, say, "It reminded me of a trip to Otto's." Otto's is Dad's favorite place for barbecue in Houston. If the meeting went all right, Dad continued, Baker should say, "It reminded me of a trip to Molina's." Molina's serves excellent Tex-Mex.

"And what if it goes poorly?" Secretary Baker asked.

"Then tell me, 'It reminded me of a tennis game with Bob Murray!'" Dad replied, referring to an old Houston tennis rival of theirs.

Afterward, Baker reported to Dad that the trip had been like Molina's—a good meeting, but we still had some serious challenges to overcome. Given Gorbachev's effective public relations blitz in Europe, Baker was primarily concerned with Dad being upstaged at a pivotal NATO meeting in Brussels three weeks later.

The stakes were high, and not just for Dad.

"Gorbachev may have been out in front of me in Europe," Dad conceded, referring to the Soviet leader's public relations blitz in Europe. "He was already talking about Europe as a 'condominium'—as a house where people could freely move into other rooms, meaning other countries. We were doing our strategic review and getting ready to talk about a 'Europe whole and free.' So we were not ships passing in the night at that point. I think there was confidence that we can move forward together."

At that first NATO meeting, incidentally, Dad was further indoctrinated into the ways of international diplomacy as president. Once all of the leaders were in place for the meeting, they went around the table, and the various leaders made remarks. Chancellor Kohl of Germany started, followed by Britain's Margaret Thatcher, France's François Mitterrand, and Canada's Brian Mulroney. Since Dad was the president of the United States at his first NATO meeting, everyone was looking at him, and he took notes during these remarks.

Most leaders kept their remarks short and to the point, and then the prime minister of Iceland was recognized for his comments. Iceland has no navy, no air force, and no soldiers in NATO. It is a member of NATO because of its strategic location in the North Atlantic. Once the prime minister started to speak, Dad politely resumed his note-taking.

"The prime minister went on and on and on and on, and President Bush looked absolutely exhausted trying to keep up with this guy," Prime Minister Mulroney recalled. "Finally, the secretary-general of NATO banged his gavel calling for a coffee break, and the president came staggering over to see me because we were sitting just opposite. He said, 'Brian, what the hell happened?' I said, 'Well, George, you just learned your first rule of modern diplomacy as president of the United States. The smaller the country, the longer the speech!'"

★   ★   ★

One of the very first public announcements Dad made as president, this one on January 21, was that two of my brothers, Marvin and Neil, were going to make up a tennis match with tennis champions Chris Evert and Pam Shriver that had been rained out in 1988.

"These women, confident of their own ability, have suggested that the Bush boys will not get over two games a set," Dad said on the White House South Lawn to members of the news media. "And yesterday, Chris Evert renewed the challenge. I am absolutely confident that the Bush boys will get over two games a set . . . And there's going to be a tremendous match right here on this tennis court [at the White House] as soon as spring is here."

The day of the renewed match, May 16, Neil couldn't make it, so Jeb was brought in as a wild card. It also rained that day, so they couldn't play at the White House. Dad, ever the great organizer, called up to the Senate and moved the match to the indoor courts on Capitol Hill, in the Dirksen Senate Office Building. Once word of the match spread, a handful of senators—including John Breaux, John Heinz, Thad Cochran, and John Warner—joined the small crowd of spectators.

"What your dad didn't care to admit was that Pam had a shoulder injury and she hadn't played in two months, and I had just come off a layoff of five weeks and I hadn't played," Chris Evert told me. "Pam and I rolled our eyes, and we were thinking maybe that was the price we had to pay to stay at the White House," after a recent weekend visit with Mom and Dad. "We had to play with the boys, who we thought were not going to be good players at all. We thought we would have to be nice to them. Because I said to Pam, should we really try our hardest? She said, 'Let's just see how it goes.' "

Once the match began, the boys quickly took the lead, much to the delight of the crowd. "I didn't realize Marvin had that big of a serve, and I didn't realize that Jeb was that good," said Chrissie. "They beat us two sets. We left the building with our tail between our legs because, honestly, before the match we were thinking about giving them games. Pam and I were red-faced when we left . . . and your dad never lets us forget it."

"After we beat them, Marvin and I vowed not to talk about it in public until after their tennis careers were over, for fear of diminishing women's tennis," Jeb teasingly told me. "Fortunately, we played indoors because the court was a lot faster and it made it possible for us to stay in the game," Jeb remembered. "In fact, we won the first set, lost the second, won the third. The court was very slick, very fast. If we were playing on the court at the White House outdoors, we would have lost because they could have killed my serve—they're great players. They almost won anyway. But the point was: it's not about me or Marvin or Chris Evert or about Pam Shriver; it's about Dad, and how excited he got. It was a great moment for Dad, and the thing that gave him more joy in sports than anything else I can remember."

★ ★ ★

Starting in April 1989 and escalating throughout May, Chinese students began to gather in Tiananmen Square in the heart of Peking (by this time more commonly known in English as Beijing)—not unlike our National Mall in Washington. The students were mourning the death of Hu Yaobang, who had been regarded as perhaps the most liberal or progressive among the Chinese leaders—a sympathetic figure open to the popular desire for political reform.

Meanwhile, a sizable international press corps had started assembling in Peking near Tiananmen Square for a historic meeting between Mikhail Gorbachev and the Chinese leadership in mid-May. Gradually, however, the media's attention was diverted from the summit, focusing instead on the students' demands for reform and their open criticisms of the Chinese government.

The early restraint of the Chinese military in the face of the student protests gave hope that there might be a peaceful resolution between the students and the communist leaders. Anyone who was alive at the time will never forget the sight of the lone, brave student stopping a column of tanks. In the end, however, the Chinese leaders had lost face and deemed the situation no longer tolerable. Appeals for restraint on all sides sadly gave way to violence. On the night of June 3, Chinese troops moved upon the temporary "Democracy Plaza," opening fire and clearing the square.

Dad was as horrified as anyone at this brutality, and needed little prompting to respond. In fact, he led the world in imposing sanctions on the Chinese government—suspending military sales and halting all military contacts. However, while many of the talking heads on TV wanted him to take more drastic action—such as declaring embargoes and cutting off diplomatic relations altogether—Dad felt such actions would only hurt the people of China and set back bilateral relations immeasurably.

"Of course, that was a very traumatic experience in China's history," Dad recalled to Sir David Frost. "It put an understandable strain on the relations between China and the United States . . . Yes, we had some critics . . . Let the critics say what they want, but I think history is going to say we did it all right . . . You don't always look back. You've also got to look ahead. But if we go back to slapping them publicly all the time and confronting them, and accusing them of seeking hegemony—we could put world peace at jeopardy. It's that big."

To avoid aggravating the tragedy, Dad appealed to his seventeen-year friendship with Deng Xiaoping, the chairman of the Chinese Communist Party. My father wrote Deng a private, personal letter outside of the normal diplomatic channels, keeping only one copy for his private file.

The letter reminded Deng of his previous statements to Dad about the need for good relations with the West and his desire to keep China "moving forward." Dad also said he was writing as a genuine *lao pengyou*—or "old friend," as Deng had called Dad years earlier. Finally, Dad told Deng he was thinking of sending a personal emissary, in confidence, to "speak in total candor to you," and asked for a reply outside of bureaucratic channels. He signed off "with a heavy heart."

Within twenty-four hours, Deng had agreed in a personal reply to Dad, and Brent Scowcroft was sent immediately to China.

"The trip was completely secret, because we didn't want at this point anybody to know we were talking with the Chinese," General Scowcroft said, explaining the sensitivities involved. "That would have caused a big public relations brouhaha. So I went over on a military aircraft, a C-141, with aerial refueling so I didn't have to land anywhere and nobody would spot me."

As the U.S. military airplane neared China, however, somebody had neglected to warn the Chinese defense forces that a special emissary was approaching. Spotting this unannounced plane, the forces sent a message into Peking asking permission to shoot it down. That's when the Chinese leadership intervened to save the secret travel party—or at least that's what the Chinese leaders told General Scowcroft and Dad.

"What that trip did was, I think, very important to the future in China," Scowcroft added. "It demonstrated to the Chinese the value we put on the relationship. While we had this crisis between us to which we had reacted fairly sharply, we thought that the relationship was extremely important—and I think it was an extremely important move for the president to make."

Deng died in 1997, and his successor, Jiang Zemin, looked back on that time, telling me: "Even when our bilateral ties suffered certain difficulties, President George Bush could still put the relationship in a strategic perspective and put the overall interests of the two countries above other considerations. Hence, he made important contributions to the maintenance and development of China–U.S. relations."

★   ★   ★

The disturbing, tragic images of the Chinese pro-democracy demonstrators being violently put down were fresh in Dad's mind as he and Mom set off for a nine-day trip to Europe a month later. In Central and Eastern Europe, similar hopes for reform—and the risk of a crackdown—were also in the wind. For Dad, the centerpiece of this trip would be his visit to Poland and Hungary, two nations loosening the Soviet grip on their societies.

Dad and Mom first stopped in Poland, where together they had visited two years prior. The Solidarity labor movement had continued to achieve a great deal of progress on reforms, and Dad and our ambassador, John Davis, had arranged a luncheon at the ambassador's residence in Warsaw attended by Wojciech Jaruzelski, the chairman of the Polish Council of State, as well as Bronislaw

Geremek, a parliamentary opposition leader and Solidarity member. After Dad spoke, both leaders offered toasts.

"It was the first time those two guys had ever sat together," Bob Gates observed. "It was fairly remarkable for him to put the head of the communist government, Jaruzelski, at the same table with one of the dissident leaders. The president showed that he was a great bridge-builder in this respect. Because he engendered such goodwill from all parties, particularly as it relates to Poland, he essentially greased the skids on which the communists were slid from power."

The following day, Dad addressed a joint session of the Polish Sejm and the Senat at the Polish National Assembly building; during the session, the entire parliament sang to him the Polish ceremonial song "Sto Lat": "Good luck, good cheer, may you live a hundred years!" Afterward, General Jaruzelski told Dad that the assembly had never done that for any other visiting world leader—not de Gaulle, not Khrushchev, not Brezhnev. The day after that, Mom and Dad traveled to Gdansk—the birthplace of Solidarity—for a truly memorable lunch with Lech and Danuta Walesa at their home. The lunch was in a tiny house with a breakfast nook; the table was covered with many wineglasses and silver; and the meal was huge. Mom and Dad and their hosts crowded in two to a side so the press could get a picture. Then they left by car to drive to the Gdansk shipyard.

"We could see people lined up alongside the roadway before we got to the shipyard," Mom remembered. "Along the way, Lech would say, 'Oh my God! Biggest crowd ever, bigger than Margaret Thatcher even!' As far as the eye could see there were people. I noticed Peter Jennings on the TV platform and later read the transcript of his program. He said something like, 'Why has President Bush had such disappointing crowds?'"

From Poland, it was on to Hungary. Dad was supposed to speak in the main square in Budapest, and as they pulled in, they saw a sea of people—nearly 100,000 had gathered, waiting patiently in the rain for hours. General Scowcroft was there, as was Condoleezza Rice of the NSC staff. Tim McBride went with Dad into a trailer offstage and discovered that Dad did not have a raincoat to wear. After a few minutes of scrambling on Tim's part, a Secret Service agent stepped forward and said, "Here, the president can wear mine," and offered him the kind of raincoat that can be folded up and carried in a pocket.

With the coat on, my father stepped out onstage with Bruno Straub, the President of Hungary's Presidential Council. The crowd enthusiastically cheered. But then they all stood and waited as President Straub gave a very long, dull speech. General Scowcroft remembers what happened when it was Dad's turn to speak: he took his speech and tore it up in front of the crowd. "He said that this was not the time for this kind of thing—and he just ad-libbed this wonderful short speech. While it was happening, the rain quit and the sun started to come down through the clouds. And the crowd went crazy," General Scowcroft said.

After his remarks, Dad left the stage and began shaking hands with the people in the crowd, with Tim McBride at his side. As he began working the rope line, he saw this elderly woman who was shivering. Dad said, "You're so cold. Here, let me give you my coat."

Tim whispered, "You can't do that, that's not your coat."

A tug-of-war ensued over the twenty-five-dollar raincoat, won by Dad.

"Later, I'm explaining to Agent Robinson why we don't have his coat anymore," Tim said. "And the president wrote the agent a check for the coat, which I'm sure was never cashed. We have a great picture of him in this coat, which he signed and gave to the agent. It was the generosity of someone else's coat."

The Europe trip concluded with drier stops at the G-7 in Paris and the Netherlands.

★ ★ ★

Our family convened in Kennebunkport for the Fourth of July weekend that year, and some mornings, Dad and I would go for a jog and talk. That weekend, I told him that *People* magazine had called and that I was worried that the press would make a big deal out of my divorce. The last thing I wanted to do was become a distraction or burden for Dad. I was relieved when he told me not to pay too much attention to the media interest.

Throughout Dad's presidency, August proved to be a month seemingly reserved for crisis management—highlighted by the Iraqi invasion of Kuwait in August 1990 and the attempted coup in the Soviet Union in August 1991.

August of 1989 proved uneventful by comparison, but productive nonetheless. Before leaving for a working vacation in Maine, for example, Dad signed the Financial Institutions Reform, Recovery, and Enforcement Act on August 9 in the Rose Garden. He had introduced legislation to fix a festering savings-and-loan crisis soon after entering office, and Congress, in keeping with the prevailing spirit of bipartisanship, had followed suit.

"Reagan sort of brushed it under the rug and postponed it, but President Bush pushed for action right off the bat," Boyden Gray remembered. "The economy still dipped into recession, but that was an enormously important piece of work that cleared the decks—allowing the economy to take off in 1991."

The legislative and economic work behind him, Dad—and indeed our entire family—were soon subjected to another, different kind of S&L crisis. Sadly, the same spirit of bipartisanship that inspired Congress to tackle the fallout from 750 failed S&Ls soon gave way to political gamesmanship, with some Democrats paying particular attention to a single Colorado S&L, Silverado, where my brother Neil at the time served as an outside director.

That December, Dad wrote our family friend Lud Ashley saying, "I cannot believe his [Neil's] name would be in the paper if it was Jones and not Bush. In any event, I know the guy is totally innocent."

Eighteen S&Ls in Colorado had failed, not just Silverado. Many more in Texas and throughout the country also failed at that time.

Yet Silverado was the only institution called to testify in front of Congress.

Dad had once felt kindly toward Congressman Henry B. Gonzalez of Texas; but that changed when Gonzalez, chairman of the House Banking Committee, subpoenaed Neil to testify on Capitol Hill—doing everything he could to embarrass and make life hell for Neil.

"They put Mom and Dad—Dad in particular—in a complex position," Neil said. "He's the president of the United States, and his son has been investigated by a federal regulatory agency. There's nothing you can do about it. He could offer his love and his support—which he did—but he couldn't intervene. Everything worked out, but the only thing I regret is how it became such a politicized issue."

The Silverado episode not only showed how complicated it was for Mom and Dad to raise kids in the public eye, it also emphasized how important it was for us to stick together. "Even though we are not physically close to each other, we're a very close family—some would say almost dysfunctionally close—because there is an abundance of unconditional love. There's so much love for our parents, and that love has been shared to the next generation, to us and to our children," Neil said.

★   ★   ★

Dan Rostenkowski, the former congressman from Illinois, first met Dad when they were both young members of the House Ways and Means Committee in 1967. While Dad left the House in 1970, Congressman Rostenkowski stayed on the Ways and Means Committee and became chairman of it during the Reagan years. He and Dad stayed good friends throughout, despite the unlikely match of a rough-and-tumble Chicago pol and my father. Regardless of his gruff exterior, the congressman is a charming man.

One day early in 1989, Dad called him. "Danny, you've got to come down here. I want to show you this place [the White House]. I'll buy you lunch." So he said okay, and soon after, he heard from Treasury Secretary Brady, also inviting him to lunch in his office. Rostenkowski tells the story of his lunch appointment:

> In the Treasury offices they've got these big high windows and you could see the thunder and the lightning and the rain. Nick Brady picks up the phone and I surmise that George Bush is on the line. So I got the phone. He says, "When are you coming to see me? My treasury secretary invites you and you go to his office but you won't come see me. Hang up the phone and come right over here." "Well, can we finish lunch?" I said. "It's raining like an s.o.b. outside." He said, "Come through the tunnel."
>
> I hang up and Nick Brady looks at me and says, "What tunnel?"
>
> So Brady calls the Secret Service, the guy outside the door. "Is there a tunnel between the Treasury and the White House?" "Yes, sir, there is." So he shows us where the tunnel is.
>
> We get over to the White House and we wind up going past the bowling alley and into the janitor's room, and the janitor is sitting there. I said, "How do we get to the president's office?" And he jumped up and said, "Who are you and what are you doing here?" I said, "I'm with Nick Brady, the secretary of the treasury." He recognized Nick Brady, so he took us upstairs, and we finally get to the Oval Office. So we walk into the office and no one is there. Patty Presock told us the president was in that little cubbyhole office around the corner. He's got John Sununu and Jim Baker in there, and I walk in with Nick Brady. George looks at the three other fellows and he looks at me, and he says, "Would you fellows mind leaving me alone with the chairman for a minute or two?" So they get up and they go into the Oval Office.
>
> He stretches over to look and see if they're out of the room. He looks at me, throws his hands up in the air, and says, "Jesus Christ, Danny, I'm president of the United States!" I started to laugh and he laughed and he says, "I've got to show you this place." He just dismissed the three of them and he took me around, showing me the White House.

★   ★   ★

Dad turned his attention to two other top domestic priorities: the war against drugs, which was the subject of his first address to the nation from the Oval Office in September, and the education summit later that month at the University of Virginia.

In hindsight, the education summit was interesting not only for what it accomplished but also because it brought Dad together in partnership with the man who would succeed him in the Oval Office: Arkansas Governor Bill Clinton, who was also then the head of the National Governors' Association.

"This whole school reform effort's been going on for more than twenty years," President Clinton said, looking back, "but it would never have had the legs it had if President Bush hadn't brought us together and supported the process. It was the first major step nationally since Terrel Bell, President Reagan's secretary of education, issued that famous Nation at Risk report in 1984."

President Clinton also recalled an argument his wife, Hillary, and Dad had during the summit dinner that first night.

"She told him that our infant mortality rate was higher than a lot of other countries," President Clinton remembered. Dad disputed Hillary's assertion and said he would look into it.

"The next day—this is so typical of him—he wrote Hillary a note and gave it to me," President Clinton said. "He said, 'Give Hillary this. She was right.' He wrote her a note thanking her for telling him something he didn't know. See, I think that stuff is a sign of strength, not weakness."

★   ★   ★

The fall of 1989 proved a pivotal turning point in the Cold War, a time when Dad's newly revised foreign policy strategy seemed to produce immediate results in Eastern Europe.

America's previous policy toward Eastern Europe, General Scowcroft explained, had been that we supported any of the satellites who stuck their thumb in the Soviets' eyes. For example, during the Reagan administration Romania was our number one satellite, our favorite. That would change.

"What we did was support those nations who were struggling for greater freedom to turn to market economies and to open their political system," General Scowcroft recalled. "So Romania went from first to last, and Poland went up to first place. We tried to encourage Poland, we tried to encourage Solidarity, and along with that, we modified our arms-control policies in an attempt to get Soviet troops out of Eastern Europe, because we thought that the Soviet troops, with their jackboots on the neck of the people, were what was probably keeping the revolution from happening."

Eastern Europe had a history of recurrent uprisings. A vicious cycle tended to play out where the Eastern Europeans would revolt, and the Russians would come in, clamp down, kill a lot of people; it would be uneventful for a while, and then it would erupt again. What Dad and his team wanted to do is keep the eruptions gradual, never to the point that the Soviets would feel they had to crack down. "The problem is," General Scowcroft said, "we didn't know exactly where that point was, but that was our goal: keep things moving in Eastern Europe, but don't give the Russians a provocation to come in."

Reading Dad's diary entry for November 8, 1989, I saw that Dad was sensitive to the criticism from some observers that things were not moving quickly enough in Eastern Europe. Any reaction by the Soviets in Poland, Hungary, or East Germany could change the perception among the American people that things were in fact moving in the direction of democracy. Dad knew that if he put too much of an American face on the internal reforms going on inside those nations, we'd be inviting a crackdown.

Then, the very next day, November 9, 1989, the East German government announced a new visa policy that essentially opened the door to the West. After twenty-eight years, the Berlin Wall "fell" in the sense that it was rendered obsolete by this new immigration policy. More than ten thousand East Germans crossed the border into West Berlin. There were mass celebrations that lasted for days, as people broke pieces off the Wall, danced on top, and crossed through the Brandenburg Gate. East Germany allowed free elections shortly afterward.

"On the day of the fall of the Wall, November 10, 1989, I spoke with President Bush extensively by phone that evening to inform him about the opening of the borders," Chancellor Kohl told me. "I also told him about two large rallies that had just taken place in Berlin: one in front of the Schöneberger Rathaus, which a left-wing mob had disrupted; and another one at the Gedächtniskirche, where 120,000 to 200,000 participants gathered peacefully and joyfully. In an address there, I thanked the U.S. for its solidarity and support, without which this day would never have happened. George Bush seemed highly interested in the events and said he was deeply impressed by the way in which the Federal Republic was handling the whole situation. It was also important to him that I had publicly praised the role the U.S. had played."

Given this dramatic development, there were many voices in Congress urging Dad to celebrate the fall of the Berlin Wall as the triumph of democracy.

"We both felt an overwhelming euphoria—a euphoria that said this was truly freedom's victory," Secretary Baker recalled. "But as a statesman, President Bush wanted to welcome the change diplomatically, almost clinically. He knew that Moscow would be watching our public statements, and watching them very closely. He was determined not to be overly emotional so that Gorbachev and [Foreign Minister Eduard] Shevardnadze would not feel, as the president himself later said, that we were somehow sticking our thumb in their eye."

In fact, according to Dad's diary, President Gorbachev had contacted Dad the day after the Berlin Wall fell to ask that the United States not overreact. Dad took a heap of public criticism for his tempered reaction, and as Secretary Baker put it, "This was an example of how George Bush would always put what's right for America ahead of what's right for George Bush."

"My restraint—or prudence, if you will—was misunderstood,

certainly by some in the Congress," Dad recalled. "Senator Mitchell, the leading Democrat in the Senate, and Dick Gephardt, the leader in the House, were saying, 'Our president doesn't get it. He ought to go to Berlin, stand on the Wall, dance with the young people to show the joy that we all feel.' I still feel that would have been the stupidest thing an American president could do, because we were very concerned about how the troops in East Germany would react. We were very concerned about the nationalistic elements in the Soviet Union maybe putting Gorbachev out. I think if we'd misplayed our hand and had a heavy-handed overkill—gloating, 'We won, Mr. Gorbachev. You've lost, you're out'—I think it could have been a very different ending to this very happy chapter in history, when the Wall came down."

"The fall of the Berlin Wall was not a complete surprise for us," President Gorbachev recalled. "Not everyone, however, was ready for the pace of German unification that the Germans on both sides of the border wanted. West Germany's NATO allies—the British, the French, the Italians—did not want German reunification, particularly a quick one. I understood this from my conversations with Mitterrand, Thatcher, and [Italian Prime Minister Giulio] Andreotti. We, too, had some apprehensions. But I believed that it was morally wrong to continue to insist indefinitely on the division of such a great nation, putting the blame for the past on the shoulders of new generations. All the parties had to act with great responsibility to avoid complications in the process of unification."

It was against this very optimistic historical backdrop that Dad and President Gorbachev met just off the coast of the tiny nation of Malta in December. Dad and his staff were onboard a U.S. Navy cruiser, the USS *Belknap*, while the Soviets were aboard the USSR cruiser *Slava*.

On the eve of the summit, President Gorbachev wanted to accommodate Dad's desire to have the negotiations onboard two navy ships. But, just to be on the safe side, he also made arrangements for a huge passenger liner, *Maxim Gorky*, which was cruising in the Mediterranean, to head for Malta. It was supposed to be a hotel for the delegation and entourage.

The day after their arrival, the two delegations awoke to the rumble and roar of a big storm. The two military ships were being thrown by the waves as though they were tiny boats. Ariel de Guzman, who worked as a navy chef at the time and has served as Mom and Dad's chef and house manager for years, remembered how Dad went up on the bridge of the ship with the captain, watching the ocean swells in the pouring rain.

Suddenly, Dad saw a silhouette of someone out on the bow of the ship. The figure seemed to be holding on to something, struggling to keep his balance and looking down toward the water. Dad asked the captain on the bridge about it. The officer explained that a sailor was standing watch on the bow to make sure the anchor lines didn't dislodge in the rough seas, causing the ship to drift into shallow water and run aground. In fact, he was on a telephone reporting back to the bridge as the "eyes" on the bow.

According to Ariel, Dad "left the bridge and went to meet the telephone talker despite the strong winds and blinding rain. He shook his hand and thanked him for helping keep the ship safe."

President Gorbachev recalled how Dad's qualities—"a serious approach to problems, balanced judgment, and the ability to put reason above emotion"—made their mark at Malta. "When we discussed the most complex issue of that time—German unification—George said, 'We will not do anything recklessly and will not try to speed the unification issue . . . At the same time, the Germans have to think about the time when the Federal Republic of Germany and the German Democratic Republic will be history. In this matter, I will be acting prudently. Let our Democrats accuse me of timidity: I will not be jumping on the Wall, for there's too much at stake here. I will not be tempted to act in a way that's flashy but could have dangerous consequences.'

"I appreciated those remarks, and subsequent actions of President Bush were consistent with them," President Gorbachev reflected.

He added, "The most important thing that I recall about Malta is that it revealed a high degree of mutual understanding and willingness to consider the unique position and interests of each other, as well as the understanding of the immensity of the global problems that required us to join forces. The handshake across the table at the conclusion of the talks was not a mere formality, but a gesture that recorded the fact that our two countries no longer regarded each other as enemies."

Dad's relationship with Mikhail Gorbachev was truly a unique one. "One contrast between our relationship and those that preceded it was the amount of contact I had with Gorbachev," Dad recalled in *A World Transformed*. "I probably had more interaction with him than my combined predecessors did with their Soviet counterparts. I liked the personal contact with Mikhail—I liked him. How many American presidents could say that about the leader of the Soviet Union? Roosevelt or Truman saying that about Stalin? Kennedy about Khrushchev? Nixon about Brezhnev? I know President Reagan felt warmly about Gorbachev, too, but he did not have the opportunities to work as closely with him as I did. Gorbachev and I found we could sit down and just talk. I thought I had a feel for his heartbeat. Openness and candor replaced the automatic suspicions of the past. It was a stark contrast to the dark decades of Cold War we were leaving behind."

Chapter 17

THE RIGHT THING

"George Herbert Walker Bush made the prosperity of the 1990s possible. Without the 1990 budget agreement, you would not have had the prosperity in the Clinton administration."
—*Newsweek* editor **Jon Meacham**

In May 1989, an international panel of election observers led by former president Jimmy Carter and Vatican officials detected massive voter fraud by Manuel Noriega's government in Panama during their national elections. The political and security situation there had steadily deteriorated to the point that, in October of that year, some members of the Latin American press had begun to ask Dad if the time for military action had come. Yet it wasn't until a U.S. marine had been killed, his wife brutalized, and Noriega had declared war against America that—on December 20—Dad lost all patience with Noriega's dangerous behavior.

As the situation escalated in December, however, General Scowcroft was worried how the operation was going to play in Latin America. He told me, "When we went into Panama, normally that would have caused an explosion in Latin America—*big brother in the North is throwing his weight around again.* But before we went in there, your dad had talked to virtually every head of state in Latin America. Not about Noriega and Panama necessarily, but just how they were doing. So while there were some complaints about our unilateral action, it went off without any serious eruption in Latin America. And that is almost unbelievable. That's the way he operated. It was just instinctive for him."

Operation Just Cause was the first time Dad put American troops into harm's way. He has since commented frequently how that decision—which only the president can make—is the most difficult thing a president can do. But Dad knew it had to be done, after all other options were exhausted.

"When I went to him to say we should take out the whole Panamanian armed force," Colin Powell recounted, "he listened carefully, some questions were asked, some issues were raised, and we went ahead and we did it. And he was very decisive."

After seeking refuge in the Vatican embassy for several days, Noriega surrendered to American forces on January 3, 1990—just nineteen days after the Panamanian National Assembly had bestowed the title of "maximum leader" on him. Thereafter, Noriega was brought to Miami for trial on drug-trafficking charges, racketeering, and money laundering. He was subsequently convicted in July 1992 and sentenced to forty years in federal prison.

Two interesting postscripts on Panama: After Noriega's personal possessions were searched, a cardboard gun target with the names Bush and Cisneros written on it was found with several bullet holes in the head region. (General Mark Cisneros was the army commander in Panama, and Noriega obviously hated him as much as he did Dad.) Dad hung the target in his office at Camp David, but it always made me uncomfortable to look at it.

Also, within weeks of the successful Operation Just Cause, Dad met a woman in Cincinnati named Sandra Rouse whose son, Private James Markwell, died on the first day of the battle. On December 18, before the operation, Markwell had written a poignant letter to his family:

I have never been afraid of death, but now he is waiting at the corner. For me, I don't know. I may walk by; he may stop me. I have been trained to kill and to save, so has everyone else. I am frightened by what lies beyond the fog, yet intrigue and curiosity have brought me through my training this far—I must go through the fog whether the other side is a plane ride home for Christmas or the fog never ends. Do not mourn for me. Revel in the life that I have died to give you.

Dad wrote to my brothers and me after meeting Mrs. Rouse and reading Private Markwell's words. In his letter, Dad said, "When I mourn our dead and wounded, when I think of their families and loved ones, I also think of the courage of our troops. I expect I'll remember PFC James W. Markwell as long as I live. I'll remember a loving mother's grief but also her pride in one young, courageous and patriotic soldier."

★   ★   ★

As Christmas 1989 approached, Dad wrote this entry in his private diary:

December 16, 1989

Ellie walked in about 4:00 am—she was sleeping in Bar's little office off our bedroom—and I was aware of her presence. I held out the blanket (we didn't say anything), pulled her in, and then rolled her over into the middle. Millie was already there, so in went Bar, Millie, Ellie and me. I said, "Be quiet, and go to sleep." We really never did go back to sleep, but she didn't say anything. She was a wiggly little thing, but she hugged me and it reminded me exactly of when Robin was sick. It was frightening, it was much the same — her little figure standing there, roughly the same age, equally as beautiful, just walking towards my bed, and standing there, just looking at me . . .

That first Christmas, our family converged on Camp David, as we did every Christmas that Dad was in the White House. Of course, the holidays are supposed to be a joyous time of the year—and we would be celebrating Dad's first Christmas as president—but the truth is, all was not well for me and several others in our clan.

In fact, I was so distraught about my deteriorating marriage, one night I curled up in bed next to Dad and sobbed. Meanwhile, Mom's eyes were still giving her problems because of the Graves' disease; and Ganny's health was not good—she was in the hospital. Then Aunt Nan's husband, Sandy Ellis, passed away, which was hard on both of my parents—and indeed all of us who knew and loved him.

On the positive side, Neil was optimistic about a new business venture; George had just finished his first season as general manager for the Texas Rangers; and Marvin had a great year business-wise, and—best of all—he and Margaret applied to adopt a second child. Their son, Walker, arrived on December 30.

★　★　★

More than just a new decade was dawning as 1989 gave way to 1990. As we moved into the last decade of the millennium, the bloody Russian Revolution of 1917 was also starting to yield to the peaceful revolution of 1989. Everywhere you looked, it seemed, freedom was on the move. Nelson Mandela was soon to be freed in South Africa; and in Latin America, one dictatorship after another was yielding to democracy. Moreover, the formerly jailed dissident leader Lech Walesa would soon be elected president of Poland; while the jailed playwright Vaclav Havel was already president of Czechoslovakia.

In the Soviet Union, 1990 saw an end to the Communist Party's monopoly on power and the birth of modern property rights—two fundamental reforms that would not have been possible even ten years earlier. While the march to freedom seems inevitable now, at the time it seemed anything but that. No one knew what was going to happen next.

The burning international question that Dad confronted in 1990 centered on Germany. The opening of the East German border in late 1989 had raised the possibility of reunification, but how—and when? After all, Rome wasn't built in a day: it had taken forty-plus years for the Soviets and East Germans to establish the institutions and systems used to divide families and isolate East Germans from West Germans.

When the issue of reunification first came up, a critical catalyst in moving the process forward was a dinner that the president and Helmut Kohl had in December of 1989 right after the Malta Summit.

"For me, it was especially important that I be informed first-hand by President Bush about the Soviet-American summit meeting, which had taken place on warships off the coast of Malta," Chancellor Kohl recalled. "George told me that Gorbachev had seemed tense with regard to the German question and thought that the Germans were proceeding too quickly, that I was in too much of a hurry. Bush contradicted the Soviet president and explained that he knew me and knew that I was cautious and would not jump the gun on this. Furthermore, he said that Gorbachev would also have to understand the German side and to accept the emotions the events had triggered in Germany."

Chancellor Kohl continued: "George also shared my view that Gorbachev couldn't manage the tremendous pace at which the developments were unfolding. At the NATO summit one day later, George Bush played a decisive role in assuring that, on the side of the West, a further important step was taken in the direction of German unity. The American president made it clear to our partners in NATO that the United States supported my policy. George Bush's plan was to become an advocate for the German cause and in return to receive our assurance that we would strongly advocate for a united Germany's membership in NATO. Both ideas had my support."

Events moved quickly after that. "The unification of Germany . . . moved so fast that nobody was really in control of it," General Scowcroft said afterward. "But the president, early on, said, 'It's going to happen, and if it's going to happen, it ought to happen fast, and I'm going to put my faith in Helmut Kohl,' and he did. At that time, the Russians were threatening force if there were any moves to unify Germany. The British and French were strongly opposed—nobody wanted Germany unified. President Bush thought it had to be done fast before all this opposition could coalesce and freeze the process or create instabilities which would be fatal for all of us."

Chancellor Kohl could see what others couldn't: he saw an opportunity ahead as the East German communists began to lose their hold, both politically and economically. Within four months of that December 1989 dinner with Dad—in March 1990—there would be free elections in East Germany. And four months after those elections, President Gorbachev—who faced his own grave political problems at home—decided to allow a unified Germany to move forward and join NATO.

On October 3, East Germany was incorporated into the Federal Republic of Germany. After forty-five years, Germany was at last united in freedom.

"The division of Germany was always unacceptable to George Bush," Chancellor Kohl said, looking back at that historic time. "He saw it as a violation of human rights. Thus, he supported wholeheartedly the process of reunification from the fall of the Berlin Wall on November 9, 1989. From the beginning, George Bush stood at the forefront of all of those who supported and encouraged us on our way to unity. We Germans could not have won the unity of our fatherland freely—at least not in the span of one year—if George Bush as president of the United States of America, and with him the American people, hadn't stood firmly at our side."

★　★　★

After separating from my husband, Billy, for a year, I moved to Washington when our divorce became finalized. I wanted to be closer to Mom and Dad. The actual day the papers were filed, Jeb drove with me to the courthouse in Maine.

Not long after, I was renting a small home near Westmoreland Circle in Bethesda, Maryland, trying to decide where to live, when Marvin, who lived in Virginia, gave me a little brotherly advice. He said, "Whatever you do, don't buy a house in Maryland. It's one of the most Democratic states in the country." As usual, I listened to my brother, weighed my options, but eventually bought a home in the Tulip Hill section of Bethesda, Maryland.

In the meantime, I started working at the National Rehabilitation Hospital (NRH) in Washington—which remains one of the greatest experiences of my life. The hospital was built and founded by Ed Eckenhoff, who was paralyzed from the waist down at a very early age. Ed still runs the hospital and knows firsthand what it is like to receive care at a facility like NRH, and he is an inspiration to the staff and clientele alike. I launched my new career in the communications and development office and was working there when Dad signed the Americans with Disabilities Act, ADA, into law. Since then, I have witnessed the monumental effect that the ADA has had on the disabled community.

I loved working at NRH in no small part because Ed and the rest of the staff were very supportive and very discreet. They knew I wanted to avoid any kind of special attention. Despite my efforts, however, I quickly discovered that being the president's daughter in Washington is quite a different story than in Maine. When people started to learn my family background in Washington, suddenly I became very popular—and started receiving invitations from people I had never met. (The second we lost the 1992 election, most of those people disappeared.)

My friend Honey Skinner swears that when I got to Washington, I was on a mission to meet someone—and she may be right. I suppose I wanted someone with whom I could share the excitement of Dad's White House years, but by the same token I wasn't looking to get married right away. In any case, I began to date.

I was lucky in that lots of people tried to set me up with eligible bachelors, but I quickly discovered that dating in college and dating as the mother of two children, one very rambunctious, was quite a different story. It helped that I had the "daughter of the president" thing going for me. In some cases, that got me in the door.

On other occasions, however, I found it necessary to use the revolving door—walking out almost as soon as I walked in. Such was the case in early 1990 when my cousin kindly set me up on a blind date. The prospect and I were to meet at the Old Ebbitt Grill very close to the White House, just across the street from the Treasury Building. It was convenient for me to park on the south side of the White House and walk over, so I breezed in to let Mom and Dad know what I was doing. Dad teased me a little, and Mom was encouraging.

Arriving at Old Ebbitt, I found the man by description, and we had a drink at the bar. It was awkward from the start. He only seemed interested in talking about current affairs and what was going on in Washington. I wanted to tell him about my children, but knew that might be a showstopper, so I engaged in the political and current affairs discussion.

That is, until he said to me, "You know, I think it's ridiculous for your father and this administration to go to South America when the drug cartels are out to get him. Don't you think that's stupid and dangerous?" I was so mad at the rudeness of his question that I stood up, politely thanked him, and told him I had to go. I arrived back at the White House less than thirty minutes after I had departed. Mom and Dad were still there and naturally asked what happened. They laughed—Dad harder than anyone—as I gave a blow-by-blow recap of the failed encounter.

★　★　★

On February 14, before departing for the first-ever drug summit in Cartagena, Colombia, Mom and Dad went out to dinner at one of their favorite local restaurants, the Peking Gourmet Inn. There they enjoyed the house specialty, Peking duck, with George and Laura, Marvin and Margaret, and Dr. Burt Lee and his wife, Ann. Dr. Lee was a New York oncologist whom Dad had asked to be White House physician.

Nerves among the group were somewhat on edge that night, as they had been throughout our family since this particular trip had been announced. After all, in a very real sense, the next day Dad would stand at ground zero with respect to the drug war—not a very safe neighborhood for any president, American or Colombian. Here in the United States, when you mention "the war against drugs," for the most part you are referring to policies—a political agenda. In Colombia, however, this war involves armed guerrillas fighting, killing, and dying on orders from drug lords and cocaine kingpins.

Dad had promised to make fighting the drug problem one of his top priorities, and President Virgilio Barco in Colombia had defied the drug lords and become a courageous ally. On those grounds alone, Dad had to attend this summit, he felt, but he was fully aware of the dangers involved. Just the day before, in fact, the Secret Service had picked up twelve shoulder-fired Stinger missiles near the airport where Air Force One would land in Baranquilla.

As dinner broke up, Dad put his arm around Ann Lee and told her not to worry about Burt. "He said he would make sure I was okay," Burt recalled, "and I remember thinking, 'Hey, I'm the one who is supposed to be worried about him!'" As they walked out of the restaurant, people from other tables expressed their support, saying things like, "Go safely" and "We're praying for you." By the time they got to the door, Dad was choked up by all the support he was receiving.

They returned to the White House after dinner, and when he heard the helicopter landing on the South Lawn, he gave Mom a hug and she told him how worried she was. Then Dad boarded the helicopter which took him to Andrews Air Force Base, where Air Force One was waiting.

The daylong conference on February 15 was held at the Colombian Naval Academy, which sat on a very exposed spit of land extending into Cartagena harbor. Hoping for the best but planning for the worst, Dr. Lee had worked with John Sununu to arrange for an aircraft carrier staffed with military and civilian trauma surgeons to be positioned offshore. At one point during the conference, all U.S. electronic communications went down for over an hour in the middle of the day due to a failure up in Atlanta—not due to some local problem in Colombia. The traveling party, however, never knew this was the cause—they only knew that the phones suddenly went down and never knew why.

Otherwise, the summit went off without a hitch—and the participants issued their "Declaration of Cartagena," a comprehensive strategy to address the drug trade as well as the underlying economic and cultural issues. The day was long and nerve-racking but ultimately successful. (It was a success despite the fact that the final press conference was delayed because one Latin American leader's zipper was stuck!)

"On return, when the F-16s peeled off from Air Force One as we entered U.S. airspace, I heaved one giant sigh of relief," Dr. Lee remembered. "I believe I enjoyed a cocktail at that moment with Jimmy Baker. But did George Bush think about canceling that very important conference because of the danger? Never."

Later, Dad told me, "Just think what a horrible signal it would have sent to all of Latin America if we had canceled out of this meeting."

We were all worried, at various times, about the threats against Dad. Within months of taking office, in fact, the Secret Service had stopped a man who clearly intended to hurt Dad at a speech in Michigan. Such threats are without a doubt the most worrisome aspect of having a family member serving as president, yet it is part of the modern reality of the presidency.

★ ★ ★

Dad has returned to the Peking Gourmet Inn many times since that night before the drug summit. You could say he and Mom are regulars there—when they're in Washington—and the walls are covered with photos of my parents' various meals there. Wagshal's Deli, near their old house in the Spring Valley section of Washington, D.C., and not far from the vice president's residence, has many photos of Dad as well. Early in 1989, Dad and Mom visited a new Tex-Mex restaurant in D.C., the Austin Grill, and thrilled the young owners with all the publicity the presidential visit generated.

Dad's ventures outside the White House bring me to a very special group of people not just in Dad's life, but in the life of any president, as well as their family. Even to this day, Dad will sometimes jokingly refer to them as "the marshals," but the rest of us know them as the United States Secret Service. Dad calls them marshals, incidentally, because back when he was vice president, they had a funny reporter on the plane who would get up and say, "Now all the marshals are going to do this, the marshals are going to do that." No one can remember the reporter's name, but everyone still remembers him calling the agents marshals.

Guarding the president has been the job of the Secret Service since President William McKinley was assassinated at the Pan American Exposition in Buffalo, New York, in 1901.

For nearly a century after that, the Secret Service was a part of the Department of the Treasury. Since 9/11, however, the agents have reported to the Department of Homeland Security. Presidents have always received round-the-clock Secret Service protection, and recently, immediate members of the president's family— including grandchildren—do as well.

Guarding grandchildren has caused quite a few unusual situations, many seeming like they are right out of the movie *Kindergarten Cop*. When Neil's son Pierce was three years old, he had a miniature motorized jeep, which he was allowed to drive around his neighborhood in Colorado. The Secret Service would follow him in their big Suburban SUV, creeping along behind Pierce in his little jeep. His sisters, Lauren and Ashley, remember purposely taking a detour through the woods while skiing. "Most of the agents were big guys, and they'd get tangled in the branches—while we were little and could squeeze through the trees better than they could. That was fun," said Lauren.

When he was little, my son Sam actually hid from the agents at first, constantly trying to give them the slip until they explained to him that they were not there to tell on him to his mom, only to protect his life. Once he realized they were not going to report his every move back to me, he was fine with it. Then, after 9/11, when he was not so little—a senior in high school—Sam viewed the Secret Service as a serious crimp in his style. The agents reminded him that they were only there to protect him, not babysit him. Over time, they became friends. One day, when Sam had come home late the night before, I asked the agents what had gone on. A resounding silence followed. Sam was happy because they kept his confidence and the agents were happy because he allowed them to do their job. And Sam was lucky he had Secret Service, because I was contemplating murder!

Having the Secret Service nearby gave me great peace of mind, but not everyone took solace from them. In fact, while Dad was president, a family in George P.'s class removed their child from the school because the presence of the Secret Service agents worried them.

Speaking from personal experience, the Secret Service agents I have known—those assigned to Dad, or to our respective families over the years—have always been as courteous as they are professional. For this reason, many of them have come to be like family. After all, you spend a great deal of time with them. In one extreme case, our nanny when I first moved back to Washington, Eileen, was so taken with one agent assigned to my children that she ended up marrying him! Sam and Ellie were the ring bearer and the flower girl in their wedding.

There is an undeniable glamour about the Secret Service Protective Division. It's adventurous work; you are always around famous and powerful people; and you travel both extensively and frequently. But there is a harder, less glamorous side to the job that the public does not see: guarding an empty hotel hallway at 3:00 a.m., the endless planning, and the days and weeks spent away from home.

That's exactly what makes the job a considerable burden and sacrifice over time—and Mom and Dad have always been sensitive to that. When they have been in Maine for extended periods of time, for example, they will have the families of the Secret Service agents over to Walker's Point for barbecues, swimming, and boating, as a gesture of thanks.

Mom and Dad also took an extra step during the holiday season.

"During the vice presidency, they would stay in Washington until Christmas Day before they would go to Houston—and that was such a big deal," recalled Special Agent Rich Miller, who headed Dad's detail during part of his presidency. "That way, most everybody could spend Christmas Eve and part of Christmas Day with their families, and I know they did that because they didn't want to take everybody away from their families during that time. Everybody appreciated that."

After Dad became president, they would go to Camp David instead of staying in the White House on Christmas Eve. Since Camp David was guarded by military personnel, almost all of the Secret Service agents on Dad's detail could enjoy at least part of the holiday season with their families.

"That's unbelievable that the most powerful man in the world would think enough of other people to delay his vacation for twenty-four or forty-eight hours just so other people could be with their families," Miller added. "That's why people would do anything for the president and Mrs. Bush."

★ ★ ★

On March 2, RNC Chairman Lee Atwater was speaking at a Washington fund-raiser for Texas Senator Phil Gramm when Lee had a seizure and collapsed to the floor. He was rushed to George Washington Hospital, where Dad's White House physician, Dr. Burt Lee (the oncology specialist), met them.

After seeing Lee briefly, Dr. Lee immediately pulled Sally Atwater aside and told her he had a brain tumor—and had about a year to live. (Sadly, this initial diagnosis proved accurate.)

The news shocked Washington. Lee wasn't even forty years old yet, his wife had just become pregnant, and he was at the top of his profession.

Part of his success, no doubt, was his charisma. For example, the event Lee had put together the day after Dad's inauguration, the Celebration for Young Americans, featured the who's who of rhythm and blues musicians—and had to be the most fun of all the inaugural events. Marvin had emceed that event, and when Dad arrived, he even strapped on a guitar and hammed it up with Lee onstage.

"When he first had the seizure—it was classic Atwater—he had everybody spin it that he was perfectly fine," Ede Holiday, who became cabinet secretary, remembers. "He told everybody in his close-knit circle that he didn't want it known how bad it was. And so everybody spun it for a long time trying to give Lee what he wanted, until it just got to be too hard, of course."

Mary Matalin remembered filling in for Lee, representing the RNC at cabinet meetings: "At one of the first White House meetings I attended, your father sent a note across the cabinet table saying, 'I know how hard this is for you and you're doing a great job. Hang in there.' Bear in mind: I wasn't walking around moaning 'woe is me.' The fact that the president would even consider what my problems were shows how in sync he is with the real world."

Dad continued to stay in regular touch with Lee, even though the progression of the cancer made Lee increasingly inaccessible. It was not just that he was incapacitated, but at times Lee didn't know who he was. He came to the White House for a visit at one point, and Ede Holiday remembers, "I went up and gave him a hug and I honestly think he was so self-conscious that he didn't want anyone to see him like that. And yet he so wanted to show that he could still connect." Through it all, Dad and Dr. Lee kept in contact with him, Sally, and Lee's mother, Toddy.

"What an impact it had on Lee's mother and Lee's wife, who was pregnant at the time, and Lee didn't know," Mary said. To those of us who were there outside the family support system, the president's involvement was the kind of thing we'll never forget." Near the very end of Lee's life, Dad and George went to the hospital together, to say farewell. Dad kissed him good-bye and choked back tears.

As he got sicker, Lee had apologized publicly to his former political opponents, including Michael Dukakis, in a *Life* magazine article. On the day Lee died, reporters asked Dad about Lee's deathbed apology, and he said, "As he took stock of his life, he wanted to make things right, heal some wounds, and that was a very noble thing. And I salute him in death as I did in life."

When I recently asked Dad about Lee's death, now almost fifteen years ago, he replied, "I think his mortality brought it home to him. He knew he was going to die, and he changed and found the Lord. He was a changed man. He saw the light. He was an emotional fellow, but he calmed down at the end and I think he died a happy, contented man."

★ ★ ★

On March 22, Dad was nearing the end of his forty-first news conference—mostly dealing with assistance for emerging democracies in Central America and Poland—when the media asked him for a statement on the subject of broccoli. Dad had recently instituted a total ban on broccoli on White House and Air Force One menus, prompting a series of humorous protests from growers across the country.

As long as I can remember, Dad has hated broccoli. I am not sure if he hates the smell or the taste more. I think it is just a total, complete aversion.

So the media had hit a nerve, and Dad could not contain himself:

> This is the last statement I'm going to have on broccoli. There are truckloads of broccoli at this very minute descending on Washington. My family is divided. I do not like broccoli. And I haven't liked it since I was a little kid, and my mother made me eat it. And I'm President of the United States, and I am not going to eat any more broccoli.

"This was one I felt strongly about, and I had to speak out," Dad later told British journalist Sir David Frost. "In the process, I liberated many four-, five-, six-year-old kids all across this country who shared my hate for broccoli. The good news was the broccoli sales went up. Two huge broccoli trucks appeared on the South Lawn of the White House, along with the second largest concentration of press for any event when I was president. And Barbara dramatically went out because I refused. I thought it would be hypocritical to go out and greet these trucks, you couldn't expect that. And so they said, 'What are you going to do with all this broccoli?' Barbara said, 'We are going to give this to the homeless.'"

Dad's public declaration generated a great deal of interest not only from growers but from other well-intended broccoli supporters as well. One such supporter, a Carlo Cacioppio of Chicago, even went so far as to send Mom a recipe for cream of broccoli that he created. Carlo assured Mom that "if you make broccoli this way, your husband will love it. Even if he doesn't, I'm sure you'll enjoy it."

Sadly, Carlo was wrong. Dad is still decidedly, virulently anti-broccoli; but like Mom, I am very much pro-broccoli and thought you might want to try Carlo's recipe:

Carlo's Cream of Broccoli

2 cups pre-cooked broccoli
3 cloves garlic, finely minced
1/4 cup olive oil
1/4 cup chopped black olives
1 pound spaghetti
1/4 cup shredded provolone cheese
1/2 cup grated Romano or Parmesan cheese
1 cup cream
2 tablespoons chopped parsley

Cut broccoli and sauté with garlic in olive oil. Cook and drain spaghetti, and toss with broccoli. Melt the cheeses with the cream and add parsley. Simmer until smooth and creamy. Combine all ingredients and serve.

★   ★   ★

In April 1989, my brother George had assembled a team of investors and bought the Texas Rangers from Fort Worth oilman Eddie Chiles. George became the general manager of the club and quickly became the public face of the team.

Early in 1990, shortly after visiting the troops that had been wounded in Panama, Dad called George and suggested he get one of the wounded soldiers from the Dallas area to throw out the ceremonial first pitch at the Rangers' home opener. George thought this was a great idea and invited a Navy SEAL named Al Moreno, who had been wounded in the head and was still somewhat paralyzed.

In a note to Secretary Cheney and General Powell, Dad recounted how this moving moment unfolded: "Moreno strides the hill amidst cheers and plenty of tears and opens the game. George said he thanked the Rangers for letting him have the honor. Janie Fricke, country singer, was dissolved in tears and George said he had to choke 'em back too. The crowd gave a long standing ovation to this young hero. Patriotism was alive and well there at the ballpark."

Just as our military's actions in Panama and Kuwait helped to restore faith and confidence in America's fighting men and women, so, too, did Dad want to strengthen the office of the president itself—the institution. He felt strongly that Congress had managed to erode some of the powers and prerogatives of the presidency, and he wanted to help reverse that trend.

That desire was evident when someone on Dad's political team came up with the idea to veto some line items in the budget. Scholars even today disagree whether the president has "line-item veto" authority, but Dad's advisers urged him to show he really was tough and unafraid to take on Congress on spending. That's when they hit on the idea to veto specific projects in the budget.

"There was a lot of political pressure being put on the president from within his own party to assert that the Constitution gave the president the inherent line-item veto," former attorney general Bill Barr, who was head of the Justice Department's legal counsel office at the time, recalled. "One day Boyden Gray and I were sitting together at a ceremony in the East Room. After the program, the president walked over to Boyden and me and commented that he was being pushed hard on the line-item issue. He asked what Boyden and my preliminary views were. I said that, while an argument could be advanced, I did not think, at the end of the day, the position would be sustained, and that I personally was not persuaded this was the framers' intent."

The president replied, "You guys know my view that the presidency has been weakened since Watergate, and you know that I want to strengthen the office, leaving it stronger than when I came to it. But I think it will end up weakening the office to make claims of power that are not well grounded and then get rebuffed. So, as you look at this, remember—I am not inclined to go down this route, unless you guys tell me that you really believe that the Constitution gives me the power."

Dad ultimately decided he did not have the constitutional standing to assert the line-item veto. In fact, after a Republican-controlled Congress gave President Clinton such authority in 1996, and after President Clinton had exercised that power on dozens of occasions, the line-item veto in that form was ruled unconstitutional in 1998.

★ ★ ★

It's interesting: Dad is more of a risk-taker in terms of life choices than Mom, yet it was my mother who found herself having to defend the choices she'd made in life when she spoke to Wellesley College in June 1990. At the time, the undergraduate women were protesting that Mom had been invited as the commencement speaker because she was "the wife of" someone, rather than a leader in her own right. Others would have backed out of the invitation, but not Mom.

I was at Wellesley that day and can attest to the tension in the air. That strain eased, however, when Mom brought another famous "wife of"—Raisa Gorbachev—and talked about following one's own dreams, not the stereotypes of yesterday and today. Then she said, "And who knows? Somewhere out in this audience may even be someone who will one day follow in my footsteps, and preside over the White House as the president's spouse. I wish him well!" The crowd, protesters included, erupted in applause.

Mom also said something that stayed with me: "Whatever the era, whatever the times, one thing will never change: fathers and mothers, if you have children, they must come first. Your success as a family—our success as a society—depends not on what happens at the White House, but on what happens inside your house."

Family first, she was saying, just like Dad always does.

★ ★ ★

During the summer of 1990, our Uncle Lou surfaced on the White House radar screen several times. In fact, two of his funnier antics warranted an actual memo from Jan Burmeister, who handled Dad's personal mail at the White House, to his assistant, Patty Presock, seeking high-level guidance on how to handle one evolving situation:

July 24, 1990

Memorandum for Patty Presock
From: Jan Burmeister
Subject: Lou Walker

Patty, we need some guidance regarding phone calls that have been coming into my office and to Debbie Romash's office regarding Lou Walker.

In June, we received a call from the Airlines saying that a Lou Walker had a last minute change in flight plans that would add a penalty to the total payment to his ticket. Mr. Walker told the Airlines that he was coming to visit the President of the United States and that he was the President's Uncle. He asked that they not bill him the extra charge. The Airlines called us wanting to confirm this.

We told them that, yes, Lou Walker is indeed the President's uncle, but that the President would NOT want any special handling. Just to handle the matter routinely. As a courtesy to the President, they did not bill the extra charge to Lou Walker.

Just last week, Debbie Romash received a phone call from a production company in New York saying they received a phone call from Mr. Lou Walker asking for tickets to "Miss Saigon." Mr. Walker was told that the play would not be in New York for at least a year and that no commitments can be made. Mr. Walker told the production company that he was the "President's Uncle" and that he wanted to have the tickets confirmed since he was bringing the President's Mother to the performance.

Do you think someone is using Lou Walker's name? Do you want to call Mr. Walker, or mention this to the President so he can discuss it with Mr. Walker.

In the future, we will refer all phone calls to you.

Thank you.

★   ★   ★

On July 26, 1990, Dad signed the Americans with Disabilities Act before an audience of invited guests on the radiant, sun-drenched South Lawn of the White House. With the single stroke of a pen, he extended fuller access to the American Dream to 43 million Americans with disabilities who had previously been essentially barred from buildings, transportation, and other means to opportunity. To be sure, that moment culminated years of work and dedication on behalf of so many who believed in this noble cause.

In 1986, Dad personally accepted a report from the National Council on Disability on behalf of President Reagan titled: "Toward

Independence." That report recommended the passage of national, comprehensive legislation that prohibited discrimination against Americans with disabilities—and the ADA was just that. Previous laws and regulations under the Rehabilitation Act of 1973 had addressed discrimination against persons with disabilities by federal agencies and contractors who had business with the federal government, but had "left broad areas of American life untouched or inadequately addressed," as Dad noted in his statement that accompanied that historic bill signing.

The beauty of the ADA is that it gave the business community a certain degree of flexibility to meet the requirements, but there is no doubt that there were indeed firm requirements required of both business and local governments that, today, we now take for granted. For example, municipal sidewalks must be "cut" to accommodate wheelchairs, and new businesses must provide ramps. Furthermore, many metropolitan bus systems today across the country also feature "lifts" to assist disabled individuals. The point is that in countless ways large and small, the bill Dad made law that hopeful day has helped to remake the face of American society—and has gone on to inspire numerous nations abroad.

A number of key leaders paved the way for the passage of such a landmark civil rights legislation: activists such as Evan Kemp, Justin Dart, and Sandy Parrino; legislators like Senators Bob Dole of Kansas and Tom Harkin of Iowa, and House members like California's Tony Coehlo; and White House staffers such as Mike Deland, Boyden Gray, and Bill Roper. Of course, there were countless more who shared in this bipartisan triumph of the democratic process, but space limits prohibit mentioning them all here. Besides, they have already had their reward: seeing their selfless efforts bear legal, federal fruit.

For me, as a new member of the National Rehabilitation Hospital that day, I was truly humbled to witness that awesome moment when my father literally threw open a door of exclusion that had previously shut out so many people. As a staff member—and later, as a board member at NRH—I saw firsthand how the ADA would become a reality, how it would affect real lives, and how it would give hope where none had existed.

Candidly, some conservatives didn't like Dad signing the ADA, but on a personal level—outside of his skillful efforts to end the Cold War without a shot being fired—I cannot think of another act that made me prouder of my father. The ADA was "kinder and gentler" in action. My dad is always willing to "walk the walk," and the fact that the ADA has been so universally accepted today speaks to the vision and collective dedication behind it.

As an avid outdoorsman, Dad was also very committed to passage of the Clean Air Act, with his able general counsel, Boyden Gray, heavily involved. Like the ADA, Dad had promised his support for the Clean Air Act during the campaign; it, too, hit a logjam (this time in Congress), and Dad personally intervened to keep the legislation moving forward.

"That's been a great success," Boyden said, "but it's never gotten the credit it deserves. It was the most sweeping environmental statute ever passed. The benefits from just one part of the bill alone—the acid rain title—are the greatest net benefits of any regulatory program ever in the history of the United States. It was the first use of emissions trading credits worldwide for achieving environmental compliance, and they are similar to what's used in global warming now. It's used in Europe and being studied in Asia. It was a huge, huge success."

That desire to make things work in Washington, however, cost Dad politically when the time came to negotiate with congressional Democrats on the federal budget in 1990. Senator Alan Simpson, then the minority whip under Bob Dole, and one of Dad's closest friends, remembers the negotiations held at a neutral site on the outskirts of Washington:

> It was called the Andrews Air Force Base negotiations, and it lasted for days. Bob Dole would come back and report that we could get things we've never been able to get—things they're still trying to get right now. Structural reform of the budget. Catastrophic health care. He had the full package together. It repre-

sented fifty years' worth of different attitude on spending. But it needed a little sweetener in the form of a tax. The president said he knew he'd get cremated on it. Dole said, "But we're going to go pass this package for you."

Nobody understands that when President Bush agreed to that [budget deal], it was the biggest act of courage that any president had ever done. We had to do this for the good of the country, and the Senate backed President Bush by a huge vote—63 to 37. It was a great bipartisan vote in the Senate. Big vote.

It went to the House, and you ought to see the roll-call vote on that. It was every liberal Democrat and every conservative Republican sticking it in George Bush's ear—liberal lefties, right-wing cuckoos. The Republicans didn't like the fuel tax in the deal, and the Democrats wanted to see him break "Read my lips," so down it went. That was a disaster. Those s.o.b.'s in the House—both sides—just cremated it.

After Republican defections and Democratic gamesmanship in the House had defeated the original budget deal, Dad followed through on his threat to veto the continuing resolution—which was only a temporary fix—and the lack of a federal budget subsequently shut the government down for three days in October. With half a million troops on their way overseas to the Persian Gulf region and Democratic majorities in both houses insisting on a tax increase, however, Dad felt pressured to get a deal done quickly and soon agreed to a new budget deal that raised taxes on the wealthiest Americans and also imposed new charges on tobacco and luxury items. In exchange, Dad got Congress to agree to significant caps on discretionary spending, as well as the single largest deficit reduction package ever enacted.

To announce the 1990 budget deal, Press Secretary Marlin Fitzwater was told to post a two-sentence statement on the bulletin board and not say anything else.

"We weren't able to frame the issue at all," White House Communications Director David Demarest noted. Shortly after the agreement was announced, in fact, David was standing with Governor Sununu when they were approached by Bobbie Kilberg,

Dad's director of public liaison. Bobbie said, "Governor, the business groups are going crazy. What am I supposed to tell them?" Sununu reportedly said to her, "Don't tell them anything."

"And that was our communications," David said.

Many of the agreement's critics suggested that Dad had failed to appreciate the political consequences of breaking his "no new taxes" pledge. Nothing could have been further from the truth. Even before he was sworn in, Dad knew this would be the toughest domestic problem he would face, and there would be consequences for breaking that pledge. Later, in one crucial private meeting leading up to Dad's decision to sign the budget deal, John Sununu said, half in jest, "Remember, there have been lots of great one-term presidents." Dad responded in a half-facetious tone, "I can assure you that is not in any way on my mind."

As Dick Darman, one of the chief architects of the agreement, noted, "We all appreciated that he knew very well that he was taking an enormous personal risk—and that, unlike most conventional politicians, he was willing to sacrifice his own political interest for what he took to be the public good."

Ways and Means Chairman Dan Rostenkowski, who was involved in the budget negotiations, said, "Your dad has to be admired for making the decision that he did, after he made that asinine statement about no new taxes, because, in my opinion, he sacrificed himself when he realized that we were going to have to balance the budget and we were going to have to raise revenue. I used to argue with your dad, saying, 'George, you've got to do this.'"

Senator Bob Dole agreed: "It wasn't that the president wanted to raise taxes, he didn't have any choice. It was either take what the Democrats were going to give us, because they had the majority, or we weren't going to get a budget. We had to keep the country moving, and you get to a point where sometimes you have to accept what the opposition, particularly when they have the majority, give you. So it was a big campaign issue. I never thought it was fair, but some things aren't fair in politics."

Years later, Dad looked back at the tumultuous time. "Raising taxes was a tremendous political mistake for me because I shot a lot of credibility. People said, 'Hey, he said he wasn't going to do it and he did it.' Even the biggest tax-raiser of all, my successor, Bill Clinton, used that to undermine my credibility. So that hurt me very much, my own going back on what I said."

Dad actually handed the Clinton administration an economy that had resumed vigorous growth before he left the White House. During 1992, for example, the economy grew in excess of 3.2 percent, and the last quarter was even stronger at 5.8 percent.

"I wish I had never said, 'Read my lips, no new taxes,'" Dad said to an interviewer years later, "because had I not made it so pronounced, people would say, 'Well, you know, he has to do this.' President Reagan raised taxes several times, but he just kept saying, 'I'm against a tax increase.' And he was very convincing about it, and for some reason, the right wing of our party that still criticizes me for a tax increase has nothing to say about the Reagan tax increase, which is good. I'm not trying to undermine his legacy. I just wish I'd been that good."

Dad continued, "My failure was not being a good enough communicator at the end of my presidency to convince people that the economy had recovered. I needed a couple of quarts of Ronald Reagan to get through the quest for change and the very effective campaign of my opponent that said the economy is in the tank. Not to make the American people believe something that wasn't true, but just to get them to understand the truth. I think I was maybe a couple of quarts low on charisma."

★ ★ ★

As tough as those decisions were and as difficult as politics at that level can be, Dad had fun with the job. Mom had already given him a nickname within our family—Perle Mesta—after the 1950s socialite whose Washington parties drew so many international types that Harry Truman appointed her ambassador to Luxembourg. There was a Broadway show written about her, titled

Call Me Madam, in which Ethel Merman plays the lead and actually sings an Irving Berlin song called "The Hostess with the Mostes' on the Ball." That would be Dad—the host with the most, always putting together guest lists, welcoming people and offering drinks, sending notes afterward.

"He just couldn't bear not to have something going on morning, noon, and night," added Laurie Firestone, Dad's White House social secretary. "If there was an evening free, we were all thinking, 'Oh, great, they finally have a night off.' Not at all. He would call me first thing in the morning saying, 'I see we have a free evening. We've got to do something. What movie can you get over and who can you invite? I'm thinking maybe you should invite X, Y, and Z to a little dinner, and watch the movie.'"

One of the perks of being president is getting to see the latest movie releases—in some cases, even before they are released in public. Helping matters in this regard is the fact that Dad and Jack Valenti, the former aide to Lyndon Johnson who used to be head of the Motion Picture Association, are good friends.

Dad was equally frenetic on the subject of state dinners, hosting a total of twenty-nine over four years—in addition to often having heads of state to the White House for what they called a "working visit." I recently came across a letter from Dad to the guests at table 8 (filled with various governors, business leaders, and VIPs) on the morning after the state dinner for Queen Elizabeth. Apparently, they had passed him a funny note after dinner begging for more dessert:

Dear Table 8:

> *It was a pleasure having you at the Queen's State Dinner. Taken as a whole, your table behaved fairly well. All the silver was accounted for!*
> *But then, horrors! I received a note from Table 8 begging for the chocolate wheels off the dessert cart. Appalling!*
> *I tried to be sure that Her Majesty did not see me reading this appeal you sent me. Down, Table 8, down!*

Next time, though you all seem united, it is better you sit apart.
Sincerely,

George Bush

One of the people at table 8 was Lenore Annenberg, the wife of Walter Annenberg. Mr. Annenberg was the founder of *TV Guide* and owned several television and radio stations, in addition to having served as U.S. ambassador to Great Britain. Mrs. Annenberg was President Reagan's first chief of protocol. In the spring of 1990, the Annenbergs graciously agreed to host a last-minute summit between Dad and the Japanese prime minister at their home, Sunnylands, in Rancho Mirage, California—on only five days' notice. There were bilateral meetings during the day at a nearby country club, and then a formal dinner that night in the Annenbergs' dining room, which seated sixty. "The dinner was quite special because we had a receiving line and we did it just like a mini–White House," Mrs. Annenberg told me. "Nothing like that had ever been done here before. It was exciting."

In addition to state dinners, there were congressional barbecues and weekends at Camp David with guests. Dad liked bringing people together so much, in fact, that he even tried his hand as a matchmaker between eligible bachelors and bachelorettes. In October 1990, for example, he purposely seated my single cousin Grace Holden next to Justice David Souter, who was a bachelor, at a state dinner for the Hungarian prime minister. "The evening was magical and memorable, and Justice Souter was engaging and a delightful speaker," Grace told me afterward. They wrote to each other briefly, and she attended some Supreme Court hearings as his guest, but not much happened after that.

That same month, Dad asked Marvin to "pinch-hit" for him at an event honoring Princess Diana, who was in the United States raising money for one of her charitable causes at the National Museum Building. Dad explained to Marvin that he would sit next to Princess Diana, and they would brief him on all the protocol issues.

"It will be a lot of fun," Dad reassured Marvin. "Margaret can go and Doro will be there and you'll just really have a great time."

Marvin agreed. "I was a little nervous because I didn't fully understand what it meant to be the host, but got a quick education when we showed up at the event itself."

After Marvin cleared through security, someone approached him and said the British ambassador, Anthony Acland, and his wife, Jenny, needed to speak with him urgently. The ambassador's wife, it turned out, wanted to make Marvin aware of a few things.

"First, she briefed me on some of the protocol, which I really appreciated," Marvin remembered. "And then beyond that, she said, 'Her Highness really likes to dance. Just after the dessert is being picked up, you'll hear the orchestra begin to play and at that time that will be your cue that you should ask Her Royal Highness to get up and dance with her on the dance floor.'"

Marvin looked over her shoulder at the dance floor, which was a fairly large space surrounded by many tables.

"I began to feel queasy in my stomach," he continued. "I really didn't quite know how to cope with this except to tell her that I was not going to do that."

Undeterred, Mrs. Acland suggested that dancing with the princess was part of Marvin's responsibility as the substitute host for Dad. Marvin told her he wasn't a very good dancer except for "freestyle dancing," then he asked what kind of dancing Princess Diana was interested in.

"She said, 'It's ballroom dancing,'" Marvin said, "and all I could think back to was the time when Mom and Dad made me go to Mrs. Simpson's dance class on Wisconsin Avenue in Washington. I wasn't very good then, and certainly very little had occurred between the time I was twelve and that particular evening to give me more confidence. And so, the long and short of it, I just ultimately told her that I couldn't do it."

During dinner, Marvin was seated to Princess Diana's left, but she spent the first forty minutes talking to somebody else—fully engaged in conversation. Margaret and I, meanwhile, kept jerking our heads and pointing toward the princess as if to say, "You need to start talking to her." The problem was that the protocol stated that you're not allowed to touch the person. So there was no way for him to get her attention.

"So I waited patiently and had a nice conversation with the person to my left but was ready to expand my horizons a little bit," Marv said. "She finally turned around and asked how I was, and we had a really nice conversation about her young children and about my young children and her life and what her interests were. It was really fun, but as I was speaking to her I started getting a little more nervous about the dance situation, because I wanted to make sure that my message had gotten across clearly to the ambassador's wife."

Just before the dessert course arrived, Ambassador Acland approached Marvin and whispered in his ear that Marvin was off the hook. Somebody else had volunteered to do it.

"Much to my surprise, it was [Transportation Secretary] Sam Skinner," Marvin added. "When the princess came back, she said, 'I understand you didn't want to dance with me.' And I said, 'Whoa. Let's get this story straight. I'm not a very good dancer.'"

The next day, Princess Diana visited Mom and Dad at the White House over tea. When Mom and Dad asked, "How were our kids last night?" Princess Diana responded, "I really enjoyed your daughter-in-law, but your son was quite naughty and would not dance with me."

A month later, Marvin received a beautiful photograph instigated by Dad and signed by the princess. The inscription read "To my reluctant dancing partner. From Diana."

★   ★   ★

That December of 1990, Dad invited me to accompany him on a five-country swing through Latin America—to Brazil, Uruguay, Argentina, Chile, and Venezuela. It was wonderful for several reasons, most of all because I would be able to spend seven solid days with Dad. Adding to the excitement: we traveled on the new Air Force One that had been commissioned by President Reagan.

There can be only one word to describe that new plane: *amazing.*

Air Force One is the name of any U.S. aircraft carrying the president on board, but since 1990 the presidential fleet has been comprised of two Boeing 747s and a 707. Each is highly customized—with medical facilities, sleeping quarters, and a real kitchen—and can fly one-third of the way around the world without refueling. It can accommodate about seventy people, including the president and his staff, Secret Service agents, and the press. The president's private suite is in the front of the plane and includes a bathroom with a shower and an office. Whenever Air Force One finishes taxiing on the tarmac, the plane comes to a stop with the onlookers gathered on the left side of the plane, away from the president's side and closer to the stairway from the door.

Air Force One is equipped with fax machines, copiers, eighty-five phones, and nineteen televisions, which enable people on the plane to watch the president on CNN in the back of the plane as he waves to the crowd and descends the stairs in the front of the plane. The fun part of Air Force One is that you can walk around freely, talk on the phone, or make a copy on the copier—I suppose because it's the safest airplane in the world. I remember one time the stewards prepared grilled beef for a meal in the kitchen, and how odd it was to smell grilled food on an airplane.

It was fun being on Air Force One. Dad and I slept overnight in the front cabin, which has two very comfortable twin beds. It was surreal to tuck in for the night, sleep well, and wake up arriving on another continent. I remember taking a shower the next morning and feeling the plane tilt forward. It suddenly occurred to me that we were getting ready to land, and I was in the shower. You never saw anyone move as quickly as I did at that moment to dry off and dress just in time to arrive in Brazil. I have seen so many pictures of presidents and First Ladies on the top of the staircase on Air Force One, and there I was with Dad that day waving to those who were waiting to meet the American president.

At each stop, we had formal dinners and toasted the presidents of each country. I was often seated next to the host presidents, and found myself clinking glasses with them. As I think back on it, it seems unreal. Somehow it was normal for my dad to be president, but to be in the company of another president seemed incredible. I remember a fun evening with President and Mrs. Luis Lacalle of Uruguay in the coastal resort of their country—in Punta del Este—and I recall jogging with Dad for a couple of miles and then jumping into the ocean together. Dad was managing the Gulf War effort throughout the trip, but one of the most tense moments came when we flew into Buenos Aires for a visit with President Carlos Menem of Argentina.

"The day before George Bush was due to arrive in Argentina, a serious military coup attempt was quickly neutralized by forces loyal to my government," President Menem told me. "In such a critical situation, U.S. security officials suggested that the president's visit be suspended, considering the high risks involved. In spite of this, President Bush—in a gesture that speaks highly of him—made the decision to go ahead with the planned visit, arriving in Argentina as scheduled. That was the first time that I met personally with the president of the United States. From that moment on, an exceptional relationship was born, not only at a personal level but also between our two countries."

Dad invited me to play tennis with him and President Menem, and in a triumph of diplomacy I am very happy to report that the U.S.-Argentina relationship survived my nervous, terrible performance! Aside from the tennis, I loved playing First Lady for a week and came to appreciate even further the demands that go with the position. It gave me a unique perspective on both Mom's and Dad's roles. Suffice it to say my respect for my parents—and all presidents and First Ladies—only increased as a result of this rare experience.

Chapter 18

A Sense of Honor

"I had the privilege of working with George Bush during the first Gulf War. I came to know a wise man, a compassionate man, a man who needed no prodding to do what was right, a man who never shrunk away from the toughest of decisions at the toughest of times."

—John Major

Shortly after midnight on August 1, 1990, two Iraqi divisions comprised of more than 100,000 Iraqi soldiers and seven hundred tanks surged southward into the tiny nation-state of Kuwait and quickly overwhelmed any resistance. The main thrust of the attack was spearheaded by Iraq's elite Republican Guard, while special forces converged on Kuwait City from the Persian Gulf—using helicopters and boats. Within hours, the invaders had established a provisional government and publicly declared Saddam Hussein, the Iraqi dictator, as its leader.

"I was having a drink with a friend in town," General Scowcroft later recalled, "and I got a call from the Situation Room asking me to come back. When I returned around 9:00 p.m., the president was in the White House Medical Office receiving treatment on his shoulders. We talked about what to do, and he decided right there we should notify the United Nations and call for a NATO meeting. I conducted a telephonic NSC meeting that night, and we set up an NSC meeting for the next morning."

Details of the invasion were sketchy that first night. Initial reports suggested that up to two hundred people had been killed in heavy gunfire and that the younger brother of the emir of Kuwait was shot dead while trying to defend the royal palace. The emir himself had escaped to Saudi Arabia. It wasn't until about an hour after Dad and General Scowcroft first spoke that initial reports such as these could be confirmed.

By the time the NSC meeting was held the next morning, however, it was clear that a genuine international crisis existed. Still, it was much too soon to decide on a strategy in Scowcroft's view, so that initial NSC meeting became more of an assessment session—a first chance to examine "where we are" and "what the situation is."

That same morning, Dad was scheduled to travel to Aspen, Colorado, and give a speech on the transformation of the military at the end of the Cold War, so the NSC meeting occurred earlier than usual. Gathered around the Cabinet Room table, Scowcroft remembered how most comments expressed a tone of acceptance: *Well, it's unfortunate, but this is a small country. It's halfway around the world. It's a fait accompli. We can't do much about it, and so what we need to do is adjust.*

When the media were brought in, Dad recalled, "among the forest of boom and handheld microphones, I was careful in my remarks. I condemned the invasion and outlined the steps we had taken . . . I did not want my first public comments to threaten the use of American military might, so I said I was not contemplating intervention, and, even if I knew we were going to use force, I would not announce it in a press conference. The truth is, at that moment I had no idea what our options were. I did know for sure that aggression had to be stopped and Kuwait's sovereignty restored."

After the meeting, Dad and General Scowcroft flew to Aspen. Because they were going to be late, Dad decided they would travel in one of the small government jets that could land at the Aspen airport. If they took the 707, they would have to land in Denver first and switch planes.

"As we flew out there on this tiny jet," Scowcroft recalled, "we were facing each other and our knees were touching. And I was scrambling to revise his speech that he was giving for the fact that there had been a big invasion. And he was already starting to call his colleagues around the world to get their take on the new situation."

On the way out, General Scowcroft confided his dismay at the tenor of the NSC meeting, feeling the situation was much more serious. "The president agreed completely, and right there on the plane he decided that the situation in Kuwait was intolerable," Scowcroft said. "So I said, 'Why don't I start off the next meeting and explain why it's so serious.' And he said, 'Maybe I ought to do that.' I said, 'No, if you did it, you will stifle discussion because it will sound like you've made up your mind. So let me do it, let the discussion proceed. And then it will come out that way.' "

Before Dad delivered his hastily revised speech, however, he went to the Aspen home of Henry Catto—then the U.S. ambassador to the United Kingdom—to make more calls and to meet with British Prime Minister Margaret Thatcher. As luck would have it, Thatcher was already scheduled to attend the same conference held by the Aspen Institute, which would give the two leaders a chance to confer in person just hours after the Iraqi aggression.

Following their bilateral meeting, Dad and Lady Thatcher held a joint press conference.

"I remember sitting on the bed in the Cattos' bedroom with the president on the phone," Scowcroft said. "He talked to King Hussein, Hosni Mubarak, King Fahd, and others. During this time, he was constantly gathering information. Afterward, he and Thatcher gave a good press conference. Someone later put out the notion that Thatcher had to buck the president up—that she said, 'Don't go wobbly, George.' Well, that didn't happen then. That was an entirely different circumstance that happened about a month later." In fact, according to her own memoirs, Prime Minister Thatcher uttered this phrase during a phone call with Dad three weeks later, on August 26. They were discussing the passage of a U.N. Security Council resolution the day before, which enabled the coalition to enforce the embargo against Iraq. "We must use our powers to stop Iraqi shipping. This is no time to go wobbly," she said. She wasn't worried about Dad's resolve—she would have been preaching to the choir—but rather wanted to make sure that the embargo was enforced by the entire coalition.

Dad later recalled how, during their press conference, Lady Thatcher "put her finger on the most important point—whether the nations of the world had the collective and effective will to implement the resolutions of the United Nations Security Council and compel withdrawal and restoration. It would be up to American leadership to make that happen."

Leaving Aspen, Dad and General Scowcroft returned to Washington and spent the following weekend at Camp David. There they met with the NSC principals, including Vice President Quayle, Secretary of State Baker, Chief of Staff Sununu, Secretary of Defense Cheney, Chairman of the Joint Chiefs Colin Powell, Director of Central Intelligence Bill Webster, as well as General Norman Schwarzkopf, who at that time headed the U.S. Army Central Command based at MacDill Air Force Base near Tampa, Florida.

While Schwarzkopf was a newcomer to the NSC inner circle, his military roots ran as deep as any—with a father who also graduated from West Point, served in World War I, reenlisted during World War II, and was assigned to postwar Iran training the national police force there (with young Norman in tow).

Now, some forty years after attending school in Iran, one of Schwarzkopf's biggest responsibilities was defending the oil fields of the Persian Gulf. He had assumed his post as a four-star general in 1988, and one of the first tasks he tackled in his new post was revising and updating the contingency plans for defending against an Iraqi attack. Little did he and his staff know, but within months Dad would call upon them to put that proposal into action.

The NSC meeting at Camp David that initial weekend after the invasion was another conceptual briefing, and again Dad didn't say much. After the NSC team departed, General Scowcroft stayed behind and accompanied the president back to the White House the following day—a Sunday.

The midafternoon summer shadows had only started to streak across the hazy South Lawn on August 5 when Marine One hovered in at 3:00 p.m. Watching on TV, I could see the somberness in Dad's face as he approached the bank of microphones staged near the Rose Garden. I sensed no apprehension, but rather a smoldering intensity in the way he spoke. Dad reflected in his diary:

Although over the weekend I had been thinking about the need to voice my determination to the American people, I had not decided when I should do it. At that moment, I just planned to fill everyone in on the diplomatic steps we were taking and the international reaction. I explained that none of our allies was willing to accept anything less than total Iraqi withdrawal from Kuwait, nor would they tolerate a puppet government. Everyone, of course, wanted to know what measures we would take ourselves to protect Americans in Kuwait, especially in view of Iraqi threats to close down foreign embassies. To this, I answered, "This will not stand. This will not stand, this aggression against Kuwait."

After the press conference, General Scowcroft's phone rang in his West Wing office. General Powell had been watching Dad on TV, and after hearing the sudden declaration, he told Scowcroft, "Well, we'll learn not to leave you two up there alone!"

But General Scowcroft recalls that the decision to set out this firm marker was Dad's—and his alone. Dad had yet to decide exactly how to kick Iraq out of Kuwait—Operation Desert Storm was still five months from commencing—but he knew what had to be done. The status quo, the situation as it existed that late August afternoon, was not acceptable to him anymore.

"No bravado—it was just a calm, quiet way of going about his business," General Scowcroft said. "He didn't pound the table and say, 'You guys fall in line,' or anything. He forged the policy by the power of his persuasion. They all think they came to the same conclusion right off the bat."

★   ★   ★

On August 16, King Hussein of Jordan visited Dad in Kennebunkport. Jordan had sided with Iraq over the Kuwaiti invasion, and His Majesty, a friend of Dad's for years, came to Maine to plead for America's understanding. Marlin Fitzwater recalls the conversation and said Dad was hearing none of it.

"You picked the wrong side," Dad reportedly said.

Then my father started to walk King Hussein down the driveway from the Big House to his helicopter. Suddenly, he stopped next to the Bungalow, shook the King's hand, and said, "My mom has been sick. I want to stop here and see her." Dad walked into the Bungalow, leaving the king to walk alone to his helicopter and the waiting press corps.

Dad was sending a signal that he didn't have time for weakness in the face of aggression.

That same day, the Saudi ambassador to the United States, the distinguished Prince Bandar, and the Saudi foreign minister, Prince Saud, also came to Walker's Point to consult with Dad. After their meeting, as Prince Bandar was likewise returning to his helicopter, my daughter, Ellie, skipped along at his side. Bandar was carrying his worry beads, which were made of onyx and diamonds, and apparently, he was so taken with Ellie that he offered her the beads.

Clearly, Ellie—who was five at the time—could not appreciate what a thoughtful and extremely generous gesture this was, because she took the beads, much to my embarrassment, and promptly threw them in the prickly *Rosa regosa* bushes that lined that section of the driveway. I will never forget the sight of Prince

Bandar, dressed in his splendid white robes, as we waded into the brambles to retrieve the beads.

In order to isolate Saddam and Iraq internationally, a large measure of Dad's success would lie in his personal relationship with the Soviet leader, Mikhail Gorbachev. For years, the USSR had supplied Baghdad all of their weapons systems. It was a major source of influence on the Middle East throughout the Cold War, and the Soviets had a lot of people working in Iraq on that fateful day in August.

"I can remember, at one point, being sent to Moscow to talk to the senior Soviet military leadership, including my counterpart, their defense minister," recalled Dick Cheney, at that time the secretary of defense. "The Soviet military was very reluctant to answer our questions. What we wanted to know was what had they provided to the Iraqis, were there any systems there we didn't know about, did the Iraqis have some capabilities we were unaware of that would be a threat to our troops. Left to their own devices, most of the Soviet military leadership would not have cooperated, but Gorbachev saw to it that they cooperated enough. That was due primarily to the relationship he had with the president."

Dad was constantly on the phone with President Gorbachev, and they also held a bilateral meeting in Finland in September where the two superpowers issued a joint statement calling for Iraq's unconditional withdrawal from Kuwait.

"We did not differ in our assessment of the invasion of Kuwait as an act of aggression," President Gorbachev told me. "Indeed, what happened was that right after the end of the Cold War a greedy and brazen aggressor trampled underfoot a small state, with its huge oil reserves. This kind of behavior could not be tolerated. Our meeting in Helsinki on September 9, 1990, held at the initiative of the president, focused on how to preserve and consolidate U.S.–Soviet partnership in the face of the crisis."

"It is good that the Soviet Union and the United States have shown the world that now, in this gulf crisis, they are together, that they stand side by side," Dad said at that Helsinki meeting.

"I appreciated his willingness to consult with us and his statement that he would not want the conflict to escalate and would prefer a peaceful solution—even though at the time many in the United States were calling for immediate military action," President Gorbachev added. "At the final stage of the crisis, the United States decided that a ground operation was necessary in order to expel Iraqi troops from Kuwait. We, however, were sure that this could be achieved through political pressure, and things were moving precisely in that direction. Nevertheless, I saw it as my main task to preserve what we had achieved in international affairs and in U.S.–Soviet relations. No one, including Saddam Hussein, could drive a wedge between us."

On September 11, 1990, Dad appeared before a joint session of Congress about the Persian Gulf situation, and spoke of a new partnership with the Soviet Union and a "new world order" where "the rule of law supplants the rule of the jungle." The speech was very well received. On the way to the Capitol, Dad rode in his limo with Sig Rogich, who was a special assistant to the president. Sig often teased Dad about his wardrobe, most of which was not to Sig's liking. In the limo, Dad asked Sig if everything was ready for the speech. Sig responded, "We are good on everything, sir, except for your tie."

Dad said, "What do you mean, my tie?"

"It doesn't match your suit, sir, and quite frankly, it's a bit drab and it doesn't send the right message," Sig replied. So Sig switched ties with Dad.

Later, Dad returned Sig's tie, along with a photo of himself in the tie making the historic speech. The inscription read, "When it was all said and done—all in the magnificent House Chamber said as one, 'Look at that tie!' It sent just the right message to Saddam Hussein. Thanks Sig—George Bush."

In early fall, Dad decided he wanted to visit the troops being stationed on and around the Arabian Peninsula. When he set the date for his visit over the Thanksgiving holiday, the Secret Service started working with General Schwarzkopf and his staff to sort out the complicated details.

"I'd been over there two trips before that to work with General Schwarzkopf to help set the trip up," recalled John Magaw, the Secret Service agent in charge of Dad's detail. "It was my job to know exactly what the president and First Lady were going to do, and the military agreed that they wouldn't change the schedule without us [the Secret Service] knowing. But the catch was: the President wanted to interface with the troops. How do you make sure that troops that are in combat one day are mentally okay to face the commander in chief the next?" Specifically, they were worried about all those soldiers with weapons being so near the president.

Schwarzkopf recalled arguing the point, saying, "These are trusted members of the armed forces. Certainly, we're going to go to war, and certainly, I'm not going to go out and take away the weapons of all of the troops that are there. It just doesn't make sense. It would insult the troops."

To solve the problem, Schwarzkopf and Magaw decided to follow the same procedure troops encountered daily at mess hall: they would bring their firearms forward, present them to show they were unloaded, and then stack all the rifles together. All normal procedures.

This time, however, a Secret Service agent dressed in military uniform would guard the weapons.

In the midst of all the planning for security and other scheduling needs, Dad remembered some of the smaller details, too.

"Going through all of these briefings, we were concerned about safety, and the generals were focused on the troops," Magaw remembered. "But at one point, the president spoke up and asked, 'What shoes should Mrs. Bush wear?' The terrain was all sand and very uneven, and he wanted her to be comfortable. I just found that to be so thoughtful, and typical, of him."

Following stops in newly liberated Czechoslovakia and in Germany and Paris, Dad and Mom landed at Dhahran Air Base on November 22, and my father addressed a crowd of air force personnel. Then they hopped into a helicopter with General Schwarzkopf and made the first in a series of flights to visit with troops.

Between stops, Dad and the general discussed the operation to that point, as well as the developing plans for the battle to come. "Through all our dealings, I sensed that he trusted me—just as he trusted Colin," Schwarzkopf reflected. "He trusted the two of us as a pair as far as the conduct of the war was concerned, and he never—ever—interfered, micromanaged, or did any of the things that just drove us crazy in Vietnam."

At each stop, Mom and Dad found the morale of the troops high. Eyewitness accounts all report the same thing: when he got up to give his speech, he maybe spoke five words before all the cheering and hollering would drown him out. During their Thanksgiving dinner at an encampment near Dhahran, moreover, the troops besieged them and took pictures with their little cameras while Mom and Dad both signed autographs like crazy.

The traveling squad next flew out to the USS *Nassau* in the Persian Gulf where Thanksgiving services were held, then back to eat a second Thanksgiving dinner, this time with marines.

"For me, this was a very emotional trip," Dad said. "Looking at the young kids, I knew some of them would be going into combat when the Storm began—and they all looked so young. Aboard the USS *Nassau*, where we attended a prayer service on the top deck, I lost it. The tears of gratitude freely flowed."

"It was just a wonderful and inspiring visit—particularly for the soldiers," Schwarzkopf said, looking back. "In Vietnam, we didn't have a lot of presidents coming over and getting person-to-person contact with the soldiers. This president let our troops know that, from a personal standpoint, he really cared—not as troops, not as a huge army, but as individuals."

During this Thanksgiving trip, meanwhile, a power struggle within the ranks of British conservatives ended with Lady Thatcher's resignation—and the subsequent election of John Major, first elected to Parliament eleven years earlier, who was currently serving as chancellor of the exchequer. Considering the time and effort Dad and his team had invested in keeping such a diverse coalition together, losing a staunch ally like Lady Thatcher at such a critical time—in the midst of delicate U.N. negotiations, for example—was a very tough blow.

"I remember going through London on one of my trips out there and stopping at Number 10 Downing to see Mrs. Thatcher," Cheney said, "and she kicked everybody out of the room and then gave me—oh, an hour, hour and a half talking about the decisions we were going to have to make, how she thought the conflict would unfold, all based on her experience in the Falklands War a few years before that. She was a great ally."

Any apprehension Dad or his team might have felt about the changing of the guard within the British government, however, would be quickly put to rest. Shortly after his election, Prime Minister John Major flew to Washington for an informal meeting, and Dad invited him to Camp David. The foul winter weather grounded all air travel, so the four of them—Dad, John Major, Brent Scowcroft and his British counterpart, Charles Powell—drove in one car.

"We started talking about Iraq and when we would be ready to begin liberating Kuwait," General Scowcroft recalled. "It started as a general conversation, but Prime Minister Major said, 'We need to start thinking about getting ready to go.' He asked the president what time frame he had in mind, and the president said, 'Well, I'm thinking about January 17.' It was dark in the car, but Major didn't hesitate for a second. Here's a brand-new prime minister just entering office, and he's about to go to war."

"John Major never flinched," Dad added. "He never said he had to check with his cabinet or needed more time to consult. Given the circumstances, one could not ask for a better ally or a better friend."

"Ideally, I would not have chosen to be drawn into a military conflict within days of taking office, but I never had any doubt about the justice of the action to be taken following the Iraqi invasion of Kuwait," John Major told me. "Nor was there much doubt in my mind that if Saddam Hussein were left to his own devices, he would turn his attention to Saudi Arabia—and possibly other gulf states—sooner rather than later. It was a clear decision on our part."

As the mid-January deadline drew nearer, preparations—both diplomatic and military—continued at breakneck speed. In November, the United Nations Security Council passed a resolution authorizing the coalition to use "any means necessary" to restore Kuwait's sovereignty. In December, Dad offered Saddam Hussein fifteen dates to meet with Secretary Baker—an offer Saddam eventually refused.

"Saddam never believed I would use force," Dad once told the British journalist Sir David Frost. "Maybe he read the 'Wimp' cover in *Newsweek*. Maybe he was listening too much to the post–Vietnam syndrome in the United States as it surfaced through the lips of some of the senators. Whatever the reason, he miscalculated."

Entering 1991, I could sense the pressure building inside Dad. At times, he seemed lost in thought—as if his mind were elsewhere. He seemed fully aware of the seriousness of the next steps if Saddam Hussein didn't change course, and that lives would be lost.

"One of the things that was great about working with him as president was he had a great sense of humor, and we had a lot of laughs," recalled Bob Gates, who was General Scowcroft's deputy during Desert Shield and Desert Storm. "He always had a way of breaking up the pressure, but that kind of came to a halt in the fall of 1990. He was much more solemn. Clearly, the burden of the decisions that he faced was wearing on him, and so we went through a five-month period—until the spring of 1991—where the old George Bush was replaced by the war president. We all felt those pressures, but it fell most of all on him. So there was a lot less joking around."

Perhaps the most contentious event leading up to the start of the war was the debate over a congressional resolution supporting the war effort. Dad had made the decision right off the bat to seek congressional approval for the coalition's objectives. They already had the support of the United Nations Security Council, but the road to success on Capitol Hill proved a bumpier ride.

A major debate had engulfed Dad's top advisers for months concerning whether the administration should even seek congressional approval if force was needed to reverse the Iraqi invasion. Both Scowcroft and Defense Secretary Cheney argued against it. But Dad had learned a great deal watching President Johnson during the Vietnam War, particularly the way LBJ went to Congress to get the Gulf of Tonkin resolution passed. Dad decided that, whether he legally had to or not, it would be best to have congressional approval for any military action he took.

"He listened to our debate," Cheney said, "but in the end he said, 'No, we're going to go up there and we're going to ask for specific authorization to use force.' It was a close vote, especially in the Senate, but it turned out to be exactly the right thing to do, particularly in terms of, I think, national support for the enterprise. The country really came together behind it. Of course, the vote took place just a couple of days before we actually launched the air force, so it was a courageous step on his part."

It was a great disappointment to Dad that the Senate majority leader, George Mitchell of Maine, made the Senate vote authorizing Desert Storm a partisan vote. In fact, the entire Democratic leadership leaned heavily on its members to defeat the measure. Even Senator Sam Nunn of Georgia, a man Dad respected a great deal on military affairs, voted no. Eventually, the resolution passed 52–47, with only ten Democrats voting in favor of it.

That final weekend before the January 15 deadline, Mom called our family friends Betsy and Spike Heminway and asked them to join Dad and her at Camp David. Spike's job, according to Mom, was to keep Dad busy.

Spike remembered, "She said, 'He's got to make this decision, and you've got to keep him occupied.' So we did everything—horseshoes, bowling, everything. At about four o'clock, however, he said, 'Come on, Spike, let's go take a walk around the perimeter.' So the two of us set out, and at one point I looked at him and there were tears in his eyes. When I asked what was wrong, he gestured to the military police around us and said, 'See these kids? I've got to send them to war, and I don't want to do that.'"

Arnold Schwarzenegger and Maria Shriver were also at Camp David that weekend. On Sunday morning, as everyone filed in for an intimate chapel service, one of the press aides approached the Heminways and asked them to sit in the front row with Mom and Dad.

"'No, no, no,'" Betsy recalled saying. "'Let the Schwarzeneggers sit there. We see them plenty.' But they kept saying, 'No, you sit up there.' We wondered what was so important about us sitting up there, and we later found out it was because there was going to be a picture of the president at chapel that day—the day before they announced what was happening—and they didn't want to have him sitting with 'the Terminator.' They were worried that some weirdo might try to make it an issue."

One interesting sidebar from that weekend involved "the great toboggan run"—make that "the *infamous* toboggan run." After church that Sunday, Betsy and Mom raced out to go down the hill behind Aspen, the president's house at Camp David, before the grandchildren got to the saucers and the toboggan first. They had monopolized them the night before, and the grown-ups thought they could have a run before the kids got dressed in snowsuits. Now, the snow had melted a little the night before and then frozen—so it was ice instead of snow. Seeing Dad and Arnold Schwarzenegger having so much fun, Mom decided she wanted to try it. The toboggan slid down the hill at breakneck speed, heading for the woods.

"I jumped on a saucer and flew, spinning on the ice," Mom recalled. "Dad saw me and yelled 'abort' and 'jump off.' I was so stunned I ended up hitting a tree and had a small break in my leg. I was lucky I didn't hit my head!"

In the aftermath of this domestic disaster, Dad decided he would send Mom off to the hospital with Betsy, while he stayed behind with Arnold. "That was a bad move on my part, something I haven't lived down to this day," Dad said fifteen years later.

A few nights later, Dad and Mom invited Senator Alan Simpson, his wife, Ann, and Lud Ashley to the White House residence for a quiet dinner. When Dad opened the curtains afterward, he could see and hear the protesters gathered just outside the North Lawn fence. Senator Simpson recalled how Dad asked aloud, to no one in particular, "How can they think that I like war? I've been in war. I don't want any more war. But, by God, we can't have this guy just taking over another country."

Dad continued talking to Ann while Mom and the senator walked Millie. Senator Simpson said, "We got in the car afterward and Ann said, 'He's going to pull it. He's going to pull the chain shortly.' When I asked if the president said that exactly, she said, 'No, but I can just tell. He's not going to let this [the Iraqi invasion] happen.'"

Meanwhile, the preparations continued—and Dad gathered as much information as he could. His late friend the widely respected *Time* magazine columnist Hugh Sidey remembered going over to see the Air Force chief of staff, General Tony McPeak, before the air campaign began.

"Do you know where I've been?" General McPeak asked Hugh. "I've been at the White House having breakfast with the president." Dad found out that General McPeak had recently been over to Saudi Arabia and flown a couple of missions in an F-16 with his fighter pilots over the desert. Dad wanted to know what it felt like to be in the cockpit, what the desert looked like down there, and the other preparations.

"I invited Tony to come over because I wanted to know if the air force was ready to fight and if he was as confident as he was a few months before when he had briefed me at Camp David," Dad said. "He assured me we were ready and that our technology would in fact be effective—that our stealth fighters could not be detected by enemy radar. I had a high regard for Tony and was greatly relieved by his upbeat report."

As Dad prepared to announce the start of the war on TV, White House Communications Director David Demarest, who had helped Dad with close to 750 speeches and remarks by this point, found out Dad was writing his own remarks for what he would say to the nation. David later learned that Dad had also asked Dan McGroarty, who was one of David's writers, to sit in the outer office outside of the Oval Office in case Dad needed to check a fact or to help with a line. David candidly confessed to me that he was hurt about that—as the head communications man, he understandably wanted to be sitting out there at this great moment in history.

"Late in the day I get a call, and the president wanted to see me," David recalled. "So I went down to the little study outside his office and he said, 'I'm working on this. What do you think about this line?' I looked at the line and I thought it was fine, but it wasn't anything particularly consequential. Right then David Valdez walked in to take a picture of me and the president working on this speech, and then David left. I went back to my office and I thought, he's intuitive enough to know that I would have wanted to be a part of this day. That was extraordinary, particularly given the moment he was about to experience. That human quality of his always came through."

★   ★   ★

On January 16, I went to the theater with Honey Skinner. As it turned out, the Simpsons were there, too. We had settled in to watch a play when Honey suddenly noticed a Secret Service agent scrunched down at the end of our row, waving at us. It could only mean one thing. "They've bombed Iraq," I whispered to Senator Simpson as we all left the show.

Honey and I left immediately and went to the White House— up to the private quarters, where Dad and Mom and my brother George were gathered. "I remember the seriousness of it," Honey reflected. "I felt personally that I shouldn't be there because I wasn't in your family, but immediately everyone said, 'Are you kidding? Get in here.'"

Billy Graham was there, too, and we watched the beginning of the air war on television. Dad remembers, "I knew exactly what time the bombers were supposed to be over Baghdad and then we were getting a report from Bernie Shaw on CNN, 'The skies are lit up and you can hear it.' I called over to the Situation Room and said, 'What's going on? It's early.' It wasn't supposed to start until later. They checked and said some of the planes had been detected early and they were shooting at them, using defensive antiaircraft artillery to get them."

Dad continued, "I remember walking over to the Situation Room to get the reports from the battlefield, and the reports were good. We didn't lose any planes. Nobody knew how fierce the battle would be, because Saddam had said it would be 'the mother of all battles.' We did very definitive targeting to avoid civilian damages as much as we could. I was worried about all these pilots and crew members going into harm's way, and then out they came in good shape. It worked out pretty well, and it was a very exhilarating time. It was a Saturday. The next day we went to church."

My friend Jodie Dwight and I went to Camp David the next weekend, right after the war started, along with Sam and Ellie. Friday night, Jodie and I went to the helicopter pad to meet Dad—he flew in very late for an intense weekend of telephone diplomacy. It was icy cold, and every star in the sky shone bright and brilliant. We were wearing the army-green parkas with fur-trimmed hoods that are provided in the cabins for the guests at Camp David. The second Dad's foot hit the ground, the marines on duty hoisted the American flag. For some reason, the image of the raising of the flag is just as vivid to me today as the stars were that night.

Few in our family would argue that the six weeks of the air campaign, and the hundred-hour ground war that followed, was the most nerve-racking time of Dad's presidency. Bernie Shaw, the CNN anchor who was holed up in a Baghdad hotel with reporter

Peter Arnett, recalled that Marlin Fitzwater had issued a statement warning all American journalists to leave Baghdad before the bombing began, as there was no way for the U.S. military to protect them. Bernie told me:

> I actually said during our coverage, "I want to thank the White House for the many warnings given us, but obviously we're going to stay here." I did that publicly for a reason—to say thank you, and that we were aware of their concerns, but we're not budging because we thought the story should be covered. But it was awfully lonely as other journalists started bailing out and we were the only ones there.
>
> President Bush called CNN president Tom Johnson to lean on him heavily, saying, "Get your people out of there." He said, "Well, Mr. President, we've got to do our job."
>
> Tom stood his ground and said to your father, "We're going to stay." And the president said, "My friend Bernie Shaw is in there. I'm concerned about him."
>
> When Tom Johnson was editor of the *Los Angeles Times,* he lost two journalists on his watch, so he was very sensitive to journalists being killed. Tom Johnson responded, "We're concerned about his safety and everyone else's safety." And that was [the end of] that conversation.
>
> Then do you know what Tom did? He picked up the phone and called Colin Powell at his office at the Pentagon. Tom asked the general point-blank, "Is the hotel a target?" And Colin Powell exploded, saying, "You're calling me on an unsecured line asking me about classified information." I think Tom said he hadn't heard that kind of cursing since LBJ talked to him.
>
> Tom used to be a right-hand aide to President Johnson, and he and General Powell had first met when they were White House Fellows together. They were friends. And then Colin Powell said, "Bernie Shaw's my friend, too."

It was a difficult time for everybody. Ellen Tolten, who was one of the military nurses staffing the White House Medical Office during that time, recalled, "When Desert Storm started, I remember him saying how he worried about all the soldiers. He wondered what their parents were thinking, and he was up late with a lot of desk work."

Being members of the military themselves, the nurses could all relate. They knew what it was like to be separated from family.

During the war, Dad rarely left the White House except to go to Camp David or Kennebunkport. In fact, he went for sixty-four or sixty-five days without formal travel because of the war. On February 1, however, he visited troops and military families at the Cherry Point Marine Corps Air Station in North Carolina.

"The morale at Cherry Point was sky-high, but the emotions ran deep as I visited with families whose loved ones were halfway around the world," Dad said. "The families were supportive of our objectives, yet all of us were worried about the safety of their husbands, sons, and dads—their wives and daughters and moms."

"One of the things that struck me from my perspective as secretary of defense was the extent to which he had a connection with the troops up and down the chain of command," Vice President Cheney said recently. "On the one hand, he knew what he was asking of them because of his own experience in World War II, because he had been shot down. That degree of understanding and empathy that he displayed for them was very important. They understood what they were being asked to do, and why. They also had great confidence in him that their sacrifice was worthwhile—and that he would not in any way, shape, or form ever treat that obligation lightly."

★   ★   ★

My husband Bobby Koch and I first met in 1990, soon after Iraq invaded Kuwait. I was working at the National Rehabilitation Hospital, and my friend and officemate Heidi Hicks invited me to lunch with Bobby and another friend who was looking for a job on the Hill. Bobby Koch worked for Dick Gephardt at the time, who was the majority leader in the House from Missouri. The lunch was really intended for the friend, but Heidi invited me along.

My first impression of Bobby, to be candid, was that he was good-looking and funny. I had reservations because he worked for one of Dad's political opponents, Dick Gephardt. Heaven only knows what he thought of me.

Time went by, however, and I suddenly began to think that Bobby might not be so bad. I began to talk to Heidi and Tom Nides, Bobby's great friend, about how I might be able to see him again—and we came up with what we thought was a brilliant plan. Since it was Christmas, I would invite Bobby to the White House to see the Christmas decorations. Tom suggested he and his girl-friend Virginia come along—that way it would not be so awkward.

The problem with the plan was that Bobby was nowhere to be found, so I ended up showing Tom and Virginia the decorations without him. It was the first of several foiled plans to get together, until one evening Bobby invited me to dinner. As soon as I accepted, though, the phone rang and it was Dad. He was calling to ask if I would go to the funeral of Peter McKernan, the only son of Governor Jock McKernan from Maine. Peter, who was twenty years old, tragically collapsed during baseball practice at Dartmouth and died nine days later. I admire Governor McKernan and was heartbroken for him, so of course I wanted to attend the funeral.

The only problem was, it was the same night as the much-antici-pated date with Bobby. So I called Bobby and asked him if we could meet at 9:30 p.m., which I'm sure he thought was odd. Following the very sad funeral in Maine, I raced back for our date at Tout Va Bien in Georgetown. The only thing I remember saying was that I loved Italian food, and he very kindly pointed out that we were at a French restaurant. But I do remember thinking he was someone special.

After that, I invited him to the state dinner for Queen Mar-grethe II of Denmark on February 20. Bobby called his friend Tom and asked why I was inviting him to a "steak" dinner, at which point Tom, known for colorful language, set him straight.

"It's a *state* dinner, you idiot," Tom delicately corrected him.

The state dinner was beautiful. My dad had nearly thirty state dinners during his tenure at the White House and saw the importance of receiving heads of states in this way. Bobby came as my date, and it raised some eyebrows among a few people—one of them being Marilyn Quayle, who knew Bobby from the Hill. She came right over to him and said, "What are *you* doing here?"

Mom heard the exchange and marched over and said, "Bobby is our guest, and we're glad he's here," which ended the conversation.

"When the president told me that Bobby and you [Doro] were coming up to Kennebunkport for the first time, he mentioned that Bobby was a Democrat," John Magaw remembered. "We were in the old house up there where the office was, talking about what he was going to do that day. But then he said, 'Listen, none of that matters. All that matters is my daughter's happiness.'"

When Bobby first met the Secret Service agents who were protecting the children and me, the agent said to him, "No horseshit tonight, got that?" What Bobby didn't know was that one time, while I was on a date with someone else, my date thought it would be fun to try and ditch the Secret Service. That night, while Bobby was driving me with the agents following in the car behind us, he made a wrong turn. Worried, he turned to me and said, "Do you think this is what the agent meant by 'no horseshit'?"

★   ★   ★

I am not a military historian, and will leave it to others to analyze the Gulf War and its aftermath. What I remember most, quite simply, is the immense feeling of relief we had when we heard the end of the war could be in sight. The conflict to that point had been as one-sided as it could be; things could hardly be going better; and the national mood was nearing elation. It was a hopeful time.

"My feeling was, we had told our allies and the world that our mission was to end the occupation of Kuwait," Dad recalled. "When forming the coalition, we told our partners we will end the aggression—at which point our mission will be complete and all of us can bring our troops home. This we did. One's word is important in life, especially when it comes to war and peace."

Prime Minister Major agrees that the war ended when it should have: "If we had gone against the U.N. mandate, the coalition would have broken up; we would have gone to war to uphold international law, only to end it by breaking international law; and it would thus have been very many years before the word of an American president or a British prime minister was trusted again in international circles. In essence, we would have won the war but lost the peace. I have never doubted that the president's decision to cease hostilities when he did was entirely right."

"I recall talk of a 'turkey shoot' among the troops," Major added. "Saddam Hussein had withdrawn his professional soldiers from the front lines so that they might encircle Baghdad. In their place, he put little more than young boys with guns in their hands. Neither the president nor myself, nor any of the military commanders, had any stomach for the bloodshed that would be entailed in the entry into Baghdad."

"It was a sense of honor," General Powell said. "We did what we said we were going to do. Maybe we can kill some more people and destroy some more forces, but we did what we said we were going to do, so let's stop. And he was absolutely right. Nobody disagreed with him at the time. There was a lot of second-guessing after the war about how he should have gone to Baghdad—done this, that, and the other—but he was right."

Dad wanted to end Desert Storm with a period, not a question mark, and he got his wish on March 3, when coalition generals from Saudi Arabia, Britain, France, Kuwait, Egypt, Syria, and other nations observed Iraqi generals accepting all of the coalition's conditions for a permanent cease-fire at the Safwan Air Base. General Schwarzkopf accepted the documents offering Iraq's formal capitulation.

At the time of the cease-fire, more than 110,000 coalition air strikes had been flown; 148 U.S. service members had been killed in action, and 467 had been wounded. We mourned those who made the ultimate sacrifice wearing our nation's uniform, yet we also rejoiced that the casualties had not been nearly as high as even the most conservative estimates predicted.

Rich Miller, a Vietnam veteran who at the time was the number two agent on Dad's detail, recalled how Dad started to acknowledge the service of Vietnam veterans in his remarks. "Of course, he saluted the Gulf War vets, which they certainly deserved, but near the end he usually mentioned the Vietnam vets—and I think that was exceptional. He did it several times after that, within about two or three weeks. Finally, I said to him, 'You're always mentioning the Vietnam vets in these speeches, and I want you to know they really do appreciate it.' He replied, 'It's about time someone said something good about you guys and what you did over there.' You talk about leadership and obtaining loyalty from people. Those types of things you just can't describe."

Dad was concerned with ending what he called the Vietnam syndrome. As a congressman in the late 1960s, he saw firsthand the ugly way in which some of the returning soldiers were treated. As president, he was glad to see how our nation had united behind our troops, and he mentioned our Vietnam veterans as much as possible in speeches—often to loud applause.

"It was magnificent for those of us who had been in Vietnam," General Schwarzkopf concurred. "I served two tours in Vietnam, was wounded over there, and was separated from my new wife for a year. But nobody ever said thank you."

That, too, would change.

On June 8, Schwarzkopf and eight thousand troops found themselves marching down Constitution Avenue before 200,000 of their countrymen, leading the Gulf War victory parade along the National Mall. The two-hour march featured bands and a display of weaponry, from the "Scud-busting" Patriot missile to the M-1 tank. An assortment of aircraft that participated in the war effort, including the Stealth F-117, flew overhead. I remember Sam and his cousin Jebby loved the parade, as we all brought the children to watch it from the presidential reviewing stand outside the White House. The boys were especially excited at all the soldiers and military gear on display.

"It was a tremendous celebration of a great victory—a great victory for the right reasons. To every single one of us that was there that day, it was a thrill that we never imagined could have happened," General Schwarzkopf added.

One person not basking in the afterglow of Desert Storm was Senator Alan Simpson. During the conflict, he had taken to the airwaves and roundly criticized CNN's Peter Arnett for his reporting from Iraq throughout the war. Arnett was a seasoned international reporter, and CNN's broadcasting from Iraq was undeniably historic. Even Dad and General Scowcroft tuned in with the battle plans in their lap, following along as if they were watching a TV movie unfold according to the script. Yet, while CNN's Bernie Shaw and John Holliman had left Baghdad early into the air campaign, Arnett stayed behind, and as a result, he had attained celebrity status among his fellow members of the press corps.

Many others, including Senator Simpson and Dad, had a different take on Arnett's performances. In fact, they were outraged by his accommodating attitude toward the Iraqi regime. In report after report, details implicating wrongdoing by the Iraqis were routinely omitted by CNN and Arnett, while even the thinnest evidence hinting at any perceived transgression by the coalition forces was hyped and beamed out to the waiting world. In short, Saddam seemed to get the benefit of every doubt, while the coalition was frequently treated as "guilty until proven innocent."

So Senator Simpson went after Arnett, and a controversy erupted.

"The media tore me to bits for attacking someone they referred to as a hero," Senator Simpson recalled. "I said, 'Hero my butt! He's being put to bed every night by the Iraqi government. He's on television twice a day. He's the only organ of propaganda that Saddam Hussein has, if you can't figure that out. All the others have left—ABC, CBS.' Anyway, I was about as low as whale crap on the bottom of the ocean. I get a call from George, saying, 'How'd you like to go to Camp David this weekend? Come down to the White House about 10:00 a.m., and we'll take the chopper.' I said, 'George, you're at the top of your game, and I'm at the bottom of mine.' He said, 'I'll see you at the White House.' So we're sitting there and he's signing letters, and Barbara is needlepointing. I said, 'George, I am fully aware of what you are doing here.' We went out on the lawn and there are all these signs—'93 Percent, We love George'—people all over, the media. He put his arm around me and said, 'There are all your friends over there'—and he pointed to this big pile of media people. He got me on the helicopter and off we went. The next day, he gets up, reads every paper, watches every television channel, gets all worked up. I said, 'Why don't you quit watching television. You just bitch about it.' He said, 'Why don't you just knock it off? I'm looking for something.' Sure enough, he found the front page of the New York Times that said, 'President and Mrs. Bush with Senator Alan Simpson and his wife Ann,' with a picture of him with his arm around me."

Dad said to Senator Simpson, "That's what I wanted you to see."

Chapter 19

ALMOST A MIRACLE

"There is no precedent in history for a major empire to collapse without there being a major war, and someday George Bush will get the credit he deserves for bringing about a basically bloodless revolution that led to the collapse of the Soviet Union."

—Bob Gates

One of the most popular fixtures during Dad's term was the White House horseshoe tournament. Now, when you think of horseshoes, you probably think of a leisurely pastime played between old friends with the score only a secondary consideration.

Not in Dad's White House.

The family horseshoe historian, my brother Marvin, believes Dad picked the game up during the latter part of his vice presidency—during a campaign trip to Ohio and the National Horseshoe Tournament. The next thing we all knew, a truck was pulling up to the vice president's residence on Massachusetts Avenue with all the ingredients to make a professional horseshoe pit.

After Dad and Mom moved into the White House, they had a pit installed next to the swimming pool. (According to Dad's diaries, on his third full day in office, he began planning where the horseshoe pit would go.) The pit was so close by, in fact, if Dad was sitting in the Oval Office and people were playing, he could hear the clanging of the shoes. Eventually, they set another practice pit up by the basketball court, far enough away from the Oval Office that Dad wouldn't always be tempted to go out and see what was happening. Both were regulation pits with all-weather artificial clay, so if the rains came, the pits could be swept and instantly ready for play.

Before the first match, Dad appointed himself "commissioner of the tournament." He loves to add a tongue-in-cheek ceremonial element like this even with our family tournaments. Then, together with the head usher, Gary Walters, they came up with the different teams—from the vice president's office, the gardeners, the nurses, and so on. Even Air Force One had a team. Then within each team, they would have a play-off to see who the two members of that team would be. As soon as play began, every time you'd walk into the White House there would be a big buzz about who beat who.

Dad and Marvin made up the family team, and during the first couple of tournaments they did pretty well, usually losing in or just before the semifinals. During one magical run, however, Marv and Dad ended up winning the whole thing, beating the housemen, Ron and Lindsey, in the finals. By this time, Dad had anointed himself "Mr. Smooth," and during that last match everyone would scream "Smooth, Smooth" as he approached the pit.

"I don't think I've ever been involved with any sporting event with Dad, or any other endeavor, that excited him more," recalled Marv, who had dubbed himself "Mr. Smooth Jr." "He may have been more excited that day than when he won the Iowa caucus, to put it mildly. He's a very competitive guy, and we had lost a couple of times when we probably shouldn't have. So there was a lot of pressure with so many people out there, and he was just elated."

Win or lose, however, when the finals arrived, Mom and Dad hosted a barbecue by the pool. They invited all the participants to bring a spouse or a guest, and Dad would usually stand up and make a funny speech before the final match. Looking back, Marvin remembers how the tournament boosted the morale of the entire White House staff, particularly during the Gulf War.

"The enthusiasm that he had for that is something that I think really helped him through some of the rough spots in the presidency because he had an opportunity to get out, release some energy," Marvin said. "It also turned that White House from an office into more of a family home because it brought together the ushers, butlers, nurses—all the different constituencies within the White House. To this day, when I go to the White House for a reception or something, someone will usually sidle over and ask if we are going to resurrect the horseshoe tournament. That's because of Dad. In a way, that tournament was not only a lasting hallmark of his presidency—it was also a metaphor for the way he approaches life."

Another morale booster for Dad personally came on July 9, when he welcomed two of his boyhood idols, Joe DiMaggio (the Yankee Clipper) and Ted Williams (the Splendid Splinter), to the White House and awarded them a presidential citation. That summer marked fifty years since the 1941 Major League Baseball season—arguably the most remarkable season in baseball history. That year, DiMaggio had his fifty-six-game hitting streak, and Ted Williams hit .406. For a baseball fan like Dad, that season—and this visit—were pure heaven.

"We arranged to have the ceremony for them on the day that the All-Star Game was played in Toronto," Governor Sununu told me. "When these legends arrived, the president presented the award to them in the Rose Garden, then we got on Air Force One and flew up to Toronto. We were with the president, the vice president, and a bunch of us from the White House just sitting there listening to these guys tell stories. It was a very memorable day."

That same spring brought with it the Great American Workout, an outdoor sports festival on the South Lawn of the White House designed to encourage people to exercise more and live healthier lifestyles. The chairman of the President's Council on Physical Fitness, Arnold Schwarzenegger, was enthusiastically leading the charge at Dad's urging. After the South Lawn event, he took the Great American Workout to all fifty states. Schwarzenegger said, "We would go always to successful schools to have 'fitness summits' and he would always remind me to go to the schools that were failing and to go to the inner-city schools, to the kids that are really disadvantaged. And we would pump them up and encourage them to stay away from drugs and alcohol and gangs. I was motivated by your father to reach out to people that need help." Arnold Schwarzenegger went on to be elected governor of California in 2003.

★   ★   ★

In April 1991, Willard Willowby passed away. Woody, as we all knew him, was a longtime White House doorman who operated the elevator in the private residence. We all loved him, and Marvin and he had gone to a few baseball games together. Dad, Marvin, and I went to his funeral and were touched to see that Woody would be buried with a George Bush button on his lapel. After Woody died, my niece Marshall told us she thought Woody's angel was in the elevator.

About a month after Woody died, Dad gave the commencement address at the University of Michigan in Ann Arbor and returned to Camp David for the weekend. Following a short nap, he went out for a jog when he sensed that something was wrong.

"I was jogging with him," Special Agent Rich Miller, one of Dad's Secret Service detail leaders, recalled, "and as we made our way down the path, he said he had a little funny feeling. So we stopped and walked back to the medical unit. I was fairly new to the detail at the time, and I just remember him sitting there as Dr. Lee checked him. When the doctor made the recommendation to go to Bethesda Naval Hospital, the president looked at me and said, 'Everybody in the world is going to hear about this. We have to think about that part of it.' The doctor said, 'Well, we'll just keep it as quiet as we can,' and I agreed to do the same. Finally, the president told Dr. Lee, 'You're the expert, so let's go.' That's the kind of trust he put in the people around him."

News of Dad's condition immediately leaked out, and when I first heard about it, I was naturally very concerned—I had no idea what an "atrial fibrillation" was. It is a condition where the heart muscles get out of sync, and as a result blood does not move efficiently through the heart. In fact, even today Dad's heart is not in "sinus rhythm," or what doctors consider normal. Yet they do not worry about this condition. He takes a blood-thinning drug called Coumadin and a few other medications, and, in his words, he feels like a "spring colt."

As it was, Mom stayed with Dad in the hospital that first night, and when I talked to him the next morning, he sounded like his old self. At Bethesda Mary Jackson, a military nurse assigned to the White House, was at Dad's side waiting to see if his heart would return to sinus rhythm when Dad complained of gas pains. Mary told him simply "Let 'er rip, Mr. President." Dad has never let her forget those immortal words.

★   ★   ★

On May 14, Queen Elizabeth and Prince Philip of the United Kingdom visited the White House for a formal state visit. Because of the traditional formality of the British throne, the visit was closely watched by the high society set.

Unfortunately, one small but important detail was neglected during the arrival ceremony.

"This was Joseph Reed [chief of protocol] making a real diplomatic bungle in the fact that I miscalculated in basic arithmetic," Joseph recalled. "George Bush is well over six feet tall, while Queen Elizabeth is five foot four. Yes, I put them at the same podium, and when Queen Elizabeth went to the podium to give her speech, all you could see of her was a hat in the shape of a 'boater' bobbing up and down."

The peculiar sight of Her Royal Highness almost totally obscured by "the blue goose," or the presidential podium, created a monumental furor with the press corps, who started referring to it as "the talking-hat incident." Dad telephoned Joseph over at Blair House and teased, "Joseph, you're in trouble. Barbara's mad at you, and you're going to take the fall!"

Joseph replied, "Sir, that's why you hired me." As a good chief of protocol, he took the blame for his blunder and then went on with the business of state. [The truth is that he had told Dad to pull out a stand on the podium after he spoke and before the Queen's speech, but Dad had forgotten.]

The formal state dinner that night was Washington at its black-tie best, but my brother George managed to inject a little humor into Her Majesty's evening. Wearing cowboy boots, he sidled up to the queen and declared, "I'm the black sheep in my family. Do you have any in yours?" Not Mom's idea of protocol.

★   ★   ★

On September 27, 1991, Dad's friend and former spokesman Pete Teeley jumped into a taxi and rushed to the hospital for an emergency appendectomy. All month long, he had felt a dull pain in the right side of his abdomen and finally had Burt Lee, Dad's doctor and an oncology specialist formerly with Sloan Kettering in New York, check it out. The doctor discovered that Pete's appendix was inflamed, and needed to come out right away. Pete packed an overnight bag, thinking his stay at the hospital would be a short one.

When the doctors went in to take out the appendix, however, they discovered a big tumor sitting underneath the appendix that had actually caused the inflammation. That night, they removed sixteen inches of Pete's colon.

The diagnosis was not encouraging: Pete had stage III colon cancer, and doctors gave him a fifty-fifty chance of survival. Making matters worse, he nearly died on the table during a second surgery, and he ended up in intensive care for ten days. Things were touch and go. The word got to Dad that Pete was dying and that he was not getting the best medical care.

Pete remembered: "So the next day, the president called the hospital and basically said, 'I'm sending over one of my personal physicians, and I want him to have access to Pete's files.' The nurses told me after that call, everything changed. All of my medicines changed, and that's when I started getting better. If I hadn't known George Bush, there's a good chance I wouldn't be here today.

"Here I am in intensive care, on a respirator, with all these tubes coming out," Pete said. "The phone rings, the nurse picks it up, and she's on the phone for a second. Then she puts her hands over the phone and says, 'It's the president of the United States. I can't talk to him. I'm too frightened.' All of the nurses were begging off, when finally the one who confessed she was a Democrat talked to him."

Mom visited Pete a few days later and declared him on his way to a recovery when she found him watching the Clarence Thomas confirmation hearings on TV. Thankfully, Pete went on to survive his cancer and write *The Complete Cancer Survival Guide.*

★   ★   ★

On Monday, July 1, Dad had stepped out of his office at Walker's Point and announced that he was nominating Judge Clarence Thomas of the U.S. Court of Appeals for the District of Columbia to succeed Justice Thurgood Marshall on the U.S. Supreme Court.

Even before the announcement was made, Ben Hooks of the National Association for the Advancement of Colored People had promised that if Judge Thomas were nominated, the White House and Thomas would be in for "the mother of all confirmation hearings," playing off of Saddam Hussein's infamous, and empty, threat to wage the mother of all battles and destroy the coalition forces that tried to remove Iraq from Kuwait.

Earlier on the day of the announcement, Judge Thomas had been

secretly brought up the driveway on the east side of Walker's Point—
away from the media—to maintain the surprise factor as long as
possible. Justice Thomas remembered what happened from there:

> Of course, President Bush introduced me to everybody on the
> deck when I arrived. Mrs. Bush was standing out there wearing a
> big hat, and she said, "Judge, congratulations." Then catching her-
> self, she said, "I guess I let the cat out of the bag."
>
> I thought I was coming up to have lunch for my interview. Yet
> Mrs. Bush was suggesting that I'm going to be nominated, so now
> I'm totally scared. Then the president introduced me to Brent
> Scowcroft and some of the others on his staff.
>
> From there, we went into the master bedroom where there
> was a little sitting area and a table with family photos, and the pres-
> ident said, "I'd like to ask you a few questions. First, can you and
> your family get through the confirmation?"
>
> I said, "Yes." Perhaps I should not have said yes, as it turned out,
> but I said we could handle it.
>
> Then the president asked, "If you go on the Supreme Court,
> can you call them as you see them?"
>
> I also responded yes to this question, noting, "It's gotten me in
> a lot of trouble, but I've done it my whole life."
>
> Finally, President Bush said, "Look, if you become a member of
> the Supreme Court, I will never publicly criticize any opinion of
> yours." He repeated that, then he said, "At two o'clock I'm going
> to nominate you to the Supreme Court of the United States. Let's
> go have lunch."
>
> That was the totality of our discussion about the Supreme Court.
>
> When things got really bad a few weeks later, I went to the
> Oval Office and apologized for getting him in so much trouble.
> Things at that point were getting totally out of control. I think I
> may have suggested then that, if he wanted, I would be more than
> happy to just say the heck with it and withdraw my name.
>
> See, I had never really wanted to be on the Court. I always saw
> it as public service, something that we're supposed to do. Never-
> theless, the president rejected my offer to stand down, saying he
> was going to be there to the end and he was going to fight it
> through. This wasn't about politics, ever. In none of the discus-
> sions we had during that time or when I was nominated was there

any discussion other than deeply personal discussion—as though you were talking to a father or an uncle.

He was in it with me as a father and as a friend.

My wife and I were so beaten down by that time. If you notice in those pictures, I had not had a haircut all summer. I couldn't go to the barbershop. I rarely went out in public. I had been studying all summer—twenty-five three-inch binders. I would read through that material all night, into the wee hours of the morning, then all day. In fact, I had not slept for sixty minutes in a row for three and a half months.

All the while, people were out to do me harm. It was like being in a jungle and people were hunting me. I thought, why? I'm just a kid from Georgia. There's nothing there. They attacked my mother. They attacked my sister, talking about her in this horrible way. We were not prepared to defend ourselves.

When you're at that point, you're beyond tears. I remember grieving about my grandparents. You sag under the weight of your grief. That's the way I felt during the confirmation. It's sort of a tearless grief. I had been pounded from July to October, over a hundred days.

Clearly, all the left-wing black groups felt they had license to do whatever they wanted to me, and they did it. Then I found out later they had focus groups to see what they could do to pry support away from me in the South. To do that, first they said I was not qualified, then they made an issue of the race of my wife.

None of it worked, though.

My mother lost thirty-five pounds during my confirmation. It finally got the best of her when we returned to the White House from the swearing-in ceremony. There was a big crowd, and my mother started feeling faint, so one of the White House physicians took her into a separate room and tested her blood pressure. They decided they wanted to take her to George Washington Hospital for observation, and you know who spent time with her until she went to the hospital? Barbara Bush. She told me, "Go on with the rest of your family and I'll look after your mom."

The president asked me, "Can you call them as you see them?" I told him I could. The oath that I took to do this job, and that promise to him, are the two things that keep me going in the difficult cases. I will not break my word to that man. I get real emotional about it. Because when you're at your lowest, you can really get the measure of the people who are there—and President and Mrs. Bush were there.

Here's what Dad had to say about Clarence Thomas: "He got brutalized in the hearing. In the view of the liberal opponents of Clarence Thomas, there's no such thing as a distinguished conservative black person. If you're conservative, they'll turn on you, and Clarence Thomas was turned on by the community. He was passed close to unanimously for the appeals court, and he served with distinction. Then suddenly, he's made into an evil guy with no morals. I found it very offensive, and the more they piled on him, the more determined I was to stay with him and to support him. I remember him coming down to the White House with Jack Danforth saying, 'Do you think it's time I got out of the race? I think it may be hurting you, Mr. President.' I put my arm around him and I said, 'You can't do that. You've got to stay in this fight, and you're going to be confirmed, I'm sure of it. You'll be a great justice.' And he has been."

Dad continued: "All this Anita Hill stuff was transparently phony, in my view. John Danforth, who was a very distinguished Episcopal minister as well as a senator, swore by Clarence Thomas. His judgment helped the votes in the Senate, but of course the most liberal media turned on him. I remember he called it a 'high-tech lynching'—and it was. They just piled on him, and lifted up this Anita Hill who came out of nowhere. She followed him around, wanted to work for him, wanted to be on his staff, wanted to be at his side, and then suddenly she turned on him."

★   ★   ★

Like the horseshoe tournament, there was another unique competition initiated during Dad's presidency, this one called the Brent Scowcroft Award for Somnolent Excellence. It grew to be a very prestigious award within the administration, even if the award's namesake and nominees did protest on occasion.

"Brent was a marvelous national security adviser, who did work long hours every night," Dad said. "Though he fell asleep regularly in daytime meetings, he didn't feel that he was worthy of having the award named for him. We all knew that that was modesty on his part, however, because he was terrific at falling asleep during meetings."

To be considered for the Scowcroft Award, first you had to fall asleep at a meeting at which Dad was present. Witnesses were required. Dad would then judge you on the soundness of your sleep and how tight your eyes were closed. Points were also awarded for "the recovery," which Dad explained using General Scowcroft as an example:

"He'd be sleeping like this in the middle of the meeting, and then he'd hear something subconsciously, so he'd wake up. He had a notepad, and he'd immediately start smiling and writing down what he hadn't heard. So recovery was part of it."

A new file was started in 1991 with Dad's hand-typed, private Scowcroft Award notes:

April 30, 1991: The challenge today mounted by Dick Cheney is worthy of total approval. He slept soundly. Everyone applauded when he woke up—a sterling performance as far as sleeping goes . . .

May 9: A fantastic challenge by Ed Derwinski [secretary of veterans affairs]. Very firm eye closure and a remarkable recovery gambit. Ed with eyes tightly closed used the seldom-used nod technique. He nodded vigorously whenever in his slumber he heard the end of a sentence . . .

May 17: Following the Queen's [Elizabeth of the U.K.] state dinner . . . the next morning Brent and John S [Sununu] jointly announced that I had made a serious challenge for the Scowcroft Award. Aware of my innocence, I discussed this important matter with Bar, who confirmed I was never out of it. Eyes open at all times, she stated. Brent's witness was Doro, who defended her father against this ludicrous charge. Though this entry is now part of the Scowcroft File it really is so fallacious a charge that it shouldn't have been brought up . . .

Eventually, the Scowcroft Award grew to be such a successful award domestically that Dad instituted an international award.

"One time a delegation from Iceland made a starring performance," Dad recalled, "because they had three people sitting at the table at this CSCE [Conference on Security and Cooperation in Europe] meeting in Paris, and all three of them were asleep at the same time. Even the guy that was speaking was asleep while he was speaking."

Describing Dad as "unmerciful" concerning the award, the harassment apparently got so bad that General Scowcroft had a pair of eyeglasses with wide-open eyes painted on them. He also noted how "his" award exemplifies why Dad is so good with people.

"Sometimes in our debates, things would get very heated and very tense," the general said. "In the middle of it, the president would come out with some joke—and you could just feel the tension breaking. That's what he used the Scowcroft Award for."

★　★　★

Of all the modern presidents, Dad was perhaps the most avid boatman to occupy the Oval Office. President Kennedy served aboard a PT boat in World War II and sailed at his home in Hyannisport, but Dad had an absolute passion for his twenty-eight-foot cigarette boat, *Fidelity*—and for driving it fast.

It was while Dad was out on his boat on August 21, 1991, that he received the news of Mikhail Gorbachev's release from house arrest following a failed coup.

Throughout July and August, there had been rumors that some of the Soviet hard-liners in the military and government hierarchy would attempt a coup to stop President Gorbachev and his reforms. When Dad visited Moscow in July, President Gorbachev had dismissed these threats as rumors; but on August 18, the hard-liners struck. TV reports indicated that President Gorbachev had resigned for health reasons, replaced by a committee of old-school Soviets.

President Gorbachev and his family were taken to their vacation dacha on the Crimean Sea, where they were held under armed guard. After four days, however, the coup-plotters were disbanded and the White House switchboard was finally able to contact President Gorbachev by phone.

"I was not satisfied with the connection we had," Special Agent John Magaw said. "I wasn't sure it would be secure. We weren't very far out [in the boat], so we turned around and, bang, the president threw it in high as he did a lot of times. When we went into the house, I stayed outside the bedroom, but I could see [President and Mrs. Bush]. The president sat on the edge of the bed, and there was tremendous concern in his voice. He said, 'Mr. President, I'm sorry to hear what's happened. Where are you, what's going on? Is your family going to be okay?' While I couldn't hear the other end of the conversation, I could see that the president was reasonably satisfied with the answers."

"At 5:45 p.m., seventy-three hours after communications had been disconnected, the connection was restored. I first talked with Boris Yeltsin, who had taken the right stand during the attempted coup, and then with other leaders of the republics," President Gorbachev said. "It was, of course, also important to resume contacts with the leaders of those countries that by that time had become our partners and to assure them that we would do everything possible to stabilize the situation, and that there was no reason for concern as to the control of nuclear weapons. In my conversation with George Bush, I was particularly touched when he and Barbara conveyed their best to Raisa, for whom those days were a terrible ordeal, and said that for three days they had been praying for us."

★　★　★

When Dad went to Kennebunkport for his August vacation that summer, it became clear to the press that fishing would be a huge part of his agenda. As Marlin Fitzwater recalled, each day's press briefing included the question, Is the president going fishing today?

"The media knew that the president often used these fishing expeditions to discuss business with staff, friends, or heads of state invited along for the ride," Marlin recalled, "so reporters asked about every detail of the fishing. Soon every briefing began with the same question: 'Did the President catch any fish today?'"

After two or three days, one of the reporters filed a pool report to all other reporters, saying it was "day three with no fish." Then it became "days four, five, and six with no fish."

Dad thought this was rather funny and soon joined in the fun by chiding himself to the press, saying, "Well, boys, it is day seven with no fish."

"But then the president's competitive instincts took over, and he started to get serious about his fishing," Marlin recalled. "Trips on the water lasted longer. He would go further out to sea looking for fish. Guests started including real fishermen."

Some horrible hand of fate had taken over, because the harder my president appeared to try, the less fish were available. He couldn't even get a bite.

"Not only that, as we got to day twelve or thirteen, his humor about the whole matter began to fade," Marlin said. "In fact, the staff didn't even want to ask him about it anymore. And I started going to the Secret Service for a fishing report, rather than upset the president."

Finally, on day seventeen, Dad caught a fish. By that time, Marlin said, the fishing report was more famous than foreign policy.

★ ★ ★

As 1991 wore on, it became clear that Chief of Staff John Sununu had an increasingly strained relationship with the media, and the political damage he sustained as a result, fair or unfair, in turn weakened his hand in dealing with Congress. There was tremendous scrutiny on Sununu especially after it was learned that he had taken government aircraft to go see his dentist. The media took to referring to this as the Air Sununu Scandal.

As the press commentary intensified, Sununu dug his heels in.

"From the Reagan days, there was a presidential order that the chief of staff and the national security adviser could not fly on commercial planes," Sununu explained. "So Scowcroft and I were always operating under that order. But when they started going after me in the press, they always seemed to bury the part about the presidential order in paragraph 73."

Andy Card, Sununu's deputy, recalled that on June 12, Dad's birthday, the chief of staff was going up to New York to attend a stamp show—but didn't disclose what his plans were directly to Andy. "At first, I heard he was going up for briefings with the General Services Administration. I thought it was a weird thing for a chief of staff to do, but turns out he was going up for a stamp show. This was during the height of the Air Sununu Scandal, and I told him, 'This is not right.'"

According to Andy, Governor Sununu defended the trip by saying, "I'm driving. I'm not taking the plane. I'm driving up. The White House driver is driving me up, and I'm going to work in the car."

That same day, Dad gave a big domestic policy speech on the South Lawn which focused on his "points of light" initiative. The event was being driven by Gregg Petersmeyer and his team in the Office of National Service, and Sununu's absence did not go unnoticed.

"That was when his relevance was significantly diminished in the White House," Andy said. "Ann Devroy, a tough, take-no-prisoners reporter for the *Washington Post*, was on a mission to do him in—and so during the summer, Sununu was seen as a damaged leader in the White House. It became increasingly uncomfortable for the staff as more people in Congress and elsewhere recognized it."

A more candid conversation about the role of the chief of staff—and what should happen—took place that August up in Maine.

"This was at the same time that the president was asked to make decisions about his campaign, the reelection campaign," Andy said. "What's the structure going to look like? Do you start things that early? What role does Bob Mosbacher play? What role does Fred Malek play? What role does Bob Teeter play? What role does the chief of staff play? So it was an interesting time in terms of both policy dialogue and campaign dialogue."

Andy thought Dad should make a decision on the chief of staff and start fresh in the fall, but perhaps owing to Dad's prevailing sense of loyalty, such a decision was not made, and Sununu continued to hobble onward as the administration moved through September, October, and November.

During the Thanksgiving holiday, Dad went to Camp David. David Bates, who later became the cabinet secretary at the White House, and Dorrance Smith, formerly the longtime producer of *This Week with David Brinkley* and Dad's head of media affairs, were up to play tennis. During that same period, Sununu's friends—like Senator Bob Dole—started calling Dad and saying positive things about the job his chief of staff was doing.

When Dad asked Andy why this sudden flurry of calls was directed at him, Andy replied, "Well, I think that they're probably calling because Sununu would ask them to call and say he should stay in there."

Dad called Andy back shortly after that and asked him to come to the White House after he returned from Camp David to meet with Boyden Gray and Dorrance—and to discuss what Sununu was doing. "We met on a Sunday afternoon at the White House, because I think the president wanted to do it when Sununu wouldn't realize," Andy remembered. "So we gathered in the Oval Office and came to the conclusion that probably Sununu wasn't contributing as much as he should, and he should move on."

A healthy discussion over how the team would deliver this awkward message to Sununu followed and finally, someone suggested Andy should do it. My brother George had a big part in resolving the matter, but at the staff level, the plan called for Andy to deliver the message, accompanied by Dorrance and Boyden.

"On December 2, we went to Sununu's office and shut the door," Andy said. "Cutting right to the chase, I said that I thought the president would accept Sununu's resignation."

Sununu replied, "No, he won't. He wants me to stay on."

Andy pressed: "Well, I think he would accept your resignation, and I think he'd like to have it."

Sununu then asked everybody to leave except Andy, and the two had a very emotional conversation. They then worked out a method to make the resignation known—doing it the next day, when Dad visited Florida and Mississippi.

"I remember the president did not come to the Oval Office that morning because he was leaving right from the residence to go on the trip," Andy said, "but he called and wanted to know what was going to happen. So I told him, and then I met him in the Diplomatic Room before they left to get on the helicopter. That's where I told him that something would happen that day. I couldn't guarantee at what point during the day, but something would happen. He thanked me, and I stayed at the White House. As they left, I told Marlin Fitzwater to stay on his toes, because something would be happening."

That morning, December 3, Sununu called Andy into his office to share the resignation letter that he had written in pencil on white lined paper. Sununu said he would deliver the letter and talk to the president about it on the trip. Sununu's resignation was effective December 15.

"I love John Sununu, and I owed him a lot," Dad said. "He is one of the brightest men I have ever met, and his sense of humor is great. I hated every moment of this very difficult decision and still love the guy."

Looking back, Sununu believes the absence of Lee Atwater was a contributing element in his demise. "If Lee had lived, I wouldn't have had to leave," he said. "I think a lot of the political problems I ended up with would have been blunted because Atwater was smart enough to deal with those crazy political things, and it put me in a position where I couldn't take care of my own political problems."

"It was difficult," remembered Sam Skinner, who replaced Sununu as chief of staff. "Number one, we were at 41 percent in the polls. The president's approval rating had gone from 90 percent after the war to 40 percent because of concerns about the economy, and everybody—except the president, it seemed—was pretty demoralized. He always had a positive nature, and he just said we're going to have to attack it. Of course, we had some unbelievable things happen over the next few months that made us feel as if we were jinxed."

★   ★   ★

I have already confessed I am no historian, and to that, let me add I am certainly not qualified to offer a scholarly analysis of the end of the Cold War. Yet I feel reasonably safe in suggesting that December 1991 will stand out in history, for centuries to come, as a period of profound—and positive—change in our world. First, on December 8, Russian President Boris Yeltsin called Dad to tell him that the Russian republics had taken the final, historic step to make their decades-old dream of self-determination a reality. Russia, Ukraine, and the other states that made up the USSR decided they would form a Commonwealth of Independent States. They were in essence casting aside the yolk of tyranny—the Soviet regime in faraway Moscow—that had suppressed them for too long.

Second, on Christmas Day, 1991, Mikhail Gorbachev resigned as leader of the Soviet Union. "Because President Bush had built such a strong relationship with Mikhail Gorbachev, he understood on a personal level what the fall of communism meant to him," Secretary of State Condoleezza Rice said. "He understood how difficult the decision was for Gorbachev to essentially manage the death of the Soviet empire. Gorbachev recognized that—and he respected it."

Then she told me of a fascinating moment: "Before the Soviet flag was lowered for the last time at the Kremlin, the final call Gorbachev made was to President Bush. He wanted reassurance from a trusted, valued friend that the decision he had made was correct, that history would judge him favorably."

"It so happened that I was making my statement about stepping

down from the presidency on the day when Christmas is celebrated in the West [the Russian tradition is to celebrate it later, on
January 6], but I nevertheless asked my assistant Pavel Palazchenko
to find out whether it was possible to contact the president," President Gorbachev recalled. They found Dad at Camp David, and
President Gorbachev recounted for me how their historic conversation went:

> I told President Bush that in about two hours I would be making
> a statement about stepping down. I also said that I had just sent him
> a farewell letter but I still wanted to take the opportunity and call
> him to reiterate once again how much I valued all that we had been
> able to achieve together—both when he was vice president and,
> particularly, when both of us were president. I expressed the hope
> that the leaders of the CIS [Commonwealth of Independent States]
> countries, particularly of Russia, understood their responsibility in
> preserving and increasing the capital we had created over these
> years in relations between the Soviet Union and the United States,
> and generally in international relations.
>
> I have on my desk the Decree of the President of the USSR.
> Due to the cessation of my duties as commander in chief, I trans-
> fer control of nuclear weapons to the president of the Russian
> Federation. I attach great importance to this matter being under
> secure control. As soon as I make my statement on stepping down,
> the decree will enter into force. So you can celebrate Christmas
> and sleep quietly tonight.
>
> As for me, I have no intention of hiding in the taiga. I will re-
> main in politics and in public life. What I intend to do is help the
> processes to get under way in our country and for new thinking to
> prevail in world politics.
>
> U.S. media people have often asked me what I thought about re-
> lations with you. I would like to say, not only through the media but
> to you personally on this day, that I very highly appreciate our coop-
> eration and partnership, our friendship. Our roles may change, and
> in fact they will change. But what we built together between the
> two of us and what we did together will remain forever.

President Gorbachev remembers Dad's reply as follows:

I want to assure you that we'll remain engaged in your affairs. We'll try hard to help, particularly the Russian republic, given the problems it is facing, which may get worse in winter.

I am very glad to hear that you have no intention of hiding in the taiga and will continue to be active in politics and public affairs. I am sure that this will help the new Commonwealth.

I have written you a letter, which will be sent today. I say in it that I am confident that what you have done will go down in history and future historians will fully appreciate your achievements.

I note with satisfaction what you've just said about nuclear weapons. This is extremely important internationally. I appreciate your attitude, and that of the leaders of the republics, in this matter. I want to assure you that we'll continue to cooperate very closely in this important regard.

Now, on a personal note: I have noted your wonderful, very pointed remarks about the relationship that you developed with me and Jim Baker. I value those remarks very highly, and they fully reflect my own feelings.

I hope our paths will cross again soon. You'll be a welcome guest, and we'll be happy to host you, after things settle down, perhaps here at Camp David.

My friendship toward you is unchanged and will always remain the same as we go forward. There should be no doubt whatsoever in this regard.

Of course, I will work on relations with the leaders of Russia and the other republics with due respect, openly and positively, and I hope on a progressive basis. We'll move toward recognition, with full respect for the sovereignty of each republic. We'll work with them on a broad range of issues. But this will in no way affect my determination to maintain contacts with you, consider your advice in your new capacity, and preserve our friendship with you and Raisa. Barbara and I cherish it.

So on this very special day, at this historic crossroad, I salute you and thank you for all you've done for peace, and I thank you for your friendship.

"*Perestroika* and President Gorbachev's *New Thought* ushered in a new era in world politics," Chancellor Kohl said of the former

Soviet leader. "His name will remain inextricably linked with the end of the Cold War, the arms race, and to the peaceful revolution in the German Democratic Republic. His level-headed actions after the fall of the Berlin Wall were decisive for the further development of the peaceful revolution. On November 10, 1989, the day after the fall of the Wall, the then-KGB forces in Moscow and the hardliners tried to persuade him to send in tanks and military units against the demonstrators in the DDR, who were supposedly storming Soviet Army facilities. But I was able to calm Gorbachev and convince him that his information was incorrect. Because of the trust in each other that we had built up in the preceding months, he believed me when I assured him that the demonstrators were peaceful and wanted nothing other than to live in freedom. We will always be grateful to Gorbachev, who—faced with the decision of sending in tanks and or leaving them in the barracks—chose the peaceful solution."

"To have that happen—to have the Cold War end and the Soviet Union dissolve without a conflict—is almost a miracle," General Scowcroft reflected. "If you had asked any American twenty years earlier how such a series of events might happen, they would have guessed it would happen by war. I mean, these things just don't happen the way it happened. Today, looking back, it seems sort of inevitable. But the president managed it in a way to reduce the tensions—not to alarm the Soviet Union with what was going on in Eastern Europe, not to excite the French and the British about German reunification. All these things he managed very carefully. It wasn't inevitable at all."

"I am convinced it was his diplomacy and his instincts that took us through a time that was far more dangerous than almost anybody recognized as the Soviet Union was collapsing," Bob Gates added, "sitting over there with forty thousand nuclear warheads and the potential for civil war, for military intervention in Eastern Europe and Poland and elsewhere. All those things were very real risks, and it was because of his diplomacy that that empire peacefully disintegrated virtually without bloodshed."

Chapter 20

A Steep Incline

"In 1992, I was deeply torn, because I liked your father so much; but we had a lot of differences on domestic policy, very few on foreign policy. In some ways it was personally very difficult for me, that campaign, because I liked him so much."

—**Bill Clinton**

Mom and Dad rang in 1992, the worst political year of their lives, in Sydney, Australia. They were on the first leg of a four-nation, twelve-day trip to Asia. In their hearts, I am sure both my parents were happy to get away from what had become a terribly unpleasant domestic political scene: conservative commentator Pat Buchanan and white supremacist David Duke had declared they would challenge Dad for the GOP nomination, while Democratic presidential contenders such as Nebraska Senator Bob Kerrey, former Massachusetts Senator Paul Tsongas, Arkansas Governor Bill Clinton, former California Governor Jerry Brown, and Iowa Senator Tom Harkin were all attacking Dad as being out of touch and uncaring.

It was a constant chorus of political critics in stereo, and we had yet to hear from one H. Ross Perot.

The daily pounding and blistering criticism not only hurt Dad's political poll numbers but also contributed to a growing—if also technically inaccurate—perception that the economy was still in a recession. Most experts today agree that the economy emerged from a brief recession in the spring of 1991; but as the calendar turned to 1992, many Americans were being told—and some clearly believed—we were heading for another Great Depression.

The Asia trip was undertaken largely at the initiative of Commerce Secretary Robert Mosbacher, who would help chair the forthcoming reelection campaign—and who was arguing for Dad to be more aggressive about getting his economic message out. Though the itinerary took them to Australia, Singapore, Korea, and Japan, the target audience for the visuals and messages the trip produced was really in swing states like Michigan and Ohio. The idea was to announce a series of new trade and commercial agreements that would, in turn, show how Dad was working to open new markets for American businesses and help create more jobs for American workers.

This was not your ordinary presidential trip, though, because also joining Dad for parts of this trip were a number of business leaders such as the Big Three car executives from Detroit—the CEOs of General Motors, Ford, and Chrysler—as well as leading representatives from other sectors such as manufacturing. It was a good mix of people, and truth be told it had been a reasonably good and productive trip—that is, until they reached Japan.

First, even before they arrived, some in the Japanese media picked up on the fact that the U.S. CEOs accompanying Dad were overpaid when compared to their Japanese counterparts. In those days, the average Japanese CEO made maybe half a million dollars, while the U.S. CEOs who would be trying to win concessions from the Japanese auto industry received many times that. So even before Mom and Dad landed in Tokyo, this news item seemed to serve as a harbinger that it would not be a smooth visit.

The news item that made global headlines from that Japan visit came after they arrived, on January 8. That night, a flu bug caught up with Dad at a formal state dinner, and he threw up on Kiichi Miyazawa, the prime minister of Japan, which we believe may be the one and only time in history a president has done that.

"All during the daytime, he was just sick as a dog," Secret Service Agent John Magaw recalled. "Doctors were telling him, you can't continue to do this. So finally around noon, we got him to postpone whatever was on his calendar, and for the next two hours or so he rested and took medication. Still, the doctors were saying it doesn't look good, so they got as much medicine as they could possibly get in him."

That night, when Mom and Dad arrived at Prime Minister Miyazawa's palace, Dad told Rich Miller, whose shift as Dad's head Secret Service agent followed John Magaw's, that he was feeling poorly. So they went to the restroom with another agent, Tom Ferrell, and Dad became sick to his stomach, soiling his tie. The agents told Dad he could not go forward with the event, but Dad insisted, telling them, "It would be a slap in the face to the Japanese to cancel now."

"I looked at Tom and said, 'If your tie matches his suit, you're going to have to give it up,'" Rich recalls. "So he does. The president got a little kick out of that, and he put it on and then he went inside."

The room was set up with a very large U-shaped table with Mom and Dad in the middle, while Rich sat eight or nine seats from them on the left side.

"I looked at him at one point, and he started looking very pale," Rich continues. "He mouthed the word to me, 'bathroom.' Of course, he was hoping it was behind the podium, but there wasn't anything back there." Dad would have had to walk all the way through the guests to go outside, so he just gutted it out. Meanwhile, he continued to get paler, which concerned Rich enough that he finally got up and started approaching Dad.

"Just about the time I got behind him, I put my hand on his shoulder and he fell to the left," Rich said. "I reached down to grab him, trying to turn the president to his left so he doesn't vomit on himself, but I couldn't turn him. I'm thinking, 'What's the story here?' At that moment, Prime Minister Miyazawa looks at me, pulls my arm, and says, 'Hey, you're pulling my leg.' "

Mom had moved near Dad by this point and was holding up a napkin to give Dad some privacy from the audience in the room.

When Rich laid Dad on the floor, he remembers that Dad was unconscious for about three seconds before the doctors and nurses revived him. Major Paula Trivette, a very able army nurse, literally vaulted over the table to get to Dad. Dr. Lee opened his tie to get him some air, then he unzipped Dad's trousers—which obviously caught Dad's attention.

"Burt, what the hell are you doing down there?" Dad asked. Hearing this, Mom turned to the crowd and said, "I think the president is going to be fine."

"I wanted to clear the room so he could go out in a way that nobody would see him," Rich said, "but he said, 'No, I'm going to walk out of here.' He had that look about him that when he says I'm going to do this, you know he's going to do what he said."

When Rich stood him up, however, Dad had also soiled his suit. Once again, Special Agent Tom Ferrell was called to surrender an article of clothing—this time his raincoat. Donning the coat, Dad walked out of the palace right by the press to the car.

Mom, meanwhile, stayed behind at the dinner—no doubt relieved to know Dad would be all right, but also left to help salvage an awkward situation. What followed was vintage Barbara Bush. At the time for Dad's scheduled remarks, Mom stood up and said:

> I rarely get to speak for George Bush, but tonight I know he would want me to thank you, on behalf of his administration and the businessmen who are here, for a wonderful visit and for a great friendship, and on my part, for a lovely day, and I think for a wonderful day for all of you.
>
> You know, I can't explain what happened to George because it never happened before. But I'm beginning to think it is the ambassador's fault. [Laughter] He and George played the emperor and the crown prince in tennis today, and they were badly beaten. And

we Bushes aren't used to that. [Laughter] So he felt worse than I thought . . .

Mom then called on General Scowcroft to deliver Dad's prepared remarks. Her comments—combined with the fact that she stayed at the dinner—helped to reassure everyone that the situation was not as serious as it might have appeared on TV.

The dinner program that night was supposed to have been closed to the news media except for an unmanned Japanese camera set up to capture the toasts. The images that camera position caught of Dad fainting and being helped to his feet were soon beamed out to the waiting world, and caused a global stir. What was left unreported was that almost half the press corps had also come down with the same flu.

I was at the other end of that beam in Bethesda, Maryland. I remember waking up early because I wasn't able to sleep, and out of habit I turned on CNN. It was there I saw, over and over again, Dad fall over at the Japanese dinner. At first, I was scared, and I immediately ran downstairs to find the agent on duty. (I had actually rented out my guest room to the Secret Service. It worked out well, as they were able to have a command post in my home, and I always felt safe.) They told me Dad was fine and that it was just the flu. Even so, the TV channels ran it again and again, and each time I saw it I couldn't help but worry. I was very glad when he and Mom came home.

One morbidly humorous postscript to what was an otherwise embarrassing and scary episode: Since the dinner that night was closed to the press, many of the working media members and camera people went to a Tokyo restaurant that night—all gathered in a single room. Clearly, there was a miscommunication as to what had happened to Dad, because the hostess entered the room and in that wonderfully formal and proper Japanese way kept saying, "Very sorry. Very sorry." When everyone quieted down, the hostess then dropped this bombshell: "Your president died tonight."

After a moment of stunned silence, pandemonium broke out as

everyone scrambled for the door—fearful that they were missing the story of the century.

★   ★   ★

Unfortunately, Dad's political year got off to a fairly lousy start as well. The problems took root even before 1992 started. In addition to the primary challengers pounding away on the right and left, his attorney general, Dick Thornburgh, lost a special U.S. Senate election in Pennsylvania in November following the sudden death of Senator John Heinz, who died in a tragic helicopter crash earlier in 1991. Within a week of Senator Heinz's death, both Lee Atwater and Dad's old friend John Tower had died, and within two weeks Dean Burch had died of cancer. It was a rough time in my parents' lives.

When that Pennsylvania race began, Dad's favorability rating was up in the eighties, and Attorney General Thornburgh, who had also served as Pennsylvania governor, had a forty-five point lead against Harris Wofford, the university president who had been appointed to fill Heinz's seat temporarily.

"You couldn't believe that you could squander something like that, but at the end of the election, George Bush's favorability ratings were below 50 percent and my lead had vanished," Governor Thornburgh recalled. "I remember going to the White House after that, where I licked my wounds. I said to the folks down there, You know, up in Pennsylvania, back when coal was king about a hundred years ago, when the miners went to the mouth of the mine every day they'd release a canary into the mine. And if the canary came back, they knew that it was safe to work in the mine. If the canary didn't come back, they knew there was trouble in the mine.

"Boys," he continued, "I'm your canary, and there's trouble in the mine."

The Pennsylvania Senate race not only introduced health care as a key 1992 issue, it was also interpreted by members of the

White House press corps and the national news media as a direct rebuke of the Bush administration for failing to act aggressively on a sluggish economy and other domestic concerns. Thus, between Wofford's stunning victory in November 1991 and the Sununu resignation the following month, the press must have felt there was plenty of political blood in the water at 1600 Pennsylvania.

The media feeding frenzy was on.

On February 4, Dad went to the National Grocers Association convention in Florida, and before he gave his speech he toured the exhibition area where he was shown the latest scanner technology. Of course, Dad knew how a supermarket scanner worked; but in one demonstration, executives showed Dad how the scanner could still ring up a product even if the bar code was torn in five different places—not your typical grocery store technology.

Unfortunately, a *New York Times* reporter named Andy Rosenthal, the son of *Times* former managing editor A. M. Rosenthal, wrote a story under the headline "Bush Encounters the Supermarket, Amazed." He went after Dad for not understanding how a basic scanner worked. Dad's political opponents seized on Rosenthal's piece to support their own attacks against my father as being out of touch, and soon this nasty fairy tale was dominating the airwaves.

"I was amazed at how much coverage this one relatively minor incident had gotten," remembered Howard Kurtz, the media critic for the *Washington Post*, "so I started making some phone calls and discovered that the *New York Times* reporter, whose front-page piece had ricocheted this story into the media stratosphere, had not witnessed the supermarket incident himself. Instead, he had written it from a couple of paragraphs in a pool report. What's more, the *Houston Chronicle* reporter who wrote that pool report thought the matter was so insignificant that he didn't include it in his own news story."

My father-in-law, George Koch, is a former president of the Grocery Manufacturers of America, and he followed the scanner episode very closely. "President Bush was one of the greatest listeners that we've ever had in the presidency. He would listen to what you had to say and would appear to be very, very interested. He would never say, 'Look, I know all this.' The reporter mistook his polite and personal way of listening with not being knowledgeable. The most important thing in this whole story was the reaction of *Newsweek,* which stated that Bush acts 'curious and polite,' but it went on to say 'hardly amazed.' Michael Duffy of *Time* called the whole thing completely insignificant as a news event—prosaic polite talk. He said if anything, the president was bored. Bob Graham, who demonstrated the scanner for the president, said, 'It's foolish to think the president doesn't know anything about grocery stores. He knew exactly what I was talking about.' "

Again, Kurtz explained how the media often assign narratives to people in public life and then look for stories or anecdotes to confirm those narratives. The example he cited was Vice President Quayle misspelling "potato" in a classroom, which was utterly insignificant in and of itself, but it tapped into the unfair "media narrative" that Dan Quayle was not an intellectual.

"In the case of President Bush," he noted, "the media narrative at the time was, nice fellow, something of a patrician and a little out of touch with the concerns of ordinary Americans who have to worry about the price of a quart of milk. That's why this scanner story took off like a rocket. It confirmed this media narrative about the president; and if the same thing had happened to some other presidential candidate, it probably wouldn't even have rated a paragraph."

Kurtz pursued the story-behind-the-story, and his story changed the tone of the coverage a little bit, but it could not slow down the tidal wave of debate about this one minor incident. In fact, the scanner reference continued to surface for years even after Dad left the White House—to his constant frustration. "I wrote Punch Sulzberger, publisher of the *New York Times,*" said Dad. "I think this was the only such letter I wrote as president. I like Punch a lot, but he was not willing to do anything about the nasty Rosenthal piece."

"The trouble is, it gets stuck in the computer, and it's still there today," Dad said. "It's just manufactured news—fake history—but there's no question that it hurt me a lot."

★ ★ ★

Dan and Laverne Rostenkowski were in the White House residence visiting one afternoon with Mom and Dad when Millie and Ranger came into the room. Ranger went right up to the chairman of the Ways and Means Committee and relieved himself on his shoe, hitting the pale carpet around it at the same time. Congressman Rostenkowski remembers, "The next thing I know, your dad's got a steward in with some soapy liquid. He tells them to leave and your dad is on his hands and knees cleaning the carpet. And I said, 'George, you're president of the United States, you're my president. Get off your darn knees.' He said, 'How can I ask a steward to clean up after the dog?' "

Later, Dad sent Congressman Rostenkowski a photo of them all at the scene of the crime, inscribed, "To Dan and Laverne. Watch out for that dog. Whoops! Anyway, welcome, welcome, welcome. George and Barbara."

Speaking of dogs, Uncle Lou often dropped by Walker's Point with his dog, Gilbert. Because Gilbert was a feisty little Jack Russell terrier, Uncle Lou was often discouraged from bringing the dog for visits.

When Gilbert died, Uncle Lou asked if everyone thought it would be okay for him to put flowers in the dog's memory on the altar at church. No one knew what to say but thought it was ridiculous, so they told Uncle Lou he'd better check with Mom, who also loves dogs. He walked right into her bedroom without knocking and said, "Barbara, you love your dogs. Don't you agree that I should put flowers on the altar in honor of Gilbert?" Mom said, "Louis, all I can say to you is, does Gilbert accept Jesus Christ as his Savior?" Louis turned on his heel, saying, "Damn you, Barbara!" and marched out, slamming the door behind him.

I think everybody was laughing, including Uncle Lou.

★ ★ ★

For both Republicans and Democrats, the first true battle-
ground of the 1992 primaries was not Iowa, but rather New
Hampshire. In Iowa, Dad's organizational strength as an incumbent president was prohibitively strong, and such was certainly the
case for the favorite Democratic son, Iowa Senator Tom Harkin.
Accordingly, most challengers chose not to invest precious time or
dollars fighting losing battles there and instead went directly to
New Hampshire.

What Iowa lacked in fireworks, New Hampshire more than
made up for. First, spurred on by the conservative newspaper the
Union Leader in Manchester, Pat Buchanan's insurgent campaign—
the so-called Buchanan brigades with their rhetorical "pitchforks"—
was making inroads against Dad. Just two weeks after Pat declared
his candidacy, in fact, one poll published in the *Concord Monitor*
in late December had Dad leading 58 percent to 30 percent for
Buchanan—an undeniably strong start for an upstart challenger.

"It was a real eye-opener," Vice President Quayle recalled. "Not
that it was fatal, because you can have these challenges and survive, but that was sort of the first sense that okay, this is going to
be a tougher race than we had anticipated."

Perhaps more sensationally, however, Governor Clinton's campaign problems first surfaced in New Hampshire in mid-January and
for a time overshadowed Dad's troubles. One of Dad's campaign
managers, Fred Malek, recalled, "It was incredible. We thought Clinton was going to kill himself, go down with a lot of that stuff. We
didn't see how the hell he could survive. But, boy, he did."

On the Republican side, meanwhile, Pat Buchanan won 37 percent in New Hampshire, which shocked and concerned all of us,
and only added to the media feeding frenzy. All political hell broke
loose that someone who had never run for office and had very
little money could do so well against an incumbent president.
After all, we were eleven months removed from the historic victory
in the sands of Kuwait and not even two months removed from

the collapse of the Soviet Union and the peaceful end of the Cold War. Dad had seemed almost invincible just a short time ago.

Buchanan's campaign suddenly had life and his supporters were emboldened, but the candidate himself was realistic about his prospects moving forward.

"After New Hampshire, I hoped there would be talk that the president really didn't want to run for a second term and that Mrs. Bush didn't want him to run," Buchanan said. "I couldn't beat the president of the United States. My hope was maybe I could do like Gene McCarthy and do well in a very early primary—and then if President Bush, like Lyndon Johnson, decided not to run, it would be too late for anybody else to get in."

The night after the New Hampshire returns hit the nation, Texas business magnate H. Ross Perot announced on CNN's *Larry King Live* that if his supporters could get his name on the ballot in all fifty states, he would run for president as an independent candidate. While the Buchanan candidacy had been somewhat surprising to Dad, Perot's announcement was more of a disappointment. Dad and Ross had known each other for two decades, and during the 1970s Perot had obviously thought enough of Dad to offer him a job after he left the CIA.

Perot had served in the navy like Dad, before founding Electronic Data Systems (EDS) in Dallas in 1962. In 1979, he paid a team of former special ops people to rescue two EDS employees in a daring mission after they had been jailed in Iran over a contract dispute. During the 1980s, however, Perot had wanted to go to Southeast Asia to look for U.S. servicemen still missing from the Vietnam War. That request was nixed by the Reagan administration, and Dad volunteered to deliver the news—a decision he later regretted. In fact, Dad said, "Perot shot the messenger."

As had Buchanan, Perot opposed the Gulf War—and he also had encouragement from an outside source (in Perot's case, it was a new grassroots organization exasperated by congressional pay raises). For all of his business success, however, Perot had never run for public office at any level; and apparently even he wasn't quite sure what to expect during his first foray onto the campaign trail.

"At the end of that first show, Perot asked me, 'Do you think we'll go anywhere?'" Larry King recalled. "And I said, 'Who knows?' Then suddenly it took off. The economy was in trouble, and along comes this little guy in Texas taking on the major parties. I think, frankly, had he not veered off and gone a little nuts, Ross might have won. He was in the right place, at the right time, and he has only himself to blame."

To manage his campaign out of the gate, Perot tapped his lawyer from Dallas, Tom Luce, who first met Dad in the mid-1960s and was also friendly with my brother George. Unlike Mr. Perot, Tom did have campaign experience: he headed SMU Students for John Tower in 1961; he had worked for the state party; he had been chairman of several different candidates' campaigns; and he had also run (unsuccessfully) for the Republican nomination for governor of Texas in 1990. Tom's first job was trying to instill some kind of campaignlike organization on a candidate who also wanted to be his own campaign manager and press secretary.

"It was a very unconventional campaign, to say the least," Luce said. "When I arrived at the headquarters to help him, there were 2,500 pending media requests and there was no staff whatsoever. So I was press secretary, campaign manager, and gradually we built up a little staff, but not much of one. As I say, Perot was a very unconventional candidate."

Looking back, most outside observers—my brothers and I included—are convinced there was an undeniable vendetta element to the Perot candidacy. He seemed to have some unknown grudge against Dad.

Larry King said, "The president used to ask me every time, 'What does Perot have against me? I knew him in Texas. I don't know any reason why he would not like me.' I would ask Perot, who said, 'This is just politics. This is just agreement or disagreement.' I don't know that I ever believed that. Something happened with the president that turned Perot off him."

Oddly enough, Perot's antagonism was not as surprising to some of us as the betrayal of Ed Rollins, a veteran Republican operative. Ed's wife, Sherry, had taken an important job as the director of the White House Office of Public Liaison, and that spring, Ed wrote Dad a very glowing letter expressing confidence he would be reelected and offering to help in any way possible. Within weeks, however, it was announced that he had joined forces with Jimmy Carter's former chief of staff, Hamilton Jordan, as one of the two new Perot campaign managers—and Sherry resigned her White House position against Dad's wishes.

★ ★ ★

In February, Dad asked me to lead the presidential delegation to the Winter Olympics in Albertville, France. I was really excited because I knew he had also asked his sister, Nancy Ellis, to go. Aunt Nan is one of my very favorite people—a dynamic woman with a magnetic personality. Her mannerisms remind me of Katharine Hepburn. A Yale friend of Dad's, Osborne Day, was also in the delegation, so I knew it was going to be fun.

I was really surprised, however, when I heard who the remaining traveling squad would be: Hollywood stars Don Johnson and Melanie Griffith! Dad really liked both Melanie and Don. At one point, he had invited them to a state dinner, and Marvin was seated with Melanie. Afterward, she wrote Marvin a note, calling him "the sexiest dinner partner in town." Marvin's wife, Margaret, who was also at the dinner, immediately contacted Don and got him to write her a note, which read, "To the sexiest dinner partner in town—two can play at that game."

We had an odd assortment of people going to Albertville. Only Dad would dream up an eclectic group like this, and off we went.

Albertville was a charming winter wonderland of a town filled with eighteen hundred athletes from sixty-four nations. We went from event to event all bundled up in our warmest winter wear, taking in the ski jumping, figure skating, ice hockey, bobsledding— always cheering on our American athletes.

While it was thrilling to be at the Olympics, I have to admit I was fascinated by Melanie and Don. One afternoon, our delegation was walking into one of the Olympic events. Even though I was the head of the delegation, it felt more natural to fall behind the movie stars as, let's face it, they really were the center of attention. Everywhere they went, cameras flashed like crazy. Both usually wore long fur coats and wonderful fur hats, and Melanie very glamorously would hold her cigarette in a cigarette holder just like a Hollywood starlet. On this occasion, an eager young man came running up and asked if he could please have their autographs, to which Don responded in his most movie-star-like way, "Later, baby, we're on a U.S. delegation."

Dad liked sending family members on delegations to other nations because "it was something you could appoint family to without paying the price of nepotism. The U.S. must be represented and should be at the inauguration of presidents and funerals. Vice President Gore did not go to many funerals, and he made a huge mistake. It was at a funeral that I met Gorbachev—after Chernenko's funeral—and I got to size him up for the president. And so delegations do some good. You can have a lot of bilateral meetings with other countries you can't have if you just wait for them to come to Washington. I liked going on delegations for Reagan and I liked appointing delegations. Having said that, however, they don't have an enormous influence on policy," Dad told me.

Meanwhile, back at home, unbeknownst to me, Bobby had gone up to Camp David the Saturday after I left to ask Dad for my hand in marriage. Mom and Dad were thrilled and were touched that Bobby would make such an effort; and Bobby, for his part, remembers Mom calling him that morning to see if he was still coming because it was snowing that day.

Bobby drove up for the day and went straight to Aspen, the presidential cabin at Camp David. As he arrived, he remembers seeing Mom and Lud Ashley throwing on parkas and rushing out to take a walk. It was obvious to everyone why Bobby was there.

Dad was sitting in front of the TV flipping the channels when Bobby entered the room, and stopped to hear what Bobby had to say. Bobby remembers Dad shedding tears of happiness over the request and saying yes.

When I got back to the United States, Bobby took Sam, Ellie, and me out to dinner at the Congressional Country Club. After dinner, Bobby took us into a private room and proposed to all three of us! He gave me a diamond ring with three diamonds— one each for Sam, Ellie, and me. Upon hearing the proposal, Sam yelled, "Yessss!"

It was very sweet . . . and very unanimous!

★ ★ ★

On June 11, Mom and Dad traveled to Panama for the first time since the restoration of its democracy in early 1990. It was a hopeful time in Panama, and it was a positive first stop for Dad before he continued on to Rio de Janeiro for a contentious, politically charged United Nations conference on the environment.

At the time of Dad's visit, the United States was viewed favorably by 80 percent of Panamanians, and friendly crowds lined the streets of Panama City as Mom and Dad's motorcade drove past. Both Panamanian President Guillermo Endara and the Secret Service were worried about protests breaking out, but after a big lunch at the Presidential Palace Dad tried to put his host at ease, joked that the "tiny, tiny handful of people that are protesting . . . ought to go up to San Francisco and get an idea of what a real protest is like."

After lunch, the Endaras and Dad and Mom went to a large outdoor event in the Plaza Porras—where some ten thousand Panamanians were waiting.

During the event, Mom remembered there were a few students throwing rocks and what they thought were firecrackers, followed by Panamanian troops firing tear gas out in the crowd. When the

Secret Service heard what they believed to be gunshots, they evacuated my parents back through the arrival area into the armored limousines.

"When I approached the president about leaving, he didn't want to because it would look bad," said Special Agent and detail leader Rich Miller. "So I mentioned to him, 'We really need to go because Mrs. Bush is on the stage with you, and we really need to get both of you back in there.' That's when it clicked for him, and we got up and evacuated back into the car."

The next stop on the itinerary was a U.S. military base. Upon hearing that the motorcade route was free of problems, the agents sent half the motorcade ahead just to make sure it was clear. Then it was time for Mom and Dad to move.

Special Agent Miller recalled, "After we got in the car, I looked at President Bush and said, 'We're not going anywhere that President Endara can go because we were going to the airport to leave the country as scheduled.' So the president looks at President Endara and very apologetically says, 'You've got to get out.' The guy looks at him like, really? I don't think he wanted to get left behind, but he was fine."

Now flash forward fourteen years. In February 2006, Dad went fishing in Panama with the president, Martín Torrijos, who was elected in 2004 and is the son of former president Omar Torrijos Herrera, killed by Manuel Noriega. While there, Dad learned that a woman named Balbina Herrera, who was in that 1992 audience— and who participated as tear gas against Dad was released—today serves in President Torrijos's cabinet as minister of housing. Happily, she is now fully committed to democracy.

When Dad heard this, he immediately wrote her a note, dated February 15, 2006:

Dear Balbina,

Excuse my informality. I just want you to know that my eyeballs are clear now!

Just kidding! Everyone tells me you are doing a great job as a very popular minister who now supports your fine President.

I understand you met my son. Now how about meeting his father—I love Panama.

Good luck,

George Bush #41

Dad asked President Torrijos if he would give the note to the cabinet minister. President Torrijos said that he would not only give the note to the minister, he would read it aloud at the next cabinet session!

★ ★ ★

After a four-month engagement, Bobby and I were married on June 27. Because I had been married before, I wanted something low-key—definitely not a White House wedding. Yet Bobby had not been married, so I also wanted to make sure he had a proper ceremony and reception. We decided to be married at Camp David, where Mom and Dad had dedicated the beautiful new Evergreen Chapel just a year before.

The presidential retreat was first established in 1942 in the Catoctin Mountains near the little town of Thurmont, Maryland. That part of Maryland is always at least ten degrees cooler than Washington, and President Roosevelt enjoyed going there to escape the dreadful summer heat in our nation's capital, which was deemed to be hard on his health. FDR soon dubbed the encampment Shangri-La.

In 1953, President Eisenhower renamed the retreat Camp David, after his grandson, and that name stuck until my brother Marvin mounted a modest campaign to have the retreat renamed, immodestly, after himself. In fact, he succeeded in convincing most members of our immediate family to refer to it as Camp

Marvin, though for the record this remains strictly an informal designation.

Several months before the wedding, Mom took me to New York to buy a dress. We went to see Arnold Scaasi, who has made beautiful dresses for Mom for years. Arnold loved the rich and, in the case of my mom, the famous, and he excitedly pulled out bolts of beautiful fabric and draped them over the First Lady, settling on a lovely lilac lace fabric.

Then Arnold turned to me and said, "Oh yes, the bride . . ." Clearly, I was not as famous or interesting! Nevertheless, Arnold also made a beautiful dress for me: salmon chiffon on the bottom topped with lace.

There were also a few unplanned fashion statements made at our wedding. For example, unknown to us, Bobby's brother Danny thought it would be funny to surreptitiously put Bush-Quayle '92 stickers on the bottom of Bobby's shoes, so when he knelt at the altar, he did a little campaigning on behalf of our ticket. We heard the laughter but didn't know what was so funny until later.

Dad had forgotten to pack a suit and was forced to wear what he had in his closet—most notably a pair of white pants with a thin blue pinstripe, exactly like the New York Yankees wear!

I am biased, of course, but our wedding was beautiful. First, we were surrounded by our close friends and family members. Added to that, Camp David features breathtaking views of the Appalachian Valley as well as a variety of majestic trees. Idyllic is the word that comes to mind. All the cabins are named after trees, such as Birch, Dogwood, and Maple, and we held the reception behind Aspen, the president's house, where tables were set on terraces on different levels and around the pool.

While guests mixed and mingled, a division of the Marine Band played country music. I will never forget the generosity of some of the White House personnel who came up to help that weekend. Because Camp David is run by a small detail of Marines primarily concerned with security, they didn't have enough people there to man a wedding, so some of the White House butlers, Laurie Firestone from the Social Office, and others volunteered to help us. Looking back, I am still touched by their thoughtfulness.

Finally, I'll always remember what George Hannie, one of the extraordinary butlers who works at the White House, said to me. As I was thanking him, George spoke up and said, "It's okay, honey, but just don't do it a third time!" Words to live by!

(Incidentally, one of the greatest joys of having the privilege to visit the White House regularly thanks to my brother George is being able to see the White House staff, many of whom are still there from Dad's time as president.)

Unlike our very private wedding at Camp David, we held our rehearsal dinner on June 26 at the White House. Traditionally, the groom's family hosts the rehearsal dinner, but the Kochs, who very much wanted to host it, understood that if Dad were to go someplace else, the entire press corps would have to go with him—and our private family event would have turned into a zoo. Since it was our desire to have a private wedding, it worked well to have the rehearsal dinner at the White House.

I remember wearing a long red chiffon dress that I had made for me. It still hangs in my closet, and if I cut myself in half, it might fit. The State Dining Room was decorated with red and pink flowers and pink tablecloths and looked as beautiful as at any state dinner. But the atmosphere was permeated by family and friends. There were some articles in the press that speculated on who would be at the wedding—which cabinet members and politicians around town. But we didn't want a "Washington" wedding.

There were toasts and lots of exuberant laughter. Sam, Ellie, and I prepared a "rap" song that we sang to Bobby which wasn't anything Snoop Dogg would approve of, to be sure. There was also dancing in the foyer to the music of the Marine Band. Known as the President's Own, the U.S. Marine Band was established by Congress in 1798, making it the oldest musical organization in the United States. They are elegant and remarkable, and, as president,

Dad loved the privilege of having them play at White House events.

Today, I often accompany out-of-town friends on the tour of the White House. Every once in a while, the tour guide will mention, among other things, that President George H. W. Bush's daughter had her rehearsal dinner in the State Dining Room. Even now, when I hear it on the tour, it still seems as if they are talking about someone else.

Bobby's being a member of the "loyal opposition" has certainly added spice to our marriage. Little did he know that he would be so outnumbered down the line by more governors and presidents! I know there have been awkward situations for Bobby to cope with over the years, but he has always handled it all with class and dignity. He has always been totally loyal to our family.

That doesn't mean Bobby has placed his political convictions in a blind trust, however. While we have the usual arguments that all married couples have, I will confess that some of them have also crossed into politics. Bobby remains unconvinced of some of my positions, but I'm working on it!

★   ★   ★

As the 1992 campaign moved into summer, the two major party candidates were shifting gears from the primary season to the general election. Dad had soundly defeated Pat Buchanan, while Bill Clinton had outlasted Paul Tsongas and was in the process of finishing off his own tough-talking insurgent challenger, former California governor Jerry Brown.

It was the Perot campaign, however, that appeared to be on a roll as Memorial Day came and went. The Texas billionaire was at or near the top of every national poll, and his campaign was close to registering Perot in every state. The national media loved this remarkable, improbable development and lavished Perot with airtime and print coverage.

Yet, as soon as Perot was possibly poised to break the race wide open, the bottom fell out on his campaign. Several weeks' worth of critical news stories throughout May and June started to take its toll on both the candidate and his standing with voters. Mr. Perot also reportedly balked at footing the bill for fundamental campaign staples such as TV advertising and yard signs. By the time the Democratic convention had started in New York in mid-July, Mr. Perot had dropped nine points in just the previous week alone—and the clash of egos and tempers at Perot headquarters boiled over, past the breaking point.

Some accounts suggested that Mr. Perot dropped out of the race because he realized that his continued success would mean his family would lose their privacy—a burden he did not want them to have to bear. If this is true, I can understand and respect that.

However, the official explanation he gave when he dropped out on July 16 was harder to follow. Mr. Perot said he was dropping out because it was clear that no one would win the election outright— which would, in turn, force the vote into the House of Representatives, delay the selection of the ultimate winner, and deny the new president adequate time to prepare the new administration. Such a development would be too disruptive to our political system, Perot said, and he did not want to contribute to that.

During all this, Dad was in Jackson Hole, Wyoming, with Jeb, Secretary Baker, and Jamie Baker for what had become his traditional getaway during the Democratic convention.

Meanwhile, Tom Luce, the lawyer for the now-defunct Perot campaign, decided to join Dad's campaign. "I felt like I had discharged my obligation, if you want to call it that," Tom Luce said. "I felt that I had done what I could do, and Ross Perot had decided to drop out of the race. I had no idea he was going to get back in the race, and in the meantime I'd committed to President Bush— so it was a simple proposition in my mind.

"My secretary came in and said, 'The president is on the phone,'" Tom Luce recalled, "and I said, 'Yeah, sure.' I thought it was one of my smart-aleck friends, but she was serious. I picked up the phone and the voice said, 'Tom, this is George Bush.' I kind of sat up straight in my chair and he said, 'I'm in Jackson Hole fishing with Jim Baker and I just heard the news about Ross Perot, and I just want to tell you that I more than most people value loyalty. I know why you did what you did, and welcome back—no hard feelings.'"

Dad asked Tom and his wife, Pam, to come up to the White House after Perot dropped out. My brother George set up the meeting.

"We had dinner with President and Mrs. Bush, George W., and Nancy Ellis, and my wife in the upstairs dining room," Tom said. "Then I went out on the Truman balcony, which was quite a thrill for me to talk to the president after dinner about what he called the Perot phenomenon."

With Mr. Perot seemingly out of the race (at least until early October), the fall campaign appeared to be shaping up as a two-man showdown between Dad and Bill Clinton—and Dad's campaign finally appeared to be getting traction. In July, they even managed to string together several days of positive coverage.

The Perot departure had created a void at exactly the moment the Democrats were conducting a successful convention in New York. To try and keep the Clinton campaign in check, Mary Matalin and Torie Clark on Dad's campaign team started putting out what they called "a lie a day" items chronicling how Bill Clinton would say different things to different crowds to win their approval.

On August 3, they put out a press release that contained twenty or so statements, including one item calling attention to the fact that the Clinton campaign had paid $25,000 for investigators to contact several women with whom Governor Clinton allegedly had affairs. Mary and Torie thought this "bimbo eruption" issue was fair game, because taxpayer dollars were involved.

As soon as the press release went out, however, the national press corps went nuts. It was the first time either campaign had formally raised the infidelity issue, and, as a result, our campaign release dominated the network news coverage. Immediately, a number of people on both sides of the political aisle were calling for Mary's head—Democrats outraged at what they said were "dirty tricks," and Beltway Republicans upset that Dad had been knocked "off message" by the antics.

"I was utterly devastated," Mary said. "Everyone at the White House wanted an apology, but that would have made the situation worse. So the president called me from Air Force One, and I couldn't stop crying. He said, 'Don't cry. It's okay. You were doing it because you were fighting. Just don't do it again.' The grass roots loved it because we were fighting back, but the Beltway crowd hated me for doing it."

The next day at the White House, there was a meeting of the senior campaign staff in the Roosevelt Room. To Mary, it seemed that everyone at that meeting gave her the cold shoulder; but when Dad came into the room, he walked all the way around the table and gave Mary a big hug.

In the meantime, Governor Clinton had selected Tennessee Senator Al Gore as his running mate and started to make Vice President Quayle an issue in the campaign, suggesting that Quayle was not prepared to be president. By then, the vice president had endured the overdone "potato" flap, but he had also made his famous "Murphy Brown" speech defending traditional "family values" and attacking Hollywood for its corrosive influence on our culture. That speech elicited howls of protest from political opponents and most corners of the media, who said they didn't need anyone from Washington lecturing them about values. Yet many of these same critics hailed President Clinton two years later when he made a similar speech about values in Memphis.

Nevertheless, some of Dad's political people started to talk about whether or not to keep the vice president on the 1992 ticket, arguing that it might help my father's poll numbers to get a new partner. Dad rejected this advice.

"You just don't do stuff like that," he told Mary Matalin.

That summer, historian David McCullough spoke at the White

House about Teddy Roosevelt. Dad invited Senator Alan Simpson to stop by the Oval Office after the lecture, and the senator had something on his mind.

"Let me tell you what I see about this campaign," the senator said. "When I'm through in this seven minutes or eight minutes, it might just be a rupture of our friendship. Stay out of the damn boat. Quit playing golf or you'll have a whole lifetime of doing that. Let the people know who you really are. They don't know who you are."

Dad took off his glasses and began to chew on the temple of them. "Well, how do I do that?" he shot back.

"Just be the same guy with the people of the United States as you are with all of us in the Senate," came the reply. "Write your own stuff."

In the end, Dad reassured his friend, "I can see you're very worried about me and the campaign. Don't worry. I'm not worried. They're never going to elect Bill Clinton to be president of the United States."

★ ★ ★

On August 13, Dad walked into the White House press briefing room and announced that he had asked his secretary of state and friend of thirty-five years, Jim Baker, to resign from the Department of State and return to the White House as chief of staff. If there was any question that Dad was determined to give his all in the fall campaign, this announcement answered it.

At this point, Dad had been the target of an unending barrage of political attacks and negative media coverage for the better part of the previous year. He remained confident of his ultimate success as he geared up for the Republican convention in Houston. Yet we knew a tough road lay ahead, particularly as we watched Bill Clinton and Al Gore storming across the country on a bus tour that kept their positive press coverage going well after the final balloon drop at Madison Square Garden.

With Perot out, and the Clinton-Gore ticket surging, the Republicans gathered for their national convention in Houston. The task Dad's team faced at the Houston Astrodome was no less daunting than the challenge they had confronted in New Orleans four years before—and hopes were high that Dad could produce a similar turnabout.

Beauty is in the eye of the beholder, as they say, and how the Houston convention went depends on whom you ask. The media, which are invariably drawn to controversy and conflict, focused on Dad's former primary opponents and made much of the more strident parts of Pat Buchanan's otherwise strong speech—and that of Pat Robertson. We featured more than 120 speakers that week, but the media focused like a laser beam on but a handful of lines from two or three speakers.

In fact, when I saw the news coverage of the convention, I felt like I had attended an entirely different event. By contrast, I remember my young nephew George P. giving a speech he wrote himself, giving it very well, and punctuating it at the end with "Viva Bush!"

I remember Labor Secretary Lynn Martin talking about the increasing role of women, and President Reagan giving what would turn out to be his final major political speech, doing so in his usual classic style. Best of all, in my view, I saw Mom and Dad stand before America that week and paint a positive, inclusive, and hopeful picture of the future. They were funny and warm, and, media coverage notwithstanding, they closed the gap with the Clinton-Gore ticket as they rolled out of Houston.

The battle had been joined, but Dad still had his work cut out for him.

★　★　★

During the first week in September, Dad traveled to Chicago, arriving at a hotel on South Michigan Avenue for a fund-raiser that evening. That afternoon, the director of political affairs at the

White House, Ron Kaufman, ran into Illinois Congressman Henry Hyde, who had been trying to get ahold of someone at the campaign or at the White House.

It turns out that, in the same hotel that same night, the Catholic League of Illinois was having its annual Man of the Year dinner in the ballroom downstairs. Many church leaders from Illinois and throughout the Midwest would be there. The Midwesterners would be there to honor Governor Bob Casey of Pennsylvania, who was one of the few pro-life leaders in the Democratic Party. In fact, Governor Casey had been denied a speaking role at the Democratic convention in New York because of his views on abortion, and as such was one of the few Democratic governors who had not endorsed Bill Clinton. (One of the others, Maryland Governor William Donald Schaefer, would endorse Dad later in the campaign.)

To Ron, stopping by this Catholic event was a no-brainer—a huge opportunity the campaign should not pass up. There was some back-and-forth as to scheduling a drop-by, but Ron thought, no problem, we'll go down after our event. "We finish our event," Ron said, "and I said, 'Okay, let's go downstairs,' and I was voted down—'No, we can't go, we're leaving.' We never went. Bill Clinton's campaign would have had him go downstairs, work every hand in that room, and kiss every nun twice on the cheek—but for some reason, we didn't. That's just how bad the 1992 campaign was."

★   ★   ★

Just as Dad had brought Secretary Baker back to the White House to help him for the stretch run in 1992, the decision was also made to make Sig Rogich, the 1988 media consultant who had recently been appointed ambassador to Iceland, a similar offer he could not refuse.

In fact, Sig was back in Washington getting ready to return to Iceland when Secretary Baker called and said he wanted Sig to come back and run the media for the campaign.

Sig recalled protesting at first: "I said, 'I can't do that. I moved everything—my clothes, my car.' To which Jim said, 'Well, I just got off the phone with the Old Man [which is what Secretary Baker called Dad in private]. Why don't you tell him you can't do it? Just put me on hold and call him—it won't take very long!' Well, Baker knew I would never do that."

After attending a White House meeting that night, Sig went to the headquarters the next morning and fired almost everybody on the campaign advertising staff. From there, Sig moved into a D.C. hotel and, from September through election day, never took a day off.

"When I came back to help the campaign of the president of the United States, we had two or three commercials in the can—and that's it. We were almost into September," Sig told me. Over the next thirty days, we produced forty TV commercials and probably three hundred radio commercials. None of that was done before, because nobody could make a decision on the advertising. It was run by committee to a degree that we just didn't get anything done."

On October 1, Ross Perot reentered the race, naming retired navy admiral James Stockdale as his running mate. The Texas billionaire also announced he would run a series of thirty-minute infomercials on the economy.

Perot's "October Surprise" came in time to get him in the three televised presidential debates that month. Meanwhile, Dad has always maintained he hated debates—"too much showbiz," he said. The three-way debates with Perot and Clinton did little to change his view. During the Richmond, Virginia, debate on October 15, for example, Dad checked his watch at one point, which commentators and political opponents pounced on to suggest Dad wasn't interested in fighting for the American people. Twelve years later, at the dedication of Bill Clinton's presidential library in Little Rock, Dad confessed that when he looked at his watch, he was actually "wondering when Ross Perot would be done speaking."

Perhaps the best summation of the final stages of the 1992 campaign appropriately came from David Bates, who had started with Dad as his traveling aide back when he was an asterisk in 1978 and was cabinet secretary in 1992:

It was a painful experience because all the cards were stacked against him. Plus his campaign, the White House, everybody, including me, should have and could have done a better job for him. Everything was unfortunately breaking against him. The economy was perceived to be much worse than it actually was. The economy was coming back and getting stronger, but it was not really apparent to people at that point.

It was almost as if it was destined not to be. He had done such a great job in foreign policy. The Cold War ended without a shot being fired. Desert Storm had gone so well. He booted Saddam out of Kuwait. Germany was unified. All the foreign policy issues were off the table. I mean, that was apparent to the average person. It was a very similar situation to Churchill after World War II when he was voted out. He was a victim of his own success: World War II ended, he had led extremely ably during World War II. Then when the war was over, the British people turned to a younger, more energetic person [Clement Atlee] who was talking more about the domestic economy. They turned Churchill out.

Buchanan ran against the president in the primaries and basically called him a liar, which hurt. You had Clinton there talking, and the media repeating everything Clinton said, "worst economy since the Great Depression." That was kind of a preposterous claim—one of the big lies of the 1992 campaign—but you had Clinton out there saying, "I'm going to focus on the economy like a laser beam."

Then you had Perot, who got 19 percent of the vote. Most of those voters came from us.

To this day, I am certain that he could have won but for Lawrence Walsh indicting Caspar Weinberger [for the Iran-Contra affair] the Friday before the election. I remember that Friday morning we had a campaign stop in St. Louis with Governor [John] Ashcroft, and the Democratic governor of Maryland, Governor

Schaefer. It was really big news, and we were really moving. I heard Jim Baker say on the Wednesday before the election he thought we were going to win it, because we were moving up. Clinton was losing support. The theme about trust was really working, and I think a lot of doubts were starting to creep in about Clinton.

Fred Steeper, the pollster on that Friday morning before the campaign, had it dead even in terms of his overnight tracking numbers. Of course, to get dead even, we were coming up and Clinton was losing support. And a CNN poll of likely voters that same morning had us back minus one. And then at 11:00 a.m. the independent counsel looking into the Iran-Contra affair, Lawrence Walsh, announced his indictment of Caspar Weinberger for allegedly lying to investigators, and the main exhibit was some note saying Bush was in the loop. It was awful. That weekend was absolutely awful.

From that point on, noon until election day, it was nonstop coverage about Iran-Contra. And I remember that Friday night in Wisconsin, we did *Larry King Live,* and George Stephanopoulos somehow got his call through—surprise, surprise.

It was a Thursday before the campaign, and we were at the Ford Museum in Grand Rapids, Michigan, at an event with the former president, and Baker said that he was walking by the press bin and [ABC reporter] Ann Compton said, "How are you feeling, Secretary Baker?" And he said, "We feel good, we're moving." And she said, "I know, but I don't think it's going to last." And then the next morning, boom.

To give you an idea of the impact of the Walsh indictment: on October 30, five days before the election, Andy Card—then secretary of transportation who had just come back from managing the federal response to Hurricane Andrew in Florida—jumped on a small plane with Secretary of Labor Lynn Martin, Secretary of Energy Jim Watkins, and Republican National Committee Chairman Rich Bond to do airport rallies in swing states. They were supposed to do four events in Ohio, three in Michigan, and end up in Milwaukee, Wisconsin.

At the first stop, the troupe landed at the airport on the West

Virginia side of the river, but the event was actually in Ohio. They got off the plane, did a press conference, went to a little rally, then got back on the plane and flew to the next city.

"We get off the plane, and the first question at the press conference was on the Iran-Contra special prosecutor," Andy remembered. "It's like you hit the brick wall. All the momentum goes. So everything that you want to talk about is gone because it's all Iran-Contra. It was very demoralizing."

They did that first rally, then we went to the next stop in Columbus, Ohio. There it was the same deal—everyone interested in Lawrence Walsh. By the time they reached Dayton, Ohio, Secretary Martin said, "This is not working. I'm not going to get back on the plane. I'm going back to Washington."

By the time they reached Cleveland, Jim Watkins said, "This isn't working," and he, too, left. Long story short: all the positive momentum that we had all felt on Thursday was gone by Saturday morning.

"You talk about a politically timed indictment, but I didn't say it then," Dad said. "Don't blame somebody else. Just get along about your business. But that was a cruel blow by a special prosecutor who I'm afraid I don't respect for no other reason than that one reason."

To add to our woes, the actual indictment was handled by a San Francisco trial lawyer named James J. Brosnahan, who worked for the independent counsel and who had a long record of making political contributions to Democratic presidential candidates and other liberal causes. In fact, Federal Election Commission records show that Mr. Brosnahan made a $1,000 contribution to the Clinton/Gore campaign on October 29, 1992, the day before Weinberger was indicted.

★   ★   ★

The Halloween before the election, we were living in Bethesda, Maryland. Sam and Ellie were attending public school, and I went to their yearly Halloween parade, standing with all the other parents watching the kids march by on the blacktop. Suddenly, I saw one of the students marching with a Clinton-Gore sign. Looking closer, I saw the student had a clown suit on and a George Bush mask. Some of the parents nearby chuckled.

I stood there without expression but was dying inside. I remember feeling so hurt and thinking how insensitive it was to Sam and Ellie. Throughout this awful campaign, they often got comments from other children, parroting their own parents. One time, Ellie took a paintbrush with red paint and ran it right down the face of a classmate who told her that her grandfather was going to lose. She was only five years old; and while she didn't understand the politics, she was hurting.

When someone you love is in political office, politics are personal. There is no way around that. We, as a family, are fiercely loyal, and whether you are five or thirty-three, as I was in 1992, those kinds of cruel moments cut the deepest.

★   ★   ★

As they neared the final stop of the 1992 campaign, Air Force One was dropping into Baton Rouge, Louisiana, on November 2 for Dad's second-to-last campaign rally—coming in from Kentucky before moving on to Houston for the night. It was late afternoon, and the Oak Ridge Boys were on the plane. Mary Matalin and Ron Kaufman were sitting up front with Dad.

"For the president, the Oaks did a medley of gospel songs a capella, ending with 'Amazing Grace,'" Ron recalled. "As they sang 'Amazing Grace,' everyone in the place started to cry—not bawling crying, just tearing. It was clear we were going to lose, and it was all over. It had been a long campaign, and that was the first time we actually admitted to ourselves, even semiprivately, that this is over." Dad thinks he and Mary Matalin were probably the only two people who still thought we would win.

As sad as that time was, we still found ways to laugh as a family. On election night, for example, we all gathered in Dad and Mom's suite to watch the returns. We were in the living room, and Mom was in the bedroom reading a romance novel. Things were not looking good at all, casting a pall over the room. Periodically, however, Mom would walk into the room and say, "What's it like to drive a car?" and then walk back out. A few minutes later, she came in and asked, "How do you buy an airplane ticket?" and then walked back out and read her book.

It really made us laugh. She was trying to lighten things up.

There was no taking the bone-jarring hurt out of the final 1992 results. It just hurt, and it hurt a lot. As a family, we had tasted political defeat in the past—but together, we had never endured an uglier, more disappointing, and ultimately helpless year than 1992. We saw a good man, and a great leader, brought down by distortion, innuendo, and fabrication.

That night, Governor Clinton became the first candidate since Richard Nixon in 1968 to win the presidency with less than 50 percent of the popular vote. Still, he won almost 45 million votes to Dad's 39 million and, most important, the 370 electoral votes he and his supporters needed, to Dad's 168, to claim the White House.

As a family, our eyes were wide open: after Dad's twelve years of success at the highest level, we knew that presidential politics was, and still is, a rough neighborhood. And as always, Mom and Dad kept us grounded during this difficult time—just as they had through the heady times. When the moment came to concede, we stood together, as always.

"Everybody had gone out onstage—all the family was out there—and the president was about to be announced," Joe Hagin recalled. "We were in the offstage announcement area waiting to go out. David Bates, the announcer, and I were the only people standing back there with him. David and I were both crying. The president reached out and grabbed us both by the neck, one in one hand and one in the other. He said, 'Boys, don't worry about this. It's been a heck of a ride.'"

With that, Dad walked out and gave his concession speech. Offstage, Joe regained his composure and surveyed the scene. "I watched a big Secret Service agent at the front, standing there stiffly. About halfway through the speech, I saw a big tear run down his face—which shows how much the Secret Service loved him, and still love him."

★   ★   ★

Without question, November 1992 had to be the worst month of Dad's life, but not because it was the month he lost the presidential election: rather, it was the month he lost his dear, sweet, amazing mother. As Dad wrote to Lady Bird Johnson a few weeks later, she was "our leader, our compass, our family's best person."

I went with my dad to Greenwich to visit his mother the day she died, November 19. I remember the date clearly because it was Ellie's eighth birthday. I had planned an afternoon swim party for Ellie with many of her classmates from Westbrook Elementary School. Dad called me the day before, however, and said, "Your grandmother is very, very sick and I'm going up to say good-bye. I want you to come." Dad knew how much I loved her and how honored I was to carry her name.

More important, I knew how much Dad loved her. Dad needed someone to be his emotional support that day, but he picked the wrong person. When I saw my grandmother in the last stages of death, both Dad and I wept unabashedly. It's still moving to think I was there when my father said good-bye to his mother, the woman who had the biggest impact on his life. I believe that to be true because my dad's life was not defined by the political system he navigated, but by the set of beliefs his mother taught him. To be kind and thoughtful and to think of the other person. To live a life of service and to honor God.

Leaving Ganny's bedside that day was one of the hardest things I've ever done. We went back to Washington—Dad to his final days as president, and me to Ellie's party. That day at 5:05 p.m., Mom got a message from Patty Presock that read:

> Nan Ellis just called. Mrs. Bush Sr. died 5 minutes ago. I thought you might want to tell the President.

Nan Ellis said that Mrs. Bush Sr. was waiting for the President and after he left today, she just let go.

If you learn by example, my grandmother set the best there could be—and Dad absorbed every bit of it. Dad and I knew that day that Ganny went to heaven as she had been preparing to do. Consider what she observed when she wrote her own eulogy years before her death on April 17, 1981:

This is a service of gratitude to God for the easiest life ever given to anyone to live on this earth and all because of LOVE. From my mother's knee I learned to know Jesus and that He would always be with me if at night in bed I would just tell Him any mean, selfish, even untrue things I had done during the day, He would lift them from my mind and I would awake refreshed, and later along the way if there was a steep incline, He would take my hand and help me up the hill. How right she was.

Chapter 21

MOUNTAINTOPS AND VALLEYS

"He did have a vision, even though people would criticize him on the so-called vision thing. It was his vision and his quiet pragmatic way of going about things that brought the Cold War to an end and put us on a better path for the future. It was a pragmatic vision of getting the problem solved and getting the job done—not just lecturing about his vision."

—Colin Powell

Even after fourteen years, the number of reasons you find for Dad's defeat in 1992 depends on the number of people you ask—because everyone, it seems, has their own convictions on the matter.

Looking back, Jim Baker thinks there were three main reasons for Dad's defeat—and the one reason that was Dad's fault was actually a product of his and President Reagan's success.

"We'd been in power twelve years," Secretary Baker said, "and it was very hard to be seen as an agent of change when you've been there twelve years and people want to vote for change. The only constant in politics is change. That may sound funny, but it's true."

Dad shares this view: "I don't see how anybody could have done it differently against this onslaught for change, change, change. And the opposition, the Clinton campaign, was very good with their war room and their young Turks throwing footballs in their campaign. They were good, very good."

Secretary Baker also pointed to Ross Perot's candidacy: "He took 19 percent of the vote. We got 38 percent and Clinton got 43 percent, and we know he [Perot] took two out of every three votes from us. You take two-thirds of 19 and add it to 38 and you get 51 percent. So that really hurt us."

The third thing that hurt Dad, according to Secretary Baker, was the negative perception too many Americans had about the economy. "We had an economy in '92 that was coming back," he said. "Many of the president's advisers told him that nothing needed to be done substantively because the economy was coming back; and, indeed, it did. But nobody realized it until October, too late for us."

Still, when you look at everything that happened during his administration, Dad's four years in office were of far-reaching consequence for our nation—and for the world. No question, President Reagan's "peace through strength" broke the back of the Soviet economy, forcing the Soviets to the negotiating table; but as we entered the endgame, the fact that the Cold War was won without a shot being fired, without conflict between the superpowers, is largely due to the leadership my father exerted during those tense, dangerous times. As the Chinese proverb states: the height of skill is not to fight and win one hundred battles, but to win those battles without having to fight.

When you look at everything Dad did in his career leading up to his presidency, it is as if everything he did throughout his life was preparing him to meet the central challenge of his time. My brother George told me, "I think his greatest accomplishment was helping to wind down the Cold War. He had a deft touch in dealing with the winners and losers. It's a lesson I've learned from him, by the way, that personal relationships matter a lot. These leaders came to trust him during this tumultuous time, because he was very steady in helping to bring order."

Dad was true to himself to the end. General Scowcroft said that every time they prepared a speech for my father with soaring rhetoric in it, Dad would cross it out. He'd say, "That's not me. I'm not comfortable talking that way." Maybe it's because, for Dad, true eloquence lies in action. He knows full well the power of words in politics, but he actively shunned anything that smacked of "show business."

As for the "vision thing," General Scowcroft said, "Did he know where he was going? Did he know how he wanted to get there? In a world as kaleidoscopic as he inherited, the answer is clearly yes. Now, would it have been better to have more vision instead of the decisiveness? Well, I presume that's a contrast, for example, with President John F. Kennedy, who had vision and expressed it. 'We'll carry any burden, we'll pay any price, go anywhere, in defense of human liberty.' And where did we go? To Vietnam."

Former state department spokeswoman Margaret Tutwiler put it this way: "Popular would have been to sever relationships with China after Tiananmen Square. Popular at the time would have been to bomb Iraq into oblivion and take Saddam Hussein. Popular would have been to stick it to Gorbachev and pop champagne on the Berlin Wall. Instead, he always chose what was best for the country, not necessarily what was easy and popular—or what would have been great for George Bush."

★　★　★

Returning to the White House with Dad the day after the election, Marvin recalled how they had to drive in from Andrews Air Force Base because they couldn't land Marine One, the president's helicopter, on the South Lawn. The entire White House staff had gathered out there to welcome Mom and Dad home, and it was too crowded to land.

"When he got there, it was the first time that I'd seen the emotion creep out of his bones," Marvin said, "and I think part of it was just the fact that he felt confident that he could continue, finish the job, be a great president in a second term. I think the emotion that came out that day was driven by the fact that he saw the lawn full of people who had given so much to him, and he felt that he'd let them down. And the great thing about Dad that is consistent with his perspective in moving forward in life is the transition from that day. That might have been the low point, but after that, he took one step at a time looking ahead."

Mom remembers that on that ride home they saw a lone runner on the 14th Street bridge stop and salute as the president's motorcade went by. That single gesture of patriotism moved Dad to tears.

A few days after the election, General Powell called Dad at the White House. "I know it's a little unusual for the chairman of the Joint Chiefs of Staff to call the president," General Powell remembered, "but he and I were so close that I just wanted to tell him that we were thinking of him. And he thanked me very much."

Within two hours, Mom called Alma Powell and invited the Powells up to Camp David that weekend. The Powells couldn't imagine Mom and Dad would want somebody "horning in on the family on that weekend," as General Powell later put it, "but we went up to Camp David and we spent the evening watching a movie, and we walked around the grounds. The president and I were in front, and since it was the fall it was getting dark early. I remember him saying a couple of times, 'Colin, it hurts. It really hurts. I never thought they'd pick him,' meaning Clinton. And I said, 'I know it does. It has to, but it will pass.' We were family from that moment on."

★　★　★

Hard feelings don't disappear quickly after a rough campaign and a tough election loss, and most in the administration felt a lingering sense of antipathy toward the media in particular, as well as Dad's political opponents. Yet Dad was determined to see his job through—to "finish this job in style," as he said at the time. When he convened his cabinet two days after the election on November 5, he talked about each cabinet officer's responsibility to continue to govern and be prepared for the transition. Dad wanted to make sure President Clinton had everything he needed to be able to do the job.

"It was a very noble speech," Andy Card, who was then secretary of transportation, recalled. "He was always about duty, honor, service; and at this meeting he was exhibiting that."

After that cabinet meeting, however, Dad had one last mission for Andy: running the Republican side of the presidential transition. Andy thought Bob Zoellick, Secretary Baker's deputy chief of staff, was going to handle the transition, but Mom and Dad wanted Andy, and they wanted him and Kathy to come to Camp David that weekend to discuss it in depth.

Andy recalled how the conversation flowed once he arrived at Laurel, the main lodge where the president's office is at Camp David, that weekend:

> The president started by talking about the transition. Specifically, he said, "I want this transition to work. I don't want President Clinton to drop the baton, so we've got to make sure he is running at full speed when we pass it to him. We want to be supportive and encouraging and have no bitter, lingering animosity."
>
> The president then talked about some of the people who should help in the transition, and some of the loose ends that had to be cleaned up in the administration—what he wanted to get done before he left. Most of the conversation centered around all the correspondence. He wanted to make sure all the people that wrote to him got answers back. He also worried about people who worked for the administration that he cared about. He offered to "clear the decks" for President Clinton so that he wasn't left with anybody that Clinton had to fire.
>
> Then we broke and we went for a walk—and it was a walk down memory lane. The president talked about the first time he ran for the United States Senate. He talked about Martin Allday, for example, and Jimmy Allison. He talked about running for Congress and serving in Congress. He talked about running for president. He reflected on the people that helped him and never asked for anything.
>
> It wasn't sad, but it was a little melancholy. It was almost cele-

brating with the recognition that he'd run his last campaign, and it didn't end up the way he wanted it to end up.

He wasn't even angry. I think that he was disappointed probably as much in himself and the campaign. He talked about all the kids, and Barbara. He talked about Lee Atwater, Rich Bond, and Vic Gold. He talked about Nick Brady and Mac Baldrige.

Throughout it all, I didn't have to say a word. I didn't even know a lot of the people or the places or the instances. He was just talking. He expressed some frustration about some people—it wasn't all "I love everybody." There was some "I'm glad I don't have to deal with this person anymore." There was also a little bit of that. But it was a sunset discussion rather than a sunrise discussion.

We just kept walking, and he did 90 percent of the talking. It was almost as if he wasn't talking to me. I just happened to be there while he was talking. He loves the people in this country, and he was grateful for the support that he had—that was evident.

He didn't say, "I don't know what I'm going to do for the rest of my life." Neither did he say, "This is what I'm going to do for the rest of my life." It was really, "What great things have happened, and what great lessons I've learned, and what great experiences I've had. I wish it wasn't a defeat that we were talking about."

In the coming weeks, Andy worked to identify where Dad's new office would be, what it would look like, and how it would be staffed. Dad really didn't want to focus on it, but he knew he had to—and he gave Andy broad latitude to work closely with Rose Zamaria, who had started working with Dad a quarter of a century before and who became his first post-presidential chief of staff, to find a suitable setup.

After one or two near misses, Andy and Rose met with Realtors and finally decided on a fairly new building not too far from where my parents would build their new home in Houston. The office space was under construction, and Andy went and called Dad from Fuzzy's Pizza, a nearby restaurant that Dad has since come to love.

★   ★   ★

While Dad has never been one to dwell on the past, in the wake of the '92 loss he was clearly doing a lot of thinking as he and Mom prepared to transition back to private life. As always, he was reaching out—and writing notes. On November 5, for example, he wrote to Vice President Quayle's daughter, Corinne. Dad even wrote on the envelope "Personal—Counting the Vice President."

Dear Corinne,

I've been doing a little thinking since the election.

I've been thinking of the effect on my own kids and grandkids. I saw Noelle, my beautiful Noelle, with tears in her eyes. She knew I was hurting inside—and I know she cared so much.

Then I said I wonder how our wonderful VP's kids are doing— and I thought of you and your brothers. I know it is not easy for you.

But soon the ache in your heart will go away and a whole wonderful future will unfold. You will have more privacy, more time with your great Mom and Dad.

Your father should stay in public life. He has so much to offer. And remember it hasn't been easy for him; because the Vice President has always gone along with the President; and he's had to take a lot of the fire that he wouldn't have otherwise taken. But he did it with loyalty and class—and I will always be grateful. Good luck to you. I just wanted you to know I was thinking about you.

Love,

George Bush

Dad wrote a lot of letters during this time, too many to include here. "He's one of the best writers I've ever known," my brother George said to me. "He is a powerful writer. He can share his heart better on a piece of paper than he can in person. He may not have been raised to be touchy-feely; yet he can be very emotional. I remember he was reading a story and he burst out in tears because he was so affected. He's got a tender heart."

People were reaching out to Mom and Dad, too. On November 10, the Republican leaders in the Senate invited Mom and Dad and the Quayles to a private dinner at the Columbus Club at Union Station near Capitol Hill. The event was set up as a salute to the president and vice president, but in his remarks Dad turned the spotlight back on the members of his team. He saved his final and most poignant comments for the minority leader in the Senate, his former political rival who had become perhaps Dad's strongest ally on Capitol Hill, Bob Dole.

"It's well known that he and I went head-to-head in tough primary days long ago," Dad said that night. "But the beautiful thing is . . . here's a guy who took on this role of leader and worked with a president with whom he had done combat in the past, but subsequently we became, again, fast friends. He never put his agenda ahead of the president, and that's the way it ought to work when you have the White House."

When it was Senator Dole's turn to speak, he also gave a very warm tribute to Dad and even broke down at one point during his remarks.

"We were all so emotional," Senator Dole recalled. "We respected the president. We knew he had integrity. We knew he did a good job, and a lot of us felt without any criticism of Clinton that Ross Perot cost us the presidency. So it was really a great evening in a way. I mean, you don't celebrate defeat, but our view was that we ought to get the president and First Lady up there and let them know that we're your friends, and we're your supporters, and we'll always be that way."

He added, "It's always easy when you're sitting in the White House or anywhere else having won, but this was only several days after the election when we had this dinner, and it says a lot about President and Mrs. Bush that they were able to come up there."

That night, Dad returned to the White House and immediately penned a handwritten note to Senator Dole:

11-10-92
late at night

Dear Bob,

When you invited me, I didn't want to come. I didn't think I could face the music. But now I am so glad you asked me.

The warmth of your generous remarks made it all so worthwhile. You have been a truly noble leader, and as I leave Washington I will take with me a friendship I value—a respect for a true leader I'll always feel. Thanks, Bob.

George

Shortly before midnight, Mom and Dad decided to go to the Vietnam Memorial on the National Mall near the Lincoln Memorial. It was the tenth anniversary of that austere black granite wall, and there was a round-the-clock program where family members and veterans were reading the names of those who didn't come home. Dad wanted to go over and read a few names, but even though he had promised the press years ago that he'd always alert them whenever he went out of the White House, he wanted to do this without notifying the media. He didn't want to be seen as "sticking it in Clinton's ear," as he put it in his diary. Dad just said, "To hell with the media."

According to Chris Emery, one of the White House ushers who accompanied Mom and Dad in the car, Dad wanted to keep this visit low-key—and he didn't seem in the mood to discuss it beyond that.

Chris also recalled how the motorcade used no sirens and even stopped at every red light, owing to the low-key nature of the visit. During the short drive to the monument, Chris also recalled how Mom and Dad talked about their house-hunting in Houston and asked him about getting their computers and accounting program set up in their new office.

When they arrived at the memorial, roughly one hundred people stood gathered in the cool evening mist.

"The only light was the moon," Chris remembered. "No press, no lights, no security, no entourage. As they approached the stage where individuals were reading the names, bystanders started to recognize them—and several widows and family members of veterans came up and hugged them."

Eventually, Mom and Dad made it to the stage. Mom stood by as Dad stepped up to the microphone and read ten or so names, then slowly backed away. Chris recalled that the crowd applauded loudly. On their way back to the car, Mom and Dad shook dozens of hands and signed dozens more autographs.

"So many of the veterans told the president how much they appreciated him and how sorry they were that he lost the election," Chris said. "A few even insulted the president-elect, but President Bush said over and over that we need to rally around President Clinton now."

During the ride back to the White House, Dad was lost in thought—pensively studying a hat given to him by one of the veterans. Then, reflecting out loud, he said he hoped that Desert Storm helped vindicate the Vietnam experience—that he felt bad for the veterans who returned home from Southeast Asia to jeers, and not the cheers and respect they deserved.

"I believe I saw a tear in the president's eye," Chris said.

★   ★   ★

On November 19, Nebraska Senator Bob Kerrey sent Dad a handwritten note that deeply touched my father—"about the nicest I have ever received," he wrote back. Senator Kerrey, of course, had run in the Democratic primary that year and had been as tough as any candidate in challenging the administration's record. In his letter, Senator Kerrey wrote:

Dear Mr. President,

　　I was terribly sorry to hear the news of your mother's passing. It is a terrible loss.
　　In spite of all the unkind and unreasonable things I said about you this past year, this is my belief: history will judge you to have been a strong, good President who did more than his people knew.
　　You have my respect, my prayer in this difficult hour, and my admiration.

　　Signed,

　　Bob Kerrey

Another generous assessment came from one of Dad's predecessors, Jimmy Carter, who told me, "I observed very closely your father's accomplishments and his moral standards, the accuracy with which he spoke to the American people. All of these things aroused a great deal of personal admiration from me. There have been a number of successors who have served in the White House since I left and he is by far the one who treated me best and with whom I had the closest possible working relationship."

★　★　★

A year or two into his presidency, Dad had invited comedian Dana Carvey and *Saturday Night Live* creator and executive producer Lorne Michaels—who were in Washington for an event—to drop by the Oval Office for a brief visit. By then, Dana Carvey had been impersonating Dad on *SNL* for several years, and my father had enjoyed seeing clips of him on TV.

Dana was in town to play Dad at an event that night hosted by Pamela Harriman, one of the grande dames of the Democratic party, at the Kennedy Center.

Dana recalled, "I remember that the president's poll ratings were so high that I came on dressed as number 41, so to speak, and was just making fun of the fact that the Democrats didn't have a chance against him. That was the sketch. So when we met him, he was just really gracious, and we took pictures and chatted a little bit. I think he assumed that Lorne and I politically were way left of him, which was not necessarily true at all."

After that visit, however, Dad and Dana did not speak again until a few weeks after the 1992 election. Then, out of the blue, Dana got a call saying, "This is White House operator number one. Hold for the president."

Dad got on the phone and asked Dana if he wouldn't mind coming down to the White House to "cheer up the troops," and invited Dana and his wife, Paula, to spend the night at the White House. The Carveys arrived the afternoon of December 6.

"It was Christmastime," Dana said, "so all the bows and ribbons and trees and lights were out. It was especially gorgeous, and then we went upstairs to the Lincoln Bedroom and your dad had left us a really nice note on the bed saying something like, 'Glad you're here and see you down the hall for a pre-dinner drink at 6:00.' As I'm holding the note, he walks in to say hi."

That night, Mom and Dad took the Carveys to the Kennedy Center Honors, where Dad's friend and jazz legend Lionel Hampton and actor Paul Newman and his wife, actress Joanne Woodward, were among the honorees. At one point during the ceremony, the emcee, Walter Cronkite, turned the spotlight to the president's box and asked the audience to "salute President George Herbert Walker Bush for his years of service to our country."

"The whole place stood up and gave a standing ovation," Dana said. "After that, we were ushered off into the elevator very quickly. So it's President and Mrs. Bush; a Secret Service agent; and my wife and me. The president was really kind of emotional. It was sort of an awkward moment. It kind of shook him up a little bit because it was unexpected."

Back at the White House, it was nearing midnight when there was a knock at the Carveys' bedroom door. They thought it was the butler, but it was Dad who walked into the Lincoln Bedroom, carrying glasses of water on a big tray. "Who's thirsty?" Dad asked before he and Mom led the Carveys on a tour of the White House. Then Mom tucked the Carveys in and took their order for breakfast.

The next morning, the White House staff was invited to assemble in the East Room, and after they played "Hail to the Chief" to announce the president into the room, Dana walked out as Dad as a surprise. As Dana remembered it: "The president said, 'You go out as me, and I'll go out as me. That way there'll be two of me.'"

Mom and Dad and Paula Carvey joined Dana onstage—whereupon Dana gave an impromptu performance. Displaying all his trademark Dadisms, Dana joked that he had even impersonated Dad in calling the Secret Service, saying, "Feel like going jogging tonight . . . in the nude."

★   ★   ★

The presidential and personal transition aside, Dad still had two months in office—and as always, he packed a lot into the time he was given.

For example, on December 4, Dad announced Operation Restore Hope to repair the food supply lines in war-torn Somalia. Already, a quarter of a million people had starved to death because of famine. The United Nations appealed to the world for help because the warring factions there made it impossible for relief workers to deliver food supplies.

For months, Mom and Dad had watched the TV reports as the suffering in Somalia deepened by the day, and finally my father could bear it no more. As he had in Iraq, Dad gave the Pentagon a clearly defined mission: end the starvation, then come home. In fact, my father wanted the troops home before the inaugural because he didn't want to saddle President Clinton with a military operation at the outset of his administration.

Roughly two weeks later, Dad signed the North American Free Trade Agreement, or NAFTA, which had become the centerpiece

Mom and Dad arrive on Air Force One in Seoul, Korea, February 27, 1989.
(GBPL/Dave Valdez)

Mom and Dad host a state dinner in 1990. (GBPL/Dave Valdez)

Mom and Dad with President Lech Walesa of Poland, July 11, 1989. (GBPL/Dave Valdez)

Dad and Prime Minister Margaret Thatcher at Camp David, November 1989. (GBPL/Carol Powers)

Dad and his vice president, Dan Quayle. (GBPL)

Dad jokes with his staff by wearing a hooded robe during a daily intelligence briefing in 1990. (GBPL/Dave Valdez)

Dad and German Prime Minister Kohl take a walk at Camp David, February 25, 1990. (GBPL/Susan Biddle)

Dad and President Gorbachev sign the START Treaty in the East Room of the White House, June 1, 1990. (GBPL/Dave Valdez)

Margaret Bush and me sharing a laugh with Princess Diana. (GBPL/Susan Biddle)

Dad with the troops in Dhahran, Saudi Arabia, November 22, 1990. (GBPL/Dave Valdez)

Dad and Prime Minister John Major hold a joint press conference at Camp David. (GBPL/Dave Valdez)

Jeb and George at Camp David, Christmas, 1990. (GBPL)

General Colin Powell gets a status report from General Schwarzkopf, while Dad speaks with Prime Minister John Major, February 27, 1991. (GBPL/Dave Valdez)

I was delighted to met Her Royal Highness Queen Elizabeth of Great Britain at a state dinner in her honor. (GBPL/Dave Valdez)

Celebration on the South Lawn to honor the baseball accomplishments of Ted Williams and Joe DiMaggio, July 9, 1991. (GBPL/Dave Valdez)

Former presidents Ford, Nixon, Reagan, and Carter join Dad at the dedication of the Reagan Presidential Library in 1991. (GBPL/Dave Valdez)

President Carlos Menem of Argentina celebrates Ellie's birthday at Camp David. (GBPL/Susan Biddle)

Sam on the conference table at Camp David with a model of Air Force One. (GBPL/Susan Biddle)

Dad, Sam, and Ellie join Arnold Schwarzenegger and the Harlem Globetrotters for the Great American Workout at the White House, May 1, 1992. (GBPL/Dave Valdez)

Dancing with Bobby to the music of the U.S. Marine Corps Band at our rehearsal dinner. (GBPL/Dave Valdez)

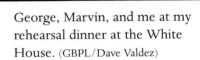

George, Marvin, and me at my rehearsal dinner at the White House. (GBPL/Dave Valdez)

I so appreciate the White House staff who volunteered at our wedding at Camp David. From left to right: William "Buddy" Carter, George Hannie, Ricardo "Sam" Sanvictores, and James "Jim" Selman. (Not pictured: James Ramsey.) (GBPL/Dave Valdez)

Mom and Dad at the 1992 Republican Convention in Houston. (GBPL)

George and me with Harry Smith, making the media rounds at the 1992 convention. (GBPL)

Aunt Nan wows the crowd at Bergen County GOP Headquarters in Hackensack, New Jersey. (GBPL/Carol Powers)

Dana Carvey cheers up the troops at the White House, December 7, 1992. (GBPL/Dave Valdez)

Former Canadian prime minister Mulroney and his wife, Mila, visit Mom and Dad in Kennebunkport. (GBPL)

Celebrating Mom and Dad's fiftieth wedding anniversary at the Grand Ole Opry in Nashville, Tennessee. (GBPL)

Paul Marchand, Dad, Freddie Couples, and Jim Nantz get ready for some serious horseshoes. (GBPL)

Dad is the first visitor to the Oval Office after the inauguration of the 43rd president of the United States. (The White House/Eric Draper)

Dad plays Carnac at Mom's seventy-fifth birthday party, June 8, 2000. (GBPL)

Robert catches a big one with Dad. (GBPL)

Gigi, Laura, Jenna, and Barney walk along the pier in Kennebunkport.
(The White House/Susan Sterner)

Laura and Gigi. (GBPL)

President George W. Bush rides
a Segway Human Transporter
in Kennebunkport. (GBPL)

Dad grabs the hand of President George W. Bush after his speech at the National Cathedral after the 9/11 attack. (The White House/Eric Draper)

President Bush and Governor Bush in the Oval Office. (The White House/Eric Draper)

Celebrating Dad's eightieth birthday at Minute Maid Park in Houston. (The White House/Eric Draper)

Gigi imitates the portrait of President George Washington that hangs in the East Room of the White House. (GBPL)

Mikhail Gorbachev at Dad's eightieth birthday, with Jebbie, Gigi, Pierce, and Sam. (GBPL)

Sam, Neil, Pierce, and Lauren getting ready to parachute at Dad's eightieth birthday. (GBPL)

Gigi holds the veil for George P. and Mandi on their wedding day. (The White House/Eric Draper)

At George P. and Mandi's wedding, Dad and his brothers and sister: Bucky, Pressie, Nancy, and Johnny. (GBPL)

Mom and Dad at the 2004 Republican Convention in New York City.
(The White House/Eric Draper)

Me, Marvin, Mom, and Sam dance the conga line on election night, November 2, 2004. (The White House)

The second inauguration of President George W. Bush.
(The White House/Eric Draper)

Campaigning with Barbara and Jenna.
(The White House)

Thanksgiving in Crawford with Jenna and Barbara. (The White House/Eric Draper)

President Bush 41 and 43. (The White House/Eric Draper)

Mom, President Bush 43, and Dad laughing on the White House lawn. (The White House/Eric Draper)

President Clinton is greeted at Kennebunkport by Gigi and Robert, and their cousins K.C. and Max. (GBPL)

Bobby and me with our children at Mom and Dad's sixtieth anniversary in the Red Room. (The White House/Eric Draper)

Placing the galley of *My Father, My President* into a time capsule aboard the aircraft carrier *George H. W. Bush*. (Kevin Wensing)

Dad parachutes in March of 1997. (Tom Sanders)

in Dad's vision of a hemisphere united by economic and political cooperation. NAFTA to this day continues to be a hotly debated issue; yet Dad and many experts believe it has been a major success.

The final foreign policy achievement during Dad's waning days as president came on January 3. After visiting American troops and relief operations in Somalia over the New Year holiday, Dad met Mom in Moscow, where he became the first American president to set foot in a democratic Russia. There, together with Russian President Boris Yeltsin, Dad signed the second Strategic Arms Reduction Treaty of his administration, called START II. This was perhaps Dad's last major act as president, but it was certainly not the least important.

Though START II has since been superseded by an agreement that my brother, our current president, signed with Russian President Vladimir Putin in 2002, START II remains a landmark step in the ongoing process to drastically reduce the threat of nuclear war and make ours a safer world.

In one of two major, final speeches, Dad went to the United States Military Academy at West Point on January 5 to warn the cadets—and the nation—against complacency in the face of the tough global challenges that remained, saying:

> We see disturbing signs of what this new world could become if we are passive and aloof. We would risk the emergence of a world characterized by violence, characterized by chaos, one in which dictators and tyrants threaten their neighbors, build arsenals brimming with weapons of mass destruction, and ignore the welfare of their own men, women, and children. And we could see a horrible increase in international terrorism, with American citizens more at risk than ever before.

Little did Dad or anyone else know, but as he was warning about American citizens being more at risk than ever, terrorists were preparing to strike the World Trade Center towers just a month later, on February 26, killing six people and injuring one hundred.

★ ★ ★

As Dad and Mom were preparing to leave the White House, the many people who worked there were preparing to say good-bye to them as well. Mary Jackson, one of the military nurses assigned to the White House, wrote to him:

> *Respecting you was so easy. We just wish every American could know the George Bush that we know—a George Bush who sends soup and skim milk down to the office of a lowly nurse, because he's afraid she's missed dinner; a George Bush who calls a young WHCA [White House Communications Agency] trooper who mistakenly introduced him as the Vice President instead of the President—and consequently, takes the heat off of the young man; a George Bush who agonizes over the loss of each pilot and soldier in a war where losses were overwhelmingly low; a George Bush who visits the Vietnam Memorial at midnight so as not to be construed as a pretentious act, but as a man truly paying respect to his fallen comrades; a George Bush who I overheard refer to himself as "the luckiest Gampy in the world" and openly displays affection with his wife, kids and grandkids; a George Bush who laughs at my dumbest jokes and on his worst days, is a better and stronger person than I have ever been.*

During Dad's final weekend as president, he and Mom hosted a cocktail party at Camp David on Saturday evening for the Joint Chiefs of Staff, the Supreme Court of the United States, and country singer George Strait. General Scowcroft also came because there was a lot of foreign policy being conducted that weekend.

But there were a few other surprise guests as well.

"Only George Bush would do this," said Prime Minister Mulroney, who stayed the entire weekend with his wife, Mila. "Only George Bush had the generosity and the magnanimity and the sense of genuine friendship to invite to Camp David that weekend the cochairs of the incoming transition team, Vernon Jordan and Warren Christopher. And they were there. Together, we had cocktails, then went over to the chapel where people spoke and a few hymns were sung. Then they all went home."

On Dad's last day at Camp David, a Sunday, he had a particularly expansive talk with his Canadian counterpart. "He reviewed his entire life with me—what had happened to him, the good and the bad," Prime Minister Mulroney told me. "He said he had been to the mountaintops and into the valleys."

★   ★   ★

On inauguration day, Dad had his final national security briefing, left a note on the Oval Office desk wishing President Clinton well, and took a final walk around the White House grounds with Mom and the dogs. That morning, someone noted to Dad that "the polls look good today. You're leaving office with people liking you." Dad thought that was pleasant, but it didn't change the fact that he hadn't finished the job—a fact that weighed on his mind. Yet he left office feeling the same sense of wonder and majesty for the presidency as he had coming into the job.

The good-byes that proved to be the hardest—the most emotional—were to the White House nurses, the groundskeepers, the butlers, the ushers, and other staff members who had become like family to my parents. "We'll make it in Houston—I know we will," Dad recorded in his diary. "We kid about her [Barbara's] cooking. We kid about no staff, no valets, no shined shoes, and no pressed suits. We did that before, and we can do it again."

Then, according to custom, Dad and Mom prepared to receive the Clintons. When President Truman handed the presidency to Dwight Eisenhower forty years earlier, in 1953, they reportedly exchanged not a word during their ride to the Capitol. Dad and President-elect Clinton—as well as Mom and Mrs. Clinton—had no such difficulties.

"On the ride to the Capitol, I told President-elect Clinton that I knew he had a tough job and that I would not be out there criticizing him," Dad recalled. "I believe I kept my word on that."

Before he took leave of his responsibilities, however, Dad had one more mission. Special Agent Rich Miller, his Secret Service detail leader, asked my father to carry his brother-in-law's Purple Heart from Vietnam during the ceremony. "My brother-in-law, Bill Ellis, was wounded in Vietnam, and was a big Bush fan from South Carolina," Rich recalled. "I thought it would be such an honor for President Bush to carry Billy's medal—as if he didn't have 200,000 things on his mind. After the ceremony, of course, I'm going to go with President Clinton. But President Bush hands me this white envelope, and in it was the little card to my brother-in-law saying how proud he was to carry the medal up there for him."

On inauguration day, I went about my normal daily routine trying to stay busy and keep my mind occupied. As I watched President Clinton being sworn in on my kitchen television, the hurt of the loss came flooding back. I had already said good-bye to Mom and Dad, but it didn't feel like a good-bye because I knew I'd see them in either Houston or Maine very soon.

When I saw them climb the stairs to Air Force One, however, it hit me. They were gone. For my parents and for all of us, life was taking a new and exciting turn into the unknown.

Chapter 22

ULTIMATE FREEDOM

"George has a flair for life that is infectious. I wish I got up every morning feeling the way George Bush does—you don't waste ten minutes because it's a wonderful life, and you've got to take advantage of every second of it."

—**Dean Burch**

I had moved to Washington in 1990 to be closer to Mom and Dad, and I was naturally very sad when they left Washington. When Dad was president, people would often ask me if I ever saw my parents; and they were always surprised to learn that I saw them all the time. "But aren't they busy running the country?" they would ask. That was true, but both of my parents have always made time for family.

They still do; but on January 20, 1993, the epicenter of my parents' life together shifted to Texas and Maine. By moving back to Houston, in fact, they surprised their political opponents and more than a few media commentators. This, despite the fact that they had lived in Houston since 1959—and in Texas since 1948. They had voted in every election in Houston; raised their kids there; Dad launched an offshore drilling business venture in Texas; and both made many lifelong friends there.

Simply put, Texas is their home. During his presidency, Dad

also brought the 1990 G-7 economic summit and the 1992 GOP convention to Houston.

"We knew all along we would be moving back to Houston," Dad said. "For one thing, I darn sure didn't want to hang around Washington writing op-ed pieces with other ex-presidents on how to save the world. There's too much to do here at home."

Still, some people weren't convinced where "home" would be.

In 1980, Mom and Dad purchased a vacant lot in West Houston next to their longtime friends Bobbie and Jack Fitch, and had planned to build a new home there when fate interceded—Dad was elected vice president. Though the lot would remain their intended home for twelve years, they took up residence at the Houstonian hotel a few blocks away, where they stayed whenever they were in town.

Throughout his vice presidency and presidency, however, Dad's political opponents would put up signs in front of the vacant lot ridiculing the thought that "this elitist could live in so modest a space" and that "Bush will never return here." They thought Dad and Mom would go back to their childhood roots in the East, or eventually buy a much bigger lot and build a palatial home.

Whatever their motivation, such speculation proved wrong.

As soon as the 1992 election results were clear, Mom in particular pivoted immediately into preparing for private life, including the long-anticipated construction of their new house. While the new house was being built, they rented a house on the same street. (Today, my brother Neil lives on the same street, right across from Mom and Dad.) When they arrived at their temporary home on January 20, and their final motorcade pulled into the driveway, all of the neighbors lined up to greet the new arrivals.

There they exchanged greetings and took bags inside to unpack. After a while, though, Dad got fidgety and said to Jack Fitch, "Let's go to the office and see how they are coming along with the renovation." So Dad and Jack got back in the limousine with all the police escorts, and off they went to the new office—just over two miles away.

"We pulled up to the entrance where the reporters and TV people were," Jack recalled. "After various interviews, we went up to the office for about an hour. When it was time to go, we went down in the elevator—and no one was in the lobby, no police escort in sight. We went to the parking garage, where only one car was left, an old Lincoln Town Car with two Secret Service men waiting. Then we joined the bumper-to-bumper business traffic going home for the evening."

Dad and Jack slowly made their way home like all the other commuters stuck in traffic, nobody bothering to look at their car. In a few hours, the president of the United States became "the guy next door."

On the way home that night, Dad told Jack, "Things are going to be different. I am going to set up the office on a 9:00 a.m. to 5:00 p.m. basis so the staff and volunteers won't feel like they have to come in early and stay late."

When Mom heard about that, she was skeptical. "Famous last words," she said.

She was right. This decree lasted exactly one week. From then on, Dad has always left the house between 6:30 and 7:00 a.m. and comes home between 6:30 and 7:00 at night—and that's when he's not on the road.

"He has the energy of ten bulls," Jack said.

★   ★   ★

On his second day as a private citizen, Dad wrote to Patty Presock, his longtime assistant, who remained back in Washington:

Dear Patty,

My office, where I am now sitting, looks out over a sea of green trees. Beyond, off to my left, is the skyline of Houston—then further right the skyline of the Galleria area.

Then, way beyond that, way beyond, off to the north and east is Washington, D.C.

I am separated out now. Away from the decisions, the attention, the majesty and wonder of the White House.

No one says, "Sign here" or "Check options 1, 2 or 3." No one says, "The motorcade is ready," or "We have 3 quick photo-ops then the Roosevelt Room signing!"

I have no doctors nearby—and woe, no nurses.

It's strange, it's very different. I feel tired like I did after Robin died—and, yet, I've done nothing.

Friends have rallied 'round—and I like that; but I don't want to go off and do things with people. I hope I'm not instantly aging.

Barbara is bustling—rental house . . . cozy and done. New house—contracts signed, building starts tomorrow—Book contract, a major one, signed up and her computer is already digesting Chapter 1. Buying a car (Taurus, maybe Sable)—busy—and she's leaning forward.

I'm different. I'll get there, but right now I don't seem to care. It's not lack of limelight; it's not even a sense of failure—it's the people in my life—people that have given, given, given.

I miss you, Patty. I loved your letter (so did BPB). But I really miss you.

Love,

GB

★   ★   ★

In March 1993, Dad returned to Washington to receive an award at a downtown hotel. There he noted how his life was different: "The last time I was in this ballroom, I had speechwriters. I had a TelePrompTer. Now I have writing paper that says 'Sam'—that's my grandson, Sam, out here where we're staying—with a picture of a basketball, a baseball, a bat, a soccer ball, and a football. Things have gone to hell, I tell you, since I left," he said to laughter.

During this first trip back, Dad asked me to host a party at my house for some of his former staff members. Dad did all the inviting, and I asked some of the butlers at the White House who were off duty if they wanted to come and give us a hand. I knew Dad would love to see them.

The biggest hurdle Dad faced was the feeling that he had disappointed everyone around him. I can't remember my father ever being so low. Still, he wanted to see everyone, see how they were doing, tell everyone he was there to help if needed. He wanted to make sure everyone got settled into their new lives after their devoted service to him.

He told Chase Untermeyer and a group of friends at the party, "I was with a carpenter who was working on the house. He was explaining to me how he could build out the closets. Not long ago, I was being briefed on the Soviets and the Chinese. But you know what? I found it pretty interesting."

After President Truman left office, he wrote a book called *Mr. Citizen* in which he suggested that former presidents be given the right to participate in congressional debates—with the right to speak, but no right to vote. While Dad deeply respects President Truman, he has had zero interest in injecting himself into some sort of formalized role in the legislature. As he saw it, he had his chance and did his best during the quarter century between 1967 and 1993—and there were plenty of strong leaders who were perfectly capable of fighting for the principles that unite Republicans.

"I don't think there should be any formalized role, because the four or five living former presidents are just as different as any four or five Americans you might encounter on the street," former president Jimmy Carter told me. "All of us have different backgrounds and responsibilities and interests. So I don't think it's possible to have any uniformity about the way former presidents should act after they leave office."

Still, if Dad wasn't going to do as President John Quincy Adams did, and run for the House of Representatives after leaving the White House, my father had to decide how his post-presidency would start to take shape.

On March 1, 1993, Dad wrote three or four close friends, including his friend Lud Ashley, and included a copy of a book titled *Farewell to the Chief: Former Presidents in American Public Life*, by historian Richard Norton Smith and Timothy Walch. The note went as follows:

> *I am trying to decide what to do with my life after a good period of thinking, catching up with family, and going to Maine for four months.*
>
> *Before fall, I'll do some speaking. I'll be talking [about doing my] Memoirs. I'll be doing no interviews, no press, very few public appearances. I have been at the Head Table and now I want not to do that so much.*
>
> *I want to do something useful . . . I'd welcome some suggestions about the future. I want to help others in some way. I need to make some money, not a ton.*
>
> *I don't want to be frantic about influencing history's judgment of what I tried to do . . .*

★   ★   ★

In mid-April, Mom and Dad accepted an invitation from the emir of Kuwait to return to that liberated country for a series of events commemorating the allied victory in the Persian Gulf War. Accompanying my parents on this trip was a group of family and friends. I would love to have been part of that group, but Bobby and I were expecting our first baby the next month.

Neil remembers the journey this way:

> The Kuwaiti government sent a specially refurbished plane to Houston to bring the delegation to Kuwait. After the plane took

off from Houston, everything in the ascent was normal, we reached cruising altitude, and everyone settled in for a long journey. Not too far out of Houston, perhaps over Mississippi, we noticed a flurry of activity, men moving hastily down the aisles towards the cockpit. It turns out that the metal stripping that covers the wings of the big plane was beginning to peel off—one strip at a time. At one point, we could actually see through the wing all the way to the ground. This would have been frightening, except that the pilot announced that even if the entire stripping came off both wings, the plane is aerodynamically designed in such a way that it would still fly. To be extra cautious, however, it was decided that the plane would turn around and return to Houston. The delegation, minus a few weaker souls, departed the next day on yet another airplane that was sent by the emir.

Once we arrived in Kuwait, there was quite a reception at the airport followed by a motorcade to the government guest palace. It was striking that the music in the limo was blaring loud Arabic music with a hypnotic cadence. What was memorable was that every once in a while the words "George Bush" would pop up. It was explained that after the liberation many people in Kuwait named their newborn babies George Bush. The songs were made to express their appreciation for Dad's critical role in liberating Kuwait.

It was a festive trip, marked by a state dinner, a visit to the Kuwaiti parliament, a tour of the war-damaged city, and a visit to a military base. Everywhere the traveling party went, they saw enthusiastic crowds.

During the trip, Dad recalled, "The most moving thing happened to me. The Kuwaitis presented me with a beautiful old door to a house. Around the side of it, they had engraved the names of all the U.S. military who had lost their lives in the war. There was also a plaque that read, 'An old Kuwaiti proverb says, "When a man gives you the key to his home it means that you are the best and most valuable friend to him; and when a man gives you the door it means that you are one of his family."'"

After they returned home, however, the intelligence services learned that terrorists had attempted to assassinate Dad during this visit. In fact, Kuwaiti authorities had detained seventeen suspects, some of whom reportedly confessed that the Iraqi intelligence service was their sponsor. The authorites also found a belt loaded with explosives, the kind a suicide bomber would use, and recovered a Toyota Landcruiser containing between eighty and ninety kilograms of plastic explosives connected to a detonator. Lud Ashley, who was on the trip, put it this way: "People were caught with all kinds of explosives that were destined to blow the living bejesus out of our entire troop."

This highly disturbing discovery set in motion a chain of events involving the CIA, the FBI, and the Department of Justice that pieced together the evidence and linked the assassination attempt to Saddam Hussein's government. When conclusive proof was in hand, the Clinton administration launched a cruise missile attack against the Iraqi intelligence headquarters in Baghdad on June 26 to retaliate. The following day, Madeleine Albright, then the U.S. ambassador to the United Nations, addressed an emergency session of the Security Council and provided evidence to the international community.

★   ★   ★

As time went on, Dad traveled and gave more speeches, and some of his 1993 commitments took him to such varied places as Taiwan, England, Puerto Rico, Morocco, Hong Kong, and Sweden. One speaking engagement shortly after leaving the White House took him to the Princess Hotel in Acapulco, Mexico. Our family friend the Reverend Billy Graham was speaking at the same event, and a prominent Mexican businessman invited Mom and Dad, along with Billy and Ruth Graham, to have lunch and spend part of the day on his boat.

Rev. Graham had to leave early for an appointment, and since the boat was only a few hundred yards from shore, he borrowed a blue swimsuit from Dad and swam to shore, planning to walk back to a friend's apartment where the Grahams were staying.

"When I got to the beach, I found out I was on Mexican Navy property and was promptly arrested," Rev. Graham recalled. "While I was waiting for the officer in charge to decide what he was going to do about me, I sat down on a bench that had apparently just been painted—and when I stood up, the suit was green!"

The Grahams sent Dad's swimsuit to the cleaners, but they couldn't get the green stripes out, so the Grahams gave it away. A few days later, they saw a man walking in town wearing the green-striped suit. That incident became a running joke between my parents and the Grahams, who have laughed about it for years.

★ ★ ★

Heartbreak hit Dad and our friend Don Rhodes when Dad's dog Ranger died shortly after my parents returned to Houston. Ranger was originally Marvin's dog, but Dad loved him so much that he came to live with Mom and Dad—and Don was just as fond of the dog. Ranger was one of Millie's puppies, the only male, and that spring they discovered he was riddled with cancer. He had to be put to sleep on April 6. "Ranger had no enemies," Dad lamented to Mom at lunch that day, as they discussed how much pain he was in and whether he should be put down. Ranger's quality of life "just wasn't worth a darn," Dad said.

Anyone who had seen Dad with Ranger knew how much that loss hurt him, yet it fell to an old friend, Ambassador Fred Zeder, to put a smile on Dad's face when he wrote expressing his condolences that Ranger had gone "paws up."

Eventually, Ranger's ashes were buried on Walker's Point along with all our family dogs.

In May of that year, my third child, Robert Daniel Koch, was born, weighing in at over ten pounds. He was Bobby's first child, and he is named after his father and Bobby's brother Danny. Needless to say, his dad was overjoyed, as was I.

Almost since birth, Robert has always loved ice cream. Years later, his cousins and he were eating so many Klondike Bars in

Kennebunkport that my mother decreed the ice cream off-limits. Shortly afterward, Mom caught Robert violating this rule, hiding on one side of the house with chocolate all over his mouth and fingers. That's when Mom actually bought a lock for the freezer door.

★　★　★

During Dad's presidency, he would often listen to music to help him relax during his neck therapy with the military nurses assigned to the White House. As time went by, the British singer Roger Whittaker became a favorite of Dad and the nurses—so much so, in fact, that they decided to start a Roger Whittaker fan club right there in the White House. Their motto was "More Roger in Our Lives."

Everyone naturally assumed Dad would appoint himself the president of this new club, but he balked. "I'm tired of being president," he joked. So instead he became the recording secretary of the club and an Air Force nurse, Kim Siniscalchi, became the club president. One had to be "accepted" into the club, and together, Kim and Dad reviewed applications for membership. The club included Dr. Burt Lee (aka the Burtser), and nurses Mary Jackson, Ellen Tolton, Paula Trivette, Debbie Beatty, and Art Wallace.

During his last days in the White House, Dad decided to invite the entire fan club to Maine that summer. What the nurses didn't know was that Dad had made T-shirts and called Roger Whittaker and his wife, Natalie—whom Dad had never met before and cold-called—to invite them up for the visit as well.

"We kept it a total secret," Dad said. "I called Roger up and said, 'You'll never believe this, but we've got a bunch of nurses here who are absolutely nuts about you and would you be able to come to Maine as a surprise?' The Whittakers accepted the invitation and arrived early on the day of the nurses' visit. When the nurses got to the gate at Walker's Point, however, one of the agents, seeing the Roger Whittaker T-shirts, said, 'Oh, Mr. Whittaker is already here.' So the surprise was blown, but we really had fun."

As you might suspect, Dad developed a very special bond with the nurses. Ellen Tolten told me, "Still to this day, I get tears in my eyes. He would think we were just as important as any dignitary, any leader in the free world. He would introduce us, 'Do you know my nurse Ellen?' He treated us like we were royalty. That was absolutely wonderful, and it was something he did after the fact."

★ ★ ★

In addition to the Roger Whittaker visit, Dad was also looking forward to spending more time in Kennebunkport in general. Throughout his presidency, he always looked forward to the day when he would be able to more fully enjoy the ocean air surrounded by family and friends. A storm that ravaged Walker's Point a year before he left the presidency almost ruined this simple dream.

In late October and early November of 1991, a devastating two-day nor'easter—known as the "perfect storm"—had battered the Maine coast and slammed Walker's Point. The storm flooded the Big House and caused a lot of damage to the property. The house was left standing, but barely. Mom and Dad thought about tearing it down and rebuilding it farther back from the waterline but then decided against it. They liked being near the ocean.

"We just restructured it," Dad said. "The house was strong and there was no damage to the foundation or the rest of the house. We did have to beef up the steel beams under the living room. It was devastating. I don't think there was a stick of furniture left. The walls were knocked down. The worst part was losing the pictures and memorabilia. You can replace furniture."

The destruction on Walker's Point was heartbreaking for Dad, but he and Mom rebuilt it almost exactly as it had been, and these days you can't even tell what happened.

And now, Dad was finally having time to pursue his passion for fishing. "Throughout the years he was president, he'd come to Kennebunkport," said Dad's local fishing buddy Bill Busch, "but when he went fishing, it was a race. He had too much going on, too many people around."

The summer of 1993, everything changed. Life for Dad was still moving at a frantic pace, but it was more manageable. His schedule was much more flexible, which meant he was really able to fish.

Bill Busch had been introduced to Dad by a talented boat mechanic in Kennebunkport, Paul B. Lariviere (aka Wazoo), who years before had heard Dad was not having much luck out on the water. Bill, who loves fishing so much that he has a tattoo on his arm that reads "Eat-Sleep-Fish," soon became a regular on Dad's fishing trips.

In his second-floor office in Maine, Dad has situated his desk and computer so he can check e-mail and type letters with a clear view of the bay—that way, he can keep an eye on the seagulls, swirls, blitzes, and other dead giveaways that fish are present. Occasionally, the little bay astride Walker's Point will fill with millions of tiny bait fish seeking refuge from the open sea, and, depending on what part of the season it is, sea bass and bluefish will come within feet of the shore thrashing about as they feed.

The combination of fishing *and* boating, however, is even more pleasing to Dad, because it marries two of his passions.

"I think that's his ultimate freedom," Bill said. "Being out there, driving the boat, just going wherever he wants to go—and going fast. If we catch a lot of fish, great. If we don't, we still have a great time. And if one of his kids or grandkids is along for the trip, he gets a whole new vigor. You can see the father and grandfather in him come out."

Of course, inherent in almost every undertaking with Dad is the ribbing, the joking. Out on the water, for example, Dad will frequently tell you, "I'm just the captain. I can only take you where the fish are. If you don't catch any, don't blame the captain."

Beyond the cool waters of Maine and the tropical waters of the Texas Gulf Coast, Dad's fishing exploits have taken him all the way to Tierra del Fuego in Argentina for sea-run brown trout, off the North Carolina Coast for false albacore, to Panama for the rooster fish and the large jax, the River Test in southern England for brown trout, and to Canada and Iceland for Atlantic salmon.

Dad has also fished from the Tree River in Canada's Northwest Territories, known for its large Arctic char. In fact, his visits to that remote corner of the world prompted an enterprising reporter named Arthur Milnes, who was working at the *Deh Cho Drum* in Fort Simpson (population 1,273) at the time, to fax Dad in 1997 requesting a "guest column" from Dad on the subject of fishing. Forget the politics, said Art, and much to his surprise, Dad accepted the offer to have his own byline. Here's an excerpt from the article my father penned:

This year the weather was perfect. We fished in T-shirts, needing a sweater or jacket only in the early morning or late afternoon. The weather up there is variable and it can get wet and very cold even in August; but not this year.

There were a lot of char in those fast-running waters, a lot of big, strong fish. My 13-year-old grandson, Jeb, from Miami, Fla., got a 25- to 30-pound fish on his Magog Smelt fly—a brown, wet fly that was very productive over the course of our whole trip.

He fought the fish for 45 minutes, following our guide Andy's instruction to perfection. The big red, finally tiring, came into the shallow waters just above some rapids, and then with one ultimate surge of energy he flipped over the edge of the pool into the white-water rapids, broke the 20-pound test tippet, and swam to freedom.

My grandson, not an experienced fly fisherman, had fought the fish to perfection. He did nothing wrong. All the fishing experts who were watching told him so, but those big fish are strong and tough and they never give up.

I had 43 fish on my fly rod, only to bring two into the shore. Don't laugh. I was proud to have kept the fly in the water, kept on casting, having the thrill of having that many fish, even for a moment, on my No. 9 rod . . .

I am a very happy and a very lucky man now. Because of time spent fishing and the chance that fishing gives me to relax and think freely, now more than ever I see clearly just how blessed I really am. I served my country. I have a close family and a wonderful wife to whom I have been married for 52 and a half years, and yes, I went to the Tree River and caught char.

Tight lines to all you fishermen!

(Submitted by this most enthusiastic amateur to whom Canada has given such joy.)

News of Dad's brief foray into journalism was wired across Canada and the United States, and earned Art Milnes a modicum of celebrity that he, in turn, credits with changing his career.

One final fishing anecdote. On three occasions, I have been very fortunate to accompany Dad as a guest of Gustavo and Patty Cisneros on a fishing trip to two very special, and very different, parts of Venezuela. In fact, it was Gustavo who taught me to fly-fish.

The first is Manaka, located near the junction of the Ventuari and Orinoco rivers in the heart of the Amazon jungle. There we fished for the powerful peacock bass—or, as it's known in Spanish, the *pavón*. During our first trip to Manaka in 2001, I remember casting a line that became caught in a branch over the water, the lure dangling a few feet above the surface, blowing in the breeze. In an instant, an alligator with its jaws wide open surged straight up out of the water and snapped up my lure!

During that same trip, Dad caught close to thirty-five peacock bass in two and a half days of fishing, but he also caught the desire to come back and catch a real trophy fish. And he did catch a trophy fish. Gustavo remembers the moment: "The president holding on to the rod as it was bending all the way, his face in disbelief. He walked all over the boat as the captain tried to keep it in a steady position, fighting against the current of the river and, on top of that, the pouring rain. President Bush fought the fish for at least ten minutes and finally landed it. It was a 16-pounder, the biggest peacock bass he had ever caught!"

By ten-thirty we had caught so many fish that Dad told the guides that it was time to "tell the divers to take a break and stop putting the fish on our hooks!" That's when Dad got the idea to break the camp record. Gustavo continues:

> At the time, the record of the camp for the most fish caught in a day was 80. When we took a break for lunch we had already caught 86 fish. Suddenly the president said, "Hey guys, do you think we can get up to 100 fish?"
>
> By five-thirty in the afternoon we had caught 97 fish and the deadline was six o'clock. Finally we reached the 100 fish milestone. I thought our day of fishing was over, but as we were getting ready to head back home, the president threw out his line one more time and, of course, got another peacock bass. "Now this team is called 'the 101 Team'" he declared.
>
> From there, we flew ninety miles off the northern coast of Venezuela to an island chain known as Los Roques to chase "The Ghost of the Flats"—or bonefish. During this trip, the president proceeded to catch forty-four fish in two and a half days. It was the largest number of bonefish ever caught by the forty-first president of the United States of America.

★ ★ ★

Fishing and public speaking aside, the summer of 1993 was a busy one for Dad. He and Mom had several visitors, including former South African president F. W. de Klerk, whom Dad respected enormously for his handling of the complex and emotionally charged transition to Nelson Mandela's leadership. That summer, Dad also started working on a book with General Scowcroft about the end of the Cold War and the other serious foreign policy challenges of his administration. Helping the twosome was a small team of trusted advisers known as the book group, including Arnie Kantor, Condi Rice (who was then provost at Stanford), Ginny Mulberger, and Florence Gantt.

Mom, meanwhile, had already started to write her memoirs. It is a matter of public record that Mom and Dad started their books at roughly the same time, but out of respect for the office of the president I am not sure it is appropriate to note who finished their book a full four years before the other!

During this first summer back in Maine following the 1992 election, my brothers George W. and Jeb separately spoke with my parents about their impending decisions to run for governor in their respective states, Texas and Florida. "I was excited and proud that both wanted to get into the arena, but I was disinclined to try to plan what they should do," Dad said. "Both had grand visions of why they wanted to run and on how to get elected."

Mom had her opinion, too: "I confess to thinking there was *no* way either one could win. Like their father, they didn't ask. They thought it out and ran."

★   ★   ★

In September, a breakthrough in the Mideast peace process brought Israeli Prime Minister Yitzhak Rabin and Palestinian leader Yasir Arafat to the White House to sign a peace accord. President Clinton invited Mom and Dad to come for the ceremony and stay the night. Mom wasn't ready to go back to the White House just yet, but Dad went and witnessed the historic Rabin-Arafat handshake on the South Lawn.

Another eventful occasion from the fall took place in another seat of power, when Mom and Dad went to Buckingham Palace. There Dad was named a "Knight Grand Cross of the Most Honourable Order of the Bath" by Queen Elizabeth on November 30 in recognition of his leadership during Desert Storm. The only other U.S. president to receive this distinguished honor was President Reagan.

The Order of Bath actually dates back to medieval times. According to the Royal Web site, the name of the honor arose from the ritual bathing, fasting, and prayers that the candidates went through before being knighted.

Fortunately, Dad did not take to wearing suits of armor. After he was knighted, though, he did ask Mom, "Tell me, darling, what does it feel like to be married to a real, live knight?" She rolled her eyes and responded, "Make the coffee, Sir George."

Of course, Mom and Dad have had a long-standing joke between them about my mother's cooking. Even their oldest son, the president of the United States, has publicly referred to Mom as "one of the great short-order cooks of all time." Mom tells a story about herself that helps to explain why: One day, she put a dozen eggs in a big pan, turned on the stove, then went upstairs to make the bed.

"I got involved in my desk work," she told me, "and two hours later the Secret Service called and asked me if I was cooking something. I raced downstairs to find the twelve eggs had exploded. The pot was ruined and the kitchen—including the ceiling—was covered with thousands of eggshells and eggs. Your dad walked in to find me cleaning up. He got on the island and vacuumed the ceiling while I swept and washed. The amazing part was that it was dry and did come up easily. This time, we went to Eatzi's and brought home a delicious lunch."

There's a method to Mom's madness: "If you built it up as a truism that you're not a good cook, then you don't have to cook." Soon thereafter, Ariel de Guzman, who had been a steward at the vice president's residence and a personal attendant at the White House, came into my parents' lives. He cooked for a month for them during the summer of 1993, then returned full-time in the fall. He's been with them ever since, and recently published a cookbook based on my parents' favorite recipes.

★   ★   ★

Dad loves to play golf—or "commit" golf, as he says these days—but playing in front of large crowds is "tension city" for him.

"As president, I spoke before a million people in Wenceslas Square in Prague with no problems whatsoever," he said. "But put a golf club in my hand and line a few hundred people up, and I can feel every muscle in my body tighten."

Dad was especially nervous the first time he played at the

"birthplace of golf," the St. Andrews links in Scotland, in September 1994. Ken Raynor, Dad's longtime friend and the head pro at the local Cape Arundel course in Kennebunkport, joined my father for what turned out to be a ceremonial round of golf—at which the new captain of the club of the Royal and Ancient Golf Club "drives" himself into office.

Ken explained that the outgoing captain hits his tee shot right before the ten o'clock bell sounds at the local church, and then right after the bell, the incoming captain plays away. There are caddies waiting and watching out on the fairways, and the first one to pick up the new captain's ball gets a gold coin.

About four thousand people were waiting for a ceremony to take place on the Old Course. Dad, a brand new member of the Royal and Ancient, was a little nervous, so he took a few practice swings before teeing off. An official came right over and said, "Excuse me, sir, here in Scotland, we don't take practice swings on the teeing ground."

That didn't help Dad's nerves.

Nevertheless, Ken told me, "the president got up there and literally hit the best tee shot I've ever seen him hit. The crowd was hushed it was so good. He probably hit it 250 yards right down the middle, and he proceeded to shoot a 39 on the first nine holes."

In 1995, Dad also played in the Bob Hope Tournament with President Clinton, President Ford, Bob Hope, and pro golfer Scott Hoch. When Dad plays golf, he likes to play fast—he doesn't throw too many grass clippings into the wind, test the direction, or "plumb bob" any putts. That round at the 1995 Hope Tournament, however, lasted six hours, which had to be excruciating for all concerned.

Incidentally, Dad's lack of patience also extends to the practice tee. Pro golfer Fred Couples once offered to cure Dad's slice if he gave Fred ten minutes for a quick lesson.

"Ten minutes?" Dad asked. "Who's got ten minutes?"

Golf is the only sport that challenges fishing for affection in Dad's heart, and it might have something to do with the fact that Dad comes from good "golf genes."

For one thing, Dad's maternal grandfather, George Herbert Walker, was president of the U.S. Golf Association (USGA) and also donated the Walker Cup—a prestigious prize awarded to the winner of a biannual competition pitting the best amateur golfers in the United States against the best of the British Isles (Great Britain and Ireland).

Dad's father, my grandfather Prescott, was a tremendous golfer in his own right: he often "played off of scratch"; he served as president of the USGA during the 1930s; he played frequently with President Eisenhower during the 1950s; and he "shot his age" at 69, a tremendous feat.

Pro golfer and golf historian Ben Crenshaw told me, "I've read so much about President Bush 41's father and grandfather. They were so well liked, and they helped lead the game. The inception of the Walker Cup matches, gosh, that was 1923. Later on, Senator Prescott Bush was president of the United States Golf Association when Bobby Jones had his grand slam year in 1930, and your grandfather was referee in his match."

In addition to Dad's own exploits on the golf course, during his post-presidency Mom and Dad have also been fervent supporters of the major international competitions, including the Walker Cup, the Ryder Cup, and the President's Cup (of which he has been an honorary cochairman).

"He has traveled to South Africa and Australia, and he's attended these major competitions on U.S. soil," said CBS sportscaster Jim Nantz. "He's spoken to the U.S. team on the eve of the final day of matches. For a solid ten years, he's been right in the middle of the competition at the highest levels of the sport, and the sport's never been graced with a presidential presence to the degree that George Herbert Walker Bush brought to the game."

★ ★ ★

In 1994, my brothers George W. and Jeb officially announced they would run for governor in Texas and Florida, respectively. It was very exciting, but also nerve-racking. At the outset, it seemed that both faced uphill challenges. First, both would have to run hard to win their party's nomination. Then, if they could hurdle that obstacle, each would go on to face tough, popular incumbents—Governor Ann Richards for George, and Governor Lawton Chiles for Jeb. They also had history working against them: only one other pair of brothers had been simultaneously elected as state governors. (It was in 1967, when Winthrop Rockefeller became governor of Arkansas and his brother Nelson, who later became Ford's vice president, was elected governor of New York.)

Given what our family endured in 1992, it might surprise some that anyone with the last name Bush might want to subject themselves to the rigors of political campaigning so soon—but not Dad.

"I knew they were interested, and they all pitched in and helped me through the years," he said, "so it wasn't as if they didn't know the process. I was very proud, of course, that they decided to get into the political arena. Perhaps the only good thing to come of the '92 election is George and Jeb probably couldn't have done it if I'd won the second term—so it was great to see them both trying."

After Jeb won a bruising primary battle to face Governor Chiles and George captured the GOP nomination in Texas, the conventional wisdom among the political commentators was that George would lose to the widely popular Ann Richards while Jeb had a chance of beating Lawton Chiles. Clearly, it was not as clean-cut as some people said.

George ran a very disciplined and tightly focused campaign centering on four key issues—civil justice reform, juvenile justice, education, and welfare reform—and ignored the sharp, and often personal, jabs coming from the witty Governor Richards.

Jeb also ran a positive campaign on the issues—namely, law enforcement, education, and welfare reform—and was locked in a tight race coming down the stretch. Then an automated phone call claiming to be from the American Association of Retired Persons (AARP)—but really originating from the Chiles campaign—

went out to 750,000 senior citizens in Florida claiming, falsely, that if elected, Jeb would cut their Social Security payments.

On election day, George won by a comfortable margin with 53.5 percent, but Jeb lost by 64,000 votes—the closest gubernatorial election in Florida history.

"I felt very badly when Jeb lost and very happy when George won—so it was a night of mixed emotions to say the least," Dad recalled. "You don't like to see one of your kids hurt."

"I remember talking to Dad that night," Marvin said, "and the first thing out of his mouth was, 'I feel terrible for Jeb.' And the beautiful part about our family is that I know that George appreciates that about his father."

My brother George also remembers talking to Dad: "He said to me, 'Great victory,' but he took Jeb's loss very hard. The victory was great—he loved it. But typical of Dad, he was more worried about the agony of the defeat in this case. During that race, I didn't feel any competitiveness with Jeb at all. Nor after I won did I feel any need to second-guess how he ran his race. He had a great race and competitive race and just had different circumstances."

★   ★   ★

Through the years, Dad has developed a reputation as the idea man—coming up with new ways of doing things, or a neat idea for getting people together.

Jean Becker, Dad's post–White House chief of staff, told me, "Your dad thinks that all things are possible. Sometimes that drives me crazy—because unfortunately, not all things are possible. But it's a wonderful quality to have. He'll have an idea and say, 'Let's invite a hundred people over tonight,' and because we're devoted to him, we'll spend hours trying to make the most ridiculous things work."

When you come up with so many ideas, however, not all of them ring true. For example, Dad has tried to convince the grandchildren that he invented "the wave" that is frequently seen at sporting events. One time, he went to a football game, his story goes, and he got ants in his pants and suddenly stood up with his hands in the air. Several other people did the same, and the rest is history—unproven history, but history nonetheless.

"He has little-boy characteristics," said Jim Nantz. "He gets very enthused about things you'd get enthused about when you were twelve years old. He loves to pull surprises, he loves to tease people. He gets excited about things that are just such simple little joys of life that, unfortunately, most people outgrow."

But Dad saves his most creative ideas for the unending string of family competitions, whether it involves all of us and naming something, or which grandchild will be the first asleep. He is competitive by nature and loves games, tournaments, and contests, no matter what the age of the participants.

For example, the "First Asleep" contests. When the grandkids were younger, Dad would pull one or two aside after dinner and say, "Do you want to enter the first-to-sleep contest? It works like this. You go to your bed, and I'll go to mine. If you fall asleep first, you call me, and if I fall asleep first, I'll call you." And off the grandchild would go. It didn't take long for them to figure that one out.

Dad's ideas and competitive streak extend to the tennis court. Four or five years ago, during a stay at the Gasparilla Inn in Boca Grande, Florida, with all of the family gathered around, Dad issued a challenge that whichever grandchild could beat him first in tennis would win one hundred dollars, or what Dad calls "folding green."

"So George P. challenged him first and Gampy miraculously beat him," my niece Lauren, Neil's daughter, recalled. "Nobody could beat him, and eventually, I got brave enough to try. We were in Maine by then, and knowing Gampy likes playing in front of a crowd, I challenged him when there weren't a lot of people around—I thought I was being sly. The first few games were pretty close, and then he put a hat on with the fish sticking through it to throw me off. At that point, it's not like you really want to beat him even—you just have fun playing with him. So, yeah, he beat me, which was depressing."

We cannot verify this last anecdote for historical accuracy, but Scott Pierce, Mom's younger brother, said one of the most important things Dad taught him was always choose the best partner. "In tennis and in golf, President Bush would always arrange the teams, and his guy was always better than mine," Uncle Scott said. "I complained about this one time, and he said, 'Okay, you can have Marvin tomorrow.'"

This pleased Uncle Scott, as Marvin was playing very well at the time and had carried Dad to victory that very day. The next day, my uncle showed up anticipating victory when Dad appeared with a guy who was carrying several rackets.

Dad said, "Scott, have you ever met Ivan Lendl?"

Chapter 23

THE SPRING COLT

"This is history—the likes of which I have never seen, and no-body else has. As you know, George Bush landed safely. Then, in a few hours, he was off for Spain with his grandson, and then to Rome to see the Pope, and then he was coming back and going to Latin America, and he was going to play golf at Augusta after the tournament was over. The life goes on. An amazing little vignette in this quite remarkable man, whatever your politics are."
—**Hugh Sidey** after Dad's first parachute jump in 1997

On January 6, 1995, Mom and Dad reached a proud family milestone when they privately celebrated their fiftieth wedding anniversary in Sea Island, Georgia—returning for only the second time to the spot where they honeymooned half a century prior. There they played golf and dined with friends Louise and Bill Jones.

When my parents returned from that weekend getaway, they attended a grander anniversary celebration at the Grand Ole Opry in Nashville that included our family—with all thirteen grandchildren (the fourteenth, my daughter Georgia Grace or "Gigi," named for her grandfather, would arrive a year later)—and extended political family, as well as my parents' friends from the entertainment industry. The program that night featured a heavy emphasis on country music stars like Vince Gill, the Oak Ridge Boys, Lee Greenwood, and Loretta Lynn. Roger and Natalie Whittaker also flew in from England, and some of Dad's political colleagues such as Lamar Alexander, Sonny Montgomery, and Marilyn Quayle offered very kind remarks about the strength of my parents' marriage.

"One might say that the catalyst in their marriage is humor," said my Uncle Johnny Bush. "They can tease and scold and banter and laugh. Even when crushed by the loss of a child, they could still find ways to laugh. Through life of constant change and uncertainty, of raising five children, frequently moving from one location to the next, of supporting her husband through over thirty years of the vicissitudes of political life, Barbara has ever and always been able to make a home for him, and in that home there is always laughter."

Adding to the laughter in their home early in 1995 was the fact that *Outlaw Biker* magazine named Mom their "Biker Babe of the Century" and described her as a "classy broad." That gave Mom, and Dad, plenty to talk about as they continued to crisscross the country giving speeches, helping a number of charitable causes, and pursuing other interests. In 1994 alone, in fact, Dad gave 111 speeches, campaigned for forty-eight candidates, traveled to twenty-two foreign countries, and visited more than half of the U.S. states.

"It's amazing," my brother Neil observed. "I love the fact that they've always been so active. They're both so youthful in their minds—proof that age is just a number. Dad worries about losing his memory, but he's got a better memory than I have now—and I think it's because they just keep moving forward, always looking ahead."

Meanwhile, the festivities from Mom and Dad's fiftieth anniversary were just settling down when it was time for the family to reconvene again—this time in Austin to see my brother George sworn in as the governor of Texas. I remember we all gathered in George's very ornate, new office in the State Capitol in Austin.

Mom remembers, "It was one of life's happiest moments. I was truly touched to see George's friends from Midland, Houston, Yale, and some from Andover. And there were Laura's friends from Austin, SMU, Houston, and Midland. That day, I took the two of them off my worry list. Faith, family, and friends are the things that allow one to accept challenges. George and Laura have all three."

Jeb, for his part, returned to Florida, where he was already the presumed GOP front-runner for the 1998 gubernatorial race. He continued working with state Republican leaders on issues ranging from "truth in sentencing" laws—making sure criminals serve at least 85 percent of their jail time—to promoting charter school education around the state. Speaker of the Florida House John Thrasher noticed that Jeb was so active, so visible, and so effective at shaping legislation that he was like a "phantom governor."

★ ★ ★

On April 1995, a truck bomb exploded in front of the Alfred P. Murrah Federal Building in Oklahoma City, destroying the building, killing 168 people, and wounding hundreds more. Among the dead that day was a federal agent named Al Wicher who had served on Dad's Secret Service detail. Agent Wicher was a husband, father, and son—and that personal connection to the tragedy only added to the shock that Dad, and all of us, were feeling during that time.

The Oklahoma City blast occurred on the second anniversary of the unsuccessful federal raid on the Branch Davidian compound in Waco, Texas, which resulted in the deaths of seventy people, including a Bureau of Alcohol, Tobacco, and Firearms agent named Steve Willis. Dad attended Agent Willis's funeral in 1993. What's more, immediately after the highly controversial ATF raid in Waco, Clinton Treasury Secretary Lloyd Bentsen named Dad's former Secret Service lead agent and friend John Magaw to head the ATF.

Given Dad's connection to Agent Wicher and the ATF, Dad was

deeply offended shortly after the Oklahoma City bombing when he received a solicitation letter from the National Rifle Association (NRA) referring to federal agents as "jack-booted thugs" and describing them as "wearing Nazi bucket helmets and black storm trooper uniforms." Though he was a lifelong member of the NRA, Dad was galled by such reckless language and tactics— attacking the reputation of our nation's law enforcement officers to raise money. The letter was so offensive, in fact, that Dad fired off a letter to the NRA's president resigning his membership effective immediately. "I have long supported many things the NRA supports," Dad told me, "but this excessive anti–law enforcement rhetoric was too much for me."

Dad's resignation made national news, and the NRA's defenders— of which there are many in Washington and elsewhere around the country—accused Dad of grandstanding to get a good headline or two. Nothing could be further from the truth. He simply could not stand by while some of the finest professional men and women he knew, with whom he worked on a personal basis, had their character dragged through the gutter.

It's a common refrain throughout Dad's life.

"The L-word, 'loyalty,' that's what they'll put on his tombstone," said Senator Al Simpson. "Loyalty to President Reagan, loyalty to his country, loyalty to his family, loyalty to his friends regardless of the consequences . . . Show George Bush a fallen dove—unless he shot it, of course—and he will go fluff the poor bird up and put it back on its feet again . . . You would want him on your side."

In 1996 Dad's friend, Illinois Congressman Dan Rostenkowski, saw his forty-two-year career in public service come to an end when he pleaded guilty to two charges of mail fraud related to his congressional office. In July of that year, Congressman Rostenkowski was sent to a federal prison hospital in Rochester, Minnesota, where he was treated for cancer and then transferred to the federal jail in Oxford, Wisconsin, in December. (In December of 2000, President Clinton pardoned him.)

During his seventeen months of incarceration, the former chairman of the powerful U.S. House Ways and Means Committee lost sixty-five pounds—but he was also reportedly not enthusiastic about receiving visitors. That didn't stop Dad from reaching out to his former colleague from Capitol Hill.

"Danny told me the story about your father calling the jail saying he wanted to talk to Rostenkowski," former Illinois congressman Marty Russo told me. "One of the officials told him, 'We don't allow calls in.' So your dad said, 'I'm President Bush. I want to talk to him.' They had to get the warden on the phone, who said, 'Yes, sir, Mr. President.'"

"Danny called me and said, 'You know what, that gives you the measure of the man,'" Congressman Russo continued. "Of course he was former president at the time, but Danny said, 'The president calls me, puts his prestige on the line to talk to me. That's the kind of friend he is. He never forgets his friends no matter what.' It was a really emotional thing for Danny to tell me that story."

★   ★   ★

When Dad was president, his perpetual penchant for inviting groups of people to come for a movie or stay for dinner or overnight didn't cause much trauma in the Bush household because Mom and Dad had the White House staff and Laurie Firestone to help magically transform these spur-of-the-moment whims of a restless mind into a seamless reality.

After he left the White House, of course, Mom and Dad no longer had the same number of hands to facilitate Dad's voracious appetite for entertaining—an appetite that only grew more ravenous when my parents reach Maine for the summer. It got to the point that Mom joked she runs the busiest bed-and-breakfast in Maine, and she may actually be right!

The guest list over the course of a typical summer ranges from family, to former and current heads of state, to pro athletes, to members of the Bush extended political family, to anyone else Dad has encountered along the way. In going through Dad's personal files, I found literally hundreds of notes to people that included an invitation of one kind or another: "We won't take no for an answer," he'll write. "It would be a joy to see you." Or simply, "Come see us."

Jean Becker, Dad's chief of staff for the last twelve years, aptly describes Dad as a "tumbleweed."

"He just collects people as he goes long," Jean explained. "I've often wondered how frustrating it must be for the kids and grandkids, brothers and sister, and nephews and nieces who really are his family, because you think you're going to spend some time with him and suddenly there's thirteen other people there at the table, or four other people in the boat. He adopts everybody."

We call some of these people "brothers from another mother." The truth is, while Dad's collection of friends grew, our circle of friends widened as well—and our lives are far richer today for it.

For the Fourth of July holiday in 1995, Dad invited Vaclav Havel, who had recently stepped down as president of Czechoslovakia, to Walker's Point for the festivities. Also invited were Governor Jock McKernan and his wife, Senator Olympia Snowe.

All during dinner, Dad was lobbying Mom to take the dinner group out on the boat after supper to watch the fireworks, but Mom was resisting. She would vary her response from questioning the logistics of moving so many people onto the boat, to the dampness and chill in the air, to changing the subject altogether, saying she preferred to watch them from the house.

"Finally, getting nowhere with Mrs. Bush," recalled Governor McKernan, "the president stated in a loud voice that he thought the guest of honor, President Havel, should make the decision on whether the group watched the fireworks from the boat or from the house. A hush came over the room, and President Havel, without missing a beat, responded, 'It is always difficult to choose between two worthy options. And while I, personally, would side with the president in viewing the fireworks from the boat, I believe it would be more appropriate for the group to accede to the wishes of our hostess and view them from the house.' "

As disappointed as Dad was, he led the applause for such a diplomatic response.

★   ★   ★

In October 1995, Dad and his Presidential Library Foundation hosted their first event in Colorado Springs—a forum called "A World Transformed: Our Reflections on the Ending of the Cold War." Journalist Hugh Sidey was there in the audience:

> I went up to a conference that former President Bush had in Colorado Springs on ending the Cold War. He had Gorbachev there—naturally, President Gorbachev talked too much, but it was nice to have him there; he was very central in that operation. There was Margaret Thatcher, who sat three hours with her ankles, her thighs, her knees, pressed together and her hands folded. British discipline. I was absolutely amazed. And there was George Bush, looking a little more grandfatherly, a little tummy there, coming up with a little more gray hair, and Mitterrand was still alive. He was a little green at that point, and he was dying. But he was still funny; he had that Gallic sense of humor. And there was Mulroney—I didn't know till I got up that close to him how much like Jay Leno he appeared. You know, he's got that big jaw. They talked all morning long, these people who had brought this about. And then it suddenly occurred to me as I watched that every single one of them had been punished by the political system that they supported: Bush, defeated; Mitterrand was in hot water over there; Margaret Thatcher, out, criticized; Mulroney, same thing; Gorbachev, defeated. Isn't that an irony? The people in this public life.
>
> A week later, I was back in Washington, and I went to the funeral of a friend of mine, John Scali, who used to be the U.N. representative under Nixon. And there in front of the church was the gathering—he was also, as you know, an ABC correspondent—of the hierarchy of television. Goodness, there was Roone Arledge, and there was Sam Donaldson and Cokie Roberts and Ted Koppel and Peter Jennings. They were all gorgeous, I mean, they had

Phoenix tans and a few of them had chin tucks, and Sam's toupee was on straight. But the sense of power and position and prestige in this group was unmistakable. I was talking to a friend of mine and I said, "Last week, I was with the people that did all the heavy lifting, and they were uncertain and a little frayed at the edges, to be honest with you. But here is this group. What is happening in our society, and in our culture, and in our politics?

Dad had broken ground on his presidential library at Texas A&M a year before that conference, and on November 6, 1997, Mom and Dad celebrated the dedication of the George Bush Presidential Library at Texas A&M University with President and Mrs. Clinton, President and Mrs. Ford, President and Mrs. Carter, Nancy Reagan, Lady Bird Johnson, former world leaders such as Lech Walesa of Poland and Toshiki Kaifu of Japan, movie stars like Kevin Costner, former cabinet and staff members, and an estimated 25,000 other friends, relatives, and Aggies.

Both Jeb, as the president of the Library Foundation, and George W., as the host governor, addressed the sun-splashed crowd; and when it came time for Dad to speak, the first thing he did was apologize to his mother in heaven.

"She always told me, 'Don't be a braggadocio, George. Nobody likes braggadocios,'" Dad recalled. "I worried how she would feel about our library, because it is a bit of an ego trip—I mean, most of the pictures and exhibits are about me."

That same fall, in September 1997, Mom and Dad also celebrated the dedication of the George Bush School of Government and Public Service at Texas A&M. Together with the library, the Bush School has become a consuming passion for Dad. He loves the spirit of the campus, the Corps of Cadets, and the friendly manner of the students. He loves their commitment to excellence and traditions and was devastated when a massive log pile for the traditional student bonfire—a tradition ninety years old at the time—collapsed inward in November 1999, killing twelve Aggie students.

Every semester, Dad invites Bush School students to the cozy apartment he and Mom have on campus or goes into a classroom and lets them ask him any question they want for as long as they want. Dad has also brought a lot of prominent political figures and business leaders from across the country and around the world to the A&M campus for the widest variety of events—speeches, conferences, award ceremonies.

"He's here quite a bit from October to May," said Texas A&M President Bob Gates, who also served as Dad's NSC deputy and CIA director. One time, for example, Dad called Bob and asked him to go to lunch in the cafeteria in the Memorial Student Center—in the heart of campus, the busiest spot and at the busiest time.

So Dad and Bob Gates walked into the cafeteria right at lunchtime, and people turned and looked and couldn't believe he was there. The twosome fetched their trays, got in line, and Dad got the barbecue plate.

By the time they made it through the food line and to the cash registers, word had spread and the cafeteria became kind of a mob scene. Dad didn't want to sit at a table for two because that was too exclusive, and there weren't any tables for four, so they sat at a table for six. Instantly, four guys from the Corps of Cadets plopped down their trays and never moved the entire rest of the lunch.

"I'll bet President Bush signed two hundred autographs while he was eating, and probably took twenty-five or thirty pictures," Bob Gates said. "Kids had cameras in their backpacks for reasons I don't understand, and he even talked to a couple of moms on cell phones. How he actually finished his meal while he did all that other stuff was a real trick."

Dad also draws a crowd of Aggies whenever he does one of several things: goes to the recreational center on campus to work out, attends one of the many sporting events he and Mom support each year . . . or jumps out of a perfectly good airplane.

★ ★ ★

Since Dad's parachute jumps, people have asked when he became such a daredevil. He has always loved driving his boat fast, but something changed during a trip to Puerto Rico in the mid-1990s.

"I thought I had a rein on your father and his penchant for pushing the limits of personal safety until he announced he was going hang gliding into the sea," recalled Jim Pollard, who led Dad's post–White House Secret Service detail for several years. "This event was a 'not normal operation' according to Service Service standards, so we set up an elaborate contingency plan to protect the president in case something went wrong. All went well, but what I did not know at that time was that this event was only the warm-up of 'not normal' things to come."

What really got people scratching their heads was when they first heard that Dad planned to make a parachute jump in March 1997. The month before, my father had dropped by a meeting of the International Parachute Association in Houston to see a friend, Chris Needels, who convinced Dad it was easy and safe. That visit rekindled a deep desire Dad had harbored since he was shot down in World War II.

When he was shot down in September 1944, that parachute jump was decidedly *not* a voluntary effort. Not only did his two crew members die, but Dad was also injured as he exited the plane. He had pulled the rip cord too early. He received a glancing blow to his head, while the chute itself had ripped when it got caught on the horizontal stabilizer; it therefore did not open fully—making for an accelerated fall into the sea.

Dad told me he wanted to make another jump in part "to show that old guys can still do stuff."

To realize his goal, however, Dad would have to win converts to his cause—and overcome the objections of family members who thought we were saving him from himself. To their credit, each of my brothers understood this desire immediately when Dad called, even if they couldn't refuse teasing Dad about having a midlife crisis at age seventy-three.

"Fine, Dad," said Jeb, "but don't change your sexual preference."

"That's great," said the governor of Texas, "but don't tell anyone about your eighteen-year-old girlfriend."

I'm afraid I was less reassuring. When Dad called to tell me the news, my first reaction was, "Oh, Dad, do you have to do this?"

"Yes, Doro," he replied. "I'm going to do it, and don't you tell anybody."

"Do you think I'd tell anybody *this*?" I gasped in disbelief. Little did I know that he'd take up parachuting as a hobby in his seventies and eighties.

Even General Denny Reimer, then the head of the army, checked in with Dad to make sure he was aware of the risks. Fully satisfied after their phone visit, General Reimer said, "I hope this doesn't lead to my getting a call from Strom Thurmond next week."

Dad's jump was being sponsored by the U.S. Parachute Association, but would be held at the army base in Yuma, Arizona, and coordinated with the U.S. Army Golden Knights, the elite parachute team. On March 25, 1997, Dad jumped out solo at 12,000 feet and fell down to 4,500 feet at 120 mph.

Dad's good friend Hugh Sidey watched with Mom from the ground below: "We're out in the desert and he's up above us. He's in a parachute, and Barbara Bush is below. President Bush brought along his orthopedist, just in case, and so we're standing down there in the desert, watching the president of the United States descend in a parachute. And the doctor turned to me and said, 'You've probably seen this before.' And I said, 'Are you kidding? This is history, the likes of which I have never seen, and nobody else has.'"

Dad still jokingly says that when safely on the ground, he asked Mom what she thought. Mom said, "I haven't seen a free fall like that since the '92 election!"

The jump made worldwide news, and soon Dad was hearing from friends around the globe. Most important, we thought he had maybe "exorcised the demon" and gotten this urge out of his system.

We should have known better.

Two years later, Dad celebrated his seventy-fifth birthday in June by making a second jump—this time at his library at College Station. The second skydive was dubbed Operation Spring Colt, and after his chute opened, it read "Making Cancer History: M. D. Anderson."

The jump did not go smoothly. Dad was tumbling and on his back for most of the free-fall descent. One of the Golden Knights, also in a free fall, helped Dad get into the proper position just seconds before it was time to open his chute. No one on the ground could tell this, but the film taken by an army parachutist shows the whole fall in frightening detail. When asked about it later on, Dad mischievously said, "Only my laundryman knows!"

Our whole family had arrived in Houston the day before for Dad's seventy-fifth birthday dinner with seven hundred of Mom and Dad's friends and an extravaganza for a thousand more featuring Bruce Willis, Van Cliburn, Larry Gatlin, Arnold Schwarzenegger, and other stars. The entire weekend raised over $10.2 million for M. D. Anderson Cancer Center in Houston.

Dad first joined the M. D. Anderson Cancer Center Board of Visitors in 1977, when he and Mom moved back to Houston at the start of the Carter administration. Since losing Robin, Mom and Dad have both always had an interest in helping in the fight against cancer, and M. D. Anderson had a sterling reputation as a world leader in cancer research and treatment. When my parents returned to Washington in the Reagan administration, however, Dad temporarily resigned from the board—but that didn't stop him from donating the proceeds from his 1987 campaign biography, *Looking Forward,* to the hospital.

After the White House, Dad reconnected with the Board of Visitors and became increasingly drawn into its work—or make that pulled. Around the time of his seventy-fifth birthday and this second parachute jump, the head of M. D. Anderson, Dr. John Mendelsohn, approached Dad about becoming chairman of the Board of Visitors. "We explained to him that becoming chairman involved two years as the vice chairman, then two years as chairman-elect, and then two years as chairman. So it's a six-year deal."

Upon hearing of the six-year commitment, Dad turned to Jean Becker and kiddingly said, "This is harder than being president!" But he agreed to accept the appointment.

Over the years, Dad has raised literally tens of millions of dollars for M. D. Anderson. He attends many events at the hospital, and he hosts an annual fund-raiser for the hospital every summer at Kennebunkport. Jean Becker said, "He makes a difference in big ways and little ways, and sometimes he'll say to me, 'Jean, I just don't think I'm doing enough. I have to do more.' And I'll just roll my eyes and say, 'How much more can you possibly do?'"

In addition to M. D. Anderson, Dad has also been actively involved in the Eisenhower Exchange Fellowships program, which he chaired for four years; and the Points of Light Foundation, of which he is still the honorary chairman. He also has been very active with First Tee, a PGA Tour–sponsored program created by Dad's friend Commissioner Tim Finchem to make golf more accessible to kids from every background.

★ ★ ★

In March 1998, Dad received a letter from his friend Vic Gold admonishing him for comments that were very critical of the national press. Out there on the speaker's circuit, Dad would frequently knock the heck out of the Beltway press—and no matter where he was, he received a standing ovation from the crowd in response.

"It felt good doing it," Dad confessed.

But Vic, whom Dad respects a lot, thought such behavior was beneath Dad as a former president, so Dad joshingly decided he would start a new organization called Press Bashers Anonymous in order to help him stay "clean."

He did very well for the first year, then my brother George declared his candidacy for president—and the last seven years have been a roller-coaster ride of relapses and recovery.

"The love/hate thing with the press has gone on forever," Dad said. "In a fit of anger in 1992—when I thought I was grossly, unfairly treated—I went back and looked at some of the things they were saying about Grover Cleveland, and it was the same thing. It's ever thus."

As for his own relations with individual members of the national press, Dad has gradually softened his hard edge against *most* members of the fourth estate. Maureen Dowd of the *New York Times* said, "I think he gained respect for me during the Clinton administration, when he realized that I treated all presidents—not just Republicans—with the same skepticism and tweaking style."

Maureen went on to tell me about the time she brought her mother to a White House Christmas party one year, and Dad kissed her mother when she came through the receiving line. "In the car on the way home, she was quiet for a while and then said in an ominous voice, 'I never want you to be mean to that man again.' She kept a framed picture of that night—with her, me, your dad and mom—near the chair she sat in for years after she lost the ability to walk or see. Her last vote in 2004 was for your brother."

My favorite Maureen Dowd column was the one she let her brother Kevin write for her one Christmas Eve. He lauded the job the president was doing. I wish she'd let Kevin write her column every day!

Dad, though angry at Maureen's attacks on the president, genuinely likes her. "I know this is a hard one to understand," he told me. "It's just a dad thing." He does, however, remain totally disenchanted with the *New York Times,* feeling the paper is merciless toward my brother and that it is guilty of editorializing.

★　★　★

For the first four and a half years after leaving the White House, my father's personal aide, Michael Dannenhauer, went just about everywhere with Dad. They had developed a very close relationship, but all that time Michael also lived with a deeply held fear.

"All those years I always wondered if the president assumed I was gay," Michael said. "Obviously, I was never going to say anything to him about it. In 1998, when he asked me to serve temporarily as chief of staff, in the back of my mind I wondered if he would want me to be his chief of staff if he knew I was gay. Would he be embarrassed by me? Would he want to fire me?"

Michael confided first in his sister Beth and then in Jean Becker, Dad's chief of staff who was taking time off to help Dad write *All the Best*. Jean asked Michael if he planned to tell Mom and Dad, and Michael emphatically shot that idea down, thinking it would be far too awkward a conversation. However, Michael was just as emphatic that Jean tell the truth if she was asked about it—just as he would.

In December 1998, Michael was in Dad's office for an early-morning meeting. Dad's longtime assistant Linda Poepsel was also in the office, and after she left, Dad asked Michael to close the door. My father was seated behind his desk, and Michael stood in front assuming it would be a short conversation. Unknown to Michael, Dad had been at his library at Texas A&M the previous day with Jean, and the two had discussed Michael.

"Now, don't be mad at Jean," Dad started the conversation. "Don't be mad at Jean, because I asked her. I asked her if you are gay."

Caught totally off guard, Michael sat down and put his head in his hands, unable to look at Dad.

"I want you to know I don't care," Dad continued. "Barbara and I love you. You are a part of our family, and it doesn't matter to us that you're gay. I am not embarrassed of you and never will be."

Michael recalled that Dad's eyes welled up and tears streaked down his cheeks.

"I hope I have never said anything or done anything in our time together to make you feel less of a person," Dad concluded. "I want you to be happy—that's what is most important."

★   ★   ★

Since the state of Texas changed the terms of office for governor from two years to four years in the 1970s, no sitting governor of Texas had ever been reelected. In 1998, however, my brother George campaigned for reelection as a prohibitively strong incumbent with 70 percent support in Texas—and growing support nationally should he become a GOP candidate for president in 2000. Everywhere he went that year, Texans and reporters asked if he would seek the White House, and when he won that November with 69 percent of the vote, the speculation over his political future only intensified.

Meanwhile, thanks to the way he handled a tough loss in 1994 and the constructive leadership he has shown on a host of issues in the interim, Jeb also found himself back on the campaign trail in Florida as an equally strong candidate for the GOP nomination—but facing a tough challenge in the general election against Lieutenant Governor Buddy McKay.

Jeb campaigned hard all fall, and not until the exit polls started coming in on election day was he fully confident of the outcome. Dad was monitoring the exit polls from Houston as well, and once the numbers looked encouraging, he decided to lease a small plane and fly over to Miami with Mom to surprise Jeb that night.

Dad recalled, "When we arrived, the campaign people asked if I wanted to introduce Jeb and I said, 'Oh yeah. I'm very proud to introduce the new governor of the state of Florida.' It was a very emotional thing to be able to do."

"I didn't know they were coming," Jeb told me. "I was pretty confident that I was going to win, and to have them there was fantastic."

Dad used to tell this funny—perhaps fantasized—story. Flying back to Houston that night, with the light of New Orleans off in the distance, Dad looked out his window and said, "This has to be the happiest night of my life."

"What about the night we were married?" Mom shot back.

"That was a very pleasant night, too!" Dad replied.

★ ★ ★

On June 8, 2000, Mom turned seventy-five years old, and Dad had planned a big surprise party for her a few nights later at the Kennebunkport River Club. There were 176 guests, including family members, tons of her friends from throughout her life, all of Mom's former aides dating back to the earliest days of Dad's vice presidency, and other special invited guests. That night, Marvin emceed the toasts, skits, and singing—it was an unforgettable night.

Like the Roger Whittaker surprise, however, Dad's cover was blown at the last minute. The day before the party, Senator Alan Simpson called and said, "Listen, Bar, I know you are too smart not to have figured this out. So I'm not going to play the whole game here. Ann and I cannot be there, but wanted to wish you a happy birthday, and hope the party is great tonight."

Mom said, "You know, Alan, I don't know what you're talking about. I think you better hang up the phone right now."

Undeterred, Dad marked the occasion of Mom's seventy-fifth birthday by presenting to her a photo of the "Ranking Committee." It was then that so many people in Dad's life would finally, at long last, come to learn the true identity of this infamous committee. Dad explained, "It is not a club. There are no members to it. Just an authority that ranks these jokes. People send them in, like yesterday I got one from Brent Scowcroft. One of them is fairly funny and the other one is not, so the Ranking Committee e-mails back, 'You get seven on the one, four on the other. Try again.' And so it's fun. We've got several people in on it."

For so many years, Dad had referred to this secret committee whenever setting up competitions, judging a competition, or— these days—evaluating the jokes he receives via e-mail. The committee's proceedings were always done in secret because "people would try to corrupt it," Dad explained. What's more, the committee's word was absolute and final, and the committee did not like the whining about its rankings.

Something wasn't quite right when we first saw the photo of

the Ranking Committee, however. The five members appeared to be diverse—there were two women and three men—but they all had the same face . . . Dad's face, to be precise.

"How does his mind work?" Jean Becker asked. "Where did that come from? And, of course, we took that picture on a day when he had a hundred things that I thought were really important—but we had to drop everything to get the local photographer up here."

Dad posed three different times—as a golfer, as a businessman in a suit and tie, and as a hard-core motorcycle biker with a bandana or do-rag on his head with dark sunglasses and a jean jacket vest. For the ladies in the photo, Dad's longtime assistant Linda Poepsel sat in one chair with her professional attire while Jean donned an Arabic robe. Dad's face was superimposed on Linda and Jean.

"The biker costume, I wish we knew where that came from," Jean said. "He left that on forever. There's actually a picture in my office in Kennebunkport of him as the biker with everyone who was in the office that day. He loved walking around as the biker person, and I finally had to tell him to go change because he had an appointment."

★ ★ ★

On June 12, 1999, in Austin, my brother George declared his candidacy for president of the United States. Then he flew to Iowa, New Hampshire, and other politically important states aboard a campaign plane dubbed *Great Expectations.* At the end of the month, his campaign announced they had raised a jaw-dropping $36 million in the first half of 1999—twice as much as Vice President Gore. George's campaign was off to a flying start.

After the sheer agony of 1992, I was awed by my brother having the fortitude to mount his own presidential challenge. True, George came to the starting line with an enviable political name; but as he put it at the time, he "inherited only half of Dad's friends and all of his enemies." He would still have to prove himself and lead a team with little experience at the national level through the killing fields of primary politics.

Looking back, George told me that he felt free to make his own decision about running for president—and not worry about the consequences if he was not successful—because of the unconditional love he has always received from Mom and Dad.

"There is an enormous spotlight on you, as well as pressure," George said. "If I sat and agonized and thought, 'Gosh, if I lose, I'll diminish the family name,' I wouldn't have run if that had been my psyche. I never thought that way. The only thing I was concerned about was, one, did I want to put my own family through this media meat grinder, and two, was I prepared to, upon victory, be in a position where there would be no such thing as anonymity—because if you win, you are forever made president."

Dad, meanwhile, was easing his way into the campaign. Of course, he was completely interested in seeing George do well and helping him in any way, but at the outset, his first and foremost concern was that he didn't want to be a burden.

"He thought that if he were to get involved early on, it would dredge up Republican fears of 1992," recalled Dad's traveling aide Gian-Carlo Peressutti, "so he really downplayed his role to everybody during the exploratory committee phase. Then that kind of morphed from 'I'm really not going to be involved' to 'I can see I can play a helpful role in raising money, and so that's going to be my role.'"

So as he traveled around the country keeping his own engagements, Dad started doing a few fund-raising events. For example, if he would give a speech to a business group in Charlotte, North Carolina, George's campaign would tack on a fund-raising event while Dad was there.

"As the primaries got closer, the president did in fact end up doing more political events," Gian-Carlo added. "The political events he did really were events to motivate the base."

Dad and Mom even surprised George one time at a campaign rally in New Hampshire, which turned out to be a very emotional event for two reasons: first, because we were able to keep it a complete surprise; and second, because it was the first time that Dad and George appeared together at a campaign event for the presidency.

As we had with Dad, our entire family threw ourselves into George's campaign. I traveled around to all the primary states for George W. with my sister-in-law, Tricia Koch. One assignment we got was to go to Dixville Notch, New Hampshire, the first town to cast the first votes in the first primary of the presidential election. The voting takes place at midnight at the Balsams Hotel in the famous "Ballot Room."

This tradition began in 1960 when Dixville Notch was granted the right to conduct its own elections. It is important to candidates because it attracts national and international media attention. Some old New Hampshire veterans would say, as Dixville Notch goes, so goes the nation—and as far as I was concerned, this was an important assignment. So Tricia and I left the main headquarters in Concord and hopped into a four-wheel-drive vehicle with a volunteer driver to head up to Coos County, which borders Canada.

The weather report called for snow, so our Texas-born volunteer driver thought it best if we stopped for "survival" supplies just in case. That was a bit worrisome, but we were on a mission to win the first votes for my brother. So we packed up a first-aid kit, water, some snacks, and headed out. Four-plus hours later, we survived whiteout conditions where we occasionally couldn't tell the road from the forest and made it to the Balsams Hotel in the White Mountains.

After we arrived, we were told that we couldn't blatantly ask people for votes, as we were in the room where votes were actually cast. Arizona Senator John McCain had already been to Dixville Notch and had handed out signed copies of his book. Had we known, I would have come armed with signed books—lots of people in my family had written books, including a few dogs. That would have been easy. Instead, we immediately felt at a disadvantage. Still, there was no doubt whom we were there for, as we were clad in George W. Bush gear from head to toe.

Another interesting rule in the Dixville Notch vote is that voters can declare or change their party affiliation on the night of the vote. So everyone was a potential vote for George W. Bush, and Tricia and I were determined to get the majority. We did everything else we could think of—winks, nods, hugs—to get the votes of the twenty-nine citizens of Dixville Notch who showed up that night.

As the night wore on, the tension built. Midnight finally came and the votes were announced. For the Democrats: four votes for Senator Bill Bradley and two votes for Al Gore. For the Republicans: twelve votes for George W. Bush, ten votes for John McCain, and one vote for Steve Forbes. (How'd we miss that one vote?)

At that moment, you would have thought we had won the entire election in a landslide. Tricia and I were bouncing off the walls with excitement. The joy carried over into the next morning on our car ride back to headquarters. We ran into the headquarters thinking everyone would be celebrating, but unfortunately, that was not the case. Early statewide polling results were beginning to come in, and things were not looking so good. The New Hampshire primary loss to Senator McCain in 2000 ended up being as hard a loss as the win in the Iowa caucus was encouraging.

But George regained his footing with a solid win in South Carolina, won nine out of the thirteen Super Tuesday states, and took a lead in delegates he never relinquished from that point on. On February 15, he won the Delaware caucus, and I was asked to make his official acceptance speech as winner. I have heard many acceptance speeches over the years, but this was the first—and only—time I would ever be making one. It was my big moment. I worked hard on the speech, practicing it over and over. As I was giving the speech, however, I realized that an acceptance speech is only interesting if it is being delivered by the person who actually won the election.

George had come into the primary fight riding a wave of great expectations, and thanks to the help of a very talented political team and thousands of dedicated volunteers, he had met them.

★ ★ ★

In August, the Republican Convention was held in Philadelphia, where George officially became the Republican nominee. In his acceptance speech, he said, "Mother, everybody loves you and so do I. Growing up, she gave me love and lots of advice. I gave her white hair. And I want to thank my dad, the most decent man I have ever known. All of my life I have been amazed that a gentle soul could be so strong. Dad, I am proud to be your son."

Coming out of Philadelphia, the Bush-Cheney ticket surged to an 18-point lead, and everyone was geared up for the bruising home stretch.

At one point during the fall campaign, I pulled into a local gas station and saw a woman at the pump who had a "George W. Bush" bumper sticker on her car. I went over to thank her, explaining that I was the candidate's sister. "No, you're not," she said to me. "Governor Bush doesn't have a sister." I politely explained that yes, he does, and I am his sister. No, she repeated, that's not possible.

At this point, I could tell she was starting to suspect that I was some kind of nut. To prove my real identity to her, I ran and got a copy of Mom's 1994 book, *Barbara Bush: A Memoir,* out and showed her a family photo. (I just happened to have the book that day; I don't always drive around town with a copy!) Anyway, I thought I had convinced her until I found out later that she called the campaign to verify who I was—she didn't believe me, after all!

When the fall debates took place between Al Gore and my brother, I went to support George. I remember thinking that I had come to the event to support my brother, and yet what on earth could I do? So I spent time in the holding room with George, Laura, and other friends and family. George was relaxed and ready, but the rest of us were miserable, nervous wrecks. I had bought an herbal stress-relieving balm from the local grocery store, and brought that along in case it might help. I shared the stress-reliever with Laura, and we rubbed it all over our "pulse points," as instructed on the label. I'm not sure if it was George's great performance or the herbal balm, but we were much calmer by the end of the debate, which my brother won.

My parents voted early on election day 2000, then made the ninety-minute drive to Texas A&M, where Dad had an event with Bush School students in College Station. While they were at the Bush Library Foundation office on the A&M campus, Jean Becker started receiving exit poll results from Ron Kaufman, Dad's former political director at the White House. The first wave of numbers was not encouraging.

From College Station, Mom and Dad drove to the Governor's Mansion in Austin. The plan called for us to have a family dinner at the Four Seasons and then go upstairs to a suite and watch the returns.

Events took a disturbing turn during dinner, however, when the networks called Florida for Vice President Gore, and I remember Jeb tearfully hugging George and expressing his regret that Florida had gone the other way.

"I felt like I let him down," Jeb said.

With the early returns not offering much encouragement, my brother George decided he would prefer to watch the returns back at the Governor's Mansion with Laura, Mom and Dad, and Laura's mother, Jenna Welch. Meanwhile, Marvin and I went to a conference room right next to the family suite with Karl Rove, Condi Rice, Don Evans, and others. The room had four televisions and a bank of laptops with people on the Internet collecting information from around the country.

On nights like election night 2000, even the most brilliant people set reason to the side. For example, I sat next to Condi, and at one point we decided to switch seats. As we did, we started winning states. From that moment forward, whenever we lost a few states, Condi and I decided to switch seats again—as if that somehow altered the cosmic order of things.

Before they pulled Florida back from being called for Gore, however, there were a handful of states that we knew we needed to win if we were going to lose Florida.

New Mexico was one of the states, and when it came across the wire that we lost New Mexico, too, I remember Condi Rice saying, "That was one of the ones we needed, wasn't it?" That stark realization sucked the life right out of the room.

Things were still looking bleak when Karen Hughes, one of my brother George's closest friends and counselors, arrived at the Governor's Mansion.

"I went up the back stairs and saw President Bush 41," she said. "He was sitting on the couch by himself. Without thinking, I said, 'Oh, hello, Mr. President, how are you?' He said very quietly, 'Not very good right now.' I felt so terrible. Here's this wonderful man just dying inside, watching in agony, concerned for his son."

Throughout the night—as she had in 1992—Mom would periodically go into the main room, watch for a while, then leave.

Back at the Four Seasons, we were still anxiously watching returns when an NBC reporter called to say, "Florida is not a done deal." They were suspicious of how quickly Florida was called, and at that point in the night they were thinking about pulling it back. As word of this critical turn spread, Marvin walked over to the window, leaned out, and said, "Condi, you can come off the roof now." Everybody cracked up.

I also remember seeing Jeb run down the hall with a cell phone on each ear as word came in that Florida was being put back in the undecided column. He was heading over to the Governor's Mansion to monitor events from there. I remained behind at the hotel, so Karen Hughes detailed what happened from there:

> Jeb came bounding up the stairs with a couple of staff members, shouting "back from the ashes." He got on the computer and started reading election returns—like the local county judge race. Jeb was convinced that we were going to carry Florida.
>
> When Fox declared Florida for Governor Bush, Jeb said, "I'm not seeing that. Where are the numbers? We'd better be sure." I felt as the senior staff person there that I didn't want us to go out and declare victory and not have it be the case. We were trying to

make certain that the numbers were backing up what we were hearing on the news.

Then Vice President Gore called and conceded. That was a euphoric moment. President and Mrs. Bush 41 hugged the president-elect, who also kissed Laura and shook hands with Jeb. There was a sudden release of tension.

Once the networks declared and Al Gore called, a lot of people came over from headquarters, including campaign chairman Don Evans and Karl. Vice President and Mrs. Cheney also arrived with Senator Alan Simpson and his wife, Ann.

Jeb, meanwhile, was still looking at the numbers. I wanted to make sure everybody had the idea this was over, so I was calling the press to make sure they knew Al Gore had conceded.

The president-elect went downstairs to get ready to go do a victory statement. Before he could go out, however, Don Evans received a call from Bill Daley, the chairman of the Gore campaign, saying that Gore was going to call back and we should wait. All of a sudden, everybody was confused. No one knew what was happening.

I walked back upstairs, and President Bush 41 and the president-elect were standing in the living room. The president-elect was on the phone and he was talking to Gore. And I remember him saying, "What do you mean you're retracting your concession?" It was bizarre.

That's when Al Gore said something like, "Don't get snippy with me."

When it was clear the election would not end that night, we decided to send Chairman Evans over to make a statement, and the president-elect said, "I'm going to bed." President Bush 41 said, "I am, too."

There wasn't really much discussion after that.

I just can't imagine much of a bigger up or down than thinking that you've been elected president—only to learn maybe you haven't. But both the candidate and his father were so stoic and so controlled. Obviously, they were feeling it very intensely, but no one yelled, no one said any bad words.

★ ★ ★

After election night 2000, the country was plunged into a thirty-five-day period of court fights, press conferences, and endless political debate—some of it acrimonious and baseless commentary. George and Laura handled this extraordinary period by assembling a superb team led by Secretary Baker to manage the recount process. Then they got out of Austin, out of the spotlight. George didn't want to get caught up in reacting to every new twist and turn, which was smart—as there would seemingly be a new crisis every day.

"He was at peace," Dad said. "He got ridiculed for being out at his ranch and not tuning in to every little up or down in that long, long, arduous process. He knows who he is. He did his best. He did all these old verities that you learn from your parents—do your best, give the other guy credit, try your hardest. I mean, he did those things."

While in Crawford, my brother George would check in with people by computer. He would instant-message me and others, "What are you doing? What's going on?" It got to the point where I didn't want to leave my desk for fear of missing a message from him. (Later, when he became president, he wrote us all a final e-mail, saying he'd have to sign off of e-mailing as he was no longer a private citizen.)

Dad was nervous, too, and called all of us more than usual.

He also dispelled a myth that arose.

"I read in the paper that I was the one that got Jim Baker to fly down to Florida, to lead that beautiful effort in the recount," Dad explained. "Jim's presence there meant everything to me, but I had nothing to do with that. I didn't know about it until I either heard it from Dick Cheney or from George. Some people didn't believe that, but it is the truth. I didn't know one single thing about it. But if George later said, 'What do you think about it?' I'd say, 'You couldn't have done better.'"

Jeb was also caught in a difficult position during the recount. He had worked his heart out for his brother, but as governor, his first priority—his duty—was to determine if the election was conducted in a proper manner and that the recount process was thorough and fair. Like George, Jeb kept a low profile and left the grandstanding on TV to others.

Lord knows, there was plenty of commentary to go around.

"When a national leader accused Jeb and George of using Nazi tactics, and the media didn't really respond to that, I was outraged," Dad said. "But it was more than just the political outrage: it was the hurt of a father who has pride in two wonderful sons who would never use such tactics. So it was a period of anxiety, but if George had lost, it wouldn't have been the end of the world for us."

From afar, Dad continued to monitor events in Florida closely through Secretary Baker and Margaret Tutwiler, and at one crucial point in the court proceedings in Tallahassee, Dad checked in with Margaret to get the latest news.

"I told him everything I knew about the matter from my perspective," Margaret said, "and then I remember saying, 'I'll have Mr. Baker call you back as soon as I can find him.' When I asked for his phone number, the area code was 517, so I asked where he was. He said, 'I'm at the Mayo Clinic getting ready to have a hip replacement.' His attention was entirely on George his son—not himself."

One day during the recount, my former husband, Billy LeBlond, was in town for the weekend visiting Sam and Ellie. We were all at my house when I received a call saying a group of people were gathering to protest in front of the house on Massachusetts Avenue where Vice President Gore lived. I jumped at the opportunity to get out and do something, as I couldn't stand being in this awful limbo. Everyone in my family laughed and said, "You can't do that. You're crazy—someone might see you there!" But I was determined, so I put together a disguise and announced I was going.

Billy and the kids were going to see the Washington Capitals hockey team play, but postponed going to the game to join me on the protest. Billy met me standing in the freezing cold, yelling very creative and very adult chants such as "Get Out of Cheney's House!" and "Sore Loserman!" and "I say President, you say Bush."

Incidentally, I wore a scarf and big sunglasses as my disguise, but this attempt at being incognito failed miserably. There I was shouting away with everyone, and random people would walk up and say, "Hi, Doro!"

On December 12, the United States Supreme Court voted 7–2 to stop a manual recount ordered by the Florida Supreme Court, saying such an order had "constitutional problems." The High Court's action essentially meant my brother would become the forty-third president of the United States.

George remembers, "An NBC News guy got a copy of the court order and started reading it on camera. As I recall, I picked up the phone and called Dad and I said, 'I'm not a lawyer, but I think this means I won.'"

The next night, Vice President Gore gave a thoughtful concession speech; immediately afterward, Dad called him to thank him for the gracious way in which Gore handled the matter that was so difficult for him and for the whole country.

"I had returned to the Naval Observatory, the vice president's residence, after making my speech downtown at the Old Executive Office Building," Vice President Gore told me. "The telephone rang and the operator put your dad through. He told me that he was personally moved by, and grateful for the content of the speech, and I was equally moved by his personal gesture in calling. It was certainly in keeping with his reputation for gestures of that kind. I was impressed by that and very grateful."

Roughly an hour later, Speaker Pete Laney of the Texas House—a Democrat—introduced my brother to the world as president-elect.

"It didn't sink in for us until he walked in and was introduced by Pete Laney," Dad recalled. "I think that was really *the* most emotional moment for your mom and me—the realization that our son was the forty-third president. I'll never forget it. We were alone—tucked into our bed in Houston, Texas. We watched, and we sobbed."

A week later, George went to Washington to continue working

on his transition, which included meetings with congressional leaders, Chairman of the Federal Reserve Alan Greenspan, Vice President Gore, then finally to the White House to visit President Clinton.

"When I saw our oldest son walk into the White House as the president-elect, sitting next to a very gracious President Clinton, I thought it was amazing," Dad said. "I had just been on the phone with George from the Madison Hotel, and then I saw that—another imprimatur of reality, as he was greeted in that office he's going to serve in for the next four years."

Chapter 24

FAMILY CONTINUITY

"It's a name that I wear with pride, but only after I became an adult did I fully appreciate the significance. In my old age I will be able to say I was named after that guy who not only was a great president but also a great human being."

—**George P. Bush**

On January 20, 2001, I attended my fourth presidential inaugural involving a direct family member. The day was cold and dreary, with a drizzly rain and temperatures just above freezing. The people sitting behind the podium weren't allowed to bring umbrellas, because the people behind them wouldn't be able to see the ceremony. Luckily, the people at the Inaugural Committee thought to put a clear plastic poncho and a package of hand-warmers on each seat where we were sitting on the West Front of the U.S. Capitol.

As for our family, we weren't going to let the rain bother us. We were all ready to celebrate my brother's and Vice President Cheney's inauguration, especially after such a grueling ordeal with the recount. His supporters had been deprived of a celebration on election night—and even later, when he was declared the winner, the mood was more along the lines of "Are you sure?" than anything else. This time, we all arrived at the Blair House proud and relieved.

The inaugural events in 2001 seemed particularly festive to me; and in addition to the regular events, my home state of Maryland hosted a black-tie affair at the Chamber of Commerce building in downtown Washington. George W. won the state in the Republican primary, but during the general election struggle for the so-called blue states—won by Vice President Gore—and the red states, won by my brother, Maryland in 2000 turned a deep blue.

A lot of people are working hard to change the Democratic leanings; Republicans in Maryland remain a very tight-knit group. Someone decided that, as the sister of the president-elect, I should be the honored guest at this special celebration. I remember the long pink and black dress I wore, and since we were welcoming a Texan into the White House, I finished off the outfit with cowboy boots as a tribute to my brother.

Mom and Dad also dropped by that night, and the crowd went wild.

"I think it was more emotional for me when George won," Dad said, comparing his experience with my brother's. "In 1988, I had been vice president for eight years at Reagan's side. I knew how the Oval Office worked. There was still awe and wonder on my part when I sat at that desk for the first time—the same feeling that the current president felt when he sat there."

"President Bush 43 learned so much about how to instill respect for the office," said Karen Hughes. "You wear a tie in the Oval Office. You don't have food in the Oval Office. You don't wear blue jeans in the Oval Office. You show respect. He knew that from day one, and knew that from watching the example of his dad."

One time, I was in the Queen's Bedroom with Dad, and he looked at his watch and he said, "Oh, I've got to run." Quickly, he showered, put on his coat and tie, and looked as crisp as if he were going to a state dinner.

I asked, "Dad, where are you going?"

He said, "I've got to run. I don't want to be late for the president."

The first picture taken in the Oval Office, on January 20, 2001, featured the forty-third president and Dad together. Dad also has a similar picture taken on January 21, 1989—his first day in the Oval Office—with his mother, Dorothy.

"So there's kind of a family continuity there," said Dad.

While George's election didn't change us from a family standpoint, it did reverse the roles between my parents and the new president and First Lady. For twelve years, it was us "kids"— George and Laura included—who agonized over each negative story and every cheap political shot directed at Dad. My father was always the one to calm us all down.

Since George and Jeb had entered the political arena in 1994, however, it was Mom and Dad's turn to worry about their sons' political fortunes—and that concern only intensified after George and Laura entered the White House. Dad continues to be a voracious consumer of political news and information, and hardly ever misses a slight against the current Oval Office occupant. Now my brother George finds himself telling Dad to stop reading the papers and to stop worrying about whatever the latest line of attack is.

"Dad pays so much attention to the criticism that when we talk he'll occasionally rehash some attack," the president said. "So I spend a lot of time comforting him and assuring him that I'm fine. People looking from the outside in on the presidency can draw all kinds of conclusions as to how you're feeling. Is the burden of the office getting to you? He, of course, has more concern than anybody because I'm his son."

"It's much worse, by far, when it's your son who's criticized," Dad said. "It didn't bother me as president because I could handle it. I know George is strong and can take it, too—but it still burns the hell out of me."

After the 2000 election, very early on, I remember George asking me to look in on Mom and Dad more often, since he'd probably be less able to with his schedule. He's always been very good about checking in with them—and still does—but he was worried enough about his impending schedule to say something to me.

George's election has had several other distinct effects on our family.

Initially, it caused a great deal of confusion to have two presidents in the family. For example, whenever Dad and my brother were in the same room and someone called out "President Bush" or "Mr. President," they both turned and answered. To cope with this problem, Congressman John Dingell came up with an informal nickname for Dad and George whereby Dad today is frequently referred to as "41," shorthand for the forty-first president, while George W. is—you guessed it—"43." Together, Congressman Dingell joked, they make "84."

To those who study the presidency and revere it as an institution, I recognize this shorthand treatment for the president seems highly inappropriate; yet at times it has proved inescapably necessary. Just ask artist Ron Sherr, who was commissioned to paint a dual portrait of Dad and George that today hangs in the Bush Library at Texas A&M. Ron was given a period of time with Dad and George in Laurel, the main lodge at Camp David. After George and Dad entered the room to begin the sitting, Ron said, "Mr. President, please turn to your left."

Both Dad and George turned to their left.

"I'm sorry, President Bush," Ron said, pointing to Dad. "Not you. I meant you, President Bush," pointing to George.

Dad told Ron he might want to use the 41–43 designations to avoid confusion, but Ron demurred, feeling it was not right. The confusion continued, however, wasting valuable time. Finally, George said, "Ron, you've got ten minutes left."

Flustered, Ron started barking out orders: "41, you do this! 43, sit like that!"

Another impact of George W.'s presidency relates to Dad's ability to speak out on the issues. Every former president is different, but for his part Dad has never had much interest in trying to shape legislation or influence events as an ex-president. He did go to the White House twice during the Clinton administration—for the

NAFTA signing and the Mideast peace ceremony—and Dad later issued a statement of support for the Clinton administration's stated goals in Bosnia.

For the most part, however, he has kept his own counsel and tried to stay out of the press. That natural inclination for discretion increased dramatically once George W. and Jeb got into public life.

"He has been there as a sounding board, as a loving father, as someone who cares about his son, but not trying to tell his son what he should do or how he should make decisions," said Karen Hughes.

"I don't want to do something that in any way—directly or indirectly—complicates the life of the president of the United States," Dad explained. "If I deviated from one of the president's policies—even if it was unknowingly—some enterprising reporter would rush into the White House press room and say, 'Mr. President, your nutty father over here is saying this and that.' The president doesn't need that kind of grief, and neither does the governor of Florida."

Like any father and son, Dad and George do speak often.

"I originate the calls and it's as much a call just to check in than anything else," the president said. "Mother says, 'Dad loves to talk to you.' Point being that he likes to be kept abreast. He likes to hear what's going on. But I think he's got enough confidence in me as the president and as a person to be able to deal with the pressures and the decision-making. I remember fishing with him one time in 1992. Sitting there on the boat, he said, 'This is a job where you make an enormous number of decisions, and I like making decisions.' It turned out to be an accurate description of the job. You've got to be able to make decisions and stand by them."

Finally, George's election also prompted comparisons between the Bushes and the only other American family to have a father and son as president—the John Adams family of Massachusetts. Dad wrote a letter to his friend Hugh Sidey about the phenomenon:

I have just finished David McCullough's book on John Adams. I loved it. I read every page carefully and with great enjoyment. I kept trying to make comparisons between the Adamses and the Bushes, though author McCullough would probably die if he thought I was doing that . . .

We both had sons who became president. Once out of office Adams largely stayed offstage, although he was more actively involved than I have chosen to be. Like Adams I am very proud of my family.

I am luckier in one sense because, thanks to TV, the telephone, and the papers, I get to see my beloved son actively involved in the problems of the presidency. Whereas by the time John Quincy Adams was elected, John Adams was very old and though sharp until the end he was not able to keep up with events and problems John Quincy was facing. Communications were so different back then.

In many ways Abigail Adams and Barbara Bush are alike. Both are very strong women, both possessed of very strong opinions, both loyal wives devoted to family.

One big difference between John Adams and me related to his education and his reading. A prolific reader, he loved the classics, prided himself on his ability to speak Latin, and had a library of extraordinary proportions.

True I studied Latin for four years—two in grade school, two in boarding school; but I couldn't wait to stop studying Latin. Big difference there between me and John.

I took eleven years of French, too; but unlike John I never lived in France and thus I am far less fluent in the language than he.

Who had the tougher role as president, John Adams POTUS #2 or George Bush POTUS #41? [POTUS is an acronym for President of the United States.]

I'd have to go with John Adams. Life was tougher back then and the press was sometimes ugly. Adams was attacked in editorial-like letters. But then again I used to be hammered in actual editorials and in the news columns day in and day out.

On the other hand, John was elected by only a tiny handful of people. He did not appear to me to put in the grueling hours I did.

He was gone from Philadelphia and Washington a lot. His name-calling evil press was sporadic, whereas mine and every modern president's press coverage was (is) a constant barrage of attacking articles.

The problems he faced were huge and he took tough positions particularly regarding France and standing up to [Alexander] Hamilton and others.

But my challenges, though different, were pretty big, too. Back then he was an original. I was just one more man in the long line; but the presidency meant every bit as much to me as it did to John Adams.

I loved the fact that toward the end of their lives, [Thomas] Jefferson and Adams overcame their differences and again became friends.

Should I make up with Ross Perot? The answer is no. Perot is no Jefferson, and I am not trying to say I am a John Adams.

Adams dealt with small numbers and big problems. I dealt with huge numbers and big problems, though my problems, unlike those Adams faced, had little do with the survival of our country.

Adams, like everyone back then, had medical problems that plagued his family, and medicines were primitive. I am spoiled by modern medicine.

Adams spoke in flowery words. I don't speak such words.

Adams had some humor but that does not appear to be a main trait for him. I love humor of all kinds; and I have the Internet to keep the jokes rolling in. No Internet for old John, and besides, I am not sure he would approve of the Monica Lewinsky limerick that has given me so much laughter.

John Adams had a son who was a real disappointment, a black sheep. I have no such son—only four wonderful men who bring me nothing but joy. They are of fine character and they are strengthened by their loving families. John Adams' daughter, Nabby, seemed close to him, but not as close as my beloved Doro is to me.

John Adams died at 90 or was it 91? I want to live to at least 90 unless of course my health is such that I become a burden on others.

When John Adams wanted to convey his pride in John Quincy, it took horses and carriages and plenty of time to get the letters through. When I want to talk to #43 I just pick up the phone and usually the president answers. As a matter of fact I just hung up from calling him. I saw him give a great speech in Missouri. I called him and in but a few minutes I got him in his car sitting there in Independence, Missouri. Amazing!

When he got older, John Adams had bad tooth problems. No crowns or drills or Novocain for Old John; but for me a broken tooth is nothing. Music in the dentist's office. A fine assistant passing the tools and pumping in the Novocain and shortly afterward a new gold crown. Lucky me, poor toothless John.

John and I both enjoyed working on matters foreign. The problems he faced as envoy and president were enormous. Mine were less formidable, but certainly they were important, sometimes urgent.

At time John Adams seemed a bit cranky. I am not a cranky guy.

So I shall end this treatise. Don't show it to McCullough for he will look at these rambling comments and say "Harvard educated, cultured, well spoken and well written, John Adams would never write such trivia. I feel I know John Adams. And I do know George Bush. And George Bush, you are no John Adams."

John Adams was reportedly happy in his later years, but he could not possibly have been as happy a man, as lucky a man, as I am.

★   ★   ★

When George W. became president, he told my brother Marvin and me that every time he and Laura go to Camp David on the weekends, we were invited. Marvin, Margaret, Bobby, and I live close by and feel lucky to be able to be a part of George W.'s presidency. When I heard the president's invitation, I thought how very nice it was, but I wouldn't dream of imposing. He was the newly elected president, after all, and would have so much on his mind.

All he needed, I thought, was his sister hanging around and getting in the way. I quickly learned, or the president and Laura quickly made me feel, that I was completely and utterly welcome.

One weekend, I was there with my two younger children, Robert and Gigi. We were sitting around the dinner table with a big crowd: the president, Laura, Dr. Condoleezza Rice (who was then the national security adviser), and other family and friends. Robert, eleven years old at the time, loves the food at Camp David and really looks forward to the dinners. The president enjoys Mexican food and southern fare, and it's usually served family-style on the table and passed around.

At this particular dinner, Robert was looking around the table to see what he might have, and I suddenly heard him say very politely to Condoleezza Rice, "Dr. Fruit, could you please pass the rice?" at which point he turned as red as a tomato, and then stammered, "I mean, Dr. Rice, could you please pass the fruit?" Everyone laughed at such an innocent faux pas.

I realized then we could provide these family moments for the president—to lighten his burden for just a moment, in the way that only family can.

★　★　★

In July 2001, Jeb visited Walker's Point, and, as usual, the agenda called for a little fishing. Jeb showed up that first morning on the dock wearing a red windbreaker and took off with Dad and Bill Busch. The fishing was as great as the weather, but before they headed home Bill decided to play a little joke and slipped a mackerel they were using as bait fish into the pocket of Jeb's coat. Bill fully expected to hear from Jeb regarding this "souvenir from Maine" before long.

A few days later, the president arrived at Walker's Point—and Dad and Bill took him fishing as well. After a good morning trip, they returned to the dock, tied up the boat, put away the gear, and headed up to the Big House for one of Ariel's great lunches.

"We came inside, passing the big closet by the door, which was open with all of its contents over chairs, on the floor, and on a rolling garment rack," Bill recalled. "There was even a fan inside the closet blowing air out toward the screen door. Everyone looked—puzzled—and continued into the dining room for lunch," Bill said.

A few moments later, Ariel passed by with a funny look on his face. He stopped and declared, "I found the smell in the closet. It was a mackerel in your pocket, sir."

Mom looked at Dad and said, "George Herbert Walker Bush! What are you doing with a mackerel in your pocket?" Bill started to sweat, as he realized how the mackerel got there. He sensed certain death at the hands of my mother and quickly came up with, "Mr. President, you didn't have to save the bait, I'll get more to-morrow!"

★ ★ ★

On September 11, 2001, Al Qaeda terrorists crashed four commercial airplanes filled with innocent men and women into the Twin Towers of the World Trade Center, the Pentagon, and a field in rural Pennsylvania. A fifth plane was reportedly supposed to crash into the White House or the Capitol building, but that attack never materialized.

Mom and Dad attended a Washington, D.C., event on September 10 and stayed the night at the White House. That next fateful morning, they kissed Laura good-bye as she was getting ready to testify on Capitol Hill and jumped on a plane bound for St. Paul, Minnesota, where they were scheduled to give a joint speech.

At 9:45 a.m., the Federal Aviation Administration grounded all air traffic for the first time in history, forcing Mom and Dad to land in Milwaukee. They were taken to a motel on the outskirts of town and started to catch up on the surreal, devastating news. Bobby, likewise, was grounded in California and was not able to get home to us for a week.

As soon as I heard about the attacks, like everyone else, my first thoughts concerned my family. Our four children were in four different schools, and there was a lot of phone calling as to whether to pick up the children or leave them at school, where they may have been safer. Some of the schools told the kids what had happened, some left that to the parents. I walked down the street to pick up Robert at school, where he was in third grade. Gigi and Ellie, meanwhile, were retrieved by friends. The only child I could not get to was Sam, whose school in downtown Washington would not release him until later that day.

Also nerve-racking was the fact that Marvin was in New York, and we couldn't get in touch with him. It turned out that he was in the subway near the Twin Towers when the attacks happened, and he had to evacuate from where the train stopped on the tracks.

Of course, "my family" also included my brother, the president of the United States, who was thrust into a crisis unlike any other since our nation was attacked at Pearl Harbor sixty years before, in 1941. God only knows how he coped with the shock and the enormity of such a catastrophe, as the world watched the Twin Towers collapse, as we saw the Pentagon in flames. And yet, while everyone was struggling to understand the meaning of these atrocities, the president was already reaching out to his advisers, assessing the information, and preparing our government to fight the global scourge of terrorism that descended from the sky that day.

Naturally, when I saw the president get off Marine One on the White House South Lawn that night, I was relieved and concerned—relieved that he and the First Lady were safe, but also deeply concerned about the awesome responsibility now set upon his shoulders.

The next day, Mom and Dad received special permission to fly back to Maine. All air travel was still grounded, so they didn't see a single plane on the way. That afternoon, Jim Dionne, who owned a fishing store in Kennebunkport and is an occasional fishing partner of Dad's, took his boat out on the Kennebunk River and headed over to Walker's Point. He encountered Dad and a Secret Service agent in *Fidelity* coming out of the cove.

"What are you doing out here, Jimmy?" Dad asked.

"I came out to see if you were okay," Jim responded.

In what would become a familiar refrain from Dad in the aftermath of the attacks, Dad said, "We're fine, but please say a prayer for my son George."

Jim then pointed to the American flag flying high on Walker's Point. "Those colors never run, sir," he said.

Dad turned to look at the flag, then told his friend, "You're right, Jimmy. They don't."

Like New York, Washington was a traumatic place to live in the aftermath of 9/11. Everywhere you looked, you saw a reminder of the new world in which we were living. Fighter planes routinely screamed overhead at all hours, and helicopters were flying low over the city. Heavily armed Humvees and antiaircraft batteries were also positioned throughout our nation's capital.

Within a couple of days, my children and I had Secret Service protection. I remember shortly after that, Robert fell on the playground at his all-boys' school. Within minutes, the Secret Service had rushed across the lot with a first-aid kit—to Robert's surprise and the teacher's chagrin. The school's motto is "Play hard, pray hard, be a good guy." Usually, if Robert falls at school, the teachers tell him to shake it off—and while he's at it, get a haircut.

There was great turmoil and uncertainty across the country as well, and my brother—and our First Lady—sought to comfort our nation while also showing our resolve to the world. I was particularly proud of Laura, whose calm demeanor and nurturing personality reassured us all. One of the media outlets dubbed the First Lady the "Comforter in Chief" for the way she helped to pull us all through, and for once I think the media got it right!

On September 14, the president and First Lady led the nation in prayer at a service held at the National Cathedral. I felt very fortunate to be able to attend that service with Mom and Dad. Also present were Vice President and Mrs. Cheney, most of the cabinet, President and Senator Clinton (with Chelsea), President and Mrs. Carter, President and Mrs. Ford, and other national and international dignitaries.

I remember sitting in the National Cathedral, where I had gone many times as a schoolgirl, and thinking how much our nation had changed since those innocent days. Our nation was under attack. There was a tremendous amount of emotion within those stone walls that day. After the president delivered his remarks, he returned to his seat, and Dad reached over to squeeze his arm in a silent show of support.

From there, the president flew to New York to see for himself the wreckage at Ground Zero. There, overcoming concerns for his safety raised by the Secret Service, he stood on the rubble of the towers and, using a bullhorn, promised that "the people who did that will be hearing from all of us soon."

Then on September 20, my brother went to Capitol Hill to address a joint session of Congress.

"I was very proud of his leadership," Dad said, "and I thought his statement to the joint session of the U.S. Congress made very clear to the nation what our priorities are and what he was determined to do. The country saw a man who was in charge, who wanted to do what is right, and wanted to do it in a just manner. He did not want to hurt innocent people in the process, but he was determined to root out this terror. And I think that statement to the country was perhaps the proudest moment Barbara and I had—sitting there watching him with tears in our eyes."

In the weeks that followed, Washington was a different town. People displayed American flags everywhere—on cars, in front of homes, on lapel pins—and people were far more courteous to each other than usual. Like everyone else, I felt the need to do what I could to support our president and our troops. That Christmas, I joined a group of friends who had figured out what we could do in our own small way: we partnered with a computer company to videotape messages from families to the troops overseas, and they made sure the tapes got to our soldiers in Afghanistan in time for the holidays. We felt it was the least we could do for the brave men and women who were protecting us.

Two quick postscripts to 9/11: About a year later, I was at the White House visiting the president with family and friends in the private quarters when a Secret Service agent approached the president. The agent had broken into a sweat, and after taking one look at him, my brother immediately asked what was wrong. The agent explained that an airplane had unexpectedly flown into the restricted airspace near the White House. The president turned to us and said, "Everyone, we have to leave right now. Let's go!"

Children were rounded up, the presidential dogs were grabbed, and we all started running as fast as we could down the back stairs of the White House to safety. I grabbed my youngest daughter Gigi's hand in a death grip and led her downstairs with the other children right behind. In the rush, Sam called out, "Hey, Mom, do you want me to grab that painting of George Washington off the wall?" He was a history major, and I guess he was thinking of following in Dolley Madison's footsteps when she rescued the painting when the British burned the White House. Sam's humor was not appreciated by his mother at the time, although now it does seem funny. Thankfully, the whole episode turned out to be a false alarm.

September 11, 2002—the first anniversary of the terrorist attacks—was a beautiful day in Kennebunkport. At 8:15 a.m., Dad called the staff office and Secret Service command post on Walker's Point and asked everyone to come to the Big House. Jim Nantz and his wife, Lorrie; pro golfer Davis Love and his wife, Robin; and the head pro at the Shadow Hawk Golf Club in Houston, Paul Marchand, and his wife, Judy, were all visiting. The night before, the group piled into Mom and Dad's bedroom at the Big House in Kennebunkport and watched a DVD about a man who lost two sons on that awful day in New York City—one a fireman and one a policeman. The film left everyone speechless.

"At 8:46 a.m., we gathered around the flagpole overlooking the ocean with the flag waving in the light morning breeze and bowed our heads for a moment of silence," remembered Paul Marchand. "There were no cameras—just a personal moment of grieving."

From there, they watched the national service that included my brother George and Laura and then the group attended a church service in Kennebunkport conducted by several area ministers. Paul noticed that, upon arriving at the church and before entering his pew, Dad genuflected on one knee and lowered his head. For maybe thirty seconds, he was lost in prayer before taking his seat.

The service was short with prayers, homilies, and hymns.

"As it happened, I was the only one to drive back to Walker's Point with the president from the service," Paul said. "In the car, President Bush's tears were flowing. I said, 'Are you okay?' He said, 'I think about the families of those who were lost and I think about George and how difficult these times are.'"

★   ★   ★

Just as Dad fulfilled a long-held desire to make a parachute jump in 1997, he also completed another special mission in July 2002 when he traveled back to the Pacific island of Chi Chi Jima where he was shot down in September 1944. Jean Becker and CNN's Paula Zahn made the journey with Dad, as did author James Bradley, whose book *Fly Boys* detailed eight navy and marine airmen who were shot down, captured, and executed by the Japanese forces on Chi Chi Jima. The ninth airman in Bradley's book, Lieutenant George H. W. Bush, escaped capture.

Before they left, Dad told Paula, "This is something I have thought about every single day since the day I was shot down."

"He said that there were all these unanswered questions that troubled him that he was hoping this trip would answer for him," Paula recalled.

Because his trip was facilitated in part by the Japanese government, Dad first visited Atsugi on the Japanese mainland, a facility near Tokyo shared by the U.S. Navy and Japan's Maritime Self-

Defense Force. From there, they flew to Iwo Jima, where they stayed for the night.

The next morning, Dad took part in raising a ceremonial U.S. flag on Mount Suribachi on Iwo Jima, site of a vicious 1945 battle where the U.S. Marines suffered some 28,000 casualties [killed and wounded] and where Japan lost some 21,000.

His hosts asked him if he would mind stopping at a memorial for the kamikaze pilots. "I felt funny at first, since my own ship had been attacked by kamikaze pilots, but I am glad I did it. Those Japanese pilots were not terrorists. They were uniformed officers who paid the last full measure of devotion attempting to save the lives of their embattled compatriots," Dad said to me.

Then the group jumped into helicopters, and some of the Japanese military officials handed Dad a map of the coastline they would be flying over.

"Once we landed on Chi Chi Jima, his mood changed tremendously," Paula said. "In the helicopter, we were in the air for about an hour and he was looking at maps of the coastline very, very carefully with a couple military officials pointing out to him what some of the bombing runs involved; and as we got closer and closer to Chi Chi Jima, they actually flew over the exact spot where his Avenger went down. I could see he was thinking very intensely about that day."

When they landed on Chi Chi Jima, roughly a hundred people with beautiful leis around their necks waved American flags, and it seemed every woman who came to honor Dad placed a lei around his neck as well. At one point, he was wearing about fifteen leis.

From the airport, the group traveled in a very small motorcade to what would be the equivalent of the island's town hall, where the local politicians held a reception for Dad and talked about his war experience.

"As I watched this lunch unfold with local politician after local politician honoring him and saying incredible things about his valor, I was trying to imagine how many of them had relatives who perhaps targeted him when he was doing his bombing runs," Paula recalled. "As it turned out, we actually united the president with a man now who must be in his late eighties who was on duty the day President Bush was shot down, training his guns on the president's plane."

The Japanese military officials did a lot of research before this trip and were able to pinpoint the exact spot where Dad's TBM Avenger was shot down—not far off the coast. So they took boats a half mile out, and Dad got into a rubber dingy by himself and floated out to the spot where he landed in the water.

"He wanted to try and remember what it was like to be in the water that day," Paula explained. "He wanted to be able to focus on the coastline, remember how far out he was and how terrified he was. More importantly, he was coming to this exact spot to pay honor to his fallen friends, John Delaney and Ted White."

Dad took a couple of wreaths with him in the rubber dingy and spent ten minutes reflecting before he very slowly placed the wreaths in the water in honor of his two fallen comrades.

"During that trip, I saw the sands on which so many gave their lives," Dad said. "I hate the word 'closure'—it's overused these days—but maybe the whole trip was about closure. It was certainly about reconciliation."

★   ★   ★

Lud Ashley once said that Dad's greatest accomplishment in life is his family. Mom and Dad now have seventeen grandchildren. I've spoken with some of the older ones while working on this book. Each of them has their own unique relationship with my father—all of them tender and sweet in their own way.

As Dad has become more computer literate, he has found that a great way to keep in touch with his grandchildren is by e-mail. He uses the technology to stay in touch with them from wherever he is in the world, and wherever they are in their lives.

"He e-mails all the time, so he's always caught up with everyone," my niece Barbara said. "He definitely knows what's going on in our lives. For example, once when I broke up with my boyfriend, he made me reenact the breakup. Gampy played my boyfriend, and I played myself doing the breakup. It was at the [Crawford] ranch. He just wanted to see how I handled that. He was curious how it went and wanted some serious details."

Dad also wrote to my nephew Jebby, Jeb and Columba's youngest son, after he got into trouble while at college.

> *Jebster,*
>
> *I, of course, was disappointed to hear about your woes. Just vow not to do it again. I think of the worries that your Dad, and probably your Mom have. But you can make all that right by making a good record as you finish out UT.*
>
> *Advice from Gampy: Remember to be a good sport when the Aggies beat UT.*
>
> *When we get back (leave here October 11) we want you to come stay with us either in Houston or up at Aggieland.*
>
> *I love you, and except for this incident, I am very proud of you. You are a good man, so don't let 'em get you down.*
>
> *Devotedly, The one, the only Gampster*

Here's a note from Dad to Lauren, Neil's daughter, who had asked if she could have a few friends from Princeton University up to Kennebunkport before the summer:

> *Darn it, darn it, darn it. The plumbing at the point is all off, no water running, no flushing, no washing. The houses do not get opened up until the second week in May when we get up there (hopefully). I am so sorry we can't have those other tigers there. I would have sung "Boola Boola" and in other ways tried to make them feel at home, too.*

How is your thesis going? How are your marks over all? Any Ables? Any Dogs?

Do find time later in the summer to come up to Kport after we are all settled in on "the Point."

This from your devoted, Gampy, with tons of love.

At the end of the summer of 2003, he wrote to George P., Noelle, Jebby, Lauren, Pierce, Ashley, Barbara, Jenna, Marshall, Walker, Sam, Ellie, Robert, and Gigi. He refers to his English springer spaniel, Sadie, at the end:

In exactly 69 minutes we drive out of the gate of the point we love so much. The trek back to Houston begins. We speak at West Virginia Monday, then fly back to Houston Monday evening.

Yesterday Bill Busch and I took a final run in Fidelity. *It was heaven. Swells but no real chop on the sea. There were tons of mackerel breaking the water but no blues, no stripers chasing them. We did see some tuna, obviously in quest of a mackerel lunch. I left Bill off on his boat here at the point then roared back to the river— going full blast. I am sure it was over 60. I felt about 19 years old.*

The only thing wrong with the last five months is that none of you were here enough. Oh I know some got to stay as long as usual, but there never can be enough of having all of you here. Next year, promise this old gampster that you will spend more time with us here by the sea.

I am a very happy Gampy. My legs don't bend too well. As you know I have had to give up fly fishing off the rocks, but there is plenty left to do—plenty of wonderful things.

I think of all of you an awful lot. I just wonder how each of you is doing—in life, in college, in school.

If you need me, I am here for you, because I love you very much. This comes from your devoted, Gampy.

PS—I never went in the ocean this year. The first time in my 78 years here (I missed 1949) that I haven't gone in. Sad am I, but I got huge kicks of seeing you dive off the pier. I got a clear shot at that from Jean's office window.

Sadie just came in. She is very nervous. She sees the bags. She knows Ariel, Paula and Alicia left a week ago. Now she prances around viewing the horrid suitcases wondering what's next for her. She'll be OK in Houston but she'll miss Kport—of that I am sure.

The grandchildren can tell how much he is enjoying life after the White House. "After he was past the presidency, Gampy just became very carefree and let all of the burdens that he had as president go," my niece Jenna said. "He loves to travel and do fun things. Gampy has given us so many opportunities after he's been president to be together as a family."

Jenna's right, and as a result the cousins have grown especially close over the years despite how public their lives have been at times. "There are always reasons for us to see each other and stay in touch, but also I think the whole political environment makes you cautious sometimes about who you trust and who you are going to choose as your friends," her sister Barbara added. "No one has ever had to be like that in our family because everyone trusted each other and everyone depends on each other. I don't really have that many issues with it, because I have really great friends. All of our family members have really great friends, too, but that's something you have in the back of your mind."

★   ★   ★

On June 5, 2004, President Reagan passed away after a ten-year struggle with Alzheimer's disease. Thousands of mourners filled the streets of Washington, D.C., after his body lay in state in the U.S. Capitol and was taken to services at Washington National Cathedral. Both my brother and my father spoke at the service, and in his eulogy, Dad said, "As his vice president for eight years, I learned more from Ronald Reagan than from anyone I encountered in all my years of public life."

It was an emotional moment for Dad, as he has a difficult time getting through any funeral, but especially for a good friend like President Reagan. Seeing the Reagan family hold up so strongly helped him get through his remarks without choking up.

After the services concluded, Dad and Mom left immediately for Dad's long-scheduled eightieth birthday celebration in Houston.

The birthday extravaganza was named "41@80" and thousands of old and new friends were invited to Houston for an elaborate celebration at Minute Maid Park. Larry King emceed, and entertainers such as Crystal Gale, Ronan Tynan, and Amy Grant and Vince Gill performed. Dad's friends from the sporting world spoke—Chrissie Evert, Greg Norman, among others. Many current and former world leaders who had been previously invited to Dad's celebration joined him at President Reagan's funeral and then came to Houston. There were fireworks, and, to the delight of the crowd, the Golden Knights, the elite skydivers from the U.S. Army, sailed through an opening in the stadium roof.

Larry King told me, "The proudest thing I did was when he asked me to host his eightieth birthday. That was the night I had to settle things when every foreign leader wanted to talk."

Larry continued, "We're running late, so I said to them all, 'Listen, fellows, why don't one of you speak for all of you?' So Mulroney said, 'Well, I know him the best. I'll speak for two or three minutes, represent all of us.' Gorbachev goes, '*Nyet!* I will speak or no one will speak.' And then Gorbachev sits down. I've got them all standing back there and now I don't know what to do. I go over to your father and I said, 'Listen, I've got a problem here. I got them all, it's running close to eleven o'clock, what do I do?'

"Your father said, 'Gorbachev saved the world. We can't dump Gorbachev. This is a diplomatic thing.' Then he said to me, 'Figure it out.' I went back and said, 'Okay, come back, Mr. Gorbachev, you speak and the others will stand behind you. You'll represent them all, two or three minutes.' He said, 'Three minutes? *Nyet*. Don't limit me to three minutes.'

"Now the world leaders are all looking at each other, like, oh, boy. Then Dan Quayle leans over and says to me, '*I told you.*' It was a comedy. Gorbachev got up, but they couldn't stand next to him, they had to stand behind him. And he gave a very witty seven-minute speech. Prime Minister Mulroney was very sporting. They all understood. They said, 'Listen, this is what we've got to do.' That was a terrific moment."

The next day, everyone boarded buses and a special Union Pacific train to College Station, where the Bush Library is located. The Oak Ridge Boys sang under a big tent, the Texas A&M Wranglers danced, and everyone ate barbecue. The highlight of the day, of course, was when Dad jumped out of an airplane with the Golden Knights.

On the day of the big jump, my niece Lauren went out at dawn with Dad for a practice jump. (Some members of our family had done a jump the day before, without Dad, and she wanted to go again.) "I drive out to the airfield and it's just Gampy and me jumping, because he wanted to prove to them that he could go alone. I'd gone the day before, so I wasn't panicked. There were all these younger guys who obviously idolized Gampy. They're in the plane, too. Gampy and I were at separate ends of the plane so it's hard to talk. It was a really special moment. It was really early, so the light was beautiful. I just liked being there with him."

Dad's big jump at the party—in front of the crowd—went off without a hitch, and the entire weekend was a great success. Overall, it raised almost $60 million for my parents' favorite charities and brought together an international cast of dignitaries.

"George really wanted me to jump with a parachute together with him on the day of his eightieth birthday," President Gorbachev told me. "I replied, half in jest, that he shouldn't subject my life to such a risk, since I had not had the same practice that he had. I promised him that after his landing I would meet him with a bouquet of flowers. I kept my promise, adding a bottle of vodka into the bargain."

★ ★ ★

George's 2004 reelection campaign was approaching, and Barbara and Jenna were thinking about going out on the campaign trail for the first time. In 2000, they were just freshmen in college when their dad ran for president. He never wanted them to be in the public eye if they didn't want to. This time around, however, they were at a good time in their lives to help and didn't want to feel that they hadn't helped if their dad lost. They traveled together and were very effective letting people know more about the president.

Many of the grandchildren were old enough to participate in the campaign. George P., who was a star in 2000, was not able to campaign as much as he wanted because of his job as a law clerk; but the campaign sent Sam and Ellie to Colorado, to put up signs and pass out brochures.

I was happy to join Jenna and Barbara on the campaign's "W Stands for Women" grassroots effort aimed at getting out the women's vote. Every vote counted. George thought the women's vote was key—naturally, because he's surrounded himself with so many strong women, like his chief political adviser, Karen Hughes, Secretary of State Condoleezza Rice, and Margaret Spellings, his former domestic policy adviser and now secretary of education, to name a few.

My sister-in-law, Tricia Koch, and I packed our bags—that way, when a call from the campaign came, we were ready to go at a moment's notice. The eight children between us whom we left behind were well taken care of, and when we were gone, they wore their George W. gear. My mother was worried about our husbands, but thanks to the miracle of microwaves and frozen food, we knew everyone would be fine. This was a close election, and as we later found out the hard way, everyone's efforts made an enormous difference.

My favorite part of being on the campaign was traveling to places I'd never been and meeting all kinds of people who genuinely care about their country. I marched in parades and rode on fire engines. Along the way, I experienced the innate decency of the American people.

Here's an e-mail Dad sent to my nieces Barbara and Jenna, George and Laura's twins, just before the 2004 election.

After leaving you I went to a good rally with Gov Jeb. Now I head to Houston on this great plane. But it is lonely here now. No twins to brighten my life. No cute and stylish introducers. No sleeping beauties to look over at saying to myself "are those 2 sleeping beauties the same two who bugged me about the aliens and sic-ed that cat on me in Austin?"

I am getting older, girls. Maybe you noticed that I walk a little different and that my hearing is less able to handle the diphthongs and the decibels.

But what you cannot possibly know is what is deeply ingrained in my heart. I tease you. I show off in front of your friends. You name it.

But you can't really know the depth of my pride in you. And you cannot possibly know how much I love you both.

I am an old man now. I hate to admit it, but one reason I want to stay alive a lot longer is to watch you go on now to your exciting lives ahead and maybe, just maybe, get to hug your kids.

Win or lose on Tuesday, and I am now more confident it is "win," I will be there for you. You have your own great Mom and Dad but if you ever need a shoulder to cry or an old guy to laugh with count me in.

I just want to be sure that you both know of my pride in you and of my love.

This from the one, the only Gampy aka The Gampster

On election night, November 3, the early exit polls looked terrible. I was so worried that I told Mom I'd rather not come down to the White House where everyone was gathering. I had been doing satellite television interviews up to the final hours and couldn't stand the thought of my brother losing. But Mom ordered me to come, in that voice from my childhood: "Get. Down. Here. Right. Now."

After 2000, the last thing my brother, the First Lady, the nation, and the rest of us needed was another cliff-hanger. After Minnesota was called for Senator Kerry at 4:38 a.m. the next day, as well as Michigan at 5:30 a.m., my brother was leading 269 to 238. Only Ohio and its 31 electoral votes hung in the balance. Thankfully, Senator Kerry spared the nation another contentious recount. He decided not to legally challenge the Ohio results and called the president at 11:00 the morning after the election to concede. Upon hearing the news, we took the kids out of school and joined thousands of supporters at the Reagan Building in Washington, D.C., for the president's victory speech.

In all the excitement of the night before, Laura remembered seeing Dad in a touching scene: "Little Kate Cheney, the vice president's granddaughter, was here. Kate was in second or third grade. She was the only little person there. Gampy had this very long conversation with her. She was telling him about her teacher who had fifteen cats. On the night of such an emotional roller coaster, here was the father of the candidate centered enough that he could have a conversation like that."

Chapter 25

CEILING AND VISIBILITY
UNLIMITED

"I can't see the notch in the hills across the ocean, the notch that I navigate by to get to Perkins Cove, so in that sense visibility is less than perfect; and yet I can confidently tell my kids my life is CAVU—ceiling and visibility are truly unlimited for your devoted dad."

—my father in a letter to his children, preparing to leave Maine for the winter

On December 26, 2004, an underwater earthquake off the coast of Sumatra measuring 9.0 on the Richter scale triggered the most devastating tsunami in recorded history, unleashing waves of death and destruction around the entire Indian Ocean perimeter. As word reached our family in Florida, where we had gathered for Christmas, the horrible news and video images shattered the Christmas calm of the holiday season in the wake of my brother's grueling reelection campaign.

The initial reports suggesting that 3,000, then 30,000, then 100,000 were lost didn't begin to tell the whole story. In the end, over 273,000 lives were lost—more than a third of whom just vanished without a trace. The physical damage to homes, schools, roads, and mosques was just as profound.

A week later, the president stood in the Roosevelt Room of the White House with Dad and President Clinton and announced that his two predecessors would team up to raise awareness of various groups helping victims recover from this catastrophe. Thus was born the political "odd couple," as Mom calls Dad and President Clinton.

Six weeks after the White House announcement, Dad and President Clinton boarded a U.S. government plane, a 757, and hopscotching to Hawaii and Guam, made a five-day visit to Thailand, Indonesia, Sri Lanka, and the Maldive Islands to tour some of the most devastated areas.

By all accounts of that trip, a genuine friendship was solidified.

"When President Bush and I took that trip, it meant something to me," President Clinton said. "Whatever there was left from the '92 campaign, it gave us a way to erase it. His willingness to do this and what we've done and how well it's worked out has been a joy to me and a personal sort of relief."

"I was very touched a couple of times when I saw President Clinton help President Bush make a hard step up or grab his elbow when we were walking over unsteady ground," Jean Becker recalled. "He didn't make a big deal of it. He just did it very casually."

Dad described the trip in a letter to his friend Hugh Sidey, which read in part:

> *About eight hours ago, we left the Maldives, the final stop on our four country swing to inspect Tsunami damage. It has been an amazing trip . . .*
>
> *Let me start by commenting what it has been like traveling with Bill Clinton. I thought I knew him, but until this trip I did not really know him. First of all, he has been very considerate of me. I think my old age had something to do with it. He always waited so we could go off the plane together, giving the greeters the old familiar "wave from the top of the stairs." You've seen that a million times. You wave even if there is no one to wave at . . .*

Clinton went out of his way not to criticize the President. He talked about the generous commitment of the USA, of our effective military support, of the money the private sector had given.

Now on to the trip of tears:

I have never seen such devastation. We started off in Thailand at Phuket. Many of the big resort hotels in Phuket are still in operation. But soon after we boarded our helicopters we began to see the real ravages of the tsunami. Many buildings were flattened. Only rubble and cracked foundations remained. Those left standing had been gutted.

We flew to tiny Pukua Pa then drove to Baan Nam Kem village. We chatted with some kids. We watched the building of some new fishing boats, the fishing fleet having been totally demolished. We saw firsthand the good being done by U.S. aid workers and NGOs (non-government organizations) of all sorts.

But it was not until the next day when we landed in Aceh (pronounced Ah-chay) that we began to feel the human side of this tragedy. Our helicopter made several turns over the hardest hit area. Where there had been hundreds of private homes, there was nothing. Much of the rubble and debris had been cleared, the bodies removed; but I kept thinking what this must be like for the families. Mostly fishermen, they lived by the sea, living humbly in tiny homes, but at least they were safe and free to make a living.

Now as we walked from the chopper a few hundred yards to our briefing point, we went through lines of people. The old and the young, men and women, all lined up as we came in. The saddest part related to the little children. I saw one father holding his six-year-old son's shoulder. He was standing, emotionless, just holding his boy and staring. I asked the translator with us exactly what happened to this man. His wife and several of his kids were all killed, only this one boy alive, with him, at his side. On and on these tales of sadness went. Kids watching their parents drown, tales of fear, tales of hopelessness. It was so moving and so desperately sad . . .

The news stories from this historic visit to the region together with the TV ads Dad and President Clinton did—to say nothing of the efforts of other nonprofit groups—helped to raise an estimated $1 billion in private donations for tsunami relief.

In the meantime, Dad—with President Clinton's approval—also started a local Bush-Clinton Tsunami Fund in Houston, Texas, that collected donations mostly from local companies, schools, and private citizens.

Dad wanted to thank everyone who gave money, so his office set up two or three days where they had everyone from CEOs who gave $100,000 to a group of kids who raised $1,000 at their lemonade stand come by. One day, twenty-six different groups came and presented their checks to Dad. One was a group of tattoo-bearing motorcycle riders who had done a bike-athon to raise funds. The Secret Service said that one of the guys had a pretty bad history involving drugs, but Dad didn't care.

"That's the kind of stuff he does all the time," Jean said. "It totally amazes me how he's so willing to give and give of his time. I've been trying for years to tell him that it really is okay to quit. He doesn't have to raise money; he doesn't have to lend his name; and he shouldn't feel obligated anymore. Every time we have this conversation, he'll totally agree with me—and then the first thing I know, we have two new projects. He'll say, 'Well, Jean, how can we say no to them?' "

In May 2005, President Clinton came to Houston, where the local tsunami fund there announced they had raised $11 million. At the Houston event, Mom joked that she had become so accustomed to seeing Dad and President Clinton together that she was going to start calling the latter "son."

"Those Bushes," President Clinton replied a few days later. "They'll do anything to get another president in the family."

At the Alfalfa Dinner in January, my brother George joked that when President Clinton had awoken from his recent heart surgery, "all of his loved ones were gathered around: Hillary, Chelsea . . . Dad."

President Clinton also sent Dad and the president copies of a cartoon that came out around this time. One panel showed the president saying, "I oppose gay marriage." The other panel showed 41 and 42 on a couch holding hands. The president sticks his head in the room and screams, "Dad!!" Later, Bill Clinton sent Dad a copy saying, "George, maybe we'd better cool it."

The banter continued in April of 2005 when the three traveled together to the Vatican, for the funeral of Pope John Paul II. They were at the U.S. ambassador's residence. The three presidents were sitting together on the couch when President Clinton, who was sitting in the middle, told my brother, "This is all your fault. You started this."

The president put his arm around President Clinton, and they took a picture of it. Dad sent a copy of the photo to President Clinton inscribed, "Bill, I don't like being jilted; but I'm still your friend."

★   ★   ★

After Dad and President Clinton started working together, a friend of mine said, "If your dad invites President Clinton to Kennebunkport, then I know he's really lost it." Fast forward to June 2005, and sure enough, Dad had extended the invitation.

As Dad told his friend Jim Nantz, the CBS sportscaster, "I've invited President Clinton to come over to Kennebunkport this summer. We've been spending a lot of time together on tsunami relief, and I thought it would be fun if he came to Maine, played some golf, relaxed—strictly a social visit."

Dad had been thinking about the meeting, he told Jim, and wanted it to be very comfortable. He wanted President Clinton to have a good time, and he didn't ever want it to be awkward. Bottom line: Dad thought it would be more fun to include another golfer, Jim, in the group. Jim enthusiastically agreed.

Typical of Dad, President Clinton's arrival had to be something out of the ordinary. A motorcade wouldn't suffice. Dad wanted to pick him up by boat at a harbor outside of Portland, Maine—a forty-five-minute boat ride in smooth seas.

On Monday, June 27, however, the conditions were anything but calm.

"The trip up there was almost frightening," Jim said. "It was raining sideways with the wind and choppy conditions. We would go up over a wave and, boom, we'd bottom out into the next wave. It took a special mariner to figure out how to get up the coast. President Bush was using all the electronics he had on board."

At a couple of points, it was so foggy and rainy that the group couldn't see the Secret Service boats that were flanking them.

"Next thing you know," Jim continued, "according to the navigation system, we were in the area where we were supposed to make a turn toward the coast. So he slowed the boat down, and we came to a crawl. With all the fog, it looked like a scene out of a movie—or a spy novel."

President Clinton had come off heart surgery the previous fall, so after he arrived, Dad explained how he was concerned that the boat ride going back might be a very rough ride, and President Clinton right away properly opted to go by car.

Walker's Point was abuzz waiting for President Clinton and Dad to arrive. Tricia Koch, who helped me with this book, came with me for this historic visit as part of our research, and our kids decided to make welcome signs. When we saw the motorcade approaching, everyone on the Point came out to greet them.

Out of the car came 41 and 42—a sight I never expected to see in Kennebunkport. Jim Nantz followed, videotaping the visit (the first time I had seen Jim behind the camera!). President Clinton smiled and greeted everyone warmly.

Upon the first ten minutes of meeting President Clinton in this private setting, everyone was mesmerized. He is engaging, and knows a lot about everything. Simply put, he fascinated us to no end.

What I love about Dad is that, whether or not his guest is a head of state, you get the same welcome—"my house is your house." That night, he and Mom hosted a small cocktail party for President Clinton. The party had barely started when suddenly Dad decided to show his special guest the "You da man" video, which I should explain.

A few years back, Dad convinced himself that he actually coined the phrase "You da man" back in the early 1960s. He maintains he was inspired to shout it to the Houston Astros' Rusty Staub as he rounded third base following a home run, and it slowly caught on from there.

Sensing that few, if any, in his own family believed him—grandchildren included—Dad pressed his case with Houston Astros owner Drayton McLane, who had a very funny piece of videotape created celebrating this unknown piece of baseball lore and played it for the crowd at Minute Maid Park during a game at which Dad was present. The crowd clearly enjoyed it.

So Dad showed the video to his distinguished visitor. President Clinton already knew that Al Gore invented the Internet, but not until that night did he know who first came up with the expression "You da man"!

Dinner that night was at Stripers, a new restaurant that is a local favorite, after which Mom and Dad retired for the night while President Clinton played cards with some staffers.

The next morning, Jim Nantz, 42, and 41 hit a few putts on the practice green right outside the living room windows near the Big House. (Jim and his University of Houston classmate Paul Marchand, now head pro at the Shadow Hawk Golf Club in Houston, had the putting green built as a present to Dad for his friendship through the years. "What do you give a guy who has given you so much?" Jim said to me.)

From there, it was on to Cape Arundel Golf Course—a course Dad has played most of his life, and where he claims to have won the 1947 club championship. Ken Raynor, the head pro at Cape Arundel, told me, "As the story goes, he took on a local by the name of Chad Brown, who was a post office worker down here. And your dad's pride was not only winning the club championship, but closing him out on the eleventh hole. But nobody quite knows whether Chaddy was really sober or not during this match, because he was known not to be. The championship may be tainted a little bit."

Anyway, on that day with Jim Nantz, Ken Raynor, and President Clinton, it seemed the entire town—and even a few members of the news media—turned out to watch the foursome tee off. The featured match that day pitted Dad and head pro Ken Raynor against President Clinton and Jim Nantz.

"After President Clinton birdied the second and third holes," Jim recalled, "I was leaning on a putter and whispered to President Bush, 'Of all the golfers you've had here through the years— Arnold Palmer, Greg Norman, Davis Love, Fred Couples, José María Olazábal—how many of them were two under par after three holes?'"

"None," Dad whispered back.

On the fifth hole, Dad pulled his tee shot onto the steep embankment that runs down the left side. He discovered his ball tangled in a thick patch of grass. To reach the green a hundred yards away, Dad had two choices: risk that he could muscle the ball out of the rough and over the creek that also ran down the left side of the hole, or pitch out safely back into the fairway.

Spying Dad's predicament, President Clinton jumped into a cart and drove to a point up the fairway. "Hit it here, George," he shouted, waving his arms at the 1947 club champion. Dad followed the advice, hit a perfect recovery shot, and went on to save par.

The match ended dead even.

Most recently, Dad and President Clinton have teamed up to help raise funds to assist the Gulf States in their recovery from Hurricanes Katrina and Rita. Though these storms raged ashore within weeks of each other in 2005, anyone who has driven through the lower Ninth Ward in New Orleans, or through Pass

Christian, Mississippi, knows it is going to be years—and possibly even decades—before some communities resume any sense of "normalcy." Together, my father and his successor have raised well over $100 million to lend a helping hand, so their productive partnership endures.

Looking back, what I noticed, first and foremost, was that Dad and President Clinton like each other. In fact, I formulated a theory about their relationship—that if Dad hadn't extended the hand of fellowship and made it okay for them to be friends, they wouldn't have what I saw to be a comfortable friendship.

Even today, however, some aren't certain whether the friendship is genuine. To be sure, the sight of Dad and President Clinton coming together as they did stunned a great many people, particularly those who worked so hard on both sides during the 1992 campaign. How could two men who fought so hard to beat each other bury the hatchet and start a working partnership as if nothing had happened?

Some also wonder if there is an element of 2008 politics involved.

To be candid, my brother Jeb maintains Dad is being used. "President Clinton's advisers have figured out that, in terms of character and integrity, a rising tide lifts all boats," Jeb said. "So I could see President Clinton's motivation. Apparently, he is a very likable person. I believe Dad does it because it was important to show the world that partisanship stops when there's a crisis, and I think the tenor in Washington is such that having a nonpartisan relationship between two former presidents is good."

Part of what makes the Dad–President Clinton relationship such a fascinating thing to watch is that they both have family members who are active in national politics. The fine line that they have to walk as former presidents—and occasional partners—is even more complicated.

"President Bush is obviously very protective of the president and Jeb," President Clinton said, "and on the other hand he knows I have to be protective of Hillary. He knows that we have to air our disagreements some, partly because we're still in the game—but I try to leave most of this stuff to her. 41 is probably better at this than I am."

"President Clinton is in a different spot than I am," Dad offered. "He's still young compared to me, and he's got a wife who's politically active, so he seeks out more press and more attention for the wide variety of causes he pursues. I periodically catch grief from family and friends and people on the right—just as President Clinton has caught hell from the left—but what we are doing together transcends politics."

★   ★   ★

A few days after my brother George launched the 41–42 partnership for tsunami relief in January, he and the First Lady also hosted my parents and over one hundred family members and close friends at the White House to celebrate Mom and Dad's sixtieth wedding anniversary. Of course, that very special occasion marked an important milestone for our family, but it was also a noteworthy historic event. No other president and First Lady had lived long enough to see their sixtieth anniversary. Abigail Adams died three days after she and President John Adams celebrated their fifty-fourth, which now stands as the second longest marriage of a First Couple.

Laura came up with the idea for the party, which touched Mom and Dad. The evening was a formal black-tie affair, and the entertainment featured the Marine Corps Band, as well as performers Ronan Tynan, Michael W. Smith, and the U.S. Army's Alvy Powell, who sang at Dad's 1989 inaugural.

The hardest job that night, assembling the guest list, fell to Dad, while my brothers and I had the easiest job that night: deciding how to salute our parents. We chose George to speak on our behalf since he was the oldest, but I'm not going to lie: the fact that we would be in the White House and he was the president *may* have also factored into the decision.

The president spoke before dinner, and after dinner he invited others to make brief remarks. One toast that stood out came from David Rubenstein, cofounder of the Carlyle Group. David started by noting he was probably the only person there who had worked in a Democratic White House—at which point a few eyebrows were raised.

"Wait a second," David continued. "If it hadn't been for me getting inflation so high in the Carter years, 41 would not have been elected vice president of the United States; and if he hadn't been elected vice president, he might not have become president. If he hadn't become president, 43 wouldn't be president!"

Both my parents gave moving remarks that night.

"To have your family around you," Mom said, looking back, "and to celebrate in the house where your son serves as president—that's not a bad deal."

That night, Dad observed that it was amazing to give a speech where you looked back at a life where you fell in love with a special girl, went to war and got shot down, got pulled out of the Pacific Ocean, and somehow went home alive. Then you married that special girl and together set out on an incredible journey marked by tremendous challenges and heartbreak and joy that led to the White House and beyond. Then, to be able to give such a speech in the White House because of what your son had accomplished . . . well, let's just say the tears flowed.

You could say that the Bush "Bawl Patrol," a phrase Dad coined referring to the fact that we cry a lot, has been on constant alert in recent years—as there have been a few weddings to celebrate.

First, in March 2004, Mom and Dad and Marvin and I were on hand to see my brother Neil remarried to a fellow Houstonian, Maria Andrews, who volunteered in Dad's office. The ceremony and reception were held at the beautiful home of Neil's friend Jamal Daniel, and the bride and groom looked radiant. This happy union not only brought three new grandkids into the family—Lizzie, Pace, and Ally—but it also meant I had another very kind, very smart, but very tiny sister-in-law! (By the way, I've learned to stand next to my tall brothers in photos, rather than their tiny wives.)

We reached another milestone in August 2005, when George P., the oldest grandchild, became the first grandchild to wed, marrying Mandi Williams of San Angelo, Texas. George P. and Mandi met at the University of Texas Law School and they make a striking couple.

The wedding at the church of St. Ann's by the Sea in Kennebunkport, where my grandparents had been married in 1921, was beautiful. The father of the groom, Jeb, said, "It was a huge day for Columba and me. Having the wedding in Maine was such a blessing, and seeing our son, fully in love, getting married in front of family and friends was one of the greatest joys of our lives. Mom and Dad were such incredible grandparents for their first grandchild."

All of the grandkids were clearly excited to see the first of their generation "take the plunge." Mandi thoughtfully included Gigi as the flower girl, and Sam and some of his cousins served as ushers. Also, in honor of George P. and Mandi's alma mater, the University of Texas, everyone in the wedding party wore tuxedos and dresses accented by burnt orange.

The new couple held their reception on a specially built platform at Stripers Restaurant, using the Kennebunk River as a backdrop, and Ariel made the groom's cake. Even though he is not a big dancer, Dad danced with the new bride.

One final wedding story: During the summer of 2004, Dad invited golf pro Phil Mickelson and his wife, Amy, to Maine for a visit that included not only golf but also a boat ride.

"We thought it would be a lovely little cruise along the Maine coast," Phil recalled. "Very quickly, we found out we had two choices: hold on tight or become lobster bait."

On our way back to the dock, Dad noticed a wedding party on the grounds of the Nonantum Hotel, and said, "Do you think we should say hi?"

The Mickelsons laughed, but the next thing they knew they were trailing along as Dad docked and shouted to the party, "I guess FedEx lost my invitation!"

"Here was the forty-first president working his way through a gathering, shaking hands, taking pictures, smiling all the way," Phil said. "Then in front of this group, he wished the wedding couple a life filled with happiness, humor, and love."

★ ★ ★

One of the great honors of my life came when Dad called a few years ago and asked me to serve as the sponsor of an aircraft carrier being built—one that would bear his name. I had no idea what was involved in being a sponsor; but if Dad was asking, again, the answer is always "yes."

On December 9, 2002, Secretary of the Navy Gordon England officially named a new carrier being built after Dad, owing to his service during World War II and his service as president. The new aircraft carrier will eventually replace the forty-seven-year-old USS *Kitty Hawk* (CV-63). The *George H. W. Bush* (CVN 77) will be the tenth and final ship in the Nimitz class, and the first carrier of the twenty-first century.

Next, on September 6, 2003, Mom, Dad, and I went to the Northrop Grumman shipbuilding yard at Newport News, Virginia, for the keel-laying ceremony. The keel is the horizontal part on the hull, or bottom, of the boat which steadies it and helps with steering. Dad went there to "authenticate" the keel by chalking his initials onto a steel plate, which was then welded and permanently affixed to the hull. As sponsor, I had to "certify the keel to be true and fairly laid."

In July 2006, the ship's huge island—its command and control center—was lowered onto the massive hull. A set of Dad's navy wings and those of the ship's captain, Kevin O'Flaherty, along with a bound set of galleys for the present memoir, were sealed into a time capsule that was then placed onboard.

To be christened in October 2006, the *George H. W. Bush* is three football fields long, weighs 97,000 tons, and carries seventy-five combat aircraft. It is among the world's largest warships, possesses state-of-the-art technology, and is powered by two nuclear reactors, making it capable of operating for twenty years without refueling.

Being a sponsor, I quickly discovered, involves more than you might think. The sponsor's spirit remains with the ship for as long as it is on the water, and sponsors develop a special relationship with their ship and keep in contact with it over the years. At the ship's christening, I will smash a bottle of champagne over the bow and say, "In the name of the United States, I christen thee *George H. W. Bush.*"

In 2008, when the ship joins the fleet and is officially commissioned, I will say, "Crew of the USS *George H. W. Bush,* man our ship and bring her to life!" The entire crew, assembled onshore, will yell, "Aye, aye, ma'am!" and sprint up the gangplanks onto the ship. The radar will start to rotate, the gun turrets will spin around, bells will ring, alarms will sound, and ship whistles will blow. The Navy Band will play "Anchors Aweigh" and the fighter jets will fly overhead. The ship truly will come to life.

Dad just can't wait. He has a model of the ship on his desk and shows it to every visitor who comes to call. The day after the keel-laying ceremony, I received this e-mail from him:

Doro,

> *Yesterday was a very happy, meaningful day in my wonderful life and that you were at my side in that starring role made it perfect, even beyond perfect. Love from your admiring devoted DAD.*

★   ★   ★

In an active life filled with change, Mom and Dad have lived in more than thirty houses during their marriage, but their home in

Kennebunkport has been the one constant. Dad has spent a part of every summer there except one—in 1944, when he was at war in the Pacific.

Just as my grandfather Prescott was viewed as the unofficial mayor of Greenwich, Connecticut, Dad has also come to support a wide range of local causes in Kennebunkport.

To give you an idea: In recent years he has picked up some local scuttlebutt at H&B Provisions, the local grocery store, that some of the newcomers to Kennebunkport felt somewhat unwelcome and were having a hard time meeting people. After he heard it a few times, Dad decided he wanted to do something about it.

He told his aide Tommy Frechette, "Let's invite everyone in our neighborhood that we've never met before and introduce them to some of the old neighbors. We'll have them all come in together."

The event was soon dubbed the Old-New Party. Everyone that received an invitation showed up, but figuring out whom to invite required Dad's staff to go door-to-door to see who lives there.

"Whenever he encounters a barrier," Tommy said, "his natural inclination is to break it down."

Dad is at his best when he's on Walker's Point. When he is not there over the winter, he gets antsy by February—talking about his boat every day.

"Let's talk to Bill Busch just for the heck of it," he'll say to Tommy Frechette.

"I know it's February and it's freezing, but how's Maine looking?" he'll ask Bill. "Are we ready to go? Any patterns on the fish?"

When people come for a visit, Dad's whole outlook changes. He gets into what I call kid mode and gets very excited. He gets everything ready, and whether the visitors are heads of state or a grandchild, he's waiting at the door for the big arrival. Then it's on to the activities, whether fishing, boating, or sports events. "Let's do something fun," he'll say. "Let's get them out here on the banana boat and we'll spin them around" or "Let's see who can jump in the cold water first."

My dad's nephew Hap Ellis sums up life at Walker's Point this way: "Nothing beats fishing the rocks at Walker's Point at all hours. And if your dad sees me, he invariably comes out on the porch and shouts to get my attention and then, in that timeless fishing gesture, holds his hands wide apart as if to ask, How big? I honestly think he gets enormous pleasure out of knowing those bass are there, and that we are out there battling for them, even though the Secret Service won't let him out there anymore. It is as if one little piece of what Walker's Point is all about for him is intact for that moment that day: family, fishing, Walker's Point . . . and then it's on to the next event.

The times Dad spends in Kennebunkport are his happiest times—not the years at the White House, or in China, or at the CIA, as much as those places and institutions mean to him. Walker's Point is where his heart is, and where he can do all the things that are most important to him. It is there that he can give back to others, he can spend precious time with friends and family, and can "get into the grandchildren business big-time." It is there he can go to the church of St. Ann's by the Sea, he can spend time on the ocean and breathe in the salt air.

One time, a friend asked Dad about my brothers' decisions to enter public service. "What is it about public service and your family? Is it something in the water up here in Kennebunkport?" he asked. "I'll tell you what's in the water," Dad said. "Bluefish!"

To Dad, life is not about looking back to the presidency, but looking forward to all the adventures still to come. Every family has its history, and most people think the most important part of our family's history involves the presidency. But we think what's significant about our family history is what Kennebunkport has come to symbolize for us: faith, family, and friends.

On that note, it seems fitting to close this chapter, and this book, with an excerpt of a letter Dad sent to his five kids:

This is my last day in Kennebunkport after almost five months of great happiness. There is something about this place that gets into one's very soul. Don't you agree?

Here's what I want to tell you at summer's end.

I had a little plaque made. It says CAVU. CAVU was the kind of weather we Navy pilots wanted when we were to fly off our carrier in the Pacific. We had little navigational instrumentation, so we wanted CAVU—"Ceiling and Visibility Unlimited."

At Gar Hole's funeral this summer—he was our exec in the Pacific—I saw a wooden plaque that read CAVU, so I had a little bronze one made up for the end of our house here, the end where the seas pound into the rocks the most, the spray most likely to weather my plaque. It will then blend nicely in and guests will no longer say "What does CAVU mean?"

When it has blended in, outsiders might not notice it—fine by me. But I will not pass by it without realizing how lucky I am, for the plaque describes my own life—as it has been over the years, as it is right now.

I used to seek broad horizons in life, and I found plenty. Now I don't care if I can't even see Ogunquit [a town thirteen miles south of Walker's Point]. Limited horizons are OK by me just so family is in view.

I don't want to sit at the head table or be honored or get a medal or have stuff named for me. That's happened and I have been truly grateful for some of the honors, but no more need come my way.

I sit on our deck, out of the wind, near the sea. And I realize that because of all five of you and yours I am a very happy man. I don't need anything. I don't want anything—only your love.

Because of your love and your caring about us and the joy your kids' laughter and even the sadness a tear reveals, I know my life has been very full and happy. And your mother feels exactly the same way.

Your mother and I sit out here like a couple of really old poops, but we are at total peace. She does crossword puzzles, real puzzles, reads a ton of books, plays golf, calls people up on the phone, writes letters, and occasionally gets mildly (to use an old Navy expression) pissed off at me. I can handle it though—no problem. I fall back on bad hearing and changing the subject. Both work.

Because of the five of you whose hugs I can still feel, whose own lives have made me so proud, I can confidently tell my guardian angels that my life is CAVU; and it will be that way until I die—all because of you.

Acknowledgments

Writing this book has been a privilege and a passion for the last year and a half. I went into this project not having any idea how to begin. I come out of this project grateful for all of the support I received along the way.

Once I decided to take on this project, the first call I made was to my sister-in-law and friend Tricia Reilly Koch. I knew she would love this challenge, and in her inimitable way she accepted my plea for help with unbounded enthusiasm. I truly could not have done this without her.

Tricia and I are grateful to Larry Kirshbaum, former CEO of Warner Books, who now runs LKJ Literary Management. Larry believed in this project the instant he heard about it and stayed with us after he left Warner Books. He was our biggest cheerleader, and his guidance was invaluable.

We could not have asked for a better publisher than Hachette Book Group USA. Our thanks go to Maureen Egen, Jamie Raab, Karen Kosztolnyik, Emi Battaglia, Jennifer Romanello, Bob Castillo, Jimmy Franco, Karen Torres, Chris Barba, and the rest of the excellent staff.

There would be no book if it were not for the special talents of Mary Kate Cary and Jim McGrath. They are hardworking, loyal, and masterful at their craft. Each contributed to this book in their own special way, and for that I am grateful. Barbara Feinman Todd was with us early on, and I appreciate her valuable contributions.

An enormous thank-you goes to everyone at the George Bush Library, especially the "Ladies at the Library," Laura Spencer, Debbie Carter, Mary Finch, Bonnie Burlbaw, and Buffie Hollis, who did research, fact-checking, and found pictures so beautifully. Also a thank-you to Robert Holzweiss, supervisory archivist, Patricia Burchfield, and Warren Finch.

Everyone in Dad's office staff in Houston was a big support. Special thanks goes to Mary Sage, who constantly found contact information at a moment's notice; and Jean Becker, who offered first-rate advice whenever I called.

It became clear that former world leaders were difficult to track down, but I so appreciate the efforts of General Brent Scowcroft, Ginny Mulberger, and Gail Turner, who made them easy to find.

Patty Presock's meticulous files were a springboard for this book, and she was instrumental in getting this project off the ground.

Susie Peake kindly helped early on with the infamous letters eventually recovered by the United States Secret Service—and so a special thanks to them too.

It's essential in life to have a computer guy. Ours was Matthew Pocarro, who can do or fix anything on the computer.

Melissa McPherson transcribed hundreds of tapes for us faster than we could get them to her.

Many thanks to Brett Orlove and Terri Lacy, who kept us legal.

Susan Biddle, former White House photographer, photographed the cover and was able to capture so beautifully how much I love my dad.

David Valdez, my dad's personal photographer during the White House days, provided many of the wonderful interior photos for this book.

Eric Draper, my brother's personal photographer, also provided more recent photos.

The list of people to thank is endless. And they all added so much to the project. I am completely responsible for all the people I left off this list.

My profound thanks go to Roger Ailes, David Baldacci, Doug Band, David Beightol, James Bradley, Mary Cheney, Gina Dellaquila, Susanne Dieper, Deborah Hocutt, Matt Hueber, Jack Janes: Danny, Reilly, KC, Max, and Jenna Koch; Christy MacCormack, Matthew McLaughlin, Jack Mills, Martina Nibbeling-Wriessnig, Louisa Sheldon, Bobby Watson, and of course Google.

I have four amazing brothers: George, Jeb, Neil, and Marvin helped me every step of the way. As did my mom, who is one remarkable woman. I love them all more than they'll ever know.

Last but not least, I want to thank my husband, Bobby, and my children, Sam, Ellie, Robert, and Gigi, for their patience and understanding throughout this project. And for bringing me joy and happiness every day of my life.

I am grateful to the following people for spending their valuable time being interviewed:

Roger Ailes
Leonore Annenberg
Lud Ashley
James Baker
William Barr
Ralph Basham
David Bates
Becky Beach
Jean Becker
Rich Bond
Rudy Boschwitz
Pat Buchanan
Chris Buckley
Bill Busch
Ashley Bush
Barbara Bush
George H. W. Bush

George P. Bush
George W. Bush
Jeb Bush
Jenna Bush
Johnny Bush
Laura Bush
Lauren Bush
Mandi Bush
Margaret Bush
Marvin Bush
Neil Bush
William "Bucky" Bush
Pierce Bush
Bill Canary
Andy Card
Jimmy Carter
Dana Carvey

Dick Cheney
Bill Clinton
Tony Coelho
Sean Coffey
Tom Collamore
Ben Crenshaw
David Cunningham
Dick Darman
F. W. de Klerck
David Demarest
Bob Dole
Michael Dukakis
Nan Ellis
Chrissie Evert
Geraldine Ferraro
Tim Finchem
Laurie Firestone
Marlin Fitzwater
Gerald Ford
Tom Frechette
Bob Gates
Dan Gilcrist
Vic Gold
Mikhail Gorbachev
Al Gore
Boyden Gray
Don Gregg
Jack Guy
Joe Hagin
Betsy Heminway
Spike Heminway
Martha Holdridge
Ede Holiday
Karen Hughes
Toshiki Kaifu

Ron Kaufman
Larry King
Hank Knoche
George Koch
Helmut Kohl
Howard Kurtz
James Lilley
Tom Luce
John Magaw
Sir John Major
Fred Malek
Paul Marchand
Lynn Martin
Mary Matalin
Tim McBride
Reba McEntire
Jon Meacham
Ken Mehlman
Dr. John Mendelsohn
Carlos Menem
Rich Miller
Jack Mills
Bob Mosbacher
Hosni Mubarak
Brian Mulroney
Jim Nantz
Sally Novetzke
Frank "Junie" O'Brien
Gian-Carlo Peressutti
Colin Powell
Patty Presock
Dan Quayle
Pat Quinn
Ken Raynor
Sig Rogich

Dan Rostenkowski
Pete Roussel
Karl Rove
David Rubenstein
Marty Russo
Carlos Salinas
Arnold Schwarzenegger
Norman Schwarzkopf
Brent Scowcroft
Bernard Shaw
Alan Simpson
Honey Skinner
Sam Skinner
Craig Stapleton

Debbie Stapleton
John Sununu
Pete Teeley
Harry Thayer
Meg Thayer
Clarence Thomas
Angus Thuermer
Ellen Tolton
Martin Torrijos
Margaret Tutwiler
David Valdez
Paula Zahn
Rose Zamaria
Jiang Zemin

I would also like to thank all those who sent letters filled with wonderful stories about Dad:

Sir Antony and Lady Jenny Acland
Princess Catherine Aga Khan
Joe Allbritton
Duane Allen
Ann Kelly Allin
Jay Allison
David Alsobrook
Hushang Ansary
Placido Arango
Bill Archer
Marjorie Arsht
John B. Ashmun
Sally Atwater
Bob Barnett
Thomas Barrow
David Bates

Bertie Bell
Griffin Bell
FitzGerald Bemiss
Bishop Ben Benitez
Mrs. W. Tapley Bennett
Lloyd Bentson
Jack Blanton
Taylor Blanton
Houston Blount
Tom Bradbury
Phil Brady
Nancy Brinker
Jim Burch
Therese Burch
Dan Burke
Jan Burmeister

Bill Busch
Billy Bush
Jamie Bush
Jeb Bush Jr.
Johnny Bush
Lauren Bush
Frank Carlucci
Henry Catto
Ellie Caulkins
Elaine L. Chao
Pat Chick
Mary Higgins Clark
Kay Clarke
Stuart H. Clement Jr.
Caroline Cole
Tom Collamore
Francine Collins
Lodwrick M. Cook
Denton A. Cooley
Fred Couples
Earle M. Craig Jr.
Quincy Crawford
Ben Crenshaw
Walter J. P. Curley
Ed Curran
Osborne Day
Tony De Angelis
Mary Delaude
Harold R. DeMoss Jr.
James "Jim" Dionne
Maureen Dowd
Phyllis Draper
William H. Draper
Jane and Murray Dwight

John and Diane Eckstein
Chris Emery
Emilia Fanjul
Brad Faxon
Betsy Field
Jack Fitch
Marlin Fitzwater
Rudy Gatlin
Steve Gatlin
Sandy and Bert Getz
Vic Gold
The Reverend Billy Graham
Shirley M. Green
Liz Grundy
Sondra Haley
John Paul Hammerschmidt
Mabel Hanson
Sarah Harding
Mark Hatfield
J. M. Hewgley Jr.
Grace Holden
Robert B. Holt
Mary Jackson
Dan Jenkins
Anne Johnson
Belle G. Johnson
Lady Bird Johnson
Bill Jones
P. X. Kelley
Jack Kemp
Howard W. Kruse
Richard K. LeBlond II
Dr. Burton J. Lee III
Bessie Liedtke

James Lilley
Debbie Longnecker
John D. Macomber
Allie Page Matthews
John McCain
John R. McKernan Jr.
Anne Mendelsohn
Phil and Amy Mickelson
Arthur Milnes
Eric and Jane Molson
Bob Mosbacher
Thomas W. Moseley
Jim Nantz
John Newcombe
Greg Norman
Phillip O'Bannon
Sandra Day O'Connor
Jack Oliver
Pierce O'Neil
Joe O'Neill
Robert Paine
Arnold Palmer
Andrew Peacock
Gian-Carlo Peressutti
Peggy Pierce Peters
Gregg Petersmeyer
Mr. and Mrs. G. H. Pfau Jr.
Richard "Digger" Phelps
Margy Pierce
Scott Pierce
Gary Player
Jim Pollard
Rob Portman
Twanna Powell

Nancy Reagan
Louise Walker Resor
Sig Rogich
Emile Roy
William Donald Schaefer
Willard Scott
James E. Selmon Jr.
George P. Shultz
Hugh Sidey
Anette Siegel
John Silber
Ray Siller
Sichan Siv
R. C. Slocum
Alex G. Spanos
Stephen Spenlinhauer
Jodie Dwight Stevenson
Dick Thigpen
Mary Holden Thompson
Sheila O. Todd
Russell Train
Paula Trivette
Takashi Tsurusawa
Chase Untermeyer
David Valdez
Jack Valenti
Wilhelm Wachtmeister
Bert Walker
Caspar W. Weinberger
Jane Weintraub
Wendy Whitworth
Stephen A. Wynn
Zahira Zahir

Sources and Other Notes

In writing *My Father, My President,* many of the observations were the collective memories of my whole family, a product of our years together. I depended heavily not only on my own recollections, but also those of my parents, my four brothers—George, Jeb, Neil, and Marvin—and my aunts and uncles as well. As I began to share some of our stories and memories with my mother and father, the amorphous themes that were to become *My Father, My President* soon took shape. My parents and I began discussing the book in earnest during the summer of 2005 in Maine, and my entire family was invaluable to me as work progressed throughout most of 2005 into 2006.

Many of the personal letters and family documents that I used came to me from the private and never-before-seen files kept by Patty Presock during Dad's vice presidential and presidential years. Unless otherwise noted, all photos herein came from our private family files: from my grandmother, my mother, and, in many cases, my own family photo album. All of these photos have now been donated to the George Bush Presidential Library. As I mentioned in the acknowledgments, the highly talented staff of the library not only provided original source materials but also helped me tremendously in tracking down specific facts and clarifying hazy memories.

I relied on the following six "Bush books" throughout many chapters of this book: my mother's original autobiography, *Barbara Bush: A Memoir,* and her sequel to it, *Reflections: Life after the White House;* my father's collected letters, published under the title *All the Best, George Bush: My Life in Letters and Other Writings;* Dad's book with Brent Scowcroft, *A World Transformed;* and Jim Mc-Grath's collection of Dad's "wit and wisdom," titled *Heartbeat: George Bush in His Own Words.* Dad's 1987 book, written with Vic Gold, *Looking Forward: An Autobiography,* was useful as well.

Among the strengths of this book, I hope, are the entries taken from my father's diaries. Some of them are available to the public through the Bush Library and some were previously published in *All the Best;* the rest will remain private until they are available posthumously. Many of the letters and documents I relied on are from Dad's personal files and our family records. Some of these papers are at the Bush Library, but many of them are not yet available to the public.

Every letter we received and every interview we conducted was tremendously valuable in the process of writing this book, each in its own way. Whether or not each source was quoted in the text of the book, every letter and interview led us to new insights, further recollections, and, many times, a few laughs—or even tears—at a story well told. I am tremendously appreciative of the hundreds of Dad's friends—world leaders, Secret Service agents, congressmen, friends—who were so generous with their time in support of this book.

Chapter 1. The End Depends upon the Beginning

In writing about Dad's early childhood, I relied heavily on observations from his siblings—Prescott Bush, Nancy Ellis, Jon Bush, and William (Bucky) Bush—and have acknowledged their contributions in the text. An interview with Nancy Ellis by Amalie Moses Kass, "The Childhood of a President," published in 1989 in *Wellesley* magazine, was the source of several quotes from Aunt Nan. For additional information about Dad's childhood, I interviewed Betsy and Spike Heminway, who were childhood friends of my parents.

Dad's letter of September 21, 1996, to my daughter, Ellie, is from my own personal files; and the May 22, 1920, letter from George Walker to his sons and Dorothy Walker Bush's inscription in Dad's Bible are from my father's personal files.

For insight into his years at Andover, I received many letters from his classmates and was able to interview Frank "Junie" O'Brien. My interview with Mr. O'Brien provided the quote that begins the chapter. The Phillips Andover Web site, www.andover.edu, was helpful in confirming facts about the school. The quote about Andover's influence on Dad's life came from his 1998 interview with David Frost, for the A&E Network special "George Bush: A President's Story." The early chapters of *What It Takes,* by Richard Ben Cramer, also helped me fill in specific details about this time.

The anecdote about Dad carrying Bruce Gelb's chair is taken from Ambassador Gelb's remarks at a conference at Hofstra University, April 17–19, 1997. Four books resulted from the transcripts of that conference, and Gelb's remarks appear in the first book, *A Noble Calling: Character and the George H. W. Bush Presidency,* edited by William Levantrosser and Rosanna Perotti, under the panel discussion "Ending the Cold War."

Chapter 2. A Wartime Wedding

First and foremost, I depended on my mother's and father's many memories for this chapter. Again, I relied on the recollections of Dad's siblings, especially my Aunt Nancy Ellis, and friends such as Spike and Betsy Heminway and Junie O'Brien in describing my parents' courtship and dating.

The reference to Dad joining the Royal Canadian Air Force came from an interview with Jim Nantz on *CBS Sunday Morning,* March 30, 1997. The information about Prescott Bush's involvement in the founding of the USO was corroborated on the official USO Web site, www.uso.org.

Of course, my father's discussions with me about his wartime experiences formed the backbone of this chapter. For additional details, I referred to the chapter on my father in Tom Brokaw's book *The Greatest Generation*, particularly Dad's description of his being charged with reading his crewmates' mail and seeing a fellow sailor killed in a plane accident on deck. My interview with Jack Guy, a member of Dad's squadron, was particularly helpful too. The letter to Jim Wyke's mother is available at the Bush Library, as is the letter from Prescott Bush to Ted White's mother. The letters between my parents and between my father and his parents are also at the Library.

The best eyewitness account my father has seen of his being shot down by the Japanese appears in F. Willard Robinson's interview of Lt. (jg) Nathaniel Adams in Robinson's 2004 book, *Navy Wings of Gold*. The details about reports of cannibalism on Chi Chi Jima also came from Robinson's book. I relied on details from Lou Grab's unpublished 1996 essay, "Fly Boy," which was in Dad's private files. Dad also discussed the cannibals on Chi Chi Jima in his 1998 interview with David Frost.

My interview with Paula Zahn was tremendously helpful, as was her making available to me the transcript of her 2003 documentary *A Flyboy's Story*, about Dad's 2002 return to Chi Chi Jima. I used a quote from my interview with General Norman Schwarzkopf to begin the chapter, and my interview with former Secret Service agent John Magaw provided the anecdote about his calling my father every year on September 2.

For the material on Dad and Mom's years at Yale, I'd like to thank many of Dad's classmates, especially Lud Ashley and Junie O'Brien, for sharing their memories with me (Junie went to both Andover and Yale with my father). The stories told to me by my Uncles Johnny and Bucky were also invaluable. I found a 1991 article from the *Daily Princetonian* by Dan Klein, "June 5, 1948: Yale Rips Tiger Baseball, 14–2. Pregame Ceremony Unites Bush with the Babe," to be helpful too.

Chapter 3. Go West, Young Man

This chapter opens with a quote from Martin Allday, taken from the Hofstra University conference transcript titled *A Noble Calling,* under the panel discussion "Molding Presidential Character: The Bush Apprenticeship."

Dad's recollections of being locked out of his own bathroom came from his 1998 interview with David Frost on the A&E Network, *George Bush: A President's Story.* His anecdote about the drunken Democrat voting in the GOP primary also came from this interview.

For the Odessa and Midland years, a letter to me from Earle Craig was very helpful, as was a good accounting of the Martini Bowl courtesy of John Ashmun. I relied on an article Dad wrote in 1986 for *American West* magazine ("Texas 1948: Some Fond Memories") in which he described the culture surrounding the Odessa–Midland high school football games. Joe O'Neill's letter to me about my father's coaching of the Little League team was very useful.

In writing about Robin's death, I relied on not only my parents' recollections but also those of their friend Lud Ashley, as well as a letter from Melinda Cox describing how Dad continued to teach Sunday school throughout this time. I also used excerpts from the previously cited 1998 David Frost interview.

Information on the Zapata companies came from the 1965 Zapata Annual Report to its shareholders (provided by Don Rhodes); Dad's book *Looking Forward;* from my Uncle Johnny's memories; and from information Dad recently recounted about his offshore drilling days. My brother George is the source of the story about my father meeting Lyndon Johnson.

My father's memories of Prescott Bush's Senate career formed the basis of that section. I also relied on Prescott Bush's official papers, which came to me from the Bush Library, and on the official U.S. Senate Web site, www.senate.gov. My interview with Governor

Michael Dukakis, while focused on the 1988 campaign, brought to light additional memories of my grandfather and the effect he had on Governor Dukakis's career.

No account of my father's life would be complete without the input of one of Dad's best friends, James Baker. My interview with Secretary Baker followed up on a long letter he had written me about my father, and both were very insightful.

Chapter 4. Jumping into Politics

Herbert Parmet's 1997 biography of my father, *George Bush: The Life of a Lonestar Yankee,* provided many of the details about Dad's role in the 1968 Nixon-Agnew campaign, as well as background information on Texas politics and the race against Ralph Yarborough. I also used the *Handbook of Texas Online,* at http://www.tsha.utexas.edu/handbook/online/articles/CC/fcosf.html, under the entry "Ralph Yarborough." Pete Roussel's memories of that period were taken from the Hofstra book *A Noble Calling,* although I personally interviewed Pete as well.

I relied on the 1965 Zapata Annual Report for the information on the losses attributed to Hurricane Betsy. I am grateful to Taylor Blanton for his responses and e-mails as I tried to clarify my own foggy memories throughout this chapter. Senator Alan Simpson was invaluable, as he recalled my parents buying his parents' home in Washington, D.C., as well as many other stories used in later chapters. I am grateful to my old friend Olivia Crudgington for sharing the letter my father wrote her when her father died, which, until this book was published, had only been seen by one other person.

The account of Dad's vote on the Housing Rights Act of 1968 came from a number of sources: a 1978 oral history of Jimmy Allison found at the Bush Library; a letter to me from Allie Page Matthews; and a November 18, 1968, *Houston Chronicle* article "Bush's Life Threatened Over Rights Vote," by Ken Sheets. President Bill Clinton's memories of my father's vote on that bill were also very insightful. I also utilized Dan Gillcrist's letter to me about Dad's visit to an African American church shortly after the historic vote.

I again relied on the oral history of Jimmy Allison for the stories about Dad selling his shares in Zapata and his writing to Paul Dorsey, the cancer patient.

I am grateful to Lady Bird Johnson for her letter to me recalling Dad's attending the Johnsons' departure from Washington. Hugh Sidey, Dad's great friend and the longtime *Time* magazine correspondent, wrote to me about this episode as well, several months before he died.

The story about Dad visiting LBJ at his ranch came from my interview with my brother George and appears in *Looking Forward* as well.

Chapter 5. Baker and Bentsen

Of course, for this chapter I utilized Secretary Baker's recollections from his interview and letter to me, as well as remarks he made at the Hofstra conference found in *A Noble Calling*. I also relied on a letter to me from Senator Bentsen for his memories of the 1970 Senate race.

For facts on Texas politics in the 1970s, I relied on the *Handbook of Texas Online,* under entries for Ralph Yarborough, John Tower, and John Connally. I also utilized Herbert Parmet's *George Bush: The Life of a Lonestar Yankee* for background information on Texas in those days.

My brother George shared many memories of the campaign with me in my interviews with him. The quote about Dad saying "We can win this race" and George learning from Mom and Dad that life goes on came from an article by David Shribman, "Casting a Long Shadow," in the January 9, 2000, *Boston Globe.* Of course, my brother was the source of the story about taking Tricia Nixon to the Alibi Club.

Pete Roussel's memories of the 1970 Senate race came from the Hofstra conference, published in *A Noble Calling* under "Molding

Presidential Character: The Bush Apprenticeship." The newspaper article that reported on me crying in the corner was titled "Bush Concedes, Wishes Bentsen 'Best of Luck,'" from the *Houston Chronicle* of November 4, 1970.

Chapter 6. Eloise at the Waldorf

The chapter opens with a quote from Secretary of State Condoleezza Rice, who wrote me a wonderful letter with a number of very good anecdotes about Dad. I'm grateful to her taking time from her busy schedule to help me. The fact that Dad had performed the hat trick of attending U.N. sessions as president, vice president, and ambassador came from a memo on the U.S. Mission to the United Nations dated January 4, 2000, at the Bush Library.

The letter from President Nixon to my grandparents on their fiftieth wedding anniversary and my grandmother's eulogy of my grandfather are both from family files and are now at the Bush Library.

Perhaps more than any other source, General Brent Scowcroft was exceptional in his support of this book. His remarks about Dad's service at the U.N. came from the Hofstra book *A Noble Calling*, under the panel discussion "New World Order: Nationalism and Internationalism."

Dad's friend Spike Heminway provided the story about going to the Mets game, as referenced in the text; Tom Lias and Arthur Fletcher recalled key votes in the United Nations General Assembly in their 1978 oral histories at the Bush Library; Dean Burch's 1978 oral history was also critically important and was the source of all quotes from him. The information on the Overrated Party came from Dad's personal files.

Chapter 7. The *Titanic* Boiler Room

The above-referenced oral histories included one from Congressman Bill Steiger, who has since passed away; I excerpted from it for the opening quote. I also used Arthur Fletcher's remarks about Watergate from those histories later in the chapter, as referenced in the text.

For the facts and chronology of events that took place during Watergate, I relied on an Associated Press document, "Watergate Break-in to Pardon: A Chronology," published on *Houston Chronicle Interactive,* June 7, 1997. Information about John Connally came from the *Handbook of Texas Online,* and the account of Congressman Whitehurst submitting Dad's name for vice president came from his 1978 oral history. I utilized a *Washington Post* article by Carroll Kilpatrick, "Nixon Tells Editors, 'I'm Not a Crook,'" published November 18, 1973, for background information on that day. I also consulted President Ford's memoir, *A Time to Heal.*

I'd like to thank my brother Marvin for his excellent recall of his photographic adventure at Jeb and Columba's wedding; the letter about Watergate to my brothers from my father is from his personal files.

Dad's Watergate diaries are available at the Bush Library. I am grateful to my friend Liz Grundy for her recollection of carpooling the day after the Saturday Night Massacre.

I found a fascinating account of the Watergate era on the Arizona State University Web site, http://www.asu.edu/lib/archives/rhodes/essay4.htm. Along with original newspaper articles, it contains a 1995 essay by former House Minority Leader John Rhodes, "I Was There" (augmented with 1974 notes kept by his press secretary, Jay Smith). Rhodes's memories of the day Dad learned about the "smoking gun" tape came from that essay. Dean Burch's memories of the "smoking gun" tape, of the final Nixon cabinet meeting, and of his observations afterward all came from the 1978 oral histories. The late Caspar Weinberger's letter to me was very useful, and I appreciate the assistance of the Nixon and Ford libraries in verifying the various accounts of that final cabinet meeting.

Dad's letter to President Nixon urging him to resign is at the Bush Library. His anecdote about Bob Strauss's phone call about making love to a gorilla came from Dad's 1998 interview with David Frost.

Chapter 8. Land of Contrasts

The quote from General Scowcroft that opens this chapter came from *A Noble Calling,* under the panel discussion, "New World Order: Nationalism and Internationalism." For recollections about the day that Gerald Ford asked Nelson Rockefeller instead of my father to be vice president, Pete Roussel and Spike Heminway were very helpful, as was my interview with former president Ford. Dean Burch's memories of Ford's decision came from his 1978 oral history.

I appreciate the information shared with me by Harry Thayer about the brunch my parents held for Chinese diplomats and, later, the incident involving the Vietnamese-American diplomat. James Lilley's memories were also very helpful, as was his essay "The Unlikely Alliance: On the centenary of Deng's birth, memories of his bond with a U.S. President," published in *Time Asia* on August 30, 2004. For background information, I used "The Beijing-Washington Back-Channel and Henry Kissinger's Secret Trip to China, September 1970–July 1971," edited by William Burr and found in the National Security Archive on the George Washington University Web site, www.gwu.edu.

"George and Barbara Bush: A Breezy Yankee Style in Peking," from *People* magazine May 5, 1975, and "George Bush Is Picked to Carry the Flag to China," also from *People* magazine September 23, 1974, were very helpful.

I'm grateful to Spike Heminway for his memories of our spending the holidays with their family that year, as well as my brothers Neil and Marvin for their accounts of our trip on the Trans-Siberian Railroad.

Dad's China diaries are available at the Bush Library.

Chapter 9. A Year at Langley

I thoroughly enjoyed my interview with Bob Gates, former director of the CIA and now president of Texas A&M University, home of the Bush Library, for his insights into Dad's tenure at the CIA. Ambassador Lilley was also very helpful in this chapter, as was Hank Knoche, Dad's former deputy and a longtime CIA employee. I appreciate Mr. Knoche taking so much time with me, and I also relied on his 1978 oral history for additional details from that time.

My father's letter to Bill Steiger was in Dad's personal files, now at the Bush Library. Secretary Baker and General Scowcroft were insightful about President Ford's "Grand Shuffle," which resulted in Dad being named CIA director. I also quoted from Dean Burch's 1978 oral history about that time.

The quote about nervousness inside the Agency came from an interview with Angus Thuermer, a former public affairs officer there. Former U.S. attorney general Bill Barr, who used to work at the CIA, was very helpful in explaining the work of the Pike and Church Commissions, and the effect their hearings had on morale. The quote from the anonymous government official came from Alexander Cockburn and James Ridgeway's article "George Bush" in *Rolling Stone* magazine, March 20, 1980.

Former congressman Rob Portman's letter to me was very helpful, as were his remarks on the day that the CIA headquarters building was named for my father.

Chapter 10. An Asterisk in the Polls

For this chapter, I relied heavily on the memories of many of Dad's longtime political friends and advisers, including Andy Card, David Bates, James Baker, Margaret Tutwiler, Karl Rove, Pete Teeley, Joe Hagin, Tom Collamore, and Becky Beach. Each of them was very generous with their time as I conducted long interviews and asked many questions, and I appreciate their support. My

Uncle Bucky and brothers Jeb and Marvin also were very instrumental.

The story of the 1977 trip to China was enhanced by the contributions of Ambassador Lilley. My brother George and his wife, Laura, were very helpful in taking time out of their busy schedules to share stories of their marriage and his 1978 congressional campaign.

Dad's stump speech, "Why I Want to Be President," first delivered in Union City, New Jersey, on February 8, 1979, is in Dad's private papers at the Bush Library. The quote from Hugh Sidey about Dad's qualifications to be president came from his remarks at the Hofstra conference recorded in *A Noble Calling* under "Ending the Cold War," which was a panel discussion. I'm grateful to *Newsweek* editor Jon Meacham for his terrific insights and historical expertise.

The details of the "I am paying for this microphone" incident came from President Reagan's autobiography, *An American Life,* and from contemporaneous accounts in the *Los Angeles Times* and *Newsday.* The story of Dad's rule about not kissing babies without permission came from John Magaw, former head of Dad's Secret Service detail. I appreciate the many anecdotes John shared with me for the first time ever. Bernie Shaw, the former CNN anchor, was also very generous with his time and memories of this campaign. Ron Kaufman and Vic Gold provided the stories about Dad raising money to pay employees after the campaign ran out of funds; John Magaw and Becky Beach helped with the stories about the day Dad withdrew from the presidential race, as stated in the text.

Chapter 11. Out of the Clear Blue Sky

Again, my interviews with Vic Gold, Andy Card, Margaret Tutwiler, Pete Teeley, David Bates, and James Baker provided the bulk of the information for this chapter, and I hope they know how much I appreciate their generosity. I have tried to accurately reference their contributions throughout the text of this chapter.

Most important, my brother Jeb's memories of the night at the Detroit Convention when Dad was asked to be President Reagan's vice president were crystal-clear, and a great help to me. The source of the joke President Reagan told on the elevator—"Charlie, can you change the heads on 13 and 14?"—was David Bates, in his interview with me.

I am very grateful to former CNN anchor Bernard Shaw for his time on the phone. His anecdote from the 1980 campaign trail in Nebraska was the first of many helpful contributions to the project.

Pierce O'Neil wrote a letter to me about his experiences with my father in Kennebunkport over the years, and the story about the broken propeller on Dad's boat came from that letter.

Chapter 12. Mr. Vice President

I began writing this book a little more than a year after the death of President Ronald Reagan, and I am saddened by the fact that his personal recollections are missing from it. The quote that opens this chapter came from his remarks at a campaign rally on August 24, 1988, in Los Angeles when my father was running for president. A copy of it is available in *The Public Papers of the Presidents*, under "Ronald Reagan, 1988." I appreciate the assistance of both the Reagan and Bush Libraries in helping me find a wealth of information on their relationship.

I found the details about the vice president's residence on the grounds of the Naval Observatory on the White House Web site, as part of an online tour conducted by Mrs. Cheney at http://www.whitehouse.gov/history/life/vpresidence.html.

Former congressman Dan Rostenkowski was exceptionally helpful to me in recounting the early days of the Reagan Administration, and Dad's role in his becoming chairman of Ways and Means.

Many of the facts about the 1989 inauguration came from the book *200 Years of the American Presidency*, published by the Donning

Company in 1989. Laurie Firestone was key in remembering some of the details of the inaugural balls and my parents' entertaining during the vice presidential and presidential years. The anecdote about Dad's talk with his new staff on the first day came from Joe Hagin. Again, Jon Meacham's perspective on the impact of the Reagan-Bush administration was terrific.

I pieced together the events that took place on the day President Reagan was shot—and my father's role in them—from a number of sources, including Pete Teeley, Chase Untermeyer, John Magaw, Don Gregg, Joe Hagin, James Baker, and Rich Bond. The story about my parents' visit with the Cameroonian couple came from Chase Untermeyer.

Lud Ashley was the source of the story about the 1982 midterm elections and Dad's campaigning in Ohio; Marty Russo told me about Dad's tennis and paddleball games on the Hill; John Newcombe shared with me the story of playing tennis with Dad in Australia. Secret Service agent Jim Burch sent me a letter with anecdotes about my father's tennis adventures, and the former head of the Secret Service, Ralph Basham, was very kind in allowing me to interview him; he provided the story of weighing Dad in the locker room.

My father's letter to my niece Lauren when she was born and my brother Neil's 1986 letter to Mrs. Resa Ward, a teacher at Breckinridge Jr. High School in Roanoke, Virginia, about her struggling students came from family files. Neil's, Marvin's, and George's comments in this chapter came from one of the many times I interviewed each of them for this book. My brothers, as always, were tremendously helpful to me.

I am grateful to former Canadian prime minister Brian Mulroney for allowing me so much time in my interview with him, and his stories added a special touch. Don Gregg was the source for the story about meeting President Mitterrand, and Joe Hagin and James Baker discussed Dad's travels during his vice presidency.

John Magaw was instrumental in his recall of Dad's initial meetings with Soviet leaders Brezhnev, Andropov, and Chernenko.

Dad's observations of the Brezhnev funeral came from his 1998 interview with David Frost. The anecdote about my parents' lunch in Zambia after the Brezhnev funeral came from remarks he made at St. Martin's Church in Houston on December 26, 1982. Excerpts from Dad's cables to President Reagan after each funeral appear in *All the Best*. I am extremely grateful to the library staff for double-checking the accuracy of the facts surrounding the three funerals.

My sources for the account of my parents' 1983 trip to Europe were Helmut Kohl, who served as German chancellor from 1982 to 1998; Ambassador Donald Gregg; and Chris Buckley (Buckley's was one of the funniest interviews I conducted during the process of writing this book). General P. X. Kelley's letter to me provided the facts for the account of the October 1983 bombing of the Marine barracks in Beirut.

The details of my family's history in Kennebunkport came from my parents and from a history of Walker's Point supplied by the Bush Library. Aunt Nan's comments came from my interview with her and from the *Wellesley* magazine article by Amalie Moses Kass previously cited. The Bush Library also helped me piece together events surrounding the nor'easter of 1978, and Tim McBride was the source of the story about the dinner with the visiting diplomats. Emile Roy's very detailed letter to me provided the anecdote about Dad not wanting him to "lose his head" during a fishing trip. President Bill Clinton was the first person outside our family whom I interviewed for this book, and one of the first stories he told me was his memory of meeting my father in Kennebunkport in 1983.

Sean Coffey had spot-on memories of the July 13, 1984, Old-Timers Game in Denver, and I also relied on a video of that game provided to me by the Colorado Republicans and Channel 9-KUSA in Denver. The video was the source of Dad's quote about the evening being a "Walter Mitty" night. Pete Teeley also shared his memories of that game with me.

My interview with Geraldine Ferraro was fascinating, and I appreciate her kindness to me. She provided me with many of the facts about her nomination as vice president. Lynn Martin was also generous with her time when I interviewed her about her key role in preparing my dad to debate Ms. Ferraro. Boyden Gray was the source for the story about the debate rehearsal session in the Old Executive Office Building. Bob Barnett, who played my father in Democratic debate preparations, was instrumental in helping me write about those debates and his postelection lunch with Ms. Martin, Ms. Ferraro, and Dad.

For background information on the debates and on the "spin" that followed, I utilized a segment from the *McNeil/Lehrer News-Hour,* "Debating Our Destiny, 1984," available on *NewsHour Online* at http://www.pbs.org/newshour/debatingourdestiny/dod/ 1984broadcast.html.

Sean Coffey supplied me with the details of the "kicked a little ass" comment and its origins. My mother provided the details of the "rhymes with rich" incident and its aftermath, and Ms. Ferraro's comments here were invaluable. I also appreciate her memories of the postelection lunch with Dad.

Chapter 13. Master of the Small Gesture

Former congressman Marty Russo was the source of the paddleball story from inauguration day. Tom Collamore told me the details of Dad's typical day at the White House, and of the grueling pace of his travel.

Ray Siller wrote me a long letter with his funny recollections over the years he has known my father, and he was the source of the story about the fake dog poop in the closet. Shirley Green's letter to me provided the details of her home being robbed and Dad's response.

Marlin Fitzwater provided the insights that created the title of this chapter and an account of the 1986 dinner in China. Chris Buckley told me of the staff meeting on the morning after a leak to the press. Marlin Fitzwater, David Cunningham, and David

Bates remembered Dad blacking out on the tennis court during President Reagan's surgery.

Tim McBride was the staff member who commented that Dad always believed in our better sides; Tim, Tom Collamore, and Joe Hagin told me stories of Dad's high regard for the Secret Service. John Magaw told me of C. Fred getting sick in the limo and of Dad's reaction to obscene gestures by roadside observers; my cousin Debbie Stapleton told me of Dad diving into the water to unsnag the propeller before the agent could. Tim McBride was the source of the story about Dad not keeping people waiting in motorcades. My brother George told me about his resulting desire to stay on time, and he provided the quote that begins the chapter in an interview with me.

My brother Marvin, his wife, Margaret, and my parents were the sources for the section on Marvin's battle with colitis. My interview with former senator Rudy Boschwitz produced many of the details about Operations Joshua and Solomon, as did Wolf Blitzer's interview of Israeli Ambassador to the U.S. Meir Rosenne, published in the *Jerusalem Post,* June 5, 1987, and an undated editorial in the New York *Daily News,* "An Act of History."

Tim McBride recalled his experiences with Dad the day of the *Challenger* tragedy; the passage from President Reagan's speech that day was from his Address to the Nation on January 28, 1986. Boyden Gray's comments to me about Dad's role as Reagan's vice president came from my interview with him, as did his story about why crack cocaine was so addictive. The facts about the drug issue came from my interview with Boyden, as well as from the second Hofstra book, *Principle Over Politics? The Domestic Policy of the George H. W. Bush Presidency,* edited by Richard Himelfarb and Rosanna Perotti. I used Boyden Gray's and Philip Brady's remarks from a panel discussion transcribed in it, titled "Civil Rights, Drugs, Housing and Education," for the details of the South Florida Task Force. John Magaw's interview with me provided insights into how my father handled intelligence matters.

The memo to Patty Presock about sending gifts to George P. at camp, as well as George P.'s letter to Dad, came from family files. My niece Barbara told me the story of Spikey the stuffed animal in my interview of her, and my sister-in-law Laura told me of Dad opening the drain to retrieve her contacts.

Marlin Fitzwater was the source of the discussion about my father's press strategy. He also told me about the beginning of the press coverage of the Iran-Contra affair. The quote from the Tower Commission report came from the *Executive Summary of the Report of the Congressional Committees Investigating the Iran-Contra Affair,* November 1987. I appreciate the help of the Bush Library staff in locating this publication, since it was out of print.

I relied on my own memories of meeting Billy Graham as well as those of my brother George, taken from my interviews with him.

Chapter 14. Pointer Man

I am extremely grateful to Governor Michael Dukakis for graciously agreeing to speak with me; his quote to me about Dad opens this chapter.

In addition to my own recollections, I used the actual cover story, "Fighting the Wimp Factor," from the October 19, 1987, issue of *Newsweek* magazine. My parents and Aunt Nan supplied supporting details to my own memories of that incident. Congressman Dan Rostenkowski, Ede Holiday, and Jon Meacham all shared their memories and opinions with me. My interview with Howard Kurtz of the *Washington Post* was particularly helpful for this section.

The details of Dad's announcement in 1987 at the Hyatt Regency in Houston were corroborated by Dad's private files and in *All the Best.* Background information on the 1988 campaign came from a variety of sources, including the *Washington Post* and *New York Times* archives, and Richard Ben Cramer's book *What It Takes.*

Roger Ailes, in his interview with me, detailed the leadership of Dad's campaign staff, and Ede Holiday also provided many specifics. My brother Marvin told me the story about "Fast Eddie" Verdeliac, and Jeb and George both told me about meeting Lee Atwater for the first time. My sister-in-law Laura described moving to Washington for the campaign, and Karl Rove explained my brother George's role in Dad's campaign.

The 1989 *Esquire* article referred to in the text was titled "One Leg at a Time," and it was discussed in John Brady's 1997 book, *Bad Boy: The Life and Politics of Lee Atwater.*

The quote about my brother George telling *Newsweek* magazine the answer to the "Big A" question came from a *Washington Post* article by Lois Romano and George Lardner Jr., dated July 31, 1999: "Bush's Move Up to the Majors."

Michael Dukakis discussed firing Donna Brazille for spreading rumors about Dad in my interview with him. Dana Carvey, in a hilarious interview with me, told me about meeting Dad for the first time and how he began his impersonation of my father. Debbie Romash Dunn provided memories of the early days of the campaign, and my brother Marvin and Ede Holiday remembered Lee Atwater day-to-day.

Andy Card and John Sununu were the source for the information about both men's initial involvement in the campaign and the New Hampshire primary. Mary Matalin told me about the Iowa campaign, and Sally Atwater's letter remembered what happened after Dad lost Iowa. My brother Jeb also talked to me about the night of the Iowa loss. Ede Holiday and Bob Mosbacher told me of the importance of winning the New Hampshire race after Iowa, and Mosbacher and Sununu told me the story of getting the "Senator Straddle" ad aired. Therese Burch's memories of campaigning with Dad in New Hampshire were priceless.

The sources for information about the South Carolina primary and the Super Tuesday primaries came from Bill Canary, the Brady book about Atwater previously mentioned, and a report by Robert

MacNeil, "The First Super Tuesday," on *NewsHour Online,* March 9, 1988, which I accessed at http://www.pbs.org/newshour/retro/super_tuesday_88.html. The results of the Super Tuesday primaries came from this latter source.

I also used an interview of Lee Atwater by Jim Lehrer, "Lee Atwater: Campaign Strategy," *NewsHour Online,* August 23, 1984, found at http://www.pbs.org/newshour/convention96/retro/atwater.html, for additional background information.

Mary Matalin's work on the Michigan primary was explained in her interview with me and in her 1994 book with James Carville, *All's Fair: Love, War, and Running for President.*

Ann Richards's remarks at the Democratic Convention came from her keynote address on July 19, 1988. Ted Kennedy's November 17, 1989, letter to my father afterward is from Dad's private files. Michael Dukakis was the source of the section detailing how the Democrats chose their VP nominee, and about his grandmother being at the convention.

Ronald Reagan's remarks came from his address to the 1988 Republican Convention. Jeb told me the story of George P. nearly throwing up onstage. Fred Malek's letter to me contained the story about Dad's friends trying to guess his VP choice. Dan Quayle added many details about the day he was chosen to be Dad's running mate.

The information on Marilyn Quayle came from Mark Hatfield's chapter on Dan Quayle in his book written with the Senate Historical Office, *Vice Presidents of the United States, 1789–1993,* written in 1997 and available on the Senate Web site, www.senate.gov.

My brother Marvin provided the account of casting the states' votes the night of Dad's official nomination as president; Ray Siller's letter to me was the source of the Pointer Man story. Fred Malek's memories of Dad the night of his acceptance address were in his letter to me; Roger Ailes's notes to Dad for the speech were in Dad's private files. Insights from my brother Jeb and Tom Collamore were essential to the section on the writing of that speech and its impact on the convention. Roger Ailes was the source of the account of Dan Rather's interview of Dad.

Roger Ailes and Sig Rogich provided me with a lot of information about the campaign ads and the strategy behind them. The quote from Lee Atwater about Willie Horton came from "What Lee Atwater Knows About Winning," by Jan Collins Stucker in *Southern Magazine,* April 1989. The briefing paper on Willie Horton that Dad sent us was written by the late White House researcher Bob Simon and was in Dad's private files.

Information about the death of Eddie Byrne and the endorsement of the Boston Police came from a video of the Republican National Convention produced by the RNC. The economic figures I cited came from a Bush campaign issues document titled *George Bush: Leadership on the Issues,* and the "line of the day" information came from Mary Kate Cary, a campaign writer at the time. Andy Card discussed opposition research on Dukakis, as mentioned in the text, and Roger Ailes told me about the debate negotiations he and James Baker conducted with the Democrats. Jeb remembered the debate specifics, as did Dick Darman in both his letter and his interview with me. The anecdote about Marvin and George going to the movie theater during the second Bush-Dukakis debate came from my interviews with Marvin and Pat Quinn. Secretary Baker, Roger Ailes, Michael Dukakis, and Bernie Shaw all discussed the actual debates with me.

The letter to Mom from Dad about their public displays of affection appears in *All the Best.* Jeb's memories of the final days of the campaign were key, as were Joe Hagin's of election night. The final line of the chapter is a reference to Dan Jenkins's 1984 book, *Life Its Ownself.*

Chapter 15. Age of the Offered Hand

The opening quote for the chapter is taken from Mom's interview with David Frost for his 1998 A&E special "George Bush: A President's Story," and the quote from President Reagan in the second paragraph comes from *All the Best.* Additionally, Tim McBride provided the anecdote about Dad's overcoat on inauguration day, and Jon Meacham gave me his insights as well. Dad's letter to President Reagan is at the Bush Library.

The information on Statuary Hall can be found on the official Web site of the Office of the Clerk in the United States House of Representatives at http:// clerk.house.gov/. Specifics on the inaugural parade were provided to me by the Bush Library; and I also appreciate all the information supplied to me by Gary Walters, chief usher at the White House.

My parents, as well as Marvin and Margaret, shared their memories of inauguration day with me. I found the transcript of Dad's first press conference in *Public Papers of the Presidents, George Bush, 1989*, volume 1. The eight-volume collection of *Public Papers* that cover Dad's four years as president is published by the Office of the Federal Register for the National Archives and Records Administration and proved an invaluable resource for double-checking facts and dates for this and subsequent chapters that touch on Dad's White House years.

The story about Wendy Robbins calling Uncle Johnny came from the latter, and Aunt Nan recalled my grandmother's reactions to seeing the White House.

The White House Historical Association provided the information on previous vice presidents' offices and the use of the *Resolute* desk. The note from President Reagan that Dad found in his desk on his first day in office is at the Bush Library. Dad's eulogy of President Reagan, given June 11, 2004, is the source of the quote about that note. Dad's January 20, 1989, note to the Reagans is also at the Library. Jay Allison told me the story of the flag on Dad's desk in his letter to me.

Dick Darman wrote me a letter that contained the anecdote about Dad's behavior in the Oval Office, while Judge Webster's observation came from his remarks to the Hofstra conference recorded in the book *A Noble Calling: Character and the George H. W. Bush Presidency* previously mentioned.

The transcript of Dad's first press conference as president-elect, on November 9, 1988, is available through the Bush Library and also the *New York Times* archives. Governor Sununu spoke with me about the transition between the Reagan and Bush staffs, and Joseph Verner Reed's story detailing Dad's first dinner party as president came from the Hofstra University Conference.

I greatly appreciate former First Lady Nancy Reagan's gracious letter to me about Dad's phone call to her husband on the first Thursday after he left office. Former vice president Quayle, in my interview with him, told me of his subsequent weekly lunches with Dad.

President Gorbachev wrote me a long letter in response to my questions about his relationship with my father, and I am grateful to him for his thoughtful responses. I have quoted extensively from them for this section and several others from Dad's White House years. I also gleaned details concerning the December 1988 Armenian earthquake from a front-page article in the *Washington Post* archives ("Bush's Son Visits Quake Victims: Injured Armenian Children Receive Candy, Teddy Bears," by John Thor Dahlburg of the Associated Press, December 25, 1988). My nephew George P. added his recollections of the visit he and his father made to help with relief efforts. Dad's letter to George P. came from our family files.

For information on Graves' disease, I consulted the National Graves' Disease Foundation Web site, at www.ngdf.org. The stories about Uncle Lou came from various family members.

The assertion that President Franklin Roosevelt was the first chief executive to have his first "100 days" analyzed was drawn from an observation made by PBS commentator Mark Shields during an April 28, 1989, broadcast of the *MacNeil-Lehrer News Hour* and corroborated by several online media sources. My interview with Tony Coehlo provided the story about Dad's first meeting with the congressional leadership.

Background information on the Tower nomination came from the *Handbook of Texas Online,* under the heading "John Tower." I quoted Dad's February 21, 1989, letter to Charles Bartlett about how vicious the Tower nomination process had become. Sam

Skinner told me the story of Senator Tower signing "the pledge" in his interview with me.

General Scowcroft told me the details of the NSC internal review of policies and the formation of the Gang of Eight. General Powell also added details. A quote from President Gorbachev's letter to me closed the chapter.

Chapter 16. Greasing the Skids

The opening quote for the chapter came from my interview with former Canadian prime minister Brian Mulroney. Dad's personal papers and published writings provided the details concerning his visit to Asia in February 1989. For background information on Emperor Hirohito's life, I consulted a documentary on General Douglas MacArthur from the PBS series *The American Experience,* found at www.pbs.org.

The source for the fact that Dad has made sixteen postpresidential visits to China was his personal papers at the Bush Library.

Much of the information on my trip to Paraguay came from the White House briefing book I was given in preparation for that trip. I also shared the memories of my friend Jodie Dwight. Secretary of State Condoleezza Rice's letter to me provided the story of Dad calling Chancellor Kohl, and former CIA director Bob Gates filled in the details of Dad's telephoning other world leaders. Through the good offices of General Brent Scowcroft, many world leaders responded to my questions, former Japanese prime minister Toshiki Kaifu being one of them. His letter to me provided the anecdotes about Dad's call to him on New Year's Day and, later, his horseshoe game with Dad.

General Scowcroft's memories of President Mitterrand's visit to Kennebunkport enhanced my own memories of that trip. Walter Curley's recollections came from his remarks to the previously cited Hofstra conference recorded in the book *A Noble Calling.*

In his personal letter to me, Secretary Baker supplied the anecdote about speaking in code if the meeting with the Soviets went well. Dad's remarks about Gorbachev calling Europe a "condominium" came from his 1998 interview with David Frost. The "smaller the country, the longer the speech!" story came from Prime Minister Mulroney in his interview with me.

My brothers Marvin and Jeb both recounted their match with Chris Evert and Pam Shriver for the record, but Chris Evert provided the bulk of the details in the book. I relied on *A World Transformed* for the historical details on China and the Tiananmen Square episode; Dad's letter to Deng Xiaoping is in the Bush Library; and General Scowcroft provided the details of his secret trip to China during the summer of 1989. I am very grateful to Jiang Zemin, the former president of the People's Republic of China, for responding to numerous questions regarding Dad and relations between our countries.

The background information on Dad's summer 1989 European trip, such as the details of lunch with the U.S. ambassador to Poland John Davis and other attendees, came from *A World Transformed*. Bob Gates also shared his memories of that lunch with me. The translation of *Sto Lat* came from the Polish American Center Web site, at www.polishamericancenter.org. Several people recalled the incident with the raincoat in the main square in Budapest; I relied on accounts of it from Condoleezza Rice, General Scowcroft, Tim McBride, and my mother.

Boyden Gray and John Sununu provided the details of Dad's work on the savings and loan crisis and his signing of the Financial Institutions Reform, Recovery and Enforcement Act. My brother Neil provided many of the facts about his testimony before Congress, and his insights on the effect the controversy had on our family. I supplemented Neil's insights with facts and figures obtained from the Federal Deposit Insurance Corporation Web site at www.fdic.gov and from a January 16, 1990, *New York Times* article titled "Where Savings Crisis Hits Hard," by Richard W. Stevenson.

I appreciated Dan Rostenkowski telling me the story of visiting Dad at the White House early in his presidency during my interview with him. President Clinton shared with me his memories of the Education Summit in Charlottesville, Virginia.

General Scowcroft explained the end of the Cold War in his remarks at the Hofstra conference, found in the panel discussion "New World Order: Nationalism and Internationalism" in *A Noble Calling,* and in my interviews with him. For background about the fall of the Berlin Wall, I referred to numerous sources, including the Newseum's Web site at www.newseum.org. German chancellor Helmut Kohl was kind enough to share his thoughts about that critical time; and the quote from my father about Senator Mitchell and Congressman Gephardt came from his 1998 interview with David Frost and numerous other speeches and public utterances. Secretary Baker, General Scowcroft, and President Gorbachev were also extremely helpful to me in writing about this crucial time in history.

For the Malta Summit, I relied on Dad's recollections and President Gorbachev's memories in his letter to me. The account of Dad thanking the seaman on the bow came from Ariel de Guzman's 2005 book, *The Bush Family Cookbook: Favorite Recipes and Stories from One of America's Great Families.*

Chapter 17. The Right Thing

The opening quote from Jon Meacham came from my interview with him. *The Public Papers of the Presidents,* Dad's many writings, and interviews with key members of the National Security Council informed my treatment of the circumstances leading up to the Panamanian invasion in 1989. The letter from Private James Markwell came from the Bush Library archives.

I relied on Dad's personal diaries, personal files, and my own recollections for the Christmas 1989 observations. The section on Europe and Germany grew out of Dad's writings and recollections and my interviews with Chancellor Kohl and General Scowcroft.

I appreciate Ed Eckenhoff and my former colleagues at the National Rehabilitation Hospital for confirming the details of my time working there. Dad's private papers and recollections, as well as a letter I received from Dr. Burt Lee, Dad's White House doctor, formed the basis for the material on the 1990 Drug Summit in Colombia.

Dad's private files and our family's collective memory also contributed to the section about Dad's travels outside the White House. I also consulted the 1946 book *Starling of the White House*, by Colonel Edmund Starling, as well as my interviews with the many agents who served on Dad's detail for the material on the Secret Service.

Dad's statement concerning his aversion to broccoli in March of 1990 can be found in volume I of his 1990 *Public Papers*, and Carlo Cacioppio's broccoli recipe came from the Bush Library archives. For the section on Lee Atwater, I relied on my interviews with Dad, Sally Atwater, Mary Matalin, my brother Marvin, and Ede Holiday, as well as John Brady's 1997 book, *Bad Boy: The Life and Politics of Lee Atwater.*

I appreciate having former attorney general Bill Barr's insights on how my father approached the line-item veto issue. The Jan Burmeister memo regarding Uncle Lou came from the Bush Library archives.

My interviews with Congressman Tony Coehlo and Boyden Gray, respectively, provided the basis for the material on the Americans with Disabilities Act and the Clean Air Act amendments. I also consulted volume II of the 1990 *Public Papers* for facts, numbers, and the key figures who shaped that legislation. On the 1990 budget deal, I solicited input from Dad, senators Alan Simpson and Bob Dole, congressmen Dan Rostenkowski and Lud Ashley, and White House Communications director David Demarest and OMB director Dick Darman. Marlin Fitzwater's book *Call the Briefing* also provided useful details.

My interview with Laurie Firestone served as the backbone for the narrative on Dad's social activities as president. I also retrieved the "Table 8" letter from Dad's personal papers at the Bush Library archives. My interviews with Lee Annenberg, my brother Marvin, and a letter from my cousin Grace Holden provided the balance of insights and anecdotes.

The United States Air Force Web site provided many of the details on Air Force One, and former president Menem of Argentina kindly responded to my questions related to our trip to South America in December 1990.

Chapter 18. A Sense of Honor

The opening quote came from the text of the speech that former British Prime Minister John Major intended to deliver in Houston, Texas, during Dad's eightieth birthday at Minute Maid Park. Because the program was running very late, however, President Gorbachev spoke on behalf of the world leaders in attendance, and Prime Minister Major never gave his prepared remarks. I am grateful that he shared them with me.

Dad's writings and recollections, my interview with General Scowcroft, and media reports by BBC and CNN formed the nucleus of the section covering Iraq's invasion of Kuwait. I also consulted the *Public Papers;* British Prime Minister Margaret Thatcher's memoirs, *Downing Street Years;* and Secretary Baker's *Politics of Diplomacy.* The information about General Schwarzkopf's background came from his biography on the Academy of Achievement Web site.

My interview with Marlin Fitzwater gave me insights into the negotiations that Dad undertook in Maine in August of 1990. President Gorbachev and Vice President Cheney also shed light on the U.S.–Soviet relationship as the Iraqi crisis deepened. Sig Rogich, John Magaw, and General Schwarzkopf also shared anecdotes from that fall when Dad addressed a joint session of Congress and visited Saudi Arabia. Prime Minister Major, Vice President Cheney, and General Scowcroft augmented Dad's recollections about Lady Thatcher's fall from power in November 1990.

Mom, Spike and Betsy Heminway, and Senator Simpson shared

anecdotes from early 1991, as the Gulf War neared. The Tony Mc-Peak anecdote came from a January 6, 1992, story written by *Time* magazine journalist Hugh Sidey, which Mr. Sidey retold during the previously mentioned 1997 conference on Dad's administration held at Hofstra University.

I am grateful to journalist Bernie Shaw, who shared his perspectives about CNN's historic broadcasts as the Gulf War started. I also interviewed Nurse Ellen Tolten of the White House Medical Unit, who detailed how the stress of that time weighed on my father; and Prime Minister Major and Secretary Colin Powell, who added their thoughts to Dad's concerning the end of the Gulf War and its aftermath.

Secret Service detail leader Rich Miller and General Schwarzkopf added personal observations about Dad's mood and the parade on the National Mall celebrating the war's end. The closing section regarding Peter Arnett arose from my interviews with Dad and Senator Simpson, with additional details from Senator Simpson's 1997 book, *Right in the Old Gazoo: A Lifetime of Scrapping with the Press.*

Chapter 19. Almost a Miracle

My brother Marvin and Gary Walters also provided much of the information about the White House horseshoe tournaments, while Governor Sununu recalled the DiMaggio/Williams visit to the White House and subsequent trip to Toronto. I interviewed California governor Arnold Schwarzenegger about his service on the Council for Physical Fitness, and I appreciate his time and helpful comments very much.

The section on Dad's atrial fibrillation came from my interviews with my parents and former Secret Service agent Rich Miller; and Joseph Verner Reed's insights about Queen Elizabeth's 1991 visit are from the Hofstra University conference. The anecdote involving my brother George and Her Majesty came from Mom.

Pete Teeley told me the story about Dad's role in averting his near-death experience, and I also consulted Pete's book, *The Complete Cancer Survival Book*, to confirm the details surrounding his ordeal.

For the section covering Justice Clarence Thomas's nomination, I spoke to Dad and Justice Thomas and reviewed the *Public Papers*. The comment regarding Benjamin Hooks, to be clear, is taken from a question asked by a journalist during the July 1, 1991, press conference in Kennebunkport at which Dad announced the Thomas nomination.

The "Scowcroft Award for Somnolent Excellence" was derived from my interviews with Dad and General Scowcroft, from Dad's private files and other writings, and from his 1998 interview with British journalist David Frost. The Secret Service boating section was drawn from my interview with John Magaw, as was part of the section recounting President Gorbachev's release following the 1991 coup attempt. President Gorbachev also provided his personal recollections from that tense period. Marlin Fitzwater gave me the details regarding Dad's fishing slump during the summer of 1991.

Details surrounding Governor Sununu's demise as White House chief of staff came from Dad, Governor Sununu, his then-deputy Andy Card, my brother George, and Governor Sununu's eventual replacement, Secretary Skinner. For the demise of the Soviet Union, also in December of 1991, I received insights from President Gorbachev, Chancellor Kohl, General Scowcroft, Secretary Condoleezza Rice, and Bob Gates.

Chapter 20. A Steep Incline

Many of the 1992 campaign details such as polling figures and key dates came from the 1993 book *Mad as Hell: Revolt at the Ballot Box, 1992,* by journalists Jack Germond and Jules Witcover.

Secretary Robert Mosbacher provided much of the background for the January 1992 Asia trip. Multiple sources shared with me their perspectives on the night Dad became ill at the Japanese state dinner: principally, my parents, Secret Service agents John Magaw and Rich Miller, and members of the White House medical unit. The Tokyo restaurant anecdote came to me from a member of the press.

The Governor Thornburgh anecdote came from his remarks at the previously mentioned conference at Hofstra University in 1997. The section about the "grocery scanner" and the *New York Times* came from Dad's recollections and writings, Marlin Fitzwater's book *Call the Briefing,* the *New York Times* archives, and my interviews with *Washington Post* media reporter Howard Kurtz and my father-in-law George Koch, who was then president of the Grocery Manufacturers of America.

The Uncle Lou story about his dog Gilbert came from my mom and Uncle Jon Bush. Vice President Quayle, Pat Buchanan, and Fred Malek talked to me about the 1992 New Hampshire GOP primary. Mr. Ross Perot declined to be interviewed for this project, so the background information on him and his candidacy came from my interviews with CNN's Larry King and Perot confidant Tom Luce, as well as multiple online sources, including www.famous-texans.com, the EDS Web site, and Mr. Perot's biography at www.perotsystems.com.

My Aunt Nan helped me recall the details of our 1992 trip to France, where I led the U.S. delegation to the Winter Olympics. My parents and husband, Bobby, told me how he went to Camp David to ask for my hand in marriage.

The recollections I gleaned from Dad and Secret Service agents Rich Miller and John Magaw about his June 1992 trip to Panama were supported by additional material from the *Public Papers.* Dad's private office in Houston, Texas, shared the February 2006 letter he sent to Balbina Herrera, and Panamanian president Torrijos confirmed the details by e-mail.

The background information concerning Camp David came from several online sources: the National Park Service Web site, the White House Web site, and www.infoplease.com.

The analysis of the Perot campaign going into the summer of 1992 was drawn from media reports and from the Germond/

Witcover book, *Mad as Hell*. The Mary Matalin anecdotes came from my interview with her, and Senator Simpson told me about his visit with Dad following the David McCullough lecture in 1992. The GOP convention section is largely drawn from my own recollections, though the Bush Library archivists confirmed the details.

Dad's former White House director of political affairs Ron Kaufman gave me the anecdote about the Catholic League of Illinois. So many of Dad's political colleagues also shared their thoughts regarding the fall campaign with me: Secretary Baker, Sig Rogich, Andy Card, and David Bates chief among them. The source for James Brosnahan's political contributions was a February 25, 2002 *National Review* article by Byron York, "American Tali-Lawyer: Defending John Walker Lindh."

My brother Jeb recounted the Election Night anecdote about Mom, and Joe Hagin shared his experience with Dad from that evening. The November 19, 1992, note from Patty Presock informing my parents about my grandmother's death came from Dad's personal files, as did my grandmother's self-written eulogy.

Chapter 21. Mountaintops and Valleys

Secretary Baker's postmortem analysis on the 1992 election came from my interview with him. My brothers George and Marvin, and Dad's longtime political supporter and aide Margaret Tutwiler, also shared their thoughts with me. General Scowcroft's comments were drawn from the Hofstra University conference.

Andy Card provided me with useful insights on how Dad handled the transition both professionally and personally. My father's letter to Corinne Quayle and senators Bob Dole and Bob Kerrey were from his personal files. I also appreciate Senator Dole taking the time to share his recollections with me by phone.

Former White House usher Chris Emery sent me a letter with his detailed diary entries recorded the same night he visited the Vietnam Memorial with my parents, on November 10, 1992. Dana Carvey's observations from his December 6–7, 1992, visit to the

White House are drawn from my interview with him. I relied on the published collection of *Public Papers* for the section covering Somalia, Russia, and Dad's final major addresses as president at Texas A&M University and the United States Military Academy at West Point.

White House nurse Mary Jackson's note came from Dad's personal files, and Prime Minister Mulroney spoke with me about Dad's final weekend at Camp David. Finally, the material for Inauguration Day 1993 arose from Dad's personal papers and writings, and from my interview with Special Agent Rich Miller.

Chapter 22. Ultimate Freedom

Dad's ever-faithful friend Don Rhodes confirmed the details about the lot in Houston where my parents built their present-day home, and neighbor and friend Jack Fitch sent me a letter detailing my parents' first twenty-four hours back home as private citizens. The letter to Patty Presock came from his private files. The Chase Untermeyer anecdote came from his letter to me for this project.

I deeply appreciate Jimmy Carter sharing with me his thoughts about the role of a former president. Dad's March 1, 1993, letter to friends came from his personal papers. Both my brother Neil and family friend Lud Ashley shared their recollections of the April 1993 trip to Kuwait with me. Also, some of the details surrounding the failed assassination attempt against my father were drawn from George Mason University's *History News Network* at http://hnn.us/articles/1000.html.

The Reverend Billy Graham wrote me a letter regarding his and his wife's encounter with my parents during a 1993 speaking engagement in Mexico. Also, the story about Ranger's death came from my parents' recollections and writings.

Dad and Nurse Ellen Tolten provided the recollections around the nurses' and Whittakers' Maine visit in summer 1993, and Dad's fishing buddy Bill Busch shared with me several anecdotes about my father's passion for the sea and fishing. Canadian journalist Art

Milnes was the first "outside" person to contact me about this project, at Dad's urging, and I appreciate his detailed letter to me. I also appreciate our friend in Venezuela Gustavo Cisneros for sharing his anecdotes from the visits Dad and I have made to his country.

My parents shared with me how my brothers George in Texas and Jeb in Florida approached their respective 1994 campaigns for governor starting in 1993. The background information about the Knight Grand Cross of the Order of Bath came from the official British royal Web site, http://www.royal.gov.uk/output/Page495.asp.

Information surrounding my family's golf heritage came from Dad, golfer Ben Crenshaw, CBS announcer Jim Nantz, and my own recollections. Information about my brothers' 1994 political campaigns in Texas and Florida came from their interviews with me. Finally, my sisters-in-law Laura and Margaret shared many of the "Idea Man" anecdotes with me, while my niece Lauren and my Uncle Scott Pierce shared stories detailing Dad's competitive nature in sports.

Chapter 23. The Spring Colt

The details about my parents' fiftieth anniversary trip to Sea Island, Georgia, came in a letter to me from resort owner Bill Jones. The information from the Nashville celebration and the yearly activities came from my parents' writings and recollections.

The background information on Jeb's resurgence in Florida and John Thrasher came from a *National Review* article titled "Gentle Jeb," October 26, 1998. The background information on the 1993 Branch Davidian assault in Waco and the 1995 Oklahoma City bombing came from the BBC Web site and www.oklahomacity nationalmemorial.org, respectively. I also interviewed my father and consulted his private papers concerning his resignation from the National Rifle Association.

The information regarding Dad checking in on former congressman Rostenkowski came from my interview with Illinois congressman Marty Russo and was corroborated by Dad; a June 12, 1997, *Chicago Sun Times* article by Michael Sneed; a January 24, 1998, *Congressional Quarterly* article by Jackie Koszczuk; and the *New York Times* archives.

The Hugh Sidey excerpt about the former world leaders is taken from his comments at the previously mentioned Hofstra University conference. The background information about Dad's involvement with the Bush School students came from his current chief of staff, Jean Becker.

Secret Service detail leader Jim Pollard also sent me his reflections on Dad's penchant for pushing the limits of his personal safety, and some of the material surrounding Dad's 1997 parachute jump came from *All the Best*. The information about the 1999 seventy-fifth birthday celebration came from Dad's personal files in Houston as well as Dr. John Mendelsohn at the M. D. Anderson Cancer Center in Houston, Texas.

Dad's comments about the news media came from a panel he hosted at his presidential Library at Texas A&M in 1999. *New York Times* columnist Maureen Dowd, who participated in that panel, was also thoughtful enough to send me a lengthy e-mail responding to questions. The anecdotes from Mom's seventy-fifth birthday in 2000 came from Mom, Dad, Senator Simpson, and Jean Becker. My brother George offered me insights into his 2000 campaign, and Dad's traveling aide at the time, Gian-Carlo Peressutti, filled in key details throughout.

I appreciate Dad's former aide Michael Dannenhauer sharing with me his very personal anecdote.

For Election Night 2000, Dad and Mom; my brothers George, Jeb, and Marvin; Dad's aides Jean Becker and Gian-Carlo Peressutti; and George's confidant Karen Hughes all offered details to drive the narrative of that unforgettable night. I relied on Dad's recollections, my brother George's, and Margaret Tutwiler's for details about the recount period and subsequent declaration of victory. Finally, I am deeply grateful to former vice president Al Gore, who shared his insights on the emotional phone call my father made to him on the night the vice president conceded the 2000 election.

The concluding quotes from Dad were taken from his December 20, 2000, interview with Paula Zahn, who was then with the Fox News Channel.

Chapter 24. Family Continuity

Dad's comments about George's victory were taken from a 2001 interview he gave to PBS's Ernie Manouse. Karen Hughes's comments about President Bush 43 in the Oval Office came from my interview with her.

The anecdotes about how my brother's election as president has changed our family all came from my parents and family members. Dad's letter to Hugh Sidey about the Adams family came from my father's personal files.

The anecdote about Jeb and the mackerel came from Dad's fishing buddy Bill Busch.

The information about the 9/11 attacks came from the official 9/11 report, from the Federal Aviation Administration Web site, from my parents' writings and recollections, and from my own memories. Another fishing friend of Dad's, Jimmy Dionne, sent me a letter detailing his interactions with my father in the aftermath of 9/11. Dad commented about George's leadership and his address to the joint session of Congress during a December 2001 interview with ABC's Diane Sawyer. Houston golf professional Paul Marchand described to me how Dad reacted to the 9/11 anniversary a year later, on September 11, 2002.

For the section about Dad's return visit to Chi Chi Jima in 2002, I relied heavily on my interview with CNN's Paula Zahn and the transcript from her historic on-site interview with Dad.

I reached out to all of Dad's grandkids for their thoughts, anecdotes, and—best of all—e-mails they had received from Dad. My father shared the emotions he felt during the funeral for President

Reagan with aide Jim McGrath the morning after the service in Houston. The information about Dad's eightieth birthday party came from his private papers, published news reports in the *Houston Chronicle*, the letter I received from President Gorbachev, and the interview I had with Larry King.

I gleaned key details about Election Night 2004 from www.us-electionatlas.org and corroborated them using published media reports. Finally, my sister-in-law Laura offered the anecdote about Dad and Kate Cheney.

Chapter 25. Ceiling and Visibility Unlimited

I consulted USAID for the facts and figures surrounding the death toll from the Indian Ocean tsunami in December 2004. President Clinton, Jean Becker, and Dad offered insights into the February 2005 trip to Asia, and Dad's letter to Hugh Sidey in March of 2005 was obtained from his personal files.

The information about the Bush-Clinton Houston Tsunami Fund came from Bush staff sources.

Jim Nantz provided key insights from President Clinton's historic visit to Kennebunkport in June 2005. My sister-in-law Tricia Koch and I were also present with our children.

The background information on Mom and Dad's sixtieth wedding anniversary celebration at the White House came from my parents and their friend David Rubenstein; pro golfer Phil Mickelson also sent me a letter with the anecdote about crashing a wedding with Dad during their summer 2005 visit; and personal aide Tommy Frechette shared the "new-old" party in Maine with me.

My cousin Hap's e-mail he sent to me captures the essence of Walker's Point.

Dad's concluding letter came from the same letter that produced the opening quote for this chapter, to each of his kids in 2001.

Every effort has been made to ensure that each reference used in the production of this book has been properly sourced and cited. My sister-in-law Tricia and I have double- and triple-checked every section to be sure we have fully adhered to the accepted industry standards for a work of this nature, and I want to thank my partners at Warner Books and Larry Kirshbaum of LJK Literary Management for the diligence they demonstrated in guiding us through this vital section of the book.

Index

Our wish for you at Christmas
        is for a world at peace-
    a world full of love
Merry Christmas from
        all the George Bushes

#8 — 5000 LONGMONT, HOUSTON, TEXAS 77027 • 5161 PALISADE LANE, N. W., WASHINGTON, D. C. 20016

A Merry Christm

George Jr.

Jeb

Neil

Marvin

Dorothy

From the Bushe

Dorothy   Jeb   George Jr.   George   Barbara   Marvin   Neil